Clean Hands, Clear Conscience

Clean Hands, Clear Conscience

Amelia Williams

Published by Tablo

Quotations

Ignorance is bliss but knowledge is power.
– Thomas Gray.

Happiness is the rarest emotion amongst
intelligent people.
– Ernest Hemingway.

If you tell the truth you don't have to
remember anything.
– Mark Twain.

This is a true story only the names have been changed.

To the best of my recollection 100% is fact. The only reason I've used a pseudonym is to avoid any publishing firm being sued for publishing it under my real name.

Not many people like a brash outspoken female who has an opinion on almost every subject. But that describes me. I am the most unconventional seventy-six year old, anyone could meet and most people can only tolerate me in small doses and that has never bothered me.

Self-analysis:

I don't suffer fools gladly I have no co-ordination between hand and foot and definitely no co-ordination between brain and tongue. I swear worse than a Trooper in the privacy of my home, very rarely in front of friends, and never in public (unless provoked). I make idle threats to intimidate.

You could lock me in a cellar for years without windows and without any form of communication and I guarantee someone would accuse me of something and everyone would believe them.

I am my own worst enemy.

I have learnt that most people would prefer to believe a pretty woman's lies than an old battle-axe who seems to be as hard as nails.

There are many things in this book that I'm ashamed of and I would love to go back in time to change. They are true accounts and I could either not share my dirty laundry in public. OR I can share with you the reader the truth of what my journey through life has been.

Everyone knows that lawyers love to get paid handsomely, they love money. Before anyone wants to bluff a No Win No Fee lawyer into believing I have slandered them only for the lawyer to realise they have wasted many hours to get paid nothing. I'm prepared to have a polygraph test to prove that everything I've written is true. I'm also willing to pay for a polygraph test for anyone else who feels they've been slandered and believes they can prove me wrong.

I realise polygraph tests are not permissible in courts of law in Australia. But I'm confident that Judges and Jurors would realise the results of polygraphs should be enough to sway their decision in my favour.

I welcome the challenge.

Chapter 1

The Living Nightmare

Detective Kennedy lowered his bulky frame onto the wool covered lounge.

'Amelia, can you identify this as the knife you used to stab Frank?'

He produced a knife from a large plastic bag and held the base of the blade between his thumb and index finger. I felt an instant flash of horror, as I stared at the eight-inch, blood caked weapon. I murmured, 'Sweet Jesus, have mercy on me.'

Norm Kennedy leaned forward and rested his massive hand on my quivering arm. His rugged sunburnt face told a story of a man who had dealt with people from all walks of life. At that precise moment, his eyes showed compassion for me as I sat almost motionless beside him. My voice broke the silence as I stammered in disbelief, 'I … I didn't think it was as big and as sharp as that.'

'What sort of knife did you think that you had picked up, Amelia?'

'I thought it was the blunt headed, ham knife that Frank had used to cut the ham. Some happy Christmas isn't it?'

I buried my face into my hands and sobbed uncontrollably, and my mind flashed back over the events that had happened in the past twenty-four hours. I wondered, what in the name of God had caused this tragedy to happen?

I could see myself sitting in our late model Ford outside the butcher shop where Frank worked. 'Please God, don't let him be drunk. Where the hell is he? The shop doors have been closed for half an hour. Don't tell me that they're all in there celebrating Christmas.' I recalled saying to myself.

I kept thinking about all the times I had waited outside different butcher shops thinking similar thoughts. My mind was in turmoil sitting in that car, remembering all the beatings I had taken. The weekends had become a nightmare of constant arguments, which had often turned into violent outbursts. I shuddered as I remembered the many agonising hours I had suffered both physically and mentally. Sitting in that car was another form of torture, just waiting and worrying. And I wondered when the hell it would all end. Look at the time, the kids will be wondering where we are. But Vivian's a fairly worldly kid for almost fourteen, she'll get the two younger ones to have their bath and they'll probably be watching TV. They'll be okay. I had assured myself.

I wondered again why Frank didn't drink in front of me anymore. I thought, he knows damn well I'm not completely stupid, so why bother to hide the obvious? I tried to comfort myself with positive thoughts. Telling myself that he hadn't had a drink in the past five weeks and I reminded myself, that's the longest time he's been sober, he's really trying to get off the grog. I kept thinking it must be hard for the poor bastard I'd hate to have to give up cream in my coffee. I wonder if I'm a coffee and cream-aholic? What a ridiculous thing to think of, Amelia, God you think idiotic thoughts, I'm glad no-one can read your mind, because they'd have you put away. Oh. Thank Christ. Here he is now. Oh shit no. He's been drinking. Oh, please God let him be in a good mood.'

'Hi, honey, had a beer with the boss, they're all in there still grogging on. This is Russell the apprentice I've told you about. I told him we'd give him a lift home. Russ this is my old woman, Amelia, she's not a bad old scout. Amelia, this is Russ.'

The drive to Russell's house was, to anyone observing, a pleasant, chatty excursion. Just three people discussing the events of the day, the weather and Christmas. Frank pulled the car into the driveway of Russell's parent's home and Russell alighted offering us thanks for the lift and wishing us a Merry Christmas. Frank drove away, tooting the horn and waving. As he lowered his arm,

Frank snarling 'What's wrong with you, ya bitch?'

I was always very aware of his change in moods, but I was really taken by surprise at such a sudden transformation and without stopping to think about the question I replied, 'Oh Frank. Why did you get on the grog? It's Christmas, couldn't you just this once have stayed sober? Every bloody Christmas it's the same, you're always drunk and in a crappy mood.'

Frank 'Don't start nagging. That's all you're good for is bloody nagging.'

Amelia 'I'm not nagging, I'm stating a fact, every Christmas you get on the grog, you get dirty on yourself so you take it out on me. Why?'

Frank 'Because you're always bloody nagging.'

Amelia 'If I'm such an old nag as you say, why do you put on a big front for your so-called friends and tell them that I'm not a bad old scout?'

By this time, Frank's face had become distorted with rage his eyes were like that of a madman. He slammed his foot on the accelerator and started driving like a maniac. I clutched the vinyl seat in an effort to brace myself for a nerve-racking drive, which I had experienced many times before. I bit my lower lip and uttered a silent prayer. I focussed onto the traffic ahead, and saw in the distance that the traffic lights had turned red. The two cars directly in front were slowing down and I knew that if Frank didn't ease off the accelerator now, he'd end up ploughing into the back of the blue Valiant. I knew not to say anything about his driving because that would only aggravate him more. I stiffened my legs and dug my fingers deeper into the vinyl seat until my knuckles turned white. My whole body was tense in anticipation of being catapulted through the windscreen on impact. As suddenly as he had accelerated, Frank jammed his foot onto the brake pedal. In doing so, he almost locked the wheels. The car veered off the road onto the left, narrowly missing the Valliant's nearside mudguard. Frank turned to me and said, 'You think you're so bloody smart and such a good driver, you can drive the rest of the way home.'

Without daring to question his peculiar sense of reasoning, I silently sighed with relief and slid behind the wheel. I had only gone a few hundred yards when his demanding, menacing, voice ordered me to drive to the nearest pub. I told him that I wouldn't.

My voice was shaky, both with fear of the consequences of what might happen for defying him and also from the near catastrophe a few minutes beforehand. Frank poked his index finger hard and deep into my cheek and said through clenched teeth, 'I said drive me to the nearest pub, bitch head.'

I replied very determinedly that I was driving us home, where our kids were waiting for us, it's almost six-thirty and it was getting dark and the kids would be worrying and wondering where the hell we were.

Frank let out a demented, taunted laugh, which reminded me of the haunted house type movies I saw as a child,

Frank 'That's a good one, you being worried about the kids. The only person you worry about is yourself. And anyhow they're your kids, not mine.'

Amelia 'Oh for God's sake don't be so damned ridiculous, Frank you know as well as I do that they're your children.'

Frank 'Oh no they're not I'm only their father but I don't own them, you've seen to that. You've turned them against me, you and that bastard of a father of yours. The great Rob Long whatever Daddy says little Amelia does cause Daddy's the boss.'

Frank continued, 'Well I'm telling you bitch your father is nothing. He's just a two-bob lair who likes to big note himself.'

His voice was almost at screaming point, and just to prove to me that he meant what he said, he aimed a hard punch to the side of my head, behind my left ear. Choking back the tears, I gripped hold of the steering wheel as hard as I could, so that I didn't lose control of the vehicle or my temper. I drove home in silence, and as soon as we walked through the back door, Vivian, Heather and Claire gave out a resounding chorus of, 'Hello, Dad.'

Vivian took one look at her father, and without erasing her smile, she glanced imploringly at me. I flashed a despairing look at her. Vivian knew instinctively what that look meant. We had often communicated to each other with facial expressions, and the look I had shown was, watch what you say, he's in a very bad mood.

Although Heather was only a few weeks off her tenth birthday, I knew not to even try giving her a warning look. Even if she knew what the look meant, she wouldn't have heeded it anyway. Heather held her own counsel and if she didn't want to do a particular thing, she just wouldn't and that was that.

Claire at four and a half was far too young to understand any such warning glances from anyone. Besides to her, her father was the greatest man in the world. She idolised him. And Frank, knowing this, showed favouritism to her. Claire put her hands up to her father to be picked up and given a cuddle. As he leant forward to lift her, he lost his balance and fell against the kitchen cupboard. Claire let out a little giggle and in mock reprimand she said, 'Daddy, have you been on the drunk again.'

Little did she realise what repercussions her innocent remark would bring. I pretended not to hear the comment and took the electric frypan from its cupboard and indicated to Vivian to get the other two out of the room. As she walked out the arched doorway into the living room, she called to Heather and Claire to come and see Santa Claus on TV. I turned to Frank

Amelia 'Do you want vegetables or salad with your steak?'

Frank snarled, 'You bitch, you put her up to that didn't you?

Amelia 'I don't know what you mean.'

Frank 'Don't give me that ya bitch, you know what I'm talking about. You told Claire to say that didn't you? Admit it.'

Amelia 'Frank, don't be so stupid, she's only a baby, and how could I have put her up to anything? I've just this minute walked in the door and I haven't even opened my mouth.'

He grabbed me by the throat with his left hand and squeezed hard.

Frank 'I oughta choke you, ya bitch.'

He then spat in my face. I struggled to get free and in doing so, I raised my arm to wipe his saliva off my face, with my sleeve. Frank then delivered a punch to my left temple with his right hand, knocking me to the floor.

Frank 'Trying to hit me were you bitch? I'll give you what for, you ever hit me.'

With that he kicked out at me. I rolled my legs over far enough to allow his boot to just graze the side of my left calf. And I scrambled to my feet screaming hysterically.

'You bastard, I hope you rot in hell.'

Frank lunged forward to grab hold of me, just as I started to run for the back door. He grabbed me by the hair and pulled as hard as he could. He lifted his hand above his head as if to strike me a backhanded blow.

Vivian terrified, screamed, 'DAD, PLEASE DAD, DON'T.'

Heather was crying and Claire had begun to scream. Frank turned towards the children and ordered to them, 'Get out or you'll all get a thrashing.'

He lowered his hand and let go of my hair and shoved me towards the children then stormed towards the back door

Frank 'I'm going to the pub and I might not be back.'

As he stamped down the back stairs, I mumbled under my breath, I hope to Christ you fall down the stairs and break your neck, you bastard.

•••

Ambulance man 'Mrs Williams.'

His soft wheezing voice broke my thoughts.

Amelia 'Pardon?'

Whilst wiping my face with a tissue.

I looked up to face the elderly, overweight, gentleman standing in front of me. He coughed a rasping, dry, hollow, sound. I gathered my thoughts and realised that this fellow was one of the ambulance attendants. I felt a sudden hot flush of embarrassment and tried desperately to stifle a broad smile as the thought crossed my mind, God the ambulance man looks as if he needs an ambulance. He sucked in air through his thick lips, in short quick gasps.

Ambulance man 'We can't turn the stretcher through the back or front doors to go down the stairs, so we won't be able to carry your husband on the stretcher to the ambulance.'

He gasped again, and the sound of air being sucked in between his teeth, made a slight whistling noise.

Amelia ' Christ.'

I pressed my hands onto the armrests of the lounge chair in an effort to levitate myself into a standing position. I could feel the blood rush to my head, as if I had just performed an exhausting physical exercise. Beads of sweat had begun to expel on my brow and upper lip and I thought for one horrifying moment that I was going to lose consciousness. I just could not believe that this was happening. I thought to myself, my whole life has been violently thrust into the outer limits of the Twilight Zone. I couldn't believe the events that were happening around me. Here I was in my own living room on Christmas Day, police from the forensic department, photographers and detectives were swarming everywhere. And standing before me was this elderly man with a severe respiratory problem, complaining that he couldn't carry my dying husband down a flight of stairs. I took a deep breath in an effort, as if to regain my sanity

Amelia 'For God's sake, Frank's dying. He's got to be taken to the hospital for medical help in a hurry. You can't just leave him on the kitchen floor.'

Ambulance man (frowning) 'We'll have to try and support him in an upright position, Mrs Williams he's lost a lot of blood. Could you get an old towel to cover the wound?'

I ran as fast as I could to the bathroom cupboard and grabbed the first towel I saw. I turned to run back down the hallway and was surprised to see Detective Keith Fletcher had followed me.

Amelia (flabbergasted) 'I was just getting this towel for Frank's wound.'

Fletcher, a young man in his early thirties, seemed to tower over me. He put his huge hand out for me to pass the towel to him

Detective Fletcher 'We have to check everything, Mrs Williams.'

Handing the towel to him

Amelia 'Please, can you get them to hurry?'

He strode down the hallway, allowing the towel to unravel as he went. I hurried behind him and then I realised Norm Kennedy was beside me. I stopped suddenly to look at him inquisitively. And as if in answer to my thoughts

Norm 'We can't let you out of our sight, Amelia, you realise the situation is serious, don't you?'

Amelia 'Y ... yes, may I go in here and get another tissue?'

He smiled sympathetically and nodded and watched me as I quickly crossed the floor of the bedroom. I pulled out a handful of tissues from the box on my dressing table. As I turned, I caught sight of my reflection in the mirror. I brushed my hair off my face as I walked back towards Norm Kennedy and said, 'I don't look too crash hot at the best of times, but I look a damn sight worse at the moment and I feel even lousier.'

He put his arm out as if to usher me through the doorway and said, 'Take it easy, we're here to help you as much as we can. Come and sit down in the lounge and we'll go over everything just as it happened.'

As we entered the living room, the two ambulance bearers walked through the doorway from the kitchen. Between them, was a near skeletal figure of a man, whose face was a pasty yellowish colour. I felt my eyes enlarge almost cat like and I stared in disbelief at Frank being half dragged, half supported through to the front doorway. I hurried across the room and held open the swinging flyscreen door.

As they all passed me, I stepped outside the door onto the front patio. I held the door open with my right hand and offered my left hand to help support Frank through the doorway. Frank lifted his arm with great effort, causing his face to contort in agony. With as much strength that he could muster, he pushed my hand away. I stood aside, still holding the door ajar, as they proceeded down the long flight of thirteen steps. Each step seemed to take an eternity to manoeuvre. As they approached the sixth step, I saw my brother Edward run towards them offering his hand to Frank

Edward 'Here mate, let me help you.'

Frank in a hoarse, throaty, gasp, 'Piss off, ya bastard.'

Norm Kennedy put his arm on my shoulder and helped me back into the house. In the background I could hear Dad and Edward talking to Detective Fletcher. As I sat down in the lounge chair, the humming sound of the ambulance's motor being kicked over filtered through the open living room window. With the siren blaring, the ambulance departed and its deafening whine could be heard as it drove away towards its destination.

Sergeant Gordon Cully entered the living room with his cap pushed to the back of his head. He was a man in his early sixties with a receding hairline.

His ruddy complexion and sparkling eyes, matched with his large protruding stomach, gave him the appearance of being an all-round good sport. He wiped the perspiration off his forehead with a large handkerchief. As he folded the handkerchief to put it back in his pocket, he pursed his lips and blew a puff of air up over his large red nose onto his forehead.

Sergeant Cully 'We've finished here now, Norm. The boys are just packing up their cameras and equipment and are ready to get back to headquarters. I'll be on duty for another hour or so, but if you want me for anything else, you can ring through to the local station. The wife and I have our quarters just at the back of the station.'

Norm 'Okay, Gordon, we'll be here for a little while yet, I'll be in touch as soon as we get through here. If you don't hear from me today, I'll definitely contact you before the week is out. Have a Happy Christmas, what's left of it.'

Norm gave a wry little smile as he glanced at his watch,

Norm 'Its three-forty-two already.'

Sergeant Cully 'Yeah, I'll go home and finish my pudding the missus had just dished it up when I got the call. See you, mate.'

He turned to walk away, and just as if he'd had an afterthought he turned back and faced me

Sergeant Cully 'Try not to worry too much, Mrs Williams, you're in good hands, everything will be okay.'

I smiled at him, totally unsure whether to believe him or not. As if he could read my thoughts, Sergeant Cully gave me a reassuring wink and nodded his head towards me. He patted my hand

Sergeant Cully 'Keep your chin up, you've got three terrific kids there, they're a credit to you.'

He turned and walked across the living room floor and out the front door.

Norm 'Gordon's a good bloke he's been on the force thirty years and is due to retire in about eighteen months. He's a well-liked and respected bloke.'

Amelia 'He seems a really nice person, a sort of grandpa type.'

Norm Kennedy roared a loud comical laugh

Norm 'I don't think he'd appreciate being called Gramps.'

Amelia 'I didn't mean yours or my grandfather I meant a child's gramps.'

Norm nodded

Norm 'I know but I couldn't help but wonder what he'd say if we called him gramps in the future. Anyhow we had better get on with this matter, or don't you want to try and recapture a little bit of what's left of Christmas?'

I frowned not to fully comprehending what I had heard,

Amelia 'What do you mean, aren't you going to charge me?'

Norm Kennedy took a long look at me

Norm 'Do you want to be charged?'

Amelia (stammering nervously) 'No … not particularly, but I didn't think, I mean, I thought, it was … um … your duty, to arrest me.'

Norm 'My duty is to ascertain the facts, not to arrest nice young women such as yourself.'

I began twisting a tissue around my fingers nervously

Amelia 'But the facts are that I have just stabbed my husband and for all you and I know, he could be dead as of this minute.'

I tried to compose myself, but I could feel my bottom lip start to quiver and I struggled desperately within myself to stop from bursting into tears.

Norm Kennedy (looking directly into my face) 'Amelia, if I thought for one moment that you had wilfully and premeditatedly attempted to murder Frank I would've arrested and charged you long before this.'

I sighed a deep heavy sigh

Amelia 'I guess that's something, if nothing, what if he's dead?'

Norm 'IF, (The thick set Detective said, choosing his words carefully) 'IF Frank dies, I'm afraid I'll have no alternative other than to charge you with murder. The hospital will ring me here, within the next hour to give me a report on his condition.'

He had no sooner gotten the words out of his mouth when the phone started to ring. I jumped at the sound, closed my eyes and drew a deep breath.

Amelia 'Do you want me to answer it, Norm, or will you?'

Norm 'You answer it, it may be a friend ringing to wish you a Merry Christmas.'

I stood up thinking God this guy has got a sick, sense of humour.

I almost fell as I ran into the kitchen to answer it. A young male voice asked to speak to Detective Kennedy and I turned to call him only to find him standing alongside of me. I stammered, 'It's for you, I … I think it's the hospital.'

'Norm Kennedy speaking, yes … I see … four … five.'

He looked at his watch and I glanced at the clock on the wall. I thought that must be the time of death. Five past four, did Norm just say five past four? Oh God, I can't think straight.

'Okay, we'll probably be there in about an hour.' I heard Norm say, then he hung up and turned to me and said, 'Come and sit back down and I'll tell you what's happening.'

My eyes ran around the kitchen as if I was just seeing it for the first time. It was a bloody mess in the true sense of the word. There was blood everywhere, some of it was congealed, some too thick to congeal and in places it looked like thick, dark plum jam that had been flung around the floor. I felt nauseous and I put my hand to my throat in an effort to stop myself from becoming violently ill. I could feel a chill run down my spine and the goose bumps, which had risen, over my body, seemed enormous. I hurried into the living room and sat heavily down on the same lounge chair I had risen from less than five minutes previously.

Norm 'That was the hospital, it's not good news, but it's not bad news either.'

Amelia (groaning,) 'He's still alive then, Thank God. What's the bad news?'

Norm They've taken him to surgery, he's lost a hell of a lot of blood, four litres to be exact. He'll probably be in the theatre about five hours.'

Amelia 'Christ, four litres?'

Norm 'Yeah it's a lot, there's only five litres in a human body so it's touch and go for him, Amelia.'

Amelia 'I know. I didn't think he'd make it down the stairs let alone to the hospital. He's a plucky little bastard, isn't he?'

Ignoring the question,

Norm 'How did you meet him Amelia?'

Amelia (smirking) 'An ex-girlfriend introduced us that's why she's an ex-girlfriend.'

Norm Kennedy laughed 'How long have you been married?'

Amelia 'Almost fifteen years.'

Norm 'Does Frank drink much?'

Amelia 'No, not really, he only has to have a couple of beers and he's in a world of his own.'

Norm "He's a two-pot screamer?'

I smiled, because I had never heard the expression before, but I thought it described Frank perfectly.

Amelia 'Yes, that would hit the nail right on the head.'

Norm 'Has he ever hit you before, Amelia?'

Amelia 'Oh God that's a good one. Yes, many times.'

Norm 'Why?'

I frowned and looked at Norm shaking my head

Amelia 'Why? Why does he drink? Why does he bash me? Why does he do any bloody thing? If I knew the answers to those questions, mate, I wouldn't be sitting here now, would I?'

I burst into tears and tried to wipe my face with the now almost shredded tissue.

Amelia 'I'm sorry, I only wish to God, I could answer that.'

Detective Keith Fletcher walked into the room followed by Vivian, Heather and Claire

Detective Keith Fletcher 'Amelia, your father and brother are going home do you want the children to go with them?'

Amelia 'Yes please, if they can unless you both want to speak to them.'

Detective Keith Fletcher 'I've already had a talk to them. That youngest one can talk can't she? She'd talk the leg off an iron pot.'

Amelia 'Has she been giving you a hard time?'

Detective Keith Fletcher 'Not at all, she's been making me laugh though.'

Amelia 'God. What's she been saying?'

He laughed a little chuckling sound

Detective Keith Fletcher 'She's been mainly complaining that it's her father's fault that she'll miss out on seeing Mary Poppins at the movies tomorrow.'

Norm Kennedy roared with laughter as I glanced disdainfully at Claire who was smiling innocently at me.

When Norm stopped laughing, I said, 'It's bloody pathetic isn't it?'

Heather and Claire kissed me goodbye and Vivian came up to me and put her arms around me.

Vivian 'I'll see you when you get back to Granddad's place.'

I fought to choke back the tears.

Amelia 'I'll be okay, love, don't worry. Where's Granddad and Uncle Edward?'

Vivian 'Just outside on the patio.'

Amelia 'Can I just say goodbye to Dad please?'

Norm 'Sure.'

Dad put his arms around me and whispered into my ear that everything was going to be alright, and not to worry about a thing.

He kissed me on the cheek and gave me another hug. As he withdrew his arm, I noticed tears filling his sky-blue eyes.

I thought to myself, Poor Dad, he should be enjoying his retirement, instead of having all this worry heaped onto his lap. I wish I could undo all the heartache I've caused him.

'See you tonight, Amelia, and don't worry too much, ring us if you need us.' He hugged me reassuringly and walked down the stairs behind Edward and his two oldest granddaughters. Claire was perched on Edward's shoulders.

As he sat down on the lounge chair

Keith Fletcher 'What a day.'

Amelia 'It hasn't been a very Happy Christmas for any of us has it? You two look as if you've missed your Christmas lunch completely.'

Keith Fletcher 'No we're right, we had just come on duty when you rang. But we'd better finish this report or you'll miss out on your Christmas tea. Just tell us in your own words what happened.'

I took a deep breath and began, 'I'd better go back to last night.'

I told them of the hair rising drive home and how Frank had demanded to be driven to the pub, then the fight that had ensued when we arrived home.

Keith 'What time did he get back?'

Amelia 'I'm not too sure, about nine-thirty, I think. The kids were in bed asleep and I ran and got into bed as soon as I heard the car. I didn't want him to know that I was awake, so I pretended to be asleep. I heard him making a hell of a din in the kitchen. It seemed like an eternity. Then he eventually came into the bedroom and told me to get up. He wanted me to put the kid's presents under the tree. And as soon as I came out he began to argue about this that and the other and I just said, 'Look, Frank, if you want a blue go back to the pub because I don't want any more fighting ever. I was pretty tired and I had a stinking headache where he'd belted me. He eventually went to bed and flaked. I was very thankful of that, but I was feeling sick and sorry for myself and I sat out watching TV. They were singing Christmas Carols and I couldn't cop that garbage, so I turned the set off and made my bed here on the lounge. I couldn't get to sleep though until about four o'clock. The kids got up at five and woke me then they went in and woke Frank. I sat up until about eight o'clock until I thought I was going to keel over. I went into the bedroom but I couldn't get to sleep for ages. I just lay there crying. I had tried to get him in a good mood but he wouldn't even speak to me without snarling. While I was lying on the bed, I kept on arguing with myself whether I should take the full bottle of Nembutals that I had on my dressing room table. I must have cried myself to sleep because the next thing I remember it was eleven o'clock. When I came out here, the kids were playing on the floor and Frank was laying on the lounge. I asked him if he would drive us down to my parent's place, but he refused. I didn't really want him to, because he and Dad don't get on, in fact they haven't spoken to each other for two years. But I didn't want him to stay here, because I thought he had some grog hidden.'

Norm Kennedy interrupted with, 'How do you mean, hidden?'

Amelia 'For some unknown reason Frank hasn't had a drink in front of me for nearly two years.'

Keith Fletcher , 'Do you know why?'

Amelia 'I think he was too embarrassed and ashamed to. He had gone into a clinic to sober up a couple of years ago and after he came out of the clinic, he's never drank in front of me. I can't think of any other reason.'

Norm Kennedy 'Where did he hide his booze, do you know?'

Amelia 'Oh. I found a couple of his hiding places, but as soon as he discovered I had pinched them, the bottles I mean, he'd find another hiding place. For all I know there could be a dozen bottles hidden all over the place right now. Once when we lived in another house, there was a bottle of vodka in a glass cabinet. I used to keep an eye on it to make sure it was still there. Until one day I noticed that the seal had been broken, he'd obviously had drunk the vodka and filled the bottle with water. He's a cunning bugger, but then I can be a bit thick at times.'

They both shook their heads at me, I'd like to think that they were thinking that I wasn't thick but they could've been thinking God how thick can you get?

Keith 'Do you drink Amelia?'

Amelia 'No, very rarely I might have an occasional Gin Squash, but generally I don't. I don't like the taste of most alcoholic drinks especially beer, it's too sour.'

Both Detectives laughed

Amelia 'Obviously you pair don't share my opinion.'

Norm nodded

Keith 'You're not far from wrong there.

Amelia 'Anyhow, I went around to Mum's place with the kids and I was only away about an hour, when I got back, Frank was as blind as a bat.'

Norm 'Was he staggering drunk?'

Amelia 'No not quite, but not far from it.'

Norm 'How many beers do you think he would have had?'

Amelia 'Your guess would be as good as mine for all I know, he could have mixed his drinks. I know for a fact that he's had Vodka with beer on occasions, and I'm almost certain he's had a go at metho as well.'

Both Detectives nodded

Norm 'What happened then?'

Amelia 'Well when I saw that he was half shot, I told the kids to behave themselves and I started to prepare the table. I got the ham out and asked Frank to cut it for me. I'm pretty useless with a knife. I usually cut myself if I attempt to slice meat up. Anyhow, he cut it up and I distributed the slices out on the plates. Whilst I was dishing out, he went to the fridge and brought out a bottle of beer. I was surprised at that.

Keith 'Did he say anything to you when he took the bottle out?'

Amelia 'Oh he had been bitching whilst he was cutting the ham, and he said something about going around to his boss's home, because there was a party going on there. He was trying to get me to bite, but I didn't answer him, no matter what I had said, it would have been the wrong thing. When he got the beer out, he said, 'Oh well. I think I'll have a beer" I think it was his way of goading me into saying something about his drinking and also I think it was his way of saying, what do you think about that?

Norm 'Did you say anything?'

Amelia 'Well I guess I looked surprised, but I can't remember if I said anything. I'm sure if I had, there would have been a blue then. He poured a beer and drank it fairly quickly, and then he went into the bedroom. I continued to dish out the rest of the food and I called the kids and Frank when it was ready. Frank came out and he had changed his clothes. He was wearing one of the shirts I had given him for Christmas. I looked up and said 'Are you going out?' and he replied, 'Yep. I told ya, I'm going to a party.' I got really annoyed about that, because the kids had practically begged me to stay down at my parent's home for the day, but I thought to keep the peace, it would be better for us to come home and try to have a family Christmas with Frank.'

Keith 'What happened then did the argument start then?'

Amelia 'Argument it was more like World War Three. I said, 'Christ, if I had've known you were going out, I would have stayed down at Mum and Dad's place and had Christmas there.' Well. That was enough fuel for his fire and it was on for young and old. One thing led to another and he even had the audacity to tell me not to raise my voice to him. Mind you, he was screaming top note himself. Anyhow, he came over and grabbed me by my throat and he clouted me across the head. I fell on the floor and was crying and the kids started screaming. I told them to get out of the room and they ran into the living room. Frank picked me up by the hair and started to thump me about.

Somehow, I managed to get away and I went into the bedroom to get a tissue to wipe my face. When I came back out, he was standing between the doorway of the kitchen and the living room. I walked out and sat in the lounge and I was crying. Frank ordered me to shut up, and I told him that I couldn't. I just couldn't stop sobbing. He took a flying dive at me and knocked me down onto the floor and he just kept hitting me and hitting me and hitting me.

As I was telling them what had happened, I was crying almost uncontrollably as I remembered my ordeal.

Norm 'Would you like a glass of water?'

Amelia 'Yes thank you.'

I attempted to stand up and Keith jumped to his feet,

Keith 'I'll get it for you, you just sit there.'

As he walked away

Amelia 'I'm sorry for being so silly I don't usually carry on like this. I don't think I've ever cried so much in my life before, as I have in the past twenty-four hours.'

Norm 'No, you're alright. You've done very well so far.'

Keith returned handing me a glass of cold water.

Keith 'There you are.'

Amelia 'Oh thanks.'

After taking a mouthful and swallowing it gasping

Amelia 'That's better, my throat was as dry as a bone, come to think of it I haven't had a thing to eat all day.'

Keith 'Do you want something to eat?'

Embarrassed,

Amelia 'Oh no thanks. I couldn't stomach a thing after what's happened, I just remembered that I never did get around to eating, that's all. I can't even remember if the kids ate either for that matter. Poor little buggers.'

As I took another sip of water,

Norm 'Do you feel up to continuing?'

Amelia 'Yes, I'm right, now, where was I?'

Norm looked at his notebook. I hadn't noticed until then that he had a notebook. And I wondered if he had written everything, I had said into it. He looked up and smiled

Norm 'I'm flat out reading my own writing.'

He seemed to realise that I had just noticed the notebook and he added, 'Oh, I'm just jotting a few things down every so often, for when I write out my report.'

I nodded, but not really understanding, I couldn't help wondering what his report would say.

Norm 'Frank kept hitting you. What happened then?'

Taking a deep breath

Amelia 'Claire came over and was pleading with him to stop and Frank was like a maniac. He picked her up by her arm and leg and flung her across the room and she landed on the lounge and bounced off. I screamed, "You fucking bastard, you could've killed her."

I thought he had broken her back because she was lying there screaming and not moving. As soon as I called him that, he kicked me in the tailbone and I rolled onto my stomach. Christ it hurt.' Then I heard Vivian yelling and I looked up and Frank had pushed her onto the ground and he punched her in the face and kicked out at her. I threw myself onto her to protect her, and Frank punched me again. Vivian got up and I told her to get Heather and Claire and run for it, meaning out the front door. They were too frightened to move. I got to my knees and crawled over to the lounge and Frank went to Claire and screamed at her to shut up. Then he started to walk towards the kitchen. I stood up and tried to carry Claire to the front door but Frank ran through the room and blocked us from going out. He ordered them to go back and sit on the lounge, and they did. Then he turned on me again, I begged him to stop. I just couldn't take any more and he laughed and said, 'That's right bitch, you beg, because I'm your master.' I was completely exhausted and practically fell on the ground and crawled over to the lounge. Frank went back to the kitchen and poured himself another beer. I wanted to run, but I knew that I couldn't. I just sat there trying to think out a plan to get out, as soon as I could get my strength, if I ever got it.'

Norm 'How did you get the knife?'

Amelia 'Frank had ordered me not to move so I sat there for oh about five minutes while he abused me my hands were sopping with sweat just as they are now.' Showing both detectives the palms of my hands my palms were bright red and the perspiration was oozing out of the pores. Without hesitating I blew my breath on my hands whilst I wriggled my fingers. And as I've done on numerous occasions, I wiped my hands down the side of my shorts.

Amelia 'Believe it or not they often get worse than this. They were worse when I was sitting here with Frank abusing me. The only way I can really ease it a bit is to run them under cold running water. I asked him if I could wash my hands and he said, 'Okay, providing you don't get out of my sight.' So, I went past him and went to the sink. I washed my hands and I looked around for the tea towel. It was over on the bench near the stove. When I picked it up and wiped my hands, I saw the knife had been underneath it. Frank was pouring himself another beer and as I dropped the tea towel down, I picked up the knife....

Norm Kennedy sat forward in his chair.

Norm 'Right, now I want you to think carefully, Amelia, what were you thinking at that precise moment?'

I took a sip of water and frowned

Amelia 'I think I was wishing him to get out,'

Norm 'Was that all?'

Amelia 'Yes, I think so Oh. I was also wishing how I could get to the back door, but I didn't want to leave the kids in the house with him.'

Norm 'Did you think, I'll kill this bastard?'

Norm Kennedy's voice had changed, instead of sounding sympathetic, he sounded as if he was accusing me.

Without hesitation, I said in a very offended tone, 'No. I just wanted to get to safety I was terrified of what he might do next.'

His voice not so aggressive

Norm 'What happened then?'

Amelia 'Frank saw me holding the knife and said come on bitch, if you're game enough.'

Norm 'What did you do then?'

Amelia "Get out before I kill you, ya bastard."

Norm 'Did you feel that you wanted to kill him then?'

Wiping the perspiration off my face.

Amelia 'No, I wanted to torture the bastard. I just wanted to give him a dose of his own medicine.

Keith 'How far away from you was he?'

Amelia 'He was still near the doorway and I was near the stove, that'd be about three feet wouldn't it?'

Keith 'About that, did he come towards you?'

Amelia 'No he never moved other than his hands he stayed in the same position. He just kept taunting me to have a go. I walked towards him until I stood directly in front of him and I held the knife up in front of my chest.'

Norm 'Where was the head of the knife?'

Amelia 'About an inch away from his stomach.'

Norm 'Was it near his naval would you say?'

Amelia 'God. I don't know I was looking at his face. I know my hand was shaking, I was shaking all over.'

Norm 'Were you excited?'

Amelia 'Jesus. You've got to be kidding, I was nearly shitting myself, and I was so scared.'

Norm 'What were you scared of?

Amelia 'HIM.'

I nearly screeched the word. I took a deep breath.

Amelia 'He had this peculiar look on his face as if he was playing a game it was as if he had a surprise in store for me.'

Norm 'How do you mean?'

Amelia 'Oh you know, as if he was waiting for me to make the first move and he would win the game with his counter attack.'

Norm 'Go on.'

Amelia 'He said, 'Go on, go on, you're not game are you, and he held his hands above his head and he stuck his stomach out. I ... I felt a sort of twitch in my hand.'

Norm 'Your hand moved you mean?'

Amelia 'I ... I don't know, it was a sort of sinking feeling as if my hand moved without me feeling it.'

Norm 'Did you know that you had stabbed him at that stage?'

Amelia 'No I didn't know, I thought the knife may have, but I wasn't sure. There was no force it was like as if the blade had sunk into thin air.'

Norm 'How far did the blade penetrate?'

Amelia 'I honestly don't know I just cannot remember. I don't remember pulling the blade out. I didn't think it had even gone in. One minute he was standing there then he was staggering into the living room. It happened so bloody fast I just can't remember.

As I was talking to Norm, I put both hands to my forehead and pushed my hair back off my face and stretched my neck backwards in an effort to think harder. Then I fell back on the lounge and gave out an exhausted moan. I shook my head slowly from side to side as if I was giving a negative answer to an invisible person.

Norm 'What happened then can you remember?'

Amelia 'Yes, I put the knife on top of the cupboard near the living room doorway.'

Norm 'Where was Frank had he gone into the living room did you think you had stabbed him then?'

Amelia 'No I had put the knife down and I was just about to gesture to Vivian to come into the kitchen so that we could all go out the back door.'

Norm 'But you said before that Frank had staggered into the living room, surely you must have realised then that he was hurt?'

Amelia 'No, Frank's one of the best actors I've ever met, one day I accidentally tapped him across the mouth like this. I gestured a light smack across my cheek, mouth and nose, with three fingers honest to God you would have thought I'd planted a haymaker on his face. He'd often over dramatize situations.'

Keith 'When did you realise that he wasn't acting?'

Amelia 'Vivian ran into the kitchen and said 'Quick, Mum, he's bleeding' and I said 'Are you sure? Vivian said, 'Yes, there's blood everywhere, you've stabbed him, Mum.'

Heather and Claire came in screaming that he was bleeding and vomiting. I ran to the phone and started dialling triple zero. I told the kids to go downstairs and to stay out of the way. I got through to the operator, I didn't know you had to speak to an operator and I just gave my name and address. She kept babbling, 'What service do you want?' and I said 'Ambulance. Then Frank slammed his fist on the phone and disconnected the call.

Norm 'What happened then?'

Amelia 'I had to struggle to get the receiver off him and I then had to force his hand off the cradle of the phone. He was bearing down as if he was on the toilet and the blood was spurting everywhere. I said, 'For Christ's sake you fool, lie down on the floor or you'll bleed to death. The stupid bastard stood there laughing. He was obviously in great pain, but then he pushed his fingers into the wound as if he was trying to make himself bleed more then he said, 'I'll show you how good I am.' and he picked up his glass of beer and swallowed every drop.

Norm and Keith's mouths were agape and they both shook their heads in disbelief.

Amelia 'By this time I was dialling again he tried to stop me but he ended up sliding down and he lay on the floor. The operator answered again and I had to give her a full explanation why I had hung up. The stupid bitch wasn't going to put me through to the ambulance for a minute she told me that I was a crank call. Then I rang Dad and told him to hurry up here.

Norm What time did you stab him?'

Amelia 'I don't know, I wouldn't have a clue, what's the time now?'

Keith 'Ten to five.'

Amelia 'God I honestly don't know. You'd have to check with the operator, she'd have to register the time she got the calls, wouldn't she? It was only a minute or so before I rang her the first time. Then it was at least another four minutes before I rang her again. It could have been two o'clock or half past, I just don't know.'

Keith 'What happened after you spoke to your father?'

Amelia 'I was only talking long enough to tell him that I had stabbed Frank and that he was in a bad way, and that I had rung the ambulance. He said that he was on his way and I hung up. I turned to Frank who was lying in a straight line directly behind me. I grabbed a cloth and started to mop his brow but he told me to piss off. I told him not to be so stupid and he said, 'If you want to do something for me pour me a beer.'

Norm (in a disbelieving tone0 'He said what?'

I nodded in disgust.

Amelia 'Yeah, he asked me to pour him a beer can you beat that?'

Norm 'Christ.' turning to Keith he said to his partner, 'You couldn't beat that with a stick.'

Keith just shook his head in total disbelief.

Norm 'What happened then?'

Amelia 'I took his shoes off him and undid his belt and trousers I don't know if I did the right thing or not. I remember reading somewhere that if a person is in distress to remove any tight-fitting garments. I couldn't take his shirt or trousers off. I wouldn't even try to. So, I just took his shoes off and I think I packed the tea towel under his head to sort of try and relieve the pain. I guess that was a bit dumb, but I was panicking. I get a bit confused when I panic.' I shuddered as

I remembered. 'I know he was vomiting stale grog and bile and that made me almost vomit on him.'

Norm 'How long did you have to wait for the ambulance?'

Amelia 'Oh. It could have been five to seven minutes, but it seemed a hell of a lot longer.'

Norm 'Who arrived first the ambulance or Gordon?' Keith asked.

Amelia 'They arrived together the police car was directly behind the ambulance. I couldn't do any more for Frank, and besides, he kept telling me to piss off. So, I just paced up and down until I saw the Ambulance. I ran out to let them know which house to come to.'

Norm 'When they came in, what did you do?'

Amelia 'I showed them to the kitchen.'

Norm 'Did you say anything to them?'

Amelia 'Yes, I said, 'I've stabbed my husband, he's on the kitchen floor, you'd better hurry, I don't think he's going to pull through.'

Norm 'Did you think he was dying?'

Amelia 'God yes there was too much blood to be just a small nick.'

Norm 'Did you go into the kitchen then?'

Amelia 'No I stood in the doorway I didn't want to be in their way.'

Norm 'Where was Gordon?'

Amelia 'He went over to Frank and said 'How are you mate?' and Frank abused him and told him to get out because it had nothing to do with the cops.'

Norm 'He told Gordon that it had nothing to do with the cops?'

Amelia 'Yes Frank said something like 'It was an accident, I did it myself when I was cutting the ham, now piss off.'

Norm 'Are you sure of that, Amelia?'

Amelia 'I'm positive, you ask Gordon, because he came out of the kitchen into the living room and said, 'He's an aggressive little bugger, isn't he?'

Norm 'What happened then?'

Amelia 'You two walked in then.'

Norm turned to Keith 'I think we'd better get over to the hospital now, hey?'

Keith nodded and stood up. I looked at the two of them inquisitively and Norm told me that they'd take me to the hospital to find out what was happening. I gave them directions of a short cut to the hospital and I thought the drive over, was incredible. I still had difficulty accepting what was happening. I kept thinking on the journey, here I am, sitting in a car that's identical to the one

Frank and I own, chatting pleasantly to two men I had only met a couple of hours earlier. These men should be arresting me for stabbing my husband, but they're not. Instead they're talking and laughing with me as if we are old friends. Surely this can't be reality.

Norm 'Which school do the girls go to Amelia?'

Amelia 'Vivian goes to high school and Heather goes to primary school. Claire starts pre-school next year.'

Keith 'Do they like school?'

Amelia 'Vivian does, but Heather hates it, I think she's nearly as dumb as her mother. I pity the teacher who gets Claire though she or he will wonder what hit them.'

Both men laughed and I pressed the fleshy part of my left arm between my right thumb and index finger. 'I am awake.' I muttered to myself.

Norm 'What was that?'

Amelia 'Nothing, I was just thinking out loud. I can't believe what's happening.'

As we drove into the Princess Alexandra Hospital grounds

Keith 'Here we are, we'll park in the ambulance zone, I doubt very much that we'll get booked.'

Both men laughed and I stifled a grin

Amelia 'I wonder if I could get away with parking in a no parking zone? My car's exactly the same as this one even the colour's the same.'

Norm winked 'Don't push your luck too far I think that after today you've run out of a bit of luck.'

Amelia 'God and don't I know it.'

I stood aside as Norm spoke to one of the many doctors in the busy casualty department. Keith Fletcher was listening to the two men as they spoke to each other and he periodically nodded to me. I had no idea what the nodding meant, but I assumed it meant, so far, so good.

I heard Norm say, 'Do you want a word with her?'

He crooked his finger at me to come over. I hurried towards them

Doctor 'Your husband is still in surgery, Mrs Williams. We won't know anything definite until tomorrow morning, though he should be out of the theatre at about eight-thirty tonight.'

Amelia 'Do you think he'll pull through?'

Doctor 'I just don't know, Mrs Williams, I really just don't know. He's in a pretty bad shape, he's lost a lot of blood and the surgeons are doing everything they can.'

Amelia 'Thank you.'

I rubbed my face in an effort to bring myself out of this nightmare.

As the three of us walked out through the large, swinging hospital doors, an Ambulance pulled up alongside the Detectives car and a swarm of medical staff spilled onto the footpath. It just seemed a normal event to us as we got into the car.

As we drove back home

Norm 'He's not feeling any pain now, Amelia, he was unconscious when he arrived.'

For the rest of the journey, we travelled in silence. When we pulled into the driveway, I noticed the curtains in our neighbour's home, move slightly. I remembered back, to when the ambulance bearers were helping Frank down the stairs, I couldn't believe my eyes. The neighbours across the street had been having a Christmas party apparently, and they had all stood two to a step watching everything as it happened. I remembered thinking at the time, Bloody ghouls I should give them all a wave and ask them if they'd like some autographed photos as mementos.

I was feeling a bit braver by the time I got home, so I waved up to the 'closed' curtains and they moved slightly again. But there wasn't any breeze.

Norm (stifling a smirk) 'Will you be okay to get to your parent's home, Amelia?'

Amelia 'Yes thanks. I'll just go up and tidy up and go straight over. I'll be there within a half hour or so.'

Norm 'Okay, we'll come there later tonight, I'm afraid we'll have to get a statement from Vivian it's just a formality, you understand.' He had said it almost apologetically.

Amelia 'Righto, what time do you think?'

Norm 'Oh! As soon as the hospital lets us know how the operation went.'

I started to walk towards the stairs and I was surprised to see Norm get out of the car and he blocked my path.

Norm 'Are you sure you're okay?'

Amelia 'Positive.'

Norm 'You realise we could be charged for leaving you in charge of a dangerous weapon, Amelia?'

Amelia 'But you've got the knife, haven't you?'

Norm 'No, I don't mean the knife, I mean your car. You won't do anything silly like trying to commit suicide by driving over a cliff or something?'

I looked at him in total disbelief for a moment and then burst out laughing.

Amelia 'You've got to be joking, don't you? I don't have the guts to do that.'

Norm 'Good girl keep smiling we'll see you tonight.'

As they drove away, they tooted the horn and I waved goodbye to them. I turned, back smiling and happened to glance at my neighbour's window and the curtains moved again. I wonder what they're thinking. They're probably as confused as me bloody sticky beaks.

At seven forty-five that night, I replaced the receiver of my parent's phone into its cradle. I turned to Dad and Edith

Amelia 'He's out of the theatre and he's on the di list.'

Edith 'Oh thank God our prayers have been answered.'

The doorbell rang out in deafening tones.

Edith 'I wonder who that could be.'

Claire 'It's probly (sic) the coppers, Grandma.'

Dad 'Don't say coppers, Claire, you should say, policemen, darling.'

Edith 'C ... come in won't you please?'

Norm 'Good thanks, Mrs Long, is it?'

Edith 'That's right I'm Amelia's mother.'

I walked forward and formally introduced Norm Kennedy and Keith Fletcher to my mother.

Edith 'Have you had anything to eat?

Norm 'No not yet.'

Edith 'Would you like something there's plenty there?'

Norm 'Thanks, Mrs. Long don't go to too much trouble though.'

Edith 'Oh it's no trouble at all.'

She scurried off to the kitchen.

Norm (turned to me) 'He's out of surgery.'

Amelia 'I know I just rang the hospital I just got off the phone when you rang the doorbell. But he's on the di list, so it doesn't sound the best does it?'

Norm 'Well I spoke to the doctor about fifteen minutes ago. He rang me as soon as he'd finished in the surgery and he said that Frank would be in intensive care overnight and that everything is going to be okay.'

Amelia 'Well they didn't sound so convincing to me, a few minutes ago.'

Edith (came out of the kitchen and announced) 'It's ready when you are, Gentlemen.'

Norm (walking into the kitchen) 'Boy, that was quick.'

Edith 'A ham and chicken salad doesn't take much time to put on a plate, I'm afraid it's only the leftovers, we've already eaten.'

Both men sat down and tucked into the food.

After they had finished

Norm 'Boy. Mrs. Long, if that's the leftovers I'd have loved to have seen what you had to begin with I can't remember when I had such a delicious meal.'

Edith 'There's plenty more there.'

Keith 'Honest to God. I couldn't eat another morsel.'

Norm nodded in agreement.

I had been sitting in the living room, just shaking my head in disbelief as I heard my parent's making pleasant conversation with the two burly men. ' I do not believe this' I muttered to myself ' It's more incredible than a Science fiction story.'

Dad 'Vivian.'

Vivian came out of Edward's bedroom where all the kids had gathered to play a game. She glanced at me as if to say, I'm scared, Mum.

I assured her

'There's nothing to be frightened of, just answer the questions as best as you can, okay?'

She nodded and slowly walked into the kitchen. Edith came and sat down in the lounge with me, Dad stood at the kitchen door listening to Vivian and the detectives as they spoke. About a half an hour later, Vivian came out of the kitchen with a big smile as if she was pleased it was all over.

Amelia 'All finished?'

Vivian (still smiling) 'Can I go into Uncle Edward's room and play again?'

Nodding, I turned to the two detectives

Norm 'Well that about wraps it up folks we'll get back to you good people if anything develops. But I honestly don't think it'll be necessary.'

Turning to me he added, 'You see that you get a good night's sleep and try to forget that this ever happened.'

They bid us all farewell and as they drove away, I turned to Edith and Dad

Amelia 'Do you believe what's happened today?'

Edith putting her arm around me 'No my dear, I don't. We'll all wake up tomorrow and find out that it's only a dream.'

Amelia 'And pigs will fly.'

I went to the hospital a couple of days later Frank's ex-boss and apprentice (Steve and Brad) were visiting Frank. They looked at me with disgust and without saying a word they walked out of the room. No one ever believes the poor battered wife theory and I wasn't even going to waste my breath telling them I wasn't the baddie here.

Frank had more tubes hanging out of his body than I'd ever seen before or since. What could I possibly say? 'Sorry I stabbed you. Sorry you've bashed the shit out of me for years. Sorry that you're a little turd.' All I could do was shake my head in disbelief

Amelia (with a smirk) 'Ya wouldn't close your eyes ya bastard?'

Frank 'Nuh, I didn't want to give you the pleasure of sayin' well that's it.'

Amelia 'Is that all you've got to say?'

Frank 'Yep.'

With that, I walked out of the hospital with as much dignity as I could muster and I was bawling my guts out by the time I got to the car.

Less than two weeks later, I was in the kitchen when Frank came to the back door, I nearly shit myself.

Amelia 'What do you want?'

With a silly smirk

Frank 'I live here, don't you remember me? Besides I've got nowhere else to go and no money, I spent my last dollar on a cab getting here.'

Amelia 'Frank, you have got to be joking.'

Vivian and Heather were a bit wary, but Claire rushed over to him

Claire 'Daddy, you're all better, come and sit here with me and I'll be your nurse.'

I assured Vivian that I'd be all right and for her to take the other two downstairs. He was in enormous pain and had great difficulty sitting on the lounge chair. I offered him a coffee and we sat and talked about what had happened. He apologised profusely for what he had done

Amelia 'It's too late to apologise, Frank, you're an absolute madman in drink and you could have killed any one of us or for that matter, all of us.'

Frank 'Don't you think I know that? I've had almost two weeks lying on my back just thinking about what I did. I can't undo what I did, but I want the chance to prove that I didn't mean it.'

Amelia 'Frank, every time you've bashed the crap out of me, you're always sorry, until the next time.'

Frank 'I promise you there won't be a next time.'

Amelia 'You can say that again. I didn't stab you purposely, Frank, but I know one thing for sure, if anyone especially you, ever lifts a hand to me again, I wouldn't hesitate in doing it again.'

Frank 'Okay, fair enough, it's a deal then.'

Amelia 'There's no deal Frank, you lift your hands to me or the kids again and that's it.'

•••

Many Christmas Days have passed since then, and I don't think one day has gone by that I don't think of that dreadful day. I would like to say that we have been blissfully happy, because you read about 'blissfully happy' marriages in fairytale stories, unfortunately this isn't a fairy story.

We live in the real world, where shit happens to everyone. We've had more than our fair share of shit since then, and we'll probably continue to battle more shit in the future.

Now that you the reader have possibly come to the conclusion of whether I'm a goodie or a baddie I'd like to take you back in time to tell you the whole story of my life.

It's a hell of a ride.

Chapter 2

The Princess

I was born on a Tuesday in the summer of the early 1940's, the youngest of three children to Rob and Edith. Rob and Edith were the average middle-class odd couple. Rob a butcher by trade was an honest strict no nonsense man who expected perfection from all of his family. Edith, on the other hand, was always quietly spoken and although she'd never admit it, she allowed herself to be a doormat.

By the time World War Two broke out in 1939, they had been married four years with a son James aged three. Rob didn't hesitate joining the army and on completion of his training, twelve months had passed before he finally boarded the Queen Mary in Sydney on Friday 13th December 1940. He arrived in Cairo on Monday 10th March 1941, and Edith had given birth to another son, Edward, in February 1941. Fortunately, Rob was only away two years, unfortunately he had been sent home medically unfit with a depressed fracture of the skull. Reading his diaries, he had been a driver in the Supply Corps and was on call twenty-four hours a day to get the supplies through and help out whenever and wherever he was needed.

On Monday 22nd June 1942, he had volunteered to help put a fire out on board the ship The Royal Emblem, which had been bombed by heavy artillery. The fire was so intense that it was impossible to douse and the order was given to drop the hoses and abandon ship. Rob hadn't heard the order and when the other men dropped the hoses the force of the water gushing through forced him down a coal hatch. He awoke in the Alexandria hospital unable to move the left side of his body. The medical staff had given him little chance of survival, but after five months of rehabilitation he was finally sent back to Australia.

James and Edward were about as opposite as any siblings could be. James was seven when I was born and because of the age difference I looked up to him as my hero. He never seemed to do anything wrong, he was funny, witty, charming, good-looking and an all-round good kid.

Edward on the other hand was gangling, awkward, and unsure of himself and always the butt end of my cruel jokes. He being almost three years older than me, had a distinct advantage strength-wise, not that this really helped him. Let's face it, I was daddy's little princess and whatever I said was law.

The earliest recollection I have was standing on the front veranda trying desperately to pick a raw peanut out of my nostril. As there wasn't anyone else around, I must have been the guilty party to pushing it up there in the first place. I heard my mother yell in a shriek, 'Amelia don't pick your nose, you dirty little girl.' Knowing my temperament as it is now, I feel sure if I had been able to talk, I would have undoubtedly said something like 'I'm not picking my nose, you silly old fowl, I'm bloody dying.' I remember it seemed like an eternity before she realised what I was doing. Mummy told me I would have only been about eighteen months at the time, but my mother's memory was not totally reliable she's the only mother in history who could forget what day of the week her only daughter was born. For years I went through life believing I was born on a Monday, only to find out through a television show that it was in fact a Tuesday. If you tried telling this fact to Edith, I guarantee she would argue with you until the cows came home. At times I felt sure I was adopted, perhaps it's only wishful thinking on my part.

I was born with a deformity of my left hand and because of this I was literally given the run of the house no matter what I said or did, much to Edward's disgust and horror. Edith would invariably justify my indiscretions by stating, 'Amelia has only got four fingers on her left hand.' I can still see Edward's face seething with rage as I poked faces at him whilst I waved my left hand in his face. In actual fact my entire left arm is deformed it's shorter by approximately two and a half centimetres and is at least two centimetres smaller in circumference around the wrist. No one has ever been able to explain it other than to say it was a quirk of nature. My personal theory is: the deformity is a direct result of my father's depressed fracture of the skull which left a weakness down his left side. My middle finger is missing and my index and ring fingers are joined at the knuckle. Both fingers are webbed together up to the second joint making it impossible for me to move either finger singularly.

Somehow, I managed to survive my preschool years unscathed. Well almost.

There were a few minor problems. Like the time I got my grubby little mitts onto all of my mother's jewellery including a particularly pretty butterfly brooch which was mummy's favourite. I recall her saying over and over with a nervous urgency, 'Show mummy where you put the pretty rings and brooches, darling. I promise you mummy won't smack you.' Boy was I ever conned. I led her down the back stairs and very proudly pointed to the drain where the laundry water went. My mother fell to her knees and tried in vain to plunge her entire arm into the pipe. After a few minutes of fruitless digging she pulled her hand from the drain and planted it several times around my buttocks and legs. I bellowed like a wounded bull and issued my favourite threat, 'I'm going to tell my father.' That evening on hearing of my dastardly deed daddy reprimanded mummy for leaving the cupboard unlocked enabling me to get at the jewellery. I was of course, rewarded with being sung to sleep by daddy as per usual, with my favourite song.

There Once Was A Frog.

There once was a frog and a wooing he would go,

With another little frog he knew.

He happened to stray in a field one day,

Where a wee little mushroom grew.

Said he what a fine little home you would make,

Providing your shelter free.

If only you would grow in the night,

I'll bring my bride to see.

So, grow, grow, grow little mushroom grow,

Somebody needs you so.

I will call again tomorrow morn, said he,

And if you've grown bigger, then you'll suit, me.

So, grow, grow, grow little mushroom grow.

There was also the time I raided Mummy's cupboards where I discovered the tin of lovely chocolates that she kept hidden under her petticoats and panties. I ate up like there was no tomorrow. Oh, chocolate was wonderful. I didn't have to worry about being caught mummy and daddy were in the kitchen with Uncle Simon Uncle Jacob and Aunty Amelia, (daddy's two brothers and Uncle Jacob's wife). Mummy was obviously aware of the deafening sounds of silence and came in to investigate. Ha, you're too late I thought, I've eaten the lot there's not one chocolate left in the tin. Do you think she wasn't upset? She was near hysterics and yelled top note, 'Rob, quickly, she's eaten the Laxettes.'

'Jesus.' daddy yelled as he swooped me up and ran through the house.

For the next two hours of my life I was head down in an empty bath whilst they all took turns thrusting their fists down my throat in an effort to retrieve their precious chocolates. The miserable buggers, I couldn't for the life of me work out why they didn't just go to the shop and buy some more.

On another occasion, I recall going to tennis with mummy. I distinctly remember this particular day because I was given the honour of choosing the cake from the cake shop window to take to tennis for morning tea. Mummy pushed me along in my striped canvas stroller and I felt very important. Tennis was always a fun day and most of the ladies were nice. One big lady in particular whom I had to call Aunty Celia used to throw the ball for me to catch. I liked her because she seemed a nice, happy lady.

Mummy asked 'Which cake will I get darling?' They all looked so beautiful but the one with the wavy chocolate and white icing was definitely the best. I pointed to the most beautiful cake I had ever seen. What a magic moment, I had made the most important decision of my entire life. Boy oh boy. I couldn't wait until morning teatime. It seemed like an eternity before they finally served morning tea and I was so hungry.

We had walked all the way over the two big hills. Well, I admit I was sitting in my pram, but I watched the ground as mummy pushed me there. Mummy and Aunty Celia hit the ball for a long time and when I awoke, they said we were going to have a cuppa. I put my little hand up high when Aunty Celia asked 'Would you like some cake Amelia'?

I couldn't believe my eyes when I was handed this horrible looking cake in a bit of paper, it had yellow icing and what I suspected was fly poo-poo embedded into the yellow goo. God, I hated Aunty Celia, no wonder she was so fat and ugly, she ate little children's special cake and didn't even give them a taste of it the rotten old bag.'

I was about two years old and I recall sitting on the grass in the backyard. My grandfather had built a chicken coop and he kept chickens and ducks, so there was always a plentiful supply of fresh eggs. Mummy was hanging the washing on the line and she had let the duck and her ducklings out to have a wander around the yard.

I picked up two or three of the beautiful yellow, fluffy ducklings and had them sitting on my lap, I turned to pick up another one and I glimpsed a black and white thing from the corner of my eye. The next thing I remember was feeling an excruciating surge of pain on the right side of my face and I heard the mother duck quacking.

The pain on my face caused me to screech in absolute agony and terror. Mum came running as fast as she could, yelling at the duck to shoo out of the way. The mother duck had pecked at my right eye in an attempt to get me away from the ducklings. I was very lucky I didn't lose the sight out of my right eye if not the eye itself. Its bill had actually missed my eye but it had grabbed the soft flesh just below the eye and had broken the skin. For the following week I was as good as blind because my eye was completely closed and as black as the ace of spades and as large as one of the eggs the duck had laid.

I was all of three the day I happily skipped along the road alongside my mother, as she held my hand, she kept telling me how much fun I was going to have. I was blissfully ignorant of the torturous barbaric ritual this woman was leading me to. I never did like Doctor Crouch. He was mean, old, fat and ugly so I was more than a bit surprised when he greeted us at the door of this great big house with all the beds in it. I was even more surprised when Mummy undressed me and put my new frilly jammies on me, it wasn't bedtime. It wasn't even dark and I hadn't even had my breakfast.

Amelia 'I don't want that black thing on my face, it stinks, where's my father, I'm going to tell my father on you and he'll get the police.'

Dr Crouch 'Amelia wake up, it's all over.'

I wanted to scream but my throat felt as if it had been ripped out through my mouth, I glared around the room and there was that traitorous woman who called herself my Mother. Mother she didn't even know the meaning of the word what sort of person would allow their child to undergo such torture?

Doctor Crouch stood at my bedside smiling down at me as if he liked me, I stared back at him and gave him my famous go and drop-dead look. He bent forward and tickled me under the chin and said, 'You'll be a bit sore for a little while but you'll be able to have some ice cream and jelly for tea.' I smiled a whimsical smile as I lifted my head off the pillow then I chundered great globs of half congealed blood all over his lily-white coat. As my head hit the pillow, I closed my eyes and waited for death to overtake my body. I drifted into a heavenly haze with the soothing satisfaction that divine justice had been done.

I was about four, and I was quite a cute-looking chubby little girl who looked as if butter wouldn't melt in my mouth. I'd like to show you the photos to prove it but I can't so you'll just have to take my word for it. I was an absolute little bitch for never wanting my photo taken. Mummy would pamper, cajole and plead with me to smile for the camera, but the more she pleaded the more determined I became that I wouldn't.

There were a number of snaps of me dressed beautifully with my hair in ringlets and ribbons and wearing a crocheted dress. In each photo I have my arms folded across my chest with the worst scowl on my face. I can recall snarling 'NO. I won't. I don't want to, and you can't make me if I don't want to.' But mummy had a secret weapon of reversing the situation turning me from a defiant little devil to a blubbering mess. Almost every week, she'd say to me 'I'm going to die one day and then you'll be sorry.'

I detested her saying that to me and for years I constantly worried myself sick that she might die soon. We always had to call our parent's friends by the title aunty and uncle. We had no qualms about that, but we only had three real aunts and four uncles. 'Aunt' Peggy took me into town to the pictures and bought me a little Golden Book. I can even remember that I wore my dark green, velvet dress with the inlay of beautiful lace on the front of the bodice. People stopped and told Aunt Peggy and myself how lovely I looked. On returning me home, Aunt Peggy told Edith that I had been a perfect angel and she promised that she'd take me out again one day. She never did though and she never stopped calling me brat face, that's a name I detest to this very day. Funnily enough, I don't ever recall being naughty in her presence so my reputation must've preceded me. If I ever hear a child being called a brat, I usually stop them and say, 'Please don't call him/her that, they may grow up resenting you.'

Believe me, I get some very strange looks.

Chapter 3

Relatively Speaking

Aunty Amy and Uncle Jacob had two daughters, Diane and May. Uncle Simon who was divorced had a daughter, Jean who lived with her mother Flora. I can only vaguely recall meeting Flora and Jean when I was very young. Mum's brother Uncle Clive and his wife Denise had Betty, Bert and Nigel. Dad's half-sister Aunty Marge had two daughters, Joan and Yvonne by her first marriage. (Quite a few years later Aunty Marge married her second husband Michael they had a son, Simon, whom I've never met). As Joan and Yvonne lived in Sydney, I didn't get to meet them until we were adults.

Dad's mother, whom we all called Ninny, would visit us at least once a year and she'd tell us all about Joan and Yvonne. Ninny used to tell me that Yvonne was her favourite granddaughter, when I eventually did get to meet Yvonne, I learnt that Ninny used to tell Yvonne that I was her favourite granddaughter. Yvonne admitted to me that she had hated me because Ninny had said that I was her favourite granddaughter, funnily enough both Yvonne and I recognised many similar idiosyncrasies we both had.

Ninny had a rather perverse habit of showing me her closed fist whenever she thought I was being naughty. In doing so, she would point to her knuckles and say, 'See them dead babies?' Mummy would almost reel in horror whenever she heard that.

I didn't see Diane and May very often, but I liked them both. They were (and still are) nice girls, I was always on my best behaviour with them. Diane is James age and May is a couple of years younger than me. My fondest memory of Diane is going over to stay at their house one weekend. She painted my fingernails and put make-up on me and I thought I looked absolutely beautiful. I fondly remember playing dress ups with May whenever she and Aunty Amy came to visit us and we'd sit under the big mango tree where I'd pour cordial from the teapot of my kitchen tea set. We ate buttered arrowroot biscuits and Vegemite, peanut paste and strawberry jam sandwiches.

So, there were rare occasions when I behaved like a civilised human child.

'Aunty' Dot and 'Uncle' Stan had known Dad for many years. Aunty Dot had gone to the same school as Dad, she was only about four feet, eleven inches (one hundred and forty-eight centimetres) tall and Uncle Stan was about five feet, six inches (one hundred and sixty-five centimetres), both were hairdressers and were a typical Darby and Joan.

Uncle Stan used to like to get into the rum a bit and Aunty Dot didn't like him drinking so he'd hide the bottles in the garden or under the spare bed or wherever he thought she'd never find it. Whenever I'd go around to their place, she'd whisper to me, 'See if you can find them love.' She'd give me sixpence (five cents) to buy an ice cream and I'd be in my glory looking under anything and everything. I'd fossick in drawers and cupboards and as soon as I'd find a bottle, I'd race in to tell her. She'd get hold of the bottle, look at how much was there she'd pour half into the sink and top it up with water and put the bottle back in its hiding place. It was on one of these seek and find missions that I found heaps of MAN magazines with various other Post, Pix and Women's Weekly magazines in their spare room. I told James and Edward about the MAN magazines with the nude ladies in them and they both came to visit Aunty Dot the next time I went there. I had to innocently ask Aunty Dot if we could go and read the books with the cartoons in them in the spare room. She patted my face and said, 'Of course you all can, sweetheart.'

We all ripped into some good educational perving at what ladies looked like without their clothes on. I adored Aunty Dot and Uncle Stan they were the loveliest couple you could ever wish to meet.

My mother's mother and father lived with us in the big colonial house in a quiet street as did my father's brother Simon. James had not been able to say the word grandma as a little boy and he called her Mama. When Edward and I were born we carried on the tradition but over the years the word was shortened to Mum. Everyone else in the house except James and Edward called my mother Edith, and I guess at the time I couldn't see any reason why I couldn't as well.

Mum and Granddad were as different as chalk and cheese they were both very hard working. Granddad had owned his own slaughter yards when Edith was a little girl. He had bought all the land for one thousand pounds (two thousand dollars) and had sold it ten years later for the same amount when the abattoirs were introduced. The land was eventually subdivided some forty years later by a large real estate company who named the estate, The Wongabell Estate at Kenmore. Anyone who is familiar with that area will no doubt think that my grandfather was not much of a businessman. The area is now and has been for many years one of the most sought-after areas in Brisbane. Actually, he wasn't really a bad businessman he had a thriving little butcher shop, in spite of the number of people who owed him for their meat supply.

Mum and Granddad were softies and could never see anyone go without, but this didn't amount to a hill of beans to the abattoirs. When the abattoirs became compulsory, Granddad, along with many other butchers during those days, went bankrupt. Granddad didn't give up trying to make it big in the business world, he leased a shop in Adelaide Street, Brisbane but that failed so he leased another in George Street just around the corner from the city's police station.

Because his surname was Ireland, he got the idea of decorating the shop with shamrocks to encourage all the Irish police to be his customers. Even in those days the bagmen were in force. The cops would hand their Gladstone bags over the counter and expect Granddad to fill it to overflowing and most of them forgot to pay.

His opposition in those days was a fellow by the name of Scarborough so Granddad erected a sign outside his shop,

DON'T GO TO SCARBOROUGH,

YOU'LL GET TAKEN BY A SHARK.

Granddad never seemed to me to be a humorous sort of person, except when he was drunk but then he wasn't trying to be funny. The shamrocks and the play on words of the other butcher's surname proved he did have a side to him that I never saw. I personally think the funniest thing about my grandfather was his name. Rupert John Thomas Paulston Hayford Hallwell Ireland. What made it even funnier is the fact that he was born on Saint Patrick's Day and the name Patrick never got a mention. To add more humour to it, everyone called him Jock.

I would have loved to have been at Mum and Granddad's wedding just to hear the minister say, 'Do you Rupert Frank Thomas Paulston Hayford Hallwell Ireland take Maisy Leggott as your lawful wedded wife?'

She and Granddad arrived in Australia in 1912 on their honeymoon. Granddad had become so ill he had to be hospitalised for nine months with some mysterious illness. Mum had to find work by scrubbing floors to pay for his medical care. They went back to England in 1919 only to realise Queensland was where they wanted to stay for the rest of their lives.

My memory of Granddad is he was always working. When he wasn't going to the abattoirs that had financially crippled him, he was either going to or coming from someone else's home where he had cut their grass and/or worked odd jobs to get extra money for Mum. He used to call my grandmother Mum as well.

It was nothing unusual to see him walking along the street with a scythe over his shoulder and a hanky with a knot in each corner sitting on his head to protect his balding head from the sun.

One afternoon Edward and I were walking over to a friend's house and we saw Granddad coming down the hill towards us. We nearly killed ourselves with laughter at the sight of him. Instead of his hanky he had about six hats on his head. Edward ran to the other side of the street to avoid being seen with him. Edward had said to me, 'God, what's the silly old bastard got those on his head for? Before I got the chance to reply Edward had run across the road. When Granddad got closer to me, I greeted him

'Granddad, why are you wearing so many hats?'

Granddad 'I had left them all at different houses and I remembered to bring them all home today.'

I felt so sorry for him both for the fact that it was a hot day and him having to walk after doing a lot of hard work, but mostly because his own grandson refused to be seen with him. A number of years later when I was a teenager and living with him and Mum. I was hurrying to catch a bus and Granddad was walking back to the house after having a couple of beers at the Regatta pub. As he approached, I remembered the incident all those years earlier. I felt a pang of guilt at the time because I hadn't taken the time to really get to know him. I stopped and chatted with him and I can still feel his hand as he rested it on my shoulder. He looked so tired and old and the thought flashed through my mind, I wonder how much time you have left.

I became aware of a man pulling up alongside of us

Stranger 'Are you alright, love?'

Amelia 'Yes why?'

Stranger 'Is that old man annoying you?'

I saw the hurt look on my grandfather's face and I wanted to scream abuse at the fellow. Instead, in my best elocution voice I said

'This gentleman is my grandfather.'

And by Christ I was so proud of that fact I was near bursting.

I cannot leave the stories of my grandfather's scientific experiments go unmentioned. He truly believed that he should have been a scientist and was always concocting something. It was a Sunday afternoon and we had all been on a rare excursion to the beach, all of us except Granddad. On our arrival home Granddad was sitting on the front steps, he said, 'You can't go in there yet, I've just sprayed the place to kill all the cockies.' After about twenty minutes Dad became very angry and started to swear and demanded entry proclaiming that no one could keep him out of his home. Granddad reluctantly unlocked the door and we all entered the house only to be almost asphyxiated by a very pungent odour. When the coughing and spluttering settled down Edith gave out an unmerciful howl and for the first time in my life, I heard her swear, 'What have you sprayed my pots and pans with, you silly bastard?'

Granddad explained that he had concocted a formula that he knew would get rid of the cockies. Edith went off her brain showing everyone how the concoction had eaten holes in every aluminium saucepan she possessed.

Granddad was quite partial to drinking stout, but he never kept it in the refrigerator. Whenever he was asked why he kept it in the cupboard he would invariably reply,

'It might be in Mum's way in the fridge.' I've been told unchilled stout is a fairly potent beverage so it came as no surprise that Granddad had more than a passing interest in requiring a good hangover cure.

He sat at the kitchen table one evening experimenting with a number of ingredients, no one really took any notice of what he was putting in the glass. After about an hour had passed, he announced he had successfully made a good pick-me-up. I remember noticing that the glass was filled to the top with dark brown fluid, like Worcestershire sauce. He held it up as if to make a toast and drank the entire contents in one gulp. He placed the glass down on the table and promptly passed out with his face almost embedded into the wooden tabletop. He was still in that position eight hours later.

He couldn't remember the ingredients on his waking but we all feel certain that he would have put Castlemaine Perkins out of business if he had only been able to patent it. His favourite saying to anyone who would listen was, 'I'm full of science.'

Dad would give me an exaggerated wink and say, 'You're full of something, you silly old fool.'

One night, Granddad didn't arrive home from work and he hadn't been seen at any of the hotels he was likely to call into to have a quick beer. After checking the hospitals etc Dad decided to go to the watch house. The cop at the gate asked Dad what name was granddad likely to be under

Dad 'Jock Ireland.'

The Cop 'Sorry no one here by that name, there is an Ireland but Jock's not one of the many names this silly old bugger has given.'

Dad 'That's him, but don't ask me what his full name is I wouldn't have a clue.'

The policeman laughed

The Cop 'I thought he was having a go at me by giving a bodgie name.'

Dad was ushered down a long corridor to the cells, and to use Dad's description, 'There was old Jock hanging on to the cell doors like Jesus Christ on the cross.'

Dad reckoned he couldn't help but burst out laughing at the sight of him.

The Cop 'He's been there like that since four o'clock this afternoon and refuses to get off.'

Granddad explained later that the cell was lice infested and the other men in the cell had either urinated and/or messed their pants and he didn't want to be contaminated by them. He had been booked for being drunk in a public place, (namely George Street, Brisbane) but he hadn't had a drink since the night before and he was cold stone sober.

Granddad had had both of his legs badly broken in an accident many years before and had walked with a swaggering limp from that day on. The police hadn't bothered to listen to his pleas as far as they were concerned, he was a silly old drunken fool and they were doing their duty by getting him off the street.

Mum was a born worrier and there wasn't a day that went by she wouldn't be worried about one of us. It was nothing unusual to hear her say as she wrung her hands together, 'Where's it all going to end? 'To which I would invariably reply as I grew older, 'When we're in our pine box.'

Looking back, I felt that we all created or at the very least over emphasised dramas solely to get her worrying. I believe now she enjoyed worrying over us and we in turn enjoyed the security of having someone as caring and loving to be there for us. Granddad would often say, 'She's a mighty woman.'

Mighty wasn't the half of it, she was bloody fantastic.

Mum gave birth to three children. Cecil (1912–1987), Edith (1915–1999), and Wilfred (1916–1916), who survived seven short days. Wilfred had been a breach birth and I've been told in those days breach birth babies were very lucky to survive. Mum never spoke about Wilfred very often, but when she did it was always with reverence and a longing in her voice.

Mum was fifty-three when I was born and in the twenty-nine years that followed until she passed away, I think I aged her by at least eighty-five years. From as far back as I can remember she worked at two jobs for at least twenty years. From nine to five, seven days a week, she was assistant cook/kitchen hand/waitress at Mt Coot-tha Kiosk and from eleven to three, six nights a week she was a cleaner at the Wintergarden picture theatre. At least three nights a week she would indulge herself, Edith and I in an outing to the pictures. Nine times out of ten she would be out like a light before the interval. She was always very embarrassed to have fallen asleep during the picture and never failed to say when awakened,

Mum 'I'm not asleep, I'm just resting my eyes.'

Amelia 'You were snoring.'

Mum 'Oh. I wasn't, was I?'

Amelia 'Yes, the people in the back were complaining.'

Realizing I was fibbing she'd say, 'I may have dozed for a moment, but I was listening and I didn't miss anything.'

Occasionally the conversation would be,

Amelia 'Did you see the part where she fell on the stairs?'

Mum 'No I must've missed that part.'

Most times when she dozed off, her head would nod forward and every so often she would nod her head back and forth as if she was agreeing with someone's point of view.

One evening we went to Her Majesty's Theatre to see the Ice Follies live on stage. 'Aunty' Lilly had accompanied us and we were engrossed in marvelling at the tremendous agility of the performers when the lady sitting next to Mum leant over and touched Aunty Lilly on the arm

Lady 'Excuse me is this lady alright?'

We all nearly died of embarrassment and laughter as we looked at Mum who had her head tilted backwards as if she were looking at the ceiling and her mouth was wide open. Aunty Lilly nudged Mum and she awoke saying, 'I'm not asleep, I'm just resting my eyes. I couldn't contain myself and burst into gales of laughter.

Mum, Aunty Lilly and Edith joined in much to the astonishment of everyone around us.

Mum loved to gamble, she'd have a flutter on the horses every Saturday, but most of all she loved to buy casket tickets. In those days casket tickets were like lotto tickets.

It was nothing unusual for her to go into the city on the nights we didn't go to the pictures just to buy casket tickets from different newsagencies throughout the city. On these excursions I'd accompany her and I'd be rewarded with my favourite delights; chips, chocolates, peanuts, chewing gum, but most of all comic books. Never a week went by that I didn't get my favourite fare. I doubt that I ever missed a copy of Archie and Jughead and Edward never missed out on his copies of The Phantom.

There was only one gift that Mum promised to buy me that she never bought, a beautiful diamante purse. It was displayed in a showcase window in the wall outside Allan and Stark's in Queen Street. Every night when we went into the pictures or to buy the casket tickets, I'd stand in front of that window and admire that purse which to me was the ultimate in beautiful possessions. Mum would say, 'I'll buy it for you when you're old enough to appreciate and look after it.' No matter how hard I pleaded and protested I could never convince her I could look after it and appreciate it now.

Many years later

Amelia 'You never bought me that diamante purse you promised me.'

Mum 'You never became a diamante person. If I'd bought it for you would you have appreciated it and looked after it?'

Amelia 'No I would've said what would I want this crap and left it in my duchess drawer.'

She just looked at me with her I knew that, look on her face.

Apart from being a peacemaker, diplomat and thorough lady, her other claim to fame was her cooking. No one in this world could ever bake an apple pie like Mum they made your mouth water. She could make a delicious meal out of scraps in the fridge, her fruitcakes were superb but her lunch time snack was without doubt her masterpiece. Two slices of bread, cheese and tomato on an old toaster tray which she put under the gas burner, they just melted in your mouth. I'd give my eyeteeth to eat one right now.

Chapter 4

Schools In

Edith had an obsession with putting my hair in ringlet curls. Every opportunity she could grab me and keep me still long enough, she'd get white strips of old sheets and wind my hair around her finger and tie the ringlets in. I absolutely detested the painful ritual of having my hair brushed and combed and tied up, then having to sleep with the rags in my hair and having the knots combed and brushed the following morning. I put a sudden stop to that sort of carry on when I was about four.

Edith was busy doing something one day and I got her dressmaker's scissors and hacked my beautiful long golden locks off to the roots. I wasn't going to take any chances I even cut my eyebrows and eyelashes. That was probably the reason I decided I wanted to be a hairdresser. I can still hear her high-pitched screech all those years ago when she discovered what I'd done. Every person who ever entered our home from that day, I bailed up and I'd brush and comb their hair and give them different hair styles, until I was about twelve. That's when I found out apprentice hairdressers were paid thirty shillings (three dollars) a week, but shop assistants got five pounds (ten dollars). I made a conscious decision then that hairdressing was not the vocation I thought it would be.

I started school at the ripe old age of five years and one month at the local preparatory school. James and Edward attended the local state school but my mother had other plans for her precious daughter. I think I saw school as being an escape from my mother's clutches, probably if the truth were known Edith was just as pleased as I was when I started school.

Miss Cobbin was not only my teacher she was also my Sunday school teacher and I can't say I was overly impressed with her at all. I guess she was quite a good teacher and knew her job, but she wasn't pretty. In fact, she was very plain with straight black hair cut in the basin cut and she had long black hairs on her legs and a thatch of black hair under each armpit. I did extremely well in my first year at school so much so I topped my class and completed preparatory one, two, three and four in one year, instead of two years and I went into grades two and three the following year. I particularly loved reading and writing and Miss Cobbin would always call on me to read out loud to the rest of the class. I hated having to do sums and if I had've had my way I would've eliminated sums from the school curriculum. I bless the inventor who devised the hand held calculator but why oh! why didn't you invent it before I started school?

My memory of my two years there was mainly of a girl called Rita. She was from a poor family and her clothes were hand me downs and grubby and I felt sorry for her. Another girl called Roslyn who had long black plaits was sometimes my friend when she had some-thing I wanted but mostly I didn't like her. A pretty girl called Penelope whom I liked because she was nice, but I didn't want to like her because she was my rival who vied for the affections of Robby, my best friend's brother and my best friend was Carol. I've always had a great fear of heights and one of my proudest moments was the day I climbed the climbing frame all the way to the top which must have been at least a zillion feet high, well six feet (two metres) anyway. I remember that day as clear as if it was ten minutes ago.

Amelia 'Look at me, Miss Cobbin,, look at me.'

I was just so thrilled at my achievement and so was Miss Cobbin who glanced up and said 'Mmm, that's good, Amelia.'

Then the realisation hit me, I had to climb back down again and that took at least another ten or fifteen minutes.

There was also the day just before Mother's Day when I was chosen out of all the children in the school to be photographed by the photographer from the Telegraph newspaper. I was carrying a big bunch of chrysanthemums as I walked across the road outside the school. I bet our family is the only one in the world who still has that photo. A couple of years or so later Bullen's Circus came to Lang Park and Edward was photographed feeding hay to the elephants, Edward's photo appeared in the newspaper the following day. Edward always had to go one better than me.

The Christmas of that year was quite memorable. I had desperately wanted a walking doll. Not any ordinary walking doll, I wanted one like the shops had on display in the windows that wore real children's clothes. I have no idea where Edith was, but James, Edward and I took the opportunity of sneaking into Mum's bedroom in search of our Christmas presents. We discovered a host of goodies for the boys including a Hornsby train set and a full-size cricket bat in the wardrobe and under the bed, but there didn't seem to be anything for me. James juggled Edward on his shoulders and Edward stretched as tall as he could to peer at the many presents hidden on top of the old wardrobe. I couldn't believe my ears when Edward exclaimed, 'Amelia, you're going to get the walking doll. It's up here in a box.' I was so excited I nearly knocked James over as I jumped around the room. Edward almost toppled off James shoulders and when he clambered to the ground, I wanted to get on James shoulders to have a look at my beautiful walking doll. Unfortunately, we heard a noise and feared that Edith would cop us so we scattered as quickly as we could. I couldn't wait for my birthday and Christmas. When my birthday arrived, I was a bit disappointed at not getting my beautiful walking doll but I kept my feelings to myself, after all I only had a few more days to wait. Christmas morning arrived and we all dived under the tree and started ripping the paper off all the presents, I have no idea what other gifts I got, but I recall opening a box containing a baby doll that I brushed aside momentarily whilst I looked around for my big beautiful walking doll.

Edith, 'Do you like your doll, love?'

Amelia 'Where is it?'

When she pointed to the baby doll, I looked at it in total disbelief and cried my eyes out, Dad picked me up

Dad 'What's wrong, little darlin?'

He patted me and consoled me and I bellowed

'Edward said I was getting a walking doll.'

Dad 'When did he tell you that?'

Amelia 'When he got on James shoulders and looked on top of Mum's wardrobe.'

Dad patted me again and quietly told me not to cry and placed me firmly on the ground. He stood up, took his belt off, grabbed both James and Edward and gave them both a thrashing and walked out of the room with his face as black as thunder.

Another happy moment in the Long household.

I received my walking doll the following year. She wasn't as big as I had hoped, but she was beautiful none the less. Carol came over to play with me and my beautiful walking doll about ten days after I received my treasured doll. Carol was kind enough to break one of the legs of my doll by snapping it in half. I wasn't ever allowed to say anything about it to her mother and father because she was the daughter of my grandmother's employers at Mt Coot-tha Kiosk. Years later I heard that Carol became a lay preacher and a Pastor's wife. I trust she confessed her sin and cleansed her soul of the crime she did unto me before she took her vows.

I woke one morning during the Christmas school holidays and decided it was a nice day so it'd be nice to visit Carol. I ate my breakfast and took off telling Edith that I was going out to play. I didn't tell her a lie I just didn't say where I was going to play. She was such a spoilsport, if I had've told her who I was going to play with, she would have stopped me. I would've caught a bus if I had had any money, or if I had known where the bus stop was.

I'd been to Mt Coot-tha a few times in the car so I had a basic idea how to get there, keep in mind in those days the road up there was a bit rough. (I recently Googled the distance from our home up to Mt Coot-tha, 5.5kilometres) I can't remember how long it took me to get to there, all I remember was it seemed like an eternity. The perspiration was pouring off me and I remember being very thirsty and covered in dirt and cobbler's pegs when I made my grand entrance through the kiosk doors. Mum almost had a multi-coloured fit when she saw me no one could believe I had walked so far in the heat. I was given the royal treatment from Mum and everyone else at the kiosk, staff and customers alike for being such a brave little girl. Unfortunately, on my return home that night Edith didn't see me as being brave I went from being a heroine to a very naughty little girl in one giant leap.

I told you she was a spoilsport.

It was around this time, I guess I was about seven, when I stood on the footpath of Coronation Drive (also known as River Road) sticking my thumb up at every driver and pulling faces at them. I wasn't trying to hitch a lift I was giving them all rude signs. When Dad arrived home, he called me into his bedroom to have a little talk, you knew you were in big trouble when he did that.

Dad 'What were you doing down on River Road today?'

Amelia 'Nothing,'

I replied with all the innocence of an angel.

Dad Very patiently, 'Someone saw what you were doing and they told me, so do you want to tell me the truth or do you want to get into bigger trouble?'

I wasn't completely stupid and I figured I'd be better off admitting my crime. Secretly I wanted to get hold of the blabbermouth who had dobbed me in. I showed Dad the hand signal and the face I'd been pulling at the drivers.

Dad 'What does that mean when you put your thumb up and down in the air?' I looked around the room very embarrassed and coy

Amelia 'Do you really want me to tell you?'

Dad 'Yes, what does it mean?'

Amelia 'It means go and get fucked.'

Dad blinked, spluttered and coughed got to his feet and in total disbelief and said, 'I don't want you doing that or saying that word again because it's very, very naughty and little girls shouldn't say those things.'

I threw my arms around his neck and gave him a big kiss and a hug, he hugged me tight and we walked out of the room hand in hand. Everyone was waiting in the kitchen and I realised they had all expected me to get a hiding. James and Edward just rolled their eyes and shook their heads in total disbelief.

One of Dad's employers, Uncle Ray was a good friend of Howard Brown the radio announcer from 4KQ. Howard was in charge of one of my favourite radio programmes *The Sunday Mail Comic Club* , which curiously went to air every Saturday morning.

As a special treat Dad and Uncle Ray took me into the city to be in the audience of the show. They gave me a ticket for the lucky door prizes, the top prize was a beautiful ice cream cake. Every few minutes Dad and Uncle Ray would check the number of the ticket and tell me not to forget it, they kept on telling me to keep my fingers crossed in the hope I might be one of the lucky ones to win a prize. Surprise, surprise my lucky number was drawn out as the winner of the top prize, how lucky was I to win. Dad and Uncle Ray were over the moon with delight at my great fortune. All the way home they kept praising me for being such a lucky girl. Naturally, I was as pleased as punch to have gotten the cake, but I just had to burst their bubble by announcing,

'I'm awake up to you pair, I didn't win at all you both rigged it so that I'd get the cake.'

They both protested they hadn't rigged it, but even at the age of seven I could tell when two grown men were trying to stifle their laughter. The ice cream cake was delicious, but I was more intrigued with the dry ice it was packed in and I was very annoyed that I wasn't allowed to play with it.

I was taken to the local Catholic School and introduced to Sister Mary Mathias later to be called Mother Mathias who was the head teacher. I was enrolled into the school and became the first and only non-Catholic child in the entire school. The reason for my enrolment was sheer genius level thinking on Edith's part. She firmly believed that because my left hand was smaller than the right one it stood to reason it was considerably weaker and needed strengthening. She concluded the best thing for my hand was for me to learn to play the piano. Someone had told her that the nuns were good piano teachers. So, there I was at the ripe old age of seven years thrust into a strict religious regime to which I knew nothing about chanting prayers every half hour.

The bell would ring three times on the hour and we'd have to stand and recite the Lord's Prayer and three Hail Mary's. On the half hour, the bell would ring once and we'd stand to recite the Lord's Prayer. Twice a week I would be summoned to report to the music room to go through the tortuous procedure of trying to master the art of pianoforte. I hadn't been there very long when my music teacher, Sister Mary Leonard, convinced Edith that I should attend elocution classes as well. My five years of piano and elocution lessons certainly paid off in the long term. *Not* .

Whenever I get my hands on a piano, I invariably play a tortured rendition of Oh, can you wash your father's shirt and See the Pyramids along the Nile. I wouldn't know a crotchet from a quaver if you paid me a million dollars and the art of speech is such when the occasion calls for it, I can speak with a plum in my mouth. Fortunately, I have never had the occasion nor have I ever been able to bring 'How Now Brown Cow' into any conversation I've ever had.

As for my religious upbringing, I became every nun's target to try and convince me I should become a catholic. My observation: being a catholic meant one thing, going to mass at six o'clock every Sunday morning. My own personal religion was to sleep as late as I could every morning especially Sundays. I would tell all the nuns that I couldn't become a catholic because my mother wouldn't let me. Perhaps this was the reason when Edith won first prize of a towel and face washer in one of the many raffles the nuns made me sell tickets for, they decided to try and stop a protestant collecting the prize.

In my first year at the school I recall having to go into church to confess my sins. We all had to sit outside a row of three boxes in the back of the church and each child took their turn to enter one of the side boxes as soon as one of the other kids walked out. I was absolutely petrified of what might happen to me in the little darkened room. When I entered, I sat down as if I was on the toilet, I said a quick Hail Mary and then high-tailed it out of there as fast as my little legs could travel. I knew I'd done something wrong by the look of disbelief on all the other kid's faces, but I never did find out who or what was in the middle box. It could have been the devil himself for all I knew.

Edith received an unexpected visit from Father Murphy, the Parish Priest, in the early summer of my first year at the catholic school. She had been cooking the Christmas puddings in the old copper boiler. As you can imagine, standing over a boiler on a hot summer's day, she wouldn't be wearing an overcoat. Edith was appropriately dressed in one of her own creations which I guess was very daring in those days. She wore a floral homemade bra with matching shorts. Her hair was tied back with a scarf to keep it out of her eyes and off her face. Father Murphy's face almost hit the floor on seeing Edith almost naked. He introduced himself and Edith greeted him cordially by introducing herself. He didn't mince words and came straight to the point

Father Murphy 'Do you always dress like that, Mrs Long?'

Edith 'Yes, Father, I do when it's a stinking hot day like today, especially when I'm busy preparing the Christmas puddings over a very hot boiler'

Father Murphy 'Don't you think it's rather risqué?'

Edith 'No I don't, not in the privacy of my own home when I'm not expecting visitors. I think it's very appropriate attire and extremely comfortable for this humid climate, but I'm sure you didn't come here to discuss my clothing, Father, so how can I help you?' **Father Murphy** 'Mrs Long, it's come to my attention that you live here with two men and that you did not marry Mr Long in the catholic church even though he's a catholic.' **Edith** 'Yes, that's right, Father.'

Father Murphy 'Do you realise that you're not married in the eyes of God, Mrs Long, and living with two men is rather unusual to say the least wouldn't you say?'

Edith looked at him without batting an eye

Edith 'Father, it was my husband's decision not to be married in the catholic church as he doesn't believe in religion and I don't think it's unusual to have my husband's brother living with us. Especially considering that he's recuperating from having surgery for Tuberculosis.'

Father Murphy rather stunned by her frankness spluttered, 'Oh.'

Edith 'Now if you'll excuse me, Father, I'm a very busy woman and I do have other chores to attend to as much as I'd like to stand here and chat with you.'

She bade him a good morning and closed the door in his face.

All hell exploded when Edith retold the story to Dad, he ranted and raved, 'How dare those bastards come to my home and question my wife about me.'

He concluded by telling Edith,

'If he ever comes back again telling you you're not married you bloody well tell him to find another woman for me to marry in his precious bloody church and he can do my time in jail for bigamy.'

With all the disruptions of learning and reciting prayers, going to piano and elocution lessons twice a week, I had no interest in school by the end of my first year. I couldn't have given two hoots where the highest mountain was or how long the longest river was or where Rotterdam was on the map. I wasn't going to climb, swim or live in any of these places so what was the use of learning about them. As for arithmetic and algebra I was hopeless beyond adding the simplest of sums, but if nothing else I absolutely loved reading and writing especially doing compositions and we had to write a composition every weekend for homework.

Every Sunday night I'd sit at the dining room table and write an event to my heart's content. If I got nine out of ten for it on Monday, I was upset because ten out of ten was my usual grade and I was so proud of this achievement. Our next-door neighbour, Dotty, would come in to help me with my maths and geography, Mum used to give her five shillings, (fifty cents) to come and tutor me. Dotty did try to earn her money, but I wasn't interested in learning at all. Ironically although I hated maths, geography and history etc I now find that rarely a day goes by I'm not calculating something, I'd give my eyeteeth to visit every country in the world and I'm fascinated by historical events.

Even if I was remotely interested in learning, James certainly stopped any desire I had. He had begun learning to play the drums and every moment of his waking hours he tapped out a constant rhythmic beat on anything and everything. Every mealtime became a musical endurance for the entire family. Knives forks and spoons became the sticks and the crockery, glassware and condiment bottles were the drums and cymbals.

On Sunday nights when Dotty came to help me with my homework James would use our heads as the drums. If we were lucky, he'd only use his hands or fingers if we were unlucky, he'd use the real drumsticks. No manner of protest would stop him, his enthusiasm with his drum practice certainly paid off not only did he become a successful Jazz drummer (if only in his own home town) he also successfully taught a number of students including his own son.

In spite of constantly being harassed to become a catholic, I liked most of the nuns especially two of them. Sister Mary Angelina and Sister Mary St Angela were both kind considerate and very patient with me. Sister Mary St Angela was my particular favourite and I was her pet. Whenever she wanted something done like going to the post office or delivering a message, she'd always choose me to do it for her. She used to arrange the flowers in the church every morning and I made a special effort the entire year I was in her class to go to school early just to empty the vases and arrange the flowers in the church with her, she made me feel very special. The other kids weren't too pleased with me because of the special treatment. I used to sit in the front of the class almost under the blackboard in line with her desk. I could peel and eat an entire orange without her ever reprimanding me, but if anyone else so much as ate half a biscuit in the back row she'd punish them by making them stand in front of her desk for ten minutes. She would reward the good children with a boiled lolly and I got the lion's share of the lollies that year.

There were about thirty to thirty-five girls and five or six boys in my class for the five years I was at the catholic school. We all had our own little groups and stuck to our own group all the way through. Gabrielle, Nancy, Jenny, Margaret and I were as close as any school friends could be. Mostly Jenny and I were like sisters as we practically lived in each other's pockets, this concerned the teachers and my family for some unknown reason. No one thought that it was a good idea for us to be associating with each other and everyone seemed hell bent on keeping us apart. But the more they separated us, the more we were determined to be friends, we were inseparable.

It would be totally unfair of me to say that Jenny suggested one day that we should wag school. The honest truth is I can't remember whose decision it was and it really doesn't matter because we were both as guilty as the other. Both of us were only too willing to have a day off. We spent the day at Jenny's house because her mother was always out working, cleaning and ironing. Her father was a railway porter at Roma Street Station on the early shift and wouldn't get home until late because he'd go to the pub and get drunk every day. We sat around drinking cups of tea and eating biscuits and playing cards and other games and we sang all the pop songs as they came on the radio. Both Jenny and I had quite good voices and I really believe if we'd had a good private singing teacher, we could've become a singing duo. In those days there was no avenue for female singers in Australia let alone Brisbane, well none that we knew of anyway.

We both nearly had heart failure when a knock came at the front door. I scurried into Jenny's bedroom while Jenny went to answer the door. It was Byron Carney, the biggest dunce in our class, Sister Mary St Angela had sent him to find

out why Jenny wasn't at school. Jenny told him she had a sore throat and started
to cough, she asked him why Sister had sent him to her place

Byron 'Because I'm the only one who knew where you lived.'

Jenny 'Amelia knows, why didn't she send her?'

Byron 'Amelia isn't at school either.'

Jenny 'Do you have to go to Amelia's house?'

Byron 'Nuh.'

Jenny 'Tell Sister I'll be there tomorrow if my throat's better.'

Byron asked for a drink of cordial because he had walked from school which
was almost a mile and he had to walk back. Jenny gave him the drink and we both
thought he was never going to leave, when he did, we both collapsed into gales
of laughter.

As I write this, I've just realised that Sister St Angela sent the dunce of the class
to go on an errand. Maybe all the times she sent me on an errand she just wanted
to get the protestant out of her class.

I headed for home at about three-thirty and we'd worked out that if I walked
a particular route home, I'd get there at approximately my usual time. I got
to within five minutes walking distance from home when my father and Edith
drove past me in Dad's work van. They saw me and pulled up. I started to panic
because it was too early for Dad to be home from work. I thought God, I'm in
for it if they've found out that I've wagged it, but they greeted me with as much
love and happiness as they always did. I climbed into the van and kissed them
both and asked where they were going Dad said he had to make a delivery up the
road. We drove up the hill I'd just walked down

Edith 'How was your day?.'

Amelia 'It was alright'

Edith 'Only alright, what did you learn?'

Amelia 'Nothing much just the usual boring stuff'

Edith 'Did you go to music or elocution today?'

Amelia 'Yes, Sister Leonard was as cranky as she always is'

Edith 'That's unusual we thought you might have been sick or something'

Amelia 'Why?'

Edith 'Because you weren't at school at all were you?'

I knew there was no point in denying it because someone had opened their
mouth and I was convinced that Byron Carney must have seen or heard me
at Jenny's place. As it turned out it was an old battle-axe by the name of Mrs

McCaully who had seen Jenny and I going to the shop to buy biscuits. She was an acquaintance of my parents and had rung Edith at nine-thirty, bloody old busy body. I had visions of putting a rock through her window but I figured she'd see who did it. She was always spying on everyone from behind her curtains. I don't recall the punishment for wagging school so it couldn't have been too severe it was punishment enough getting found out. The shame of disappointing them and Sister Mary St Angela was punishment enough. Jenny and I had always been really nice to Mrs McCaully, up until that day. After that whenever we passed her house, we'd stick our fingers up in the reversed V for victory sign, but if we saw her in the street, we'd keep a good distance from her trying to make sure she didn't see us. But she probably did.

Chapter 5

The Brady Bunch

Edward and I were always looking for new and exciting adventures to be involved in. In all probability it stemmed from us being avid listeners to such radio programmes as The Adventures of Hop Harrigan, Superman, and Biggles. My all-time favourite show was Yes What, we called it Greenbottle after the main character. Listening to those programmes every afternoon was a definite must. The only time we missed an episode of any of the shows was when we went into 4BH studios to be in the audience of The Coca Cola Bottler's Club. The announcer was an absolute shit of a man who used to swear and abuse all the kids for no apparent reason other than he probably didn't like kids. Any kid that was well behaved was chosen to read the ads. Edward and I were always very well behaved and good at reading so we were nearly always chosen. It wasn't for the egotistical high or the prestige of speaking on the radio we just wanted the payment of lollies, ice blocks and drinks that were given out. We may not have been geniuses, but we sure as hell weren't complete dills.

All told in our street there were about twelve homes, but there were sixteen kids from three families. The White's across the road was a noisy household with eight kids but only the two youngest ones were James and Edward's age. Joey was one of Edward's mates and he was a gangling drongo of a kid whose only real interest in life was birds and getting into mischief. Frankie was a quiet sort of a kid like James and they used to muck around together a bit. The rest of the family Mary, Paddy, Peggy, Theresa, Una and Tony were between two and ten years older than James, so by the time we were all school age they were all in high school or going to work. Mrs White was a nice little lady but her husband was a big loud ex-cop who frightened his own kids when he yelled, so you can imagine how intimidated outsiders felt about him especially Edward and me. Sometimes Joey would invite Edward and me to play in his backyard and to look at all his pigeons. Mr White would come out and bellow, 'Youse bloody kids git on home or I'll take me belt off to youse.' We wouldn't argue, we'd be off like Flash Gordon and sometimes he'd chase us yelling, 'Go on and if youse come back again I'll boot youse in the arse.'

Yes, he was a good Irish Catholic. Full of love and good cheer to all.

When he died, he was laid out in the front room for all the relatives and friends to come and view the body and pay their last respects. I went over because I'd never seen a dead'n before but they wouldn't let me into the front room so I was a bit annoyed about that.

The Ballard family lived next door. Mr Ballard was a funny man who originated from Scotland. He'd been in Australia for years but his accent was as broad as if he'd arrived off the boat the day before. I liked him as he was always nice to any kid who came to play with his five kids and more times than not, he was always half shot. He'd often burst into song, singing all the old Scottish songs. I remember him always trying to make me laugh by saying funny things. One particular day he was trying to teach us all to talk with a Scottish accent, 'It's a broad brit moonlit nit tonit, always remember, it's not the way you wriggle your tongue it's the way you wriggle your R's.'

Mrs Ballard was also a funny person not funny ha-ha though, she was funny peculiar. Peculiar in the sense that she would cross to the other side of the street with her head down, rather than say hello to any of her neighbours. She was friendly enough once you got talking to her in her own home but if you saw her five minutes later in the street, she'd avoid you like the plague.

Hannah, the eldest of the family was exactly one month younger than Edward. She had olive skin, black hair and brown eyes and was a very attractive girl with a lovely dimpled smile. People who didn't know her mistook her to be Italian or of foreign extraction.

Dotty was eleven months older than me she was fair skinned and rather plain. She had a habit which I have always detested she bit her nails right down to the base of the quick. She was mousy and most like her mother in nature.

Lorna was about two years younger than me she had olive skin and black hair and she too was a timid sort of person yet with a rebellious streak which came to the fore as she got older. You'd be forgiven for mistaking Lorna as being part Aboriginal except for her lips which were very thin giving her a rather downtrodden look about her.

Annie was about two years younger than Lorna and was blonde, blue eyed, fair skinned with an attractive face and bright personality. She was a lovely girl.

Jimmy was about a year younger than Annie and he too had olive skin, brown eyes and black hair. He was a typical little boy who annoyed the living daylights out of all the girls, but he was a nice enough good kid.

Everyone who saw all the Ballard kids together could not believe they were related. Someone, I don't remember who, told me that Mrs Ballard's grandfather was a South Sea Islander hence the dark skin of Mrs Ballard and three of the kids. Or as Edith succinctly put it, 'They're throw backs' Whatever that meant.

Lorna was an easy target for my terror tactics, it's not a bit of wonder she became rebellious in her teenage years I probably drove her to it. I'll never forget the day that I lured her onto our front veranda on the pretext of wanting to play a game with her. I had one of Edward's cowboy guns hidden behind my back and when she came onto the verandah, I pointed it at her and told her it was a real gun and that I was going to kill her. I thoroughly enjoyed watching her squirm and I made her beg me not to kill her. She pleaded and cried but I told her it wasn't good enough and I cocked the barrel and shot her. The poor little bugger almost died too but of heart failure. I swore her to secrecy to never to tell anyone or I'd load the gun with real bullets next time.

Living directly behind us was a little girl about two years younger than me, her name was Stephanie and the only time I ever saw her was from a distance. She was never allowed out to play. I used to call out to her through the cracks of the old grey wooden paling fence but her mother wouldn't allow her to stay out talking for very long. When she first arrived there, she had her head shaved and wore a scarf around her head in the same fashion that the blacks in the cotton fields. I asked her why her head was shaved and she said she had ringworms. Edith held the theory that she had nits and told me to keep away just in case I caught them.

Hannah, Dotty, Lorna and I all went down to the Brisbane River near the Regatta Hotel one particular afternoon. I think we were sailing paper boats on the water or some such silly adventure. Hannah waded into the river, I think she must've thought it was only waist deep all the way across and all of a sudden, she went down like a stone. I thought Lorna was going to have a heart attack she panicked so much she screamed her lungs out for Hannah to come back. The current started to take Hannah further out and I began to fear that she'd end up drowning. Fortunately, though she managed to get back to the bank and drag herself out. It was an incident that could quite easily have ended in tragedy. Even at my tender age I learnt that day to never underestimate the power of the water.

I rather fancied myself as being a brownie and saving the world from itself so I joined up and went along every Saturday morning. Edward went to scouts and he seemed to enjoy them more than I enjoyed the brownies. Edith and Mum took great pains buying the uniforms and sewing our first patches on. To use Edith's terminology, 'Once the uniforms had been bought, she became a nine-day wonder and stopped going.'

I had to beat a hasty retreat from Brownies when I found I had to tie knots in pieces of string and ropes. My hands were nearly always permanently wet with perspiration and I always managed to make the string and rope a sodden mess. The same with my piano playing, great globs of dirty sweat would splosh all over the keys as I was trying to play. I always had to stop and wipe the keys with my hanky which was completely useless because more often than not it was saturated from me having wiped my hands on it before I started the lesson. I can't ever remember a day in my life that my hands weren't hot and sticky and I'd have to blow on them or wipe them on my dress or handkerchief. It's eased up in the last few years but even as I write now probably thinking about it, my hands have been dripping wet and my feet have joined them in sympathy.

Every so often Hannah, Dotty, Lorna, Edward and I would arrange a secret rendezvous at midnight in our special hidey hole. We'd raid the ice box and kitchen cupboards getting as many goodies as we could get our mitts onto and we'd have our midnight feasts and plan all sorts of adventures. None of which ever saw the light of day. I think we'd all read too many Enid Blyton books about The Famous Five and The Secret Seven because our planned adventures always included looking for smugglers.

The best part about those rendezvous was that our parents never knew about them.

I went to tap dancing and ballet classes for a while I was the only kid who could cheat in ballet class. We had to sit on the floor with the soles of our feet together and press our knees onto the floor to enable us to learn how to do the splits. I'm double jointed in the upper part of my legs and I found this to be a particularly painful exercise. So, I'd sit in my comfortable position with the tops of my legs together all the way to my knees with my lower legs facing outward. Anyone who has seen me sitting like this nearly break their legs trying to copy me. It's something like frog's legs trying to swim.

The best part about my tap-dancing days, immediately after my dance class I'd go to the pictures. I'd always be a couple of minutes late so I never had time to change my shoes. I'd run down the aisle of the pictures in my taps making a hell of a din during the first cartoon or the serial. Everyone always knew when little Amelia Long arrived at the pictures. A few times after I'd stopped going to dance classes, I'd wear the taps just to make a grand entrance and annoy the other kids as I ran past them click clacking all the way to the front row. I got more lollies that way. I wasn't above picking up the many Fantales, Jaffas and Minties off the floor that the other kids pitched at me when I sat down.

Every Saturday afternoon in the Long household the black roller blinds were pulled down and sometimes a blanket would be draped over the heavy curtains as well so no one could see inside the house as they walked past. Dad and Edith would sit near the telephone taking many calls and writing messages on the top of the marble phone table. Dad would give us kids two shillings (twenty cents) every Saturday and say, 'Hop Out.'

Two-bob was a lot of money in those days. It was nine pence (approximately seven cents) to get into the pictures and that left us with one shilling and three pence (about twelve cents) to spend. Most kids only had three pence (two cents) or if they were really lucky six pence (five cents) to spend. So, the Long kids thought they were millionaires. It never dawned on us to try and save some of the money. Who'd want to put money in a tin when there were lollies and drinks to be bought?

Dad and Edward never got on terribly well, Dad was always very strict in his ideas but he seemed to be more so with Edward. One Saturday for lunch we had brawn and salad, I managed to hide the fact I didn't eat mine but Edward wasn't cunning enough he just announced, 'I don't like brawn.' Dad saw red and made him sit and eat it, Edward forced himself to eat and made himself vomit which only angered Dad more and he copped the strap into the bargain. I used to have to tell Edward what to say or not say in front of Dad to save him from getting into trouble. I could get away with blue murder but Edward would get into trouble for the least little thing. Most Saturdays on our way to the pictures Edward would tell me how much he hated Dad he'd say,

'Bloody old bastard, I'll kill him one day.'

One particular Saturday we got down the street and Edward started to hop on one leg he hopped for about twenty feet (seven metres)

Amelia 'What the hell are you doing, you simpleton?'

Edward 'Come on, hop.'

Amelia 'What for?'

Edward 'That silly old bastard's always telling us to hop out so I'm hopping.'

Another Saturday which was memorable we arrived home from the pictures and Edith told us to be extra good and quiet because Dad was in a very angry mood. When we asked why

Edith 'The police raided us.'

I had no idea what was going on

Amelia 'What for?'

Edith 'Never mind it's nothing for you to worry about.'

James 'Did they get anything?'

Edith 'No.'

Amelia 'What didn't they get?'

Edward 'Shut up'

Amelia 'No you shut up. Tell me what the cops didn't get or I'll tell Dad I know what you're all whispering about.'

That's when I learnt that Dad was an S.P. Bookmaker and the messages he wrote on the phone table were the bets. Dad had never wanted us to be in the house on Saturday's just in case he was raided. If we had've been there and they found the bets on the premises the likelihood of us kids being taken away and put in a home as wards of the state was quite on the cards. The police apparently came in through the windows like bull elephants and frightened the living daylights out of Granddad and Edith. Dad was too smart to get caught he just wiped the marble table top with a wet cloth and erased all trace of the bets which were written in pencil. He probably lost a few quid that day and that's why he was in such a bad mood. Dad got caught on another occasion but not by the police. In those days there was no direct broadcast of the southern state races, the races were always delayed by about five minutes. On this particular occasion Dad received a phone call from one of his regular customers a couple of minutes before the start of every Sydney and Melbourne race and placed rather high stakes on each winner. At the end of the day when he realised how much the fellow had won, he knew he'd been conned somehow. He had no alternative other than to pay up and shut up. He later found out the fellow had gained the names of the winner by telephoning two friends in New South Wales and Victoria, that's when Dad found out that the southern races were delayed broadcasts. It was a costly lesson of two hundred and fifty pounds (five hundred dollars) a king's ransom in the early fifties. That doesn't sound much in this day and age but when you consider a weekly wage in the 1950s was about ten pounds (twenty dollars), imagine how you'd feel if you lost six months wages in one afternoon.

I think Dad's interest in horse racing must have had a big influence on his three kids because none of us showed any interest whatsoever in wasting money on the nags except for the Melbourne Cup, of course.

CLEAN HANDS, CLEAR CONSCIENCE

Chapter 6

Urban Terrorists

Near our street was a Railway Station, beyond that was a big eerie building that would've made an excellent location for a monster's castle in a horror movie. It was Legacy House where all the orphans of World War Two were housed. The building has been altered with extensions and improvements in recent years and is now a Hospital. Occasionally we'd play in a little park alongside Legacy House which we called the oval. It was large enough to have a football game or a basketball court but for some unknown reason the Legacy kids weren't allowed to play there.

Many years later I met a young woman about the same age as myself and she told me she recognised me as being one of the kids whom she always wanted to play with. How cruel of the powers that be denying children the basic rights of little kids to interact with other kids simply because they forgot what it was like to be a kid themselves.

The Mulvihill family lived down around the corner from us opposite the railway station. John was James age, Michael was Edward's age, Ray was about a year younger than me and Malcolm was approximately three years younger than me. John and Michael were brutes of kids. They'd always muck up any game that was started and if they didn't get their own way, they'd start a fight especially with Edward. Michael was a fair little swine. Ray was a fairly quiet kid and Malcolm was the one whom we all felt sorry for, when he was four, he climbed up to look out the window he overbalanced and fell on his head on the cement footpath twenty feet (three metres) below. Well that's what we were told. He never seemed to have any control of the mucus in his nostrils because of the damage caused by the fall and he always seemed to have permanent green candlesticks streaming onto his top lip. Recently Ray (now deceased) has been named as the murderer of a cold case of Sharron Phillips back in the 80's. It makes me wonder now if he pushed Malcolm out the window.

At the top of the hill of our street was a twenty-foot high brick wall, which encompassed a huge area of land where the Carmelite Monastery was built. No one was ever allowed in there because the Carmelites had taken a vow of silence.

Savage dogs patrolled the land and anyone walking down the street near the fence would invariably be frightened almost half to death by the dogs barking at them.

All the kids would stir the dogs every time we went anywhere near the fence by calling out or whistling. As soon as the dogs began to bark, we'd toss sticks and stones over the fence and yell at them to shut up.

On the other side of the Carmelite Monastery lived another boy of Edward's age Billy McCulkin, Billy made Michael look like the Archangel Gabriel. He was such a bad egg of a kid that Dad forbade us kids to have anything to do with him. The police came around to tell Dad that Edward, Joey and Michael were in Billy's company whilst Billy ran around the streets with a 303 rifle shooting birds from the trees. In 1974 Billy's wife and two daughters mysteriously disappeared. Since then two associates of Billy were convicted of their murders.

Billy's name has been linked to the Whiskey AU Go Go fire which killed 15 people.

We had the choice of the paddock at the bottom of our hill, the Legacy oval, the local park or the chalk dump opposite Stephanie's house to play in. The chalk dump was good to get as much white chalk as we wanted for the rest of our lives. I have no idea where the chalk came from or why it was dumped there, but it was something that none of us kids ever thought about. We just accepted it as a natural part of everyday living to have a chalk dump in the street behind our home. Eventually it was cleared and the Chinese Association was built on the site.

The paddock was a good flat area of land to play tiggy or throw a ball to each other, but as it was only at the bottom of our street, it was too close to home. Our mothers could call us home to go to the shop or to have our bath early so we all preferred to play in the park. Not only was it further from the house, it had a hill with a rough road we could drive our billy carts down full pelt. There were plenty of trees in the park to play hide and seek and on the other side of the park was the football oval and swings, seesaw, roundabout and slippery slide. Best of all we loved to spy on the couples who parked in their cars near the railway line. It was surprising the many cars that would park there in broad daylight. We'd give the poor buggers heaps by peering into the cars and when they told us to P.O.Q. we'd take off and grab a handful of goolies (stones) and toss them at the hapless couple until they drove off. Sometimes but only occasionally the men would give us all the change in their pocket and we'd leave them alone in peace.

There was one odd-bod who'd often come into the park to talk to us kids. He wasn't a child molester or anything like that he was just a poor simpleton who loved kids. He always wore a rope around his waist with about six tennis balls hanging off it on pieces of string. As well as the tennis balls, he had a spoon dangling on a piece of string. He spoke with a foreign accent and would repeatedly tell us,

'Childrik drenk planty mulk,'

Whenever he came around, we'd stop whatever games we were playing to talk to him. He'd stay for about ten minutes and then keep walking to wherever he lived and we'd resume our game.

At the top of the hill on our side of the street lived a wonderful old lady by the name of Mrs Ward, all the kids liked her and it was obvious that she loved kids. She would often give biscuits to the kids but none of us went to visit her specifically to get biscuits. We all genuinely liked her and it was a pleasure to go and talk to her. Directly across the road from Mrs Ward, next door to the White's house lived an old battle-axe by the name of Mrs Stanley. We all called her old mother Stanley among other names. As much as Mrs Ward loved us kids old mother Stanley hated us double fold, we in turn felt likewise. She had an orange tree in her backyard that none of us, that I knew of at any rate, ever raided. But that didn't stop her from putting big chunks of glass and barbed wire along the top of her fence obviously to stop the kids from jumping the fence.

Her house was always locked up like a tomb and on one particular summer day I decided on the spur of the moment as I walked past to remove the glass and put it in the gutter. I removed about thirty pieces of the jagged chunks placing them in the gutter. Out of the blue, the back door flew open and old mother Stanley stood peering down at me like a vulture. I got such a shock seeing her I nearly shit my pants. I said in my best elocution voice, 'Hello, Mrs Stanley, look at what some naughty child has done. They've put all your glass in the gutter and I'm just putting it back on the fence for you.' I placed all the pieces of glass back and took off for the lick of my life. I told Edward and Joey what had happened and they decided to get even with her for me. They both went over to the park and found a dirty old used frenchie (condom) that had been left on the ground. They picked it up and wrapped it in a bit of old newspaper and just before dark they placed it on the footpath just outside her front gate.

The following day after checking to see it was still there, we all played out in the street just waiting and watching to see if she would find it. At long last she came downstairs to do a bit of gardening. We all scattered to strategic hiding places behind lamp posts, up trees or crouched behind parked cars, anywhere as long as we could see what she'd do. We didn't have to wait long she came out of her yard as fast as her old legs could move and she had a little garden fork in her hand which she stabbed the frenchie with. She carried the offending frenchie at arm's length and scurried over the road and stood below the Carmelite Monastery fence. To our astonished delight she tossed the fork and frenchie as hard as she could, high up into the air and straight over the fence. The dogs howled their obvious disapproval as we all gathered around absolutely pissing ourselves with delight. Whenever we walked past old mother Stanley's place after that, we'd always yell out,

'Ya filthy old bitch, we saw ya throw the frenchie over the Carmelite's fence.'

Then we'd take off as fast as we could. It wasn't long after that she removed the glass and barbed wire off her fence and we stopped calling out to her.

Our other neighbours were Professor and Mrs Robinson they had two sons who were studying at University to become Medical Practitioners. Professor Robinson was a Professor of languages and taught at the Queensland University at St Lucia. Both he and his wife were lovely people and spoke with an upper-class English accent. They were the type of people whom you would expect to be stuck up and toffee nosed, but they were the exact opposite. They would always stop and talk to all of the kids and ask us how we were. We all liked the Robinsons and even though they were elderly we could never work out why the Professor carried a walking stick. He didn't appear to need it to help him walk and he seemed to be quite capable of walking up and down the street without the aid of a cane. We came to the conclusion that it was a hollow stick where he hid millions of pounds worth of diamonds. For ages we'd sit around and plan how we were going to hit him on the head to knock him out and pinch the cane full of diamonds. We figured we'd have had enough money to live happily ever after. I know it sounds as if we were completely nuts, but I guess in the fifties kids had very vivid and wild imaginations.

The Robinson's sons were as crazy as loons. It was nothing unusual to see them running around the backyard in lap laps beating tom toms as if they were Africans or natives from New Guinea. We'd often sit at our window hiding behind the curtains and watch them. Looking back, I think they must've discovered something stronger than marijuana, failing that they really were a couple of basket cases. (they both became Drs.)

I've often wondered if their antics were the cause of James telling Edith and I to stay in the kitchen one day because he wanted to show us something. He could draw any painting or cartoon character with extreme accuracy. When I was in the fifth grade Sister Mary Leonard asked the pupils if we knew anyone who could draw. I volunteered James name and before we could blink, she had a canvas backdrop sent to our home which James transformed into an absolute masterpiece. He copied a picture of a Gondolier in a gondola in Venice from a picture in the grade five reader onto the thirty-foot long by eight foot (ten metres by three metres) high canvas. It was absolutely fantastic and it was used as the backdrop in our school concerts. I've often wondered whatever became of the painting.

Anyhow Edith and I were waiting in the kitchen expecting to see one of James works of art when he came prancing through the house stark bollocky naked with his penis hidden between his legs. He did a pirouette around the room with his hands above his head like a prima ballerina and said, 'Do you think I'm too sexy for films?' Edith and I cried with laughter for about ten minutes. He was about seventeen at the time and I was ten and I thought the sun and moon shone out of him. He was a wonderful brother to Edward and me. Ever since I can remember he called me Fatso because I was always quite plump as a kid when I went down to six and a half stone a few years ago he continued calling me Fatso. Unfortunately, it's a name I've grown back into. James had charm, personality and the funniest sense of humour. Edward on the other hand was very manipulative and often quite cruel to me. I know I was verbally cruel and abusive to him on many occasions, but his behaviour went beyond being mean and unkind. Edward sexually assaulted me not long after my eighth birthday and for many years I carried the burden of guilt blaming myself. The nuns had taught us that any wrong doing in the first seven years of our lives was not classified as a sin, but any wrong done after our eighth birthday was sinful and if we didn't confess it to the priest, we would pay for it in hell. I also felt that if I'd told Dad he would be extremely disappointed in me and I didn't want to lose his love for me. I was convinced he wouldn't love me anymore. I thought too that he'd kill Edward (I wouldn't have minded that) but I most certainly didn't want Dad going to jail for murder. I eventually told my mother five months before she passed away, although she knew I was speaking the truth, I know she had difficulty accepting it because I think she felt that she had failed in her duty to protect me. I've lived with a certain amount of self-loathing since. For some inexplicable reason even though I hated Edward for what he did to me, I still felt a certain amount of sympathy for him because he never seemed to be quite right in the head. He was eventually diagnosed with schizophrenia when he was nineteen and I guess in a way I made his illness as his excuse. Since 1999 after Edith passed away, I've finally grown to forgive him for what he did. I guess in a way I've come to realise that his behaviour is no longer my responsibility regardless of his mentality. I hope by my making this public, others will learn from my mistake of not speaking up all those years ago. Unfortunately, it caused a rift between James and me. I think perhaps James didn't want to believe it happened or maybe he may have thought the problem will disappear by ignoring it and me.

...

Most of the girls in my class were nice kids, but there were two or three that needed a good boot up the backside. One of the nicest girls in the class who was extremely popular with everyone, suffered the most tragic episode any child could possibly endure. Her father, a prominent businessman, blew his brains out one night on the front lawn of their beautiful home. I overheard Dad tell Edith the night it happened. I went to school the following day and told most of my classmates. The nuns got wind of me spreading the news and rang Dad and told him that I'd been telling the other kids. He apologised to the nuns, they in turn punished me with the strap and warned me that I was not to spread the story any more. They told the class that I had made the dreadful story up and that the fellow's death was from a heart attack. It's a mortal sin for a catholic to suicide so it had to be hushed up and the little Protestant was made out to be a liar, that was my first taste of hypocrisy and I can't tolerate it now any more than I could then.

As I grew older my face became a horror story on its own, I had gold fillings in my front teeth but even that didn't improve my looks. One fateful day whilst I was at a football match, I rubbed my tongue over my teeth and to my horror I discovered a hole where my gold filling should have been, I found it had landed in my lap. I was ushered back to one of the cruellest dentists in the world, Dr Rolland. He hated me with every fibre in his body, but not as much as I hated him. Whenever I was in the chair, he would pinch my cheeks hard and lift my mouth open by putting his fingers in my nostrils. He'd force my mouth to open by just pulling my nose back as hard as he could with the tips of his fingers still in my nose. He'd purposely hit my gums with the drill and make them bleed, but only enough to make them really sting there was never any permanent damage. It was pointless telling my parents because let's face it, he was a grown up and grownups just didn't do things like that.

So, it was with great trepidation that I went to have the gold filling reinserted. I sat in the chair and before I could even get the chance to open my mouth to avoid any nose pulling and cheek pinching, he said, 'Open your mouth, you little bitch.' That was it. I was determined not to until I was good and ready. He pressed his thumb onto my top lip forcing it against my teeth. I could feel the pressure of the skin being flattened and I knew it wouldn't take too much more effort on his part to bust the skin. He released the pressure allowing me to curl my top lip up in a sneer like grimace showing my teeth clenched in a snarl. Then he put the tip of his thumb under my overlapping top teeth and proceeded to force my head back until my head felt as if it was resting on my back. I dropped my lower jaw and his thumb went into my mouth so quickly that it didn't stop until the knuckle joint was inside my mouth. That's exactly where I hoped it would stop and that's when I slammed my teeth together as hard and as fast as I possibly could. I held it there for what seemed like an eternity, the taste of his thumb wasn't the best, but by Christ I enjoyed that mouthful as if it was fairy floss melting on my tongue. I thought he was going to backhand me, but he must've realised he'd gone too far and that any more torture would have caused bruising. He put the filling back in and told Edith that if it came out again, he wouldn't be able to replace it without extensive treatment he said it was because I had too much acidity in my mouth. No need to be told the filling fell out again about a week later and Edith rang to make another appointment to have the extensive treatment. She was told that it would cost fifty pounds (one hundred dollars) which was more than a month's wages and that was totally out of the question. There wasn't any second opinion in those days so instead I was taken to the Children's Dental Hospital at Mr Rolland's recommendation whereby every tooth with a gold filling was extracted. I came away with five teeth missing and I had to wait almost six months before I received my first set of dentures. Over a period of time the wire clasps on those dentures wore holes in my other teeth and four years later they too were extracted. I've still got all my lower teeth and quite a few dentists over the years have remarked how strong they are. None of them have been able to understand how or why I should have had my upper teeth extracted. I guess nibbling the mongrel's thumb was a big no-no.

Edward and I used to fight like cat and dog just about every day of our lives, yet if he got into a fight with Michael or Billy, I'd be in like Flynn to throw a few punches and kick their groins. I remember him getting done over like a dinner at his school one day and he told me about it that night. I felt so sorry for him and I vowed I'd get the two boys responsible at the swimming baths the following Sunday. Both Brian Butler and Ross Saxon were there when we arrived and they obviously planned to do Edward over again.

What they didn't bargain on was his kid sister, I came out of and anything I could think of I did. I was like a rabid dog and both boys took off as fast as they could. Just about every kid within a five-mile radius was there that day and if any kid so much as looked like picking a fight with Edward after that, he'd warn them, 'I'll go and get my sister onto you.'

Edward's nickname at school was Longa the Donga, my nickname at the baths was Little Longa and whenever we arrived at the baths after that fateful Sunday the kids would call out, 'Longa the Donga's here, oh shit watch out here comes Little Longa.'

Most of them would stay up the deep end, because even though I was a fairly strong swimmer it was too deep for me to tread water for very long. Dad had insisted we all learn to swim and for two mornings a week he'd drive me to the baths before school to have swimming lessons. I loved swimming and I still do, but six in the morning was a bit much. Edward was an exceptionally good swimmer, but his lessons were after school nearly every afternoon. I don't know that he was good enough to go into the Olympic Games but he certainly could beat the living daylights out of any other kid as far as swimming was concerned. He had been kept in at school one afternoon and when he was finally let out, he started to run down the street to get to his swimming class. It had been raining earlier in the day and as he ran, he skidded on a wet patch on the side of the road. He lost his balance and ended up in the gutter with a fractured elbow. Not only did it stop him from swimming that season it stopped him from ever swimming competitively because his elbow was left with a permanent kink in his arm. I used to tell him that his elbow matched his brain because both of them were warped.

I too had a slight accident whilst practicing my diving expertise one afternoon. The only problem was I wasn't diving into the water. For that matter I didn't even have my swimmers on, I was showing off in front of Lorna telling her what a good diver I was. I was standing on the edge of the footpath that led to our front steps from the gate. I faced the steep hilly side of our front yard standing on my toes I lifted my arms up behind my back and in perfect formation, I thrust them straight out in front of myself whilst tilting myself forward. I got so carried away with my own importance I couldn't stop the inevitable and I plunged head long down the hill. I slid the entire length of the yard approximately fifty feet, (fifteen metres) and landed heavily on my skull as I came to an abrupt halt when my head hit the fence. It served me right for being such a smart arse.

We always had a few chooks or ducks kept in a big pen down alongside the back fence. They were supposed to be in the pen, but Edward and I would let them out to run around the yard.

We both loved all sorts of animals but it wasn't our kindness that caused us to let the chooks out. The pen was covered by a big choko vine, which provided us with the perfect place to hide and smoke but we didn't smoke cigarettes. We were 'smarter' than that we used to smoke thin brown hollow reeds that grew near the chook pen. Your guess is as good as mine as to what damage we were doing to our lungs. In all probability we were in fact ingesting chook and duck shit into our bodies. I suppose the reeds weren't any better or worse than tobacco anyway.

Chapter 7

Weekends and Holidays

One night we got a call from Dad's cousin, Muriel, and her husband, Albert, who lived in Sydney. They announced that they and their three children would be arriving in the next two hours or so, to stay for a three-week holiday. Dad seemed to be pleased, he hadn't seen his cousin for years, but he was the only one who was pleased though.

Dad's relatives had a bad habit of lobbing on the doorstep unannounced and ended up staying for months at a time. I remember an uncle Ned and an uncle Ted. One of them only had one arm and the other used to whistle all the time. They'd both settle in for lengthy stays at different times much to our disgruntlement. So, when Edith woke us at about 9.30pm and said we had to play musical beds to accommodate an entire family we were most upset to say the least. To make matters even worse the whole family were turdy toads as far as us kids were concerned.

Claire was a bit older than James Jimmy was slightly younger (about halfway between James and Edward's age) and Raymond was a year or so younger than me. Jimmy was the only one that any of us liked. They made a regular habit of coming up each year for about five years afterwards then Muriel and Albert came on their own. Each year without fail, I'd say to Edith, 'Tell them to bugger off, you can't stand a bar of them, so I don't know why you put up with them. They're nothing but bludgers.'

But she would never admit to not liking them. She'd just suffer them in silence and be a good hostess and slave to all their beck and call.

Muriel had had a bowel operation and she had to wear a colostomy bag for years. The smell of her used to make us all want to vomit. Normally we would've had a great deal of sympathy for her, but she wasn't a very nice person. What I like to describe as having the personality of a cane toad. I, of course, got up her nose by refusing to call her aunty. I maintained she was not my aunty and I had no desire to call her that.

She thought children should be seen and not heard and that naughty children should be sent to bed with their bums smacked. That was her favourite saying to me and I'd look at her in disgust

Amelia 'Well, why don't you give your own kids a belting then?'

Dad 'That'll be enough of that.'

Amelia 'Well, it's true, and anyway when are they going home, because she stinks?'

Aunty Lilly worked with Mum at Mt Coot-tha Kiosk and lived in the flat next door to Aunty Dot and Uncle Stan. When I was about three, she had commented to me that she'd like me to come and live with her because I was such a good little girl. I didn't need any encouragement I immediately went into my bedroom put a couple of my panties, socks and a dress into my little cardboard school bag, walked out and told her I was ready. When Edith told me that I couldn't go I threw myself on the floor and had a tantrum, declaring my undying love to Aunty Lilly. A few years later I overheard my father telling Edith he'd have to get rid of my beautiful blue cattle dog, Ballie just because Ballie was supposed to have bitten the postman. Ballie wouldn't have hurt a fly and I told them so. Dad wouldn't hear a bar of it, he'd made up his mind and Ballie had to go. I packed up all my junk and wrapped it in an old sheet and staggered down the street dragging the sheet filled with all my worldly possessions with Ballie trotting alongside. I had to stop near the paddock and sit in the gutter to catch my breath. Edith was totally oblivious to my departure and I was feeling rather pleased about my escape.

As I sat there, I planned to go to live with Aunty Lilly, I knew she'd take Ballie and me and look after us, even if she didn't, I'd go to Aunty Dot's place. All of a sudden, a cab came down the hill and I knew the jig was up. Mum had arrived home from work and saw me sitting there. She asked me what I was doing and I told her that I was running away to share myself with Aunty Dot and Aunty Lilly. (Wouldn't they have been pleased?) Poor old Ballie was taken away from me and probably put to sleep and I cried my guts out.

I can't remember a period in my life when I haven't had at least one pet to love and care for. I remember every one of them and their idiosyncrasies but I'd be writing forever if I were to mention them all. Suffice to say they were all a major part of my growing up and still are. I unashamedly confess I have adored them all. So, imagine how many heart-breaking weeks I've had throughout my life, when they've died and either been skittled or baited by some nut case. If there aren't any animals in Heaven I'm not going. I'd rather trust a savage animal than some humans any day.

Our local shops consisted of three grocery stores, a chemist, a butcher shop and a cake shop. An elderly man and his wife ran Cullum's corner shop. I think Mrs Cullum may have been a Fuzzy Wuzzy, she had olive skin and very tight little black curls which was always cut very close to the scalp. They were both lovely people, but very slow in walking and their shop was always so dimly lit it was always difficult to see anything properly. That's what gave Edward the bright idea of cheating them out of ice creams drinks and lollies without actually stealing them. Edward was a cunning little sod he got all our pennies and half pennies and painted them with silver frost. In a dimly lit shop to elderly shopkeepers who had poor eyesight they looked like one shilling and two- shilling pieces (ten and twenty cents.) Poor old buggers, they never stood a chance.

Mr Noble, the chemist next door to the Cullum's shop, was also quite old and was renowned for his concoctions for all ailments. He had his own mixtures for whatever ailed you and you could guarantee that it would do the trick. He was a nice enough old coot and never did me any harm, but I found out many years later he molested at least two girls whom I knew very well. I can't for the life of me understand how they allowed it to happen because apparently, he made it a regular habit. He probably knew not to try anything with me because I doubt that he'd have been able to concoct a cure for his mangled balls and massacred penis.

Mr and Mrs Alley (I now believe thinking back that their name was in all probability was spelt Ali as they too had olive skin) were the owners of the second grocery shop. They were also very nice people and Mum would often give me one shilling (ten cents) to get a bag of broken biscuits from them. Honest to God the brown paper bag would be approximately nine inches deep and six inches (twenty-two centimetres and fifteen centimetres) wide and the bickies would be overflowing.

Directly next door was Harry Steven's Butcher shop where Dad had worked for a number of years. Harry's first wife had died less than thirty minutes before I was born and this apparently had given me star status in Harry's eyes. He'd often say to Edith, when one person departs this world there's always another person to take their place and as far as he was concerned, I was his wife's replacement. Whenever I went into the butcher shop I was always treated with the utmost kindness from the old man.

Across the road was Griffith's corner store. It was the 1940s version of a supermarket whereby you could get your own groceries off the shelf and pay as you left. Not everyone liked going in there, they preferred the shopkeeper to serve you at the counter and get the groceries for you. I liked going in there to buy the foot-long American bubble gum and the giant size liquorice straps. Edward would often ring Griffith's store

Edward 'Is that Mr Griffiths?'

Mr Griffiths 'Yes'

Edward 'Are you on the tramline?'

Mr Griffiths 'Yes'

Edward 'Well you'd better get off because there's a tram coming.' He'd hang up and roll around the floor screaming with laughter. Another trick of Edward's was to ring the taxi company about eleven o'clock on a Saturday night after coming out of the pictures. He'd order six cabs in a Chinese accent for Mr Who-Flung-Dung and company at the Chinese Association. He and Joey would then hide and watch the cabs pull up honking their horns outside the Chinese Association.

One Saturday morning Edward was all dressed up in his scout's uniform ready to go to a special meeting. He had been eating oranges all morning and he came to the fence and was talking to Hannah and me as we sat on her front steps. He was drinking a pint of milk and generally making a big pig of himself and I told him so. He lifted his fingers in a pretend gun and shot me as he belched a very loud burp. I challenged him to do it again and he said, 'I'll go one better than that.' He pointed his gun fingers at me again and lifted his leg and farted. There was no noise but he had a very startled look on his face and yelled, 'Oh no, I've just shit myself.' The yellow diarrhoea poured down his legs into the tops of his green and gold scout's socks. Hannah and I nearly fell down the stairs as we screamed with laughter with Edward last seen running upstairs bellowing like a wounded bull.

One Christmas school holidays we were in the house by ourselves whilst Edith went Christmas shopping. Edward had been left in charge to look after me. That was like leaving Hagar the Horrible in charge of Attila the Hun. Edward was about thirteen and I was about ten. I had been quietly minding my own business colouring in and one of my pencils broke. I got Dad's butcher's knife from the kitchen drawer and proceeded to sharpen the pencil. If he had've asked me properly I would've given it to him, but he hadn't he had demanded it

Edward 'Give me the knife I want to use it.'

Amelia 'No, I'm using it first.'

He grabbed for my arm to twist it to make me drop the knife, but instead I moved away and I pointed the knife at him

Amelia 'Take one step closer and I'll cut your balls off.'

He panicked and grabbed the blade and I pulled it back. The knife slashed into the fleshy part of his right hand between the thumb and the index finger and the blood spurted everywhere. The pair of us nearly died of shock. I had no idea what to do. The first thing I could think of was to get a bucket of water and get him to put his hand into it. I ran around getting towels and cleaning the blood off his hand, but as soon as I'd mop it more blood would spurt out. Edith came home minutes later and she nearly had heart failure. Edward was rushed to the doctor and he received several stitches in the wound, the doctor told him that he was a hair's breadth off cutting the tendon and that he could've gotten lock jaw. The top of his index finger is permanently bent downward at the first knuckle joint because of the wound.

Another day I was listening to some records on the radiogram and Edward came into the lounge room and turned it off, it wasn't because it was loud, he just didn't like me enjoying myself. I started to swear at him and he told me to stop swearing or he'd tell Edith. I pushed him and he shoved me back onto the lounge chair which made me swear even more. He went off his rocker grabbing me by the throat and started to choke me. I punched him and bit his arm as hard as I could and he let go. I ran to Edith's sewing table and got the scissors and went downstairs to where his gold Malvern Star racing bike was. He'd saved and saved for that bike by selling papers and doing odd jobs and it was his pride and joy. I got the tubes out of the tyres and cut them in half. Not content with that, I walked one and a half miles to the police station and reported his attempt to murder me. The police drove me home in the side basher of the bike and by that time Edith was home. Edward told them that I was swearing for no reason and that he had put his hand over my mouth to stop me swearing and that he hadn't tried to choke me at all. The cop reprimanded me, Edith gave me a hiding and Edward was as happy as a pig in shit. Well for about an hour or so until he discovered his precious bike.

In the early part of the fifties Friday nights in the Long household was spent sitting around in the lounge room listening to the fights on the radio. Dad would bring home a huge tin of roasted peanuts and we'd hoe into them as if we hadn't eaten in weeks. On some Sundays, Uncle Stan would come around and quite often he'd bring big Sam Burmester a fairly famous wrestler who was a family friend. Usually other friends would turn up and before long there'd be a party in full swing. Other Sundays, Dad would bundle us into the car and we'd head off to Jimboomba pub approximately thirty-five miles (fifty-five kilometres) south-west of Brisbane. There was no Sunday trading in the pubs in those days, except the country pubs. Pub patrons had to be bona-fide travellers and would have to have driven at least one hundred miles (one hundred and seventy kilometres) before they could be served. Dad used to give his correct name, but he'd tell them he'd driven from the Sunshine Coast so as to gain entrance and allowed to have his beloved *amber nectar of the Gods* as he called it. Uncle Stan was a barber by trade but he should've been a comedian. He would give the hotelier a bodgie name such as Charlie Killfoppingbird or Charlie Honeystick and tell them he was an Englishman on holidays. He looked a bit like Leslie Phillips from the Carry On movies. Of course the staff got to know them as regular customers but Uncle Stan would still sign himself in under a bodgie name. I used to love going to the Jimboomba pub, I was always assured of having plenty of soft drinks and bags of Smith's crisps. Edith would often play the old piano there and everyone would gather around and have a sing-along. One Sunday the cops came in to check the registry book to make sure all the patrons were bona-fide travellers. Uncle Stan dived under the table which had a heavy tablecloth over it. The cops had a look around the lounge where we were all sitting and came up to our table. Dad stood up to address the cops and in doing so moved away from the table. He had a lit cigarette in his hand which he was smoking and I noticed smoke billowing up from under the table. I darted my eyes back and forth signalling to Dad that Uncle Stan was still smoking. Dad immediately placed his cigarette in the ashtray for it to burn down and thus giving a reason for smoke to be billowing from the table. After the cops had gone, I was rewarded with a packet of Fantales from Dad and a box of Jaffas from Uncle Stan for being such a smart kid. Driving home from the Jimboomba pub was always a little bit risky even though there was no such thing as random breath testing in those days. I'd always be on the lookout for anything that resembled a carload of police. One particular occasion Dad was going exceptionally fast and I said to him, 'If you go a bit faster, Dad, we'll all be able to get the best beds in the hospital.' Edith looked at me in total disbelief her eyes were as big as saucers because I'd had the audacity to say something like that. She closed her eyes and waited for Dad to go off the brain. Instead he laughed and said, 'You're absolutely right, little darlin.' He slowed down to a sedate thirty-five miles per hour (sixty kilometres).

We always enjoyed our long drives no matter where we went and we'd all sing at top note. No drive was complete without at least one rendition of Carolina in the Morning, Am I Blue, Five Foot Two and many more. On the Sundays we didn't have the parties or go to Jimboomba or BBQ's, Dad would take Edith and me to Fortitude Valley to a Chinese restaurant for dinner. The proprietors knew us extremely well and didn't even wait to take my order. Within minutes of being seated my entree was served, half a dozen fresh oysters in the shell followed by a small serving of curried prawns and rice and a small serve of fried rice. It's still one of my favourite meals.

I was about two and I was walking down George Street with my parents. I apparently wanted something and Dad said I couldn't have it so I threw a tantrum. I can't remember the belting he gave me but Edith assures me it was a 'good' one. When I was about eleven, we were on one of our many Sunday outings to the country with all of Dad's friends and their families. There were at least ten carloads of people and we'd go to a farmyard with acres of land and a running creek. I'm not exactly sure where we were, but I have an idea it was out at Upper Brookfield. In those days the area was classified as way out in the sticks but now it's almost an inner suburb. We'd have a BBQ and everyone would bring a plate of food and the men would chip in and buy a keg of beer and soft drinks. I had been sitting in a deck chair on the slope of the creek embankment dozing off to sleep in the sun. Jack Hillier the barman from the Regatta Hotel who was renowned for always being drunk came up behind me and pushed me down the side of the embankment. I rolled right down skinning my hands and knees and nearly ended up in the water. He laughed at me and sat down in the deck chair I was absolutely livid. I got up raced over to him and said, 'You drunken old bastard' I grabbed the few hairs on his head and reefed them all out. Dad found a tree branch that was about an inch thick and took me over near the car and hit me at least ten times on my backside and legs. The welts were bright red and raised to such an extent if they weren't so sore too touch you could've pinched the flesh between your thumb and forefinger. I couldn't sit down properly and Edith had to pack all the towels together for me to prop myself onto for the drive home. She also applied heaps of ice to try and get the swelling down. I couldn't go to school for three days because of the pain, it took me years to forgive my father for that belting and he lost my respect for a long time because of it too. I know I deserved a hiding on many other occasions but not that time. I think what made it more unacceptable was that he hit me in defence of a drunken old sot.

Chapter 8

Misadventures

I don't know what it was about me that seemed to entice child molesters like bees to a honey pot. Perhaps I was extremely unlucky or there were more offenders around than what was reported. I think I was about nine when the first incident occurred. Mum, Edith and I were on our way to the Regent Theatre. I hurried off down Queen Street approximately twenty feet (three metres) in front of them, and quite a few people were walking up and down the footpath. All of a sudden, a man stopped right in front of me and as I stopped to wait for him to move away, he thrust his hand fast and hard between my legs and squeezed hard. I was momentarily stunned beyond belief and I screamed as loud as I could and he let go and ran across the road towards Albert Street before Mum and Edith were able to reach me.

The second incident happened when I was about twelve. We were about the last ones inside the Metro theatre, and there weren't three seats available together and we were scattered in three different rows of seats. We were only a few feet from each other, my seat was the second seat from the aisle, there was a man sitting on the end of the row closest to the aisle on my left-hand side. Edith was approximately six seats along, but in the row directly behind and Mum was approximately three seats down but five rows back from me. The lights went off in the theatre and I felt the man's leg rub against mine, I moved my leg slightly and in doing so I smiled at him as if to say, no offence. The movie started and I became engrossed in the plot and the next thing I felt something go up my skirt and touch me on the leg and at the same time, I became aware that his right arm was around my shoulders. I jumped up and screamed, 'Mum, this man's touching me.' The fellow took off up the aisle like a bat out of hell. The picture stopped, the theatre lights went on and Mum and Edith must've flown with wings on their heels to get to me as quickly as they did. The guy had disappeared and the usherettes shifted the patrons around to allow Mum, Edith and I to sit together and we tried to settle down to watch the rest of the picture.

The third incident happened not long after that, I was walking down the street behind our house toward the paddock. I was just about to go through the paddock into our street when a hand touched me on the shoulder from behind, I turned around expecting to see a familiar face and I saw a man about my father's age. I looked directly at his face and enquired, 'Yes?' He never said a word but he had this peculiar look on his face and he glanced downward. I followed his glance and I saw he had his penis in his hand. I said very disgustedly, 'Oh put it away its bloody ugly and so are you ya, dirty old bastard.' He turned and walked away and I ran as fast as I could through the paddock. I saw the same man about twenty-five years later when I was at the R.S.L. club with my father.

Amelia 'Dad, do you know that man over there?'

Dad 'Yes, he's a mongrel.'

Amelia 'Why?'

Dad 'He's just no good he's a bad devil that's why. Why do you ask?'

Amelia 'I very rarely forget a face, Dad, and I'll never forget his as long as I live, he's the one who flashed himself at me in the street years ago.'

Dad looked at me and his eyes flashed a look of death, kill and maim.

Dad 'Are you sure, darling?'

With as much confidence as any person could possibly have.

Amelia 'I'd swear on any Bible in any court of law throughout the land.'

I looked back to where the fellow had been sitting and he had gotten up and was walking out the club through the back door. It was obvious he had recognised me and he knew I had recognised him. Nothing more was ever said about the fellow and I don't know if Dad said anything to him or if he ever dared to go back to the club after that day.

I had a big crush on Lloyd Rivers; he was so good-looking his hair was so blonde it was almost white. His father and Dad were fairly good friends, both had been in the war and they used to drink together at the Regatta pub. It was nothing unusual for Mr Rivers to put on a party for no apparent reason and half of the suburb would be there. It makes me wonder now how anyone could afford to throw a party in those days especially the Rivers, they weren't rich by any stretch of the imagination.

Mrs Rivers used to work at Edward's school as a cleaner to help pay the bills. In those days women with children very rarely went out to work unless their husbands were unable to. There were seven kids in the Rivers family the three eldest ones were older than James but still living at home. Rodney whose nickname was Ooie was Edward's age, Edward and I didn't like him but we used to tolerate him for Dad's sake. Lloyd was my age possibly a few months older.

Trevor and Gilbert (Gillie) were the funniest set of twins you could ever meet they were about three years younger than me. Quite often Jenny and I would meet up with Lloyd and the twins and some of Lloyd's schoolmates at the swings in the park. Other girls would join us and before too long there'd be a swag of us kids running around like lunatics.

We were always aware that Mrs McCaully lived across the street so we'd be shouting out to her to pull her bloody head in away from the closed curtains. It wasn't unusual for us to go over the far side of the football oval where there were huge sewerage pipes, which had been there for years waiting for someone to put them into the ground. We'd all hide in the pipes and smoke, talk, and tell dirty yarns. A few times, but alas only a few we'd pair off and have a kissing and cuddling session. All very innocent stuff, but of course that was enough for me to believe I was going to marry Lloyd when we got older. Unfortunately, the kissing and cuddling sessions were very short lived because Trevor and Gillie would always come looking for us and tell us that they wanted to be kissed as well. They were always saying and doing something really funny. Both of them were born comedians and I don't think there was a kid within a five-mile radius (six and a half kilometres) who didn't like them.

During the Christmas holidays in 1955, I visited Gabrielle, one of my school friends, at her home. I met Greg a young fellow who was on holidays staying with relatives living down the street from Gabrielle. We got on like a house on fire and Edward came to meet him the following day and we went crabbing in the Brisbane River. I had never caught a crab in my life before, but I had often eaten them when Dad had brought them home for Edith to cook. All told we caught about six of the delicious treats on the riverbank Opposite Park Road. We had had a bit of difficulty putting the twine around their claws, but with a bit of perseverance we managed to get five tied up. We divvyed them up in hessian bags three to Greg with two in another bag for us. The three of us were trying to get a good grip on the last one, which was the biggest one of all. The crab started to thrash about and Edward kept saying, 'Watch out that it doesn't toss its nipper.' So, muggins me, tried to wind the twine around it's nipper as fast as I could. My hands were slimy with mud and I think my hand slid along the nipper and the big mongrel of a thing latched onto the little finger of my left hand with one gigantic crunch. The pain that seared through my hand was excruciating I thought as sure as eggs it had chomped through the bone. I was screeching in agony and Edward and Greg were panicking not knowing what to do.

Edward 'For Christ's sake throw your arm upward and you'll be able to flip the cunt of a thing off.'

He had yelled over my voice.as I screamed at him,

Amelia 'I can't move my arm, ya stupid bastard, it's too sore.'

Greg got hold of the crab and started to jab at it with Edward's hunting knife, which only seemed to make it crunch harder. By this time, I was almost beside myself with worry and agony, not knowing what to do and thinking I was going to have one less finger on my left hand. Edward yelled instructions to Greg to jab the crab in its eyes and after a few good pokes in its eyeballs the crab let go of my finger. There was blood everywhere and I was sure that I would lose my finger. I was very lucky, the finger was a bit mangled but I didn't even go to the doctor, but I'm positive I should have had at least one stitch in it.

I learnt a valuable lesson that day, don't ever go crabbing, just buy them from the fish shop already dead and cooked.

A couple of weeks or so later I decided to experiment with Dad's razor by shaving my legs for the first time. I have no idea why I wanted to shave my legs, because I have very fine, fair hair on my arms and legs which can't even be seen. But I had to be grown-up and I shaved my arms as well. I was quite pleased with myself at doing such a great job and I sat in the bath admiring my handiwork. All of a sudden, I felt a stinging sensation on the lower part of the back of my left leg. I lifted my leg out of the water and the blood began to flow freely. Dad always kept a packet of Tally-Ho cigarette papers in his shaving cabinet for when he nicked his skin when he shaved. I dried my hands and grabbed the papers and placed one over the cut. I might as well not have bothered because no sooner had I placed it on the cut, the paper was a red sodden mess.

I tried again and again and by this time my hands were dripping with perspiration as I desperately tried to stem the blood flow. I managed to wrap a small gauze bandage around it dried myself and got dressed. I limped out to Edith and told her a story that I had climbed through a barbed wire fence earlier in the day whilst trying to pat a horse and the bath water had knocked the scab off the wound. I was rushed to the doctor and was given a tetanus needle because horses and barbed wire fences were a lethal combination for tetanus.

Serves me right, I had outsmarted myself once again.

The following August, Edward and I went to the Brisbane Exhibition (known by Queenslanders as 'The Ekka') on the last Saturday to buy heaps of sugar cane from the fruit pavilion. The farmers sold their fruit and vegetable displays to the public very cheaply and the giant stalks of sugar cane were broken into approximately two-foot lengths. I sat on the front steps attacking one piece of the juicy cane trying to take the skin off but to no avail. I went under the house in search of one of my grandfather's gardening implements and discovered his machete.

Back up onto the steps, I very gingerly gave the sugarcane a couple of whacks but the cane kept rolling around as soon as I hit it. I held the cane in my left hand and gave it a bit of a tap and I managed to split the skin slightly. I sucked at the juice and it was sheer bliss tasting that sweet nectar. I was spurred on to give the piece of cane a harder whack. This time I lifted the machete higher and plunged it down harder, it broke the skin all right unfortunately it was the skin on my hand.

You'd be correct if you guessed that it was the little finger of my left hand. Once again, I was extremely lucky the machete wasn't very sharp but it mangled my finger almost in the same place that the crab had crunched. I was beginning to get the feeling God was trying to tell me something and I made a momentous decision that the third time would be unlucky and I decided to be more careful in the future.

One night about two weeks before Guy Fawkes Night in 1956, with Edith's permission, I went for a walk with Hannah over to the shops near the railway station in search of crackers. By the time we got there, the shop that sold them was closed. We walked all the way back to the shops near the local picture theatre to see if any of the shops there were still open. We bought quite a few for the money we had and we walked up the hill towards our homes. As we walked over the crest of the hill, I noticed a pale green F. J. Holden it was the same make and model as my father's car. Very casually Hannah said, 'There's your father's car across the road.' By this time, we had walked past it and I looked back and said, 'No, it's not Dad's car but it's like it though, isn't it?' 'It is your father's car.' Hannah insisted. We kept walking and we got to the bottom of the hill and around the corner. The next thing a car came screaming around the corner practically on two wheels and came to a screeching stop. The door flew open

Dad 'You, get in the car.

I was shocked

Amelia 'Can Hannah come too?'

Without even looking at her,

Dad 'Get in.'

We practically flew down the street around the corner and up our street in deathly silence except for the roar of the car's motor. Hannah ran to her house and Dad hurried me up the stairs. Edith came out to see what the commotion was

Dad yelled, 'I found her wandering the bloody streets.'

He looked at his watch

Dad 'It's twenty to ten she should've been in bed hours ago.'

Edith went to say something and he interrupted her and said, 'I'm going out, I'll see you about her later.'

With that he turned and took off in a flurry and flew down the street in the car and disappeared around the corner. I was expecting Edith to go off the brain at me. Instead she very calmly listened to my explanation. I think I must've gone over the exact events of the evening about ten times. I gave her the exact location where I thought I saw Dad's car and she queried over and over about Hannah insisting that it was Dad's car. The following night Edith got dressed in an olive-green blouse and black skirt and flat-heeled shoes. Aunty Lilly turned up in similar dark clothing and they both left with torches in their hands. They arrived back about an hour or so later. They had gone past the house and Dad's car was parked in the side street. Edith had crept up alongside and as she got closer, she could see two people sitting in the car. She shone the torch through the open window and saw an olive-skinned woman with dark hair pulled off her face as if she wore it in a bun at the back of her head. According to Edith she had a long beak of a nose. Apparently, Dad said to the woman something that sounded like, 'Wind the window up, lambie.'

Edith 'What right have you got, to take a man away from his wife and children?

The woman 'It depends on the age of the children.'

I forget what else was said, but Aunty Lilly and Edith didn't stay there very long and they came straight back home. Uncle Simon told us later that the affair had gone on for nearly ten years. This meant that I was only two when he started going out with her. None of us wanted to have anything to do with him, as far as we were all concerned, he was already finished. James and Edward wanted to kill him. Edith had been humiliated in the worst possible way and she didn't deserve that at all. She'd been a good wife and mother all those years and he had treated her with utter contempt. To make matters worse only a few months before, he had told Mum and Granddad that they had to leave the house and find their own place to live and that had shattered me. They had lived with us since before the war and I felt as if my world was being torn apart when they left. They moved into a flat about five minutes walking distance from our house, but it wasn't the same. I had pleaded with them to take me with them, but I wasn't allowed to go. Three months later they bought a house, they had only been there two weeks when the flat that they'd occupied burnt to the ground from an electrical fault.

I continued going to school for another twelve months and Edith had to find a job to support us all. She hadn't gone to work for an employer for more than twenty years. She had no skills and no formal education but she took what employment she could find. She got a job as a milk bar attendant in Chemist Roush' soda fountain parlour, at the top of Queen Street, Brisbane. That suited me down to the ground, I loved lime sodas and strawberry malted milks and I'd go into town to see her at work as often as I could.

Years later on 60 Minutes there was a story about a heroic nurse who had served in Egypt during WW11, she had a similar sounding name to the woman Dad had had the affair with. I'll go to my grave believing that she was Dad's girlfriend.

Edith had often said to me, when I'd been particularly cheeky or naughty, 'You're in for a rude awakening one of these days, young lady.' I'd been sleeping in her bed and I awoke one morning to see her standing in the bedroom with only her panties on. She was bent over putting her bra on and her breasts were swinging like pendulums. I bit my tongue as the thought went through my mind, this must be the rude awakening she's been talking about for years.

As Dad wasn't around, I figured my chances of getting a belting was fairly high, if I'd said it to her. So, I kept my mouth shut just for once in my life.

Chapter 9

A Fate Worse Than Death

I was very reluctant to leave Sister Mary St Angela's class, but I had to move on. I figured that each nun had shown me kindness so the new nun who had replaced Sister Mary Marietta (the one I had feared) would be a pushover. Sister Mary Marietta was a really cranky, red-cheeked woman but quite attractive really. All the kids called her the painted doll (behind her back of course) because her cheeks looked as if she always applied rouge. She used to be in charge of sports days and was renowned for forcing everyone to participate. I always hated sports and I was the best asset the opposition had, no matter what the game. So, she wasn't exactly thrilled with me because she was so competitive.

I was very relieved when Sister Mary Enda kept smiling at me the first morning, I entered her class. I smiled sweetly back at her each time that she smiled at me. Just before little lunch, she called me out to her desk. I was more worried than surprised, because she hadn't actually said, Amelia, will you come to my desk please.

Her exact words were, 'Long get out here.'

I stood at her desk and she picked up a feather duster with a cane handle, she held the feathered end in a vice-like grip and whacked the cane across my left arm three times and told me, 'That should wipe the smile off your face.'

She then told me to get back to my place and pay attention. Everyone in the entire room was in total shock. I went back to my desk with tears welling in my eyes and my jaw set determinedly. I sat there willing the tears to go back to wherever they had come from. I could feel every pair of eyes looking at me and I was more than relieved when the bell rang for us to go out to play. I think everyone from class came up to me to ask me what I had been doing to cop the cane. 'Nothing, I did absolutely nothing. She kept smiling at me and I smiled back at her and that's all I did.' We all found out that same day that she wasn't smiling she was snarling and grinding her teeth.

Worst of all, she not only taught the seventh grade (the class we were in), she also taught the eighth grade at the same time as well. That meant I had her as my teacher for two whole years. I never found out why she singled me out to vent her hatred, I can only assume it was because I had wagged school the year before or the fact that I was a Protestant or perhaps a combination of both. I won't say I did nothing in those two years to warrant punishment, but truthfully, I was wrongly accused of many things during that time. I copped the cane on a regular basis and if she couldn't grab the cane quick enough, she'd punch me in the back with a closed fist or grab me by the shoulders and she would shake me like a rag doll. I wasn't the only one in the room who copped her verbal and physical abuse though. Quite a few of us did.

Nancy's sister, Quinn, who was in the eighth grade, did something wrong one day. Sister Mary Enda got hold of her and shook the living daylights out of her then flung her about twenty feet (six metres) across the room and through the doorway onto the veranda. Fortunately, Quinn skidded to a stop against the brick wall that surrounded the balcony. If she hadn't stopped, she would've no doubt gone over the wall and down about twenty feet, to the cement below.

Everyone absolutely detested Sister Mary Enda. She was definitely a mean evil witch of a woman who should never have been a nun let alone a teacher. She made me sit amongst the boys as punishment, at first, I hated it but we learnt to accept each other. All the boys treated me as one of them instead of being the enemy. The one thing I didn't like about sitting amongst them, I had to sit next to Timothy Finch. Timothy used to pick his nose and eat it and it would make the flesh on my back crawl. Even thinking about it now, I get a cold shiver running down my spine.

A few years ago, I heard that he became a doctor. I just hope he mastered hygiene. God help his patients if he didn't.

I had been a bit keen on Leo Wyatt, whose family owned an extremely well-known business. The Wyatt's were not only prominent business figures, they were also known for their kindness and generosity. What a pity they didn't teach Leo a few more manners. He took great delight in spitting in my face one day in the playground and he lost all affection I had for him. I met him a few years ago, he became a barrister and his body odour was putrid.

Someone sitting behind me had been talking in class one morning and Sister Enda accused me. She flew down the aisle and punched me between the shoulder blades. I got such a shock, that without thinking I said

'What was that for?'

She ground her teeth at me

Sister Enda 'Talking'

Amelia 'You're wrong again, because it wasn't me.'

She ground her teeth again, curled her lip up like a monkey and sneered,

'Long, you'd give cheek to the Pope.'

Amelia 'Well bring him along then.'

The entire room erupted with laughter, so I was sent out to stand on the verandah for the entire day. Whatever interest I had in schoolwork went out the window the day I entered her classroom. As far as I was concerned, I was there solely as her punching bag. She said a very curious thing to me one day, which took me at least five years before I worked out what she meant. She said, 'Long, in years to come, no doubt you'll be holding up the street corner.' I thought she meant I'd be a lazy bugger, leaning on the wall watching the world go by.

Obviously, she meant that she thought I'd become a prostitute.

We walked into the schoolroom one morning and she was in a mood fit to be tied.

Whenever we entered the classroom, the first thing we'd do after looking at her to see how frothy her mouth was, we'd check the blackboard for the lesson. On this particular day, the board was almost wiped clean. The letters A.M.D.G. were still there which were a permanent fixture and meant All My Duty to God, but some wag had written in bold writing directly underneath, Aunt Mary's Dead Goat.

No prizes for guessing who got the blame. The funny part was even if I had stood on a chair with at least two cushions, I wouldn't have reached the writing.

On the first morning of the eighth grade, she put me in the back row at the top of the class. It definitely wasn't because I had finally become a genius. She had obviously no desire whatsoever of teaching me, and this was her way of keeping me as far away from her as possible, but it didn't stop her from throwing the blackboard eraser at me. Actually, I think she probably thought I was an easier target there and the chances of me ducking, and her hitting another kid was reduced. She'd also get her exercise by walking up behind me, and giving a good clout wherever her hand landed, just for practice. Sitting next to me was Diane. She was a nice girl and I'm very ashamed to admit that I pinched sixteen shillings (one dollar and sixty cents) of her raffle money from her desk one day. I hid the money (all in coins) in my sock and I had a hell of a job walking to the tram terminus shops where my friends and I bought our favourite lollies and drinks and stuffed ourselves senseless. I was under suspicion but nothing was proved. I bumped into Diane's mother about eight years later and she told me that she knew it was me who'd stolen the money and hidden it in my socks. Obviously one of my friends who had enjoyed sharing the ill-gotten gains, had dobbed me in.

In recent years, I was stunned to learn that Diane's brother was one of the barristers in charge of conducting the Fitzgerald Inquiry. Which was the biggest Queensland Government scandal that caused a number of politicians and the police commissioner to be sent to jail.

There was a newspaper honour box at the tram terminus it was a rickety old tin contraption that was very unstable. One afternoon we were running around playing tiggy, and me being an awkward little bugger, ran headfirst into it and knocked it over. Apart from all the Telegraph newspapers blowing around the street, all the money inside the money box section went spilling all over the footpath. At first, we were all embarrassed at the accident and we scrambled to pick up all the coins to replace them into the moneybox. Then we realised how easy it would be to keep some for ourselves. So, we counted it out thus, one for the tin one for us, one for the tin four for us, none for the tin and the rest for us. It was really strange how we all took it in turns to accidentally knock that honour box over on a regular basis after that. Good little Catholic school girls we were.

Sister Mary Leonard, the music teacher, had not been very popular in my books. She was not a cruel woman like Sister Mary Enda, but she wasn't too frightened to give her pupils a good clout or a push if she thought they deserved it. Most of us didn't think we deserved the amount of clouts and pushes she dished out. We were all practicing for our annual concert on one particular occasion and we were singing our little hearts out. All of a sudden, she stopped playing the piano and jumped up and called out rather aggressively, 'Who was that?' We all looked at each other rather quizzically. None of us seemed to know what she was on about, and then she said, 'That high note, who was that. Who hit that high note?' No one owned up for fear of getting into trouble, then when she realised that everyone was too scared to speak up, she smiled and said, 'Whoever it was they've got a lot of potential, so now who was it?'

Some of the class pointed at Jenny and some pointed at me. She looked at the pair of us and said, 'Okay, which one of you was it?' We both pointed to each other. As it turned out, it was the both of us, and we were both encouraged to sing together. For the concert we were positioned on the opposite ends of the stage in the choir, so that our voices balanced and coordinated with the rest of the choir. On another occasion Jenny and I ventured into the music room to speak to Sister Leonard, but she wasn't there.

Leo Wyatt's family had loaned their beautiful Xylophone to Sister Leonard to use in the concert, it was just standing there begging us to play it. Unfortunately, the sticks were nowhere to be found, so Jenny and I looked around for something else to use to belt out a tune.

Still nothing, so Jenny took out a comb from her pocket and the two of us scraped the comb up and down on the keys. Later in the day, Sister Mary Leonard told the singing class that someone had wilfully damaged the xylophone keys badly and the only way to repair it was to have all the keys totally replaced. She asked for the culprit to come forward and own up after class. No need to be told, she never found out who the guilty party was. I must say in our defence though, we didn't wilfully damage it, we were just too bloody stupid to know any better.

Later in the year, I, along with about ten other kids from our school, went with many hundreds of other children throughout South East Queensland, to attend an examination in theory of music. I had passed my piano playing examinations each year and had been awarded Certificates of Merit on each occasion. But I wasn't confident of getting a pass in the theory of music. When the results were to be read out in the music room, we all stood there almost wetting our pants with fear. Sister Mary Leonard called our names alphabetically and as she handed out the certificates, she'd shake the kid's hand and say, 'Congratulations, you passed with seventy-three percent' or whatever the percentage was. My hands were dripping with perspiration from fear of what my percentage was going to be. I felt sick to the pit of my stomach and I wished I'd never come to school that day. I honestly thought I was going to vomit when she glared at me and said, 'Amelia Long,' I stepped forward after secretly wiping my sweaty hand on the side of my uniform. She handed me my rolled certificate, which was tied in the centre with a little pink ribbon, 'Amelia, your percentage is,' she paused and looked at me and then said, 'ninety-one percent, you topped the class.' Everyone gasped in shock as Sister Mary Leonard threw her arms around me and gave me the biggest hug and kissed my cheek and said, 'Congratulations, love. Good on you, well done.'

I loved Sister Mary Leonard from that magic moment on. I couldn't believe it, me the dill of the year, had done something right for once. I wouldn't know a crotchet from a quaver if my life depended on it now.

Who said that a little knowledge goes a long way? Not in my brain it doesn't.

Chapter 10

The Real World

Jenny started to come to school with a lot of pocket money to spend and she confided in me that her mother had encouraged her to sneak into her father's bedroom whilst he was in a drunken stupor and she would pinch his wage packet. For her efforts, Jenny's mother would give her five pounds (ten dollars). Well, that's what Jenny had told me! Looking back with hindsight, I would say that in all probability Jenny had withheld the money from her poor mother or she just pinched it for herself and her Mother got nothing.

Jenny would quite often buy me gifts which I could never let Edith see, so I would hide them in a little hiding spot in the paddock. After the wagging incident, I was forbidden to see Jenny after school and I wasn't supposed to associate with her at school either, however, whenever I could, I'd go over to Jenny's house, mainly on Sunday afternoons.

Her father wouldn't allow me inside the house, to be honest I don't think he allowed anyone past the front door so Jenny and I made a secret signal. Whenever I walked past her house, I'd whistle the tune Stand Up and Fight from the operetta Carmen. Then, when I knew for sure that she'd heard me, we'd meet over in the park, where we'd smoke her mother's cigarettes and make eyes at the boys. A couple of times, we went along with Nancy and Quinn and met up with other kids from the area. We'd go to a secluded swimming hole at the foothills of Mt Coot-tha and go skinny-dipping. It was a little area directly behind Anzac Park. It was a beautiful place, a real Shangri-La in a rainforest under the noses of everybody however, it went undiscovered for years. Eventually, the Brisbane City Council discovered it and they built a planetarium and car park there with a freeway alongside of it. They threw water lilies into our lagoon and called it a lily pond. So much for progress, personally speaking I preferred it the way it was.

On one of the occasions after we'd been skinny-dipping, we all congregated in Anzac Park to have a feed of chips lollies and drinks and of course a couple of smokes. We'd been there for about half an hour and we were just about ready to pack up and go home when we heard a distant roar and someone exclaimed, 'Oh shit, it's the cops.'

We all looked over and saw the police bike with the side basher approaching. The cigarettes were stubbed out and all the cigarettes including the butts were hidden as fast as was humanly possible. We were all very surprised and pleased to see a new cop to the area, and not the old pig we called Baby Face who was hated by everyone. This cop was blonde, blue eyed, good-looking and had the cheekiest smile. I doubt that any of us stood in fear of this handsome specimen of manhood. He stopped the motor of his bike and asked us, what we were doing.

Quinn 'Having a party, do you want to join us?'

He smiled and all the girls just about melted.

Police Officer 'No thanks but it's nice of you to ask.'

He then asked us our names and we told him. I couldn't believe my ears

Quinn 'More importantly, what's your name?'

Police Officer 'Constable Potlick'

We all burst into gales of laughter.

Quinn 'Potlick?' 'Which pot do you lick the one on the stove or the one under the bed?'

That was it for me, I was in fits. He laughed, and because I was still having a good chortle, he turned to me 'Well, Amelia, you seem to be enjoying yourself, perhaps you can tell me why your hair is wet.' I was struck dumb momentarily, but fortunately I came up with, 'We had a water fight.' He then asked where the water was and once again, I was floundering for an answer. Fortunately, Quinn saved my bacon by pointing to the far side of the park and proclaimed, 'There's a tap over there.'

We all knew he didn't believe that, but he didn't question us anymore. He chatted with us for about ten minutes and left. We never went skinny-dipping again for fear of being caught by the cops. I was only twelve/thirteen at the time and very naive in many ways, but if I was older, I wouldn't have objected if Constable Potlick had've caught me naked.

Quite a few years ago I was watching a television talk show and I was reminded of my own teenage years. The show had four teenage girls and their mothers, the mothers were complaining about how un-lady-like and uncouth their daughters were. Each girl behaved like ill-mannered Neanderthal cave women. They chewed gum like cows chewing their cud, spoke in loud voices and sat with their legs spread wide open, in the most un-lady-like manner. Although I was nowhere near as bad as these young girls, I know that I was aware of my unusual behaviour at their age of twelve to fifteen. So much so, that I was almost convinced that I was schizophrenic.

I thoroughly enjoyed dressing in widgie style clothing, which was classified as being totally unacceptable. Olivia Newton John gave a certain amount of respectability to the trashy widgie style in the movie Grease twenty years later, but in the fifties, it wasn't classified as respectable. Nice young girls didn't wear their hair with a kiss curl on their foreheads, nor did they wear tight peddle-pushers and skin tight sweaters. Any girl that did, was regarded as being a tart. On the other hand, I also enjoyed dressing up to the nines, wearing a conservative style dress, stockings, patent leather shoes and gloves. The contrast was so striking I could only liken it to Dr Jekyll and Mr Hyde.

I remember going to a rock and roll picture at the Wintergarden with Jenny and we were flicking cigarette ash on the heads of the two young fellows who were sitting in front of us. Both Jenny and I were swearing like troopers and trying to act really tough.

The boys were inoffensive young chaps who were trying to be nice to us and we treated them with utter contempt. We just wanted to be anti-social little misfits. The following week, I went to see a love story movie at the Rex picture theatre in Fortitude Valley on my own, dressed up to the nines. I sat in the darkened theatre and behaved in the manner as I was dressed, like a well-behaved, good-mannered, young lady. The lights went on during interval and I nearly died a thousand deaths when I recognised one of the young fellows from the previous week. He came over to where I was sitting

Boy 'Hello, don't I know you?'

I replied in my best elocution voice,

Amelia 'I don't think so.'

He looked directly at me

Boy 'I'm sure I've met you somewhere.'

I put my nose in the air with all the haughtiness of a stuck-up little prig

Amelia 'I'm sure I'd remember you.'

I gave him a coy, little smile, and all of a sudden his face dropped open like a mineshaft **Boy** 'You're the one who sat behind me last week.'

I shook my head as if I had no idea what he was talking about.

Boy 'I can't believe how different you look it's as if you're two different people.'

I couldn't contain myself any longer, I just burst into laughter. We sat and talked for a few minutes until the second feature. On leaving the theatre at the end of the film, I was as pleased as punch with myself that I had made someone else as confused about my changeable behaviour as I was.

Towards the end of our last year at school, I thought it was time to be honest with Edith and Mum. So, one night at the pictures instead of sneaking off to the toilets for a smoke I lit one whilst sitting between them. It was an eerie feeling having two pairs of eyes peering at me in disbelief. They never said one word. I guess sitting in a darkened theatre wasn't the time or place to throw a multi-coloured fit.

I would have liked to tell the mothers on that television show to try not to despair and to try not to force them to conform. The girls probably won't outgrow their tomboyish behaviour, but I feel sure that they will eventually modify their behaviour somewhat as time goes by. I think that they'll never be wilting wallflowers and never be afraid to speak up for themselves. Probably to everyone else's horror.

Jenny began sneaking out of a night time and meeting older boys whom we had talked to at in the park on our Sunday afternoon meetings. The fellows were members of a motorcycle club and were all in their late teens. Jenny's reputation went from bad to worse and unfortunately, I heard rumours that I too was being branded as a low-class moll as well, all because I was her friend. I disapproved of Jenny's night time activities as much as everyone else did. I ended up having a big argument with her and I told her that if she wanted to lower herself to that level that it was her prerogative to do so. But I sure as hell wasn't going to be dragged through the mud with her.

Mother Mathias had been transferred to another school about two years after I started at the catholic school but she had donated her lethal weapon to Mother Romanus, a thick rubber strap which was actually a strip off the floor covering from the church. It was approximately eight inches long and two inches wide and was as thick as two wooden rulers glued together. Anyone who got hit with it would remember it for the rest of their lives. I had copped it for spreading the story about my classmate's father committing suicide and on several other occasions. On my last day of school, I snuck into Mother Romanus' classroom and took the offensive weapon from her desk. I did what every kid in the school had wanted to do with it. I cut it into very tiny pieces and took it back and placed all the pieces back in her desk. I am very proud of that achievement, I believe I prevented a lot of kids a great deal of suffering. As a last act of defiance, three or four of us climbed up to the big church bell and pulled the rope to make it toll our happiness of our first taste of freedom.

In retrospect, looking back at my childhood, I was considerably lucky really. I had all the opportunities any child could ever want. I found out months later that Jenny fell pregnant and because of her age she had been taken through the courts. She refused to give the names of the fellows she had slept with but the police had charged some chaps with carnal knowledge. Their solicitors proved in court that she had accepted cigarettes and a bottle of Coca-Cola during their liaisons with her and she was proven to be a prostitute for accepting these items as payments. Jenny gave birth to a baby boy the following November and the baby was adopted out.

Hannah had arranged for me to work at Barry and Robert's Supermarket in the city during the Christmas holidays. My job entailed filling the shelves when the stock started to get low and being a general dog's body. My main memory of my six weeks working there was wearing a grey and red uniform that was at least two sizes too big for me. Being only five feet tall, I've always had problems getting clothes to fit me and Barry's uniform department was no different. Co-workers and customers alike often had a good laugh at seeing me scampering around in a uniform that should have only reached below my knees but instead it flowed around my ankles. At the end of my six weeks I had become quite attached to everyone who worked there, not to mention becoming attached to my wage every week.

On Dad's insistence, even though he was no longer living at home, I was enrolled at Stott's Business College in the city to learn typing, shorthand, and business principles. As with piano playing, the keys on a typewriter were absolutely impossible for me to master. The harder I tried, the more agitated I became, the more agitated I became the more my hands sweated. The result being a soggy mess everywhere, three months of that form of torture was more than enough for me. So much to my parent's dismay, I beat a hasty retreat and got a job as a shop assistant at Penny's Department store. I was put in charge of the toy department, which was second only to being in charge of the lollies and chocolate department. In those days the toy department was like a little house separated from the rest of the other departments. All the counters were around the entire length of the four walls with the exception of the three doorways to allow the customers to enter. The area between the counters was supposedly for the customers to walk around to look at the goods on display. It was nothing unusual for me to be on the floor on all fours crawling around playing with different toys. Of course, if I was copped by the floorwalker Mr Mac (as he was affectionately known), I would invariably come up with the story that some naughty kid had been playing with it earlier and I thought the kid had broken it and I was just testing it out. Toys weren't wrapped in boxes with cellophane or plastic in those days.

I'll never forget the day I saw a little boy of about nine put a dinky car in his pocket. I rang the bell on top of the cash register three times for Mr Mac but to no avail, he didn't hurry in as he was supposed to. I was pacing up and down behind the counter trying to pretend to be unaware of what the boy had done. I nearly had heart seizure when I saw him walk towards the door to leave the area. I walked up to him and grabbed him by the arm and told him he was under arrest. The poor little bugger almost shit himself with fright. Just as I had made the arrest Mr Mac walked in

Mr Mac 'What's the problem, Amelia?'

Amelia 'I've just arrested this kid for shoplifting; he's got the stuff in his pocket.'

I announced as proud as punch,

Mr Mac looked at me in total disbelief and shock. Slowly he turned to the terrified kid and very quietly said, 'Do you want to show me what's in your pockets, son?'

The little boy hesitantly emptied his pockets and to my surprise he had a bag of marbles, a pocketknife and two dinky cars. Mr Mac took the goods and placed them on the shelf behind the counter and asked the lad to accompany him outside the toy department. As they walked out, I started to follow but Mr Mac stopped me by telling me that it wasn't necessary for me to go with them. I was surprised and somewhat annoyed that I was going to miss out on all the action. A few minutes later Mr Mac walked back in and he was furious. He took a deep breath,

Mr Mac 'Never do that again.'

Amelia 'Why not?'

Mr Mac 'If that boy had've known the law, we would've been in big trouble. When I asked him if he'd like to empty his pockets all he had to say was 'no' and then he could've gone home, told his mother and she could sue us all for wrongful arrest and assault.'

He went on to explain that, two floorwalkers had to witness a person taking two things. He made me promise that if I ever saw anyone stealing again that I would ring for assistance and wait and let the floorwalker's deal with it.

It wasn't long after that incident I was transferred to the lolly and chocolate department and more importantly I was put in charge of the drink machine. I had it made.

I had a regular customer who came in every day without fail. She was what we would call a bag lady these days. She wore the same clothes every day with a fawn coloured lightweight overcoat, rain, hail or shine. Over her straggly peroxide hair, she wore a huge black brimmed hat adorned with flowers and black netting. On her arm she carried an extremely large, black handbag. Every day at about eleven o'clock she'd march hurriedly down the aisle of the shop from the Adelaide Street entrance and slam a one shilling piece (ten cents) onto the silver topped counter and yell at top note at me, 'Two ginger beers.' As soon as I poured them for her, she would throw them down her throat in rapid succession, then slam the disposable cups down onto the counter and she'd march away. I tried to make conversation with her a couple of times, but to no avail, she did not or would not respond. The poor old chook totally fascinated me.

One morning whilst working at the drink machine, word filtered through the shop that Buddy Holly, The Big Bopper and Richie Valance had all been killed in a plane crash. Within minutes, there were teenagers ten deep, milled around the record counter, all of them were weeping and wailing whilst the staff played their dead hero's music over the loud speakers. I can remember thinking at the time that they were all nuts. I couldn't for the life of me, understand why anyone could weep and wail for people they had never met, let alone seen. I still can't understand it. I feel saddened by something like that, and I get tears in my eyes at hearing sad news, but to weep hysterically and wail over someone you don't know. Not me, I think those people, must live boring meaningless lives.

Lori-Anne Bailey worked at Penny's. She and I became friends and we began going out to dances or the movies on Friday and Saturday nights. One night we'd both been invited out to a drive-in movie with a couple of fellows whom we'd met at the Railway Institute dance on the Friday night. I can't remember where we'd arranged to meet them, but I do know we never got to the drive-in. We were driven to a lonely deserted area on the outskirts of nowhere to a place we later learnt was called The Blunder.

We were informed by those wonderful specimens of manhood that if we didn't come across, we could get out and walk. Both Lori-Anne and I didn't hesitate, without even consulting the other, we both opened our doors in unison and hopped out of the car and started our long walk home. I had no idea where we were, let alone where we were heading or if we were heading in the right direction. The two fellows kept shouting abuse at us that we were prick teasers, to which I yelled into the night, 'That's better than being pricks like you, you rotten mongrels.'

We finally found our way out of the dense bushland area and onto an unsealed road. We were exhausted and thirsty but there wasn't a house to be seen. After about another two hours of walking, we finally came to a darkened house and we were both too frightened to go in and ask for help. Lori-Anne said, 'We're passing Archerfield Aerodrome',

I had to believe her, because she had a little bit of knowledge about the area. We could've been on Mars for all I knew. All I could see was a vast area of pitch black nothing. Finally, after about three hours of walking, we came to an intersection but there wasn't any traffic to be seen. Lori-Anne said Ipswich Road was up to our left. We walked for about another ten minutes and came up to the main highway. There was still no traffic in sight and we were debating if we should continue on up to where Lori lived or to walk in the other direction to my home. Either way we were in for a long walk. Out of the blue a car pulled up alongside of us, the driver was middle aged but obviously an angel in disguise. He asked us if we were all right and we told him where we had walked from. Although I'd been warned never to accept lifts from strangers, I was secretly praying this man would invite us into his car. I asked him where he was heading and he replied, 'Ipswich.' My heart sank because I didn't want to go to Lori-Anne's house which was on the way to Ipswich, I wanted to get home to my own bed. But most of all I wanted to see my family. Lori-Anne was supposed to be spending the night at my place and I sensed she too didn't want to go to her place probably because she'd have to answer too many questions from her parents. The man then asked us where we were going and dejectedly, I told him where I lived.

Without even hesitating he said, 'Get in I'll drive you home.'

It was after one in the morning before we finally crawled into bed. Fortunately, everyone was in bed asleep when we got home. I knew I wouldn't have gotten any sympathy from Edith if she'd seen the state we were in. We were absolutely filthy our legs were almost black from the bush and we had cobbler's pegs all over our clothes. As far as Edith was concerned, she thought I was a defiant little bugger who went out looking for trouble. Funnily enough for some inexplicable reason, she honestly believed, that because I was going out with a girl from work, that I was safe from harm. Ironically had she known that Lori-Anne lived at Inala, I wouldn't have been allowed to associate with her because Inala had a reputation for being a bad place. It still hasn't lost that stigma. The more things change, the more they stay the same.

After that night though, Lori-Anne and I never went out together again. I have no idea why not. Perhaps I subconsciously blamed her and her upbringing for getting me into that situation. I honestly don't know why. I also don't know why I had an uncanny knack of getting myself into difficult situations. As the old saying goes I didn't look for trouble, it found me.

Chapter 11

How to Win Friends

I met Roslyn and Carmen Thompson and started to go out with them. Roslyn was my age and her sister, Carmen, was a year or two older. Roslyn was a nice girl but Carmen had the reputation of being easy, but that didn't stop me from enjoying their company. I recall going to a party with them and on that occasion, I got my first taste of alcohol in the form of a bottle of Brandivino. In the early part of the evening I vividly remember all the females at the party gathered around the record player to listen to Elvis Presley's new record Old Shep. There was not a dry eye amongst us. I don't know if this is what caused me to drown my sorrows, but I gave that bottle of Brandivino a hell of a nudge. I was offered a lift home, which I gratefully accepted. As was my practice in those days, I got out of the car at the top of the hill near the Carmelite Monastery to walk home so that my family didn't know I'd been in the company of boys. Walking was not on the agenda that evening. I alighted from the car, stood in the gutter and farewelled my friends with all the dignity of a young lady. As the taillights disappeared around the corner, I slowly slunk to the ground. I never had a hope of finding myself in an upright position again, so I manoeuvred my way down our street in the middle of the road, in the most dignified way that I could. I walked on my backside with the aid of my arms as wobbly crutches. I somehow managed to push my legs ahead of me. It was a very slow process. When I finally reached the bottom of our front stairs, I assessed the situation and gradually levered myself up the stairs by crawling on all fours. Somehow, I got to the bathroom and I lit the gas geyser without blowing myself up. I sat under the shower for what seemed like an eternity. I have no idea where the rest of the family was, but I was very thankful that no one was at home. I put my pyjamas on and staggered blindly to my bedroom with the aid of the hallway wall. Just as I reached the door to my bedroom, the front door opened and the hallway light was flicked on. I was pleased to see it was only James arriving home from a drumming engagement and I smiled sweetly at my oldest brother. He took one look at me and said, 'You're drunk, Fatso, get to bed, I'm telling Mum in the morning.'

I started to protest my innocence but gave up in disgust. I staggered to bed and flaked out. I had to face the music the following morning but I managed to convince Edith that I was not drunk, 'I was extremely tired I'd been in bed asleep when I heard a noise and came out into the hallway when James turned the light on me and nearly blinded me.'

Another Saturday night I went to the pictures with Roslyn and Carmen. After the movie a whole mob of us decided to walk to the local school which was at least two kilometres away. There was about twenty of us I guess, we were all laughing and joking and singing and we decided to link arms and spread across the entire width of the street. Some of us had our arms around each other's waists, others placed their arms around the shoulders of the person next to them. We got about three quarters of the length of the street away from the picture theatre when I placed my arm around a girl by the name of Pat. As she was at least six inches taller than me, my arm rested on her backside. I could feel that she was wearing a corset and I patted her bum and said,

'Are you wearing a corset?' She was quite a big girl, certainly a lot thicker set than I was. She shrugged away and snapped very aggressively, 'No, I most certainly am not.'

She shrugged my arm off her and moved away from me. I being a stirrer caught up with her and patted her again to make sure I did feel a corset and I said, 'You are so. Hey everybody, Pat's wearing a corset.' Everyone laughed and the next thing I felt a surging pain on my face. Pat had punched me with a fist right on my nose. I staggered back and I could feel a stinging, burning sensation all over my cheeks. My eyes were involuntarily streaming with tears. I didn't stop to think I just dived at her like a front row forward and tackled her to the ground. Legs, arms and fists were being thrust around like violent whirligigs whilst the crowd stood back and encouraged us with advice of where to punch next. I knew I was winning because I had landed the most punches and the crowd was chanting my name. Pat took her stiletto heeled shoes off and was about to hammer one into my head. I somehow managed to knock the shoe from her hand. As she struggled to grab hold of it again, I kicked my own shoes off and proceeded to hammer the two-inch high, thick heel onto her head with several hard blows. Someone grabbed me and pulled me away from her. The crowd congratulated me on a job well done and they said that she deserved everything I had given her and more. It was then that I learnt that she wasn't very well liked. No one had bothered to tell her to bugger off because she had a very bad habit of turning nasty. I managed to sneak into the house without waking anyone and I slept like a baby even though my entire body felt like a steamroller had hit it.

On waking the following morning, I could hardly move without wincing in pain, but I managed to get dressed and walk to the breakfast table as if there was nothing wrong. As I sat down, I could feel everyone's eyes staring at me. I looked around

Amelia 'What's wrong?'

James broke the silence, 'Where did you go to last night?'

Amelia 'To the pictures.'

Edward (laughing) 'Pull the other leg it plays jingle bells.'

I was stunned by the fact that they didn't believe me and I looked around at Edith and she had a disgusted look on her face. James and Edward were smirking and continued to just sit there and stare at me.

Amelia 'What? What's wrong with all of you, why are you all looking at me like that for?'

James (laughing) 'How did you get the black eye, from looking too hard at the screen?'

I jumped up and ran to the bathroom and looked at my face and I nearly fell over in shock when I saw that my right eye was almost as black as the ace of spades. I went back to the kitchen and told them the entire story. Edith shook her head in disgust and was horrified, but James and Edward were in their glory and they encouraged me to tell them every move blow by blow. The more I told, the more they laughed. I loved that Sunday morning, hearing my two brothers laugh made me feel good.

I managed to hide most of the bruising of my eye with make-up and I didn't miss any time off work. Although my co-workers knew that I was hiding a black eye, none of them bothered to ask. A customer came up to me a few days later and asked if I was Amelia Long, I replied that I was and she introduced herself as being Pat's Mother. She told me that I had fractured Pat's skull when I had hit her with my shoe and that she was going to see a solicitor to press charges against me. I was sick with worry and my hands were dripping wet with perspiration, but I very calmly told her that her daughter had attacked me first and that I had to defend myself and that I had about twenty witnesses to prove it. Everyone in the shop heard our discussion, which embarrassed me more than anything, but still no one said a word. About two weeks went by and the Ekka was on. Roslyn, Carmen and I went, and we saw Pat. She had found a couple of new friends to hang around with, and she challenged me to a rematch because she reckoned that I had fought dirty. I was absolutely terrified of her seeing her in daylight as I realised how big she was. She was about five feet six inches tall and weighed at least twelve stone. I was five feet tall and was flat out being eight stone. But I didn't want to appear to be chicken, so with as much bravado I could muster I said, 'You name the time and the place and I'll be there,' We agreed to meet two weeks from the following Saturday at the little park alongside the Fire Station near where we had fought. I packed death for the next two and a half weeks. I bought myself a big knuckle duster ring from Woolworths. I remember the setting had six small pink stones set in thick chunky silver. I had figured that a large stone could fall out on impact and the claws holding the stone could turn and cut into my hand. I wanted a strong thick metal that could withstand a pounding, as well as add weight to my hand. The ring I bought was wide, thick, solid and ugly. I wore it for about ten days to get used to the feel of it on my hand. Every waking moment I thought about that fight and I would imagine myself blocking her punches and what I could or wouldn't do if she hit me in certain places. All the while I secretly prayed that she wouldn't show up and the thought crossed my mind several times that I wouldn't show up, but deep down I knew that neither of us would want to be called chicken. The big night finally arrived and as I arrived at the little park, I could not believe the size of the crowd that was waiting there. The word had spread the length and breadth of Brisbane, Ipswich and Redcliffe that there was to be a catfight. There were motorbike gangs from just about every area. There were at least two hundred people there to watch me thrash it out with this overgrown Amazon of a girl. We stood there facing each other, if you could call it that. She towered over me and someone instructed us to shake hands and come out fighting. We both refused to shake hands but I noticed that she was wearing a ring with a stone the size of the rock of Gibraltar when she thrust her fist towards me. She missed me by a country mile and I moved to the side and dived into the air as if I was on the springboard at the baths. I grabbed her hair and entwined it around my fingers and kept pulling and pulling as hard as I could. I brought her to her knees and she was screaming top note to let go. There was no way I was going to, I knew if I did, she would've overpowered me and that would've meant goodnight nurse for me.

I managed to punch her with my left fist but that would have had the impact of a dab of melted butter. She twisted herself around and lifted her hands to claw at my face and eyes. I felt her nails go down my cheeks and just as I had done a

CLEAN HANDS, CLEAR CONSCIENCE

few years earlier with my dentist, I opened my mouth and sunk my fangs onto her thumb. I held onto her hair and my teeth clasped her thumb as tight as a grey nurse shark. She was screaming and the crowd was cheering. The next thing, I felt more than heard, a large cracking noise. I was biting with such ferocity that my false teeth snapped in half. I let go of her thumb and yelled, 'I've busted my false teeth,' Someone yelled above the roar of the crowd, 'Spit them out.' But I wouldn't and I said, No one sees me without my teeth, I'm giving up.' The crowd went wild telling me not to give up because I was winning. They tried their hardest to make me spit my teeth out with promises of, 'No one will laugh at you.'

But I was adamant, I'd had enough taunts when I was younger and I'd made a secret vow to myself that no one would ever see me without my teeth ever again. I said to Pat, 'I'm giving up and you can claim victory, okay?' She agreed only too readily. I let go of the grip on her hair and it took five minutes to untangle it from my fingers. The crowd roared its disapproval at my decision because most of them had backed me to win. Pat and I shook hands and she said, 'You are one hell of a fighter for such a little person.'

Her thumb was in a sore and sorry state and we both apologised to each other and went our ways and never saw each other from that night onwards.

Carmen visited me one Sunday arvo a week or so later and after she had left I discovered my beautiful gold watch Mum had bought me had gone as well.

It wasn't long after the second fight that I received a visit from my father. He walked up to the counter and said, 'Hello, little darlin' how's my princess today?' I was still very angry with him for the way he'd treated Edith and I wanted nothing whatsoever to do with him. I just glared at him and said, 'What can I do for you, little man?' I knew that remark would hurt his feelings more than anything and I enjoyed humiliating him. A few days later, Edith told me that Dad had been in touch with her. He told her that he had seen me and that he was coming back to live because he believed I was becoming too wild and out of control, he had said that I needed to be disciplined more. Neither James, Edward or I wanted him back, but we had no say in the matter.

Not long after that, I had arrived at work and was busy arranging the stock and getting the order ready for the disposable cups. I had my back to the counter and I became aware of someone standing in front of the counter. I turned to see the store manager standing in front of the counter. I smiled sweetly but he was stony faced and held up a canvas bag and said, 'What's this doing here?'

I blinked in disbelief as I recognised the cash register float bag. I had completely forgotten to put it in the register. The following pay day I was dismissed. It had been the longest drama packed five months of my life.

I went through a number of jobs in rapid succession after that, I was a slave in a laundry for three weeks. I had to start at six in the morning and work like a slave until three o'clock with only half an hour for lunch. I was dismissed for yawning too much. The woman who owned the business was a fair dinkum slave driver. I reckon if she had've had her way, we three girls who worked for her would've been chained by the ankles to the presses and only given bread and water once a day.

Then I worked for a corner store at Ironside for about a month, but the woman who owned the shop didn't like the way I swept the floor. It wasn't that I left the floor dirty she wanted me to hold the broom the same way she did. I didn't realise that there was a law preventing people from holding the handle of a broom differently to others. But apparently there was, because I got swept out the door with the rest of the rubbish.

I worked at a milk/sandwich bar in Adelaide Street for a while. I can't remember why I didn't stay there for any length of time, but I do remember the man who owned the shop wanted desperately to take my co-worker into the back room. She was a very beautiful girl with olive skin and jet-black hair. She was nineteen, which in my opinion then, ranked her as being a sophisticated woman of the world. She goes down in my history book as having made the quote of the twentieth century. I can still here her saying to me about our boss, 'He's got no chance, the greasy old bastard. Christ it would be like putting a marshmallow into a money box.'

I finally landed a job making sandwiches and milkshakes and selling cigarettes and lollies. You didn't have to be Einstein to figure out that the family who owned this business was not Mr and Mrs Average. They were far from being a normal, healthy, wholesome family. There was Mr and Mrs Grady and their two adult sons, one daughter-in-law with a three-month old baby girl and the Grady's daughter who was in her early twenties. Nothing wrong with that, but this family was decidedly odd, to say the least.

In between serving customers and making sandwiches I was required to tend to the baby, which included feeding and bathing her. Every morning without fail I was made to put a suppository in the baby's bottom. Now keep in mind that I had just turned fifteen and I had no knowledge about babies whatsoever. Every

Wednesday like clockwork, Mr and Mrs Grady and their two sons, daughter-in-law and granddaughter would go out leaving Sonia (their daughter) and me to look after the shop, but not for long. About half an hour after the Grady's left, Sonia's 'boyfriend' would arrive and they would disappear into the back of the shop to her bedroom and they didn't emerge until lunchtime. He would leave after having a passionate farewell with her in the doorway of the shop, she telling him that she wished he could stay longer, and he telling her that he didn't want to go. She'd watch him walk away until he had disappeared out of sight then she'd hurry through to the back of the shop and emerge twenty minutes later with her long blonde hair still wet from the shower.

Ten minutes later at twelve thirty on the dot, her second 'boyfriend' would arrive. She greeted him with as much passion as she had farewelled the first 'boyfriend' and they would go to the back of the shop and wouldn't surface for air until three o'clock. She would again go through the process bidding this poor sap a fond farewell. Then she'd go back to the shower and alight as fresh as a daisy. A few minutes later, her parents, brothers and sister-in-law would arrive home.

Whoever said the fifties were the innocent years were sadly mistaken.

I would've beaten a hasty retreat from that job within the first week but for one reason. The second day I was there a handsome familiar face came in and I was transfixed as I observed from afar, how friendly and at ease he was with all the members of the Grady family. Mrs Grady told him that they had employed a new girl and called me over to meet Tony. He was more handsome than what I remembered him from our first meeting eighteen months or so previously, when he had introduced himself as Constable Potlick. He didn't show any signs of recognising me but he gave me a beautiful smile and a wink of approval as if he liked what he saw. I knew I looked older than what I was but I secretly wished I was at least two years older. I was given strict instructions by the Grady's that Tony was a good friend and that I had to make sure that I didn't muck up his lunch order. I had no intentions of mucking up his lunch order, he was going to get Rolls Royce treatment from me full stop. After he had gone, I asked if his last name was Potlick. They all laughed and told me his name was Tom Ermiston, but that everyone calls him Tony, but why did you think his name was Potlick?' I told them the story about our encounter with him at Anzac Park and they laughed and told me that Tony probably would've joined in and had a smoke with us if you had invited him. He's a really lovely bloke, and everyone around here thinks the world of him.'

Later in the day Tony came back into the shop to get another of his favourite malted milks and Jim Grady said, 'That'll be one shilling and six pence (fifteen cents) to you, Constable Potlick.' I could have willingly choked him on the spot. Tony looked at him and said, 'What made you call me that?' Jim pointed to me and said, 'Amelia thought that was your name.'

I was totally embarrassed and I knew he would know that I wasn't as old as what I looked when he realised that I was one of the kids he'd spoken to in Anzac Park. He looked at me with a very approving eye

Constable Potlick 'You sure have grown I wouldn't have recognised you in a million years.'

Amelia (cheekily) 'You'll never be a detective then, will you?'

Constable Potlick 'God I hope not.'

Amelia (Feeling more at ease with him) 'You should be a criminal instead of a cop, giving people false names.'

Constable Potlick (laughing) 'I knew you were all up to no good and I figured if you could tell me fibs, I was entitled to tell you fibs too.'

From that day, I made it my business to have lunch with Tony at the police station every day he was on duty. Except on Wednesdays when Sonia entertained her 'boyfriends' because I never got a lunch break on those days. Tony was a truly lovely young bloke and I enjoyed his company and our lengthy conversations. I would have given my eyeteeth (if I had any) to go out with him and I always had the feeling that he would've liked to ask me out too. If only I had been another two years older. All good things must come to an end though, and after I'd been with the Grady's about six months, I felt enough was enough. When they tried to get me to do all their housework as well, I figured that before too long they'd expect me to jump into bed with them all. So, I left whilst the going was good.

I was invited to go out to the movies with a fellow whose name escapes me. I had nothing better to do, so we went to the local pictures. I wasn't particularly interested in the fellow or the movie for that matter. So, at interval when I met up with two friends whom I hadn't seen for a while, I was only too pleased to stay with them and talk. We walked up the hill towards the cemetery away from the pictures on the other side of the road. We recognised a car, which belonged to another local bloke whom we all knew fairly well. The car was unlocked and one of us suggested that we should sit in it and talk in comfort. We saw no reason why we shouldn't have been there we weren't doing any harm just sitting and having a chat.

We were there for about twenty minutes or so when another fellow, Paul, whom we all knew, came staggering up the hill. It was obvious he'd been drinking but he was harmless enough and in good humour. He came over to the car and started talking to us. All of a sudden, the fellow I'd come to the pictures with, came up and accused me of two timing him with Paul. There was a lot of yelling and swearing and Paul threw an empty beer bottle, which hit the car smashing the window.

The old lady in the house nearest where the car was parked called out that she was calling the police. Everyone scattered and ran to the milk bar opposite the theatre. The police car arrived and of course no one knew anything about the car up the road being broken into. I hid behind the majority of the crowd but it didn't do me any good. I heard Tony's voice say, 'The young lady standing in the back there, I'd like to have a talk to you, would you step this way please.'

Very sheepishly I walked out onto the footpath and Tony said in a hushed tone, 'Righto, Amelia, what's the story?'

Out of fear, I stammered, 'I don't know, Tony. Honest to God I don't.'

'Don't give me that, love. I can't help you unless you help me.'

I confessed that I had been sitting in the car but I wouldn't say who else was there other than that two guys started to fight and one of them threw a bottle.

He said, 'Baby face is in charge of this, I'll give him the information and I'll get you home, away from all of this.'

I didn't know if to cry with relief or cry with fear because I was relieved to be out of the mess. Being driven home in a cop car was going to be a bit difficult to explain to Edith and Dad. Tony drove me to the top of our street and as he pulled up, he said, 'I could lose my job for doing this, Amelia, by rights I should take you directly home and speak to your parents.'

I promised him faithfully that I'd never tell anyone and I kept that promise. The following morning, I was walking past the local taxi rank on my way to meet a friend when a car full of demons (detectives) pulled up alongside me. One door flew open and the biggest Bull cop I've ever seen, growled,

'Are you Amelia Long?'

Amelia 'Y ... y ... yes,'

Bull cop 'Get in the car.'

Perhaps I had seen too many Edward G Robinson films

Amelia 'I don't even know who you are. You could be gangsters for all I know.'

Bull cop 'Don't be a little smart arse.'

He grabbed my arm and dragged me into the big black car. They drove me home, and on the way, they told me that Sgt Neilson' (Baby face) had found my diary which had fallen out of my handbag in the back of the car. I had also left a beautiful black cardigan with silver lurex thread through it, which I'd borrowed from Edith. Neither of which, was ever returned. I'll bet London to a brick, that the Bull's wife wore that for a long time.

I found out later that Tony had tried to stop Baby Face from contacting the Demons but to no avail. His co-workers hated Baby Face, as much as the teenagers who lived in the area hated him. Because I wouldn't name names, the Demons wanted to charge me with wilful destruction of property, which of course would have resulted in me being sent into a girl's home, if I was found guilty. That was a big possibility. The only thing that stopped them was the little old lady who had rung the police. She had told Tony that I had tried to break up the fight. It didn't matter a hill of beans that I was innocent, or that I was a victim of circumstances, my mother and father judged me guilty, and that alone was punishment enough.

Years later I rang police headquarters and found out that Tony was still in the force and had been promoted to sergeant. I went to the station where he worked, and we had a good long chinwag over old times. He hadn't changed one iota he was still a lovely bloke. He even confessed that he had been interested in me and would have loved to have taken me out. But as I had suspected, my age had been a big deterrent. He also told me that Baby Face had had heart surgery and that the doctor had replaced his heart valve with a pig's valve. We both pissed ourselves with laughter when I exclaimed, 'How appropriate.' I thought at the time what a pity the Queensland Police Force couldn't clone Constable Potlick. In the last twelve months I 'tracked down' Tony and I was given his mobile phone number. I rang him and we had a lengthy chat. He had become an Inspector and had retired many years previously. I asked him why he had chosen the alias Potlick and he replied that was my wife's maiden name. He had given me enough information about his life that I was able to work out that he was twenty-eight years old when I was fifteen! My lifetime of wondering what my life would have been like if I'd married him was shattered in that lengthy phone call as I realised how close I came to a possible predator!

I became a bottle blonde and quite a few people commented that I looked like Doris Day. I tried to pretend that they were exaggerating, but I secretly thought I did too and every time she changed her hairstyle, I'd try and copy her. My only wish was that I could sing as good as she could and have the money she was earning. Bridget Bardot, Marilyn Monroe, Diana Dors and Jayne Mansfield were enjoying the limelight as sex

sirens. Two girlfriends, Lesley and Veronica, who lived around the corner from my grandmother's home, talked me into allowing them to dye my hair ash blonde like Jayne Mansfield. It didn't matter that I didn't look like Jayne Mansfield or for that matter I didn't even have long hair. Veronica honestly believed that she looked like Bridget Bardot and would tell people to call her Midget Bridget. Midget was about as much like Bridget Bardot as Jerry Lewis looked like Elvis Presley. Anyhow she and Lesley, equipped with the correct blonding emulsion, fervently went to work to perform a miraculous transformation of my crowning glory. They added the precious purple drops to the liquid, as the instructions stated. Carefully wiping the mixture on my head almost strand by strand, they chatted away animatedly telling me how good it was going to look, and then the chatter became muttered whispers. I heard Lesley issue instructions to try some water and Midget whispered back, 'No that's not right.' A bit more whispered muttering and I eventually asked, 'How's it looking does it look okay?' More mutterings and Lesley exclaimed, 'Shit, Amelia, its purple.'

I laughed and said, 'Don't bullshit. Is it looking alright?' Midget said, with urgency in her voice, 'This is no bullshit, mate, your hair has turned purple.

'Quick get me a mirror.

Lesley took the little mirror off her bathroom wall and handed it to me. I stared hard into the mirror and blinked hard, as I tried to focus in the dimly lit room. My hands poured with perspiration as I witnessed my crowning glory in the deepest shade of mauve I have ever seen. I cried out not caring who heard me, 'Oh shit, one of you race down to the shop and get a bottle of peroxide quick.' Midget said, 'It's after eight o'clock, they'll be closed,' I said, 'I don't give a stuff if they're in bed fast asleep, you just get me the bottle of peroxide or you're going to be bald.' Lesley took off and was back within five minutes with two bottles of peroxide and we poured the contents of one over my head and kept rubbing it through my hair until all the purple turned yellow.

Two days later my grandmother took me into an exclusive hairdresser on the fourth floor of the Penny's building and instructed the owner, 'I don't care how much it costs, please get that dreadful peroxide out of her hair the best way you can.'

I came out with Henna coloured locks. I must say it suited it me very much, I learnt my lesson from that experience, and I have never put a colour through my hair since.

I believe I can claim the infamy of being the first person to ever have purple hair.

Of course, it became popular with the elderly many years later and with the punks in the eighties. But I would've been locked up if I had walked out in public with purple hair in 1959.

It wasn't too long before I found another job. This time it was Johnston's cake shop in Fortitude Valley. Apart from the two brothers who owned the shop, there were a couple of bakers and the head woman, Ethel (who was having an affair with one of the brothers,) and three other shop assistants. Thelma came from a poor background and although I felt sorry for her, she lost all the compassion I had for her the day she used my brush and comb and gave me a head full of nits. Edith wasn't overly impressed either because she caught them from me. We spent a great deal of quality time de lousing each other.

Marilyn was a bit of a twit. She was a nice enough person, but she tried so hard to be everyone's friend that it was sickening. I used to be highly amused every time I heard her tell a customer that sausage rolls cost fourfpence (four pence, approximately three cents).

Leone was a lovely girl and I liked her from the moment I met her. She was an attractive looking girl and would have won a Sophia Loren look-alike competition hands down. Leone lived on the northside and had many friends who lived in the area. All the teenagers of that surrounding area would congregate in The Hub Cafe at the tram terminus. It was such a great place with a fantastic atmosphere and it became my regular haunting place too. I used to enjoy every moment I ever spent at The Hub. Though on reflection, there were two occasions that come to mind that I wouldn't want to relive in a hurry.

There were at least thirty teenagers who regularly went to The Hub and probably just as many who called in occasionally. I knew most of them reasonably well and I like to think that I was fairly popular with most of them. It was a big shock to the system, (to say the least) when one of the occasional regulars came in one night whilst I was talking to a group. He had obviously been drinking and he said very loudly, 'What are you talking to that bitch for?' Someone said, 'What's wrong with you?' He replied, 'That Amelia, she's nothing but a moll.'

He went on and on what a low-class slut I was. Quite a few people tried to shut him up, but he kept up the abuse until I walked over to him and said, 'I don't know what's eating you, mate, but I think you've got a kind and likeable face, --the kind I'd like to throw shit at. The entire cafe went absolutely wild with applause and laughter and someone said, 'Mate I think you'd better apologise to Amelia, she's a good kid. The Amelia you're thinking of comes from northside and this Amelia lives near the southside.' The fellow came up to me and apologised profusely to me and offered to buy me a coke or a malted milk or anything I wanted. I declined his offer and he put his arm around me and said, 'Sorry, sweetheart, I was completely in the wrong, but Jesus that was the best line I've ever heard, you really put me in my place. I thought you were complimenting me and you made me feel like a real mongrel.' I patted him on his face and with a smirk a mile wide I said, 'That's because you've got a head like a robber's dog.' Every time he saw me after that night, he'd come up and give me a cuddle and tell me what a good sport I was.

The second incident happened on Boxing Day. Leone and I were walking along the footpath towards The Hub when a fellow whom we'd never seen before pulled up alongside of us and asked us if we wanted a lift. We both said, 'No thanks.'

We kept walking and talking and trying to ignore the fellow who kept his car in motion at the same pace as what we were walking at. He kept calling out questions such as where we were going, if we were meeting someone and we kept ignoring him. He then started to yell at top note, 'Who the hell do you think you are, ya stuck up bitches?'

I replied, in my best-spoken voice, 'She's Sophia Loren and I'm Doris Day.'

We kept walking and talking and we were just so pleased that we'd gotten rid of him. We finally reached The Hub but it was closed, so we sat down on the tram seat outside and were deep in conversation when the fellow in the V.W. came up alongside of us again and yelled, 'You pair of bitches have got tickets on yourselves haven't you?'

I had had about as much of this fellow as I could stand. I knew if we ignored him, he wasn't going away so I said in an exasperated tone, 'Look, mate, go and take a running jump at yourself will you, you're too bloody ugly to be bothered with.'

He jumped out of the car grabbed me by the throat and shoved my head several times against the brick wall. I thought I was going to lose consciousness and could feel my head starting to spin and I could hear Leone's voice screeching at top note telling him to let go of me. He jumped back into the car and took off towards the city as fast as he could move. Leone memorised the first three numbers of his number plate and as groggy as I was, I managed to remember the last three numbers. Leone rang the police and one young cop turned up about twenty minutes later.

We gave him the number of the car, the make and colour of the car and a very good description of the fellow and he drove away in hot pursuit. We sat there waiting, and a couple of the boys who were regulars at The Hub came along. When we told them what had happened, they were absolutely ropeable. They wanted to go and sort the fellow out there and then and they reprimanded us for not ringing them instead of the cops. I knew that if we had've rung them instead of ringing the cops the guy would've needed an ambulance. We told them that the cop would be back at any time and that they'd better bugger off. The cops never needed an excuse to pull up any teenager to question what they were doing and why they were there, even if they were only waiting for a tram. They didn't need to be told a second time, especially when they saw the cop car approaching.

The young cop said, 'The number you gave, doesn't correspond with a Volkswagen, so I'm afraid there's nothing that can be done.'

Fortunately, two of us had a brain and one wasn't the cop. Leone and I asked to see what number he had written down and he had written the wrong number down. He phoned through to headquarters and they got the fellow. Apparently, he pleaded guilty in court a couple of days later and went for a three-month holiday at Her Majesty's Prison at Boggo Road.

Chapter 12

Tolerance is not my Virtue

I didn't stay at Johnston's Cake Shop for more than six months or so but I associated with Leone and The Hub crowd for about twelve months, before moving on to meet other friends. Apart from my friendship with Leone, the memories that stick in my mind of my time at Johnston's were two customers who came in at separate times during the day. Stink Bomb as we had so eloquently named him was a poor old alcoholic derelict who wandered the streets of Fortitude Valley by day and slept in the cattle trains at night. He would come in to the shop to buy a pie with peas every midmorning, usually when there was a shop full of customers. Of course, he would always be served first otherwise the other customers would exit faster than a speeding bullet. He absolutely reeked of stale grog, dung and vomit. As much as I felt sorry for the poor bastard, I couldn't serve him because I would dry retch as soon as I got a whiff of him. He got a bit obstreperous one morning and Ethel ordered him out of the shop. In a well-spoken, obviously well-educated voice he said, 'I will take my business elsewhere and I shall not return.' But he did return a month or so later but Ethel chased him out of the shop with the millet broom.

The other customer was old mother Scot, so named because she had a strong Scottish accent. She wore an old petticoat with an unbuttoned lightweight coat over the top of it and a pair of old, scuffed, slippers on her feet. She would come in and say, 'I want thruppence worth of meat for me carts.' (In English, 'I want threepence worth of meat for my cats.')

We'd all take it in turns to serve her and every day we'd say, 'Sorry we don't sell sausage meat try the butcher shop down the road.'

She would shuffle out the door and down the street out of sight, until the following day. I said to Ethel one day, 'I feel sorry for the poor old bugger, don't you?'

Ethel looked at me in disbelief and said, 'Poor bugger be blowed, she's one of the wealthiest women in Brisbane. She owns at least six homes in the Fortitude Valley and South Brisbane areas and is collecting more money in weekly rent than what you'd earn in six month's wage.'

Flabbergasted, I said, 'But look at the way she's dressed.'

Ethel replied, 'That's nothing, you should see where she lives. In a dirty back room of one of the block of flats that she owns. She's got no bathroom or toilet facilities and she keeps at least six cats in the room with her.'

The next time she came in, Marilyn said to old mother Scot, 'I'm sorry we don't have any sausage meat but we've got sausage rolls and they're fourfpence.'

The old lady bought the sausage roll and when she left, I said to Marilyn, 'You're a nut, what did you do that for?' She replied, 'I'm sick of the silly old bag coming in and asking for sausage meat.' I said, 'Smart thinking, brainstorm, she'll probably come in to complain tomorrow.' Three days went by and we never saw hide nor hair of old mother Scot. When she finally came in, Marilyn went up to her and said, 'Hello, may I help you?' The old girl put the familiar paper bag with the Johnston's Cake Shop writing on it, onto the counter and said, 'I bought this here sorsage roll for me carts and they dinner lark it, so I want me money bark.' I was the only one who was game enough to tell the old girl to P.O.Q. but I didn't. We all hid in the back room absolutely pissing ourselves with laughter, whilst Marilyn tried desperately for about ten minutes explaining why she couldn't give the old girl her money back.

I was quite keen on a blonde-haired, blue-eyed fellow by the name of Rodney Grainger who lived at Chermside. We didn't go together in the true sense of the word. My idea of going with a boy was to have him pick you up at your front door or at the very least arranging to meet you at a particular time. Rodney and I never had that understanding. A whole mob of us would arrange to be at The Hub to go to the movies or a party and we'd pair off. This arrangement went on for about three months, until Rodney announced that he was going to Sydney to live.

I was really upset, but I managed not to show it, it was against my nature to allow anyone to see me cry. I was made of tougher stuff than that. I was quite shocked when he pleaded with me to go with him. Considering that we'd never been intimate, I considered that to be his way of saying that he really cared. I was very tempted to go with him and I gave the matter a considerable amount of thought before declining. I came to the conclusion that my family meant more to me than to run away from them. Besides, I thought Rodney might change his mind if I didn't go with him. He had made up his mind and left for Sydney leaving me broken-hearted.

Such a heart wrenching tragedy and I hadn't yet turned sixteen.

Chapter 13

Sweet Sixteen

I've often wondered why I bring out the worst in people. Is it because I'm short that people think that they can treat me like shit and get away with it? Or is it because I'm so brutally honest in my comments and they can't handle the truth? (I know that honesty is not the best policy, because I've proved time and time again that when someone asks for an honest opinion they are really saying, tell me what I want to hear.) Perhaps I've got the type of face that only a mother would love. I've never thought I was good-looking and I still get a sixth sense about some people and I know they don't like me just by the way they look at me. Some may call this paranoia I call it gut instinct.

I don't know what it was that turned a party I went to into a near riot. We were having a BBQ on a secluded block of land out Stafford way when another girl called Pat took a sudden dislike to me. (What is it about these girls called Pat?) She had been making snide comments about me for the best part of an hour and I was getting very pissed off with her. But I thought, keep your trap shut, Amelia, or you'll end up getting your head kicked in or at the very least walking home on your own.

I would've kept my trap shut too, except Pat came up to me and told me that she hated my guts because I was so bloody ugly. I replied only too readily, 'You're no oil painting yourself and you're a fat slob.'

That was it we got stuck into each other, no holds barred. I made sure she threw the first punch, because there was no way in the wide world that I wanted to be accused of starting the blue. She was a big lump of a girl with long blonde hair, which was a distinct advantage for me. I didn't hesitate to get a good grip on her hair and twisted many strands around my fingers and pulled as hard as I could. She punched me several times in the stomach and breasts and I knew I was losing the fight and my grip. I decided to go for broke and I kneed her in the crutch. As she fell, I fell on top of her, with her hair still knotted in my hand. My face landed onto her arm and I thought, Oh well! here goes the teeth again. I sank my fangs into the fleshy part of her upper arm. People were running around yelling instructions, some were saying, 'Let them go.' Others were screaming, 'They'll kill each other.'

Somehow or other we stopped fighting and the party broke up. Two weeks or so later, whilst a number of us were waiting for a tram to go to the city, a voice yelled out, 'Amelia'. I turned around and nearly had heart failure as I came face to face with Pat. She smiled held out her hand for me to shake

Pat 'No hard feelings, mate'.

Amelia 'Yeah, no hard feelings, mate'. As I shook her hand I said, 'I'd rather shake your fist than feel it in my gut'.

Pat (laughing) 'You've got bloody strong teeth I can tell you that, have a look at this'.

She turned her arm towards me to show a distinct T scar where I'd bitten her.

Amelia (horrified) 'Jesus, I'm sorry. T for teeth huh?'

Pat 'No T for tough, you're as tough as old boot leather'.

The tram came along and we said our goodbyes and I never saw her from that day to this. Teenagers in the fifties were certainly a very strange breed of animal.

I was about to turn sixteen and I had to plead with Edith to allow me to have a birthday party. I invited most of the regular crowd from The Hub to attend. I didn't expect too many of them to arrive because I lived so far away from their area. Most of them had to rely on public transport which meant a change of two trams to get to my place, then a ten-minute walk from the tram stop. I was like a Jack in the box the entire day waiting the time of the arrival of my guests, I was so nervous.

Finally, they started to arrive a few at a time and within half an hour there were so many kids flooding through the doors Edith said, 'How many more are coming? I don't think we've got enough food for them all'.

A few of the older fellows arrived on their motorbikes and had brought a couple of bottles of beer with them. I asked Dad for his permission to allow them to bring the beer in but he was adamant that they couldn't. I was really angry with him for that, but the fellows weren't a bit upset by Dad's decision. They said that they could understand how he felt and they stayed and enjoyed the party anyway. I only wish I could have enjoyed the party as much as everyone else, I was still so nervous about everyone enjoying themselves I was running around like a chook with its head cut off. So much so, that I kept changing my clothes about every half an hour or so. The one thing that stays in my mind about that night was, all the girls exclaiming how lucky I was to have so many beautiful clothes to choose from. As per usual I was unable to take a compliment and all I could say was that they were nothing but old rags.

Mum had baked me a beautiful birthday cake and Edith had iced it. Unfortunately, the icing left a lot to be desired. Edith could cook, crochet and sew, but icing cakes was not one of her best qualities. I, being the ungrateful little bitch that I am, had to make a big song and dance about it, telling her that I didn't want the cake because everyone would laugh at me. Fortunately, one of the girls told me not to be so silly and the cake was hungrily devoured and enjoyed by all. I only wish I could remember more of that night because I know it was one of the happiest nights of my life, typical of me to only remember the worst moments of it.

Chapter 14

Charmed I'm Sure

Edward had been going with a girl by the name of Beth whom Dad could not stand a bar of. I won't be unkind enough to repeat the nickname he called her behind her back, but I can assure you it was not complimentary. Dad was less than impressed when Edward announced she was pregnant and that he wanted to marry her. As far as Dad was concerned Edward was marrying below his standing. Be as it may, they were married and I was their bridesmaid.

Beth had arranged for me to apply for a job at Golden Investments, which was the head office of the Golden Casket agency. She had been with the office for a short period of time before I started there. Working with her gave me a better insight of what she was really like and I knew that this girl was more trouble than what she seemed. I remember overhearing her telling one of our co-workers that Edward had ruined her life because she was pregnant. I may have been ten months younger than her, but I still knew I had more common sense than what she had shown. For a start, I wasn't that naive that I didn't realise that it took two to tango, and secondly, I had more self-respect than to sleep with a fellow whom I'd only known for a few weeks. She and her friends always tried to make me feel as if I was dirt beneath their feet. Maybe I was, but if I was, at least I didn't try to blame someone else for my downfall. I think it would be a fair assumption to say that the entire Long family, with the exception of Edward didn't approve of Beth, however, we tried our hardest to tolerate her for Edward's sake.

Working at Golden Investments was different to say the least. There were approximately thirty girls working in one large room, each of them was as different as chalk cheese and chips. Our job entailed writing out the casket tickets for interstate and overseas customers. I can assure you that the majority of the customers had sick perverted minds, if their choice of syndicate names were any indication. Pennytration, Mickey Dripping, 041 Nought E, and I've got a l-o-n-g'n for u. These were just some of the requests that come to mind. All of us would have a good laugh at some of them, the more suggestive, the louder we'd laugh. One of the girls who worked near me was a girl by the name of Diana, she and I got along fairly well. We had one particular thing in common, she disliked Beth as much as I did, probably more. Well, actually there were quite a few who disliked Beth, but no one dared show it because Beth was on very friendly terms with the head girl of the office. Of course, when there are more than three females in one office for any length of time, there's bound to be a certain amount of bitchiness sooner or later. Believe me, not one day went by that at least one girl wasn't being talked about. One particular girl really sticks in my mind, because her nocturnal habits left everyone agog. In all fairness to her, it would be unkind of me to say that she wasn't a full quid, but she certainly stretched the strange barrier. Betty washed her black hair in Rinso a common brand of washing powder in those days to try and make it whiter and brighter. She was a very plain looking girl who dressed in child-like dresses and she always wore black school shoes with white socks. Her hair was black straight and cut in the basin style. Most days she would come to work looking like something the cat would refuse to drag in. She would invariably give anyone who was prepared to listen to her, a blow-by-blow description of her sexual prowess of the night before. At first when I heard her telling her stories I thought, she's got to be kidding. She was not by any stretch of the imagination a very pretty sight. My theory proved to be totally wrong someone had observed her on a number of occasions out with different fellows. Diana and I came to the conclusion that she would have to put a bag over her head before any fellow crawled into bed with her. She certainly had the entire office whispering when she started pumping No Doze tablets down her throat to keep herself awake after a particularly heavy night. It wasn't long after Edward and Beth were married that I was given my marching orders. According to the boss, the head girl, I won't even give her the satisfaction of a fictitious name had reported me for swearing too much. I didn't argue with his decision, but I couldn't help but smile to myself when I thought of the double standard irony. Hypocrisy by another name. For six months I had been exposed to reading and having to write lewd and suggestive sayings and listening to an obviously overactive, pill popping, nymphomaniac. Yet I wasn't allowed to say an occasional shit or bloody because it supposedly offended a big fat stuck up bitch who didn't like me.

Ah well. You win some you lose some.

My losses seemed to be far out numbering the wins though. My luck was bound to change soon though, surely to God.

I loved to dance and going to Cloudland ballroom on Saturday afternoons and to the Railway Institute on Friday nights was the most important thing in my life from the time I left school. I can't remember what year it was when Johnny O'Keefe arrived to play at Cloudland. He made a big Cecril B de Mille production of an entrance, pushing his way through the kids on the dance floor, wearing a lime green and lemon suit. I took one look at him and said with my usual panache, 'Oh shit.' He heard my exclamation and with a swish of his arms he replied, 'The fans rushed me, I didn't have time to change'. Without batting an eye, I retorted, 'I wouldn't piss on you if you were on fire'. I know that some people may be offended by that comment, because O'Keefe is a rock and roll icon in Australia. But the truth of the matter is he was also an egotist. And as far as I'm concerned, he couldn't sing to save himself, he was a screamer and a showman. It was around the same time that I went to a big rock concert at Milton Tennis Courts where I saw Johnny Cash, Gene Vincent and Col Joye on the same programme. I went down to the back of the stage along with hundreds of other screaming fans and we all stood in hope of meeting some of the stars. I couldn't believe my luck when both Gene Vincent and Col Joye came down and signed autographs. I stood at the wire fence separating them from the fans, and instead of leaving as soon I got their autographs I stayed and talked to them for what seemed like an eternity. I was thrilled out of my brain when they asked me if I'd like to go to a party at Oxley. They gave me the address and told me it was Johnny O'Keefe's home for when he stayed in Brisbane. I would have given my right arm to go, but I figured that they might have wanted more than my charm and personality to entertain them that night. I declined the offer.

I walked into the Railway Institute one night sporting my first perm which I had paid an absolute fortune for. It had cost me an extra two pound to have a secret formula poured on my head to prevent the perming lotion frizzing my hair. I had arranged to meet Diana, and on seeing her, I walked up to where she was sitting and stood in front of her. She looked up at me and when she showed no signs of recognition, I smiled and said, 'It's me'. She looked at me and said, 'I'm sorry I don't know you'. Thinking she was joking I said, 'Ya silly bugger'.

She looked at me again and absolutely roared with laughter and screamed out at top note, 'What went wrong, did you put your hand in the light socket.?'

'It's not that bad is it?' She wiped tears from her eyes and said, 'Not unless you plan on joining the Fuzzy Wuzzys.' It was many years before I dared to have another perm.

I met Robin and her sister, Ellen, through a girl whom I had met at Stott's Business College. I had known them awhile and I would occasionally bump into

them at dances. Robin was the same age as me and had a bit more get up and
go than Ellen who was about a year older. Ellen always seemed to me to be a
bit on the shy side, she was certainly a lot quieter. Anyhow, Robin had made
arrangements with me to go to the Gold Coast on this particular Sunday. After
much pleading with Edith she finally consented to my staying at Robin's home
on the Saturday night so that we could get a good start the following morning.
I had been to the Gold Coast with Leone on the train a few months earlier and
it had been the longest, most boring trip of my life. We had spent most of the
journey pretending we were cowboys shooting out of the windows at Indians,
just as we had seen on Wagon Train every week on TV. So rather than be bored
senseless again, Robin and I decided to travel by bus. We got to the highway in
plenty of time and waited for over an hour. When we finally realised that the bus
wasn't going to show up, we were just about ready to go back to Robin's home
when she said, 'Let's hitchhike to the Coast'. I was not keen on the idea at all.
It had always been drummed into me from an early age never to get into a car
unless they were family or close friends of the family. (Even though I had taken
the risk by getting into a stranger's car in the dead of night, a year or so earlier.)
When I said this to Robin, she said, 'That's for kids, come on don't be chicken.
There's two of us, they'd have to be pretty good to beat the two of us together'.

Reluctantly I agreed. It wasn't too long before an old guy in an old utility
pulled up alongside of us. I didn't like the look of him, but Robin had accepted
the lift before I could protest. She opened the door and said to me, 'Do you want
to sit in the middle?'

'No, I better sit near the window because I suffer from car sickness.' I sighed a
quiet sigh of relief as she scrambled in first. It was true that I suffered car sickness,
but that wasn't the reason I chose the window seat. I may not have been the
brightest kid in the world, but I had already figured that if this old coot was going
to try any funny business, I had access to the door and I would have been out
and up the road faster than John Landy. We got about halfway to the Gold Coast
then he announced that he had to make a delivery of a parcel to a house at the
end of an old dirt track. My hand went slowly over near the door handle and I
never missed a stone on that dirt track. Robin seemed to be totally oblivious of us
being in any imminent danger. Fortunately, he was true to his word and he took
a parcel into an old farmhouse and got back into the ute and drove us directly
to Southport. We got out and we thanked him profusely. I was shaking like a

leaf in a westerly wind, both with fear of what could have happened and with excitement that we'd arrived safely.

I made a secret promise to myself that I would definitely not be hitchhiking back to Brisbane or anywhere else for that matter. I told myself, if the worse comes to the worse, Amelia, you'll catch the train back and shoot the bloody Indians as you go.

We headed to Surfers Paradise and ended up at one of the beer gardens. I'd learnt my lesson from drinking that bottle of Brandivino twelve months or so earlier, not to drink alcohol again. Besides I hated the taste of all alcohol so I stuck to drinking lemonade. Not so Robin, she was sinking them back like a wharfie at the six o'clock swill. We met up with some fellows who lived in Brisbane and they promised us that they'd drive us back to Brisbane after the session closed at six o'clock. I didn't want to appear to be a worrywart, so I figured I'd take them at their word. But I had a bit of a panic attack when I remembered that the last train to Brisbane left at five o'clock.

I thought to myself, what the hell am I going to do if they change their minds. Sitting in the beer garden was giving me the shits, and I reminded Robin that we'd come down to the coast for some fun and I sure as hell didn't think sitting there all day was my idea of fun. The lunchtime session finished and we went for a drive in their car, but that was about as much fun as we had because we all ended up back at the beer garden for the afternoon session.

Finally, closing time rolled around and we all piled into the car. I said a few silent Hail Mary's as thanks and a few Jesus, Mary and Joseph's to protect us from harm. Someone suggested that they were hungry and wanted to get a hamburger. We drove around looking for a good hamburger joint.

My navigational skills in those days were very limited, however, I think we were at Burleigh Heads and by the time we found a suitable place waited for the burgers to be cooked and actually ate them, it was seven-thirty. By this time, I was really packing death with worry about what time we'd get home. Trying to sound very casual, I said

'When are we leaving?'

Robin 'Not until tomorrow morning'.

Totally flabbergasted, I yelled, 'What?'

She replied very casually, 'We've decided to sleep on the beach'.

I could feel the tears stinging the backs of my eyeballs as I fought as hard as I could to stop them spilling down my cheeks.

Amelia 'W … when d … did you decide this?'

Robin 'When we were in the pub and you were in the loo'.

I could feel my heart pound as hard as the surf and as I looked out the car window wondering what the hell I was going to do? A light shower of rain began to fall, tears welled in a flood and about two hundred feet from the car I saw a taxi pull up and a solitary figure alighted and ran to get out of the rain. I grabbed my beach bag, opened the door and ran as fast as my legs could move. I held one arm in the air and shouted, 'Taxi, Taxi'. The cab driver held the door open and I dived in. I burst into tears and absolutely sobbed. When I finally managed to speak, I said, 'How much will it be to drive me to Brisbane, driver?' The cabbie turned around and tried desperately to calm me down and I began to cry again. Still sobbing, I told him what had happened. We looked over to where the car had been parked just in time to see them drive away. The cabbie said, 'I think you've done the right thing, sweetheart, I just hope we don't hear on the news tomorrow that your girlfriend's body has been found in some deserted area'. I arrived home at five past midnight and I had to go into Edith and ask her to lend me five pounds (my entire week's wage) to pay the driver his fare. Edith went off her brain telling me that she wasn't going to give me a penny for the fare and reprimanded me for not being home hours earlier. I couldn't even begin to tell you how much she harped on about how thoughtless and inconsiderate I was. I yelled, 'Would you prefer that I should've spent the night on the beach with Robin and those blokes and possibly been raped and murdered?' There was no immediate reply just a look of disgusted disbelief. I then added, 'By the time you muck around, the cost of the fare will be up to six quid' That struck a nerve, she scurried off to get her purse and handing over the fiver she said, 'You're going to have to pay me back at the end of the week'. Terrific, her only daughter escapes untouched and unharmed from a fate worse than death and all she can think of is that I have to pay her, her precious bloody fiver by the end of the week. To add insult to injury she added, 'And lower your voice or you'll wake your father'.

Jesus. I couldn't win even if I was the only competitor. Lunchtime the following day, Robin came in to see me at work. She had the audacity and gall to try and borrow some money from me. She was still wearing her swimmers and her hair looked as if it hadn't been combed. I was so angry I just wanted to punch her into the ground. In my most disgusted and disgruntled tone, I spat,

'Robin, get out of here before I do something I'll enjoy'.

You would think that I would have learnt my lesson with Robin and steered clear of her the moment I clasped eyes on her again wouldn't you? Not me. Approximately six months later, I went to the Railway Institute dance on my own and Robin was there by herself as well. We sat and talked and she apologised for what she had done and I accepted her apology. I had a few dances and talked to a number of people whom I knew and at the end of the night I was offered a lift home, which I declined. I started to walk to the gates of the Edward Street entrance of the Railway Institute on my way to catch my tram in Adelaide Street when Robin ran up behind me grabbing my arm and said, 'Come on, we'll give you a lift home'.

I declined but she persisted. 'I know these fellows, they're okay. They're giving me a lift and they said they'll drive you home too'.

I asked very suspiciously, 'Where do they live?'

Robin 'Not far from me'.

Amelia 'But that's nowhere near where I live it's too far out of the way'.

Robin 'No, I've already told them where you live and they said it's okay. It's not too far to go'.

Again, I suspiciously asked, if she was sure they were reliable as I didn't want to have to catch another cab again. I only had two-bob on me and the old girl would kill me if I had to ask her to lend me money again.

She promised me faithfully that they were genuinely nice boys and totally trustworthy. Like a fool, to save a 1/3 (twelve cents) tram fare I got into the front seat alongside of the driver. Robin got in the back seat and as we started to drive out the gates, both the front and back passenger doors flew open and two other fellows jumped in. I turned to Robin

'Thanks a million, you bloody stupid bitch, when I get my hands on you I'm going to kill you'.

The driver 'Calm down, they're friends of mine and I'm going to give them a lift home too'.

Amelia, 'Well as long as you don't think you're going to get anything, because you've got another thought coming'.

The driver 'I'll take you straight home, I promise'.

I relaxed a bit when he asked for directions. I told him to follow the tramline right to the terminus. (A few months previously we had moved into Judge Jeffery's home near the tram terminus and my old school, whilst we waited for our own home to be built.)

As we approached the turn, I told him that he could turn left at the next street, that'd take us to the tram terminus'.

When he didn't turn into the street I said, 'You've got one more chance to turn left at the next street and continue following the tramline'.

He jammed his foot on the accelerator and started the ascent to Mt Coot-tha. I said, 'You are only wasting your time, because you'll get bugger all out of me. I'll walk before I'd give in to any of you. I can fight and I bite.'

He took no notice of me and kept speeding up the mountain. By the time we got to the kiosk all of the others were singing the latest songs. As we careered down a particularly curvy section of the road towards the television channels, I recall the words of the song were, I'm Falling and a split second later the driver miscalculated a hairpin bend and we really were falling. Actually, not only were we falling, we were soaring sixty feet over and down the side of the mountain.

I felt my head hit something and the fellow sitting on the passenger side held me close to him to prevent me from flying out the open window alongside of him. I remember seeing a huge trunk of a light grey coloured tree. Then I was sitting on the ground holding my head and an ambulance officer said, 'Lie down, sweetheart, you've got head injuries'.

I put my hand to my face and head and I couldn't feel anything wrong and I said, 'No I'm alright. What do you want me to do, is everyone else okay?'

Another ambulance officer rushed over as I started to get to my feet, he placed his arms around my shoulders and waist and gently lowered me back onto the ground in a sitting position. As he did this he said, 'Sit down, darlin' we're getting you a stretcher now'.

I insisted that I was fine, but that my arm was just a bit tender. He persisted and insisted that I stay sitting down. When I again told him that I was okay he said, 'You've been out like a light for at least twenty minutes. Now just take it easy and just sit there for a while, okay?' He added, 'We'll tend to your face in a minute'.

The driver of the car started to moan and yelled, 'Forget that bitch, what about me?'

The ambulance man said to me 'He's a real charmer, what garbage bin did you drag him from?' I looked around and it looked like a war zone. Robin was strapped into a stretcher and was carried up the hill to a waiting ambulance. The others were either lying or sitting holding different parts of their bodies in an effort to stop the pain. I was placed on a stretcher and as they carried me up the side of the mountain. I realised that one of the stretcher-bearers was Brian Cahill, the Channel Seven newsreader. He had apparently arrived at the scene of the accident just as we went over the mountain and he had telephoned for the ambulance. Luck had been on my side, if Mr Cahill hadn't witnessed the accident God only knows what the outcome would have been. As far as I'm concerned, he saved my life.

The fellow who had been sitting alongside of me said 'God your face is a mess'

I put my hands all over my face, but I couldn't feel anything wrong with it, 'What's wrong with it?' 'Just wait until we get to the hospital and ask them for a mirror'.

I asked him what injuries did he have and he replied, 'Internal, you hit your head on the top of the steering wheel and your jaw on the bottom of the steering wheel and as the car started to flip, you started to float out the window and I had to grab you to hold your head into my gut otherwise you would've been flung against a big gum tree. Your skull has busted something in my gut'.

I thanked him for saving me and he replied, 'That's okay'.

I was put into the ambulance and whisked away to the Royal Brisbane Hospital, I was told on the journey to the hospital that Robin was the one with the worst injuries she had a suspected broken pelvis, and shattered leg. It was approximately eleven-thirty at night when we got to the casualty of the RBH (Royal Brisbane Hospital) and the first thing I asked for was to notify my parents and if they could give me a mirror.

One-thirty rolled around and I think everyone in the greater Brisbane metropolis had come to gawk at my face. Everyone but my family and me, they had forgotten to notify my family and hadn't bothered to bring me a mirror. At two-fifteen Edith and James walked in and on seeing me

Edith 'Oh my God, look at your face'.

James just looked in total disbelief and said, 'Shit.'

Amelia 'Quick, give me a mirror please, I haven't seen myself yet, these bastards won't do a thing for anyone'.

As Edith fossicked in her handbag looking for a mirror, I told her and James what had happened.

Edith 'What time was the accident?'

Amelia 'About five past eleven'.

Edith 'Don't give me that, they rang me at about five to two and said that you had just been brought in and that the accident had happened thirty minutes ago'

Amelia 'Bullshit, I've been sitting here since eleven-thirty pleading with them to call you, ring Channel Seven and ask Brian Cahill, he was the one who rang for the ambulance'.

I could tell by the look on her face that she didn't believe a word I said.

Edith 'They said you'd have to stay in under observation, because of your head injuries'.

Amelia 'Pigs bum I am, I'm not staying here one minute longer, I'm going home right now'.

Edith then handed me her little make up mirror and I nearly died of fright at the sight of my own reflection. I had a huge bump the size of a large duck egg on the right side of my forehead. Both my eyes were as black as the ace of spades, but my jaw was unbelievable. As Edith had described it later, it was the size of a big pineapple, but instead of it being yellow/orange it was totally black. It was swollen to three times its normal size and it sort of stretched down towards my chest.

My other injuries consisted of a broken collarbone and a dislocated right shoulder. The nurse strapped my shoulder and put my arm in a sling and I high-tailed it out of that hospital as fast as I could. When I arrived home, Edith went in to tell Dad that we were home. He was so angry with me that he refused to come out and talk to me let alone to look at me. That upset me more than being taken up to Mt Coot-tha against my will. He believed that I had willingly gone up to Mt Coot-tha, at one-thirty in the morning with four fellows.

The following day on the front page of the afternoon paper The Telegraph there was a photo of the crash. The write up made it sound as if I had been in the car with five fellows. Robin's name was listed with the other four and my name was separate from theirs. I visited Robin in hospital a few times and she had multiple injuries to her pelvis, hip and leg. She had to have a pin inserted in her thigh and was in traction for weeks. I never saw Robin again after she was discharged from hospital and I never saw the fellows from the crash again.

If I live to be a hundred, I never want to see the driver again, unless I'm carrying a meat cleaver. I didn't keep a copy of that newspaper report because it had the name of that bastard who obviously had no respect for anyone. His name has been removed from my memory, hopefully forever.

The mind is a wondrous thing, it can memorise and regurgitate at will, or it can choose to eliminate and forget. Unfortunately, my mind gets somewhat confused and I tend to remember most of the things I should forget and vice versa. Hopefully one day I will get it right. But I doubt that it will be in this lifetime.

Chapter 15

Getting to Know You

Frank Williams was born in the November of 1938 to Mabel and Jack. His mother had often commented that she would like a son and that she would like him to grow up to be a jockey. When Frank arrived into the world the doctor who delivered him commented, 'Well, Mrs Williams, you've got your little jockey, but I think the only thing he'll be riding is elephants'.

Frank tipped the scales at ten pounds and ten ounces (six kilograms). Anyone who ever met him would find that hard to believe, he grew to five foot, seven inches (a hundred and sixty-eight centimetres) and weighed 9st.4lb (sixty kilograms) dripping wet. Frank was the second child of three, his sister Rona twenty months older and his brother Marvin twenty months younger.

I first saw Frank in the November of 1960 approximately two weeks after the accident. Both my eyes were still swollen and they and my jaw was green from the bruising and my right arm was still in a sling. I had met up with Jenny again and she had told me about her new boyfriend Carl. On this particular day, I had been standing at the door of Harry Hughes TV and Electrical shop where I had worked for the past few months as a shop assistant.

I noticed Carl and his flatmate getting off the tram about fifty feet up the street and I ran inside and grabbed a broom and pretended to be very busy sweeping the footpath outside the shop. I never gave a moment's thought to what I looked like. I felt as if I looked quite inconspicuous going about my business just unobtrusively sweeping the footpath. Carl and his mate had gone into the local shop and it seemed an eternity before they finally came out.

I don't think I could have swept that footpath any cleaner that day and my poor shoulder and collarbone were aching from the rigorous exercise of thrusting the broom back and forth. Both young men strolled past and I nonchalantly kept sweeping. Out of the corner of my eye I noted that Carl was rather short. He was quite nice looking and he walked with a rather unusual cocky gait, as if he wanted everyone to know that he was Carl the boxer and he was someone to be revered.

The other fellow was slightly taller his hair was bleached by the sun. He had fairly wide shoulders and a slim tanned body. My immediate thought was, Ooh. I prefer the blond he's much nicer looking than Carl.

My thoughts were rudely interrupted when I heard Carl say, 'God, what, happened to you?' I was dumbstruck and they both began to chuckle. Carl's mate turned back to face me and said, 'What does the other bloke look like?' I could feel my face go bright scarlet as he laughed. I tried my hardest not to laugh out loud, as I thought to myself, you cheeky bugger.

Another two weeks or so went by and I had made arrangements to meet Jenny outside Woolworths Supermarket in Adelaide Street where she worked. I remember vividly as if it was yesterday, as the tram pulled up outside the City Hall, the clock struck nine-thirty, and I was totally unaware that my entire life was about to change in two hours and five minutes. All I knew was that I had two whole hours before the shops shut and that's when Jenny knocked off work. I also knew that she was going to introduce me to her boyfriend Carl, and I was looking forward to that. I was hoping that his mate would be there too, but I figured that more than likely he wouldn't be. I killed time by window shopping and checking my watch every few minutes. Finally, at eleven-twenty I stood outside Woolworths waiting for the doors to shut. I could see Jenny standing behind the counter of the fruit section serving the customers she glanced out and I gave her a wave and we smiled at each other and I mouthed the words, 'I'll wait here'. It was a typical stupid statement that only a silly teenage girl would say, after all that's what we had pre-arranged. I watched the people as they walked in and out of the shops and up and down the footpath. Everyone seemed to be hurrying to get their last-minute shopping done before the shops closed for the weekend.

All except the three fellows standing outside the Queensland Book Depot.

I recognised two of them immediately, but the third one I had never seen before. I could feel three sets of eyes watching me and I pretended not to notice, but I felt as if the whole world and his dog could sense the rush of excitement I was experiencing. I was particularly pleased, because the good-looking blond fellow, whom I had seen a couple of weeks prior, was there. I thought very smugly, I'm going to meet him in the next few minutes. I tried to check my reflection in the shop window to make sure that I looked okay, but it was impossible because of the milling crowd. I also tried not to let them see me looking them over. I was convinced they knew who I was and why I was there. Especially when I saw them all look at each other and burst into laughter together, I turned the other way and pretended I hadn't noticed them. I thought my heart would never stop pounding in my throat and I cursed myself for having agreed to come into town to meet Jenny and Carl now. I just wanted to go and catch the tram and go home.

I thought to myself, God you're stupid. What's the point of being here, you're only going to make a fool of yourself and then go home and kick yourself for being so stupid. I decided the best thing to do was to ignore them until Jenny introduced us, then I'll leave her with them and I'll go home. Yep, that's what I'll do, I told myself.

'Hello, I'm glad you came in to meet me, Oh. There are the boys up there, come on I'll introduce you to them'. I was very nervous as I walked towards them, I felt as if I would faint. My hands as per usual were dripping wet with perspiration and I prayed that none of them would want to shake hands with me as Jenny introduced us. I heard Jenny greet them all and I vaguely remember her introducing me to them one by one. Trying not to sound awe struck I said to Frank after the introductions were over, 'Happy Birthday for yesterday, Jenny told me it was your birthday'. He looked surprised and quite shyly thanked me. As I looked at him, I thought, he's better looking than what I remember him at our first encounter. Carl interrupted my thoughts very abruptly by asking me, 'Are you going out tonight, Amelia?' I was stunned, I looked at Jenny and she was absolutely stunned too. I thought, My God. What am I going to say to him? I knew Jenny was very keen on Carl, she had told me that she had been out with him three or four times, and I knew that was a record for her. I stammered, 'N ... no, I, um, I, ah, haven't made any plans for tonight'. I was embarrassed to admit that I didn't have a date and as equally embarrassed that my friend's boyfriend was asking me out.

Carl 'Would you like to go out?'

Very sheepishly,

Amelia 'Y ... yes'.

By this time, I was not only embarrassed, I was also very flattered. Looking around at everyone I don't know who was the more shocked, everyone seemed at a loss for words. I was just coming to grips with the realisation that I had agreed to go out with my friend's boyfriend in front of her. But I was in shock that Carl had actually had the audacity to ask.

Carl broke the stunned silence with, 'That's good, Frank hasn't got a date either, so you can go with him, we might as well make it a foursome, hey?'

Frank nodded in agreement and said, 'Yeah, okay'. He didn't sound too enthused about the prospect of going out with me, but I can tell you I was thrilled out of my brain to be going out with him. I was also relieved that I wasn't going out with Carl, not that I didn't think he was a nice bloke he just wasn't my cup of tea. I could tell that Jenny was more than pleased and Carl looked like the cat that had swallowed the canary. I remember looking at Tom, the other fellow and thinking to myself, poor bastard he's been left out, but thank God that Carl didn't put me on the spot to go out with him.

We made the arrangements to meet that night but I couldn't remember a word of our plans. Jenny and I caught the tram back and, as we found out later, Frank, Carl and Tom caught a cab back to the same area. On the way home Jenny told me that we had made arrangements to meet outside the City Hall at six-thirty. Jenny only lived around the corner from where Frank, Carl and Tom shared half a house. I lived approximately a mile from them near the tram terminus.

I took great pains getting myself ready for that first date with Frank. In those days I always took pride in wearing good quality clothing, it was nothing for me to have a number of dresses made by a professional dressmaker. I had a beautifully tailored, strapless, form fitting dress with a matching bolero, which I'd never worn before. I had only picked it up from the dressmaker a few days previously. Edith was an expert at putting my hair up in either a French roll or cute ponytail, whichever my mood warranted. This particular night I wanted to look sensational so I got her to put my hair in a French roll. After I had applied my make-up and gotten dressed with my white stiletto shoes on, even I was surprised at how grown-up I looked. I felt that no one would have guessed that I still had another four weeks to go before I turned seventeen. I look a lot older, I thought, at least eighteen.

I caught the tram and paid my fare into the city, as we rattled past the street the boys lived in. I looked down their street and I saw three figures walking towards the tram line, I had a feeling that it was Jenny, Frank and Carl but I couldn't be certain. I knew that if it was them, they would have at least another ten minutes to wait before the next tram came along so I got off the tram and walked down their street. To my delight I discovered it was them.

Frank seemed pleased at what he saw and he didn't seem to recognise me as being his date. He grabbed my hand as we walked towards the tram stop. I could feel my hand get clammy as usual and I feared that he would pass comment, which would have only made it worse. We walked past Harry Hughes TV and electrical and Carl and Jenny were discussing which picture we should all go to. Frank turned to me and said, 'Where do you work?' I pointed to the shop and said, 'In there'.

He looked at the shop, and then looked back at me and all he could say was, 'W … w … w'. He pointed to where I had swept the footpath. I burst out laughing at his obvious embarrassment and said, 'Yes.' Carl and Jenny had no idea what we laughing at, and I said to Carl, 'I work at Harry Hughes'. That sort of broke the ice and I then explained for the next ten minutes how I had ended up looking as if I had gone ten rounds with Jimmy Caruthers. The movie we chose to see was a dead loss and we decided to leave the theatre at about nine-fifteen. When we got outside, we had a discussion about what we should do and someone came up with the idea that we should buy some bottles of beer and go back to the boy's place. The only problem was the old bat who owned the house they lived in, lived on the other side and she had banned Jenny from ever going into the place. We would have to be very quiet by sneaking down the side of the house and up the back stairs. We caught a cab after Frank and Carl bought the beer and we instructed the cabbie to let us out two doors away from their house. We slowly edged our way down the side of the house, squeezing between the house and fence. Jenny and Carl went first and both scurried up the back steps like rats up a drainpipe. Very nervously I followed them down the side with Frank directly behind me. It had been raining quite heavily for at least an hour and had eased down to a miserable drizzle.

I was glad that I had a jacket to cover my bare shoulders, as the rain and night air had made me feel wet cold and uncomfortable. We crept closer to the end of the house and I could feel the wet leaves of the overhanging tree brush against my face. I couldn't see a thing in front of me and I put my hands up to protect my face from the tree branches. In doing so, I lost my footing and fell heavily on my backside and slid sideways down the reddish shale at full bore. Typical of my finesse, sophisticated young lady to a bumbling blob in one split second. Frank gallantly helped me to my feet and we hurried up the stairs as quickly and as quietly as was humanly possible. He took me into the bathroom and I nearly died when I looked down at my dress. I was absolutely covered in red mud all over my skirt. It was all down my legs. It looked as if I had pooped my pants, it had run down my legs and I had then rolled in it. Frank tried to wipe the mud

off unsuccessfully and for the second time that night he started to stammer and
stutter

Frank 'W … w … w'.

Amelia 'No, I'll keep my dress on, thanks all the same'.

We wet a towel and somehow between the two of us we managed to wash
the bulk of the mud off my skirt, much to my total embarrassment. We went
into the lounge room where Carl, Jenny and Tom were sitting and I was offered
a beer.

Amelia 'No thanks, I don't drink'.

Everyone laughed

Tom 'If you're a friend of Jenny's you'd have to be a drinker.'

With that he went into the kitchen and returned with the largest glass in the
house, which held ten ounces. I couldn't believe the size of the beer that he put
in front of me.

Amelia 'Honestly, I don't drink'.

Carl 'You've got to have a beer to be sociable'.

I looked at the beer and thought the only way I'm going to drink that is to
swallow it in one go. I lifted the glass to my lips and Jenny watched in total
disbelief as I sculled the contents without moving the glass from my mouth.
When I finished it, Tom said, 'Oh no, she doesn't drink, not since guzzling came
in to fashion.'

We all sat and talked and told jokes and generally got to know each other over
the next hour or so, and then Tom went to bed. Frank turned the light off and
Jenny and Cal went into another room, Frank and I sat in the darkened room
and did some very serious kissing and cuddling. I was very pleasantly surprised
that at no time did his hands ever wander, he was a thorough gentleman. I had
never been alone with a fellow who hadn't tried to put his hands all over my
breasts or tried to run their hands up my dress. Another hour or so went by and
I very reluctantly suggested that I had better get home before I got into trouble
for getting home too late. Frank walked me home and we made plans to meet
the following day at eleven o'clock outside Harry Hughes. I got up early the
following day and dressed appropriately in shorts and blouse and after applying
my make-up, I insisted that Edith put my hair in a ponytail. I wasn't known to be
an early riser and I had to come up with a good excuse as to why I was going out,
without Edith getting suspicious. I told her that I was going to visit Edward and
Beth and baby Eddie in their flat near where we had grown up. I figured that I

had better make an appearance at Edward's place to cover my tracks, and I could leave his place early in time to meet Frank.

On my way to Edward's place I could go past Frank's place and take a short cut through the park. I figured that if I was really lucky, I might get a chance to see him as I ran across the road near his house. As I approached the intersection of the three streets between the park and where Frank lived, I crossed my fingers and hoped that Frank might see me. Without making it obvious I had a quick look towards his house and I was disappointed when I couldn't see him. I crossed over the streets and was halfway across when I heard a wolf whistle, I felt my heart pound but I pretended not to hear. Then when I got to the other side, I felt a pang of panic because he didn't call out nor whistle a second time. I was just about to stop and pretend I was checking my sandshoe laces, when I heard him whistle again. I looked over with a surprised smile as Frank walked up towards me. As he greeted me and asked where I was off to, I feigned great surprise at seeing him and hurriedly told him that I had to visit my brother and his wife. I explained it as if I were on an emergency errand delivering them a very important message. I felt like kicking myself for gross stupidity as soon as I had said that. It went through my mind that I should stay with him just in case he didn't turn up at eleven o'clock. After all, I had no burning desire to see Beth or Edward for that matter. Any chance to see my nephew I grabbed with relish. But not today, today was different. I reluctantly bade him farewell and as I walked away, I realised I hadn't confirmed our eleven o'clock meeting and that worried me. I arrived at our meeting place and was thrilled to see Frank standing outside my work place waiting for me, but I was also rather disappointed too because he had another mate with him. He introduced me to Stewart and after some discussion about what to do, we all agreed to going for a walk. Stewart had bought a big bag of cherries and the three of us walked up past the cemetery and around the back streets. It wasn't what I would call the most romantic stroll, but then again there wasn't very much to do in good old Brisbane in 1960. I was very pleased that Frank held my hand from the moment we started on our walkabout. Stewart seemed a nice enough sort of fellow, but I secretly wished he would go and find something else to do. As we walked along, we talked about anything and everything and ate the cherries with great gusto. I love cherries and I particularly enjoyed eating those sweet fresh cherries as we walked in the hot sun. I didn't want to appear piggish by eating too many of them even though I think I could have eaten them all on my own. Frank and Stewart obviously had not had any breakfast, because every time Stewart offered Frank the bag full of the putple fruit he would say, 'Would you like a cherry Frank?' Frank replied each time, 'Oh I would love a cherry.' Or he would say, 'Boy, would I ever like to have a cherry'.

(It wasn't until years later that I learnt that a woman's virginity was also called a cherry.) When I found out I felt so naive and stupid and if I could've turned the clock back, I would have kicked their heads in. But I did have a laugh and saw the funny side of my innocence.

From that fateful day in November, Frank and I saw each other every day, over the next eight months. Looking back, eight months doesn't seem a very long period of time, but when you consider that most couples in those times only saw each other once or twice a week at the very most, our courtship wasn't as short as it seemed. We were almost inseparable. When we weren't working, the only time we weren't together was when we went to bed. Edith, Dad, James and I shifted into our own home two days later. The only problem was the home was built all the way out at in the backblocks of never never. The area is only about three miles (approximately seven kilometres) from where we grew up, but in those days three miles was about as far away as the moon. The only form of public transport was and still is the City Council buses. But in those days, they were very few and far between.

My relationship with Dad was very strained, he was very domineering and I felt very stifled by his rules and regulations. He and I were very much alike, but in those days, I could never see the resemblance in our ways. I couldn't cope with all his orders so I packed my bags and left home. I shifted into a dingy little room in a dingy old boarding house and for the first time in my life I was totally reliant on myself.

I went from being awakened every morning with several time calls and finally dragging myself out of bed ten minutes before my bus was due, to sleeping in and arriving at least half an hour late for work each day. Not only that, I had to share a kitchenette and bathroom with at least twenty other young women. I soon found out that they weren't all honest because within five days I had lost food, toothpaste, shampoo and most of my underwear from the clothesline.

I was only too pleased to beat a hasty retreat from my independence to the sanctity of my grandmother's home. Of course, I wasn't going to let on that I was desperate to move in with her and granddad. I had to pretend that I enjoyed living in squalor and that the only reason I eventually agreed to shift in with her was to stop her from nagging me.

When I eventually relented to her pleading to come and stay with her, I made her feel that I was doing her a favour by stopping her from worrying about me. Now, I was not only getting three square meals daily, and all my washing and ironing done and anything my little black heart desired, I was only a ten-minute walk away from work. Best of all, I could see Frank twice a day instead of just in the evenings, because I had to walk past his house on my way to work.

It was around this time that Frank injured his back whilst wheeling a wheelbarrow full of cement up a plank of wood, whilst working as a brickie's labourer. He had apparently lost his balance and in trying to steady himself and the wheelbarrow, he twisted all the muscles in his lower back. The orthopaedic surgeon told him that the back muscles were like pieces of elastic and that Frank had stretched his to the full extent and that he would never be able to return to employment that required heavy lifting again.

He applied for Worker's Compensation and until his cheque arrived, he had to live on what little savings he had and the generosity of Tom and Carl to help carry him through. Whilst Tom and Carl went to work and paid the rent and groceries, Frank did most of the cleaning and cooking although Tom was the better cook of the three of them. I recall that Tom seemed to be able to make a meal out of anything that was in the fridge and cupboards. I remember him lamenting one particular day about the fact that he couldn't bake a nice chocolate cake. Because I quite often went to their place to have an evening meal with them, I thought, the very least I could do was to offer to bake them a chocolate cake. About a week went by

Tom 'Righto, silly bitch, (that was his nickname for me) when are you going to bake this cake that you promised?'

Amelia 'I'll bake it now if you like'.

They were all as pleased as punch that I was finally going to show them my worth. Tom went to the cupboard and got the flour, cocoa, milk, eggs, butter and baking dish out for me and said, 'I'll have to go next door and get some icing sugar and the instructions how to make the icing, from the landlady'.

Amelia 'Look on the packet, it should tell you on there. Where's the packet?'

Tom 'What packet?'

Amelia 'The chocolate cake packet I can't bake a chocolate cake without the instructions on the packet.'

They all groaned in disgust and Tom turned to Frank,

Tom 'I hope to Christ for your sake that she's good in bed, mate, because she sure as hell aint a fuckin' genius.'

We all collapsed and absolutely howled with laughter at his succinct usage of the English language and my inept ability of the culinary arts. I had grown to like Tom, he was down to earth, though quite often crude, but you always knew where you stood with him. He spoke his mind and you could always rely on him, no matter what.

Carl on the other hand was a self-centred little upstart he was moody and too good-looking for his own good. He thought he was God's gift to women and that women were only put on this earth for one reason, to have sex with. He was two timing Jenny behind her back, and although he never did me any harm, I didn't have a great deal of respect for him because of the way he used Jenny. Tom was the one I felt a bit sorry for, he wasn't good-looking and he had a certain roughness that most women would find repugnant, but I always hoped I would find a nice girlfriend for him. I did introduce him to a girl whom I feel sure he would've loved to settle down with, but unfortunately, she was looking for her prince charming.

My birthday and Christmas were only a matter of days away and Frank wanted me to go to Eukey to meet his mother. I can't remember what I told Mum, Edith and Dad to enable me to go away that Christmas. I think it was that I was going camping with a girlfriend. They probably didn't believe me anyhow, but I think that they only agreed to my going because they probably thought I'd shift out into another sleazy room again. I had no intentions of telling them that I had a boyfriend, but I couldn't keep the secret for too long.

One afternoon, Frank and I were standing outside of his place and Frank had his arms around me he bent down and kissed me goodbye. As I turned to walk across the road, I saw my father in his work van waiting in the traffic to turn the corner. I nearly had a heart attack. I quickly turned back to Frank

Amelia 'Shit, there's my father. I hope to God, he hasn't seen me'.

As I had my back to my father, Frank gave me a running commentary of Dad driving away out of sight. I breathed a sigh of relief believing that if he had seen me, he would've stopped the van and come over.

When I went to their home to get my birthday and Christmas presents

Dad 'I want you to keep away from that fellow down there, he's no good'.

Amelia 'What are you talking about?'

CLEAN HANDS, CLEAR CONSCIENCE

Dad 'You know as well as I do what I'm talking about. I saw you making a holy show of yourself out on the footpath in front of everyone'.

Amelia 'I wasn't making a holy show of myself at all, and what do you mean he's no good?'

Dad (in his usual bombastic way) 'He's a criminal.'

Amelia 'He's not a criminal at all. What makes you say that?'

Dad 'I know his family, they're all criminals the lot of them in that house'.

Amelia 'Dad, you don't know his family you don't even know who he is.'

Dad 'I know the Churchill's all right, they're all bad devils.'

Amelia 'Dad, he's not a Churchill. He just rents half a house from them. They live on the other side, and he's definitely not a criminal'.

Amelia 'Same difference if you hang around with criminals, you're as bad as them'.

No matter what I said I couldn't convince my father that he had gotten the bull by the tail once again.

Frank had made arrangements with his brother Marvin to pick us up at four in the morning. Marvin was driving from North Queensland so we weren't really sure what time to expect him. Frank thought we had better get there two hours early just in case Marvin got there earlier. Although it was only a couple of days before Christmas it was a bitterly cold night and I thought I was going to freeze to death just sitting on the side of the road waiting. To make matters worse, the police station was just across the road from where we were sitting. There were no police on duty at that time of the morning, but because I was still under age and out with a fellow at that time of day I felt sure I would be unlucky enough to get caught. Considering the fact that my father was so strict in his ways, God only knows what the outcome would have been if a cop had ventured along. As far as I was concerned, Dad and the cops had a lot in common, both would have jumped to their own conclusions and I would have been found guilty and no explanations would have been heard. Frank still behaved as a thorough gentleman, he had never once tried to put the hard word on me, and I trusted him implicitly. Dad and the cops wouldn't have believed that. Marvin finally turned up nearly two hours late, so by that time, I was almost beside myself with worry that we definitely would get copped.

The first night I had gone out with Frank he had told me that he had originally came from Eukey a small town out west and that's where his mother still lived.

I had never heard of the place and I kept asking him, 'What's the name of that place again?'

To me, going to Eukey was a big adventure. As far as I was concerned, I was going to a far-away city near the New South Wales border. Frank had told me it was only a little country town, but I had figured that he had under estimated the place.

By the time we arrived there, it was almost lunchtime and the three of us were completely buggered. Marvin had been driving all night and Frank and I had been awake just sitting on the side of the road for most of the night. Their mother was out when we arrived, Marvin lay on his bed and Frank told me to go and lie on his mother's bed because he wasn't sure which bed, I would be sleeping in. Frank lay down alongside of me and we both fell asleep almost immediately with him cuddling me. When I awoke Mabel had arrived home, Frank introduced us, and I had an awful uneasiness that she had suspected that we were doing much more than just sleeping on her bed. I sensed from that first meeting that there was something terribly amiss with Mabel and I knew instinctively that she didn't like me at all. I tried everything I could think of to please her, but nothing seemed to make her happy, other than Marvin. It was painfully obvious that whatever Marvin said or did, she seemed to agree with and if she didn't approve of something, he would invariably alter his 'mistake' to suit her.

Frank on the other hand didn't go out of his way to seek his mother's approval. It seemed to me, that he had given that up years beforehand. Whenever Frank was not in earshot, Mabel would make a comment toward me to try and belittle me or unnerve me. One particular question that she asked me was, 'How many legs does a chicken have?'

I couldn't believe that a grown woman could be so childish to ask such a stupid question. Especially considering that the question came out of the blue for no particular reason. I thought, I might as well go along with her and humour her so I said, 'Four'.

She took great delight in retelling the story to Frank, Marvin and Roy later that day. Roy was the boarder (she had told me), but Frank had told me that Roy was his stepfather. It was obvious that Frank was trying to be diplomatic by covering up the fact that his mother cohabited with Roy. I had spent more than five pounds (more than my weekly wage) on perfume and talcum powder for Mabel's Christmas present and for the first time in my life I regretted having bought someone a gift. Frank tried to console me by telling me not to take any notice of her by saying, 'She can be a warbly old bitch don't let it get to you'. Although I was pleased to be spending the Christmas with Frank, I would have much preferred to have spent it elsewhere than in her God forsaken house. Apart from the chilly reception and hospitality, the weather was also inhospitable. I had never experienced a colder climate than Eukey was that Christmas, I thought I would freeze to death. Of a night I would wear my corduroy slacks and winter, long sleeved, shirt with a thick bulky knit jumper. Over the top of those, I donned an overcoat and I wore thick woollen bed socks. I had no less than seven blankets on the bed and two hot water bottles and my teeth still chattered from the chilly night air. I was very pleased to arrive back in Brisbane on the eve of New Year's Eve. We caught a bus back and I remember wanting to discuss the prospect of our becoming engaged, but I thought Frank may have forgotten that he had proposed the night before we went to Eukey. Or worse still, that he may have changed his mind. I had gone to his place the night before we were to meet Marvin. Frank and I had been lying on his bed having a rest in readiness of catching the cab at one-thirty to go to our pick-up point. We had been making plans for our trip and out of the blue

Frank 'Let's get married'.

I was so thrilled at his romantic approach, I said

'Yeah, okay'.

We had sealed our betrothal with lots of kisses and he promised to buy me an engagement ring on our return to Brisbane. During our stay at Eukey we had visited the nearby townships of Tenterfield and Stanthorpe and in both towns, I had tried to drum up some enthusiasm by steering him near the jeweller's windows, but he had shown no sign of interest. I had told Mabel that Frank and I were going to get engaged and her reaction was to tell me that there were better fish in the sea than him. I was horrified that a mother would say such a thing about her own son.

When we got back to Brisbane, I very casually broached the subject

Amelia 'Oh by the way are we going into town tomorrow to buy my engagement ring?'

After all I didn't want to appear too anxious to scare him off. He was very enthusiastic

Frank 'Yeah I guess so'.

We thought it would be a good idea for Frank to meet Edith and I figured that it would be wiser for Frank not to meet Dad for a little while though. I wasn't too sure what Dad would say or do and I wanted to avoid a confrontation for as long as possible. I rang and told Edith that I wanted to see her. I knew she was curious by the way she spoke, though she didn't come right out and ask why I wanted to see her.

She had been working at the hotel bottle department on Friday nights helping out a mate of Dad's who was the publican and I made arrangements to see her there at seven-thirty that night. I'm not a complete dill I knew that if she was going to give me a lecture, she sure as hell couldn't do it in front of the customers. I introduced her to Frank and she greeted him cordially with a kiss,

Amelia 'I've got something to tell you'.

Edith 'I've been expecting this'.

I knew instinctively that she suspected that I was pregnant and I felt like screaming at her, I was so angry. But instead

Amelia ' What are you expecting?'

Edith 'You tell me'.

Frank 'Amelia and I want to get engaged and we'd like your approval'.

That really knocked her for a sixer and I couldn't resist a big broad smile.

She was so relieved she looked at Frank as if she were studying him and very slowly and precisely

Edith 'Well I guess that would be all right'

Before she could say that he'd better meet Dad and ask his permission as well, we thanked her and told her that we were getting the ring the following morning. It was then, that I told her that I had been to Eukey to meet Frank's mother and she said, 'I knew that you weren't going to where you said you were'. I never did find out how she knew, I was just pleased to get over that hurdle, once having done that, the world was my oyster.

We went into Wallace Bishop's at about nine-thirty the following morning and Frank insisted that I choose whichever ring I wanted. Knowing that he didn't have much money and that he had to pay the ring off on time payment, I didn't want to put him into too much debt. So as much as I wanted to choose a beautiful sparkler that would knock your eyes out. I was very practical some might even say I was stupid. But I chose one that I needed a giant magnifying glass to see the diamond. It cost twenty-seven pound and ten shillings (fifty-five dollars), and although that doesn't sound very much it was a small fortune to us. Frank kept insisting that I choose a better one but I was just as insistent that I wanted that particular ring.

That night we went out to paint the town red to celebrate our engagement and the New Year. We met up with some people who invited us to a party out at Chermside. We were there about an hour or so when Rodney Grainger walked in. I had told Frank about Rodney when I first started going out with him. Frank was not impressed at all at Rodney's appearance. The funny part was, Rodney didn't recognise me at first, but when he did, he came over to give me a hug.

Frank stood up as if he was about to punch Rodney's lights out, but he quietly walked out of the room. I followed him out to see if he was okay and he sort of shrugged and grunted like a little schoolboy. He said he'd had enough of the party and wanted to go. I went in to get my handbag whilst Frank waited for me at the front steps. Rodney grabbed me by the arm and tried to stop me from leaving. He pushed me against the wall and tried to kiss me. I told him that I was engaged but that meant bugger all to him, he refused to let me go until I kissed him. I was terrified that if Frank came in and saw this scene that he'd either start a fight with Rodney, or he'd get really angry with me. Either way, I knew there would be hell to pay. I crossed my fingers, kissed Rodney and ran out of the house as fast as I could.

Frank and I caught a cab into the city and Frank refused to talk for the entire journey. He eventually snapped out of his sulky mood, but it wasn't the last I'd hear of Rodney Grainger although it was the last time, I ever saw him.

Dad and Frank finally met, though I don't recall the occasion, so it wasn't an unpleasant encounter. I do know that Dad didn't like Frank and that was that. Nothing was going to change his mind. Dad had made up his mind that this bastard was not good enough for his little princess. To be perfectly honest, I've always thought that unless I married a doctor or solicitor or someone of equally high standing in the community, they wouldn't have been good enough in my father's eyes.

Both Mum and Grandad liked Frank and he liked both of them, so that was something. Edith and Dad held an engagement party for us in the February and all of our friends kept asking when we were going to get married. Frank still hadn't been paid any money from Worker's Compensation and he was solely reliant on Tom and me for his survival.

By that time Carl and Jenny had long parted company, we all still maintained a keen interest in his boxing career, but that was fast becoming a part of history. He tried to keep to a strict diet and training regime, but he failed dismally.

Carl was scheduled to fight the Queensland Flyweight Champion of Queensland Jackie Treschman Jackie was without doubt one of the gentlest and nicest young men I have ever met. We all became quite good friends with Jackie and on the night of their big fight, Frank and I sat front row ringside. Before the fight I had kissed both fighters on their cheeks and wished them both, good luck. They both declared to me that they weren't going to let their opponent land a punch where I had kissed them. I was the only member of the crowd that night who sat with her hands over her face. I was unable to watch two friends pummel the shit out of each other.

Carl took a hell of a beating that night, Jackie kept telling Carl to give up and lie down but Carl refused. Carl kept saying to Jackie, 'Come on, do it, do it'.

Jackie kept trying to knock him out, but Carl kept refusing to give up. Carl's boxing career ended that night. Frank and I came to the conclusion that the little bastard was mad for the pummelling he took, but we couldn't help admire his courage.

Chapter 16

Double Standards

I was dismissed from Harry Hughes TV and Electrical because his business was fast going down the drain. Harry spent nearly all of his time playing golf and leaving Jimmy Jackson the apprentice electrician and myself to run the business. It was nothing unusual for a customer to bring an electrical appliance in for repairs only to have it sit there unattended for weeks. Finally, I took it upon myself to repair toasters, irons, jugs and radios. Sometimes Harry would test them to see if they were working but the majority of the time, he would just put the price of the repair on the appliances and beat a hasty retreat to the golf course.

As for rewiring of houses and big business premises, Jimmy used to have to do them on his own without any supervision what so ever. Fortunately, he was a bloody good kid who knew his job, but he was still only sixteen and he carried an enormous responsibility for one so young. I often worried that our repairs and rewiring may cause electrical fires even deaths and that we would be charged with murder or manslaughter.

I was also terrified of being charged with theft as an accomplice after the fact. Frank, Carl and Tom would often call into the shop to visit and talk. I used to enjoy their company because it was quite boring sitting there all day every day with only one or two customers a day. I never noticed anything unusual in their frequent visits. Then one night whilst visiting their place I noticed a wine decanter and six, matching, wine glasses on the shelf.

Amelia 'Oh. they're like the ones we've got at work'.

Tom 'Are you sure that's like the one you've got at work?'

Amelia 'Yes. I'm positive, it's exactly like it'.

Tom looked at Carl and Frank and shaking his head he said, 'Silly bitch.'

They all burst out laughing, and I screeched, 'You rotten bastards.' I was absolutely mortified, and by this time they were all in fits of laughter. I looked around the room and noticed a lot of knickknacks and bits and pieces that they had taken whilst I wasn't looking. No need to be told my hands started to drip with perspiration at the thought of what might have happened if they had gotten caught. I started to worry about how on earth I was going to get all the stuff back in the shop without being seen. Within a split second, I realised that was the least of my worries. There was a knock at the door, it was Jimmy. I had invited him to come around for a few drinks and I knew that he would recognise most of the stuff as having come from the shop. Jimmy did recognise it and laughed it off and said, 'Harry deserves to be done, it'll serve the lousy bastard right'.

I took the decanter and wine glasses back along with a few of the other bits and pieces but I felt I was taking a huge risk of being caught, so I left a lot of the items at the boy's house. About a week or so later the shop was broken into and my first concern was that it wasn't the boys. I knew by the way that Harry was questioning me, that he suspected their involvement. I had a sneaking suspicion that Jimmy had told him of the things that had found their way to Frank and Tom's house. The boys disposed of all the remaining things from the shop on the off chance that the police might have gone to their home to have a look. They all denied any knowledge of the break in and I had no reason not to believe them.

I got a job in the city as a shop assistant in a newsagency. The owner of the shop was an Italian who took great delight in mauling me and the other two girls who worked there whenever we walked past him. In those days there was no such thing as sexual harassment. It was a matter of steering clear from him as much as possible, and if you were unlucky enough to get touched you kept quiet or took the consequences of being sacked. It was imperative that I stayed employed because Tom had lost his job and he and Frank were living solely on Tom's unemployment benefit. Frank would occasionally come to my place for a meal, but mostly they lived on tinned food that they bought on credit from the shop across the street from where they lived. I was only earning five pounds a week but I would help them out as much as I could, mainly with tram fares when Frank had to go to the specialist on Wickham Terrace (Brisbane's answer to Harley Street London). Every time he went into the compo office, they would tell him that his claim was still being processed.

I hated having to go into work for that filthy man and I was fast losing my patience with him. I could see the day coming soon when I was going to kick him in the balls or spit in his face. On one particular day he sent me upstairs to where the storeroom was, and told me to clean it up. He came up and I knew he was going to go for the grope but as luck had it, his wife came into the shop and he took off like a bat out of hell. I spent most of the day up there tidying up and stacking the many cartons of cigarettes stored up there. I came to the conclusion that he wouldn't miss a carton or two, so I wrapped them in a huge piece of brown paper and shoved them into my shopping bag. I was shitting razor blades that I would get caught when I walked out of the shop with them.

I became quite adept at it and I made it a Friday ritual to get a carton each week for Frank, Tom and Carl. They all thought it was Christmas every Friday afternoon. I don't know whether it was because I was able to avoid my bosses wandering hands or if he suspected I was pinching his cigarettes or perhaps a combination of both, but I got the sack. I was quite relieved that my criminal days were at an end. I certainly didn't like myself for stealing, I really don't believe that two wrongs make a right but although I felt guilty, I still had a deep-gutted feeling that it served the dirty mongrel right. I hope his wife caught him out eventually.

I got a job as a shop assistant at another electrical store at Spring Hill. It was also a sub branch for the Commonwealth Bank. I had to do a test and get approval from the bank to become a teller and I had access to all the keys of the safe. To the best of my knowledge I was one of the first females in Brisbane, certainly one of the youngest, to hold the position of female teller. It had always been a male dominated role.

Apparently, the powers that be in those days thought that females should be kept in the kitchen and bedroom only. The job was quite interesting really, besides being an electrical shop and sub branch for the bank, we also sold casket tickets, cigarettes, lollies and drinks. We were also an agent for a dry cleaner and laundry. It was quite a busy shop with a lot of regular customers who were from varied walks of life.

Spring Hill was never known as up market then, but if I had been asked to describe it, I would have to say that it was cosmopolitan bordering on sleazy. There were a number of entertainers living in the area, two of whom were regulars on Channel Seven's Theatre Royal. If I had've had the courage in those days, I would have tried to get into show business. Both of the entertainers tried to talk me into taking up singing and dancing lessons. I knew I could hold a tune, but I was only interested in becoming Frank's wife by then.

He had begun to get a bit shitty, having to rely on Tom and myself to support him. Worker's Compensation was being completely pig headed in their attitude towards him, but worst of all I was refusing to sleep with him. I still insisted on waiting until we were married. Frank has never been known to be romantic and in those days, he wasn't any different. He would say things like, 'You've got to try before you buy you know?' And 'If I went to the markets to buy a black pig and the fellow told me I could have the one in the bag, I'd want to look in the bag first, because he might be tricking me into buying a white pig'. I used to laugh at some of the outrageous analogies he'd come out with, but my standard answer was always an emphatic, 'No'.

One night I will never forget as long as I live, because I still classify it as being one of the most embarrassing things that has ever happened. Frank and I had been to the local pictures and we were walking home, a distance of approximately half a mile. I was absolutely bursting to pass wind but I felt that if I did it might be a bit smelly. I kept walking, holding the cheeks of my bum together as tight as I could. We walked past Frank's house and I debated with myself if I should excuse myself, and race into the toilet, but I decided to wait until I got home. We got to the corner of the street leading up towards my grandmother's street and Frank excused himself saying he wanted to go into the park to have a leak. I walked across the street and I was so relieved at having the opportunity to release the wind and I relaxed the stranglehold to allow it to escape. The noise of that fart was so loud I swear as God is my witness it was like a clap of thunder. I have never in my life made such a noise before or since. I wanted to have a good laugh but I was so embarrassed all I could think of was, God. I hope Frank didn't hear that. He finally walked across the road and we continued walking up the hill and nothing was mentioned about the dreadful noise. The following night we went for a walk and we ended up sitting on a bench seat in the church grounds opposite Frank's house. We'd only been there a few minutes when Frank lifted his leg and farted rather loudly. I was stunned and disgusted and in a horrified tone I said, 'I beg your pardon?'

He burst out laughing and said, 'If it's alright for you to drop your lunch, bugle arse, it's good enough for me too'. I wanted the earth to swallow me, but I laughed so hard I nearly wet my pants. I might add that after that night, Frank never stopped having repeat performances.

Tom's mother and sister Marianne came to visit Tom and Frank for a week or so. Mrs Vid was a huge woman who would have easily weighed eighteen stone. She had an unusual squeaky voice and just about every sentence she said, she would end with the word 'like'. I found this to be rather fascinating and amusing. Frank had often spoken highly of her saying that she was like a mother to him. I'm afraid I couldn't share his affection for her. Her daughter Marianne was an equally large girl of fifteen. Well, not quite as large as her mother, but she certainly would have given the scales a hell of a fright when she jumped on them. Frank had warned me that Marianne could fight like a man and that he had witnessed her pummelling the shit out of two fellows who had annoyed her one night. He said she had thrown one bloke head first into a brick wall and had held the other one in a headlock and kept punching his head in. The bloke who had hit the brick wall ran away never to be seen again, she certainly fit the bill of a Sumo wrestler. I made a mental note that if she looked like getting nasty with me, I would race home and grab Edward's cricket bat to tap her on the head a few times.

Surprisingly, I didn't mind Marianne, she wasn't likely to become my best friend, but I sure as hell wasn't going to make her my worst enemy. Mrs Vid went back home to Byron Bay after the week was up and Marianne stayed to try and get herself a job. I had no vision of her being successful though. She had no work experience her art of speech was of considerably low standard and she was very partial to sleeping in until after eleven o'clock. It was very obvious to me that she was very keen on Frank and I had more than a sneaking suspicion that Mrs Vid had hoped that Frank would eventually become her son-in-law. Frank and Tom had told me that when they lived in Byron Bay twelve months earlier, Frank had reached over to light Mr Vid's cigarette and Mr Vid had said to his wife, 'Hey, Mum, by the smell of Frank's fingers, I think we've got ourselves a new son-in-law.' I was absolutely stunned that any father would say such a thing about his own daughter. When Frank and I were on our own, I asked him what he had said when Mr Vid had said that. He said, 'What could I say? I denied it, of course. I wouldn't touch her with a barge pole'. Still stunned I said, 'But what did Mrs Vid say?'

He replied, 'They all laughed'. Apparently, Mr Vid had said it in front of the entire family and they had all thought it was humorous. It was then that I really appreciated my own family regardless of their idiosyncrasies. I could never imagine my father saying shit or poop for that matter, in front of his family. You can only guess how horrified I was at hearing about the Vid's conversations.

So much happened over the next three or four months, it's difficult to remember which incident came first. Frank had told me about Tom having a very hairy arse and I was forever pestering Tom by saying, 'Show me your hairy arse Tom'. Imagine my shock one sunny afternoon outside their home when I again jokingly asked him and he dropped his shorts in front of me, and all the traffic. I laughed fit to kill myself. I was absolutely stunned by his actions and agog by how hairy his bum really was. Tom went back to Byron Bay to visit his family and on his return, he said, 'Hey silly bitch, have you ever been embarrassed to get into a car before?''No why?' Tom and Frank, both grinning like Cheshire cats, took me to the top of the hill and made me keep my eyes closed. In unison they said, 'Okay, you can look now'. When I opened my eyes, I saw a bright, lolly pink 1934 Ford Roadster with lime green and black fleck seat covering. I couldn't believe my eyes and I said, 'Not until now, but today's the day.''Jump in'. They both urged, as they scrambled into the front and only seat. I said, 'No way, besides there isn't a seat for me.' With that Tom released the boot to display the dicky seat.

I covered my face for fear of being recognised whenever we went for a drive. But at least it was transport, even if we did have to use two and a half gallons (ten litres) of sump oil for every fifty miles (eighty-five kilometres) we travelled.

We approached Dad and Edith to get their approval for our marriage to take place on James's twenty-fifth birthday. Edith, who probably couldn't wait to get rid of me, readily agreed, but Dad said, 'No I want you to wait at least another twelve months.' I was furious, I could not see any reason in the wide world why we'd have to wait and I told him so. I pleaded for his reason and all he could come up with was, 'Because I said so, that's why.' I said to Edith, 'He's nothing but an old bastard, he just wants to show that he's king pin all the bloody time, well if necessary, I'll take him to court and get approval that way'. I knew in my own heart that I'd never do that, but I also knew that I wasn't going to wait twelve months either, just because my father said so. I told Frank, 'We'll get married whether he wants me to or not'. Frank wasn't as sure as I was, he had heard through the grapevine how pig-headed Dad could be. Frank said, 'How do you think you're going to change his mind?''I'm going to get pregnant'. I replied, with as much determination in my voice that my father had displayed when he had told us to wait twelve months. I could not describe the look of happiness that swept over Frank's face probably not so much at the prospect of us becoming parents. More for the joy of experiencing what a pregnancy entailed. You wouldn't need to be a mind reader to know that he was prepared to start there and then. A few weeks went by and Jenny, Marianne and I all went to the pictures together to see the controversial movie Butterfield 8 starring Elizabeth Taylor. After the picture ended, we all walked to a bus seat outside the Salvation Army Girl's Home and sat and discussed the film. I could sense something was wrong with Jenny and Marianne but I didn't know what. Eventually Marianne said she was tired and said goodnight and walked down the hill to where she was staying with Tom, Carl and Frank. Jenny said to me, 'I've got something to tell you'. I was totally unprepared for the bombshell that she dropped. Very quietly Jenny chose her words carefully, but all the stammering in the world couldn't soften the blow of hearing, 'Marianne told me that she slept with Frank a couple of weeks ago'. Knowing that I had fallen asleep alongside of Frank on several occasions without us being intimate I said to Jenny, 'What do you mean slept with him?' Jenny looked at me as if to say, Amelia, you don't want me to spell it out for you, do you?

I said, 'She's bullshitting Frank wouldn't touch her with a barge pole.' Jenny replied, 'Yeah I thought that too but I thought you had the right to know what she had said'.

I knew Jenny too well and I knew that she believed that Marianne had been with Frank. I asked Jenny, 'When was this event supposed to have taken place?' To my shock she named the day of the week, the time and the room where it had happened. Even stating that it was the night after Frank had arrived home from taking me to my parent's home for dinner. I could feel my entire stomach churn because that was the same night, I had finally plucked up enough courage to be intimate with Frank for the first time. To add fuel to the fire, although I wasn't positive, woman's intuition told me that I was certain that I was pregnant. The following day on my way to work I didn't bother calling out to Frank to wake him as was my usual habit. I somehow managed to get through the day without any major problems. I called in to say hello to all of them on my way home from work and I called Marianne aside and challenged her about her allegation. I had come to the conclusion that if she chose to punch my lights out, she couldn't hurt me any more than what she had done already. She didn't try to deny it instead she very matter of factly said, 'Yes it's true'. I didn't get angry I knew that would be pointless, she would have only wiped the floor with me anyway. I just looked at her with total distaste and thought to myself, you big fat ugly moll. I closed my eyes slowly and ran my tongue around the inside of my mouth as if I were ridding myself of a foul taste. I turned on my heels and walked away. As I walked to the front door Frank hurried towards me and tried to slip his arm around my waist. I shrugged him away and said, 'I want to see you at Mums later.' Very innocently he said, 'What's wrong?' I again repeated my request and walked out. Frank arrived just as we were finishing our meal, and as per usual Mum offered to cook him a meal as well. He touched his stomach and told her that he had eaten but added, 'I won't say no to a cuppa, though'. I avoided looking at him as he chatted to Mum and Grandad. We went for a walk after we had finished our cup of tea and I tried to keep as cool, calm and collected as I challenged Frank about his indiscretion. At first, he tried to deny everything by laughing at the extreme stupidity of Marianne's imagination. I said, 'Don't insult my intelligence, Frank. You're as guilty as sin and everyone knows it'. Knowing he was backed into a corner he admitted it had happened and he apologised profusely. I said, 'Not good enough, you've taken something from me that I readily gave to you with all my love and you've made a bloody mockery of me by sleeping with that low-class slut the same night'. His next words to me were so unbelievable that I laughed hysterically for about five minutes and through my tears

Amelia 'Do you honestly expect me to believe that?'

Frank 'I swear it's the honest truth, I didn't root her she rooted me. I didn't make love to her like I did with you I was asleep in bed and she got into bed with me. She got on top of me and served herself'. I laughed again in total disgust

Amelia 'Pull the other leg, it plays jingle bells.'

Frank 'You can believe what you like, but I'm telling you the truth go and ask Carl what she's like'.

Amelia 'Oh, for Christ's sake, don' tell me Carl was holding up score cards, next you'll be telling me that Tom was standing in the corner cheering.'

Frank 'I told Carl what happened and he said that she had done it to him while her mother was still staying with us'.

Amelia 'Oh yes. I can imagine how hard he would fight her off too'.

Frank 'Think about it, Amelia, her brother is my best mate. He was asleep in the next bedroom she comes in to me and starts serving herself and I am only human. I'm not bloody likely to scream rape and suffer the consequences of facing the entire Vid family screaming marriage or carnal knowledge, am I?'

Almost sixty years have gone by and I still have difficulty believing that story. Frank and I discussed the subject occasionally, we'd laugh about it and I'd taunt him with, 'Liar, liar, pants on fire'.

But he never wavered from that story and he emphatically stated 'she thought I was Woollies Supermarket and she served herself.'

Marianne went back to her parent's home before the week was over. I never forgave either of them for what happened nor did I accept it. I just chose to ignore the incident after issuing him with this warning: 'If it ever happens again, I promise you you'll sing soprano forever and I don't mean maybe.'\

I had discussed with him previously about how my father's affair had affected me and how I never would accept infidelity so he knew that I would never tolerate that in our marriage.

A couple of weeks went by and Frank went with Tom to the Vid's home for the weekend. Tom wanted to apply for a job for the upcoming whaling season. I wasn't at all happy about the arrangements but I had to pretend that I didn't mind and show Frank that I trusted him. Besides, Tom would have thought it strange if I protested about Frank being in the same place as Marianne. Jenny and I decided to go out and enjoy ourselves, on the Friday night. I can't for the life of me remember where we went, but we met some fellows who had motorbikes and they took us for a drive down to Redcliffe and we got a flat tyre. I remember that they were really nice fellows and they drove us back home as soon as they were able to get the tyre repaired. We didn't get back home until about two o'clock in the morning, and as we pulled up near the shop diagonally opposite where Frank and Tom lived. A car full of cops pulled up and they took our names and addresses. They wanted to know where we were going where we had been etc. It was par for the course to have the 'bulls' question you for no particular reason in the fifties and sixties. On the Saturday, I went up to Edith's place and spent the weekend there. I was thrilled out of my brain when Frank and Tom arrived up there unexpectedly on the Sunday afternoon. Imagine my shock when Frank demanded to know, 'Where the hell were you on Saturday morning at two o'clock?'

Amelia 'At home in bed asleep.'

Frank 'You're a bloody liar you were whoring around on a motor bike with Jenny on another motorbike'.

I lied like a pig in mud to save my own neck

Amelia 'Jenny went out with another girl called 'Marlene Sheldon'.

Frank 'You were seen being questioned by the cops, Mrs Churchill saw you and so did Mr and Mrs Parker (the local shopkeepers) as far as I'm concerned the engagement is off'.

I finally told him the truth and explained that I had done nothing wrong. He relented and forgave me my sins but I still can't help but wonder about the double standards for men and women's behaviour. It was okay for him to be serviced, but for me to be on the back of a motorbike I was categorised as whoring around. As far as the Parkers and old mother Churchill was concerned. I was the slut of the town.

Chapter 17

All's Fair in Love and War

Tom arrived home from the Labor Day march with a dirty little half-starved, rat like, twerp of a fellow by the name of Sid Moore. Tom had struck up conversation with him at the march and had taken pity on him. He was down on his luck and had been kicked out of his lodgings. Sid had told Tom that his dole cheque was due and that he would chip in and pay half the rent and food bill as soon as he got his cheque. None of us liked him from the minute we clapped eyes on him. Not only was he dirty looking, he was a lazy little shit who slept in until eleven o'clock every day. He always seemed to have money, but despite his promises he never paid a penny towards the rent or food. After a couple of weeks everyone began to complain about an ungodly stench in his bedroom. After doing a thorough search, Frank and Tom found two pairs of sheets shoved behind the wardrobe. Sid had obviously pissed the bed and instead of washing the sheets, he had disposed of them by stuffing them behind the wardrobe. One thing he had in his favour he had managed to sweet talk Mrs Churchill into reducing the rent. She was quite taken with him and would even prepare meals for them all after Sid had chatted her up. He would often do the gardening and different odd jobs for her. He had been there about six or seven weeks, when I arrived there after work one afternoon and Mrs Churchill told me that the police had been there and taken Frank and Sid away for questioning. I started to panic and barraged her with questions as to why, when, where and finally I asked where Tom was, she replied, 'I don't know, he went out at about ten-thirty and hasn't arrived home yet'. She explained that the police had arrived there at about one pm and they eventually took Frank and Sid away at about three-thirty pm. I was panic-stricken and I paced the footpath not knowing what to do. I prayed that everything would be all right and I wished and prayed that Tom would hurry up and get home. He finally turned up at about ten past six, as soon as I saw him, I started to bawl my guts out and I bellowed

'They've taken him away'.

Tom 'Who's taken who away'?

Amelia 'The cops have taken Frank and Sid to the CIB'

Tom 'What the fuck for?'

Amelia 'Wah. I don't know, Mrs Churchill said they took them at three-thirty'. Trying to cheer me up

Tom 'Oh. Is that all, for a minute there you had me worried, I thought the green cart had taken him to the loony bin for being with you.'

Tom was on crutches because he had damaged a cartilage in his knee and he hobbled up the stairs two at a time.

Laughing through my tears at his loony bin line,

Amelia 'Well why are you hurrying then?'

Tom 'I think the bastard's wearing my shoes'.

We practically flew along Coronation Drive into the city in the old Roadster. There wasn't anywhere to park legally, so Tom double-parked directly outside the CIB headquarters front entrance. I sat and watched in total disbelief as Tom ran into the building on crutches. It seemed like an eternity just sitting there waiting, but I guess it was only about five minutes before both Tom and Frank came out with grins a mile wide.

I just about flew out of the car to greet Frank. I kept hugging and kissing him as if he had been imprisoned for years.

Tom 'Get in the car, silly bitch, and let's get out of here before they change their minds. If they see him with you, they'll lock him up for the rest of his life for fuckin' insanity'.

We all roared with laughter as we took off in a cloud of jet-black smoke. Tom and I couldn't believe the story that unfolded as Frank retold the events of his day.

Sid had gotten up early for a change and had gone into town to put his form in for the dole. He had arrived back at about midday, Frank said that they had both had their lunch and Frank dozed off to sleep while Sid watched TV. The next thing Frank said he was awakened by a swift kick and a loud voice bellowing, 'Get up, ya lazy bastard', I opened my eyes and there were demons everywhere' and I said, 'What's going on? And the bull that booted me said ' Never mind what's going on, what's your name and how long have you lived here?' Before I could open my mouth, they were pulling clothes out of cupboards and drawers and throwing everything everywhere. One demon grabbed me and almost flung me through to the lounge room. They kept firing questions at me. How long have I known Sid? How long has he lived here? Where did he put the diamonds?'

Tom and I yelled together, 'What diamonds?' Frank said, 'Hang on, let me catch my breath and I'll explain as best as I can'.

He started to laugh and said, 'Two of the demons were in my room and another one was questioning me and one of them yelled out from the hallway, 'Whose drawers are these?' without looking up I said they're mine and he said again, 'No whose drawers are these here?' I again called out mine, that's my room in there, the cupboard and drawers are mine. The demon's voice got angry and he snarled, these fuckin' drawers ya silly bastard, and I looked up and he was holding up a pair of your mother's knickers, Tom'.

We fell about with laughter because Mrs Vid's knickers were a sight to behold, and had to be seen, to be believed. They were the size of a man's T-shirt. Frank went on to explain that the police had been looking for Sid for the entire time he had been staying at their home. A couple of weeks before meeting Tom, Sid had rung the York Private Hotel in South Brisbane and had told the manager that he was Dr Anderson from Wickham Terrace. He had told the manager that he had a patient from Kingaroy, by the name of Mr Sid Moore arriving in town, and he needed accommodation whilst undergoing extensive medical treatment. Sid had then asked the manager to put his patient up for the time that he was in Brisbane and that he would guarantee his accommodation bill. The unsuspecting manager was only too pleased to be of service. When Sid arrived to book in, he got the red-carpet treatment. After he had been there a couple of weeks, the manager began to smell a rat so Sid did a moonlight flit. The day he left the place, the safe was burgled of thousands of pounds worth of diamonds. He must have walked over the bridge from the York and met Tom within the hour. Over the next few days, Tom spent quite a few hours digging in the garden looking for the diamonds, but to no avail, he never found any. We heard on the news a couple of days later that Sid had pleaded guilty to false pretences and received three months free accommodation at Boggo Road. The funny part was Mrs Churchill reckoned she knew all along that Sid was a little con artist. She said, 'I never trusted him and I was worried that he might corrupt my boys'. She meant Tom, Frank and Carl when she said, my boys. We all had a good laugh at that, the silly old battle-axe.

Carl went back to live with his mother. A week or so later, Tom was notified to go to Byron Bay for the whaling season. Frank had no alternative other than to find cheaper accommodation elsewhere. He shifted into a dingy room next door to a couple that he knew from Byron Bay. I had accumulated a number of items for my glory box, which I gave to Frank to use when he shifted to Highgate Hill. Judy and Alan didn't have any appliances at all and were borrowing the jug, toaster and iron every day. Frank would meet me after work every day, and come home with me to have dinner with us. One particular afternoon he arrived quite agitated and reluctantly told me that Judy and Alan had shot through owing a month's rent, and that the landlady had confiscated my iron as payment in lieu. I said, 'Did you tell her it was my iron and that Judy had only borrowed it from you?' 'Yeah, but she wouldn't listen to me she wanted payment and they had left the iron in the room so she claimed the iron'. I was furious, but I had to wait until the weekend, before I could go and see her and demand the return of my iron. When I confronted her and explained again that the iron was mine, she told me that she couldn't care less who owned it, she was owed money, the iron was in her possession and that was it. I very quietly and coolly said, 'Now listen here you snotty nosed old bitch, I'll give you five minutes to give me my iron back and if you don't I 'm going to ring the Health Department first thing on Monday morning and tell them that this place is rat infested. I'll also notify the authorities that this dump is a fire hazard and I'll have the taxation department investigate your income'. She went inside and returned with my iron in less than twenty seconds flat.

We had approached father Lawrence O'Neil the Catholic Priest at the church where I went to school to tell him that we wanted to get married. I had gotten my own way over my father and although he tried to persuade me to have an abortion, he finally had to give in and consent to allowing us to be married. Father O'Neil proved to be a harder customer to convince that we should marry than my father, though. He insisted that we attend religious instructions twice a week for three weeks before he would even consider marrying us. I was totally honest with him and told him that I was pregnant and a non-Catholic but that I had attended the school for years. He told us that it was imperative that he spoke to us separately before we started our religious instruction lessons. He ushered me into a waiting room that was similar to a doctor's surgery waiting room and there I sat for what seemed like an eternity whilst he talked to Frank in another room. When they finally came out over an hour later, Frank rolled his eyes around and around as if to say, Oh my Godfather. This bastard is off his head.

Father O'Neil beckoned me to go into the room with him and the moment the door closed behind me, he bombarded me with questions, mainly about my sex life. How many times had we had sex? How often per week did we do it? Did I enjoy it? I thought, this old bastard is a pervert, nothing surer.

Father O'Neill 'Just because he shows his animal instincts on you doesn't mean he loves you'.

Amelia 'But I know that he does love me, Father'.

Father O'Neill 'That's where you are wrong, because animal instinct does not mean love'.

He ushered me out of the room and as soon as I saw Frank, I rolled my eyes around and around, as if to say, Yes you're right this bastard is off his head.

Father O'Neil 'What will you do if I refuse to marry you'?

Frank 'Suits me, Father, I didn't want to come here in the first place, this is Amelia's idea not mine. I'm quite happy to go to the Church of England, its downhill, I've got to climb the hill to get here. Or we can go to the Registry Office that would suit me down to the ground I couldn't care less where we get married'.

Father O'Neil told us that we were to come to him every Tuesday and Thursday evening at eight o'clock and our lessons would be for two hours each evening. He gave us a booklet each, which we were to study and learn. Frank had a minimal education and was a very poor reader, his writing and spelling was even worse. No need to be told his book never saw the light of day, never mind being opened. I on the other hand memorised the book from cover to cover, parrot fashion, fat lot of good that did me. Father O'Neil made us sit there like a pair of dunces for two nights without him even entering the room. On the third night we went there, I took a packet of raw peanuts for us to nibble on. No need to be told, he entered the room just as I had put a fistful into my mouth. He sat directly in front of us and said, 'If an army marches on their stomach, what does a Christian march on Amelia?' I knew the answer was, their soul, but I couldn't answer for all the peanuts that I had stuffed in my mouth, so I just shook my head, trying not to laugh. 'Do you know, Frank?' Frank sat bolt upright as if he was in school and without batting an eye, he said in a clear well-annunciated voice, 'A Christian would march on their feet, Father.' I sprayed the room with peanuts and nearly choked myself into the bargain. The tears just streamed down our faces, we laughed so hard. Father O'Neil was not impressed.

Father O'Neil insisted that we attend mass on Sundays. On the first Sunday, I managed to get Frank up to the door of the church. Just as we were about to enter, Frank did an about turn and said, 'There's standing room only, we'll have to go home'.

No amount of persuasion was going to change his mind, so we went home.

On the following Tuesday, Father O'Neil said, 'I didn't see you at mass on Sunday, Frank, where were you?'

Frank 'We were there father, but there weren't any seats available, so we had to leave'.

Father O'Neil 'Did you try at the later mass?'

Frank 'No, Father, we attended another parish'.

Father O'Neil 'Oh, where did you go?'

Frank 'Um, er, ah, Clayfield, Father, we went to the St Rita's Church at Clayfield'.

Father O'Neil 'What was the mass about?'

Frank 'Dunno, Father, we were sitting in the back row and the priest spoke softly and we couldn't hear him at all'.

Father O'Neil 'I hold a special mass every morning for the people who are on their way to work I want you to come to the worker's mass tomorrow morning at six o'clock. Will you be there?'

Frank (looking very sullen and grumbled,) 'Yes, Father, I'll be there'.

At six o'clock the following morning, Frank turned the corner of the street leading to the chapel and started climbing the hill towards the Presbytery. He caught a glimpse of Father O'Neil scurrying from the top of the hill, directly outside the Presbytery into the little chapel. Frank had a sinking feeling that he had been conned. He entered the chapel to see Father O'Neil and one lone altar boy waiting for him to take a seat, so that they could commence Mass for the one and only worshipper. Frank later commented how pleasantly surprised he was that they hadn't passed the plate around. Father O'Neil made it abundantly clear that he was not at all happy about mixed marriages. When I told him that I was prepared to become a Catholic, his reply was, 'You can't change your religion like you change your coat'. I thought to myself, well, you can stick your religion. I had to promise him faithfully that I would have all my children of the union Christened and brought up in the catholic faith. What sort of double standard is that? Here we were, a catholic born agnostic who wanted nothing to do with any religion and a non-Catholic who believed in Catholicism, but wasn't welcome in the catholic faith. And we were being forced into agreeing to bring up our offspring as Catholics, just so we could be married. It didn't make any sense then, any more than it does now.

He had very definite ideas about photographers, under no circumstances were any photographers allowed to enter the church or the vestry.

Imagine the shock on our faces, on our wedding day, when a knock came to the vestry door as we were signing the marriage certificate. As he jumped to his feet and ran to the door Father O'Neil said, 'That will be the photographer he'll want to get a photo of me giving you the certificate'. I feel sure we were right when we assessed him as being off his head. He was a real nut case. Because we had to attend his religious instructions, we couldn't get married until three weeks after James birthday. The only other hitch was Frank arrived at the Church as full as the Marist Brother's College. He had arrived at the pub at opening time and stayed there until five minutes to two, flew home got dressed and arrived at the church at a minute to three. He had to have one of the guests arrange the orange blossom onto his lapel before he staggered down to the altar to take his place. Father O'Neil said to him, 'What sort of state do you call this? You should be in the state of grace.' To which Frank replied, 'Don't know what state I'm in father, but I'm in some bloody state.' Then the wedding march began and I entered the church.

I had only ever seen Frank drunk on two other occasions prior to our wedding day, the first was three weeks after we met, I had been three hours late arriving at his home. He took himself to the pub and arrived back two hours later. His behaviour at the time seemed to me to be overacting his drunkenness. He was flinging his arms around, taking his watch off and giving it to me and telling me he wanted me to have it and generally making an idiot of himself. I had said to Tom, 'Is he for real?' Tom replied, 'Yeah, he's a fuckin' idiot in drink.' The second time, he had stormed off to the pub after we had an argument. On his way home, he bought some fish and chips, Jenny and I met up with him as he was staggering outside the park. I was horrified to see how awful he looked in his drunken state and I was ashamed to be seen with him. When he saw me, I expected him to greet me cordially I didn't anticipate the reaction I got. He abused the living daylights out of me calling me all the rotten bitches unhung. I retaliated with a few well-chosen words of my own and the next thing I copped a lump of battered fish splat on the back of my head as I walked away from him. He was full of apologies the following day and I was naive enough to accept his pitiful excuse for his disgraceful behaviour.

On our wedding day his drunkenness took on a playful persona, he was happy and high-spirited. Not the ugly drunk who threw things in anger or the half-wit who wanted to give all his possessions away. As we walked back in front of the altar to head down the aisle and out of the church, he turned to Tom and said, 'I want you to meet the old cheese'. He playfully swiped me with his gloves. Tom's hands were caked with grease and dirt from the whale blubber and no amount of scrubbing would get them clean, so he had to wear gloves to cover his hands. It would have looked a bit odd if only the best man had worn gloves, so Frank had to wear them as well. My cousin Fay was my bridesmaid. I've often wondered what Father O'Neill would have said if he had found out that neither the best man nor the bridesmaid was a Catholic. We had to promise Father O'Neill faithfully that we would choose only good catholic people as our attendants. Father O'Neil had told Frank that there was no fee for marrying us, but he added hastily, 'However, most people usually give me upwards of ten pounds. Oh. and it'll be another ten pounds if you want the bells rung'. I had to stifle a belly laugh as I remembered my last day at school, and we both said together, 'No bells thank you, Father'. Father O'Neil must have been bitterly disappointed when he opened his envelope for his ten pounds. Frank had placed a one-pound note and a ten-shilling note in the envelope before going to the pub and handed it to Tom to deliver to Father O'Neill after the ceremony. I must confess that I thought he was overpaid, by the way he raved and ranted at us for the three weeks leading up to the wedding. It was painfully obvious that he was waiting for an invitation to the reception by the way he kept hinting. He would have to wait until hell froze over as far as I was concerned. When we arrived at Edith's place for the reception, Tom handed Frank a ten-bob note.

Frank 'What's this for?'

Tom 'I opened the priest's envelope and saw that you'd given him too much, so I took the quid note out and left him ten-bob. I figured that we'd split the difference, so you get ten-bob back.'

A month before the wedding, Frank finally got a letter from Worker's Compensation, but not what he had been expecting. After all those months of going without, borrowing money, depending on others etc. to keep a roof over his head and food in his belly the letter said, 'We reject your claim for worker's compensation'.

Frank was absolutely ropable. He marched into the compo office and instead of taking a number, as was the routine, he flung the letter onto the desk and said, 'I've come to see about this'. The fellow behind the counter obviously knew what the letter contained, and without even looking up, he replied, 'Nuthin' I can do about it, your application's been rejected'. Frank snarled, 'I haven't come to talk to you, ya pen pushin' bastard, I want to see the pen pushing bastard who sent me the letter'. Frank was ushered into a small office and when the fellow who occupied the office entered, Frank almost grabbed him by the throat. The fellow said, 'How can I help you?' Frank told him how he had been unable to work for months, what the orthopaedic surgeon said, how he was penniless and destitute and that he had a pregnant wife to support and all the fellow said was, 'I'm sorry, take this docket to the cashier and she'll give you something to go on with'. Frank was shattered, the last thing he wanted was charity and all he could think of was how the hell am I going to be able to care for a wife and baby as he handed the woman the docket. She looked at the docket and said, 'I'm sorry sir I won't be able to pay you in full today'. Frank frowned at her as he tried to understand what on earth she was talking about. She went on, 'I can only give you ninety-nine pounds (one hundred and ninety-eight dollars) today, sir. That's the most we can pay you we'll send the remainder to you by cheque, okay?' Frank said it was as if a huge lead weight had been lifted off him and he was able to breathe again for the first time in months. He walked out of the compo office and headed towards the first cafe he could find and bought himself the best mixed grill that he had ever tasted.

He paid off the engagement ring, bought my wedding ring, a suit and shoes for the wedding, all the bills that had accumulated over the past seven months, so he hardly had any money left by the time our wedding day rolled around. Of course, he'd spent a bit giving himself Dutch courage on the morning of the wedding.

The week before the wedding, we had been invited to a party and I wasn't all that keen about going to it. I didn't know any of the people at the party, as they were mainly friends of an ex-workmate of Frank. Being two months pregnant, I didn't feel like partying on, not that I was suffering from morning sickness, I just felt exhausted most of the time. Frank thought I was being a party pooper, so, against my better judgement, I went, but after about two hours or so I wanted to go home. Frank was getting into the party mode so I told him to stay and that I would find my own way home. Although he wasn't drunk, he was certainly well on the way.

Rick, the host of the party, called out to some fellow and asked him to see that I got home safely. Without batting an eye, he said he would. The fellow grabbed his keys and he assured Frank that he would get me home in one piece and we left. I couldn't help but wonder what Frank would have thought if he had known that I was getting a lift on the back of a motorbike. I was terrified that I would miscarry and I asked the fellow to drive as slow as he possibly could and to avoid any potholes. Fortunately, I arrived home safe and sound and I thanked the fellow profusely. The following afternoon I saw Frank and he looked like death warmed up.

Frank 'I made a complete fool of myself this morning'.

Amelia 'Why, what happened?'

Frank 'I crashed out on one of the beds and slept there the night, I wouldn't have a clue what time it was or even if the party was finished when I crashed. When I awoke this morning there was a body lying alongside of me and I thought it was you, so I put my arms around her and cuddled her'.

I thought to myself here comes the bullshit story.

Frank 'I cuddled her for quite a while until she woke up and she rolled over and went to cuddle and kiss me and we both nearly shit ourselves when I realised she wasn't you. She was a he and he thought I was his sheila'.

Amelia 'What did you do?'

Frank 'We both leapt out of bed saying 'Sorry mate' and there was a whole mob of blokes sitting around watching and waiting for us to realise what was happening'.

We had found a flat and Mum had paid the first fortnight's rent and stocked the cupboard with groceries for us. God bless her cotton socks Grandad was right when he said 'She's a mighty woman'.

We didn't have a honeymoon we went straight from the reception at Edith's place to the flat by cab. I didn't even have a honeymoon night, Frank was too full to stand up, let alone do anything else. When we got to the flat, he flaked out on the bed in full marching order. I ended up taking his shoes off because I didn't want to be kicked to death during the night. I somehow managed to take his suit off him as well. He lay there in his shirt, underpants and socks and he was thrashing around like a shark out of water moaning and groaning. I tried to go to sleep alongside of him but it was impossible, so I curled up on the settee and had a very uncomfortable first night of marriage. The landlady was an old witch of the first degree. When we had first looked at the place, she had said, 'No children allowed here and I don't like drinkers or loud parties or pets of any kind'. Frank had whispered to me, 'No farting either.'

We had only been there about a fortnight, when we were awakened by loud shouting, at about two o'clock, one morning. 'Frank Williams, you dirty bastard, get off the nest and get out here'.

Amelia 'Who the hell is that?'

We listened for a while longer and again loud voices shouting Frank's name.

Frank whispered 'It's Carl and Stewart, the stupid bastards.'

Amelia 'Go out there and tell them to shut up, they'll get us both kicked out of here if the landlady hears them'.

Frank 'No, bugger them, let's pretend that we don't hear them and they'll go home'.

The noise finally died down and we snuggled up and we both dozed off. The next thing, there was a loud pounding on the door.

'Frank Williams, open the door, this is the police, put your hands above the sheet we're coming in'. The door handle rattled and there was a great deal of fumbling and bashing against the door and a voice said, 'They must be up to no good, the doors locked'.

Frank got out of bed and opened the door and said in a hushed growl,

'Shut up, you mad bastards, you'll get us all kicked out of here'. Nothing we said to them would shut them up. Eventually Frank said to me, 'I'll go with them to shut them up otherwise we're going to be in deep shit'. It was about five-thirty am before he arrived back and he was as full as a state school. He flaked out on the bed and when he awoke later in the day he said, 'Those bastards are mad, especially that Stewart, he's off his friggin head, he nearly had us all shot. We got in the car and they had a bottle of rum and Carl drove around for a while and we ended up over at Enoggera Army Barracks. We were sitting there drinking, and Stewart saw a soldier on guard duty. The soldier didn't worry about us being there until stupid bloody Stewart kept poking fun at him. He kept yelling out, 'You're a cut lunch cowboy and a Queen Street soldier,' he was just being a bloody idiot. The soldier got jack of being abused and he came over and said, 'I'll have to ask you to leave'. Then Stewart said, 'Go on you bloody ratbag, ya couldn't fight your way out of a wet paper bag'. The next thing the soldier said, 'You're on Crown land and if you're not gone in one-minute flat, I'm going to shoot you'. He cocked his gun and held it to Stewart's head. I said to Carl. Let's get out of here we can leave this fuckin' idiot here to be shot. Stewart was still pushing the gun away telling the soldier, don't be a fuckin' hero.'

I couldn't believe how brainless Stewart had been and how damn lucky the three of them were, that they didn't get their heads blown off. Later that day the landlady came up to me and complained about the noisy people we'd had in our flat

Amelia 'They were uninvited pests.'

Landlady 'Humph, your husband didn't seem to mind going out with them'.

Amelia 'My husband only went out with them to get rid of them so that they wouldn't wake the neighbourhood'.

She studied me for a while

Landlady 'Are you pregnant?'

Amelia 'I don't know what business it is of yours, but yes, as a matter of fact I am'.

She prodded her sharp bony finger into my chest

Landlady 'I told you, Mrs Williams, I don't allow children into my establishment'.

I grabbed her arm and held it firmly by the wrist and I snarled in her face,

'I have no intention of bringing a child of mine into a brothel like this and if you ever put your slimy, little, snot picking hand onto my body again you old bat, I'll beat your face to a pulp'.

She apologised and told me that I could stay there as long as I wanted to. I wouldn't have touched her if she hadn't poked me in the chest and the threat was really a hollow one but she didn't know that. We didn't want to stay there any longer than that night, but flats for pregnant people were not readily available in those days. Not ones that we could afford, which wasn't anything at all because it was impossible for Frank to stay on Worker's Compensation even though his back wasn't getting any better. It was obvious he could never go back to being a brickies labourer, not unless he wanted to go into a wheelchair early in life. He had a talk with the orthopaedic surgeon and he advised Frank to get a desk job, he said, 'You'll never do heavy lifting again, not unless you want to kill yourself'.

Frank was almost illiterate, but he would never admit that to anyone but me, so of course he wasn't qualified to become a pen pusher as he called anyone who worked in an office. He had, had experience as a knife hand at Wallangarra, Byron Bay and Ipswich meatworks and when I saw an advertisement in the paper for a slicer at Playfairs Smallgoods factory about a mile away, Frank applied for and got the job. We thought we were multimillionaires when he brought his first wage packet home. We went from living on mince and sausages to T-bones and eye fillet steaks in one foul swoop.

There I was the granddaughter, daughter and wife of butchers and I didn't know a pork chop from a beef sausage, even if they had hit me in the face. One afternoon Frank arrived home and said, 'What's for tea, I'm starved'.

I replied, 'T-bone steaks and they're beautiful, I picked them out myself'.

I got them out of the fridge to proudly show him how smart I was. He looked at the steaks

Frank 'Where did you get them from?'

Amelia 'Around in the local butcher shop. Why?'

Frank 'How much did you pay for them?'

I handed him the docket

Amelia 'What's wrong?'

He studied the price and shook his head, looked at his watch

Frank 'C'mon let's go'.

Amelia 'What's wrong, what've I done?'

Frank 'You haven't done anything the butcher has diddled you'.

Amelia 'But I gave him the right money'. I said, as we almost ran to the butcher shop.

Frank 'These aren't T-bones, they're Y-bone steaks but he's charged you for T-bones. These should be a lot cheaper. What made you think they were T-bones?'

Amelia 'The sign on them said T-bone steaks.'

When we got there, the door of the shop was locked but the butchers were still serving some customers. One butcher called out, 'Sorry, mate, we're closed we can't serve you, because it's after five o'clock'.

Frank 'You either open this door and let us in or I'm going to kick it in, you can't keep those customers locked in there forever'.

Reluctantly the butcher opened the door.

As we entered the shop Frank whispered to me, 'Which one was it?'

I pointed to the butcher who had served me and Frank threw the steaks onto the counter along with the docket

Frank 'Remember serving these to my wife today?'

Butcher 'Yes she chose them herself'.

Frank 'Where's the tray that they were on?'

The fellow brought the tray out from the display cabinet and the sign, T-bone was still on top of the meat.

Frank 'How would you like the D.P.I. to close you down and the cops to charge you with theft and fraud?'

The butcher stammered, 'W … what do you mean?'

Frank 'These aren't T-bones they're Y-bones, and you know damn well that they're a lot cheaper cut of meat'.

The fellow tried to get Frank to calm down and it was obvious the other customers were more than interested to hear what Frank was saying. Frank turned to them and said, 'I'll bet you're all getting diddled too'.

The butcher offered us our money back plus two giant T-bones at wholesale price and as we started to walk out, Frank swung around to face all the butchers

Frank 'Remember my wife's face you fellas and if she ever comes in here again, make sure she gets top quality and top rate service or else'.

We left them all nodding like the toy dogs that some people used to display in their car's rear windows.

I was too embarrassed to ever go back to that butcher shop again and I made a promise to myself that if I live to be a hundred and ninety, I would never buy anything from a butcher shop unless Frank was with me. But that still didn't stop the confusion. A couple of weeks later, Frank went to Lang Park to watch his favourite pastime Rugby League Football. I thought, now's my chance to bake him a lovely roast dinner. As I had never baked a dinner before, I decided to make sure I did it properly by doing everything step by step so that there wouldn't be any muck up. Every fifteen minutes I would baste the rolled roast carefully and I would turn it regularly, checking the meat that it wasn't burning. After two hours, the meat still wasn't anywhere near cooked. As a matter of fact, it was surprisingly raw inside and still bloody. When Frank arrived home after five pm, I was very distressed and I burst into tears

Amelia 'The roast won't cook and I've had it in the oven for over four hours,'

Frank looked at me quizzically

Frank 'What roast?'

I took the roast out of the oven and showed him the now blackened piece of meat

Amelia 'It's overcooked on the outside and still bleeding on the inside but I've kept the heat down on low'.

He patted me on the head and put his arm around my shoulder and burst out laughing. I started to laugh too, but not knowing what he was laughing at. When he finally settled down enough to speak

Frank 'Amelia, the roast you've been lovingly baking for four hours, isn't a roast, it's a rolled brisket, that's a piece of corn meat and you're supposed to boil it in water not bake it. I was going to show you how to cook it tomorrow for my sandwiches for work'.

I burst into tears and made him promise faithfully that he would never tell anyone what I had done no matter how long we lived.

We shifted from the dingy flat to the other side of the city. The first flat we lived in was only a one bedroom, kitchen, and dinette and we had to share the bathroom with all the other tenants. To make matters worse, every time the couple in the front flat made love, we could hear their bed squeak. I had no desire to be heard by anyone else and every time Frank felt romantic, I would always tell him to shush.

The flat at West End was huge and we had our own bathroom and plenty of privacy. It was a big block of flats, three stories high. The old fellow, who owned them, lived in the block of flats next door. He absolutely loved kids, he had even put a big playground full of swings, seesaws and slippery slides in the front yard. There was always a tribe of kids playing happily in the yard. We had only been there a week or so and we were awakened in the middle of the night by a drunken brawl in the middle of the hallway. There were two fellows and a woman involved in the fight and the woman was flung down the flight of stairs, the ambulance was called and she was taken to hospital. Both Frank and I were upset about the incident and we were frustrated at not being able to do anything. We felt sorry for the lady but we feared repercussions if we had've interfered.

We asked Tom to come and help us unpack all of our wedding gifts, which we had been unable to use at our first place. Edith also came over to help unpack, and I will never forget this incident as long as I live. Edith was standing on a chair placing the crockery and glassware that Tom, Frank and I were passing to her. We were all chatting away and joking and laughing and getting the job done in record time. Tom winked at Frank and me. I could tell by the twinkle in his eyes and the look on his face that he was going to say or do something that would no doubt shock Edith to her back molars.

Frank and I almost fell over in gales of embarrassed laughter and Edith just about fell off the chair in shock when Tom said to her, 'I think you had better cross your legs, Mrs Long, because your breath stinks'. Surprisingly she took the joke quite well really, and she had a bit of a chuckle as she mock reprimanded him for being a cheeky devil.

We were only at the second flat about three weeks when we gave the landlord notice that we wanted to leave. We couldn't tolerate the incessant drunken brawls outside our flat at least twice a week. We weren't getting enough sleep and we both felt that the people living in the flats were peasant class and that we didn't want our child to be brought up in that type of environment. The landlord pleaded with me not to leave. He offered us one week's rent, free, if we stayed and I declined his offer, telling him that I was sorry but it was out of the question. He asked me to get my husband's opinion before giving him a definite 'no' answer. I knew what Frank's answer would be. The landlord bailed Frank up the following day and asked him what his decision was

Frank 'No mate, I'm sorry but my wife's health is more important than a week's free rent'.

The Landlord 'You're the best tenants that I have ever had and I don't want to lose you. I've told the trouble makers that they've got to go, so things will be quieter now, I'll give you two weeks rent free'.

Before Frank could say no thanks, the old man said, 'Talk it over with your wife before you give me your answer'. I went to him the following day and thanked him for his offer

Amelia 'I'm sorry but we've decided to leave.

Landlord , 'I'll give you a month's rent free if you stay, I've been looking forward to the birth of your baby'.

I felt so sorry for him, I thought, Oh. The poor lonely man, he mustn't have any family.

When I told Frank

Frank 'Oh shit. Its tempting isn't it?'

Amelia 'No, it's sad but it's not tempting, I'm the one that's stuck here twenty-four hours a day, I'm a prisoner in a war zone of peasants. I'm not tempted to spend another week let alone another month'.

Chapter 18

Vivian

We shifted out of there and into a really huge four roomed flat that took up the full-length of the back verandah of an old colonial home. The home was owned by an elderly couple by the name of Foley. They were in their late seventies / early eighties. Both of them were Bible bashing, sticky beaks, who wanted to know the ins and outs of the duck's bum.

There was another elderly couple, Mr and Mrs Smith, who rented a smaller section of the home and they were absolute sweethearts. Mr and Mrs Foley made it their business to regularly check out the flat by wandering in and out of the rooms whenever it suited them. Admittedly it was during the day when Frank was at work, but they'd never knock or call out. I was very tempted to abuse them on several occasions and looking back I can't for the life of me work out why I didn't. I think it was because I had a lot of time and respect for Mr and Mrs Smith and I didn't want to disgrace myself in their books. I used to say to Mrs Smith that I felt like telling old mother Foley a thing or two, especially that I didn't have to go to church if I didn't want to. I can recall Mrs Smith's reply as if it were yesterday. 'Take no notice of them, dear, they're not worth bothering about. They've got nothing better to do with their lives than making others suffer their misery'. On the subject of religion she once said to me, 'It's not necessary to go into a manmade building to worship God, whenever I'm troubled, all I have to do is walk into the garden and see the trees, flowers and grass and I know that He is watching over and caring for me'.

A few incidents remain memorable from our stay at that place. It was a particularly hot summer's night early in December and I only had a month to go before the baby's birth. To cool down, Frank and I got into the old bath, filled with cold water and we just sat and soaked in it and cooled ourselves down. I really don't know how we both managed to fit into it, to be honest, because I was so huge. We heard a tapping sound outside and Frank reluctantly went out to investigate the noise. He dried himself off and wrapped the towel around himself and went out onto the veranda. He had no sooner closed the door behind him and the next instant he let out the most blood-curdling scream I've ever heard anyone yell in my entire life. Knowing that Frank is not frightened of anything, my heart leapt to my mouth as I envisaged in my mind's eye that an axe-wielding madman was murdering him. I grabbed the towel and nearly broke my neck as I raced out to hold him in his last dying moments. I couldn't believe my eyes as I rushed out the door and saw him bouncing around flinging his arms up and down and around in a frantic frenzy.

He screeched at top note, 'It's got me, Amelia. Get it off me for Christ's sake'.

I somehow managed to calm him down, and I discovered what it was that had made him go into a mad hysteria. There, clinging onto his throat was a giant coddler moth, its body was the length and thickness of my thumb and without a word of a lie its wing span was fully expanded and was the size of my hands. I swear I nearly gave birth then and there. The Foley's must have had their TV up full blast not to hear the commotion. They probably would have asked us to leave, if they had seen the two of us nearly naked, except for the towels draped around us, thrashing about trying to get rid of the moth from Frank's throat.

The other memorable event was waking at five-twenty in the morning with the most excruciating contractions. They began every seven minutes and increased to four, three, and two-minute intervals. By six-fifteen I started to moan and Frank, awakened by the noise, was concerned enough to say, 'Shut up'.

As he pulled the pillow over his head in an effort to deaden the sound

Amelia 'The baby's coming'.

He groaned,

Frank 'Are you sure?'

Amelia 'Of course I'm sure, the contractions started an hour ago and they're two minutes apart'.

Frank 'Jesus.'

He jumped out of bed and raced around the bedroom like a man possessed,

Frank 'I'll ring your old man and the taxi and the doctor and the hospital, anyone else?'

Amelia 'No just the taxi they'll get me to the hospital and the hospital will get the doctor.'

As we didn't have a telephone, it meant he either had to go to the public telephone down the street or wake the Foleys to ask to use their telephone. Frank chose to run to the public phone, the least the Foley's knew the better. I got up, got dressed, tidied up, made the bed and got my bag out ready to go. Frank had no sooner gotten back, and Dad arrived. He seemed hell bent on taking me to the hospital, but I assured him I was okay. Fortunately, the taxi arrived otherwise I envisaged having to keep my father calm until I had given birth.

Hospitals didn't allow husbands into the delivery rooms in those days, so it was pointless Frank coming with me. Instead, he came half way to the hospital and got out at Playfairs and went to work. Dad had paid sixteen pounds for my confinement at the Royal Women's Intermediate Hospital and all I can say is it was a waste of sixteen pounds. I reckon a dog at a veterinary clinic would have gotten better treatment.

Vivian was born at five-twenty pm and weighed 6lb 15oz.

About half an hour after she was born, a young nurse came into me and asked me if I would like something to eat. I was absolutely starving as I hadn't eaten since lunch the previous day.

Nurse 'It's only fish patties I'm afraid, because it's Friday'.

Amelia 'That sounds great to me'.

Another half an hour went by and she came back

Nurse 'No fish patties left, will scrambled eggs do?'

Amelia 'Yes, anything will be fine by me'.

About ten minutes later she came back with a plate

Nurse 'I'm sorry this is all I could get for you, there weren't any scrambled eggs either'.

I took the silver lid off the plate and there in the middle of the plate was what could be best described as something that the cat had thrown up. It was a plateful of fried onions, but on tasting them they seemed to me that they had been boiled not fried. I ate them because I thought I would be sick if I didn't get some food into my stomach. By the time I had finished, it was getting close to seven pm, which was visiting hours. I couldn't believe it when two wards men came in and one said, 'Okay, love, we're going to take you up to your room now'. I still had a green gown on and no panties and there was no sheet to cover me with and the under sheet was covered in blood.

Amelia 'Could you at least get me some sort of cover?'

Wards man 'Sorry, love, there's nothing here'.

Amelia 'Well where's my bag?'

Wards man 'Up in your room'.

I was still very sore from the twelve-hour labour and quite exhausted but I managed to lift myself up and drag the blood soaked under sheet to cover myself. As they wheeled me out the door, I nearly died a thousand deaths. I was wheeled through the foyer to the lifts and we waited amongst all the visitors who were also waiting for the lifts to take them to the wards upstairs. I just covered my hands over my face and wished the earth would swallow me up. I got a glimpse of Frank hurrying towards me and I started to cry.

Frank 'W … w … w,' he stammered.

Amelia 'A girl, 6lb 15oz, didn't they ring you?'

Frank 'No'.

I was so angry I wanted to punch heads in. He gave me a big kiss and cuddle

Frank 'I'll ring your mother and father and your grandmother, hey?'

I nodded and just as he turned to look for a telephone, they all walked in.

Frank 'It's a girl, 6lb 15 oz'.

Edith 'Yes we know'.

Frank's face fell to the floor he was so upset that they knew before he did.

Frank 'Oh did you ring here before you left home?'

Edith No the hospital notified us.'

It was a double whammy for Frank, I knew he felt as if he had been excluded from enjoying the news with the family and I could have willingly choked Edith there and then for opening her mouth as if to gloat, ha-ha we knew first before you did. I was wheeled into the two-bed ward and placed on the bed.

The Sister of the ward had insisted that the family stay outside until everything was organised, I was just as insistent that Frank stay with me as they wheeled me in. The wards-men left and I turned to Frank and said, 'I feel as sick as a dog'.

No sooner had I said that, I chundered all the boiled onions all over the floor. The nursing sister yelled, 'Oh my God. You could have called for a tray. I don't know, you young ones –' Before she could finish her sentence I roared, 'You bloody old hag, you wouldn't know what it's like to give birth, and you never will either you withered up old maid. You're supposed to administer care to the sick, not abuse them for it'.

She was completely lost for words. I doubt that anyone had ever put her in her place before, and I was so angry that if she had said another word, I feel sure that I would have bitten her head off at the kneecaps.

I didn't see my baby until the following morning, when a young nurse brought the babies around to their mothers at six o'clock. She walked in, handed me the little bundle and walked out. I looked at the baby and pressed the buzzer immediately. The nurse came in with an exasperated look on her face

Amelia 'Nurse, this is not my baby'.

Nurse 'Don't be silly, Mrs Williams, of course it's your baby'.

Amelia 'I am not being silly this is not my baby.'

I had only seen Vivian for a few moments before they took her away after the birth, but I knew that the baby I was holding was not the one I had given birth to even though it was a gorgeous little blonde like Vivian. The nurse and I argued for a few minutes before she finally checked the nametag, on the baby's arm. I can't remember the name now, but I recall that it was a little boy. Without any apology the nurse took the baby, I can only assume to his rightful mother, and returned within a few moments with Vivian. When I told Frank, who had desperately wanted a son, he said, 'Why didn't you keep him?'

It was at that hospital that I learned how to eat rolled oats for breakfast, (a meal that I had previously detested,) because the meals were revolting pigswill and the rolled oats were the best of the worst meals on offer.

One good laugh that I had whilst in the Horse Hospital (that's the nickname my father called the Royal.) was when my entire family including my aunts and uncles, came to visit me. My doctor had advised me an hour or so beforehand that I would have to ask Edith or Frank to bring some firm brassieres for me to wear in bed. My well-endowed breasts had swelled to almost football proportions.

When the entire family arrived, I thought, it's no use whispering to Edith or Frank to get me new bras, because that would be so rude so I very nonchalantly said, 'Could you bring me a couple of bras when you come to see me tomorrow please?' To which James replied in his loudest voice so that everyone could hear, 'Yeah Fatso, what size, eighties or a couple of chaff bags'. I still get a good laugh out of that. No need to be told we were all in absolute fits of laughter. It's a wonder we weren't all kicked out for making too much noise.

Edith went to the flat to give Frank a hand to tidy up before I arrived home. Mr Foley almost broke his neck coming over to see who the strange woman was with Frank. The old perv seemed rather disappointed when Frank said to him, 'This lady is my mother-in-law'.

Chapter 19

Friends and Neighbours

The credit squeeze of 1962 took its toll on Frank's job when Playfairs announced that they had to cut down on staff. Jobs were (for the first time since World War Two) hard to get. Dad knew a big wig in the Brisbane City Council and he made arrangements for Frank to have an appointment with the fellow and he pushed Frank's application forward for Frank to become a tram conductor. No sooner had he met with the fellow and Frank was offered the job within two weeks. He was to begin work at Light Street Depot, Fortitude Valley. That meant we'd have to find a flat closer to his work as we had no transport of our own. Some mornings he would have to start at four-thirty and on other shifts he wouldn't finish until after midnight.

The day after I gave the Foleys notice that we would be leaving, I was in the bedroom breastfeeding Vivian. Frank had just sat down on the side of the bed in his underpants when the bedroom door flew open and old mother Foley stood there with her husband and another young couple. The young couple were amazed and obviously very embarrassed as the Foleys explained, 'And this is the bedroom'.

I glared at the old bag and when the young couple apologised, I said, 'You weren't to know, but this is what you can expect if you take it'.

I'm willing to bet pounds, crowns and bars of gold that they never took the flat.

The big old home we shifted to was a block of five flatettes and one self-contained flat. We were the youngest tenants in the building and our flatette consisted of one bedroom and a kitchen/dinette. We had to share the bathroom and toilet with all the other tenants.

Betty was the landlady and she occupied the front flatette with her de facto husband Bob, who was a forklift driver on the wharves. Betty was a fairly fat lady in her late 40s although she never did me any harm, I didn't like her very much. There was something about her that I didn't like, but I couldn't for the life of me pinpoint anything in particular. Apart from the fact that she was always in her nightie and dressing gown until about half an hour before Bob arrived home from work. Bob on the other hand was a really nice bloke he was about twelve years younger than Betty and we could never understand why he stayed with her. He had been married and had a daughter aged ten, whom he never saw. He fell head over heels in love with our darling baby and he nicknamed her 'The Champ' as far as Bob was concerned nothing was too good for The Champ. He would have done cartwheels in hell if necessary, just to have the opportunity of nursing her. He had a hairy chest and Vivian would grab hold of the hairs on his chest and pull hard, but not once did he ever complain or even untangle her fingers from the hair. We'd often watch in amazement at the sight of this big man who would quite often be reduced to tears of sheer joy just watching Vivian gurgle and smile up at him.

The couple directly opposite us were funny buggers, Gwen was in her forties and Fred was about sixty. Gwen could be best described as being a rough diamond. She had a rough as guts, cut to the quick tongue without being too rude crude and ugly. Fred was an inoffensive type of bloke who was always telling a joke and trying to make us laugh. His one big claim to fame was that he would pour pepper over his food. Not a word of a lie, he would eat two large tins of pepper on his food per week.

Apart from the school teacher who lived in the back flat these two couples were the main focus of interest and played a fairly big part in our lives over the following twelve months or so. I must briefly tell you about Mr Henderson, the school teacher, he was definitely a froot-loop short of a breakfast. Every morning he would worship the sun at dawn, and then he would walk around the yard picking up imaginary things off the grass. Of an evening he would stand and meditate at the moon. His wife, who was a lovely lady, would confide in us that he had a number of odd idiosyncrasies in the confines of their flat, but she'd never go into detail about them. She'd say, 'He really frightens me at times.' Years later there was a Mr Henderson at the High school Vivian went to, and Vivian would often say, 'Henderson is definitely nuts, Mum, he acts really strange all of the time'. I often wondered if it was the same man.

Frank's behaviour became more erratic after Vivian was born. He began drinking more and was often drunk after work, on weekends and days off. Whenever he was drunk, he would become aggressive and defensive. No matter what I tried to say or do, I was always in the wrong, and he blamed me for his wanting to stay and have a few beers with the boys.

When Vivian was twelve weeks old, she was to be christened at the local Catholic Church. We had chosen James as her godfather and Dotty and Jenny as her two Godmothers. Jenny had come over to spend the weekend with us in readiness to go with us to the church. She told us about a BBQ party we had all been invited to on the Saturday night, but I wasn't all that keen to go and I told her so. I said, 'If you want to go you can'. I thought to myself that she wouldn't, because I believed she would consider that it was bad manners to go to someone's home for the weekend, and then go out to a party elsewhere. It began to rain and that confirmed it, I wouldn't take a baby out into the cold night air, especially not to a BBQ in the rain. Frank became extremely angry and abused the living daylights out of me for being a wet blanket. Out of the blue he said, 'Well I'm going to the party to enjoy myself'. With that he got ready and both he and Jenny left for the party. They arrived home about midnight and Frank was as full as a tick and Jenny was more than a bit tipsy. I pretended to be asleep and Jenny got into bed alongside of me, as we had arranged, and Frank crashed on the settee.

The following morning, Frank was extremely apologetic, as was his usual habit when he had been an absolute mongrel to me. I seethed with anger inside and only made conversation with the two of them when I felt it was necessary. I vowed and declared to myself that my friendship with Jenny had come to a dead end the moment she had walked out of my home the night before.

At the christening, the priest asked for the names of the godparents, James, Dotty and Jenny were standing at the font waiting to take part in the ceremony. I told the priest that Frank and Dotty were to be the godparents, and Jenny stood there like a prize gooseberry. The priest asked Jenny to go and sit down with the rest of the congregation and I know she would have been totally embarrassed and humiliated at having been rejected in front of everyone. Frank looked at me in total disbelief at what I had done. If I could have, I would have humiliated her more, and I would have given my eyeteeth and right arm to push Frank's face into the font for a ten minute dip.

Frank stayed out all night after doing the late shift a few weeks later. I had made a habit of waiting up for him with a hot meal when he was on the late shift. When he hadn't arrived by two am, although I was sick with worry, I crashed from sheer exhaustion and awoke at six am to feed Vivian. Frank arrived home about a half an hour later, he told me he had gone to sleep in the car down near the wharves, but I didn't believe him. I accused him of being with a woman, and then I discovered lipstick on his collar about an hour or so later. I had rung Edith and she arrived at the flat before nine o'clock, I think she must have had wings on her feet that morning to get there so quickly. Between the two of us, we grilled Frank over and over, he kept playing a cat and mouse game about the lipstick until finally he produced one of my lipsticks and said, 'Check the colour, know it all, and see whose bloody lipstick it belongs to'. Because I had accused him of being with a woman, he had wiped my lipstick on his collar when I went to ring Edith. Later that day, Bob had come in to see if Frank was okay and when I asked him why, he said, 'I saw him in the car near the wharves this morning when I was on my way to work'. I knew that Bob wouldn't cover for Frank, if anything Bob would tell Frank to wake up to himself if he thought Frank was stepping out of line. Bob would often say to Frank, 'You've got a great wife and a wonderful baby. Always do the right thing by them, if you don't, you're a mug.'

Another day after we had a big argument, I returned home from shopping and when I opened the door, I was surprised to smell a strong smell of gas. On walking into the kitchen, there was Frank with his head in the oven and the gas was turned on. The ambulance was called and the ambulance bearer said to me, 'It wasn't a genuine attempt because he had the good sense to leave the windows open. If he was fair dinkum, he'd have had all the windows sealed tight'. I remember Gwen saying to me at the time, 'That little bastard needs his neck broken, what's the matter with him, did his mother drop him on his head, in the pisspot at birth?' Then she told him, 'You don't know when you're well off, you rotten little bastard, you've got a good wife and a lovely baby and you treat them like shit, I've got a good mind to kill you myself.'

On Anzac Day night, one of the TV stations had sent a crew to Dad's R.S.L. Club to do a story about the returned soldiers and Edith and Dad were on the show. I remember that I wanted to watch the programme on the other station and I said to Frank, 'I can see Edith and Dad any day of the week and anyway the cameras will probably only flick past them'. The following day Edith rang to ask if we had seen them on the show and I told her I had forgotten about it and had watched the other channel. I was surprised that she didn't get on her high horse like she normally would.

Edith 'Well I've got a bit of good news to tell you'.

Amelia 'Oh yeah, what is it?'

Edith 'You don't sound too interested.'

Amelia 'I'm just waiting to hear what it is'.

Edith 'I don't want you to get hysterical'.

Amelia 'Oh for God's sake spit it out and be done with it, will you?'

By this time, I felt like hanging up in her ear. Edith had an uncanny knack of dragging a conversation out and making it into a Cyril B De Mille production.

Edith 'Your father has just rung to tell me that he's won first prize in the 6/- Casket'.

I nearly fainted on the spot, almost instantly my arms were dripping with the perspiration running from my hands. I had a stream of sweat pouring onto the telephone down my wrist to my elbow as I held the phone to my ear. Seven and a half thousand pounds (fifteen thousand dollars) it was a dream come true, an absolute fortune.

When I got off the phone, I felt like kicking myself for not watching them on TV the night before and I felt very guilty about it. Dad bought Casket tickets regularly each week, usually from the same newsagent but he very rarely put the tickets in his right name. He used to say, 'If I ever crack the big one, I don't want all the Gigs, Posses and Galahs knowing about it'. Sometimes he would put the tickets in the name of Rocky Stone of Pebble Road Rocklea.

On this particular occasion he had put the ticket in the name of L Rob (his name in reverse) of Ann Street, Brisbane (his work address.) The only problem with that was there was a L. Rob who also worked in Ann Street and he tried to claim the prize. He told the Golden Casket Office that he had misplaced the ticket. Fortunately, for Dad, the newsagent knew him very well and vouched for the fact that Dad was the rightful owner of the ticket. God only knows what would have happened if Dad had bought the ticket at a place where the newsagent didn't know him from Adam.

Dad paid the house off, that he and Edith had built through War Service and he gave five hundred pounds (a thousand dollars) each to James, Edward and me. I remember meeting Mum and Edith in the city, the day the money was handed over to me it was like the changing of the guards and double-checking the vaults at Fort Knox all rolled into one. Edith had given me the money inside the Commonwealth Bank on the corner of Adelaide and Albert Streets and I was going to pay it over to L.J. Hooker Real Estate for a block of land that we had chosen. The three of us had to walk two or three blocks down the street towards Fortitude Valley and into Queen Street. Edith and Mum were my bodyguards, they walked alongside of me every inch of the way and I clung onto that handbag like grim death.

Frank and I had looked at three blocks of land, the first one was at Aspley and was five hundred and fifty pounds. The second one was at Kenmore and was five hundred and twenty-five pounds. The third one was at a new suburb Acacia Ridge, on the Southside, and was four hundred and seventy-five pounds. Anyone who is familiar with Brisbane knows that Kenmore and Aspley are both excellent suburbs.

Acacia Ridge in 1962 was just a large area of land that had just been newly subdivided. When we looked at the block, I asked the salesman what the unusual thing was diagonally across the road and he replied, 'I don't know, but it's not unsightly is it?' We all had to agree, it was very tidy with nice lawns and the tubular 'thing' that continually spun around, reminded me of the hurdy-gurdy ride in the kid's playground area. We chose the Southside block and no need to be told, the area became one of the largest Housing Commission rental home areas in Brisbane. Everyone knows that Housing Commission homes have a stigma of being slum areas. As if that wasn't bad enough, the not unsightly thing across the road turned out to be a sewerage plant. But that was typical of our luck for the next fifty odd years, every golden opportunity we ever got seemed to magically tarnish before our eyes. We could reduce a huge chunk of gold into a brass farthing in two seconds flat before you could blink your eyes. I reckon that if we could catch the goose that laid the golden egg, not only would it be constipated it would be unable to fart as well.

Frank bought a 1948 Ford Mercury car for sixty pounds (a hundred and twenty dollars), we only had it a few weeks and he drove up to Mt Coot-tha after we had another argument about his drinking and he drove it straight over the side of the mountain. He hardly got a scratch on him but the car was a write off. To add fuel to the fire, it cost sixteen pounds for the towing company to winch it up and take it to the wreckers. That was a full week's wage. Frank's attitude towards everyone became worse, in particular, towards me. No matter what I said or did it was always the wrong thing. His drinking became more frequent and more often than not, whenever we argued he would give me a few clouts as if to prove that he was the boss. I've never been the type who could ever be described as a wilting wallflower, so whenever he hit me, especially if he knocked me to the ground, I would invariably sink the fangs into his legs as soon as I hit the deck. Over the next few months, Frank attempted suicide no less than seven times.

We shifted to a block of flats where we met a couple who would have an impact on our lives both directly and indirectly for the next thirty years. Tim and

Andrea were a couple of Poms around the same age as ourselves and they had a son Richard who was two months older than Vivian and they were expecting their second child. Within a matter of two or three weeks of moving to the flatette, quite a number of events took place.

James arrived at around ten o'clock in the morning days after our first anniversary to break the news that Grandad had died after suffering a massive heart attack on his way to work. Grandad had walked his usual mile to catch the tram, instead of catching it at the nearest stop to their home. As the tram rattled down the hill, he went to stand up, but instead he just slumped sideways onto the pavement alongside the seat. A nursing sister, on her way to work, saw him fall and ran to assist him but she discovered that he was already in God's care. He was seventy-four years of age and what a phenomenal man he had been. Not only was he one of the hardest workers I have ever known, (he had been a slaughterman at the Cannon Hill Abattoirs for more years than I had been on this earth) but also, he was one of nature's true gentlemen. Frank and I had been around to visit Mum and Grandad at their home only two days previously and Grandad had been in bed with a heavy dose of flu. When we left, I started to go into his bedroom to say goodbye to him but Frank insisted that I let him rest saying, 'You know what it's like when you're crook, you don't want people annoying you, so let him sleep.' It was quite a long time before I could forgive myself for not having said goodbye to him. His funeral procession was so huge, that the funeral home had to notify the police to get an officer on duty outside their premises to direct the traffic. I can still see the policeman in my mind's eye as we wended our way from the chapel to our local cemetery. As the hearse slowly edged its way past the cop he stood to attention and saluted the coffin as if a Royal dignitary had driven by.

I was awakened another morning to the news that Marilyn Monroe had died. I remember saying to Frank at the time that I thought there was more to the death than what met the eye. Sometimes I amaze myself I think I should've been a prophet of doom.

The sirens of the fire brigade awakened me another morning and when I looked out of our window, all I could see was an orange glowing sky. At the time I thought it must have been an old large house nearby that had caught on fire. As it turned out, it was the Paddington tram depot, which was situated about a mile up the road. That fire was the beginning of the end to Brisbane's trams. There had been a lot of speculation prior to the fire as to whether the Lord Mayor

(Clem Jones) would abolish the trams and when many of them were destroyed they were never replaced.

Although the flat was only two rooms, a kitchen and a bedroom it was a huge flat in comparison with the previous flat. We had to share a bathroom which was down the back stairs, what was different than all the other flats we'd lived in, we had to pay a shilling (ten cents) into the meter to get hot water for the bath. Fourteen bob a week for the two of us to have a bath every day of the week was too expensive. We soon learnt to share the bath water.

I always made sure that Vivian and I had our bath first before Frank had his. As a joke I would say to Frank as I got out of the water, 'I only peed in it twice today'. The first time I said it, momentarily his eyes widened in deep shock, then as he realised it was a joke, he said, 'Good oh. It's good for my complexion'. Quite a few times when he came home as full as a goog I was very tempted to try and crap in the water..

Frank and I nearly cried with laughter and disgust when Tim and Andrea told us that they and Richard all got into the bath together twice a week. They would often skite that it only cost them 2/- (twenty cents) a week to have a bath. The funny part was, Tim used to work restumping houses and would always come home covered in mud and grime and smelling like a polecat.

Chapter 20

Happy Holidays

We decided to invest in a second-hand, semi-automatic washing machine, which we purchased from McWhirters second-hand shop in Fortitude Valley. We'd had it less than twelve hours and it flooded our kitchen and almost the entire block of flats. I rang the store, and they promised to send a repairman out the following day. A week went by and many phone calls later and the repairman finally came out and declared that there was nothing wrong with the machine. I tried washing another load and again the water flowed everywhere. I rang them again and told them that either they send someone out to repair it properly, or they can come and collect it after I toss it out onto the tramline. The following day I arrived home from getting the groceries and Andrea told me the men had taken the machine away. I don't know how they had gotten in, because the door was still locked and the landlord had said he hadn't let them in. I rang the store to find out how long it would be before it would be repaired and returned and I was told that the washing machine would not be returned, because it had been repossessed. When I asked why, I was informed that I was behind in my repayments. I explained to the woman that I had paid a thirty-pound deposit off the ninety-pound machine and I had entered an agreement to pay the balance over twelve months.

Amelia 'I haven't had the machine two weeks so how the hell can I be behind in my payments?'

Woman 'Don't use that language with me'.

And with that she slammed the receiver down. Apparently, the word hell was the language she referred to. I went into the store about a week later to ask for my deposit back, but to no avail. Whilst I was there, I went to have a look at their range of second-hand goods and there was my washing machine on sale with a SPECIAL price tag of a hundred and ten pounds (two hundred and twenty dollars) on it.

Tim had drawn and painted a big mural of Disney characters on their bedroom wall for Richard. It was their belief that they would be there for a number of years. I was in awe of Tim's ability of doing such a fantastic drawing, but I was also amazed that he had the gall to deface someone else's property and think nothing of it. He couldn't see my point of view that he had defaced the wall. He was of the opinion that he had improved the property and what is more he thought the landlord should reduce their rent. The irony was, not long after he had finished the mural, they shifted out to live in their 'air-conditioned penthouse' at South Brisbane. I've never thought of it until now, in all probability he probably asked for a reduction in rent and when the landlord saw what he had done he probably turfed them out on their arses. Their 'penthouse' was in actual fact, a run-down cockroach-infested dump of a flat on the third floor of a slum dwelling. Tim had bought himself a second-hand fan, thus giving their 'penthouse' flat the prestigious title of air-conditioned. I kid you not, the cockroaches were the biggest I've ever seen and the place was so infested with ants that Tim had to put the legs of the cot into jam tins filled with water, to stop the ants from crawling over Richard and their new baby Chrystal. Just before Chrystal was born, we shifted into a flat above a shop. The owner of the building a Mr Wyatt lived by himself in an adjoining flat, he also owned and repaired the photo vending machines around Brisbane. Whenever the machines broke down, Mr Wyatt would ask for Vivian and me to accompany him to go and repair them. He would use us as models to make sure they were working properly. We had dozens of strips of four passport size photos taken, most of which I have lost over the years.

Not long after shifting into the flat, Frank had received a considerable sum of money I think it may have been back pay from when he became a bus driver. I know that it was a Saturday and I had been down to the shop under our flat and had bought a few groceries and we'd had an afternoon nap. When we had awakened, we decided to go to the pictures that night which was a rare treat indeed. After much discussion we chose the movie we both wanted to see and I decided to buy some eats to take to the pictures. I went to get my purse and it was nowhere to be found. For the next three hours, we practically demolished the flat in search of the elusive purse and the money. I was sick to the pit of my stomach and on the verge of hysterics. No amount of Frank's patting me on the head and shoulders could console me. I was a complete babbling wreck. We somehow managed to eat tea and finally around midnight after we had exhausted ourselves from searching every possible nook and cranny, we got ready for bed.

I said to Frank, 'I won't sleep a wink tonight from wondering and worrying where I've lost the purse'.

I flung the bed covers back and there as large as life was the purse. I had put it on the bed when I got back from the shop and I had even fallen asleep on it, but as if that wasn't bad enough, I'd even made the bed over the purse into the bargain. That was a lesson I learnt from that experience always be aware of where you place your valuables. I never want to go through another episode like that again. I can assure you that I slept the sleep of the dead that night.

Another night at that flat I was reading a magazine prior to going to sleep. There was a photo of a large snake that had swallowed a sulphur crested cockatoo and the photo depicted the snake with its bulging girth which obviously was the poor hapless cocky. I awoke to a hard slap across my face and Frank yelling, 'Wake up, wake up'.

I had been dreaming that I was walking along Coronation Drive and snakes appeared everywhere. They came from nowhere and seemed to multiply at a rapid rate until the entire road was absolutely covered in the squirming mass. There were at least ten deep and I was trying to walk through them. I must have become hysterical in the nightmare and I started to claw at Frank's face. That's when he slapped me to try and wake me. Well that's my version and I'm sticking to it.

I was delegated to mind Richard when Ann went into hospital to have Chrystal. Richard was fifteen months and Vivian was thirteen months, both were blue-eyed blondes and very beautiful babies. It was quite an experience to take them both out, no matter where we went, we would be stopped on a regular basis and everyone seemed to think they had a God given right to offer advice on childcare to birth control. It was a hundred times worse when I babysat both Richard and Chrystal at the same time. I used to hear people tsk-tsk behind my back and on one occasion I overheard a stranger telling her friends, 'That poor girl's husband should be castrated'. I thought, I can wholeheartedly agree with you lady, but not for the same reason you think.

One thing that did worry me for years was when Tim picked Richard up after Ann's confinement Tim asked me a few days later how Richard had gotten the cigarette burn on his back. I know it wasn't there when he left my care but I felt that I was under suspicion or made to look as if I was the one who gave him the cigarette burn. I always thought that Andrea was very heavy handed with Richard because he was a real live wire.

From the moment he took his first steps, he didn't walk he just took off running wherever he wanted to go. God he was a funny little kid. I thought at the time that Andrea had possibly burnt Richard and tried to cover her tracks be implying to Tim that it was me.

As mentioned before, Frank had become a bus driver after qualifying for his test at his first try. He had to drive the bus halfway up Mt Coot-tha and stop. The inspector then placed a matchbox behind the back wheel and Frank had to drive forward without letting the gears crunch or allowing the bus to roll back and crush the matchbox. After passing that part of the test, he then had to reverse the bus from about three quarters of the way up Mt Coot-tha to about halfway down the mountain. With the promotion came a pay rise, but not a great deal especially considering the extra responsibility and pressure that came with it. He already had the reputation of being a surly little bastard, so the increase in responsibility didn't exactly turn him into Mr Popularity, although he always seemed to get on well with his co-workers.

We shifted to a half a house in the next street, both sides of the house had their own private facilities but we had to share the laundry. When we first shifted there, there was a couple in their thirties with a little girl aged about eight in the other side. They warned us that the Italian owners of the house made a regular habit of going through both sides of the house whenever the tenants weren't there. I said, 'They won't want to go through my side whilst I'm out, or they'll learn a few words of English that they won't find in the dictionary'. The couple told us that they were looking around for a better place because the owners had been through their side several times. It was only a matter of a couple of weeks before they shifted out and an older couple (Carmen and Ned) with four or five of the best-behaved kids I have ever met, moved in.

I had only been there about a month when I heard a knock to the front door. On answering the door, I was confronted by a middle-aged couple. The man said, 'Are you Mrs Williams?' I looked at them rather suspiciously, wondering what religion they were bashing, and very hesitantly I replied, 'Y … yes. He smiled and held out his hand and said, 'How do you do, I'm Mr Williams.' I looked at him in amazement at first, I couldn't comprehend straight away what he meant. Then all of a sudden it hit me like a ton of bricks, that this man was Frank's father. He then introduced me to the lady with him, his girlfriend Jo. Within minutes of inviting them in and offering them a cuppa, I felt as if I had known them both for years. We got along like a house on fire, probably because he flattered my ego by continually thanking me for keeping his son out of the gutter. He (Jack or J.W. as he was known as) said, 'The last time I saw him I thought to myself that the next time I see you, son, you'll be in the gutter a hopeless drunk'. I was quite taken aback by that remark and couldn't understand for the life of me how or why he had come to that conclusion. We had a good long natter getting to know each other and we vowed that now we had finally met that we would always be good mates. I feel that we would have been the best of mates for years J.W. and I but unfortunately, he died of throat cancer less than three years later. Because he and Jo lived in Caloundra and we didn't own a car our visits were few and far between, but when we did get together, I remember them as being very happy times.

Frank and I went to Sydney for a week or ten days whilst we lived at that half house. We had contacted Muriel and Albert months before the trip and asked them if we could stay at their home whilst we were in Sydney. They were the ones who made a regular habit of arriving unannounced with their three kids Claire, Jimmy and Raymond and bludged off Edith's hospitality. When we hadn't heard back from them a week before we were due to depart, Edith rang Muriel and asked her if she had received my letter. Muriel very matter of factly replied, 'Yes but we don't have the room here to put them up'.

Edith was livid. She said to me, 'After all the years I put up with her and her brood for bloody four weeks at a time and she won't put you up for a lousy week, doesn't that beat the band?' I couldn't resist saying to her, 'I told you so'.

Uncle Simon told us that Muriel had a big home with plenty of room but she was a bit on the shy side when it came to repaying a favour especially if she thought she might end up out of pocket in the long run. All was not lost as it turned out Edith had also put up another distant cousin of Dad's and her husband on their honeymoon, when I was about eight. Edith figured that even though we hardly knew them, they could reciprocate by showing us the same courtesy. A hurried phone call was made and hey presto we had our accommodation with Nita, Alf and their three children.

Our first trip to Sydney was quite an experience to say the least, certainly a memorable event. We were booked on the six-thirty pm. Redline coach and Frank was to meet me at the Roma Street departure point at five-thirty. He hadn't arrived by six-twenty pm and I was almost frantic. As luck had it, an announcement was made over the loud speaker that the bus would be delayed in departing because the driver had called in sick. We had to wait for the bus from Sydney to arrive so that the driver from that bus could take over to drive us to Sydney. Frank finally arrived at six thirty-five pm and announced that he had been involved in a five-car pileup. He had swerved his bus to avoid a collision with one car and had managed to plough into another car which had concertinaed into the other cars. To this day I still don't know if he was sober at the time of the accident. He certainly wasn't sober when he arrived to go to Sydney.

We finally started off on our journey only to be told that we had to go down to Surfers Paradise to pick up a passenger before coming all the way back to Brisbane to go cross country to the New England Highway. What really made that part of the journey most upsetting was the fact that the passenger we had to pick up was as full as a boot, and never stopped complaining about the bus being over an hour late.

We got to Moonbi between Armidale and Tamworth at about 3.30am and the bus began to play up. The driver pulled over onto the side of the road and turned the motor off and proceeded to check all the points etc. He suggested that we all get out to stretch our legs and to go to the toilet (the toilet being the great outdoors) with blades of grass as paper.

The driver pushed the starter button but nothing happened, he tried it again, still nothing. After the third try he said, 'I'm sorry folks, you'll all have to get back out and give the bus a push to get it started'. The drunk we had picked up at Surfers Paradise had finally gone to sleep at about midnight. We weren't too happy to have to wake him up to ask him to help get the bus mobile. We took a vote and decided to leave him to sleep it off. After we got it rolling, the driver was able to kick start it and we all jumped back on the bus, quite proud of our efforts. The driver had only driven about fifty feet down the road and out of the dead of night came the voice of the drunk,

'All we need now, is to hitch a couple of fuckin' horses to this heap of shit and we can really call it a Cobb and Co. Coach'. Everyone on the bus was practically in tears of laughter at his honest assessment of the situation.

Because of severe flooding a lot of the roads had been cut and we had to back track and detour in many places. We finally arrived in Sydney at seven pm, twenty-four hours after leaving Brisbane, which must have made it the longest bus trip between Brisbane and Sydney on record. During our stay in Sydney, we were shown great hospitality by Alf and Nita. Alf took us to many places of interest and generally made us feel very welcome.

One incident, which marred our stay in Sydney, occurred in the dead of night. Vivian, who was about eighteen months old, had been extremely good on the trip down. She was always a good baby, but when we got to Alf and Nita's home, there wasn't a cot for her to sleep in. The only beds for all of us were two single beds and a small foldaway camping stretcher.

On our second night there, Vivian awoke at about two o'clock and I had quite a bit of difficulty getting her to settle down to go back to sleep. Frank awoke angry with me, and the rest of the world, for being disturbed from his sleep. He grabbed Vivian from my arms gave her a shake and half dropped and half threw her onto the stretcher with a thud and told her to shut up and get to sleep. I was so angry with him that I reached over and took a swipe at his face, dragging my nails down his left cheek. If we had've been at home I probably wouldn't have done it, although he had never hit me when he was sober. But I knew that he definitely wouldn't retaliate in someone else's home.

A few hours later when daylight came filtering through the window, I got the shock of my life when I saw his face, he had four deep scratch marks from his left temple right down to his chin. Everyone at the breakfast table stared in disbelief at Frank's face but not one word was mentioned. I apologised for Vivian's crying and told them I hoped she hadn't disturbed their sleep, but I think they were in too much shock to hear anything that I said that morning. The evil, wicked, bitey, lady had blotted her copybook again. Poor Frank, he's such a nice, quiet fellow too. It wasn't just my imagination thinking that, I knew by the look on people's faces that that's how they saw Frank and me.

We'd had enough bus dramas to last us half a lifetime so we opted to catch the train back to Brisbane. Anyone who has ever sat in those old rattlers for more than an hour would know that the nightmare trip on the bus would be classified as five-star travel in comparison with the train. When we got to Wallangarra, we had to change trains because of the different sized gauge of the tracks between New South Wales and Queensland.

Whilst we waited for the changeover, Frank rang his sister in Stanthorpe twenty miles away, and told her that we'd be passing through her town in about an hour's time. When we stopped in Stanthorpe for a few moments, I was introduced to my sister-in-law for the first time, through the carriage window. Rona seemed a really nice person and in the brief time we had, it was surprising the amount of conversation we were able to make. I promised her faithfully that I would write to her regularly and keep her up to date on our wellbeing now that we had finally met. The thing that stuck in my mind about Rona was the way she had referred to her mother as Hectors mother-in-law'. (Hector was Rona's husband.) I had a good chuckle to myself all the way back to Brisbane each time I thought about it.

On our arrival home, I was informed by Carmen that the landlady had not only been through our side of the house, but she had taken a whole tribe of the Italian community through on a guided tour as well. So, the next time she came to collect the rent, I gave her the full vent of my wrath.

Landlady 'No speaka the English'.

Amelia 'If I tried to diddle you out of some of the rent, you'd soon know more of the English. If you ever come through my home again, I'll get the police onto you'.

She beat her chest

Landlady 'Itsa my home'.

Amelia 'Not while I'm living here and paying the rent, itsa my home'.

Landlady 'Youa goa leava now'.

By this time, I was fuming

Amelia 'I'll go when it fuckin' suits me, now piss off and don't come back.'

As soon as we found another place, we were out of there faster than greased lightning.

But there was some unfinished business that we had to attend to on our return from Sydney. A week or so before we went to Sydney, Carmen and I had been out at our front steps talking when a fellow approached us and said, 'Which one of you ladies is Frank's better half?' Carmen's husband was Ned, that narrowed the field down somewhat and I said, 'I am'. He introduced himself as being Paul Davies a workmate of Frank. He went on to explain that there had been a death in his family and that he had to get to Toowoomba for the funeral.

Paul 'Frank told me that you'd be able to lend me a few quid until I get back the day after tomorrow'.

I was annoyed that Frank would tell him that, especially when we were always broke ourselves but I felt sorry for Paul and I've always had a soft heart for a sad story so I invited him in and got my purse

Amelia 'I'm sorry, Paul, I only have two-pound, (four dollars) on me and I really need that to see me through until pay day on Friday'.

He was really devastated

Paul 'What about your friend next door, could you get some off her do you think?'

Amelia ' No I wouldn't borrow money for myself, let alone you, I just wouldn't ask'.

I felt so sorry for him and I reluctantly took the money out of my purse and said, 'I'm up the creek without a paddle if you don't bring it back on Wednesday morning, because I've got to get milk for the baby'.

He handed me 10/- (one dollar) back

Paul 'I'll just take thirty bob and I'll borrow the rest of the money off someone else'.

Amelia 'Are you sure?'

I must confess that I was very relieved that he didn't take all the money,

Paul 'Yeah don't worry about it, I'll be right'.

He then asked for a cold drink, which I gave him, and he left promising to place the money in an envelope and that he would put it under a rock beneath the front steps on his way to work on Wednesday morning. Frank was on the late shift all that week, and I forgot to mention it to him that Paul had been and gotten the thirty-bob off me. On the Wednesday I got up bright and early and went down the stairs, no envelope. God I was upset. I went in and shook Frank awake,

Amelia 'Paul didn't leave the money'.

Frank 'What?'

Amelia 'Your work mate Paul, he hasn't left the money under the stairs'.

Frank 'Amelia, I've got no idea what you're talking about'.

Very slowly I went through the scenario of Monday's events after he had gone to work. He shook his head

Frank 'I don't know anyone by the name of Paul'.

I was sick in the guts to think I'd been sucked in by some con man. I was also so angry that if I had've seen the fellow again I felt as if I could have killed him. But worst of all I was worried sick and angry at my own stupidity for letting the fellow in and thus endangering my baby and my own life. A cold shudder went through me at what could have happened.

Frank remembered a fellow stopping him on his way to work as he walked to work.

Frank 'He told me he was going to start work at the depot this week and he wanted to get to know some of the blokes. I told him my name and where we lived'.

I rang the police and a young cop came around from the New Farm station and when I told him the entire story, he shook his head in disbelief at the fellow's audacity

Cop 'Did this 'Paul' have a moustache?'

Amelia 'No he was clean shaven'.

Then I went into great detail about his height, weight, manner etc I asked why he wanted to know if he had a moustache.

With a smile a mile wide

Cop 'Well it's a bit of a surprise really, because all the con men I've ever seen in the movies always have a thin moustache and oily slicked back hair'.

I told him not to give up his day job and to leave the comedy to Jerry Lewis. On our return from Sydney, there was a message from the CIB requesting me to go into their headquarters and look through their mug shots book to see if I could recognise Paul. I was taken into a dark musty room and one of the detectives brought a couple of big books into me

The detective 'We've already caught Paul but we want to make sure it's the same bloke, we don't want two of the buggers running around pulling the same stunt'.

I found Paul's mug shot without any difficulty

Amelia 'That's him'.

The detective 'Are you sure?'

Amelia 'I never forget a face'.

The detective 'Yeah that's him all right, but I've got to tell you some bad news for you, you won't be getting your 30/- back'.

Amelia 'I knew that'.

He then said something that really upset my whole peptic system, 'Oh, another thing, Frank didn't meet him in the street on his way to work Paul said that he had met your husband in the bar of the local hotel. Your husband obviously didn't want you to know that he went to the pub before work'.

That hurt me more than losing the 30/-, knowing that Frank was drinking before work at 1.30 in the afternoon. When I confronted Frank with this revelation, he denied it saying that Paul must have gotten him mixed up with another driver. Of course, there must have been at least a hundred bus drivers by the name of Frank who lived in the same street and who was heading to work at the tram depot at one-thirty on that particular day. How silly of me not to believe Frank.

Frank still maintained for years that Paul stopped him in the middle of the street and that's where they had the conversation. Frank said at the time and again 50 odd years later that he was with Merv Grogan at the time he had the conversation with Paul. Perhaps Paul had struck up conversations with a number of drivers in his search for victims and he linked Frank as being the one he spoke to in the pub. Whatever the truth is, it just goes to show that giving a stranger too much information can lead you into all sorts of deep poop.

Chapter 21

How to Win More Friends

I kept in touch with Rob and Betty and Fred and Gwen by visiting them as often as I could. They had accepted Vivian as their adopted Grandchild and looked forward to our visits. The front flat, which was the only one that was self-contained, became vacant and Betty offered it to us. It had been previously rented out at ten pounds a week, which was way out of our price range and we reluctantly had to decline. Betty had obviously anticipated that, and she quietly told me that she would reduce the rent to seven pounds ten shillings a week. That was still two pounds ten shillings more than we had ever paid before, but at that price it was a bargain and it had recently been painted and was fully carpeted. The only floor coverings we had ever had in all the places we had stayed at, was lino and a few moth-eaten scatter rugs. We practically broke our necks accepting the offer. Not long after shifting in, Tim and Andrea came to visit us in our beautiful flat and I can remember being so house proud as I showed them through the large spotlessly clean rooms. Imagine my total disbelief when Tim said, 'There's a chip of paint missing off the kitchen ceiling, I'd ask for a reduction in rent if I were you'.

I couldn't resist retaliating with, 'You should be careful that your landlord doesn't charge you extra rent considering that you've got all those ants and cockies as boarders.'

It was at this flat that Vivian had decided to do a bit of painting of her own style. I went into her room on one particular morning after she'd had her morning nap and her entire cot and the surrounding wall had been painted with poop. I had never seen a mess like it. I called Betty and Gwen in to witness the event and we all went into gales of laughter. I really didn't think it was all that funny two to three hours later when I was still scrubbing the wall and cot down.

I most certainly didn't appreciate the joke the following day when I again went into her room and Vivian was standing in her cot with poop from head to toe. She had it in her mouth on her eyelids up her nose, what wasn't on her body, was smeared all over the wall and cot, ten times worse than the previous day.

She was laughing with glee and clapping her hands, obviously thinking that because everyone had enjoyed it yesterday that it would be doubly enjoyable the second time around. At the ripe old age of eighteen months, much to Gwen and Betty's protests, Vivian copped her first taste of discipline. She sobbed her little heart out but she never painted her cot again.

Also, during our time in this flat, I was pushing Vivian in her pram on our way to the local shop, when I was stopped by a woman passer-by and she demanded to know, 'Why do you wear your wedding ring on your right hand?'

The question wasn't asked as a matter of curiosity, it was said in an aggressive authoritative manner as if the enquirer had every right to know. I was quite taken aback by her brusque manner and I retaliated with, 'What business is it of yours?'

She ignored my question and again repeated her question adding, 'Are you German?'

Thinking back now, I guess if I had've been quick enough I should have given her the Nazi salute and kept walking but I indignantly replied, 'No I'm Australian and even though it's none of your business, I'm deformed in my left hand'.

I thought that should make her feel totally embarrassed, I was wrong. 'Show me'.

I looked her fair and square in the eye, smiled sweetly and said, 'Piss off'.

I kept walking to the shop and as incredible as it may seem, she followed me into the shop and continually pestered me to show her my hand. I eventually gave in, just to get a bit of peace, because I felt totally humiliated in front of the shopkeeper. No sooner had I shown her, I practically ran home and cried my guts out.

Another similar incident happened in Queen Street. I was pushing the pram from Edward Street to Albert Street on the opposite side to where the picture theatres were and as I reached Albert Street and about to cross at the lights, an elderly lady grabbed my left shoulder from behind. I turned around and she very sweetly smiled and said,

'I want you to know that I admire you cripples.'

Very indignantly I said, 'I'm not a cripple.'

And she said, 'What's wrong with your arm then?'

'Mind your own bloody business you old bag.'

She opened and closed her mouth like a big cod as if she was trying to think of something to say and I yelled in her face, 'Get stuffed, you old bitch.'

I could feel dozens of eyes just glaring at me and I marched across the road with all the aplomb I could muster, holding my head erect and ready to attack and kill anyone in my wake. I was totally embarrassed on both occasions for having retaliated in the manner I had. I felt that not only had I degraded myself but I had lowered myself to their low life level.

You may be thinking, oh they were only acting out of kindness, well think again, because I've experienced too many similar incidents over the years and I couldn't in my wildest dreams ever classify gutter level rudeness as kindness.

I would dearly love to know where the hell these people think that they have the God given right to accost others in the middle of the street just to satisfy their insatiable curiosity? I know I'm outspoken, but Christ, I'd no more do that to a mongrel dog let alone another human being, than fly to the moon.

Another incident that happened whilst I had Vivian in the pram, I struggled to get onto the tram, I had Vivian under one wing, a nappy bag over my shoulder, parcels in a shopping bag, my handbag and of course the pram in the other hand. Not one soul offered to help me, but somehow, I managed to struggle on. Unfortunately, in the process, the wheel of the pram accidentally tipped an elderly lady's lace up boot. Before I could apologise, she yelled top note at me, 'Mind out, I paid a lot of money for these shoes and I'm an elderly and sick lady'.

In my loudest and best elocution voice I replied, 'If you are so elderly and so feeble, why don't you go home and get into bed and wait for death you stupid old hag.'

I gave my children strict instructions that if I ever become a crabby old frustrated hag like those old crones, they have my permission to put a bullet through my brain. In recent years they have indicated that the time is rapidly approaching. I must hurry to finish this epic as quickly as possible.

Betty had become too much of a sticky beak for my liking, she was always sticking her nose in everybody's business and running with the hares and holding with the hounds. Gwen and Fred had had enough too and when they told us that they were shifting, we decided that it was time to move as well. I liked Fred and Gwen they were good company, both of them were rough diamonds. I really liked Bob and I hated to say goodbye to him, but I couldn't have stayed there another minute longer with Betty as our landlady, she really was a major pain in the arse.

Bob had tears in his eyes as he said goodbye to Vivian, I read in the paper about fifteen years later that he had won a huge amount of money. I sincerely hope that it brought him happiness, he deserved it.

One of Frank's co-workers, who had been widowed for a year or so, offered us his two-

bedroom home to rent at McKellar Street Teneriffe for less than what we had been paying for our luxury flat. We jumped at the chance even though the house was dark, dreary and miles from public transport and local shops.

We took Vivian to the Ekka, on the Friday night after we moved in. As per usual, Frank was as full as a boot, and he tried to big note himself with the washing machine salesman on the electrical appliance stand. I tried to shut him up, but oh no, he had to give the fellow our address and he made arrangements for someone to come out to give me a demonstration of the latest fully automatic washing machine. As we walked away Frank said to me, 'That silly bastard won't be around. They love ya to bullshit to them, they've got nuthin' better to do than to talk to all the old bags that pretend they want to buy a washing machine'.

The following afternoon Frank arrived home blind out of his brain and promptly flaked out on the bed. I thought, I'll get a half an hour's nap whilst he and Vivian are asleep, and I lay down on the bed alongside of Frank. No sooner had I closed my eyes, there was a knock on the door. On answering it, there before me, was the washing machine salesman from the previous night. I tried to break the news gently to him that he had wasted his time coming out. But this fellow was the salesman from hell and insisted that my husband was very keen on me having the demonstration. And come hell or high water, he was going to give it to me.

The laundry was a tiny room under the back of the house. The only way to get there was via the back stairs. And so, Operation Washing Machine Demo began.

The salesman and the truck driver struggled, sweated and strained to manoeuvre the washing machine through the narrow hall and out onto the back landing. They then had to twist and turn and practically turn themselves inside out to try and get the machine down the stairs and into the laundry. The salesman then spent the next half hour setting the machine up, removing the removal bars from the machine and fixing the hoses etc. Finally, he started the machine and water spurted from the tap and hose connection. Thus, giving me the perfect excuse as to why I didn't want the machine.

Both men had to go through the process of packing the machine back in the box and manoeuvring it up the stairs and back through the house. By the time both fellows had gone, almost two hours had lapsed and I was completely exhausted. As tired as I was, I still felt as if I'd have enough energy to kick Frank's arse. I certainly would have liked to. Instead, I lay down thinking to myself, five minutes rest is better than none.

I closed my eyes and the most revolting stench hit my nostrils and I snapped my eyes open, twice as fast as they had closed. I knew the stench was of stale grog vomit, but where on earth was it coming from? I got off the bed and walked around to Frank's side and checked every nook and cranny but I couldn't find where on earth the smell was coming from. I must have looked for at least fifteen minutes.

I got back on the bed and the smell became worse. I rolled over to the edge of the bed and I was nearly on the verge of throwing up myself, the stench was so bad. I lifted the scatter rug on my side of the bedroom floor. The filthy little bastard had lifted the rug and spewed, placing the mat over the vomit in an effort to conceal it. This was the quiet, unassuming, fun loving, man of my dreams whom I had married twenty-five months previously. His mother's words, "better fish in the sea" and his father's words, "I thought I'd see him in the gutter a hopeless drunk," rang deafeningly through my ears that Saturday afternoon. But I have a very sick sense of humour and I must confess that I had to see the funny side of the situation. The dirty little turd.

One of the most curious mysteries of my life occurred at McKellar Street. I had decided to make us a culinary delight of homemade pikelets with strawberry jam and cream one evening after tea. I mixed the ingredients and added the egg, and lo and behold the mixture turned a pale shade of green. I've never been the greatest cook in the world and I know I never will be. But I think I would have to be the only person in Australia, if not the universe who has ever made a batch of green pikelets without even trying. They tasted good though.

I answered a knock on the door one morning and there in front of me was a Minister of Religion in a brown suit with a white dog collar. I thought, Oh no! a bible bashing's the last thing I need today.

As I started to close the door I said, 'We're all Catholics in this house, so you're wasting your time and mine'.

He smiled and said, 'I'm a Catholic Priest'.

I didn't know whether to laugh or cry, I was trapped by my own lie. I burst out laughing and said, 'I'm sorry, Father, I tell a lie, I'm not a Catholic at all I just say that to scare the unwanted callers away'.

He said, 'That's okay, I'm used to hearing stories, but could you tell me what religion you really are?'

Truthfully, I replied, 'A mixture, Father, I'm a Church of England who went to a Catholic school. My husband's a Catholic who went to a State school. And our daughter is a Catholic who's not old enough for school'.

He said, 'That is a mixture. Tell me did your husband go to Mass last Easter?'

'No, Father, the last time he went to church was for my grandfather's funeral and that was a non-Catholic service. My husband says he's an atheist and refuses to go into a church'.

He thanked me for eventually giving him an honest answer then bade me a good morning and left me to chuckle to myself for the rest of the day. And quite a few times since.

Les, (Frank's work mate who owned the house) had a few problems with the relatives he had shifted in with, so after only a few weeks we were on the move again. I was getting a bit sick and tired of shifting from flat to flat and I was also getting more than a bit cheesed off with the Housing Commission. As soon as we bought our block of land, we made an application for Housing Commission finance. We were told that the maximum wait was twelve months. Fifteen months had gone by and there was still no sign of them starting on building the house.

We found a brand-new flat at Jordon Terrace Bowen Hills the only problem was it was unfurnished. We bought our first bedroom, lounge and dining room suites and shifted in. We should have been the happiest couple in the world. Frank had a good steady job we owned our own block of land and we would be homeowners in the not too distant future. But most importantly, we had a beautiful, healthy, little girl. Yet for some unknown reason Frank seemed hell bent on destroying everything including himself.

His drinking binges were definitely getting worse, and his fits of depression and suicide attempts were becoming more frequent. Prior to shifting into the Bowen Hills flat, he had attempted suicide five times. Four of those were by placing his head in the gas oven and the other was by drinking a concoction of Ratsak poison and water. Somehow, I managed to be strong enough to cope with all the drama. Looking back, I shake my head in amazement and wonder how on earth I didn't crack under the strain and pressure as well.

At the time, there were a few times I got very angry with Frank and the thought had crossed my mind, I'll wait an hour or so, before I call the ambulance. I knew I'd never be able to live with my conscience if I'd done that. I also had the urge to kick the bastard's head in. Or just give him a dose of his own medicine. His clouts to show me who was boss were becoming more frequent and I would've liked to even the score.

What used to stick in my craw was the fact that only a couple of people outside my family would believe me. Everyone who knew Frank thought he was a fantastic bloke who wouldn't ever do anything wrong. They saw the side of him that I had fallen in love with, gentle, witty, good-natured and an all-round good bloke.

If ever I tried to get some advice from his co-workers about his behaviour at work, they would look at me as if I was stark, raving mad. I'm sure they used to think to themselves, poor Frank his wife is a froot loop short of a breakfast. And that he was all the more-better, for sticking by me and putting up with my ravings. My family also thought I was a screw loose, for putting up with his antics. There was one of his co-workers who believed me and still liked Frank in spite of all his carry on, a fellow by the name of Nelson Smythe. He used to refer to Frank (behind his back of course) as The Ratsak Kid.

When Frank took the Ratsak concoction, he was admitted into Ward 16 at the Royal Brisbane Hospital and transferred to Goodna Mental Hospital (now named Wacol Special Hospital.) He underwent Psychiatric tests for three weeks there. During that time, I went to Stanthorpe and stayed with Rona for a week. I wanted to find out from her, their grandmother and aunty, what Frank's childhood had been like. What I found out in that week, made my blood boil.

His Gran told me, that her daughter Mabel (Frank's mother), had given Rona away to her (Gran), for her to rear, when Frank was born. Apparently, Mabel disliked girl children. She was so fanatical about the sex of her children that she had arranged for Marvin to be adopted, if he had've been a girl. She also told me that Frank had been ill-treated as a child and that Marvin had been treated like a prince. Mabel's sister, Myrtle confirmed what Gran had told me. Myrtle's next-door neighbour Deidre told me that Frank had been Mabel' pride and joy until Marvin was born but after that, Frank couldn't do anything right in Mabel's eyes

Deirdre told me, 'Mabel used to hit Frank with a stock whip from the age of four.'

When I returned to Brisbane and asked Frank if all this information, I had learnt was true, he shrugged and said, 'Yeah, so what?' I was astounded that he didn't want to hear anything bad about his mother. But when I mentioned about the thrashings with the stockwhip, he shrugged, 'I probably deserved them'. My heart just bled for him and I wondered what other atrocities the poor bastard had endured, that no one else knew about. A few days later, Mabel arrived in Brisbane with Roy to confront me as to why I had gone to Stanthorpe to make inquiries about her son. She told me that I should have notified her that her son was in a psychiatric hospital. Unfortunately, for Mabel she had confronted me in my parent's home in front of Dad and Edith. For the first and only time my father ever said a kind word about Frank was that day. He jumped to his feet and slammed his fist down onto the laminated, kitchen table and yelled top note at Mabel, 'You wouldn't know what the word mother means, you've never been a mother to that lad and you should hang your head in shame'. He really laid into her and gave her the worst tongue-lashing I've ever heard. After having said his peace, he calmed down and invited both of them to stay for dinner. The following day, I took her to visit Frank in hospital and then around to show her our block of land. As we drove away from the land, (she was driving, and I was sitting in the back seat directly behind her) she began to denigrate Rona and myself, calling us both a couple of sluts. I didn't stop to think, I just automatically punched her in the back of the head twice. Both punches were thrown with as much force as I could muster and I said, 'You can call me anything you like, but don't ever call your own daughter names in my presence again'.

I have relived that moment in my mind many times over, and my only regret is I didn't knock the old bitch out.

It wasn't long after that, that J.W. came to visit us again. I told him what had happened and he said, 'Amelia, she destroyed everything that I loved, that's why I had to leave. When Rona was a little girl, I would buy her lollies and presents, and Mabel said to me, the only reason you're spoiling her now is you'll only want to go to bed with her when she's older'.

He continued, trying to fight back the tears, 'I haven't seen Rona for more than twenty years. I'm frightened to approach her, because I don't know what she has been told about me'.

I wrote to Rona explaining what J. W. had said and I'm very proud of my achievement of being instrumental in their reunion after such a long absence.

On one of his rare days off, Frank had volunteered to drive one of the Brisbane City Council buses to Redcliffe, taking a busload of kids from one of the orphanages on their annual picnic. Every year, the tramway employees would pick up the kids in the different orphanages and crippled children's homes around Brisbane. They'd take them to a set venue and supply them with lollies, drinks, balloons, watermelon and a picnic lunch. And at the end of the day, they would give each kid a present from Santa Claus. Frank said that wives and families of the employees could go as well.

I wasn't really in the mood for fun because Frank had tried to suicide for the sixth time only a week or so beforehand. And I was still trying to come to grips with that. However, I thought it would be a good outing for Vivian although I wasn't too sure what sort of a day we were in for.

We caught the tram from down the bottom of Jordan Terrace at 5.55am to go to the depot to collect the bus. Nelson was the conductor on the tram and he wasn't his usual happy-go lucky self. He said, 'Have you heard the news?'

'No, what is it?'

'President Kennedy has been assassinated'.

A cold shiver went down my spine and I remember thinking, Jesus, this is it, we're all doomed, and world war three will be on for young and old. There was nothing that any of us could do, except console each other. Everyone was in absolute shock and total disbelief. We had to put our grief aside and get on with trying to make the most of such a sad day. There were hundreds of kids relying on us to show them a fun time on their special day.

Despite the tragedy of the century, the children's picnic was one of the best outings that I have ever experienced. I wanted to adopt every child I came in contact with that day. Especially a little girl called Margaret. She was about eight years of age and she wasn't going to let go of my hand that day even if her life depended on it. If Frank had've been more stable I would have definitely tried to adopt her, nothing surer. I'll never forget her and I hope that she found a wonderful mother who was able to give her the love and happiness that she deserved.

Dad and Edith had booked a house at Coolangatta for a three-week holiday and they had invited us to go with them. I was looking forward to going, even though it had been less than twelve months since we went to Sydney, it seemed like a lifetime ago. So much had happened, in that time, most of it bad, and I knew that the rest would do Frank the world of good. I remember the following, as if it was yesterday.

It was a Tuesday around five-thirty pm Frank had come home not drunk but not sober either. He was in a very argumentative mood and I thought to myself, bugger you, boy, I'm not going to cop this sort of shit tonight, I'll take Vivian into the bath with me and we'll have a splash around. We had only been in the bath a short while and I could hear Frank making a din out in the other rooms and I convinced myself to ignore him. I kept saying to myself, let him go, let him do whatever he's doing, just ignore him.

I was singing to Vivian, 'Splish splash we were taking a bath'. Vivian was laughing and hitting her little hand onto the water and the bathroom door was flung wide open. I didn't look up I just kept playing with Vivian and hitting my hand on the water as well.

Frank said, 'Look at this'. I looked up at him smiling and my heart went up into my mouth. I wanted to scream but something stopped me and a voice within said, stay calm. He had one of his butcher's knives, from when he worked at Playfairs embedded into his left wrist. I could see that it was the long thin bladed knife that was razor sharp. But I couldn't see how deep the blade had penetrated, because the blood was dripping everywhere. I very coolly and calmly said, 'Get out you stupid bastard, go and bleed to death somewhere else. I don't want you in here, and don't drip blood on the carpet as you go, either'. He turned, walked out and closed the door behind him. I calmly finished bathing Vivian and myself before emptying the bath and drying and dressing both of us. I wiped all the blood off the bathroom floor before going out and getting Vivian her bottle and putting her into her cot. I then wandered around cleaning all the spots of blood off the carpet and the white tiles in the kitchen. I followed where the drops of blood were, out onto the front veranda and down the stairs. There was Frank lying on the path directly beyond the bottom of the steps. There was a thin rope around his neck and the other end of the rope had been tied around the railing of the verandah. The rope had snapped from his weight.

I can't remember where the knife was, I think it may have been on the verandah. There was blood pouring from his wrist. I calmly walked down the stairs and I gave him a good swift kick in his arse and said, 'I hope for your sake you've done a proper job this time, you bastard'. I then went to the nearest public telephone and rang the ambulance. When the ambulance bearers arrived, one of them said, 'Not this bastard again'.

Turning to me he said, 'How many times is it now?'

Very matter of factly I said

'Seven'.

Ambulance bearer 'Is it his lucky number?'

Amelia 'Christ, I hope not'.

The other Ambulance bearer said, 'And we've attended to him every bloody time it's becoming a bit of a habit isn't it?'

Frank was rushed off to hospital where he underwent three hours of surgery to repair the damage inflicted into his wrist. He spent the night in intensive care and the following day he was under observation for psychiatric evaluation. He was discharged on the Thursday afternoon. We went to Coolangatta on the Saturday and Frank had to have his wound checked by the Coolangatta ambulance officers every second day that we were on holidays.

It was around this time that an extraordinary thing happened and I have no proof other than in my memory. The Beatles had arrived in Brisbane and we had to go into the city to sign some documents pertaining to the building of our new home. We had to plough our way through hundreds of screaming teenagers who were standing outside Lennon's Hotel in George Street where the Beatles were staying. Pushing Vivian in her pram through all those kids was not an easy task at all it was an endurance test to say the least. We were definitely not fans of the Beatles in any way shape or form. We thought the teenagers were completely off their heads for standing around for hours in the hope of getting a glimpse of the dirty long-haired Poms (as everyone over the age of twenty called them.) After what seemed like an eternity getting through the crowd, we finally got around the corner into Adelaide street and proceeded towards our destination at the corner of Edward Street. We only got a few feet down the footpath and we had to stop to allow a large black car driving down a laneway from the back entrance of Lennon's Hotel. As the car drove past us the windows were wound down and we were under whelmed to see the four dirty long-haired Poms smiling and waving at us. Vivian was the only one of the three of us who waved back. We couldn't have given two hoots about the Beatles in those days but we thought it was really ironic that the fans that were desperate to see the Fab Four missed out on seeing them. On the news that night it was reported that they had gone to the Gold Coast for the day. Obviously, we saw them as they were heading down there.

Finally, work began on our home. Edith and Dad suggested that we shift into their place with them until our house was completed. Another major disaster decision, three weeks on holidays was fun, but three months under Edith's rule, was one huge nightmare. Without going into minute detail, Frank and I likened it to living under Hitler's regime, only with more rules and regulations. As if that wasn't bad enough, we had major delays and hold ups with the builders and painters. I was left to choose the colour scheme for every room. Whenever I consulted Frank, he would invariably say, 'You please yourself'. By the time I had chosen the colours for each room, I'd run out of ideas for the bathroom. When a friend suggested duck egg blue I settled on that colour. For years after that Frank complained that he had no decision in the colour scheme of the house. Whenever we had an argument, he would always accuse me of having consulted with strangers and not asking him. We went out to inspect the result of the completion of the paint job we were disgusted to find that the painter had painted Vivian's room blue and the spare room pink instead of visa versa. I went right off the brain. I told the painter that I could have found a retarded baboon that could have done a better job. Not only had he stuffed up the colour scheme, he had slopped paint all over the floorboards. Both rooms had to be repainted and the floors had to be sanded again, because we were having polished floors in every room. One thing I must say about the Housing Commission, the inspectors went over every inch of that house with a fine toothcomb. They found eighty-one faults in the home, mainly minor things like a screw missing and a spot of paint where it shouldn't have been. But they made sure those faults were rectified before handing us our keys. We vowed and declared that if we lived to be a hundred, we would never build another house again. We shifted into the house in April 1964.

Chapter 22

Les Miserables.

I knew we were in trouble when our neighbours' first words to us were, 'The reason we bought this block of land we thought we wouldn't have neighbours for at least another two years. And you've built almost on top of us the moment we shift in.'

Ron and Rene were the most miserable couple I have ever met in my entire life, miserable in every sense of the word. They complained about anything and everything and they were so miserable with their money, they would not spend one penny unless it was at least one thousand percent necessary. In fact, they made Scrooge look like a spendthrift. They wouldn't buy a TV set for the first twelve months that they were there, instead they chose to invite themselves over to our place and watch ours. Frank and I had decided to prepare the laundry floor for the black and white tiles we had bought for the job. Instead of telling Ron and Rene not to come over that night, we closed all the doors and purposely didn't turn the TV on. We were in the laundry and we were in the midst of making sure all the nails were embedded thoroughly into the floorboards when the back door was opened. Both Ron and Rene walked past us and I said, 'Oh. Sorry, we're not watching TV tonight'. Ron replied as he walked into our lounge room and turned the set on, 'That's okay'. Frank and I just looked at each other in total shock and disbelief. I picked up the hammer and started to bash the living crap out of any nail I could see. It didn't necessarily mean that the nail needed to be bashed into the floor. I just wanted to make as much noise as was humanly possible. I was going at it like a madwoman possessed and the next thing Ron put his head around the corner and said, 'Sssh we can't hear the TV'. And that is the honest to God truth.

I used to buy the Women's Weekly magazine every week and Rene would borrow it rather than buy her own. I had no problem with that, though I would have thought she could have bought it once in a while. One Monday morning I inadvertently burnt our Sunday papers and I realised that there was an article that I wanted to read. I asked Rene for her copy. She handed it to me and said,

'I won't charge you for it'. I laughed and said, 'Oh gee. Thanks'. The following Thursday she said, 'When are you going to return my paper?'

I apologised and said, 'I thought you'd finished with it, so I put it in the burner a couple of days ago'. Very indignantly she replied, 'Well, I might have finished with it, but you should have returned it. After all, I didn't charge you for it'. Whenever Frank had an early morning start, he would get a lift with Ron to the local Mobil garage and Frank would have to hitch hike the rest of the way. The entire journey Frank travelled with Ron was about two kilometres. Ron used to charge Frank 2/- (20cents) every time, to cover the cost of the petrol even though Ron had to drive past the garage on his way to work. On one such morning, Frank had left home without any matches, Ron wasn't a smoker but Frank asked him if he had any matches. Ron reached over into the glove box, shook the box that he'd retrieved and said, 'It's only half full, so I'll only charge you a penny'. Frank was so disgusted he threw a threepenny piece into the glove box. When he went to light his cigarette whilst waiting for a lift, Frank discovered there were twelve matches in the box but only three were live ones. In those days a box of fifty matches cost tuppence (two cents). There are dozens of stories I could tell about that couple, but time and space are limited. Perhaps I should write another book, just about them.

I fell pregnant the following May when Vivian was nearly three and a half. I had a very good pregnancy. As a matter of fact, my three pregnancies were trouble free. I was one of the rare breed that never had one moment of morning sickness, however, not so Vivian. All during my pregnancy she went from being a healthy robust little girl to a very sick, bed wetting child who suffered excruciating stomach cramps. She would quite often go into a coma like state, just falling limp in our arms. It was frightening to witness her having these turns. Fortunately, we were in a medical insurance fund and I had been taking her to an excellent paediatrician for regular check-ups since her birth.

Dr Kenneth was my hero, not only was he a fabulous paediatrician, he was a genuine gentleman and someone whom I could trust. He was as worried about Vivian as Frank and I were, but he was completely baffled by her symptoms. She had to undergo so many tests it was unbelievable.

One afternoon Vivian was downstairs playing with Ron and Rene's little boy Michael, when I heard Rene screech at top note, 'Ooh you dirty little girl, get on home or I'll turn the hose on you'. I ran to the dining room window and I could see Vivian and Michael sitting on the ground, and Rene was standing over them. I called out, 'What's she done?'

Rene looked up and said in a very disgusted voice, 'She's taken her pants off and is flaunting herself and exposing her private to my little Michael'. I was flabbergasted and said, 'Rene, she's only three and Michael's only two, I doubt that she was flaunting and exposing herself. I think you'll find that she's wet her pants and taken them off because they're uncomfortable to wear'. Under my breath I mumbled,

'You mad moll, you ought to be certified'.

Edward arrived at my home one afternoon just after lunch and announced that he had just died at work. I had no idea what he was babbling about and thought he was either going to tell me one of his many pathetic jokes or that he had gotten a bit of a fright of some sort. Edward was a plumber and worked for the Public Works Department.

I asked him to explain

Edward 'I died in the morgue grounds this morning, there was a gas leak in one of the underground pipes and Scotty (Edward's boss) asked me to find where the leak was coming from. I dug down to where the pipe was, and while I was in the trench the fumes overpowered me and I died'.

Amelia 'Bullshit you died, you just passed out'.

Edward 'I'm telling you I died. Scotty dragged me out of the trench and he couldn't get a pulse. There was a copper on his way to the morgue, he came over and he checked my pulse and he called for the morgue attendants who carried me over and put me on the slab. I'm fair dinkum, I was on the slab for about twenty minutes and a bloody doctor started to undress me and that's when I woke up. He and the morgue attendants nearly shit themselves'.

Amelia 'You don't really expect me to believe this crap, do you?'

The following day on the front page of the newspaper there was an article about how Edward had died, and awoke in the morgue.

Chapter 23

Patience with Patients

Vivian was hospitalised on two occasions to undergo tests. The first time she went into the RBH (Royal Brisbane Hospital) and was in there for the best part of a week under observation. On the day she was admitted, Dad drove me home after visiting hours and Frank rode his new 50cc Suzuki motor scooter that we'd bought a couple of weeks earlier. I had no sooner gotten home and Henry Walsh, whose nickname was Rogue, called in to see Frank. Frank had met him when they both lived in Byron Bay. Rogue was, as his name suggested, he was a bad bugger with a criminal record and I didn't like him at all. He had taken to calling around to see Frank on a regular basis and generally becoming a pest. Rogue decided to wait for Frank, much to my annoyance. I made a cup of tea and the minutes ticked by. After a half an hour of waiting I really began to worry. Rogue had one good thing in his favour, he didn't drink and he said to me, 'You know what these bloody drinkers are like when they get into a pub, they're in there for hours'.

I said, 'I don't think he's gone to the pub he didn't have any money on him to drink'.

All the while I was thinking 'If the little bastard's in the pub I'll bloody kill him when he gets home'. Rogue laughed and said, 'You don't know Frank too well, he doesn't need money. He can borrow off dozens of blokes until pay day he does it all the time'.

That made my ears prick up. I was curious to learn more. Frank always managed to buy grog but he never kept any money out of his pay packet. Without fail, he would give me an unopened pay envelope every fortnight and I'd give him enough money for the petrol to get him to and from work. I was about to start asking a few questions, which had me baffled for some time. If I had've asked Frank, I would've only been abused and told to mind my own business. I would've copped a few more clouts, the next time he was drunk into the bargain. I knew I had to be as discerning as possible in getting the answers to Frank's drinking money. So rather than jumping in feet first I thought I'll bide my time. I was more interested in solving the mystery of his whereabouts at that point in time. Rogue drove me up to the nearest public telephone and I rang Frank's two favourite pub haunts. He wasn't there. I rang the police, all the hospitals and the watch house but to no avail. It seemed that he had just disappeared off the face of the earth. We got back home and I was now convinced that he had gone to another pub. I was just about to start asking Rogue questions about how Frank got his money for grog, when I heard a car pull up outside. It was almost eleven pm and I was fit to be tied. I heard Frank call out and I very nearly didn't bother to look out, but curiosity got the better of me. There was Frank in the back of a taxi and I could see that he was struggling to get out of the car. On seeing me at the window, he said, 'Can you come and pay, I haven't got any money'. I was just about to say, 'Stiff shit, you can go to jail'. Then he swung a heavily bandaged leg out onto the footpath, hotly followed by a pair of crutches. The story that followed was incredible to say the least. He had been hit by a hit and run driver outside the Woolloongabba police station on his way home from the Royal Brisbane Hospital visiting Vivian. He was taken to the Princess Alexandra Hospital and had undergone treatment in the casualty department. He was then admitted under observation. He had asked both the hospital and police to notify me of the accident and he had been told, 'We've got better things to do than run errands.' He discharged himself and caught a cab home. His leg was twice its normal size and he was in so much pain that he had tears welling up in his eyes. The following morning, the newspaper reported the accident on the front page. I found this to be quite curious that the newspaper thought it was newsworthy to put in print. Yet the hospital and police couldn't make a telephone call to either Edith or a neighbour so that they in turn could notify me. I had to take Frank back to the hospital the morning after the accident, because of the pain he was in. At first, they refused to admit him, because he had discharged himself from their care. When I explained to them how the police and hospital staff had refused to make a lousy telephone call yet the newspaper had notified the world, they had a sudden change of heart. I think they may have been worried that a six-month pregnant woman's photo on the front page slamming the hospital's heartlessness may have been too much for them to handle. Frank was in hospital for almost six weeks. I was never officially notified of the accident, however the police did come out about two weeks after Frank was discharged. They issued him with a summons for not carrying a licensed pillion passenger. The irony is that if Frank had've had a pillion passenger the pillion would have been killed instantly. The driver had hit the back of the bike and ran over the wheel. If Dad hadn't offered to drive me home, I would have been the pillion. The hit and run driver, was never found and I doubt that the police would have even bothered to look anyhow.

Frank had broken his journey from work, to visit Vivian in hospital, so he wasn't entitled to Worker's Compensation. He had to sue through the nominal defenders and was eventually awarded five hundred pounds approximately a year later. I nearly ran myself into the ground, especially the first week after the accident. I was racing from hospital to hospital visiting both Frank and Vivian. Frank couldn't eat the slop food at the hospital and I'd take him his baked dinner every night, the other patients would moan and groan with delight when they smelt the food and the poor sods would watch Frank sit up eating like a king. Whoever said ' women get it easy' is an idiot.

Vivian underwent a cystoscopy at St. Andrew's Hospital to see if there was any abnormality causing her to bed wet. But, as with all the other tests, they proved to be negative. She went into a coma like state one afternoon and Frank drove us the sixty-kilometre round trip to Dr Kenneth's home. As we carried her into his home, her eyes were rolling and her eyelids fluttering. Her entire body had gone completely limp. Dr Kenneth gave her a complete physical and finally he said

'I think Vivian is suffering from phantom pregnancy pain in sympathy with you Mrs Williams'.

I was dumb struck momentarily

Amelia 'But I'm not having any pain in the pregnancy I've had no problems whatsoever'

Dr Kenneth 'That doesn't matter, Vivian is concerned with your wellbeing. She thinks you're suffering and she's enacting the pain for you'.

He advised that if she displayed any of the symptoms again, instead of sympathising or rushing to seek medical advice try giving her a good hard smack. We walked out of Dr Kenneth's home in a daze. I didn't know what to believe. A couple of days went by and Vivian had one of her turns again. I was panic stricken and very concerned and not all that convinced Dr Kenneth's theory was right. Reluctantly, I gave her a good hard smack on her buttocks and told her how naughty she was. She had a miraculous recovery and she never had any more turns of that nature again.

Chapter 24

Rogues and Idiots

One Sunday afternoon I reluctantly went to Inala with Rogue, to verify an alibi for him. He had met up with a young Dutch girl Anna and was having an affair with her. He would tell his wife Liz that he was down at our home visiting Frank and me. It wasn't a total lie, because he would call in before and after visiting Anna. As we drove down the main street on our way home, Rogue saw two young girls of about thirteen years of age waiting at the bus stop. He asked me to try and talk them into getting into the car and that he would drive them to where ever they wanted to go. I was shocked but I started to laugh because I hoped that he was joking. He pulled up alongside of them and started talking to them, trying to encourage them to get into the car. Fortunately, they had no desire to get into the car. If they had, I don't know how I would have discouraged them without getting Rogue too angry. Although he had never displayed a violent side to his nature, I was quite frightened of him. He was a huge man, not all that tall, but he was around fourteen stone of solid muscle. I was convinced that he was more than capable of at least maiming someone if not killing them with his bare hands. After having seen him trying to lure those two young girls into the car, I knew that he was definitely not to be trusted in any way shape or form. He came around one evening and said he had to go to South Brisbane to see a bloke who owed him money. He asked Frank to go with him, Frank agreed to go and I was not happy at all. I was convinced Rogue had plans of other things. I wasn't too sure if it involved going out thieving or looking for girls. I decided to invite myself along for the drive. Neither of them protested so I got Vivian out of bed put a dressing gown on her and we all got in the car. We went to an address in South Brisbane and Rogue knocked on the door. The place was in darkness and it was obvious no one was at home. As we drove back towards home, Rogue said that he was getting low on petrol and asked us if we had any money. When I told him that we didn't he told me that we would have to milk someone otherwise we'd to be stranded. I was really angry because I knew then that this was the reason he had come out that night. I gave Frank one of my famous I'm going to kill you, when we get home, looks. I had a fair idea Frank knew what Rogue was up to. Rogue pulled up near one car and got out.

Frank said to me, 'I'll give him a hand and as soon as we get a gallon, I'll tell him to drive us straight home'. Rogue got back in the car and said, 'That one's no good it's got a locked petrol cap'. We stopped near a few more cars, but each time there was a reason why they couldn't get any petrol. The overhead streetlight was too close, a dog barked, a light went on in the house across the street. I didn't mind in the least, the only thing that concerned me was, if we were going to get back to our home before we ran out of petrol. I started to breathe a little easier as we got closer and closer to home. By the time we got to the corner leading to our place. I was almost laughing, even if we did run out of petrol now, I thought we've only got about half a mile to walk home. Rogue drove past the street instead of turning into it and I was panic stricken,

Amelia 'Where are you going?'

Rogue 'We'll just try down this road, it's a lot darker there and there aren't so many nosy neighbours.'

We drove down about another two miles and Rogue said to Frank, 'I just spotted a Zephyr in a driveway'. He pulled up on the gravel on the side of the road and they both got out. Frank said to me, 'If anyone comes near, either beep the horn or whistle, but make sure you keep the doors and windows locked'. I don't mind telling you I was packing death. My hands were wringing wet, my heart was pounding and every leaf that rustled in the trees seemed almost deafening. It seemed like an eternity sitting there. I kept looking in the rear vision mirror and out through the back window, but all I could see was pitch-blackness. All of a sudden there was a tapping at the driver's window and I looked up and I could see Frank peering in. I reached over and unlocked the door and he slid in behind the steering wheel.

With urgency in my voice

Amelia 'Where's Rogue?'

Frank 'He's back there'.

Frank started the car

Frank 'We've got to get out of here, 'Rogue's pinched the other car he's driving it to the bush. He's going to take the tyres off it, because this thing needs new tyres.'

He swung the car around doing a U turn and as we took off back towards our home.

I was completely petrified and screaming

Amelia , 'You fuckin' idiots, you're both fuckin' mad, ya bastards'.

We drove deep into the bush following Rogue driving the stolen Zephyr. As soon as we pulled up, both Frank and I got out and I went off my head. I abused the living daylights out of Rogue for being such an idiot and all he could do was laugh this loud bellowing guffaw. Frank tried to calm me down and kept telling me to get back in the car and stop worrying about it. I tried to reason with him that no one deserved to have their car stolen. He agreed with me and added, 'But it's too late now, what's done is done'.

He tried to convince me that the owner would be reimbursed it would be covered by insurance, because it was a fairly new car. As if that would make a world of difference. I was disgusted and even more so when I realised that whilst we were arguing Rogue had started taking the tyres off the Zephyr. He was yelling to Frank telling him to hurry up and give him a hand. I walked back to the Falcon and sat in the back seat with Vivian and cried my heart out. I could hear them both scrambling about like demons possessed. Frank wheeled the tyres over to the Falcon and assured me they wouldn't be much longer.

Amelia 'If you've already taken the tyres off, why aren't we on our way home?'

He replied that Rogue wanted to get the radio out of the Zephyr as well. Frank scurried away into the night, leaving me to really get myself churned up. I waited another ten minutes and got out of the car and walked to the Zephyr. I issued the ultimatum that if they didn't take me home now, I was going to start walking back with Vivian. The one thing I was thankful about that night was the fact that Vivian was sound asleep throughout the entire evening.

Frank 'Get in the car, we've got to wipe our finger prints off everything we've touched and then we'll be on our way'.

I got back in the car and Frank loaded the tyres into the Falcon boot and into the back section between the front and back seats. I sat huddled behind the front passenger seat cuddling and nursing Vivian. Frank finished loading the tyres and walked back to the Zephyr. He had no sooner walked over there and he was back again with a handful of spanners and screwdrivers. He placed them and a little black box on the front seat. Very quietly he said, 'That's the radio'. He looked at me with a forlorn expression and whispered, 'Rogue's going to burn the car he thinks he's left too many prints all over it. He reckons he can't afford to take the risk of being found out'.

I can't remember what I said at that point, all I recall is feeling nauseous and numb. I was in deep shock and absolutely horrified at hearing those chilling words. I vaguely remember seeing Frank and Rogue standing near the Zephyr and then witnessing a blazing inferno. They ran to the car and in a matter of a few minutes we were back in the comfort of our home.

I don't know how, but I somehow managed to continue on in a normal existence, though the burden of guilt lay very heavily on me from that night. Not only did I lose a lot of self-respect and sense of self-worth, I felt that I was unable to mix with society because of the shame within me. Whatever respect I had for Frank went down the gurgler that night. Deep down I still loved him, but I disliked myself for it. Although it was never discussed, I feel sure that Frank lost a lot of self-respect. Though unlike me, he didn't even try to improve his image to himself or me. He seemed hell bent on destroying everything that he held dear to him. He and Rogue would often go out knocking off petrol together and for the life of me to this day I still cannot work out why Frank would go. He never gained anything from it, we didn't have a car and it was only a very rare occasion that Frank had borrowed the car from Rogue to take me anywhere.

One night a couple of weeks before Christmas, Rogue arrived and announced that he had found a poultry farm in the bush. He and Frank made plans to go and get a few chooks for Christmas. They left home at about eleven pm and I went to bed worried sick that they would get caught. Yet on the other hand, I secretly wished that they would get caught. I had this idea that Frank might come to his senses, if he was humiliated thoroughly for his actions. I awoke to the sound of Rogue's bellowing laughter in the distance. I hurriedly put my dressing gown on and walked out into the kitchen. It was two-fifteen and Frank was sitting on the kitchen floor on newspaper and he was plucking and gutting seven chickens.

Amelia 'What on earth are you doing?'

Frank 'Well what does it look like?'

Rogue bellowed with laughter

Amelia 'But what do you propose doing with them, when you've finished shoving your fist up their arses?'

Frank 'We'll keep three and Rogue can have four'.

Amelia 'Well why isn't he on the floor like a mongrel dog plucking and gutting them too?'

Frank shot me a look that could only be described as, one more word out of you lady, and I'll pull your head right off your shoulders. He thrust his hand into one of the chooks to pull its innards out, and exclaimed,

'Christ, this is hard I can't get my fingers in, let alone my fist'.

He kept pushing and prodding and eventually he removed a large yellowish ball, the size of a newborn baby's head.

Amelia 'What the hell is it?'

Frank 'An abscess, I've never seen anything like this in my life'.

I bent over to have a closer look and I heard a gurgling noise behind me. I looked around and both Frank and I burst into spontaneous laughter. Rogue, the fourteen stone, built like a tank he man, was hanging out of our dining room window heaving his heart out, because he couldn't stand the sight of the abscess.

Later, after Frank had plucked and gutted all the chickens, he handed Rogue four, making sure that Rogue got the one that had had the abscess. The irony was, out of all the chooks, apparently there was only one tender one. All the rest were as tough as old boot leather. As for the poultry farm, I found out later that they had gone to the wrong place. They had gone to the place next door and taken every chicken in the coop.

To make matters worse, Rogue had no idea how to grab a chook and wring its neck. Frank had said that it was like a massacre to begin with. Rogue had wrung one poor bird's wing causing it to squawk its lungs out.

Frank had then told Rogue, 'I'll wring their necks and you can hold them'. After he had wrung each bird's neck, he handed them to Rogue and when they got back to our home Frank discovered that every chook's head had been crushed. Rogue had thought, that when Frank had said that he'd wring the necks, that he meant that he would quieten them from squawking. Rogue figured in his little pea brain, that the best way to kill them was crush their heads with his bare hands. That's what Rogue had been laughing at, which had awakened me. Fortunately, not long after that night, Rogue stopped coming around and I couldn't have been more pleased if I tried.

Chapter 25

Heather

On the afternoon of a Tuesday in February 1966 a thunderstorm hit suddenly, sending me flying through the house to shut all the windows. As I ran down the hallway, I tripped landing heavily on my nine-month pregnant tummy. Apart from seesawing in the middle of the hallway I also skidded along with my legs at right angles, causing my shins to connect with either side of the walls, skinning both shins.

I awoke at about two o'clock the following morning to discover that I had wet the bed. I woke Frank and he very begrudgingly got out of bed whilst I changed the sheets. I got back into bed, only to discover that I had wet the bed again. I again woke Frank who became extremely angry at being awakened for the second time. Again, I changed the sheets, but of course this time I was too worried about my not being able to control my bladder because of the fall. Even though I had already given birth to Vivian four years previously, I knew nothing about my waters breaking. I grabbed a bucket and went into the lounge room and sat on the lounge with the bucket directly under me. The water ran out of me in a steady flow for ages. About every ten to fifteen minutes or so I would hurry to the toilet to empty the bucket. I would have to mop behind me as I walked. What a strange sight it must have been to anyone, if they could have seen me.

Finally, at about four-thirty, when the flow had eased off, I went into the bedroom and woke Frank, 'Oh Jesus. What is it now?'

'Look, I don't know whether you've noticed or not, but I'm pregnant and I'm about ready to give birth. Well it's either that or my bladder has sprung a leak. Would you be so kind as to go and ring me a cab and I'll do the rest on my own as per usual'.

He heaved a loud sigh of disbelief and went and rang the taxi.

By the time he came back I had awakened Vivian to tell her that mummy was going to hospital and for her to be a very good girl and that I'd have a little baby for her very soon. The early morning air must have brought Frank to some of his senses because he started to act more humanly. That's if you call someone running around like a chook with its head chopped off as being 'more humanly'. Why do men behave like complete morons when they realise that one of their offspring is about to arrive in the world? 'Have you got everything? Do you want me to come with you?

Will I ring the old girl? Have you got enough money until tonight?'

'Yes, no, yes please, I'm not going shopping.'

As I got into the cab, I looked at Frank holding Vivian in his arms and both of them waving goodbye and I thought to myself, I'm going into hospital to have my third child, and my other two kids are standing there, waving bye-bye. (Frank being my first child.)

On my arrival at the Mater Mother's Hospital, a nurse greeted me. She placed me into a wheel chair and took my bag off the driver. She mistook the driver to be my husband, telling him he could come with me. When I told her that my husband was at home probably back in bed sound asleep

Nurse 'The Rotter.'

I thought, you must know him

Amelia 'He's looking after our daughter'.

Nurse 'Ah, well he can be forgiven'

Without answering her, I muttered under my breath, 'Hopefully one day he can.'

The nuns and nurses treated me like a queen whilst I was in the delivery room. There was hardly a moment that they weren't fussing over me making sure that I was comfortable and if I needed water or ice on my brow etc. I kept on thinking, 'I wonder if they've got me mixed up with another patient and they think I'm a private, paying patient'. I could hear another woman in another delivery room screaming and yelling for the nurse every couple of minutes then I heard her yell, 'Mamma Mia, Whya Mia, I'ma dying'. A few seconds later a nun came to the door and said to me in a beautiful Irish accent

'Are you comfortable, sweetheart?'

Amelia 'I'm fine thank you, Sister, but the lady next door is in a lot of pain'.

Nun 'Oh to be sure, she's in no more pain than you are dear, it's just that she's Italian and she thinks she feels it more. And what's more she just wants us all of us to suffer as well'.

I had to stifle a good belly laugh and I grabbed my tummy and the nun was beside me in a split second holding my hand and comforting me.

Heather arrived into the world at exactly nine-thirty am weighing 7lb.11oz. She had a mass of tight black curly hair. Her cheeks were so puffy she looked as if she had at least two packs of bubble gum in each cheek. Her nostrils were dilated and her chin was sort of squat. The nursing sister had held my hand throughout the delivery

Nurse 'Isn't she beautiful?'

Amelia 'Get your glasses, Sister, she is ugly.'

Heather was whisked away to be washed and weighed and her birth recorded, and I was eventually wheeled up to the ward where all the other new mothers were.

The babies were all brought around at the two o'clock feeding time but not Heather. When I asked why my baby wasn't brought to me. I was told that she had had a lot of mucus in her nostrils and that she was upstairs under observation.

I started to get out of bed to go to wherever she was kept but I was told not to be alarmed that she was in good hands, and that she would probably be brought to me at the next feeding time. Because I had had such a hard time with breastfeeding Vivian, I had opted to bottle feed Heather. I was put on some tablets to dry up all my milk. Although I wasn't going to breastfeed her, it didn't stop me from fretting that she wasn't getting fed by my holding her. They kept giving me excuses that everything was okay and that I shouldn't worry.

I was told, 'I can assure you that if anything was wrong, you would be the first to know. Babies are often kept in the observation ward, sometimes for a couple of days.'

When she wasn't brought to me at the six am feed the following morning, I told a nurse, that if my baby wasn't brought to me at the ten am feed, I'd go right off my head, and then they'd have their hands full. Heather was brought to me and I was again assured that all was well and that there was nothing to worry about. I was never given a satisfactory reason as to why she was kept under observation for twenty-four hours.

For that matter I was never given any explanation at all. When she was two weeks old, I was sitting in the lounge room giving her a bottle and all of a sudden, she caught her breath and started to gasp for air. She threw up all over me and turned the darkest shade of purple. I put her over my shoulder and tried to help her get her breath back, but she wasn't responding. I became panic

stricken and screamed hysterically to Frank, 'Quick she's purple, for Christ's sake
do something'.

He grabbed her from me, patted her back harder than what I had, but there
was no response. To my utter horror and amazement, he held her by her legs
upside down, and hit her on her back. To this day, I have no idea if that was
the correct procedure to take, but it certainly did the trick. She got her breath
back and started to cry and I will never forget how relieved we both were at that
moment.

Heather was an unusual looking baby to say the least, nothing like Vivian at
all. Vivian had blue eyes and blonde hair. Heather's eyes were dark, and her hair
was a mass of black curls. I recall saying to Dad when he visited me on the night
of her birth, that Heather had his shaped nose and that it sort of spreads across
her face. He beamed as if he was as pleased as punch. Then I added that she had
the Williams weak chin. The smile left his face and he had an expression of horror
as he seriously said, 'Oh it's too early to tell yet'. God! I laughed, it was okay for
her to have his awful shaped nose, but we had to wait for God knows how long,
before we judged her chin to be like the Williams family. By the time she was
five months old I was more than a little bit concerned about the size of her head
and obviously so was Dr Kenneth Instead of going to a GP with my girls I would
take them to Dr Kenneth for their check-ups or if they got a sniffle etc. I figured
that if I was paying to be in a medical fund I might as well be getting the best
medical care in the world for them. Who better than a specialist, whom I knew I
could trust, and rely on, as far as I'm concerned that decision was the best one, I
have ever made in my life. If Dr Kenneth had've said to me to place my hand in
the fire, I would have without hesitation. In fact, I would have asked how deep
into the fire he wanted me to push it. That's how much faith I had, in his ability.
Whenever Dr Kenneth saw Heather, he would measure the size of her head.
Although it appeared to be a lot larger than it should have been, it was always
within the 'normal' range limit. She was also born with an umbilical hernia, her
naval protruded so far that it looked as if she had penile erection protruding from
her stomach. We tried to rectify it, including strapping it down with a penny
taped onto it but to no avail. Nothing but surgery was going to stop that navel
from popping out. It was arranged that she would enter St Andrew's Hospital to
undergo surgery when she was ten months of age.

I witnessed the most extraordinary sight, about half an hour after she had
been given her pre-op needle. I was sitting there with her just holding her hand,

crooning a song and trying to keep her calm. All of a sudden, she just did a complete somersault. The strange part was she did it in slow motion. I feel sure that my eyes must have been as big as dinner plates as I watched her in absolute stunned amazement.

Unbeknown to me Vivian had climbed up on to a trolley in the hallway and to the delight of the cleaning staff, placed her hand on her head and cried, 'Mamma Mia, whya Mia, I'm a dying'. She had obviously overheard me telling others about the lady in the other room. One of the cleaners came up to me later to tell me that she thought Vivian would become a good actress one day.

Heather's operation was a complete success and she was soon discharged and back home safe and well. I will never forget her hospitalisation at that time, not just because of her operation or Vivian's little acting performance either. There had been another baby in the hospital that I will remember until the day I die. He was a month older than Heather and he had been in the care of the nursing staff at St. Andrew's since his birth. He had been born without a top lip or palate and his mouth and nasal passage was just one gaping hole. He had a feeding tube strapped across his face entering the orifice and other life supporting tubes in his arm. He was in a bouncinette each time I visited Heather and I thought his little body seemed out of proportion. I passed comment to one of the nurses how sorry I was for the poor little mite and her reply stunned me beyond belief. The Nurse very matter of factly said 'Yes, he's quite a battler, he has a hole in the heart and a lot of internal problems including his hip deformity, he stopped breathing a few weeks ago but we managed to revive him'. I desperately wanted to scream out Why, for Christ sake? Instead I just looked at the poor little bugger and thought: mate I hope they don't prolong your life for too much longer. His parents didn't want to take him home after he was born so they just arranged for him to have the best medical help whilst he continued breathing, but why in God's name did the hospital have to prolong it? The more I think of it, the more I'm convinced it wasn't to give the child life it was a matter of money.

Chapter 26

The Sins of the Father

It wasn't long after Heather's operation that Frank was sacked from the Brisbane City Council for theft. He had been collecting presold tickets that had been discarded in the bus and reselling them to other passengers. The mystery of where he had gotten his drinking money from was solved. He was subsequently charged and appeared in court and fined. A few months after he had appeared in court, Colin Campbell, the local cop, came knocking on the door and accused Frank of stealing petrol from a car a couple of nights previously. The car had been parked in the street approximately a block or so away from our home. The owner of the car had heard a noise but didn't take any notice until the following day when he discovered he'd been milked. He reported it to the police and they put two and two together and came up with the answer Frank Williams. As Frank didn't own a car and we hadn't seen hide or hair of Rogue for the best part of twelve months I knew they were barking up the wrong tree. I heard Frank say, 'It wasn't me you can ask the missus, I was home in bed. Constable Campbell was an arrogant little turd and I didn't like him any more than Frank did, but I wouldn't have lied to him to cover Frank's arse after what I had witnessed Frank and Rogue doing months previously.

Constable Campbell 'Was Frank home in bed on Wednesday night around nine o'clock'

Amelia 'No, he wasn't'.

I thought Campbell was going to kiss me. His face had the biggest smirk all over as if to say, I've got the little bastard this time.

Amelia 'He was sitting there watching the Mavis Bramston Show and I'll bet he could repeat every smutty joke from the show word for word'.

Campbell was absolutely furious

Constable Campbell 'You're a smart arsed bitch, aren't you?'

Amelia 'Maybe I am, but I am telling you the honest to God truth'.

Frank 'Yeah, I bet if I couldn't account for my movements, you would've fitted me for it. It's true what they say once you've got a record the cops hound you for anything and everything'.

Frank had found a truck driving job with, of all places, Mayne Nickless. Fortunately, it wasn't with the armoured car section of the company or I reckon they would've been in deep shit. It seemed to me that all the truck drivers from all the different companies were heavy drinkers. It was frightening to hear them all tell stories about their daily drinking habits. Their favourite drinking holes were the two hotels at Rocklea and Thursday and Friday nights were their pay nights. T.N.T drivers were paid on Thursdays and apparently Frank would borrow money from some of the drivers and pay them back on the Friday. The irony was though, he always gave me an unopened pay packet each week as per usual. Your guess is as good as mine as to where he got his drinking money from this time.

Over the next two years, I practically wore a track going back and forth to my parent's home in the removal van. The pattern was always the same. Frank would come home drunk, pick fault with anything and regardless if I retaliated or not, he would then grab me and bash the crap out of me. I would wait until the next day and I'd pack up and move out. On one occasion in particular, he went completely berserk. After smashing me around for a while he grabbed every glass in the kitchen cupboards and threw them at me smashing them all to smithereens. To this day I still wonder how I didn't get cut from the many jagged pieces of glass that flew through the air. Not content with that, he went into the lounge room and picked up one of the single lounge chairs lifted it above his head and hurled it through the closed double glass doors. I managed to get the two kids outside and our new neighbours Dawn and Harry called out and asked if I was okay. I told them that I needed an ambulance because Frank had landed a few heavy punches around my left kidney area. Both Dawn and Harry disappeared from sight momentarily and when they returned to their back patio, Dawn invited me to come over and wait with them until the ambulance arrived. As I sat down in their living room, Dawn told me that she had also rung for the police. As we waited, she explained that she was a nursing sister and that Harry was an engineer. Both tried to make me feel as comfortable as was possible but I was in so much pain I was almost passing out. The police arrived and I went back over to explain what had happened. The officer in charge was so aggressive and rude to me I couldn't believe anyone could be so callous. Frank had placed the lounge chair back in its usual position and was sitting on it, casually drinking a bottle of beer and watching the television.

In a very gruff voice, pointing to all the broken glass

The cop 'Who did all this?'

Amelia 'My husband'

The cop (pointing to Frank) 'Who's he?'

Amelia 'My husband'.

The cop 'He did this? How?'

Amelia 'He threw the chair he's sitting on through the closed doors.'

The cop 'Oh don't give me that. He couldn't even pick the bloody chair up let alone throw it. Besides he seems a quiet sort of bloke just enjoying a beer. The story we got was that the bloke who was here was on the rampage, this young fellow's too quiet to have done this.'

I was holding my side and almost doubled up in pain trying not to pass out as I told the cop that this was the same bloke who less than a half an hour earlier was on a rampage.

The cop 'Yeah well he seems all right to me'.

Then pointing to my side

'You're bungin' it on a bit aren't ya? You're not that bad, you haven't got any bruises and you're not cut, so I'll cancel the ambulance 'cause you won't need it'.

Amelia 'I'm not bunging it on and I do need the ambulance'.

The cop 'Suit yourself, there's nothing more we can do here'.

He then turned and went to his car and drove off. I could hear Frank laughing like a madman as I stood outside and waited for the ambulance. I was in the Princess Alexandra Hospital for three days under observation. I had blood in my urine from the severe bruising to my left kidney, and I hobbled around for over a week unable to walk properly. Dad and Edith had driven over and picked Vivian and Heather up from Dawm and Harry's home and after I was discharged from the hospital I again shifted into my parent's home. I wanted desperately to go over to Frank and smash his head in with an iron bar or an axe. I also would have gotten a great deal of satisfaction if I could have tapped the cop on the head with a hammer a few dozen times as well. I have often wondered what sort of marriage he had and if he had also been a wife basher too. I'll bet London to a brick he was.

I had been at my parent's home a couple of months when I received a telephone call from Harry that Frank had had an accident at work. My immediate thought was that he had been drunk and had hit a car or a pedestrian. Instead, he had been lifting a ninety-pound high-pressure valve off the back of his truck, his back had given way on him, he had lost his footing stumbled and the valve had fallen on his hands squashing them underneath its sheer weight. I wasn't going over to see him even if my life depended on it. As far as I was concerned, it served himself right. He deserved everything he got and more. He had lost the top off his right index finger and he had squashed the right middle finger and the left index and middle fingers. He was in hospital for a couple of weeks. On his discharge he had to try and fend for himself as best as he could with both hands bandaged. I kept thinking how difficult it would have been for him and before too long I started feeling sorry for him, someone would ring me to give me a report on his wellbeing and invariably tell me that he was still on the grog. That was enough to keep me away. Then on Heather's second birthday he brought a beautiful Koala around for her. He had gone through the Christmas/New Year period without any money other than the handouts that the St. Vincent de Paul charity had given him. Workers Compensation as usual, had taken their time processing his claim. This time it had only taken them four months to process his claim. He had spent most of his first pay on the Koala and other presents for the kids for their Christmas and also Vivian's birthday. When I saw his hands, I felt like the bitch of the century for not going back to try and help him. I looked at his clothes

Amelia 'You look as if you've been on the piss and slept in them for a week'.

Frank 'These are the cleanest and best stuff I could find to wear'.

He then went on to say, that even if he could've managed to iron them without hurting his hands more, he couldn't because I had taken the iron.

With a bit of a smirk, 'Ya took the bloody washing machine as well and once I manage to swirl the clothes around in water it's a bit of a bugger getting them on the line'.

Amelia 'I wouldn't have, if you weren't such a little turd'.

Frank 'I might be a turd but you still love me, don't ya'.

I didn't answer him I just looked at him shaking my head in disbelief. I kept thinking to myself why can't I be like most people and just turn my back on him. Why do I allow myself to live through this heartache?'

We sat and talked and he explained how he had to manoeuvre the toothpaste onto the toothbrush and then try to brush his teeth but worst of all, was how he had to try and bathe himself. I knew then that I couldn't turn away from him, regardless of what he had done to me, he needed help in more ways than one and I was the silly bunny who was going to weaken and volunteer. The house was a complete shambles when I went back. The bedclothes he had on the old bed that St Vincent de Paul had given him were absolutely putrid. They hadn't been washed in the six months they had been on the bed. My first chore was to take them and put them in the burner and set them alight. Everything went along quite smoothly for a while, but Frank soon slipped into his old ways. All the promises of staying off the grog and waking up to himself all fell by the wayside. Before too long he was back in the same routine of slowly destroying himself and me along with him. He came home one afternoon as full as the Marist Brother's College, driving an FE Holden sedan that he had bought on time payment. He couldn't for the life of him work out why I wasn't thrilled out of my brain with delight. He eventually got caught for drink driving and lost his driver's licence for three months. This meant he had to change from truck driving to butchering. I had to admire him for that at least. He had never worked in a butcher shop in his life before, although he had worked at meatworks and could use a knife, butchering is totally different to the meatworks. He was able to learn the trade by watching his co-workers. If he wasn't sure how to go about doing a particular chore, he would praise one of his co-worker's capabilities and ask the butcher to show him his way of doing it. The butcher would be flattered to think that the young fellow was praising him, plus willing to learn his expertise. Frank traded the Holden and the Suzuki motor scooter in on an automatic 1963 Ford Falcon station wagon. The only problem he had to overcome clinching the deal, was getting the Suzuki to start to prove it was worthy of being a trade in. The fellow was due to arrive to come and inspect and collect the bike and Frank spent the best part of two hours trying to get it started. The Suzuki had died almost two years previously and had just been left unattended all that time. Any petrol that was in the bike would have soured many months previously. Nothing Frank did could start that bike, and my heart sunk to the pit of my stomach as I realised that we wouldn't be keeping the Falcon. The fellow arrived in due course and my heart soared when he told Frank to wheel it onto the trailer. Frank got to the back of the trailer when the fellow said, 'Oh you'd better kick it over to make sure that it's in working order'.

I felt my stomach churn and I thought I was going to throw up. My emotions were really being put through their paces that day. I couldn't believe my eyes or ears as I watched Frank press his foot down on the kick start without any force and the motor started to purr like a kitten.

The fellow nodded his approval, 'That'll do me'.

Frank turned the motor off and I nearly dirtied my pants when I heard Frank say

'Would you like me to start it again and you can take it for a spin if you like'.

I couldn't handle that, and I almost ran inside so as not to hear the fellows' response. Frank came in a couple of minutes later with a grin a mile wide, and tossed the keys of the Falcon to me

'There you go a piece of cake really.'

Every time I got into that car I felt like a princess. Frank was offered a position working at a small slaughter yard at Beenleigh. The pay was a lot better than a shop butcher paid and he jumped at the chance. Everything was going along swimmingly until one Friday he rang me from his work to say that he was bogged in the mud and wouldn't be home that night. If nothing else Frank had taught me through experience to never believe anything he said unless I saw it with my own eyes. I rang Dad and told him the story and he didn't believe it either. We went down to Beenleigh in search of the supposed bogged car. After searching in the moonlight for what seemed like hours, we were amazed to find Frank in the car and lo and behold the car was in fact bogged to its back axles. Surprisingly enough although it was bitterly cold, Frank was reluctant to come home with us. He kept insisting that he would stay with the car and get it out of the bog at first light. We managed to eventually talk him into coming home and that we'd get someone to drive him back down the following day to get the car home.

The following morning, I had hardly finished putting the breakfast dishes away when there was a knock on the front door. Two young men wearing suits stood before me when I opened the door. You would have to be a village idiot not to recognise that they were detectives. I pretended to be a village idiot as I bravely put on a broad smile across my face

Amelia 'Good morning, how are you this morning?'

The Detective 'Mrs Williams, I'm Detective Jack O'Connor and this is Detective Kevin Ryan we're here to have a little chat with your husband Frank, if he's at home'.

Amelia 'What's he done?'

The Detective 'Oh. We don't know that he's done anything, Mrs Williams, we just hope that he can help us with our enquiries'.

Amelia 'About what?'

The Detective 'Just a minor thing really, is Frank there?'

I went up the hall into the bedroom and told Frank that two demons were at the front door wanting to ask him some questions. Frank pointing to the tiny space between the wardrobe and wall he whispered

'Tell them that I must've gone out the back door, I'll be in there'.

Amelia 'I'm not telling them anything of the sort, if you don't get your arse down there now, I'll bring them up here and show them where you are. By the way are you going to tell me what you've done, or is it going to be a surprise later on in the day?'

He went out onto the front verandah and spoke briefly to them and then popped his head back around the door

'I won't be too long they want me to go to the 'Gabba CIB. There's nothing to worry about I'll get it sorted out'.

I walked to the front door towards the two detectives

Amelia 'Is he under arrest? If so, what's the charge?'

The Detective 'No, no, everything's all right, Frank's just helping us with our enquiries. We'll bring him back as soon as we've finished interviewing him. We shouldn't be too long'.

About four hours later, the two detectives arrived back minus Frank. They told me that they had arrested Frank for stealing his boss' car jack, and that they believed that other tools in the car wasn't Frank's tools either. They said that because this was Frank's third conviction, the magistrate would probably send him to jail. I asked where he was being held and they told me he was in a cell at the Beenleigh courthouse. They explained that he would be there until his case was heard on Monday morning and that I wouldn't be able to see him until then. The detectives returned the car to me later that afternoon. It was covered in mud inside and out.

At eight am on the Monday I went to the courthouse and spoke to the police officer on duty and asked him to give Frank his suit, white shirt and tie and shaving gear. The officer said I could give them to him myself but I wasn't allowed to give him the shaving gear. The cop stood alongside of me as I handed Frank his clothes. I shook my head in disgust at his stupidity.

Frank 'This is bullshit. I bogged the car going across the paddock and I went back to the work shed, to get the industrial jack. It got bogged too, so I threw it in the back of the car. I wasn't going to lug it all the way back to the shed, I was going to try and get the car out of the bog the following day. I went back to the farmhouse the boss had gone and his wife let me ring you. Then you and your old man came and insisted that I had to go home'.

Amelia 'What the hell were you doing in the paddock in the first place?'

Frank 'I thought it would be a quicker way to get home than going all the way around on the roadway'.

Amelia 'The demons told me that you confessed to stealing the jack'.

Frank 'I bloody well had to, because the smart arsed bastards were going to charge me with stealing all my own tools that were in the car. They're after me nothing surer once you've got a record, they'll fit you with anything'.

The young cop then told me that I'd have to go.

I went around to the front of the courthouse and waited until the doors opened.

Instead of a magistrate, there were two Justices of the Peace on the bench. Frank was brought through the little side door at the back of the courtroom, his hands were handcuffed and he looked dishevelled and grubby despite wearing his suit, white shirt and tie. A big burly detective stood up and introduced himself to the two JP's and told them that he was second in charge at Woolloongabba CIB. He explained that both officers, who had arrested the prisoner before them, were both on their days off. He told the court that Frank had stolen the jack whilst in the employ of the owner, and that Frank had eventually confessed when he realised that the evidence that had been gathered against him was too great to deny.

One of the JP's asked Frank if there was anything that he wanted to say

Frank 'No, nothing, Sir'.

I stood up

Amelia 'May I approach the bench, Sir?'

Frank turned around and rolled his eyes as if to say 'Oh Christ. Here we go'.

The second JP 'And you are?'

Amelia 'Amelia Williams, the prisoner's wife, Sir'.

He told me to approach the bench and I stepped forward to the long brass railing that separated the legal profession from the general public. I could feel my legs start to go all wobbly and I feared that I was going to faint. I felt very light-headed and I was more than aware of the perspiration that was pouring from my hands in great drops onto the floor. I grabbed hold of the railing and held on for grim death.

One of the JP's 'What is it you want to say Mrs Williams?'

I took a deep breath and in doing so, I could feel my heart pounding inside my chest. I felt sure that it was going to jump out between my breasts. I had absolutely no idea what I was going to say.

Amelia 'Sirs, before you pass sentence on my husband, I'd just like to tell you that he has a problem with alcohol and I really believe that he needs psychiatric help. I don't know if you're intending to send him to prison or not, but if you do, I was wondering if you could order him to have psychiatric help. I don't think he is a really bad person I think he needs help and medication. Thank you, that's all I wanted to say'.

They both thanked me and told me I could go back and sit down. As I sat down both men were deep in conversation with their heads bowed for what seemed like an eternity. When they finally looked up, they looked directly at me and one of them said, 'We're going to have to adjourn the court for ten minutes whilst we deliberate what you have said'.

Twenty minutes went by, before they reappeared

One of the JP's addressed me 'We have given this matter some considerable thought, Mrs Williams. We realise you must have undergone some considerable distress to feel the necessity to address the court. Unfortunately, we are unable to order your husband to seek psychiatric help however, we can strongly recommend it. We are also unable to give your husband a non-custodial sentence, taking into consideration the seriousness of the charge'.

They then turned to Frank and said, 'We sentence you to one month's imprisonment and we both strongly recommend that you seek psychiatric counselling whilst you're serving your sentence'.

I walked outside onto the veranda of the old courthouse and I could see the big burly detective undoing the handcuffs on Frank and placing one side of the cuff on his's arm and the other onto his own arm. They walked out of the courtroom with another detective whom I hadn't noticed until that moment. The burly demon walked up to me half dragging Frank as he strode towards me. He looked at me as if he wanted to swat me like a pesky insect snarling

'You fuckin' bitch if you hadn't opened your big fuckin' mouth ya little cunt, this little cunt would've gotten at least six months'.

I couldn't believe what I had just heard and I just stared at him in total disbelief and shock. I glanced at Frank and I could see the helplessness in his eyes. The cop then turned to Frank

'Do you feel all right? You don't feel funny in the head, do you?'

Frank 'No I feel fine, what about you do you feel a bit fuzzy?'

I thought the demon was going to punch Frank's lights out. I thought to myself You silly little bastard but at the same time I couldn't help but admire his guts. The cop turned and strode off forcing Frank to run to keep up with the big brute. I heaved a huge sigh of relief as I watched them walk to the police car.

I almost jumped out of my skin as I heard another voice

The Second Detective 'I'm sorry he spoke to you like that, Mrs Williams, he had no right to say what he did'.

I turned to see who had spoken, and he placed his hand on my shoulder and gently patted me twice before hurrying off to catch up to the burly cop and Frank. I walked over to our Falcon station wagon that we had bought only a few months before.

As I started the motor, I couldn't help but wonder how the hell I was going to pay the mortgage and feed the kids, let alone make the car payments as well. I drove off waving to Frank, thinking and hoping that his imprisonment would help him to come to his senses. I was somewhat disappointed that the two JP's couldn't order him to get psychiatric treatment. But I lived in hope that he would heed their recommendations.

Jack and Colleen, two friends of Frank's and mine had accompanied me down to the courtroom and as we drove along the highway, they praised me how well I had spoken on Frank's behalf. They both thought I had said what I had, in an attempt to get Frank a lighter sentence. How wrong they were. I wouldn't have minded if he had gotten five years, as long as he had received the treatment he needed. I was convinced that his mother was off her rocker and that somehow Frank had inherited her psychiatric problem. I also feared that our daughters might inherit whatever plagued Frank and his mother. I had never discussed the matter with Frank, but it was a thought that never seemed to leave my mind. Jack and Colleen kept talking, trying to keep me from worrying too much about what the next month would be like for me. They mainly focussed on some of the funny times we had all enjoyed. Jack reminded us of the Easter weekend a few months previously. I had taken the girls to Dad and Edith's place for the weekend and Colleen, Jack, Frank and myself went to Scarborough on Good Friday. We had hired a boat and went out fishing and crabbing. We never caught a bloody thing, probably because I was the only sober one out of the four of us and I was the one who was in charge of everything. I had absolutely no idea what the stern or the aft was, and I couldn't row the boat to save myself. We had dropped anchor about two miles out and when it started to get dark, we decided to head for shore. Colleen was as full as a boot but she insisted on rowing. She rowed and rowed for the best part of an hour and a half and when she finally stopped rowing, Jack stood up to assess how far we had gone. He lost his balance and promptly fell overboard. I was panic stricken but Frank and Colleen had thought it was a hugely funny thing to have happen. I could see Jack below the surface and he somersaulted in the water and went under the boat. I thought as sure as eggs that he would either up end the boat or hit his head and knock himself out. I asked Colleen if he could swim

Colleen 'Like a stone, love, like a stone'.

This announcement obviously delighted Frank and he cackled

Frank 'Well, I think he's gunna be successful, because he's heading down at a rapid pace.'

Jack somehow managed to surface on the opposite side to where he had fallen much to everyone's delight. Mainly because he was still wearing his glasses and he looked like an overgrown codfish. We somehow managed to drag him on board and it was about another twenty minutes later that we discovered the anchor was still in the water.

When we finally got to shore, we all piled into the car and drove down to Byron Bay where we slept on the beach and got eaten alive by sand flies and mosquitoes.

Having Jack and Colleen with me to cheer me up comforted me a lot. I hated losing control of my emotions, and I knew that if I had been alone in the car, I would have been crying my guts out instead of laughing. I had been driving the car since we bought it. It was an automatic and I was surprised how well I managed to handle it, especially considering it was a station wagon. Frank had tried to teach me to drive the old Holden twelve months or so previously but I could never master changing the gears and work the clutch at the same time. I had come to the conclusion that I must have had a co-ordination problem, as well as a difficulty with my balance. As a child I could never learn to ride a two-wheeler bike either. Frank used to get furious with me whenever he tried to teach me in the Holden, I always managed to stuff up. On just one particular lesson, I almost skittled a postman and nearly wrapped the car around a tree in the back streets of Kenmore. He had started yelling instructions, put your foot here, hold the wheel straight, do this do that, I got so confused I slammed my foot on the brake turned the motor off and got out screaming, 'Stick the fucking car up your arse'. I walked about two hundred and fifty metres down the street, before he drove up and yelled at me to get in. It was at least five kilometres to Edith's place and I knew that if I didn't get in, I would've had to walk. We got to the bottom of the street where Edith lived, and he offered me another chance to get behind the wheel again. I crunched the gears and he yelled, 'Are you fuckin' stupid or somethin?' This time I didn't bother putting the brake on, I just bailed out of the car and let it take off. I got quite a kick out of watching him scramble across from the passenger seat into the driving seat while the car was spearing across the road. At the time, I kept thinking, if he kills himself, I'll be free.

Whenever anyone asked me if I could drive, I'd always say that the world was a safer place without me being behind the wheel. It was a different matter with the automatic. Frank took me out for about an hour and I learnt everything including reverse parking behind another car without a hitch. It was pure magic and I couldn't wait to get behind the wheel again. I lacked self-confidence to go and get my licence. I figured that I would do it one day, but in my own good time. I used to drive through peak hour traffic across the Story Bridge numerous times, without a care about ever having an accident. I felt as if I was queen of the road.

About four months of driving around Brisbane I finally plucked up enough courage to book myself in for one driving lesson and I instructed the company to book me in to get my licence straight after the lesson. They probably thought I was a nut case. On the day of the test, the instructor told me I was a very good driver, but he warned me that the inspector would fail me, because they never gave licences on the first try. I refused his suggestion of booking in for three more lessons. The inspector got me to drive around Fortitude Valley, I had to reverse park behind a car on a steep hill and I didn't bat an eye. As we drove back to the parking lot at the Department of Transport, the inspector screwed up my permit and threw it on the dashboard. I felt like a million dollars. I was twenty-four years of age and I had finally achieved what I thought was an impossibility. As I walked out of the office twenty minutes later, the inspector was just getting into the car with another learner driver. He waved and smiled as I walked across the parking lot. But his jaw almost dropped to the ground as I opened the driver's door of the station wagon and the realisation hit him that I had driven in as an unlicensed driver.

As Jack and Colleen continued to reminisce, I realised that so much had happened in the past year. Colleen's son, Les, was a huge interstate truck driver and he had often come around to visit us whenever he was in town. On one occasion when he visited, he brought two young men around who were looking for a place to stay until they could find their own flat. Tony and Tom were really nice kids in their late teens. I, being the silly bunny that I am, agreed to letting them stay with us. Tony warned me that he was an epileptic who was prone to taking Grand Mal seizures. I told him that it didn't worry me because I knew a girl years ago who used to take them too. Well, I knew **of** her. She was the sister of one of the boys who used to hang around The Hub at Chermside. She had taken a turn in the picture theatre one night, and I was about twenty feet away from her. That was my entire knowledge of epilepsy. Tony would often sit and talk with both Frank and me, he absolutely idolised his father and would often speak about him. His mother had died when he was a baby and his father had remarried. He didn't like his step-mother too much, probably because he had only recently found out that she wasn't his real mother. I have no idea what made me ask him what he'd do if he found out that his father wasn't his father? He laughed and said, that it wouldn't be possible because we are the spitting image of each other.

Tom had an American accent and although he was always polite and well spoken, I always had my suspicions about him. I used to tell Frank and Tony that I didn't think Tom was an American. They both thought I was nuts and took no notice of me.

Tony and Tom had been staying with us for about three months when Tom came running in breathless telling me that Tony had collapsed in the middle of the yard. In his panic, he forgot his American accent. After getting Tony stabilised, we all sat down to have a cup of tea, we were all relaxed, and out of the blue I challenged Tom as to who he was and where he came from. He told us that he came from a wealthy family who lived in an exclusive part of Sydney. He had run away, just because he wanted to. He told me his real name and that he had used the name Tom after a radio announcer in Sydney.

Tom 'You were never fooled by me, were you?'

Amelia 'No, the others thought I was mad when I used to tell them I didn't think you were who you said you were'.

Tom 'I always had to be on my guard around you, you're a lot smarter than what you even realise, Amelia'.

Amelia 'Yeah, that's why I'm married to Frank and living in this suburb.'

I contacted his father who came to collect him the following day. His father wanted to give me a reward for locating and caring for his son. I refused, because I thought it was reward enough being able to reunite them.

Tony eventually found a flat of his own, he had found work in a warehouse in the city and we kept in touch for a while. But many years later I bumped into him in the GPO. He wanted to get married but he had discovered that the man who raised him wasn't his father. Apparently, there was no record of his (Tony) ever being registered at birth. He looked at me with a very sad expression

Tony 'Amelia you were right, I was just handed over, like a bloody book for Christmas'.

Sometimes I amaze myself at what I think about and ironically the thoughts come true.

I asked Jack and Colleen if they wanted to come over to my home for a cup of tea, both declined and I said, 'As soon as I pass these two caravans, you'll have to give me the directions to get to your place from here'.

I was in the right-hand lane and I overtook the first car towing a caravan and was halfway past the second caravan when Jack yelled, 'Look out, love, this silly bastard's coming over into our lane'. I started to brake, but I realised that the other vehicle was changing lanes too quickly for me to stop in time. I pulled the steering wheel over to the right and got onto the gravel. I sounded the horn and the driver looked over at me in total shock and disbelief. I think as he looked at me, he must have pulled his steering wheel over to the right instead of to the left. I felt the impact and heard the deafening sound of metal on metal. The station wagon was forced further over to the right and came to a sudden stop when we plummeted into the embankment wall. Without that embankment I would have been facing the traffic going toward the Gold Coast. The car towing the caravan continued on up towards Brisbane and Colleen screamed 'He's not even going to stop, the fuckin' mongrel'. We watched in disbelief as the car continued up the highway for another two hundred yards and all of a sudden, the caravan started to wobble and crashed onto its side. I asked Jack and Colleen if they were okay and they assured me they were. We all scrambled out of the car and as I felt my feet touch terra firma, I could feel my legs start to wobble for the second time that day. People seemed to materialise from thin air and were running around like ants at a picnic. Someone had said that they had rung for the police. They had no sooner said that, and the two detectives who were at the

Beenleigh Courthouse pulled up with Frank sitting in the back seat. The young cop who had apologised for his superior officer's rudeness. walked over

Young Detective 'Are you all right, Mrs Williams?'

Amelia 'Yes thanks I'm fine, but the car isn't'.

Young Detective 'It's not your day today is it?'

As I shook my head no, the burly cop bellowed, 'Is everyone else okay?'

Frank was still seated in the back seat and called out, 'Are you sure you're okay?'

Amelia pretending that Frank was also a cop 'Yes thank you, Sir, I'm fine'.

Everyone seemed to be looking at the detectives and me as if they were trying to work out how they knew me. All I could think was, oh God how bloody embarrassing. The police who had been called to the scene finally arrived. They acknowledged the detectives and spoke quietly with them for a moment, before turning to me, 'Have you got your driver's licence on you Mrs Williams?'

The detectives eventually drove off with Frank and the young detective waving me goodbye. I couldn't help but see the funny side of the event. After we gave all the details of the crash, the tow truck drivers offered to give us a lift to Brisbane in the tow trucks. I organised one driver to take Jack and Colleen to their home and the other fellow drove me to Dad and Edith's place. The tow truck driver absolutely roared with laughter when I explained the circumstances of the detectives knowing me

Tow Truck Driver 'Love, you should write a bloody book'.

Amelia 'Not bloody likely, I don't want the world knowing this, anyhow no one would believe it.'

To add fuel to the fire when I went to see the insurance company, the insurance fellow told me that the other driver had denied responsibility and that his insurance company was suing for damages.

Amelia 'Tell him and his company they can burn in hell'.

The Insurance Fellow roared laughing 'I can't do that would you believe he's a Minister of Religion'.

Amelia 'All the more reason he should be told and that he should burn I hell, and tell him to pray to God for the money to pay for the damage to my car, as well as his bloody van, while he's at it'.

By the time Frank was released, the car was still being repaired. I have no idea what our insurance fellow said to the driver of the other car but he and his insurance company accepted liability.

Chapter 27

More Front than Myers

About six months went by and Carmel and Jack (the neighbours who lived three doors up the road), asked us if we could accommodate Jack brother Jock and Carmel's sister Coral. Carmel and Coral were sisters and they had married Jack and Jock who were brothers. Carmel and Jack had four kids and didn't have the room to accommodate Jock and Coral because they had three kids.

I know I'm an idiot and shouldn't ever allow my heart to rule my head, but I couldn't see the kids go homeless. I thought to myself, It'll be only for a few days until they can find another house. I didn't know when I agreed to allow them to stay, that they had a houseful of furniture as well.

Frank must have done at least thirty trips that night going back and forth loading wardrobes and beds etc in the back of the station wagon. I almost had a blue fit when I realised how much furniture they had. We somehow managed to stack it all in our lounge room. Somehow or other Jock had managed to crack the side window in the car as he was pushing the furniture down squeezing more stuff into the back. He was extremely apologetic and promised to pay for a new window in the next few days.

They were with us for about a month before I went off the deep end. It was bad enough that it was in the midst of winter and they used all the hot water before we had our bath. It was also bad enough that Coral never hung the baby's clothes out on the line. Instead, she used to dry them in front of my heater, which she never switched off from morning til night. It was equally bad enough that I had to go out every day to get away from her and then arrive home and find the house was like a tip. But. I really lost my cool when I witnessed in disgust and horror that after she changed the baby's dirty nappy, she pushed the shit down the drain hole in my kitchen sink.

Amelia (yelling top note), 'You filthy, filthy, bitch, that's where I wash my crockery and cutlery you dirty slut'.

Coral (looking stunned) 'There's nothing wrong with what I've done'.

Amelia 'No of course not, not for a slag like you. I want you and your old man out of here tonight. I don't give a stuff if you sleep in the gutter you've lived in the lap of luxury long enough'.

Coral 'I wouldn't call this place the lap of luxury'.

Amelia 'Maybe not, but it's the best you'll ever enjoy. You've bludged off us for a month, without contributing one penny towards the housekeeping and you wouldn't work in an iron lung'.

When Frank came home half tanked, I thought, anything could happen now, it all depended on whether he was in a good mood with me or not.

When I explained what had happened, he went off the brain. He had been waiting for Jock to pay him for the broken window. Because he hadn't even offered to pay a penny, this was Frank's chance to have his say. Jock had arrived home before Frank, and as soon as Coral had told him what I had said, they went to get Jock's parents and a family friend to help them shift. They all turned up just as I finished telling Frank what had happened.

Frank 'No one is to step inside my yard if you do, I'll have you charged with trespass'.

He turned to me and whispered, 'I'm going over to get big Les. Lock the door and don't let anyone in until I get back'.

Amelia 'They'll all freeze to death out there,'

Frank 'Good, it'll serve themselves right'

Frank returned an hour later with big Les who was over six feet tall and about sixteen stone. Les stood at the front door with his arms folded as if he was the bodyguard. Frank then went down to Jock

Frank 'When you pay me the money for the window you broke, you can start taking your furniture out of my home'.

Jock protested that he didn't have the money nor could his parents get it because it was Friday night and the banks wouldn't be open until Monday morning.

Frank 'Stiff shit, no money, no furniture'.

They all jumped into their cars and came back about twenty minutes later with ten dollars.

Frank 'I want the amount in full, not in bloody instalments I'm not a bloody Walton's store its forty dollars or nothing'.

They all went away again and when they returned three carloads of police arrived with them. One cop had more braid and buttons than General Macarthur. He strode up the front steps

Braided cop 'What game do you think you're playing at?'

Frank 'I'm not playing games, but you look as if you're playing dress ups.'

The cop ignored the remark

Braided cop 'You're stopping this man from getting his furniture. Why?'

Frank 'Firstly, can he prove it's his furniture?'

Jock (calling out), 'Yes, I have a receipt.'

Frank yelling back, 'Well show it to me. Have you got it there?'

Jock 'It's in the bedroom wardrobe.'

Frank (cackling like a chook) 'You're an unlucky bastard aren't ya?'

Braided cop 'Now come on, Frank, don't be silly give him his furniture.'

Frank 'I'm not being silly the bastard owes me forty dollars for the window he broke in my car. When he gives me the money, he can take the furniture'.

Braided cop 'For Christ sake give the little bastard the money and let's all go home.'

Jock and his family got in a huddle and handed the cop the money.

One of the fellows with the family was wearing a pair of white overalls and he kept on telling Frank to wake up to himself. Frank referred to him as Whitey because of his overalls. Whitey seemed to be the one with all the money. I think the real reason Frank took such a dislike to him was the fellow's overalls were too clean.

As the cop handed Frank the forty dollars Frank said, 'I also want five dollars for the rubber I can't have the window installed without new rubber'.

Braided cop threw his arms up in despair and said, 'Give the prick the five dollars.'

I heard a stifled laugh and looked up toward Dawn and Harry's kitchen window. Although the house was in darkness, I could see their silhouettes and I shook my head and thought, God what must they be thinking? Once Frank got the money, he grabbed a broom and drew an imaginary line across the top of the steps

Frank 'If Whitey crosses that line, I'll send the bastard to kingdom come. Jock and his brother are the only ones allowed to come in and get the furniture, all the others can stand out on the footpath and watch.'

Both Jock and Jack carried everything to the footpath and the rest of the family carried it all in relays up to Jack's home whilst Frank and Les sat on the stairs and supervised. The following day Harry and Dawn congratulated Frank for standing his ground. They said it was the best night's entertainment they had ever had.

Not long after that episode, Jack broke into the Inala Hotel's lounge room and stole every table and chair in the place. I don't know how many trips he would have had to make going back and forth to the hotel to get the furniture, but it must have been a few, because he only had a little VW sedan to carry it all. But the stupid little bastard went back and took the carpet off the floor as well. I have never been in the Inala hotel, so I can only imagine that the room is quite large. My imagination is not that good, that I can work out what the hell Jack was thinking, when he took the stuff. But whatever was going through his brain at that time, it must have been a consistent thought, because, believe it or not, he not only got the carpet but he went back and pinched the drapes as well. As he was removing the last of the drapes, the publican's wife walked into the now very bare lounge room and passed out onto the wooden floor. Jack being a gentleman revived her. She started screaming her lungs out and he ran out and jumped into the car. The car stalled and the police arrested him. They nearly had hysterics when they went back to his house and found the treasure trove of goods. Jack of course went for a 'holiday' in Boggo Road prison.

After all the 'excitement' died down Frank was soon back to his usual happy self of wife bashing. The kids and I went back to Dad and Edith's place and I was determined that enough was enough. I had had more than enough. It was obvious Frank wasn't going to come to his senses, and I was still harbouring a hell of a lot of guilt about the burning of the car.

Chapter 28

Cleansing the Soul

I walked into the Woolloongabba CIB and asked to speak to Detective Jack O'Connor. I was ushered through to a desk and asked to take a seat and told that Detective O'Connor and Detective Ryan would be with me shortly. Both of them greeted me as if I was an old friend. I had made them laugh on several occasions previously when they had come around to 'have a chat' with Frank and I had said things like, 'You can take the little bastard away, lock him up and throw away the key'. This time it was different, this time I was barely able to smile. I felt frozen and heavy deep within me. I kept repeating over and over to myself, 'I have to do this for the kids and myself to have a normal existence and hopefully for Frank to seek the help that he so desperately needs.' I told the detectives everything that had happened that fateful night when Rogue had stolen the Zephyr and as I spoke, they took it in turns to interrupt me to ask me certain aspects of the crime. They seemed to me to be more interested in getting more information about Rogue than of the crime he and Frank had committed. One question led to another and before too long I told them about the time that I had accompanied Rogue when he went to Inala and he had wanted me to try and encourage the two girls into the car. I remember the intense look on their faces as they sat there in stony silence. Then finally, one of them uttered in disgust, 'So, this little bastard's a pants man hey?' I had never heard the expression before and for a fleeting moment I thought to myself, isn't every bloke a pants man? But I said, 'He's not little, he's a big bastard. He's the size of a gorilla he looks like one, acts like one, and has the mentality of one too.' I have no idea how long I was at the police station, I don't even remember leaving or arriving home. I was completely numb and oblivious to the entire world. A small article appeared in the newspaper a few days later stating that the police had arrested a man for the arson of a car in October 1965. The way that the article was written, it made it sound that the police had finally cracked the case after many years of investigation. I now know that the crime had been reported and the file had been placed in the too hard basket along with the myriad of other unsolved crimes.

That night as we sat watching television, a loud knocking on the door broke the silence.

Dad hurried to answer it and a couple of moments later came back into the lounge room and said to me, 'There's someone to see you, love'. When I asked him who it was, he whispered, 'I don't know, but he's a bad lookin' devil. Be careful, he looks dangerous.'

I opened the door and was confronted by a very dishevelled and worried looking Rogue. He had read the article in the paper and had realised that the police had arrested Frank. Rogue bombarded me with questions as to how the cops had found out and all I could manage was to continually stammer, 'I have no idea'. I knew he didn't believe me, but I couldn't care less about what he believed or disbelieved. All I wanted to do was close the door and get away from him. I finally managed to close the door and on returning to the lounge room, Edith started to bombard me with questions. Before I could open my mouth to try and get a word in edgeways Dad hurried out from his bedroom. He had been watching Rogue from the darkened bedroom. The bedroom window overlooked the patio where Rogue had stood and Dad had had a bird's eye view of Rogue as he had talked to me. He hadn't been able to hear everything though because the window was shut tight. Dad told us how he had been worried sick that the mongrel was going to hit me. He kept repeating, 'God, he was a bad lookin' devil, and the size of him, he was like a bloody ape. I thought for sure he was going to punch you he kept on clenching his fists and his hands were the size of plates of meat.' Edith was agog at the description of Rogue, and she ran around the house making sure all the windows and doors were locked and bolted. She was convinced that Rogue was going to come back and murder us all in our sleep. I laughed telling her that he wasn't going to come back, and I didn't know why she was worrying for. I explained that even though he was huge he had the courage of a dingo and I reckoned that he'd be on the outskirts of Brisbane by then.

I was eventually notified by the police and told the date of Frank's court appearance. I agonised for days as to whether I should go into the court. Edith kept telling me that I should stay well away because anything could happen. She was convinced that the entire underworld had me in their sights as a prime target, and that I was going to become another statistic. On the morning of the court appearance I made up my mind to go into the George street courthouse.

I dressed myself to the nines and on arriving at the courts I enquired which courtroom Frank would appear in and waited outside in the sun.

About twenty minutes of pacing, a group of men appeared seemingly from nowhere. I could see from the distance the first man was in a smart neatly pressed brown uniform. A group of about six men dressed in crumpled grey shirts and trousers walked in single file directly behind him, another man also in the same uniform as the first man followed close behind the group. When they got within a stone's throw from where I stood, I could see that the second fellow behind the guard was Frank. As I recognised him, he looked over at me and his eyes seemed to enlarge like a startled rabbit as he focused on me. I knew instantaneously that his look of surprise was not at just seeing me there it was a look of disapproval of the Mavis Bramston hat I was wearing. I immediately felt like kicking myself for wearing it, and I wanted to run and hide. But then in a split second I realised that handcuffs on each arm linked all the prisoners. I was overcome with shock, horror and shame for the both of us. I just wanted the earth to open and swallow me up, and I had an overwhelming urge to throw up. I took a few deep breaths as they filed into the courtroom and when I was satisfied that I wasn't going to be sick I walked in and sat in the back of the dimly lit courtroom.

The first prisoner's name was called and a slightly built, middle-aged man jumped to his feet and stood to attention. The charge of grievous bodily harm was read out and my mind fleetingly went back to a few years previously when James had been charged with the same offence.

James had been driving around a corner into the main street of Coolangatta and there was a semitrailer parked in the middle of the street. He didn't have time to brake and the car's nose went under the tray of the semi. The tray of the semi ploughed through the windscreen like a knife into melted butter. James's mate who was in the passenger side had his eye gouged out on impact. Although it was an unavoidable accident and James's mate confirmed this James was still charged.

Naturally James fought the charge and although the headlines screamed the horror of the crash and that he had been charged with grievous bodily harm. When he was acquitted of the charge, a tiny article of about ten words appeared on page twelve stating that he had been acquitted.

I was more than interested in this man's plight. The Crown Prosecutor told the court how the man had been driving along a suburban street and a kiddie on a tricycle rode out in front of the fellow's car. The man was unable to stop in time and he hit the two-year old child. At the mention of the accident, the man's shoulders slumped, his head bowed and his entire body began to shake uncontrollably. His sobs were inaudible, but everyone in that court could hear his deep breaths as he tried to compose himself. When the judge asked him how he pled, the man replied quietly, 'Guilty, your honour'.

I wanted to yell out to him to fight the charge as James had done but like the rest of the people in the courtroom, I sat silent. Without even looking up at him, the magistrate said, 'I sentence you to eighteen months'. I was engulfed by a wave of disgust at the magistrate and heartfelt sympathy for the man and I couldn't help but think, is this justice? How the hell will this man be able to cope?' A few more men faced the magistrate and were duly sentenced but I was too stunned to hear their crimes let alone their sentences. Frank's name was called and the Court Prosecutor read out the charges of theft of a motor vehicle and of arson of the same vehicle. When the Prosecutor mentioned that the thefts took place in October 1965, the magistrate looked up from his desk and stared directly at me. I felt as if he had been told that I had informed on Frank and that he was judging me more than he was Frank. His eyes seemed to burn right through to the very core of my being. Although I felt intimidated by his stare and I wanted to run out into the sunlight and breathe the fresh air, I sat rigid and fixed my vision directly at his eyes. It was as if we were both trying to fathom out what the other was thinking.

Glancing away from me, he looked at Frank

The magistrate 'How do you plead?'

Without any emotion in his voice

Frank very matter of factly replied, 'Guilty'.

For a fleeting moment the magistrate hesitated, pursed his lips as if he was surprised, pondered with, 'Hmm'

The magistrate 'I sentence you to three years on the theft charge, and a further three years on the arson charge'.

He paused, glanced over at Frank, then locked his eyes into mine again momentarily, then turned towards Frank

The magistrate 'Both sentences to be concurrent and to be suspended after twelve months, with time off for good behaviour'.

I walked out into the sunlight and lit a cigarette. My hands were wet and I was shaking, more like a shiver than an actual shake. The prisoners emerged Indian file, as they had when they arrived, linked by the handcuffs their escorts at either end of the group. As Frank walked out and caught sight of me, he said, 'G'day, how ya goin'?'

I can't even remember if I replied, but he then said, 'Where did ya get the hat?'

I suppressed the urge to laugh then he asked, 'Are you going to come and visit me?'

I still didn't answer but he continued with, 'Well, will ya write to me then?'

By this time, they had all walked about fifty feet away from me and I just stood there watching them. I was about to turn and walk away, when I heard him call out, 'See ya'.

Then they disappeared out of sight. I turned away and walked towards the bus stop in Adelaide Street. I kept shaking my head in total disbelief of what I had just witnessed during the past ninety minutes.

Over the next few weeks, I concentrated on being the best mother I could possibly be, to my two daughters. I still had the constant worry of Heather being slow in developing her motor skills. I seemed to be spending as much time at the paediatrician's surgery as I was at home. Nearly every time I took them to visit the doctor, he would inevitably order further tests for Heather to undergo. I was determined not to shirk any of my responsibilities either as a parent or of our financial commitments. I rang Custom Credit the organisation Frank had borrowed the money from for the Falcon and I told them that Frank was in jail but that I wanted to continue paying the vehicle off. Ever since we had gotten the car, I had made sure that I not only paid the instalments on time, I paid a few dollars extra so that we could own it sooner than the due date. I was approximately two to three months ahead with our repayments. I had nothing to worry about in that respect. All I had to do was retrieve the car from Frank's mother's home in Eukey. I had planned on catching a train or bus as soon as possible. The fellow from Custom Credit asked me where the car was, and I told him and explained that I was going down to collect it. He told me that that would be okay and that as long as I kept the payments up, there wouldn't be a problem. Two days later I received a phone call from Custom Credit and they informed me that they had repossessed the vehicle. I was absolutely shattered. When I asked why, they informed me that the vehicle was not in my name so therefore I had no claim on it. Within the week I received a letter from Custom Credit demanding money for their repossession fees, the cost of a replacement window, (which they had smashed to gain entrance into the car) repair costs to the front end (which they had damaged getting the vehicle onto the trailer) plus their towing fees from Eukey to Brisbane. I immediately rang them

Amelia 'Whilst my arse points to the ground, you will never get one penny out of me or my husband for that matter'.

The fellow I spoke to tried to frighten me with threats of taking me to court

Amelia 'I'd like to see you try, pal, because I would have a field day with your lousy company. For a start, you've already informed me, the vehicle was not in my name and that I had no claim to it. On top of that, you repossessed a vehicle illegally because it wasn't in arrears, and I've got every receipt to prove that'.

Custom Credit guy 'B … but your husband's in jail and he can't make the payments'.

Amelia 'How the hell would you know if he couldn't make the payments? Did you enquire? NO. And besides, for all you know, he may have only been sentenced to a week's imprisonment and if he gets out tomorrow, you'd be in deep shit. As far as I'm concerned, you and your company can take a running jump. I'll look forward to seeing you in court'.

Approximately twenty years later we met a friend of a friend whom I took an instant dislike to. When I found out he was a manager at Custom Credit that confirmed my reason for disliking him. I told him about our experience with Custom Credit and that they had ruined my credit rating for a number of years. I don't know if it was his way of having a joke but I received a letter a couple of weeks later telling me that they wanted me to come in to sort out a financial debt which had been owing for some time. I rang Custom Credit and went off my brain about the letter. I never saw the friend of a friend again nor did I hear any more from Custom Credit. I hope the sod got into deep trouble over his 'joke'.

Chapter 29

The Jinxed House

In the meantime, I had to continue finding the repayments for the loan we had borrowed from the Queensland Housing Commission or else they would end up repossessing the house. I didn't want to get offside with the QHC so I approached them to enquire about getting permission to rent the property out. The gentleman I had to see was a lovely kind-hearted man in his late fifties, early sixties. I sat down with him and poured my entire story out to him. Mr Moggeridge was a lovely man and I felt very much at ease with him, he was like a grandfather/counsellor and was extremely genuine in his concern for my children's and my wellbeing. Whenever I had to go back to the office for advice etc the other QHC staff would refer me to Mr Moggeridge. He would greet me as if I was his long-lost granddaughter and say things like, 'Here she is my pinup girl, what can we do for the princess today?' Just by those kind words, no matter how bad I had been feeling, he always managed to make me feel that I hadn't had a care in the world. I really think he had missed his vocation in life he really should have been a counsellor. No need to be told I had obtained the almost impossible from the QHC in those days, their permission to rent the house out. I rented the house to a lovely young couple. Tom was in the army, he and his wife shifted in a few days later. Every fortnight without fail Tom would pay the rent in advance to Harry and Dawn who had agreed to keep an eye on things and collect the rent for me. A few weeks went by and Harry asked me where Tom's wife was. I looked at him in stunned silence, when I finally found my tongue, I told him I didn't know and that I thought she was in the house with him. Harry said that neither he nor Dawn had seen Tom's wife for at least two or three weeks. He went on to say that Tom was a nice bloke and that he was looking after the house but he was curious as to why his wife wasn't there. He thought that I would've known her whereabouts. I had agreed with Mr Moggeridge to abide by the QHC rules that only married couples were allowed to rent the home and that I was to notify them of any changes. I asked Harry to tell Tom to ring me, and when he rang the following day, he explained that his wife had ran away with his best friend and that she had emptied their savings account.

He was living from fortnight to fortnight on his pay packet. Tom pleaded with me to allow him to stay in the house because he didn't have enough money to hire a van to shift. Unfortunately, rules are rules and Mr Moggeridge had explained that under no circumstances would the QHC let a single person, male or female to occupy the home.

Mr Moggeridge had to send Tom the letter to vacate the premises and I was terribly sad for the poor man. It was another one of the biggest mistakes I've ever made. I should have kept my mouth shut tight and just let Tom stay there. But if I had, and the QHC had sent someone out to inspect the premises, as was their right to do so, I would've been the one who was in deep poop. As it was, I was about to get into deeper poop.

I advertised the house in the newspaper and received a reply from a man who had five children. I apologised to him and said that the house wasn't big enough for that many children. He said, 'Lady be honest that's not the reason you won't let the house out to a family with five kids, it's because you think they'll wreck the place. Well I just hope you never find yourself in my position. You don't bloody well deserve to own a home if you can't be kind to a homeless family.' I should have stuck to my original statement, but oh no, I had to allow my heart to rule my head once again and I agreed to allow them to have the place without even seeing them. The moment I clapped eyes on them I knew I wouldn't get a penny of rent from them. They had been there for about three weeks and of course as I had suspected I received no rent at all, not even a hollow promise of paying something as soon as they could. Dawn rang me and said that she was concerned about the children in my house. She said none of them seemed to go to school, their hair is never combed and she had never seen them in clean clothes and she had definitely never seen clothes on the line. But worst of all she had never seen anyone carry any groceries into the house. I went over to the house and although I couldn't gain entrance, I could tell by just looking around the outside that the place was a complete pigsty. I told Mr Carter, the father that he would have to pay the rent or vacate the premises. He didn't seem to care what I said to him, I got the distinct impression that he was going to stay there indefinitely. As soon as I got back to Edith's place, I rang the Department of Children's Services and told them that they had better go out to investigate the family. I rang the electricity department and asked if the Carter's had paid their deposit for the electricity to be connected in their name. They informed me that the electricity for those premises was still in Tom's name. I explained who I was and told them that Tom had vacated the premises more than a month previously and that I didn't have his forwarding address. I also explained about the new tenants being non-payers and that they were obviously using Tom's electricity. I asked for the electricity to be cut off and the account sent to me and for them to put the account in my name. I also requested that they not reconnect the electricity until I gave them the permission to do so. No sooner had I asked, they turned off the electricity almost immediately.

Three weeks went by and the tenants were still there. Dawn and Harry kept a close eye on all the comings and goings in the house but at no time did they ever witness anyone that even resembled a staff member from the Department of Children's Services. Finally, the family packed their meagre possessions into their old bomb of a car and left. When Dawn rang me to tell me the good news, I practically had kittens I was so excited. I went over to the house armed with cleaning cloths, disinfectant and Ajax. Dawn stood on the front patio with me as I placed the key in the door. I pushed the door open and the most pungent stench filled our nostrils. We looked at each other pulling faces from the stench and very gingerly stepped into the lounge room. Without looking around to find where the worst of the smells were coming from, I raced through the laundry to the back door and flung it open as wide as it would go. I then hurried around unlocking and opening all the windows in the kitchen dining room and lounge room. In doing so, I had to step over piles of rubbish, which was littered throughout the four rooms. Dawn followed me down the hallway and we were almost overpowered by the stench we were both in deep shock at the state of each room. The filth was indescribable, but the main bedroom was the worst. There was human shit that had been wiped over every wall and on the ceiling. Someone had pissed on the walls and had let it cascade onto the floor. There was dry, white, dog's crap on the floors. Vomit was dried in clumps throughout the house. Dawn is, as I have already explained earlier, a fully qualified certificated nursing sister and midwife. You can imagine that she has witnessed some horrific scenes, but what she saw on this particular day really tested her inner strength.

She had to run as fast as her legs could take her, out through the back door, where she dry-retched for about five minutes. Dawn was unable to come back into the house and apologised for not being able to help me clean up. I couldn't blame her either I still amaze myself when I think about how in the name of God, I managed to clean it up.

It took me days of constant cleaning before I could get the house back into a liveable state. I think I would have had to burn it and rebuild it to get it back to normal.

Harry and Dawn decided that it would be a safer bet for them to choose the next lot of tenants. It was obvious to all and sundry that I allowed my heart to rule my head and that I'd end up getting ripped off. I arranged that I would pay for the advertisement but Harry and Dawn would choose who would be their next neighbours. Harry rang me a week or so later to tell me that he had rented the place to a family who originated from Belgium and that they had four children. There was a girl of thirteen, two boys aged twelve and ten and a girl of four who was in a wheelchair. Every week without fail they paid their rent, on time. Both Dawn and Harry raved about how wonderful each member of the Jehutz family were. Dawn reported that not only were they immaculate in their dress, they were a very loving family towards each other and the house was kept so clean you could eat off the floor. I was so pleased not just for the fact that the rent was being paid and the house was being looked after, but for Dawn and Harry's sake too. They were terrific people and deserved to have good neighbours and a bit of peace and quiet as well. The Jehutz family had been there about three months when Dawn rang one night very distressed. It was obvious she had been crying and was in a state of shock and bewilderment. When I asked what was wrong she stammered and stuttered, 'Jehutz has been arrested. He's in jail'. My immediate thought was that he was an illegal immigrant, and that he would probably be allowed to stay once he proved he was of good character. However, Dawn went on to say that the reason he had been arrested he had been sexually assaulting all of his children and he had forced his two sons to have sex with their sisters as well. I was in total shock and all I could say was, 'The little handicapped one as well?' She replied, 'Yeah, it's just unbelievable isn't it? Francine came home from work and found him having sex with the eldest girl and she's just about on the verge of a nervous breakdown'. I asked where the children and mother were. Dawn told me she wasn't sure and that after she had rung the police, they were all taken away. She thought they'd probably be still at the police station answering questions. The mother eventually came back to the house packed up all their belongings and shifted out of the house. None of us ever found out what became of any member of the family after that day. I hadn't even had the opportunity of meeting them and yet I felt so sorry and sickened for them.

The next couple who occupied the home were very keen on buying the premises. They had their solicitor draw up a contract whereby they had to pay $500 into a trust account as a holding deposit. I was so pleased that someone was going to buy the place that I would've agreed to anything. What an absolute idiot I was. I had signed an agreement that the contract would be finalised six months from the date of signing. What I didn't realise was that the contract also stated that Bryan and his wife could stay there rent-free until the contract was finalised. I took the contract over to Boggo Road and got Frank to sign the papers to agree to sell. He insisted that I should get my solicitor to prepare an agreement whereby that I could have the sole proceeds from the sale of the property. He wanted to make sure that Vivian and Heather and I had a little nest egg to fall back on. A couple of weeks went by and Harry rang to say that there were problems with the new tenants. He explained that they were having rowdy parties on a regular basis and that the wife wasn't anywhere to be found. Harry said they hadn't seen her let alone met her. In fact, she hadn't shifted in. I asked Harry to get Bryan to ring me, but to no avail. After about two weeks of waiting and a few more distress calls from Harry that the parties were getting worse, I went over to see Bryan. He explained that he and his wife were different religions, Bryan was a Catholic and his wife was a Jehovah's Witness they had been married for a couple of years and hadn't had any problems until the day before they were to shift into the house. She had been brainwashed by her parents that she had one of two choices to make. Either break up her marriage to Bryan and return to her family and their religion, or her family would disown her. She had asked Bryan to give her a couple of weeks to think things over, but when he tried to contact her after the fortnight, the parents refused to allow him to see or speak to her. In a way I felt sorry for him but I knew that Dawn and Harry wouldn't have complained unnecessarily about the parties so I told him that he'd have to leave. He replied rather aggressively, 'No I don't, and you bloody well can't make me shift either, I've paid you $500 and I intend to stay until the contract runs out'. I knew then that he had me over a barrel and that at the end of the contract he would get his money back and I'd be up shit creek without a paddle. What I didn't realise, was, how deep that creek was. I tried in vain to speak to Bryan's solicitor. But my requests to finalise the contract fell on deaf ears. Bryan's father was a wealthy man and it was his money that had secured the place for his son. There was no way that a poor, prisoner's wife was going to beat his wealthy client's every whim.

As far as they were concerned, I was just a peasant and had no valid reason to want to renege on the deal. For the next six months I had no alternative other than to keep my mortgage repayments to the Q.H.C. up to date. And to worry and cringe every time Dawn and Harry rang to tell of the latest events in the house that was obviously jinxed.

Chapter 30

Clearing the Air

In the meantime, I had met a fellow by the name of 'Joe' who had two children Gary nine and Sharon eight. Joe was a very kind caring man and it was obvious that he absolutely doted on his kids. His wife had left him and the kids for another man and he had to hire an elderly live-in housekeeper to cook, clean and care for the kids.

Mrs MacDougal was a lovely person and she was more like a grandmother to her family as she referred to them. Apart from being a good cook etc the most remarkable thing about Mrs MacDougal was, she had suffered from severe frostbite when she lived in England as a young woman and had to have her big toes on each foot amputated. As the two large toes are necessary to keep one's balance, it was a miracle that she was able to stand let alone walk. Both of Joe's kids were absolutely fantastic. Not only were they well behaved and good mannered, they were great fun to be around. Joe was a factory worker whose job it was to spray paint venetian blinds. He didn't really like the job that much but he didn't hate it either. It was a job that paid the bills and put the food on the table for his family with a little bit left over to take the kids to the beach every so often. Vivian got on very well with Joe's kids and they all tried to include Heather into their games even though she was a lot younger than they were. We always tried to take the kids out for picnics or to the beach every weekend and no matter what we did or where we went, we all thoroughly enjoyed ourselves. Joe started to talk marriage within the first couple of weeks into our relationship. Although I was very flattered, and I enjoyed his company, and absolutely loved his kids, I was still very uncertain that that's what I wanted. Something deep within was nagging at my conscience. Even though Frank had used me as a punching bag, I still felt that I was cheating on him. I don't know when the realisation hit me, that regardless of Joe's kindness and in spite of Frank's stupidity and cruelty towards me when he was drunk, I knew that Frank was the only man I could really love. But how the hell was I ever going to break off our relationship without hurting him? I really loved Joe, but more as a wonderful friend. The only fault I found against him was, when we had first met, he had told me he was thirty years old then a few weeks into the relationship he admitted that he was thirty-seven which meant he was twelve years older than me. And I absolutely detest people telling me lies.

I really couldn't picture being married to him for the rest of my life. The longer I took to break the relationship off, the harder it was going to be for all of us. He deserved a better deal in life than what he had already been given and now I too, was about to shatter his dreams. The same week I had made the decision to break off the relationship, he became very moody. When I asked him what was wrong, he said that his work was introducing electric spray guns and he'd have to do a special course the next week to learn how to use them. I couldn't see what the problem was and I asked him if he feared that the firm was going to put him off. He told me No, but eventually he'd have to leave and find something else, but he wasn't qualified for anything. I still couldn't understand what the problem was and I asked him why would he have to find another job, if they wouldn't be putting him off. He said he was terrified of using an electric spray gun and if we're going to be married in the next couple of years or so, he'd need a good secure job and that I would too. I looked at him in total disbelief. I had almost burst out laughing when he said he was terrified of the electric spray gun but his hands were shaking so badly that I realised he wasn't joking. But I couldn't believe that he was making a decision for me to find a job. As far as I was concerned, it was my decision to be a full-time, stay at home, mother. If I thought it was necessary to get a job, then I would go out and scrub shit off walls. I was certainly capable of that but, it would be my decision and my decision only certainly not because it was expected of me. One thing I knew for sure, Frank didn't fear anything, especially not an electrical appliance. And, he as sure as hell wouldn't expect me to go out to work under any circumstances.

I know this sounds very mercenary, but I had bought Joe a casket ticket for his birthday a few weeks previously and I thought, it would be just my luck to dump him and he'll win first prize and I'll still be as poor as a church mouse. I waited until the day after the casket was drawn before I broke the news to him that I didn't love him enough to marry him. The look on his face was pathetic and I felt like the bitch of the year. He was almost in tears and kept shaking his head and saying, 'I knew it was too good to be true'. Then out of the blue he looked directly at me and said, 'You waited for the casket to be drawn, didn't you?' I could feel his eyes burning through me and I stammered, 'Y … yes, I did'. That's when I felt like the bitch of the century. He drove me home in silence, we said our goodbyes and we didn't see each other again.

I did see him on two or three occasions from a distance, over a period of about twenty years. The last time was in George Street about thirty odd years ago, but I made sure that he didn't see me. Funnily enough, I wanted to go up and say hello to him, but I thought it would be totally inappropriate.

I had met up with Gwen who was by then a widow and living in a dingy little flat on the south side of Brisbane. She was working as a cleaner in the State Government building on the corner of Adelaide and Edward streets, the same building I had worked in when I was with the casket office. Gwen had told me that I could probably get a job as a cleaner too, and advised me where to apply. Before too long I received a letter asking me to go for a medical at a surgery in South Brisbane. On my arrival, I was absolutely shocked at the surgery. It was a sleazy little room in an equally sleazy looking building. I doubt that hygiene had been heard of, let alone practiced. Fortunately, and curiously, my medical consisted of looking through a book similar to a child's colouring book. Each page had a multitude of coloured spots and I was asked to look at the pages carefully and tell the doctor if I could see anything other than the coloured spots. I had only looked at about four pages and had discovered a different number in the centre of each page, before the doctor took the book and told me the department would let me know if I was a successful applicant for the job or not.

Being a stickybeak, I asked what the book represented and he replied, 'It's to determine if you're colour blind or not, because if you are, you wouldn't get the job. If you get a job in the railways, they don't want you being squashed by a train because you couldn't tell the red from the green traffic lights.' What that had to do with holding a lowly cleaning job in an office is still a mystery to me. I was duly appointed the position of cleaner for the architect's office on the seventh floor and also the photographic department on the roof. The hours were great, I had to start at 4.30pm and finish at midnight. That suited me to the ground. I was at home for the girls when they needed me the most, and I saw Vivian to and from school and I could spend the day with Heather. I had no guilt at leaving them of an evening, because they would be well cared for by Edith. The only problem was there was no bus service after 11.10pm. After the first couple of weeks of getting used to the routine, I joined the ranks of the other women cleaners and departed the building at eleven o'clock. None of us feared being caught knocking off early, because of the lateness of the hour. Besides, we had all come to the conclusion that we were the only ones who actually worked in the building.

The office staff were regarded as the laziest bunch of bastards that were ever allowed to draw breath. The waste paper bins bore obvious testament to that. The office girl's bins mainly consisted of tissues that had been used to blot their lipstick. I reckon they must have applied lipstick at least twenty times a day. The architect's waste bins mainly consisted of varied forms of origami. Though of course, that form of art wasn't recognised by the western world in those days. Their origami mainly consisted of differing types of aircraft. It was from one of the architects that I learnt how to make a paper turd. I arrived into their office one afternoon and began the task of emptying all the bins and sweeping the floor. I used to have to wait until all the office staff had left, before cleaning the desks and polishing the floors. Because of this, I used to alternate my starting point between the photographic and architect's office every other day. Although I didn't know many of the architects by their names, I would have a bit of a chat to some of them as I went about my business. On this particular afternoon a couple of them seemed reluctant to go home. I was getting a bit annoyed because the longer they stayed, the later I would be finishing at the end of the night. One of them called me over and asked me if I would do him a big favour and clean out all the rubbish in his top drawer. Reluctantly, I agreed and opened the drawer. I absolutely screamed with laughter when I saw this huge turd sitting on the top of some books that were neatly stored in the drawer. That certainly broke the ice between the architects and the lowly cleaner. I insisted on him showing me how he had made it, because I just had to make one for the ratbag staff in the photographic department and one for Dad, just to see him squirm. Basically, all the turd consisted of was a little brown paper lunch bag, which is soaked in water until soggy, and then scrunched into the desired shape. I placed my homemade turd on the floor of the photographic department and they almost had heart failure on seeing what they believed was a real turd. When I got home that night, I put my origami turd on the carpet for Dad to find. It didn't take him long to almost break his neck trying to avoid stepping on it. Both Dad and the photographic staff enjoyed the joke as much as I did. The photographic staff were always good for a laugh. There were seven men there and I don't think there was one day that I didn't have a good laugh with them. There was one fellow, Norm, whom I didn't particularly like because he was a creepy sort of fellow and I was very wary of him from the first time I clapped eyes on him, however, I always tried to be as nice as I could without being too friendly.

I recall one particular afternoon I arrived at work earlier than usual to avoid the obviously impending storm. Norm, who was always eager to make conversation with me commented that the rain would come down in buckets within a few moments. Without Norm noticing, I winked at the others and I said 'I'll bet you ten dollars that it doesn't rain for a month'. Norm, who loved to gamble, couldn't believe his ears. He thrust his hand out grabbed my hand, shook it and said, 'That's a bet.' He had no sooner said that, and the sky just opened up and the rain teemed down like a massive waterfall. He rubbed his hands with glee and put his hand out like a monkey waiting for a peanut

Norm 'That's the easiest ten dollars I've ever won'.

Amelia 'You haven't won ten dollars.'

He looked at me in total disbelief

Norm 'You just bet me that it wouldn't rain for a month and its bloody well pissing down right now, so you owe me ten dollars.'

Without batting an eyelid

Amelia 'Norm, it's only been raining a couple of minutes. I bet you that it wouldn't rain for a month. The month's not over yet, but if it continues to rain for the month, I'll pay you the ten dollars.'

Well the others were absolutely killing themselves with laughter. But Norm was so furious I honestly believe that he would have smashed me to smithereens if he had had the opportunity. About a week or so later, one of the other blokes asked me if I would clean the dark room first, because they had had a spillage of chemicals. I absolutely hated going into the darkroom of a night on my own. It was an eerie room and even now, I get goose bumps just thinking about it. I looked around at Mr German, the chief photographer, and he had a smirk on his face. I said, 'You're not playing a joke on me, are you?' He shook his head and then confirmed that the room was a mess and that they had tried to clean it up but it needed to be mopped as well as swept. On entering the room, I realised just how messy it was and proceeded to sweep. All of a sudden, the lights in the dark room went out and the door closed and I heard the lock click into place. Anyone who has ever been in a darkroom will testify that it is pitch black and you can't even see the end of your nose. I was absolutely petrified and I called out, 'If you don't open this door right now, I'm going to scream so loud your bloody ears will ring for hours'.

I could hear their muffled laughter and I yelled, 'Come on, you pack of bastards, this isn't funny. Let me out.' I waited a moment and then I had a sickening fear that I wasn't in the room alone. I knew instinctively that it was Norm and said, 'If you lay one hand on me, you filthy old turd, I'll rip your fuckin' head right off your shoulders'. I could hear his laboured breath and I held the broom handle as tight as I could and started swinging it like a baseball bat, with as much force as I could muster. In doing so, I started to scream all the obscenities I could think of at top note. It seemed like I had been in there for at least five minutes before the door opened and the lights came on. I ran through the doors so fast I reckon I would've beaten the Lithgow Flash. All the others were standing just outside the darkroom laughing, and I went right off the brain at them. I was still abusing them when a man I had never seen before came around and asked what was going on and if I was all right. I said, 'These pack of bastards just locked me in the darkroom with that dirty old turd. That's what's going on and no I'm not alright'. I was still shaking like a leaf. I looked around at the photographic staff and by this time they were ashen faced. The fellow whom I didn't know, told Mr German he wanted to see him in private. As they both walked into Mr German's office, the others all apologised telling me they were only playing a bit of a prank on me and they didn't think I would get so upset. One of the chaps Mr Rowlandson who had always been a thorough gentleman asked me if Norm had hurt me in any way. I told him that Norm wouldn't be breathing if he had. Mr Rowlandson told me that he was terribly sorry about the incident, and that he certainly didn't think it was funny and he wouldn't like it to happen to his daughter. I asked him who the other fellow was and he told me that it was the chief engineer from the sixth floor, two floors below. He had heard my screams and had come up to investigate. I subsequently found out that my screaming could be heard down on the first-floor level. Mr German came back and apologised and assured me nothing like that would ever happen again. I told him that I never wanted to be left alone in any room with Norm again and that if I was, woe betides the lot of them.

The industrial polishers proved to be just as dangerous as old Norm. I was only about forty-five kilo at that time and trying to manoeuvre those polishers around, really pulled the guts out of anyone, especially someone of my size. I used to ache from head to toe morning, noon and night and I figured that before too long, I'd be as irritable as the old crone who worked as a cleaner on the sixth floor. She never had a nice word about anyone. It was common knowledge throughout the building that when she opened her mouth, she was going to complain about all her problems. She also knew more gossip than anyone I ever knew and I couldn't help but wonder where the hell she got to hear it all. One thing I do remember her telling us all, that the kids at a well-known high school, had discovered a new use for glad wrap. Apparently, according to her, they used it as a condom. The thing that amazed me, how in the name of God had she found this information out. I had no desire to become a warbly old bat like her. So, when my doctor told me that the work was too heavy for me, and I was looking at serious ailments before too long. I reluctantly handed in my resignation.

Chapter 31

All Talk No Action

I wrote Frank a letter telling him about Heather's medical problems and how both kids were coming along. I was surprised to get a reply within the following week.

I practically had to go through the third degree from Dad and Edith wanting to know what Frank was writing to me for.

The letters from the prison were very easy to recognise, because they were in small yellowish/brown envelopes with the big black lettering O.H.M.S. written on the top. All other Government letters were in the large white envelopes. I used to think that the Government wanted to embarrass the families of prisoners. I know I was certainly embarrassed at getting the envelopes, but I was always pleased to read the contents.

Frank's spelling mistakes were a challenge to decipher at times. All of his letters showed no animosity towards me for having dobbed him in. In fact, he said he understood why I had done it and he apologised to me for putting me through so much heartache. In each letter he sent, he kept asking me to come and visit him. But I was still too unsure of him and myself to want to go over to Boggo Road.

Each letter he wrote which was one letter every fortnight, meant that he'd miss out on a visit. The way the prison system worked in those days was, a first offender was allowed one weekly visit or they could send one letter a week. A second time offender (which Frank was, because he had already spent a month inside a couple of years previously) was only allowed one visit per fortnight or one letter a fortnight, however, they were allowed to receive as many letters as was sent to them. But the screws censored every letter that went in and out of the prison.

In those days, I thought nothing of writing at least ten foolscap pages to a number of friends. I began writing lengthy letters to Frank. Every so often I would receive a phone call from a released prisoner who would give me a private message of undying love from Frank. The caller would inevitably urge me to go and visit Frank adding,

'Mate, you have no idea how lonely it is in there without visits.'

I figured what the hell at least if I thought I had made a big mistake going there, I could always stop writing and not visit him again. I remembered him telling me the last time he had gone inside was that boob tobacco tasted like shit scraped from the cockies cage and that toothpaste and soap was like a King's ransom. I bought tobacco, toothpaste soap and shampoo, and after ringing the prison to get permission for a visit, I presented myself at the gate.

The screws were quite nice to me, but then I made sure I dressed up to the nines, I didn't want to go there looking like a prisoner's wife. They of course knew that I was, but I remembered my grandmother's adage; 'It's one thing to be poor, but it's another thing to dress and act poor. Always have a clean, well ironed dress and your hair combed and neat and tidy'.

I'll never forget the look on Frank's face as the guard ushered him into the visitor's cage. I hadn't told him I was coming to visit and he didn't know who was there to visit him. He told me later that when the guard told him he had a visitor, he thought it might be my solicitor serving him with the divorce papers. He said that he very nearly told the guard that he didn't want a visit, but curiosity got the better of him.

The visitor's room was a fairly narrow hallway with a counter the full-length on one side of the room. The counter was partially petitioned off for each visitor to have a little bit of separation from the other visitors with their prisoner. I have no idea why, because we could still hear their conversation and they ours. There were guards patrolling behind the prisoners and also behind the visitors. If anyone tried to whisper, they would be told to speak up. If anyone objected, the visits would be terminated.

I later found out that if the guards felt it necessary to terminate a visit, the prisoner would be on an internal charge. That could lose them their privileges such as tobacco etc for a week or possibly longer. From the top of the counter to the ceiling was a sturdy wire mesh partition, which prevented the prisoners from any physical contact with the visitors. On the prisoner's side of the counter there was a wire partition separating each prisoner from the other. I could only assume that this was to stop the prisoners handing notes or contraband to each other. The visits were only of twenty-minute duration, I don't recall anything of the conversation now, other than Frank asked me to come back in a fortnight and to bring the kids as well. I continued going back and in those few visits, I became aware that some of the wives were able to slip notes to their husband's when the guards were pacing past with their backs slightly turned. There wasn't a drug problem in those days, so I guess the notes were just harmless love letters.

Frank was subsequently transferred to Wacol Prison because he was a model prisoner. He had been looking forward to that because the rules and regulations were a bit more lenient at Wacol. The visitors were allowed to greet their wives and family with a kiss and a hug on arrival and departure, but no physical contact was allowed during the visit.

My first visit there was memorable for two reasons. On my arrival and giving my name to the guard on duty at the gate, he greeted me as if I was his long-lost relation and said,

'You're the famous letter writer. God you write a good letter, I enjoy reading them'.

I thanked him for the compliment, which I genuinely meant, but I couldn't help but think You big prick, my letters weren't meant for you. Go and mind your own bloody business. I felt a bit awkward greeting Frank, but he had no hesitation in embracing me in a very tender way and he gathered the two girls in close, to have a family hug. Both Vivian and Heather wanted separate hugs and kisses and the guard turned a blind eye. We had no sooner sat down at the picnic type table and Vivian exclaimed in total shock,

'Oh no Dad your poor fingers haven't grown back on'. Everyone around us had heard her and I think we all laughed for about five minutes. Even the guards joined in.

From that first visit at Wacol I noticed one prisoner whose uniform stood out from the rest. Both his shirt and trousers were immaculately ironed whereby the other prisoner's uniforms looked as rough as chaff bags. I said to Frank nodding in the direction of the immaculate prisoner, 'Does he work in the laundry or is he the Governor's bum boy or something?' Frank sneered and said, 'No he's the rotten copper 'Wade' who got five years for theft'. I knew whom he meant, because his trial was front-page news for weeks. I said, 'Has he got a cushy pen pusher's job on the front counter, is that why his uniform is perfect?' Frank replied as if he had tasted something foul in his mouth, 'Yeah, the bastard just sits around on his arse in the office shuffling papers. He doesn't do a thing around the yard, he gets better tucker than the rest of us, and his uniforms are always freshly laundered and ironed. He's absolutely hated by the other blokes here. If he had've been treated like the rest of us he would've been accepted by everyone'.

I said, 'How long has he been here?' 'Since his sentence, he never spent one night in Boggo Road. He's doing it easy because he was a cop'. A few weeks went by and at each visit I noticed that Wade's wife and kids were always allowed in at least ten minutes before any of the other prisoner's families and they were always still visiting long after the other families were told that the visiting time was over. This I knew for a fact because we all had to wait at least ten minutes for a shuttle bus to take us down to the station to catch our trains back home, and Wade's wife never came out while we were waiting for the bus. I, in my inimitable style decided to do something about this injustice. I rang 4BH's programme Open Line and spoke on air to the three members of the panel Ivor Hancock, Wendy Mansfield and Don Seccombe. I told them and all their listeners how I thought it was a grossly unfair that a certain prisoner was receiving preferential treatment. I gave them a brief outline as to what I meant and Don Seccombe promised to look into my allegations. I said, 'Don, this isn't an allegation, this is fair dinkum'. At that point my call to them was terminated. Later in the programme, Wendy Mansfield asked for me to contact her off air when the programme finished. I rang her within five minutes after the programme ended and she asked me if I was prepared to come in to 4BH to give more details. I went in the following day and I was totally amazed that Wendy ushered me into a cramped little office and conducted the interview herself. I was overawed by her genuinely kind demeanour and I thought she was a flawless beauty. She immediately went to the top of the tree in my estimation, as a fair dinkum, classy lady in every sense of the word. The following day I was stunned to hear Don Seccombe refer to me as an unmitigated liar. He said he had thoroughly investigated my allegations and that there was no truth whatsoever in what I had said. He went on further to say that I had caused undue duress to the wife and family of the prisoner whom I had castigated. I could feel my blood boil and the tears in the back of my eyes were stinging as if I had rubbed pepper into them. I was just about to turn the radio off when Wendy interjected with 'Don, I happen to believe that lady. I met her yesterday and spoke at length with her. I thought she was totally honest and very brave for coming forward. What she has told me is abhorrent and I think that there's a cover up'. Don made a sound like a mumbled mutter and they went to a commercial break. I tried to compose myself as I dialled the open line number again and again. Whilst I continued, I listened to a male caller who virtually called me a criminal because I was married to a criminal and therefore, I shouldn't be trusted or believed. Finally, I got through and without giving my name I told them that I was the caller from the other day. Don Seccombe bombarded me with accusations about how much trouble I had caused. He went on about how the prisoner I had accused had used the old army technique of placing his uniform under the mattress to press his clothes. Ivor Hancock agreed with Don. I managed to say that the other prisoners ironed their clothes in that manner, but that this particular chap was immaculate. But Don and Ivor wouldn't have a bar of what I said and protested vehemently. Finally, Wendy interjected by telling them to let me have my say. To which I thanked Wendy and I replied, 'Firstly to the gentlemen of the panel especially you, Don, I just want to say there are none so blind as they who cannot see and in your case he who doesn't want to see'. I continued, 'To the gentleman caller who branded me a common criminal, I say, He who is without sin should cast the first stone'. Wendy had a good chuckle and they went to a commercial break. Every so often I would ring the panel to speak to Wendy on air and let her know how I was getting along. She would always say that she knew who I was and would always thank me for calling. Then one day about twelve months later she sent me a beautiful ham for Easter with a note that read 'Just a little ham from the ham panel' and she signed it Wendy Mansfield. I thought that was a wonderful gesture on her part and the ham just melted in our mouths. I've often wondered whatever became of her once she finished with 4BH. The outcome of the prisoner getting better privileges than the rest, well nothing happened to him, he kept living the life of Riley. But the other poor buggers had their mattresses turned over and their uniforms were taken out, crumpled up and thrown on the ground and trampled on by the guards for the next couple of weeks or so. The guards never found out whose wife was the 'fuckin' smart arse bitch' as they so succinctly referred to me as. All the prisoners knew though, and they thought it was a huge joke. Frank was transferred to Numinbah Prison Farm in the Numinbah Valley, which is in the hinterland directly behind the Gold Coast. The area is renowned for its picturesque beauty and the prison farm doesn't have high fences or guards patrolling the land with guns. It's commonly known as a low security detention area for non-violent, model prisoners. As idyllic as it sounds, it was, and still is, bloody miles from civilisation. The only way to get there is by car, and I didn't have one.

Chapter 32

What a Set Up

I had heard about the Fortuna Club a group being run by ex-prisoners for assistance to prisoners and their families and to rehabilitate ex-prisoners. Although I was very wary of meeting the organisers I went along to find out as much as I could and to see if they could arrange transport for me down to Numinbah. The first day I went there, I was met by a couple of the committee members Dave and Ken. They explained that the president, Lee and his girlfriend Kris, who was the secretary, were in another room having a meeting with the Criminologist Paul Wilson. I immediately felt more at ease with the knowledge that someone with a bit of credibility was taking an interest in the group. Both Dave and Ken seemed nice enough sort of blokes, I particularly felt sorry for Ken who had great difficulty walking. I subsequently learnt that he had been in a fatal car crash that had killed his best mate. Ken had, had his spine broken along with multiple other injuries. As Paul Wilson emerged from the room and started to walk past me, he focused on me and seemed to be studying me as if he was trying to work out who I was and why I was there. I got a creepy feeling from the way he looked at me and I didn't like the way he looked at me! Lee and Kris welcomed me into the club and explained that it was a voluntary organisation. Everyone helped with different chores and that it was expected of every member to attend a court hearing if another member was arrested, just to give them moral support. I went over to the clubhouse every chance I got and helped fill envelopes, prepared meals and generally mucked in. It was painfully obvious that they were short on funds and household items. As I had all my crockery, glasses and cooking utensils packed away gathering dust, I offered the club the use of them until I needed them back. I recall one night attending a party one Saturday night to raise money for the club and I met Dennis Walker the son of Aboriginal poet Kath Walker a famous Aboriginal Poet and activist (Later to be known as Oodgeroo Noonuuccal.) Dennis had been in prison and had a bit of a reputation in those days as being a bad boy. I found him to be a really nice sort of bloke to talk with and he and I stood around the record player singing along with the latest hits. He insisted that I sing the Mama Cass hit, *Dream a Little Dream of Me* about six times.

By the end of the night my favourite song had almost become my most hated song.

I was always a bit wary of Lee he seemed to me to be a smaller version of Rogue though he never displayed any signs of being a pants man.

As for Kris, there was something that I disliked about her too. I had noticed her watching me from the corner of her eyes on a few occasions. Quite a few times both Lee and Kris had asked me to let Vivian stay at their place but there was no way in the wide world I would agree to that. Vivian thought it would be a great adventure to sleep over but my answer was always a definite. 'NO'. No one at the club was able to provide me with a car to go down to visit Frank, so I saved up enough to hire a car and I picked up a gleaming brand new Fairlaine from the hire company. I felt as if I was the Queen of England driving that beautiful car and the kids and I went down the highway towards the Gold Coast as if we owned the world. Numinbah Valley was as beautiful and as peaceful as I had imagined and the prison farm seemed to me to be the perfect place to have a holiday. From that observation I always referred to Frank as 'being on holidays at the farm' or as 'being at his holiday ranch'. The visiting area was more like a big under cover picnic area and everyone sat around chatting with whomever they liked. The only time the guards were seen was when the visitors pulled up and gave their names and asked to see the prisoner they were there to visit. The guards would then point the visitors in the direction of the visiting area and they stayed outside. Visitors would show what they had in their bags, which were usually cakes and flasks of tea. Any cigarettes and toothpaste were handed over and the prisoner's names were written on the parcels and were distributed at a later time. Everyone had enjoyed a wonderful time even the guards seemed to enjoy all the kids asking them questions the entire time we were there. But all too soon it was four o'clock and everyone had to depart as the two-hour visit, had come to an end. I was on such a high leaving the farm that day I was totally oblivious to the speedometer as I drove along the highway.

I think it was around Beenleigh where I had had the accident that I glanced at the speedo, and nearly shit myself. I was cruising along at one hundred and twenty kilometres an hour. I can tell you I slowed down very smartly but it seemed like a snail's pace just keeping to the speed limit. Even now, if I get up to one hundred and twenty kilometres an hour which is quite easy with the way the traffic moves, I start to panic. Lee rang me early one morning to say that one of the members had been arrested for theft and was to appear in court that morning at ten am.

He asked me to attend and said there would be other members there as well. I was a little bit nervous about going, as I didn't know the member all that well. And besides, I hated court sessions they really gave me the heebie jeebies. I made the excuse that I didn't know if I could get Edith to look after Heather and he suggested that I could take her over there and he and Kris would mind her. Hey presto, Edith had just come into the room and said she would look after Heather. Actually, Edith had been only too happy to babysit anytime I wanted her to. She would have dropped any plans she had made, if necessary.

On arrival into the court, I discovered that James's father-in-law was the magistrate who was hearing the case. Out of consideration to my family, I declined on entering the courtroom. I didn't want to embarrass Magistrate Fenton any more than I didn't want to embarrass myself. I sat outside to listen to the proceedings unobserved by Mr Fenton. I'd only been there a few minutes when Detective Ryan and another Detective whom I recognised by face but didn't know his name, sat down almost opposite me. Detective Ryan glanced my way and as soon as he saw me, he opened his mouth and eyes in a comical mock shock/horror and said 'What are you doing here, what have you been up to?' I said, 'Gee thanks for the vote of confidence. I'm here to give moral support to someone in there, but I can't go in because my brother's father-in-law is the presiding magistrate'. Both cops burst out laughing and then Keith said, 'I didn't think you'd be up on a charge'. He then turned to the other cop and said something to which the other cop nodded. I can only assume that he had told him that I put Frank in. Detective Ryan then asked, 'What's your friend done?' I explained that I had become a member of the Fortuna Club and that I didn't really know the guy, but as a member I was required to attend to give any member who went to court, moral support. Detective Ryan again whispered to the other cop and then they both nodded. Detective Ryan stood up and walked back past me and nodded indicating for me to follow him out onto the other veranda. When I did, he bent down to my height and whispered, 'Get out of that club NOW, they've been under investigation for quite a while and they're not the sort of people that a lovely young lady like you should be mixed up with'. He then added, 'They're into drugs, and I haven't had this conversation with you. For Christ sake get out now, and go home to your kids'. I was bug-eyed and I could feel the sweat pouring from my hands and feet I said, 'I've loaned them my crockery and stuff, I'll have to get that back first'. 'Well get it out today and don't look back'. He then said, 'And remember you didn't hear this from me'.

He turned around and walked back to the other cop and sat down and they both began whispering and nodding amongst themselves. I again sat down and neither cop looked towards where I sat. It was only a matter of a couple of minutes before the members of the Fortuna Club emerged from the courtroom and we all walked out of the building together. I went with everyone back to the clubhouse and I told Lee and Kris that I needed to take my stuff back. I'm hopeless at telling lies, and I've always felt that when I tell a fib, the person I tell it to can read it all over my face. I said, 'I felt embarrassed about being at the court today and I don't think I can contribute anything to the club or its members.' Everyone protested how good I was for the club and how I was just over reacting to a difficult situation. But I was insistent that I wanted my gear and I knew that Lee realised it was more than what I was telling him. He told me that I'd have to come back on the weekend to collect the stuff. I really didn't want to go back there again considering what I'd been told. On the Friday night I rang the club and prayed that Dave would answer and not Lee. I was very relieved to hear Dave's voice and I said, 'Don't mention my name, pretend I'm an ex-prisoner making general enquiries and just answer yes or no okay?' He agreed and when I asked him if Lee or Kris had packed my belongings, he told me, 'No'. I asked if he thought I'd ever get my stuff and he replied, 'No but that's okay, don't worry about it' After what seemed like an hour but would have only been a couple of minutes of playing this silly game, I was able to establish that Lee had branded me as a traitor to the cause and was a person not to be trusted. I told Dave that I had had an uneasy feeling about Lee and for him (Dave) to be careful. He kept saying, 'Yes, that's right' and 'okay.' Frank had heard on the grapevine too, that the Fortuna Club wasn't what it was supposed to be and he had gotten a released prisoner to ring me to tell me to get out. I explained to the guy that I was having difficulty getting my stuff back and he said, 'Leave it to me.' About an hour or so later I got a telephone call from Kris telling me that I could pick up my gear as it was already packed in boxes ready to go. I phoned for a cab, collected the stuff and got the cab to drive me back home. A couple of days later on Wednesday 31/12/1969 to be exact, I received a telephone call from a social worker at the prison informing me that Frank had been returned to Boggo Road prison. Frank had applied for the new work release programme that had been introduced only a few months previously. I asked the caller if Frank had finally been given a job in the programme and he seemed very vague as to why Frank had been brought back. I had no sooner hung up from the call and the phone rang again. This time it was a man who only identified himself as Brian. He said, 'Amelia I've got a car for you for the weekend'. I thanked him and then told him I wouldn't need it. He then went on to say that I could have it for the entire weekend so that I could take Frank out on Saturday night.

Amelia 'What?'

Brian 'You know what I mean, you can get the car and smuggle Frank out again on Saturday night, like you did the other week, when you hired the car'.

I was totally flabbergasted

Amelia 'I have no idea what you are talking about'.

Brian 'Are you denying that you hired a car a couple of weeks ago to get Frank out for the night?'

Amelia 'No I'm not denying that I hired a car.'

Before I could finish my sentence, the caller hung up in my ear.

On Saturday afternoon 03/01/1970 I received a phone call from Dave. He whispered that he couldn't talk for long and that he just wanted to warn me that Lee had set me up because I had taken my gear from the club house. He said,

'There's going to be a write up in the Sunday Mail tomorrow about how you hired a car and took Frank out of Numinbah, I heard Lee ring Brian Bolton the crime reporter the other day and I wanted to contact you then, but I couldn't.' I told Dave about the social worker ringing me and then the mysterious caller offering me a car and he said, 'I'll bet that that was Bolton' He then said, 'I've gotta go'. I just managed to thank him before he hung up. But I never spoke to him again so I have no idea if he heard me or not or if Lee heard any of his conversation. I was sick to the pit of my stomach with worry, wondering what heap of bullshit Lee had told the crime reporter. I kept going over and over in my mind what the mysterious caller had said regarding the hire car. I couldn't for the life of me think of why Lee would lie through his teeth all because I wanted to take my own belongings back. Especially considering the amount of time and work I had given the club. On the Sunday morning I read the article of Brian Bolton's on page two and I couldn't help but think, if the matter wasn't so serious, it would be laughable. I thought too, that the public in general must be a pack of nut cases if they swallow this man's crap. I soon found out that the matter was more serious than what I had imagined.

Frank was not only brought back to Boggo Road, he was being held in what was known as the cages. That was the area where the dangerous murderers were held. He wasn't allowed visitors, however, I continued writing long letters every day giving him hope and encouragement that he still had a family who loved him and was thinking of him. I went through a living hell not knowing what was happening within the walls of the prison. I didn't know at that stage that he was being held in the cages, all I knew was that he was on an internal charge and all his privileges had been taken from him. As if things weren't bad enough, the following Saturday (08/01/1970the Gold Coast Bulletin had a front-page story claiming that allegations had been made to the police and prison authorities that: Without naming us we were burgling homes on the Gold Coast and hiding the goods in secret caches. We were smuggling liquor and money for gambling into Numinbah prison farm. A number of wives and girlfriends were meeting prisoners after lights out at ten pm twice a week and going on trips around the Gold Coast and returning the prisoners before the guards came on duty at five am. I didn't know whether to laugh or cry. One thing was for sure, I knew I would find it hard to believe another newspaper report again. About a month later, I received a letter from the Comptroller General of Prisons, Mr Stewart Kerr, telling me to make an appointment to meet him in his office in George Street. I duly went in and was confronted by an overweight balding creep whose very memory of him now, still makes my skin crawl. He questioned me at length about hiring the car and I gave him all the details of the firm make of car and the period of time I had hired the vehicle. He then began asking me details about taking Frank and another prisoner out of the Numinbah farm. To which I replied I had no knowledge of. He asked me the same questions over and over about six different ways. Then he said, 'If Lee was lying why would he lie?' I wanted to say, Perhaps the bastard found out that I had spoken to Detective Ryan regarding his involvement with drugs. But I knew I couldn't. Besides, not wanting to get Detective Ryan in the shit, I figured that the mere mention of drugs and they'd probably jump to the conclusion that Frank and I were dealing in drugs as well. I had been in the office about an hour and the big pig had been walking around the room behind me whilst questioning me. All the while, I had tried to keep a watchful eye on him as he circled me. Then unexpectedly, I felt his slimy hand on my right arm. He caressed my arm with his fat hand and I could feel the backs of his fingers slide up and down on my right breast. Under any other circumstances I would have jumped up and poked my fingers into the bastard's eyes.

But I felt absolutely powerless to be able to resist, for fear of what he may order the guards to do to Frank. He slid his arm around my shoulder and in doing so he said, 'A nice looking woman like you doesn't deserve to be married to a criminal you deserve the finer things in life. Perhaps you should consider finding someone who can afford to give you the things you deserve'. I couldn't make up my mind whether I wanted to vomit over him and kick him in the balls or just put a bullet through his brain. Instead I smiled sweetly and looked him fair and square in the eyes and for the first time in my life, I lied through my teeth as if it was the most natural thing to do and I said, 'Thank you that's the nicest thing anyone has ever said to me, and to think I was feeling so scared to come and see you. You're a very nice man and very easy to talk to'.

He said, 'Well I hope it won't be the last time we talk, my office will always be open for you and thank you for coming in so promptly'. I couldn't get out of that room quick enough, however, I walked slowly to the door and turned to give him another flattering smile. He said, 'Oh before you go, I meant to have asked you not to write such long letters because the guards are having difficulty reading all your mail'. I knew then that the slime ball was reading my letters himself and I said, 'Okay, perhaps I might be cutting down on them from here on in'. I gave him a coy smile, whilst underneath my breath I was saying 'Ya big fuckin' maggot I hope ya die, and soon'. On arriving home, I went straight to the bathroom and took a long hot shower, even though it was a scorching hot, summer day. I just wanted to scrub myself clean, because I felt disgustingly filthy from him having placed his hands on me. After the shower, I sat down and wrote to Frank telling him that I had had a meeting with Mr Kerr and that I had found him to be such a sweet man. I said 'It was such a pleasant surprise because I expected him to be as sour as lemons. He was a truly lovely gentleman'. For the second time that day I wanted to puke, when I read back what I had written. The letter obviously had a good impact on the silly old fart because Frank was finally released from the cages and taken back down to Numinbah. All told he had spent seven weeks in the hellhole known as the cages. I didn't fully realise how inhumane the cages were, until much later.

They consisted of four separate 10ft by10ft cages that one would expect to see in a zoo for the wild animals. They were exposed to all the elements with only the bars for the walls and a 5ft by 5ft galvanised ceiling for shelter. Every morning after breakfast, at between 8 am and 9 am, the four prisoners were escorted, under armed guards, into the cages. There they stayed, until between 3 pm and

4 pm, rain, hail or shine. In one corner of each cell, was a galvanised bucket with
a lid. Each prisoner was expected to urinate and defecate into these buckets each
day. Their waste stayed in the buckets in the searing heat until they were escorted
back to the cells where they slept, each evening.

As if that wasn't enough degradation and humiliation for the men to endure,
they also had to squat on the concrete floor to eat their lunches each day. It didn't
matter where they chose to sit, they were all surrounded by the stench of each
other's shit bins. They were only allowed to have one tin jug of water each day,
and the luxury of the week was to have a ten-minute shower each Sunday. When
I learnt of the treatment Frank and the other prisoners had received, I wanted to
get hold of all of the guards in the prison service and have them charged with
inhumanity to mankind. What made it all the worse was the fact that Frank
hadn't even been found guilty of any crime, in fact he wasn't even charged. He
was just the victim of a drug dealer's pathetic vengeance.

Now you would've thought I'd have the good sense to keep away from hiring
another car for a while, wouldn't you? Wrong.

I had met up with my old neighbour Lorna she and she and I decided to go to
the Gold Coast with the kids for the Easter break. I had caught the bus down on
a week day and found a grotty, little, one room joint at Southport for us to stay
at. It was such a hovel I think wewould have been better off pitching a tent on the
foreshore. But it was all I could afford and I was determined to have a good time.
I had gotten the phone number of a car hire firm at the Gold Coast and rang to
order a car for the Sunday so that we could drive out to Numinbah. I explained to
the fellow that I wanted a small car but that it had to be an automatic as I didn't
have a licence to drive a manual car and I had to send him a holding deposit.
When he sent back the receipt, he enclosed a letter stating that I would have to
get the vehicle on the Saturday afternoon, as his hours of business didn't include
Sundays.

On arrival at the car hire place, I paid the balance owing, signed all the relevant
papers and was then shown the vehicle. It was a gleaming VW manual sedan. I
protested 'I can't drive that I don't have a licence for a manual car.'

He replied, 'Well that's the only vehicle I have in the yard, it's either that or
nothing. It's not hard to drive.' I kept insisting to him that I was incapable of
driving a manual car and that I wanted my money back. He was just as insistent,
that I had absolutely no hope of getting my money back. I either took the car or
left it in it the yard, it didn't worry him one iota. Lorna had a manual licence,

but she was a very nervous driver and I thought to myself, I'm doomed either way, if I don't take the car I lose my money, and if I do take the car I'm likely to lose my sanity if not my life. So, after saying a couple of prayers, I put the kids in the back seat and reluctantly got into the passenger seat, which of course is known as the death seat. Lorna sat in the driver's seat, nervously checking every button and switch a dozen times, before finally starting the motor. She drove forward and narrowly missed hitting a family of four who in her words stupidly walked in front of her along the footpath. Without batting an eye or for that matter, looking either right or left, she continued out onto the Gold Coast Highway. But for the grace of God and the other driver's good driving skills, we were almost annihilated. I immediately realised that God was playing a game of Russian roulette with me and that it was his way of paying me back for my cruel joke of pretending to kill Lorna all those years ago. We had only gone about five hundred yards up the road and Lorna had managed to crunch the gearbox at least three times. I was on the verge of asking her to leave the gearbox in the middle of the road and we could pick it up on the way back, when the car started to kangaroo hop and then died. The cars behind us started to bank up until one driver came to our assistance and pushed us over, alongside the gutter. We waited until the traffic subsided before trying to start the car again. It kicked over without any problems but as soon as she tried to take off it would conk out again.

Eventually she got it mobile and she drove back to our room without too many problems. We walked to the nearest fish and chip shop and bought our meal for the night and we decided to take a drive to Surfers Paradise a distance of about two miles. We managed to get there without too many problems, though I was getting slightly pissed off with Lorna and the car, as we continually chugged along in a kangaroo hop. After attempting to park the car between two cars in a car space that would've accommodated a semi-trailer Lorna jumped out to tumultuous applause from passers-by only to discover that she was about two feet from the gutter. Unperturbed, she looked at the space and said, 'Oh fuck it'. She promptly locked the doors. Which disappointed me no end, I wanted her to leave it unlocked so that some enterprising car thief could come along and take it off our hands. After walking around window shopping for an hour or so in the dazzling glitter of Surfers Paradise we felt it was time to go back home and try and get a good night's sleep. We had envisaged driving around sightseeing on Easter Sunday morning but that thought had long gone from my mind since the moment we took possession of the car. Lorna took off and promptly got lost driving around the little back streets of Surfers. I tried to navigate, but whenever I told her to turn left, she would invariably go right. True to form, the car conked out in a dimly lit back street, where I jumped out and threatened her with every form of violence I could think of. It was there that we agreed that I would do the driving and she would manoeuvre the gears and I would work the clutch. We drove around the darkened street for about five minutes testing this skill out before getting out onto the highway. The car drove like a dream.

I headed towards Southport and was feeling very smug with myself and as we crossed the bridge between Surfers and Southport, I became aware of the car directly behind me flashing its headlights on and off high beam. I mentioned it to Lorna who turned around and exclaimed in fear and trepidation, 'Amelia, it's the cops, they want you to pull over'. I had to keep going across the bridge before I was able to pull up safely. They asked me for my licence, and as I handed it over, I told them the entire story of our adventures since 4 pm that afternoon. Both of them stood there amused and bewildered and one cop took his hat off scratched his head and laughingly said, 'For Christ sake, just swap over, and Lorna before you kangaroo hop down the road, turn the bloody lights on this time, will you?' Lorna and I chugged off and she said 'I have never in my life, heard so many words flow out of anyone's mouth in such a short space of time as what you said explaining our predicament'. With that, we absolutely pissed ourselves with laughter all the way home. The following day we arrived at Numinbah safely with plenty of time to spare. It had rained fairly heavily during the night but the sun shone brilliantly and the trees and grass were glistening and showing their true beauty after their well needed drink of water, however, the car parking area at the farm was a bit muddy and we had to be careful not to skid along the slippery surface. Naturally I was doubly careful not to fall arse over in the mud. All I could think was it would be just my luck to end up flat on my face with mud from head to toe again. Lorna had decided to meet Bob the other fellow who had been accused of leaving the prison farm in the dead of night. I hadn't met him either and he hadn't had any visitors since being incarcerated because his family lived in NSW. Frank had told me a little bit about Bob, on the only day I was allowed to visit him in Boggo Road before he was transported back to the farm. Bob had been a teller at a bank and he had discovered a customer's account that had been unused for many years and he defrauded the bank by closing the account by forging the customer's signature. Lorna and I put our names down at the office and asked to visit with Frank and Bob and the guard gave me a nod of acknowledgment and said mischievously, 'Have you hired any cars lately?' Lorna and I burst out laughing and I said, 'Don't talk to me about bloody hire cars.' As we sat waiting for Frank and Bob, I explained what we had experienced the night before. He shook with laughter and told us that he hoped we hadn't parked anywhere near his car. We walked into the visiting area after being told that Frank and Bob were already waiting for us. As we walked through the door of the picnic shed every prisoner and their visitors stood up and applauded. I looked around wondering what the hell was going on and I realised they were clapping me. I think I went a very bright shade of red and I said, 'What's this for?' Frank said, 'They're showing their appreciation for you showing Stewie Kerr up as the shit he is and beating him at his own game.' I looked over at the guard who had come in to see what the noise was and he roared with laughter shook his head and walked out which brought another round of applause. Everyone was calling out things like 'Good on ya,' well done,' and 'hope the mongrel rots in hell'. Frank gave me a welcoming kiss and held me tight. I sat down at the table and Frank introduced Bob to Lorna and me. Lorna seemed to be more than happy to meet Bob he was quite nice looking with sandy coloured hair and a broad impish grin. They both moved over to another table and started to talk as if they had known each other for years. All too soon our visiting time was over. I was very surprised to see Lorna farewelling Bob with a very passionate lingering kiss. Frank's eyebrows shot up almost over his forehead and his eyes went as large as saucers on seeing them in their clinch. Frank whispered in my ear, 'She'll be pregnant before she leaves here, at this rate'.

We got down to the car and everyone had begun to drive off. All the other prisoners had waved their love ones off and had turned and began walking back to their huts. Frank and Bob stood waiting with the guard as we got into the car. Lorna started the motor and went to drive off but the wheels just spun in the wet shale. We were bogged, and at the rate Lorna was spinning the wheels, I figured she would dig our way to China before nightfall. Frank, Bob and the guard came down, but neither of them were able to get behind the wheel for obvious reasons. They all started to issue conflicting instructions, which only confused Lorna more. I got in the driver's seat and somehow reversed the car to everyone's great delight except Lorna, whose face was as white as a ghost. She seemed not only to be in deep shock but also on the verge of passing out. I said, 'What's wrong with you?' She said with a stunned look on her face, 'You just drove over my foot.' I burst into absolute fits of laughter and I had tears just streaming down my face as I tried desperately to apologise. She was able to somehow, get in the car and she kangaroo hopped the car towards Southport as the guard, Frank and Bob walked away shaking their heads in complete disbelief. Fortunately, Lorna had only broken her big toe. As much as I felt sorry for her, I still couldn't help but wonder why she stood so close to the car as she had. And why in the name of God, didn't she yell out in pain as the car drove over her foot?

Chapter 33

Truth in Sentencing

I had moved out of my parent's home and because the tenants from hell still occupied our home, I found a half/house just a stone's throw from the new Shopping Centre, which was nearing completion. I didn't have enough money to have the gas connected, so I had to fill my electric frypan with water and place the vegetables or eggs or whatever I wanted to cook, in a cooking pot filled with water. I had to place the pot with the food, into the frypan and try to cook the meals that way. Believe me it was a bloody slow process but the kids and I tended to appreciate our meals more than what we normally would have. I had a bit of a struggle paying the rent and electricity, as well as the mortgage on the house. The week before Frank was due for release, I rang St Vincent De Paul to see if I could get a few groceries to tide us over.

Two gentlemen arrived at my door the following evening to find out why I needed assistance. I was so embarrassed at calling them I told them that I had changed my mind. I didn't like to think that I had brought them out on a bit of a wild goose chase and I apologised for inconveniencing them. I must have had a pathetic look about me as they insisted on coming in to have a chat.

In the course of the conversation I told them about not having the gas on, of course by this time I had been treating it as a huge joke and I was laughing about it. They asked me to explain how I had been preparing the meals. As I did, they sat in stunned silence finally they asked how long I had been doing that for. When I told them, it had been for about six weeks they shook their heads in horror. They went out to their van and brought in the biggest hamper of food I had ever seen. I was absolutely flabbergasted and couldn't thank them enough, but before they left, they told me that they would be contacting the gas board and arranging for the gas to be connected. They made me promise that if I ever needed their assistance again, I wasn't to wait until I couldn't cope, I was to ring them immediately. They were so kind and considerate and they made me feel as if I had won the lottery. Fortunately, I never had to ring them again needing their assistance. I vowed to myself that one day I would repay their kindness somehow.

Recently I donated a houseful of my furniture that I had stored in my garage. It took me 40 years but I kept the promise I'd made to myself. Which I'm very glad to have done.

The people who occupied the other side of the house were a French couple with a little girl Joanna who was Heather's age. Joanna and Heather got on like a house on fire, which surprised everyone because neither child could understand the other. Quite often Heather would march around the backyard like a soldier telling Joanna to salute and Joanna would obey the command. Both her parents spoke some English but most times it was a bit difficult to communicate with them, however, in the short time we had been there I had begun to learn a few of their expressions.

One particular day I will never forget, Christian (the father) came running in to me to tell me that he had just called out to both little girls to come inside. He was so excited about the fact that he had actually called out to them in French and Heather had answered the call before Joanna had. Yvette (the mother) was a hairdresser and a damn good one at that however because of her limited English she was unable to secure a job. Every week she would wash and set my hair just to keep in practice but wouldn't take any money for it. More often than not, she would do my hair in the latest styles of Paris most of which hadn't yet been seen in Australia. I always felt like a princess without a crown waiting for Prince Charming to take me out. I had to be content to just walk to the local shops to buy a bottle of milk to show off my hairdo. Eventually Yvette came home from the city one day very pleased with herself she had applied for a position with Stefan and was to start the following day. Unfortunately, though, after she had been there for a few weeks she told me that she was going to finish up because she was stuck in the wig section. She said that wigs were unsatisfactory to her because she missed the personal contact with clients. She wanted to find a little shop to start her own business. The last I heard, she was working on the Southside of Brisbane, I just hope she achieved her goal.

Frank was released at 6 am one morning after completing nine months of his sentence. He had stayed in there longer than that, because he had been kept on remand before he appeared in court for sentencing. I didn't have any transport to go and pick him up and I had no desire to go out and hire a car not even if I had've had the money.

It wasn't until after his release that I learned the details about his seven weeks in the cages. Even though the conditions were nothing short of barbaric, there were incidents during that time that were quite humorous.

Frank had been escorted to Stewie Kerr's office, in the prison grounds, almost every weekday, during the seven weeks. Kerr and/or Sochen questioned him. (Sochen was Kerr's underling.) They would question Frank for ten or fifteen minutes about him and Bob escaping from Numinbah on a regular basis. Each time, Frank would tell them that he knew nothing about any escapes. On one such interrogation Sochen said to Frank, 'Tell me about the fun and games at the farm.' To which Frank replied, 'Oh. You mean the go cart racing?' Sochen's face turned puce with rage and screamed at the guard to take Frank back to the cages. Frank hadn't even had the chance to sit down to answer any questions.

On another occasion Kerr and Sochen had brought a magistrate into the prison at the taxpayer's expense, of course. The magistrate said to Frank as he entered the room, 'I know more about this, than what you think I do.' Frank said, 'Thank Christ, will you tell me, 'cause I know nuthin about it'. The magistrate ordered him to be taken back to the cages once again. Frank reckoned he knew what a ballerina felt like, he said that he was spun around so fast he felt like he was pirouetting.

One of the other occupants of the cages was a young fellow who had committed a very ghastly double murder a few years previously. Because of the calibre of his crime, the young fellow was regarded as extremely dangerous and had spent his entire sentence in the cages. Frank said that the young guy was a genuinely nice bloke to speak to and obviously had a genius intellect. He had explained to Frank the entire details of the night he had committed the murders. It wasn't as cold and calculating as what it appeared to be, but that's his story and if he wants to share it with the world, he can write his own book. The young fellow was often asked questions by the other prisoners and guards alike, on a range of subjects. He apparently had the answers to any question asked of him, and was never proved wrong. His answer to Frank when asked how he had coped so long in the cages was, 'They only have my body incarcerated within these walls they can't lock my mind away, each day my mind escapes over the walls and I travel to anywhere in the world'. He went on to say that the mind is the most wonderful part of the body because it contains the imagination. He had thrust his hand in an outward motion and asked Frank what he saw in it. When Frank told him that he couldn't see anything the young guy said, 'That's where you're wrong, Tom Thumb's there, and I can dress him in a top hat and tails or in a pair of swimmers. That, my friend, is the art of imagination'. Frank also told me about young kids who should never have been in prison because they were first offenders of petty crimes, and were overawed by the older, more hardened criminals. He said it was pathetic to see them actually idolising blokes who had been sentenced for more than twelve months. These kids revered Frank because, not only was his sentence classified as being for six years, but because he was in the cages for seven weeks. On at least two occasions within the year after his release, Frank was approached in public and slapped on the back and offered cigarettes accommodation etc by young fellows. They honestly looked up to him as if he was a hero. Frank was extremely embarrassed by their recognition and promptly told them to piss off before he kicked their arses. They, in turn apologised profusely to him as if he was the godfather of the Mafia.

On the day before Frank's release, Kerr told Frank, that the next time he was sentenced, he (Kerr) would see to it personally that Frank would spend his entire sentence in the cages. To emphasise that he meant business, Kerr had added, 'Even if you come back after I retire, I've written it in your file that you will remain in the cages at all times'. All this, because a little two-bit criminal got shitty at me wanting my own belongings returned. Kerr must have resigned a very unhappy chappie, because Frank never went back to prison again. But the irony of Frank's sentence due to my guilt was Rogue never spent one moment behind bars for the crime. Even though he was the one who set the car alight. He was arrested, but not for arson or theft. He apparently raped a young woman and was sentenced to five years. As for the other crimes, there was insufficient evidence.

Many years later I was told that Rogue had died from liver failure. He had gone from being a non-drinker to a bad alcoholic and had literally drunk himself to death. At learning of his death, I remarked, 'The world is a better place.'

Frank had only been home a couple of days, when he applied for, and was successful in getting a job as a butcher in the new shopping centre. The centre was to open within the next couple of weeks and Frank and a couple of other butchers were instrumental in setting the store up, in readiness for the grand opening. He was making a genuine effort to keep on the straight and narrow and of keeping away from the hotels. I was genuinely proud of his achievements and naturally I hoped that it would last. I even sent a letter to Bob in Numinbah, telling him that Frank had gotten a job. Along with the note I wrote a little sign with the heading,

'LOCAL BOY MAKES GOOD'

Which I suggested should be plastered on the noticeboard. I learnt much later, that the boys in Numinbah including the screws thought that it was huge joke. A couple of months after Frank's release, I had a visit from two detectives. They had stated that they had received a telephone call from Frank telling them to come around and collect some stolen property he had in his possession. I, of course, freaked out. I emphatically told them that there was definitely no stolen property on the premises, and that they were more than welcome to search the premises. When Frank arrived home from work that afternoon, I told him about the detectives, he insisted that we should go straight down to the local cop shop. He was almost beside himself with anger and worry at being set up again. Neither of us had any doubt what so ever that the phone caller was Lee.

Frank practically pleaded with the cops to come and search our home and garden because he definitely didn't want to be fitted for possession of drugs. He explained the entire situation to the Sergeant, who was extremely understanding. The sergeant said that it wouldn't be necessary to search our home, however, he would endeavour to have Lee investigated and that if it was proved he was involved Lee would be charged. We never heard any more about Lee after that day. The incident certainly had a detrimental effect on Frank's confidence. On top of that, we still had the problem of the wayward tenant in our home, but fortunately his free accommodation was fast coming to an abrupt end.

Chapter 34

Another Touch of Evil

We finally got Bryan and his cohorts out and we couldn't believe the damage that they had done to the house. They had used one of the laundry walls as a dartboard and the power point for the washing machine was the middle of the target.

There were many holes in the walls and doors, throughout the house where they had been either kicked or punched. Every light bulb had been painted, red, purple green, blue or yellow, no two were the same. There was a deep puddle of water in the front yard that obviously had been there for some time. We soon discovered that Bryan and his friends had used the yard as a racetrack and their constant wheelies had broken all the pipes to the septic tank.

We had several quotes for the repairs and all told there was over $2,000 worth of damage. Considering that the average wage then, hadn't even reached $50 per week, it would be like having to pay more than $50,000 today, in comparison with today's wages.

We had no alternative other than to repair the damage ourselves as best as we could.

I went up to the local cop shop to put in a change of address on our licences. I had been dreading having to go there, knowing that the police knew us and were aware of Frank's behaviour etc. It was with great trepidation that I entered the building. I was convinced that I was going to be scrutinised mercilessly. As I handed over both licences to the young cop, whom I had never seen before, I told him that I wanted to change the address on both licences back to our home address. He mumbled something about having to get someone to check it out. I rolled my eyes with an exasperated and disgusted expression and thought to myself, here we go.

Colin Campbell walked out and said to my absolute amazement, 'Mrs Williams thank Christ you're back, welcome home'.

I said, 'Well that's a greeting that I didn't expect'.

He laughed and said, 'I never thought two years ago, that I'd be welcoming Frank back on my territory either, but after your tenants, Frank's a bloody angel.'

I passed some comment about Bryan and his cohorts and Jehutz, and Campbell looked at me with his eyes as round as saucers and said, 'And the others.'

I frowned, not quite knowing what he was talking about and he said surprised. 'Don't you know about Carter?'

I replied, 'No, know about what?'

He said, 'That bastard killed his little girl.'

My eyes opened wide in anticipation of hearing more. He went on to say that Carter had punched the little girl several times in the stomach when they lived at my home and that he had been charged with her murder.

He said, 'Your house has been mentioned in a murder trial. Carter's defence was that she had fallen off your patio around the same time that he had hit her. The jury couldn't determine if she died from the injuries from the fall or from the blows to her stomach. They found the bastard guilty of manslaughter. He should've been hung.'

All I could do was shake my head in total disbelief and repeatedly exclaim, 'Shit. Shit. Shit.'

He then went on saying, he had no idea what had become of Jehutz or his family but added, 'I hope the mongrel gets everything he deserves.'

When I mentioned Bryan's name, Campbell exclaimed, 'Yeah and he's another one that should be castrated. We were called to your place so many times because of his orgies. Apparently, there weren't enough bedrooms in the house so they used their cars and parked across the road as extra bedrooms.'

I looked at him in total amazement and said, 'So our home is a brothel as well as a haven for paedophiles and murderers.'

He said, 'And bloody gangsters. Bryan and his mates were seen running around with guns in their hands on more than one occasion. But when we got there, the guns were never found on the premises.'

By this time, I just cracked up with laughter and said, 'I can't believe this, Frank is actually being welcomed back by the local constabulary.'

Campbell replied, 'With open arms. If I thought he wouldn't use it, I'd give him the keys of the city.'

I felt like a million dollars as I walked out of the cop shop that day, and to think that less than an hour beforehand I had dreaded walking in.

It wasn't long after we shifted back home that I realised that I was pregnant again. We had to go through the process of establishing a good credit rating once again. We knew that after the fiasco of Custom Credit repossessing our much-loved Falcon station wagon, we had an uphill battle on our hands. We bought an old beat up Falcon that was overpriced and very dodgy mechanically, from an independent finance company operating at Rocklea. We knew we had been sold a lemon, but we were desperate to get our good credit rating back and we thought that this was the only way to do it.

That bomb nearly sent us completely broke replacing all the parts that were in desperate need of repair or replacement. Every week without fail I would pay the instalments to the American (Hughes) who owned the company. We had, had the car about two months and the steering began to shudder and black smoke billowed from everywhere. I said to Frank, 'That's it. When I go to pay the instalment on Friday, I'm going to have a go at Hughes and I don't give a stuff if the bastard repossesses it.'

Frank agreed, he was getting very frustrated with having to throw good money after bad in a fruitless attempt to keep the bomb mobile. I drove into the caryards car park and parked outside the office. I was told by the fellow behind the counter that Mr Hughes was out and he asked me if he could be of assistance. He introduced himself as John Gillespie and said that he was Mr Hughes business partner. I explained in great detail all the problems we had encountered with the vehicle in the short time we had owned it. I added that if the car couldn't be repaired satisfactorily, I would take further action. I had no idea what further action I could possibly take, but I thought it sounded good at the time.

He said he would look into the matter and he excused himself saying that he would be back shortly. About ten minutes later he came back and told me that he had successfully repossessed the car. I cannot even begin to tell you how relieved yet angry at the same time when I heard him say that. But all I could do was burst out laughing at him and I told him I had expected him to do that and that he had just done us an enormous favour. Gillespie was absolutely livid especially when I said, 'You can take us through every court in Australia but you won't get another penny from us.'

As I turned to leave, I gave him a big cheesy grin and said, 'See you in court.'

When Frank got home that night and I told him what had happened he immediately quizzed me about what Gillespie looked like. I gave him the description and Frank said, 'I think I know that bastard, he was in the road (Boggo Road) for fraud, if it is the same bloke, he is a genuine grub, a real smart arse, and everyone hated him'.

I had to convince Frank that we should go to the fraud squad and report him and Hughes because what they had done to us was fraudulent trading. Reluctantly, he agreed, and the following afternoon we walked into police headquarters at North Quay.

I nearly died of embarrassment as we entered the building because Frank put his hands above his head as if someone was about to shoot him. Believe me, if I had've had a gun, I would've been very tempted. We asked to speak to someone from the fraud squad and we were ushered into a large, cluttered office that overlooked the Brisbane River. We gave the detective every detail that we could think of including the fact that Frank believed that he knew Gillespie from Boggo Road. The cop suggested to Frank that it must be a new experience for him to be in there reporting a crime and not for committing one. Frank replied, 'Yeah, by the amount of time I've been in here talking to you, I've usually had at least two kickings, and been forced to sign a jumped up confession.'

The cop looked at him in total disbelief then absolutely roared with laughter.

As we gave the cop all the details, I was mesmerised by all the photos of criminals that lined the wall behind him and I asked if they were all on the wanted list. He said they were and in the next breath he asked me if I would be able to identify Gillespie in a line up. I replied, 'Yes of course, but I don't think I'll need to.'

Stunned, he asked me why, and I pointed to a photo directly above his head and said, 'There he is there, looking over your shoulder.'

He took the photo down looked at the back of it and said, 'Christ, I'll be buggered, it is him. You could become a good detective.'

To which Frank threw his arms in the air in mock horror and exclaimed, 'Jesus. For Christ's sake, don't encourage her.'

The cop wouldn't tell us what Gillespie was wanted for but as we left, he couldn't thank us enough.

Not long after that the finance company owned by Hughes and Gillespie folded, but we never found out the outcome of Gillespie's fate.

About two years later, two burly brutes came around to our new home and tried to repossess another car that we had bought. They maintained that Hughes had sent them to collect the vehicle in lieu of the monies he claimed we owed him. The house was a high set place with a balcony overlooking the driveway. After I had told them to leave, I grabbed the heavy electric frypan and ran out onto the balcony just in time to see them trying to open the front door of the car.

I yelled, 'If you don't get your arses off my property NOW, I'll toss this at your skulls'.

I couldn't hit the side of a barn door with a tank, but they didn't know that. I've never seen two big men move as fast as they did.

It's common knowledge now, that many years later, Gillespie was involved in the infamous Fine Cotton scandal which was the biggest racing scandal in Australia. He and others had swapped a slow horse with a fast horse by painting the fast horse's hooves white. Gillespie was duly sentenced to a few years back in Boggo Road.

We had bought another Falcon that was navy blue and white and looked as if it belonged in the scrap yard. But unlike the other bomb this car was in tip-top condition mechanically and Frank would proudly boast to anyone who was prepared to listen, 'It maybe a bomb to look at, but it's got a good donk (motor).'

We had tried everything we could think of to repair the damage to the pipes in the ground that the idiots had broken, but nothing seemed to work. We had priced the cost of the clay pipes that we needed, but they were far too expensive so we had to make do with trying to keep patching the old ones up.

Then one night, Frank said he was going out to see a mate and that he'd be away a couple of hours. He never went out of a night, especially not to visit mates. Although he had been having a few beers after work, he had genuinely been trying to keep his grog intake to a minimum. The mere fact that he was going out made alarm bells ring and I was fearful of the consequences. Being pregnant didn't help my nerves in any way either.

More than three hours went by before Frank finally got home and I dreaded the state that he would be in. As he walked in the door, I held my breath in anticipation and almost fell over when I realised that he was still stone cold sober. Excitedly he said, 'Come down to the car and see what I've got'.

In the pitch dark I could just make out differing lengths of white pipe that were tied to the roof and protruding through the windows and overflowing out of the boot. I said, 'Where the hell did you get that?'

He said, 'It doesn't matter where I got it it's just the stuff, we need to replace the old pipes.'

He didn't want any of the neighbours to see the pipes, so he decided to dig the old ones out and replace them with these new ones immediately. I went to bed, leaving him to do the job. I knew that it was pointless of me to object, because he was hell bent on doing it anyway. He finally fell into bed at about four am. When

I got up to get the kid's their breakfast, I looked out the window and there wasn't a sign of water anywhere and the grass and soil didn't even look as if it had been touched. I went down the front steps and saw all the broken clay pipes stacked under the house.

I couldn't help but stare in amazement at how he had managed to do all that on his own in such a short time. A couple of days went by and I had certainly likened to the fact that our broken pipe problem had been solved. We were sitting down having a cup of tea when there was a knock on the door. I glanced out onto the patio and my heart sunk as I recognised the two detectives standing there. I told Frank that it was Jack and Keith and he just said, 'Shit.'

As I opened the door I said, 'I hope this is a social visit.'

They both laughed and said, 'Sorry, we'd like to say it was, but we can't.'

They nodded to Frank and asked him how he was.

'I'd be a lot happier if you bastards weren't here. Have you got a thing about me or her?'

They both laughed and shook their heads and said, 'You know, Frank, out of all the crims we see, you're the only one we like and feel sorry for.'

Frank said, 'Well seeing as you like me, do me a favour, bugger off and don't come back.'

Jack replied, 'We wish we could mate, but you know as well as we do why we're here. It's no use denying it and don't give us the run around again. We know you took the pipes, where you got them from and that they're in the ground so come out and dig the bastards up and we'll put in a good word for you.'

Frank went down and started to dig and he said, 'Come on, I'll be here all day by myself take your coats off and roll up your shirt sleeves and give us a hand ya big cream puffs.'

I wish video cameras were around in those days because I would've had the best footage of the three of them all digging out the pipes together. Neither of them would say who it was but they said that they had received a phone call telling them that they had seen Frank laying the pipes. I said, 'You don't have to say, we know that it would be Rene and Ron from next door.'

Jack and Keith didn't have to comment, we could tell that we were right and all Jack said was, 'Only for the fact that one of our colleagues had received the report that some pipes had been stolen from Zillmere and had said that it must be connected to the report that we had, we wouldn't have come out. But we had to respond once he got involved.'

Frank said, 'You could've resigned and became human beings.'

I thought they were going to fall over in the mud they laughed so much. As good as their word, they spoke up on Frank's behalf and instead of going back to jail, he got off with a fine. We never saw Keith again, but years later Frank saw Jack at Lang Park at a State of Origin football match. Jack had a broken arm in a sling and was trying to juggle a couple of meat pies and a beer. Frank said to him, 'G'day mate, do ya need a hand?'

Jack greeted him cordially and told Frank that a helping hand would be much appreciated, to which Frank replied, 'Well I hope someone comes along soon.'

Having said that, Frank promptly walked away.

The distance between our home and Zillmere was approx. 30klms each way.

Chapter 35

Claire

In April 1971 I awoke rather early in the morning with severe contractions and knew that it was the day I would be giving birth to our third child. I had had another trouble-free pregnancy however, I had experienced some very odd cravings, which had convinced me that I was having a son. Without fail each day of my pregnancy, I had to have at least one packet of Fruit Tingles. I also had the lion's share of strawberry malted milks in those nine months. But the oddest craving I had every night when I had my bath, I had this insatiable urge to bite and eat the cake of soap.

I fought the urge successfully for months but it finally got the better of me. I knew that it was madness to even try to lick the soap but still I had to give it a go. God it tasted vile and I thought I was going to be violently ill in my own bath water, but it cured me from craving it again.

The other women at the ante natal clinic at the Mater Hospital all agreed that my baby was definitely going to come into this world holding a packet of Fruit Tingles and a strawberry malted in his hand. I got Vivian and Heather off to school and called out to Rhea, the neighbour who lived in the house behind Dawn and Harry, and I asked her if she would look after Vivian and Heather after school until Frank got home. She almost had a blue fit when I told her that I had had a show and was experiencing rapid contractions.

I tried to assure her that I was okay but she wasn't convinced. It certainly didn't stop me from doing a couple of loads of washing and hanging it on the line. I figured that I had better get the washing done, because I'd have enough washing to do after the baby was born without having that pile as well. I finally rang for the ambulance around ten o'clock and was told that it would be at least an hour's wait because there were a number of people needing transport into the hospital that morning. That gave me plenty of time to make sure that I had everything organised properly.

When the ambulance finally arrived, I was disappointed at seeing that it was a mini bus and not the usual ambulance where the patients can relax in the back. The driver and all the other patients were agog when they saw me standing patiently waiting on the side of the road. The driver hadn't been told that he had to pick up a nine-month expectant mother and started to radio for another ambulance. I assured him I was okay and I promised him faithfully that I wouldn't be giving birth in his van. There were other patients to pick up, so I didn't get into the hospital until 12.30 pm.

On my arrival, there was a flurry of activity of nuns and nurses rushing around getting me into a bed and making sure I was comfortable. I kept telling them that this child had a mind of its own and would arrive only when it was good and ready. They all told me that I was the calmest person they had encountered. I lay on the bed in the ward for the rest of the afternoon with the most excruciating back pain I had ever endured. Each contraction I had felt like a thousand burning spears piercing my lower spine. Finally, at about five o'clock I said to one of the constant parade of nurses, who kept asking me if I was ready to go to the labour room yet.

'I think you'd better arrange for me to go down now.'.

I had no sooner gotten the words out of my mouth and all the nurses were buzzing around wishing me all the best. I was wheeled away down the corridors with what seemed like a motorcade of nurses and nuns running in front alongside and behind me. By the time I got into the labour room, all the contractions stopped. Even though my spine was still excruciatingly painful I was convinced that this child was not going to arrive that night if at all. I said to the nursing staff 'You can all go and have your meal break, because this child is not going anywhere for a while yet.'

Finally, at 6.30 pm Claire arrived into the world. She was the exact image of Vivian and weighed 6lb 15oz the same birth weight as Vivian had been. Only for the fact that there was nine years and three months separating their age, they could have quite easily been classified as identical twins. I asked one of the nuns to tell Frank. I had been told earlier that he was out in the waiting room. She came back and said that he had gone home after being told that I had said that the baby wasn't arriving tonight. I gave them Dawn and Harry's telephone number as we still couldn't afford the luxury of having a phone installed. I found out the following day that they didn't telephone until after nine that night. Frank was in bed asleep when Harry yelled out from his back balcony. Frank apparently put his head out the window and said 'You don't have to tell me we've got another wedding to pay for haven't we?'

Harry laughed and congratulated him Frank thanked him and went back to sleep. Obviously, he had had a traumatic time with the birth of his third daughter and needed the rest.

From the moment Frank saw Claire he was totally besotted with her. Every moment he got, he was nursing her and doting on her. She had been born with a heart murmur and spent the first few days in intensive care. When I was discharged from the hospital four days after her birth, I went home empty handed and that nearly broke my heart. I was sick with worry that she might not improve or that she may need to have heart surgery. I had to go to the hospital each day not because I had to but because I wanted to. I'd sit with her for hours talking to her and telling her how much I loved her and it nearly tore me apart each day when I had to leave her to go back home.

Fortunately, she was given a clean bill of health when she was nine days old and we were able to bring her home. She had been put on a formula of carnation milk and water for some unknown reason. When she was discharged, they gave me the written instructions of the amount of milk and water I was to give her every three hours. I thought the proportions were very odd but I carried the instructions out to the exact measurements as was written on the paper.

I made an appointment to take her to Dr Kenneth for her first check up and as luck was on my side, I was able to get in to see him twelve days after her discharge from hospital.

In the meantime, she had developed a severe cold and I kept her in the pram alongside of me every night. She had very laboured breathing and I'd lie awake worrying that she would be okay. I awoke in fright one morning at about two o'clock and I couldn't hear her breathing. I jumped out of bed calling out to Frank telling him that Claire had stopped breathing. I shook the pram but she didn't murmur I swooped her up into my arms and vigorously patted her back. We both slumped back on the bed when she finally took a deep breath and started coughing. I got her back to sleep, but I never closed my eyes again that night. I just lay there listening to her breathing and waiting for her to wake for her next feed. When I took her into Dr Kenneth he examined her thoroughly and I told him that she had been very constipated and I was very concerned about her. He asked me what formula I was giving her and when I told him he looked at me in total disbelief.

Dr Kenneth had a habit of raising one eyebrow when he showed concern and I saw his eyebrow shoot up, although his expression never altered. I took the piece of paper the nurse had given me at the hospital, out of my handbag. I watched his eyebrow raise skyward again. He said that they had written the wrong proportions down and that I had been giving her four times the normal strength.

He telephoned the hospital and spoke to one of the staff which obviously denied any knowledge of the mistake. For the third time in less than ten minutes his eyebrow lifted high on his forehead and he said into the phone, 'Well I can assure you, I've seen the piece of paper with the instructions written on it and I have no reason to disbelieve, Mrs Williams. All I'm suggesting is that the nursing staff should doubly check their instructions in future.'

I had a guilty feeling for a long time after that because of the incompetence of that nurse I could have quite easily done untold damage to Claire's intestines. If it were in this day and age, I would probably have a good case of negligence against the hospital. But back then this sort of mistake was swept under the carpet.

Chapter 36

More Fun and Frivolity

It could have been the pressure of having another daughter being ill, even if only for a short while, or it could have been the pressure of everything and anything which set Frank off getting himself drunk on a regular basis. Who knows? The fact remains that he would come home as full as a boot and flake out in a complete stupor. God only knows what the hell he used to drink to get himself in the state that he did.

One Sunday afternoon I arrived home with the kids after visiting Dad and Edith and he was flaked out on the floor with his head propped up against the seat of the lounge chair. I cooked the evening meal, fed and bathed the children and myself and put the kids to bed and Frank continued to sleep.

I was tempted to wake him as his neck was in a precarious position and I thought he might damage a nerve or something. The chances of him waking, and being abusive was very high so I thought, bugger him, let him stay there and if he hurts his neck it'll serve himself right, the dopey bastard.

I watched the Sunday night movie and Frank never moved, he just stayed in the same spot snoring his head off. I threw a blanket over him and went to bed. Vivian came into our bed not long after I had gotten into bed, and I allowed her to sleep with me.

About two o'clock I heard the bedroom door open and Frank was fumbling around in the dark trying to find his way to his side of the bed. I told him that Vivian was asleep in our bed and that he'd have to go and sleep in her bed. He staggered and fumbled his way out, and for about ten minutes I heard all this thrashing and crashing in the distance. I very quietly tip toed down the hallway and flicked the kitchen light on. I couldn't believe the mess of the room. The fridge door was open and all the contents were strewn onto the floor. A dozen eggs were smashed on the floor and swimming in the milk that had spilled, the entire room looked as if a bomb had hit it. Even the kitchen and dining room curtains had been dragged down off the pelmets. The stove had been pulled away from the wall and somehow had toppled over without actually damaging the wires connecting it to the wall. Stuck between the sink and the stove, there was

Frank crumpled in a complete heap, out cold. I knew he hadn't been hit by the stove falling on him, but I thought he may have had some sort of seizure whilst getting something to eat from the fridge.

I wasn't sure but I thought he may have staggered and fallen hitting his head and dragging the stove over whilst trying to steady himself. I knew he couldn't possibly have still been drunk, because he had slept for at least nine hours I was sure of that. He had lost all power in his arms and legs and was barely able to stand let alone walk.

I half carried, half dragged him into our bed and lay him out like a corpse. I then had to carry Vivian into her room and put her back into her own bed. By the time I got back to our bedroom Frank hadn't flinched or moved a muscle I rang the ambulance and had to wait for what seemed like an eternity. I took them in and showed them where Frank lay and they shone a torch in his eyes and proclaimed him to be in a drunken stupor. They then admonished me for ringing them and bringing them out on a wild goose chase in the dead of night. I protested that they were wrong there was no way known that he could still be drunk and had wrecked the kitchen like he had. I knew him too bloody well the only time he'd smash things was in anger at me.

I knew he wouldn't just get in a rage on his own in the dead of night I cleaned the mess in the kitchen and finally got into bed just before dawn.

I awoke with a start at seven and took one look at Frank and knew he wasn't any better and he could hardly move his arms or legs. I rang the doctor and he came as soon as he could. He diagnosed that Frank had injured a nerve in his neck from being in the one position for too long and Frank had to spend the next few days in bed being waited on hand and foot. If I could have gotten the two-halfwit ambulance bearers I would have willingly choked them. They should never have assumed that just because a person reeked of grog that they were drunk. There's an old saying that to *assume* means to make an *ass* out of *u* and *me* .

Another occasion, Frank was painting the house and I went over to Harry and Dawn's to have a chat. Vivian and Heather were over playing with some of the other neighbourhood kids. When I went back home, I discovered Frank was in a dead drunken stupor. I had no idea what he had drunk but I thought he might have attempted suicide by drinking some sort of concoction. He was rushed to Princess Alexandra Hospital where he was refused treatment. He was then taken to the Royal Brisbane Hospital where he had to wait over an hour before he had his stomach pumped.

He was eventually admitted to the psychiatric ward and the staff assured me that the psychiatrist would see him at ten o'clock the following morning. I arrived back at the hospital before 9.45 am only to learn that he had been discharged twenty minutes previously. Everyone complains about our hospital system these days and blames the Government of the day. In my opinion it was just as bad back in the good old days.

Frank had kept in constant work, though he was always changing his job. He could never settle down with the same firm for more than a couple of months at a time. I somehow managed to keep all the bills up to date but we never seemed to advance at all. He started to work in the butcher shop in Myers at the shopping centre where he worked when he got out of jail. About a week later he came home and said that Myers was looking for staff for the deli counter and I decided to apply.

I started on a casual basis for a couple of days and absolutely loved it. I had only been there a few days when the manager called me aside, I thought, this is it I can't be doing the job to their satisfaction and they're going to turf me out on my ear. To my surprise he told me they had been watching me and that they were very pleased with my work and would I be interested in a full-time position. I reckon my face almost split in two with the smile I gave him and I couldn't say 'yes please' quick enough.

That was at nine o'clock in the morning by nine-thirty I was in an ambulance being raced to the Mater Hospital's emergency room. After speaking to the manager, I served a customer who wanted some sliced meat. Unfortunately, I tried to give her more than I intended. I had placed the meat onto the slicing machine turned the machine on and started slicing. All of a sudden, I noticed blood, and I casually turned to one of my co-workers and said, 'Pat, can you pass me a bandaid please?'

I had no sooner uttered the words when another co-worker, Jill, grabbed me in a bear hug from behind, pinning both my arms and holding my right hand up as high as she could. I thought, what in the name of God is she doing? Before I could even open my mouth, she lifted me up and literally bounced me along through all the shoppers until we reached the lifts. She refused to let me go until we got up to the Nursing Sister's room on the second floor. The nurse bandaged it with enough crepe bandages to cover a mummy in Egypt and all the while she kept telling me that I'd be okay.

I'm not joking I thought everyone had taken leave of their senses, all I had was a bit of a cut or so I thought. As soon as I got over to the Mater the doctor unwrapped the bandage contorted his face into a grimace and called for assistance. He told me not to look at my hand in case I fainted and I laughed at him. Then he started talking about preparing me for surgery and calling for the anaesthetist. I said, 'Hold it right there, mate this little black duck isn't going to have anaesthetic, if my hand needs stitches you can do it here thanks and I'll watch.'

He explained that my finger had been cut right to the bone and that I had severed the tissue and nerves and I needed microsurgery to repair them and that I'd need a skin graft to cover the wound. I told him that if the operation can be performed in the emergency room, I would really like to see it being done. For the next hour or so I watched with great interest as he sewed and snipped and dabbed and repaired the damage. Then to top it off, (no pun intended) he took out a scalpel and sliced a piece of skin from the inside of my right forearm approximately two inches long and one inch wide and very delicately sewed it onto my finger. It was an absolute buzz for me, to watch this masterpiece being created. I had my hand bandaged for two weeks and the skin graft had worked perfectly. I can't for the life of me work out why Myers wouldn't let me return to work.

The 'funny' thing I heard much later was a rumour that was circulating that I had done it purposely. Let me tell you something, this kid only has nine digits on the two hands she's got and she treasures each and every one of them. Anyone who believes I sliced one of them purposely I would suggest very strongly that they receive psychiatric help *now* .

I had kept up correspondence to Tim and Andrea who had long gone to live in New Zealand. Andrea had written to tell me that her seventeen-year old brother Reggie had been getting into trouble with the police because he was hanging around with the wrong crowd. She asked me if I would be prepared to provide him with accommodation because the welfare department had said that he needed to be sent away to someone who might be able to straighten him out. She had written that he had been charged with converting a car. I couldn't think why he would be charged with that, I thought, if anything he should be congratulated and encouraged. In my mind converting a car meant to take the top off the car and make it into a convertible. I learnt later that in New Zealand car conversion was car theft.

Reggie arrived and I had high hopes of trying to help him even though I had told Andrea that I couldn't make any promises. As it turned out the biggest task ahead of me was to get Reggie out of bed of a morning. He would've been one of the laziest little sods God ever let draw breath. Every morning I would get the newspaper and scan the employment column and mark off every job within a ten-mile radius that I thought he would have a hope of getting. I'd mark them off, make him his breakfast, and knock on his door to wake him and nothing. The little sod would continue to sleep, sometimes into the afternoon. This went on for about a fortnight when I told him that if he didn't get a job in a hurry or at least try to get one I would put the hose on him to get him out of bed.

This brought me the second biggest task, getting him to take a bath. I won't say he was dirty or was allergic to water but to put it kindly he being a thief I had no concerns of hiding any valuables under anything that even resembled soap.

About three months of having the pleasure of Reggie's company I gave him his marching orders and he went to live with the Woodley family, who lived a couple of streets away. They had five of the worst behaved kids in captivity. Reggie lasted ten days there before heading off to try his luck in Sydney. His luck ran out because within twenty-four hours he had been arrested for pinching a car and he spent the next twelve months of his life in Grafton prison.

I felt another bout of guilt because I had failed to keep him out of trouble. He was deported back to New Zealand on his release date. Which was pure luck on his part really because if the authorities had've done their homework they would have found that he was born in England and had never become naturalised in New Zealand. He didn't have any relatives in England so if they had sent him there, he would have been in very deep poop.

•••

Edith had found herself a job at Donut's Galore in the new shopping centre, and became more money hungry than ever. I had long regarded her as a tightwad. Not that I tried borrowing from her you've heard the old saying about a fish being watertight. Well, Edith was tighter than that again.

It became more apparent to me that the more money she got the more she loved it. I had said to her on a number of occasions that I thought she treated money as her God.

Mum on the other hand would think nothing of spending whatever was necessary on any of us as long as she thought it would please us. I had often borrowed small amounts from Mum but I always made sure that I paid her back in full even when she had said that it wasn't necessary. I had to borrow five hundred dollars to pay for the sewerage to be installed. Mum never batted an eyelid when I asked her even though I considered it to be an enormous amount. All she had said to me was that I'd have to wait until the following day before she could give it to me as she had to go to the bank to get it out.

What Frank and I found hysterical was when she handed me the money we looked at it and then at each other in total disbelief because she had paid me with twenty-five brand new ten pound notes. I thought to myself this is 1971 and decimal currency has been in since 1966 how the hell could she have had this much stashed away for nearly six years?

Instead of saying anything straight away I decided to play a little trick on her. Mum had always gotten confused with the changeover to decimal currency. Every time she saw something she wanted to buy, she'd always try to convert the price to the old pounds shillings and pence. For example, if she saw something for $3.98, she'd ask me, 'Is that nearly two pound or four pound?'

I'd say to her time and time again 'Don't worry about trying to work it out in the old money, if you want it just buy the bloody thing.'

On this particular morning I threw my arms around her and thanked her and promised faithfully that I'd pay her back as soon as I could. As always, she replied, 'I know you will whenever you're ready love there's no hurry.'

I winked at Frank and I said, 'There's only one problem Mum, you've only given me two-fifty not five hundred'.

I counted it out and she exclaimed, 'Ooh I say, I have, too. I'll have to go back to the bank and get some more.'

Frank and I burst out laughing and I said, 'I'll come with you if you like. What bank do you go to?'

She said, 'No it doesn't matter I'll go there myself and I'll get the rest to you tomorrow.'

I said 'Mum, now listen to me, you're not fooling anybody here these bloody notes haven't been in circulation for nearly six years. You've either got a stash somewhere or you've got your own printing machine'.

She coughed and spluttered and tried to convince me that the bank had paid her the notes. When she knew that I wasn't going to swallow the story she told us that she had had a few of the old notes but these ones were the last ones she had.

I said 'You're not fooling me, so get rid of whatever you've got left before they become obsolete and worthless.'

The following day she and Edith went to every bank in George, Adelaide and Queen Streets in Brisbane and exchanged at least two ten-pound notes in each bank. God only knows how much she had stashed away.

You'd think that choosing a drainer to connect the sewerage pipes would be like falling off a log, wouldn't you? Not for me it wasn't. I had gotten three quotes and of course I chose a drainer who didn't know a sewerage pipe from a bloody Jerry can. The fellows he employed probably didn't know too much either but at least they did try to do their best.

As it turned out the boss was Chris Leon a fairly well-known hypnotist who had his practice over at Mt Gravatt. Every day he would come over and oversee his workers to make sure they were in fact working. I'd hear him ask them why they had done a particular job. After they had explained their actions he'd come and tell me what they'd done and that he thought it would probably cost me a little bit more than what he'd quoted. After about a week of this sort of nonsense he came and told me that I'd have to pay him before the job was completed. I told him that I would give him half of his money after the Inspector had been to inspect the work and had given his approval and that I would pay the balance when the job was completed.

I have never been hypnotised in my life and I probably never will be but I know when someone is trying to hypnotise me. This bastard was doing everything in his power to hypnotise me so I excused myself telling him that I would be back in a moment. I went up to my bedroom and came back and he started talking to me very carefully and deliberately I placed my sunglasses on and in my very best voice I said,

'You'll have to excuse my glasses, but my eyes are very sensitive, especially to the sewerage that's coming out of your mouth'.

He became very angry and was screaming abuse at me. I ordered him out and told him never to come back in my yard again.

The Inspector came out that afternoon and told me that he couldn't possibly pass the work because it was not up to standard and advised me not to pay any money until the job was done satisfactorily.

When I rang Leon and told him what the Inspector had said, I added that if he wanted the money, he had better get qualified men to finish the work. The job was finally completed, and I sent him the amount that was on the original quote. Instead of getting a receipt we got a summons to appear in court to pay for his extra expenses. We appeared in court and the Magistrate awarded in our favour. Leon had to pay his barrister and our solicitor's fees as well as court costs. My biggest regret was paying Leon the money, I reckon I could have gotten the work done free of charge with that Magistrate.

I had suffered six prolapses of the uterus since having an I.U.D inserted into my womb after Heather was born. I didn't connect the prolapses with the mosquito coil, which I referred to it as. I thought it was due to the fact that I was born with an introverted womb. I had asked my Gynaecologist to remove the device in 1970 after I had suffered three prolapses. When I became pregnant with Claire I just thought that the pains I endured were from the weight of the baby. A few years later many American women were awarded millions of dollars for having the I.U.D. inserted. There were no law suits of that nature in Australia at the time!

After Claire was born I suffered another three prolapses and I can only describe the pain as almost unbearable. I used to feel that if I could walk on my knees I wouldn't suffer as badly. I know that sounds mad but that's how I felt. My gynaecologist used to insert a rubber ring for three months to hold my uterus back in place but within a week of its removal it would prolapse again. Eventually after the sixth prolapse, he said 'You're going under the knife if you have another prolapse, lass'.

No need to be told, I was back in his surgery suffering excruciating agony once again. Because I trusted him implicitly even though I was terrified of surgery I agreed to have a hysterectomy. Edith refused to take one lousy week off work to look after Claire for me because her money was more important to her. This was a woman who owned her own home and didn't have any debts whatsoever. Dad was by that stage working as a security officer at the wharves and no doubt gave her more than sufficient housekeeping money.

She was also receiving board money from Edward so it wasn't a question of her having to go out to work to keep the wolf from the door. As far as everyone was concerned, it was a matter of her being a very greedy woman who couldn't have given a shit about her only daughter.

Chapter 37

Mum

Mum, at the age of 82, God love her, volunteered to care for Claire, and I was so proud of her for that I could have burst. On a Saturday in March 1972 I went into theatre at 8 am and I recall looking at the clock at 8.30 am when they called my name. I said to them 'I'm not asleep yet I can still hear you'.

The nurse replied, 'No, it's all over, Mrs Williams, we're taking you to the recovery room'.

I have always referred to the Gynie since then, as Quick Draw McGraw. He had told me just before the operation that he was going away fishing for the weekend as soon as he had finished the surgery. He assured me that another doctor would come in to see me on the Sunday. I was fairly groggy at that stage from the pre-op needle but I recall thinking, Gee that's great, I'm paying this bugger a small fortune and he's off gallivanting.

That afternoon, Mum brought Claire up to me, as I lay in bed with drips hanging off me from seemingly every orifice, and I learnt that Edith had gone to a wedding of a distant friend. I was so angry with her, that if I had've been physically capable, I would have gotten out of bed and gone and punched her lights out.

The following morning a doctor came in and asked me how I was. When I told him that I was fine, he then told me that Quick Draw McGraw would be in to see me on Monday. That consultation cost me an extra twenty-five dollars as I found out a couple of weeks later when the bills rolled in.

In the afternoon, the lady in the bed alongside of me had a visit from her Gynie. I heard her tell him that she was fine but that she was worried about me because she apparently thought I was a funny colour. He came over to me checked the whites of my eyes, asked me if Quick Draw McGraw had ordered a blood test on me before my surgery. When I told him 'No' he hurried outside. Within seconds, I had nurses running around me, like chooks with their heads cut off. I was told that I was very anaemic and that I needed a transfusion. But what surprised me the most was, the Gynie who had ordered the blood was not only very concerned about me, he was absolutely livid with Quick Draw. All told

I was given three bags of blood over the next day or so, which of course I had to pay for. I subsequently learnt that I should never have had a hysterectomy at all. In fact, all I needed was to have had my uterus sewn into place, which I believe is the usual practice.

I'd dearly love to give you Quick Draw's real name so that every other woman in Queensland could stay away from him. He would've no doubt retired from performing unnecessary operations by now. But I can't stress strongly enough that if you're told you have to have surgery, get a second opinion, and a third if necessary.

It must have been a hell of a lot of work for Mum that week. But each day she would bring Claire in beautifully dressed, and smelling as sweet as a rose. She had to rely on public transport or come by cab if Frank couldn't get over to pick her up. Frank of course had taken time off to look after Vivian and Heather and he was at my bedside with them, as often as was humanly possible. Edith came up once on the Sunday, but Dad called in every day.

I wanted to pay Mum her money back as soon as I could, so I found myself a job at the Sunday Sun newspaper in Fortitude Valley. They had created a new column called The Reader's Mart which consisted of advertisements selling anything from unwanted household goods to motorcars. My job was to answer any incoming calls which in the early days, wasn't many and writing out the advertisements for publication. My main job was to telephone people who had their adverts in the Courier Mail, and find out if they had sold their articles. If they hadn't, I had to try and talk them into advertising with the Sunday Sun. I didn't mind the job, but it was regarded as a bit of a joke in the newspaper world. Hardly anyone ever read the adverts in the Sunday Sun, but I couldn't have cared less. I did more than my fair share of the work, which is more than I could say for some of the other women there. I only had to go in there from Wednesdays to Saturdays. The money was good, so I couldn't have given a continental if they did their work or not.

All told, there was about eight of us in the original Reader's Mart staff and at least three of them, wouldn't have worked in an iron lung. To hear them talk used to make the rest of us laugh. Another woman whose desk was next to mine would ask me for marital advice about how to keep her man interested. If only she knew the turmoil my life was in, she would've thought twice before even asking me the time of day.

Mum had a bad fall outside her house and had cut her hand on the footpath needing twelve stitches. I was sick with worry about her, but she was very independent and refused to go and stay at Edith's place. Edith didn't really want her to go and live with her anyway, because of wanting to stay at work.

At least once a week I would have a screaming match with Edith telling her it was time that she gave the bloody job away, to look after Mum. I might as well have gone and shoved my head in a bucket of shit for all the good it was. Edith's God, the almighty dollar, came before everything.

I'd call in to see Mum as often as I could and I managed to pay her $400 of the $500 I had borrowed almost twelve months previously.

A few weeks after her fall, she again lost her balance and although she hadn't injured herself this time, she reluctantly agreed to stay with Edith, Dad and Edward. But Edith still refused to give up working. Every Monday and Tuesday I would drive over to Edith's approximately forty-kilometre round trip to see if she was okay. As the weeks went by, I saw her deteriorate. So much so, that she could hardly get out of bed. Every chance I got I would abuse the living crap out of Edith, telling her to give up work to take care of Mum. Nothing I said would change her mind or attitude. Her way of solving the problem was to tie a rope pulley to the end of the bed so that Mum could pull herself up to go to the toilet and get herself some lunch whilst Edith was out earning her money. It got to the stage that whenever I pulled up outside the house, I would sit and wait for at least five minutes, before getting the courage to go in. I was absolutely terrified that I was going to find her dead in bed or at the very least that she had collapsed or fallen over again.

Edward had been separated from Beth for some time, and in August of 1972 they were divorced. Edward had had a number of nervous breakdowns and had been hospitalised and had shock treatment far too many times to even count, since the age of nineteen. He was eventually diagnosed as being schizophrenic. By this time, he was thirty he was just a mere shell of a man. He was devastated by the breakup of his marriage and he missed seeing his two sons. His son Eddie was about twelve and Mike was two years younger. Everyone worried that the separation and subsequent divorce would eventually tip Edward over the edge and that he'd be back in hospital before too long.

When he was in the hospital, Beth hardly ever visited him. She was far too busy shopping and socialising, and leaving the two boys in Edith's care. But that's another story.

Edith had indicated on a number of occasions that she blamed Beth for Edward's breakdowns, however, Mum, being a very reserved woman, didn't say a word against Beth. But it didn't go unnoticed that she hadn't said a word in Beth's favour either, and Mum was a firm believer in giving praise where praise was due.

Edward was far too upset to go to the divorce court to hear what Beth had to say against him. Instead, he asked me to represent him and report the outcome to the family that night. Beth had chosen cruelty as the reason for her divorce. In those days you had to have a valid reason for getting a divorce. The two main ones were given the titles of cruelty, and mental cruelty. As long as you could provide sufficient evidence or were extremely good at acting, you won your divorce.

Now I'm not saying that Beth lied, or that she was a damn good actress, however, she did get the decree nisi without any proof of cruelty whatsoever. When she stood in the courtroom, she looked around at anything and everything, except at me. When she told the court that Edward had punched her in the breast on several occasions and that he had told her that he hoped she would die of cancer, it took all my inner strength, from screaming out, Bullshit.

As she and her solicitor left the courtroom, I stood aside and let them pass, without me uttering a word. The lift arrived, and they both entered, and just as the doors began to close, I ran in too. I stood on one side of the solicitor and Beth was on the other. She never took her eyes off the door, as I stood there just glaring at her. When the door finally opened, she bolted out like a stallion and I called out to her. On hearing her name, she turned to face me and I gave her the best sneering smile that I could, and said, 'We all know that Edward didn't punch you on the breast, but on behalf of the entire Long family, I'd like you to know, that we all hope you die of cancer'.

When I went back and told everyone what had been said, Edith replied, 'Ooh, I don't think you should have said that'.

I said, 'Why not? I was only speaking the truth.'

To which Mum replied, 'That's right, Ooh, She's nothing but a vixen.'

We all fell about with laughter, because that was the first and only time Mum had ever said anything bad about anyone.

Calling Beth a vixen was the ultimate insult. For a long time after, if Beth's name was ever mentioned, one of us, if not all, would inevitably say, 'Ooh, She's nothing but a vixen'.

For my sin of saying that to Beth, she had her solicitor send a letter to Edward stating that whenever he had access to the boys, he was not allowed to let me see them. In fact, he was supposed to take them out of the home, if by chance, I called in to visit. Of course, this didn't amount to a hill of beans. I saw the boys almost as regularly as Edward. However, we all let her think she had us over a barrel.

About three years later, Beth tried to get more money out of Edward. She told him that her solicitor had advised her to contact Edward and tell him that if he didn't pay her more, they would take him to court again. Edward rang Beth's solicitor only to learn that Beth had not consulted him about her wanting more money. She had just tried to bluff him into thinking he had to pay her more without a court order.

Edward and I went to get advice from a solicitor. The solicitor was horrified at the injustice of Edward's divorce, especially at the amount she had demanded and was being paid, for maintenance. Especially considering that she was working full-time. He nearly fell off the chair when we told him about the letter regarding me. He asked me if I had any criminal convictions and/or if I was a prostitute. When I told him 'No', he sent Beth's solicitor a very stern letter stating that we would fight them in court. We never heard anymore regarding the matter again.

Edith rang me after I'd finished work on Saturday 07/10/72 and very matter of factly informed me that Mum had been admitted to hospital. She said that Mum had fallen and had broken her hip. When I asked her what had happened and when it happened, she replied, 'Last night at about five-thirty'.

I said, 'Why didn't you ring me before this?'

'Because there's nothing you could have done, we had everything under control and she's in good hands now, and being looked after by experts.'

I bit my tongue and stopped myself from saying something I may have regretted. Instead, I again enquired how it had happened. She was very hesitant and was obviously trying to choose her words very carefully, and said, 'You know what your grandmother's like, she heard your father and Edward arguing in the lounge room and she jumped out of bed and ran into the lounge to stop them. They started to throw punches and your grandmother got in the way and she fell.'

I yelled, 'Got in the way and fell, be buggered. How the hell could she jump out of bed and run? She could hardly move, and where in the name of Christ were you?'

Edith explained that she didn't know how Mum had gotten out of bed and ran as fast as she did, and that she must have panicked when she heard the commotion.

I said, 'Oh that's just fuckin' great they've probably killed the poor old bugger. What were they blueing about anyway?'

She explained that Edward had arrived home from work and had gone in to see how Mum was and he was sitting on the bed talking to her when Dad arrived home. Dad had had a few beers and apparently told Edward to get out and stop worrying Mum with his worries about Beth. Edward had raced out and yelled at him that he wasn't worrying her, that he was only talking to her. One word led to another and a couple of punches were thrown, Mum raced out and Dad had accidentally pushed her out of the way. She lost her balance and fell, and her hip snapped. I hated Dad at that moment and wanted to smash his head in.

We went to see Mum the following day and I knew that we would never get her home and it took every fibre in my body to stop myself from screaming and crying like a banshee. Her speech was very difficult to understand, it was as if she had something in her mouth stopping her from forming her words properly and she also spoke in an almost inaudible whisper. I went again on the Monday and Tuesday and I could see that she was slowly slipping away. There were workmen building extensions to the front of the hospital and each time the jackhammers were started, she almost jumped out of her skin. I went to work on the Wednesday, but I wasn't able to concentrate on my work. Although my boss had suggested that I go home, I stayed around until about one o'clock and I rang the hospital to see how she was. They told me that I had better get there as quickly as I could because they didn't think that she would last until night. They also informed me that her kidneys were failing and that it was only her heart that was keeping her alive. Edith arrived around the same time as I did, and Mum was already in a coma. I sat with Mum just holding her hand and telling her how much I loved her and that I didn't want her to die. Even if she had've been awake, she wouldn't have heard me, because the jackhammers continued to rat-a tat-tat their incessant noise. About an hour went by and I bent down and kissed her goodbye and told her I would see her later. I lied to her, because I knew I couldn't stand to come back and watch her leave this earth. This beautiful, most wonderful lady who had nurtured, cared and loved me with all my faults for twenty-nine years, was getting ready to leave me forever.

On the following Sunday night 15/10/1972 I lay in bed thinking to myself that perhaps if I donated one of my kidneys to her it might give her at least another year of life. The high-pitched screech of the telephone caused me to almost fly out of bed. It was 11.25 pm and Edith broke the dreadful news to me that Mum had gone. I cried so hard and so long I thought I would never stop. My heart was completely shattered, and I thought I could never again, be as heartbroken as I was that night.

More than a hundred people turned up for her funeral. The little chapel at the Fortitude Valley Metropolitan Funeral Home was packed and there were people standing in the foyer and spilling out onto the footpath. Her coffin was open, and as we filed past, James said, 'She even died with a worried look on her face.'

And I couldn't but wonder if she had been worried where I was and why I hadn't come back to visit her in the hospital. It's a thought that niggled me for years.

•••

After the funeral, driving home after picking the kids up from Edith's next-door neighbour's place, we got halfway along our street and Frank, who had not had a drink all day, burst into uncontrollable sobbing. He pulled to the side of the road and his tears fell like pouring rain. In the twelve years I had known Frank, I had never so much as heard him whimper, not even in pain. We must have sat there for a good ten minutes before he was able to compose himself and he said with such pride and reverence, 'She was my Mum too, and she was the best Mum in the world'.

A few weeks later I penned the following poem in her honour.

MY GRAN

When I needed help you were always there
To lend a hand with loving care
Whenever there was work to be done
I would call for you and you would run
I depended on you to always be there
But I failed to tell you how much I did care
You worried for me like no one else would
And you helped me in every way that you could

To hear you say 'Hello love'

Is my wish from heaven above

I've searched into the faces of my fellow man

But there's not one to replace my loving gran.

A few weeks went by and Edith told James, Edward and me that Mum had left her house and furniture to her and Uncle Cyril. That was no surprise, what shocked us all was the fact that Edith got the lion's share. Edith had the option of buying Uncle Cecil's share from him at probate price which virtually meant that Edith got three quarters, and poor old Uncle Cecil only got the remainder. I know that Mum wasn't overly keen on Aunty Dorothy, but I didn't think that she'd go that far, so that Uncle Cecil dipped out as well. According to Edith, the will was made out like that, because Mum didn't want Edith to be homeless. Well maybe that was the case in the earlier years, before Dad won the casket, but the way I saw it in 1972, Dad and Edith were a hell of a lot better off than Uncle Cecil and Aunty Dorothy. Edward called me aside and said, 'If mum and dad leave you and James a bigger share than me, I'll bloody well dig up their bones and kick them all over Brisbane'.

I laughed and said, 'Well I wasn't going to tell you, but you'd better learn how to use a pick and shovel'.

That same day Edith called me into her bedroom and said, 'I know that you still owed your Grandmother one hundred dollars when she died, so you now owe it to me, and you can pay it to me as soon as you can'.

I looked at her in total disbelief and I thought to myself, is she fair dinkum? When she didn't smile, I said, 'Lady, whilst my arsehole points to the ground, I will never pay you that money. I did owe Mum the money but the debt died with her. I don't owe you a bloody penny.'

She told me that I should show her some respect and that I did owe her the money. To which I replied, 'I only show respect to people who deserve it and you don't and if you honestly think that I owe you Mum's money you can take me to court. And even if you won, I still wouldn't pay you.'

She stood there with her mouth agape as I stamped out of her room.

Frank and I did find a way of paying Mum what we owed her. We paid for the inscription on her headstone and for the white marble stones to cover her grave. Every year until we shifted out of Brisbane in 1988, both Frank and I would regularly maintain the grave. We'd paint it and keep the weeds off it, but we would have done that anyhow. Uncle Cecil would also go and visit the grave as often as he could, until he had a stroke. Edith on the other hand only lived about a mile away from the cemetery and never visited the grave more than three times. Not even when we offered to drive her.

That Christmas Dad drove Edith over to give us our Christmas presents. Dad had not spoken to Frank for a couple of years, so he sat in the car while Edith played the Santa Claus role of delivering the gifts. Whilst Edith and I talked Frank disappeared momentarily. As soon as I noticed he had gone I looked outside to see him and Dad standing on the footpath talking. I was thrilled out of my brain when they both walked in and Dad said, 'It's all settled, you'll be coming up home for Christmas.'

The kids threw their arms around their grandfather whom they absolutely idolised and Vivian said, 'Does this mean we'll get more presents then?'

We had the best Christmas we had had in a long time and I recall saying to everyone, 'Mum mightn't be here in person, but I reckon she's still acting as the peace maker'.

Chapter 38

Just a Change of Scenery

Two months later, we finally signed the contract to sell the house. Around the same time, I resigned my position from Sunday Sun.

There was not going to be any problem with the sale this time, because a real estate firm had bought it as an investment. As I didn't have a very high opinion of real estate agents, I thought it only fitting that another one should get lumbered with the joint. In all the time we had owned the place, I had regarded it as the biggest jinx on this planet.

We bought a similar style home just around the corner from Dad and Edith's home. I had enrolled Vivian and Heather in their local state school twelve months earlier, because Vivian had had problems with at least three schools on the Southside near where we lived. She had attended the local school, but she didn't like it there. I enrolled her in the nearest Catholic School but to no avail, she wasn't happy there either. Then I enrolled her at Moorooka State school, the biggest school in the area where she insisted the headmaster was an old pig. I must confess that I found him to be a very unapproachable man. I think he thought himself to be well above everyone else because he had written a school textbook. I never read the book, but someone had told me it was quite good.

Heather's first day at Moorooka State School was memorable. She had put on a very brave front for weeks pretending to look forward to going. On the morning of her first day, I had tried desperately to convince her that she was going to have an absolutely wonderful time. We arrived there with plenty of time to spare and we watched all the other children arriving. Some were laughing and playing others had a few tears but were easily comforted by their mothers. Heather just sat watching and waiting, not commenting or smiling, she just sat there as if she was watching a movie on television. The teacher called us over, I signed the necessary papers and got the list of the schoolbooks she would need and then it was time to say goodbye. I gave her a big kiss and cuddle and she responded in the manner she was accustomed to, she just turned away and walked with the teacher holding her hand.

I stood there watching as they walked up the stairs to the classroom and true to form, they got halfway up and Heather's little foot slipped on the step and she stumbled and fell on the third step. She didn't fall hard it was just a momentary stumbling motion. But that was all she needed to let forth her every emotion. She screamed, kicked, punched, roared like a bull and threw the biggest, loudest tantrum I've ever seen anyone throw. I ran to help her and the teacher, but the teacher was so frazzled that she ordered me to go. I ran to the car with tears stinging my eyes I was so upset for the poor little bugger. But by the time I opened the door, I was absolutely pissing myself with laughter as I visualised the scene again, in my mind. I thought to myself those poor bloody teachers they have no idea what they're in for.

Heather was not only a very unusual child, (to say the least) she could be very lovable one minute and extremely chokeable the next. Vivian informed me that afternoon when I picked them up, that Heather had cried almost non-stop all day. Vivian had gone over to Heather's classroom during the lunch break and she said, 'Mum, I could hear her from the playground, and as soon as she saw me, she screamed louder begging me to take her home to you. The teacher told me to get out, and I had to run as fast as I could'.

I almost choked myself trying to stop the tears and laughter at the same time. I felt so sorry for her, but I could still see the funny side as well.

Vivian would often come home and tell me about the awful things Heather had done at school and no matter what I said or did to Heather she didn't seem to care. One afternoon as we were driving home, I could smell something burning. When I looked around to see where the smell was coming from, I discovered she had found a box of matches and had proceeded to burn the upholstery of the car.

Vivian would also tell me about the other naughty kids in her own class. One particular afternoon she told me that one girl used to ring people at random and threaten to kill them if they didn't send her one thousand dollars. Reluctantly, Vivian gave me the child's name and I rang her parents. The child's father answered and he listened intently to what I had to tell him and I was absolutely shocked at his response.

He said, 'Mrs Williams, I think you'll find that you've got the wrong child. It's not my daughter who's been making the phone calls, you'd be best to ask your daughter for more information'.

I thought, this guy is in denial about his kid, he obviously doesn't want to believe that she'd do something like that. I tried to talk some sense into him. I don't know what it was that he said to me that made the penny drop that he was giving me a subtle hint that it was Vivian whom he thought was the culprit, however, I still thought, this bastard's as mad as a hatter.

I hung up and pondered his words for a moment and Vivian was very anxious to learn what had been said. I looked at her innocent face and thought no way, she wouldn't have done something that bloody stupid. But without even knowing what I was going to say I blurted out, 'You bloody silly little fool, why in the name of God did you ring those poor defenceless people for?'

With all the innocence of a newborn baby she denied having made any of the calls.

I was so angry I grabbed her arm dragged her over to me and I slapped her backside about six times as hard as my hand could wallop her. She burst into tears and kept saying, 'I'm sorry, Mummy, I won't do it again. I promise I won't do it again.'

I was so disappointed in her I could have cried a gallon of tears. I was also so upset with myself, I had only ever smacked her on her hand on about four occasions previously. Vivian, to me, was the epitome of everything that was good and I would never have believed that she could have been so naughty. Instead of her actions ringing alarm bells in my brain, I dismissed it as being a silly stunt similar to the phone calls that Edward and I made when we were young. Although I put the incident out of my mind, I would, every so often, think back and wonder what ever possessed her into doing that sort of thing. Not once, did I ever imagine that it wasn't a one-off incident. I was so besotted with Vivian that for years I would tell everyone I met, 'Every mother should have a daughter like Vivian'.

I likened our relationship as being not just as a very close mother and daughter, Vivian was also my best friend. She helped me in the house or looked after Heather and Claire like a little mother, whenever I was busy doing other household chores. There was nothing that I wouldn't have done for her or given her, she was just so special to me. Don't get me wrong, I didn't spoil her more than the others. I loved them all equally and I made sure that they all got the same equality. The way I saw things was, Vivian was special because she was my firstborn and because she seemed to be so knowing and mature for her age. Heather on the other hand was always into mischief.

There were many times that I thought that Heather would drive me to an early grave. That was, of course, if her father didn't kill me first.

I recall telling Dr Kenneth one day that Vivian had all of Frank's and my good qualities, Heather had all our bad qualities and Claire had a mixture of both. Considering that Vivian used to be always well behaved, Heather would almost wreck his surgery and that Claire had just kicked him fair in the gut after smiling sweetly at him, he agreed wholeheartedly.

Frank had begun working as a casual butcher through a butcher's employment agency. What I mean by that is, he would work at any butcher shop throughout Brisbane on a casual basis either relieving staff whilst they were on holidays or having days off etc. He proved to be so popular that the fellow who ran the agency once rang me to tell me that Frank was the best in the business. I should have been proud, but I wasn't. Many people used to tell me how lucky I was for having such a lovely bloke for my husband. I used to smile and nod in agreement and underneath my breath I'd say, 'Yeah, he's such a good bloke that he came home the other day and punched the shit out of me again, as he does most weekends'.

I know for a fact that most people thought of me as a sour little bitch and I could almost read their minds ticking over what the hell does such a nice bloke stay with a bitch like that.

Apart from being a top bloke and a good worker, he also knew never to punch me where the bruises could be seen, and he never but never ever hit any of the kids.

Of course, the following day he was always full of remorse and would remain sober for the rest of the week and the best husband and father, until the next time.

He had been offered a number of permanent jobs but he always knocked them back because a casual's pay was higher than a permanent butchering job. But when he was offered a permanent job, he decided to accept because it was only a five-minute drive from our new home and the job included free meat. It was also a big help that Frank really liked Frances the owner of the shop. We had only been in the new house about four months when Frank came home extremely late one Saturday afternoon.

I had taken the kids around to Dad and Edith's place because I thought for sure he would be in a hast tasty mood. I cannot remember what the blue was about, sometimes I only had to sigh deeply, and that was enough to set him off. What I do remember is, grabbing my purse and running for the lick of my life. Anyone who knows me knows that I can't run for love nor money, but this particular day I reckon Frank Landy in his heyday couldn't have beaten me. I literally flew around to Dad's place.

I had only managed to gasp that Frank had thumped the crap out of me, when he pulled up outside in the car. He came charging into the house like a stampeding bull. Edward and Dad stood at the front door and tried to block his path. But Frank just ploughed past them and lunged at me grabbing me, and proceeded to thump me again. Edward grabbed hold of Frank and got him in a head lock, Frank was squirming around trying to free himself by thrashing his arms trying to land as many punches as he could. Edith and I stood back in horror and fear, that Edward wouldn't be able to hold him for very long. I hadn't noticed Dad race past us into his bedroom, but I couldn't help but notice him when he came back with a rifle in his hand.

The next thing, they were all outside on the patio and I could hear a lot of thumping and moaning and groaning. I then saw Frank stumbling up the stairs towards our car and Dad and Edward were directly behind him. Frank's white T-shirt was soaked with blood all over his chest. The three of them stood there just yelling at each other and I could hear Frank saying, 'Okay I'm going, you both won, so I'm going alright?'

I ran up to Dad and took the rifle off him and he told me to put it in his wardrobe. I noticed there was dried blood and hair all over the butt of the rifle and when I got into the bedroom, I saw an old bag on the bed. I wrapped the rifle in the bag and hid it in Dad's wardrobe. I looked out the window and saw Frank was just opening the door of the car when about six cars and an ambulance pulled up. There were at least a dozen detectives running everywhere and I nearly shit my pants, I got such a fright. I ran out and as I passed Edith, I heard her say, 'Oh dear God. What must the neighbours think?'

I yelled as I ran past her, 'Who gives a shit what they think?'

By the time I got outside I heard Dad saying to a couple of the cops, 'No, mate, he wasn't shot, no there was no gun involved.'

Frank had to be coaxed into the ambulance and was eventually driven to the Royal Brisbane Hospital. All the detectives, except two of them, got into their cars and drove off.

The two that remained came into the house and Dad introduced one of them to Edith, Edward and me saying that he was a drinking mate from the club.

I thought, Christ, I don't believe this. The two detectives sat down and Dad offered them a beer, but they declined stating that they were on duty. Dad chuckled and I knew that he felt like saying, that's never stopped you before. They asked me what had happened and I went over the entire scenario of what had transpired after Frank came home from work, until they arrived. But I didn't mention anything about Dad having a rifle.

The detective said, 'We received a call from a fellow who drove past, and he said he saw someone holding a rifle, who had the rifle your father or your brother?'

Before I could open my mouth Dad laughingly said, 'No there wasn't any gun, I admit I gave him a bit of a kicking and although he deserved it, I know I shouldn't have'.

The cop looked at Edward and then at me and asked us if we agreed to that. We both nodded, and the cop looked at Dad and then at his soft leather slippers and said, 'And you would have been wearing those shoes at the time, Rob?'

Dad chuckled again and said, 'Yeah, that's right I haven't had time to change them.'

The cops closed their little note books and said,

'Well that about wraps it up, it sounds as if the little bastard got what he deserved, we'll leave you good people to have your dinner'.

After they had gone Vivian and Heather came up from under the house and said, 'Have your friends gone, Grandad?'

Edward rolled his eyes skyward at me and shook his head and said, 'Its pitiful isn't it?'

Claire had been asleep in her cot in my old bedroom and none of the kids were even aware how close they were of having a potential catastrophe ruin their lives an hour or so before hand. After dinner I drove the kids home gave them their baths and put them to bed. I had my shower and settled down to watch a bit of TV and I nearly had heart failure when I heard someone creeping up the front stairs. I peered out through the drawn curtains and could see a car parked in the driveway with its headlights on and I saw the shadowy figure of someone standing near the front door. I called out asking who was there and a familiar voice said, 'It's me can you let me in and give me some dough I've got to pay the cabbie'.

I felt like saying, 'Stiff shit. Go and bite your arse'.

However, I didn't, I opened the door and I had never seen such a pathetic sight, as he was that night. After I paid the cab driver, I walked in to see Frank struggling to take his blood-soaked shirt over his bandaged head.

All I could say was, 'Now you know how it feels'.

He had had his head bandaged by the ambulance bearers and had sat in the emergency room for about four hours waiting to have his head stitched. He decided to come home because he got sick of waiting. When I looked at the wound a couple of days later, I estimated he would have needed at least ten stitches. One thing I must say, Frank had the constitution of at least ten oxen, and he never missed one day of work due to the bashing he got.

A few weeks went by and even though he still had a few drinks he somehow managed to control his temper with me. Not so with Edward though. Vivian and Heather would go around to Edith's place of an afternoon after school, if I thought I might be late getting home.

On one such afternoon Frank pulled up outside Edith's place just as Edward was about to drive away. Edward had accused Vivian of taking his two slices of bread a few days earlier and had complained to Frank and I about it. Frank of course had had a couple of beers and hadn't forgiven Edward for getting him in the headlock. Frank stood in front of Edward's car stopping him from leaving, and Frank told him to wake up to himself and an argument ensued.

Fortunately, no punches were thrown, but of course there was a hell of a lot of yelling and shaking of fists. The irony of this incident was, many years later Edward's youngest son Mike recalled witnessing the incident happening. Not only did he recall seeing the event he maintains that it was the same day that Frank got bashed on the head with the rifle butt. The funny part was, Mike never witnessed either incident, because he wasn't there. The bread incident had occurred on a school day and Mike only came over on weekends. Dad had made sure that all the kids were hunted down under the house so that they wouldn't see what was happening, when Frank was bashed with the rifle.

I heard about a clinic called Pav 4, which was the alcoholic's ward at the Royal Brisbane hospital and I suggested that Frank should ring them up and see what they could do for him. He wasn't overly keen on the idea so I took it upon myself to ring them. I was told that they held meetings every Tuesday night starting at 6.30 pm.

I told him I was going along even if he wasn't. I was very surprised when he said he would attend. We had a very interesting evening and were surprised by the amount of people who had turned up.

We were interviewed by Dr Ruth Smout the resident psychiatrist who was the daughter of Sir Raphael and Lady Cilento and the sister of the actress Diane

Cilento. Ruth was a very caring person and told Frank that if he was really interested in helping himself, he'd have to book himself into the hospital for two weeks. At the end of the meeting, he told Ruth that he would book in, and he was told to present himself at the ward on the Friday morning. The following morning, he told Frances that he had to go into hospital and undergo tests and that he needed two weeks off. Frances agreed for his time off and Frank went into the clinic as promised.

Because of the extensive counselling, we were only able to visit him at certain times. Mainly during their group sessions which suited me fine. After the two weeks were over, he came out with all the confidence in the world of being able to stay sober. For the first weekend in our entire marriage, he stayed at home and never even thought of having one sniff of alcohol. On the Monday morning, when he returned to work, Frances told him that he no longer required Frank's services. When Frank asked him why, Frances replied, 'You didn't tell me the real reason you were going into hospital'.

Apparently, he had rung the hospital to find out what ward Frank was in. We think that the word alcoholism may have pricked his own conscience, because he was quite partial to a few too many beers himself. Frank was quite upset at being sacked for attempting to do the right thing, but I kept assuring him that it was probably for the best, and that he had to learn to overcome these hurdles. He went back to working as a casual, and a few weeks later I suggested that we should go away for a week's holiday at Surfer's Paradise. It was in the middle of winter when the price of accommodation was a lot cheaper. It was the first holiday that we had had since we went to Sydney eight years previously. We had an absolutely wonderful time, even though it rained most of the time we were there.

Frank and I continued to go to the Tuesday night meetings and we met some really nice people and we thoroughly looked forward to seeing them each week. Only one of the counsellors was really interested in everyone's well-being. Her approach was, as one of a friend the others were always trying to cause a confrontation between the partners and/or other couples. Mrs Selleck on the other hand, had won everyone's confidence and we all found her to be very approachable. I don't know whose decision it was that Mrs Selleck was taken off us and we ended up with the biggest bitch at the clinic, as our counsellor.

We were sitting in the room waiting for Mrs Selleck and when Miss Sourpuss entered and announced that we had been assigned as her permanent group.

Frank and I stood up and announced we were leaving. There were about twenty others possibly more and each of them stood up and filed out behind us, in protest. We all demanded that Mrs Selleck should be replaced as our counsellor and we were told that it wasn't possible that night, but that they would discuss the possibility for next week. We all went home very disgruntled and the following week when everyone's names were called, we discovered that we had all been split up into other groups. We refused to go in to the group we had been placed with, because Mrs Sourpuss was assigned as our counsellor. Ruth told us that she regarded us as the ringleaders of the rebels. And she said we had to conform or leave. We, along with most of the others, left.

We made arrangements to have a grog free party at our home the following weekend it would have been a fantastic night only for one thing. Frank chose that day to hit the grog for the first time in seven weeks, and he made a complete holy show of himself. I was the only one who was embarrassed and upset, all the others were very sympathetic and supportive towards me, but that didn't ease the hurt one little bit.

From that day on, Frank never brought alcohol in the house he chose the option of hiding his grog and sneaking a drink whenever he could. I think he must have thought what the eye doesn't see, the mind won't know. The one good thing though, the bashings had stopped, and that was a blessing in disguise.

Chapter 39

The Best Boss

Frank was offered a job with a really nice butcher called Steve. Frank had worked for him on a fairly regular basis relieving the other butchers when they had their holidays. Steve was the sort of guy who could have easily got God and the devil to shake hands and let by-gones be by-gones. Everyone liked him, he was funny, cheeky, irreverent and an all-round good bloke. Steve asked me if I would be interested in doing the deliveries of a Friday, and I readily accepted.

The fellow whom Frank had replaced had been doing the deliveries for about three years and he thought he was the best thing since sliced bread earning himself the nickname The Star. Steve warned me that I would no doubt come across some angry customers who were used to The Star doing the deliveries. The Star used to be away for hours because all the old dears wanting him to have a cup of tea or a chat. But there were also about three customers who would ring Steve and complain that the meat order had something wrong with it.

When I arrived back within a couple of hours, Steve thought that I must have gotten lost and had come back for directions. I told him I had finished all the deliveries and he was in shock. He then asked if any of the customers were unkind or rude. I told him truthfully that everyone was extremely kind and all had commented how nice it was to have a lovely young lady doing the deliveries. He rolled his eyes in disbelief, and said, 'Obviously, The Star must have gone walkabout on the deliveries.'

I handed him the money and asked him to count the float and the money I had collected to make sure the tally was right. It was my turn to roll my eyes in disbelief and shock when he said, 'I don't know how much was in the float, if I thought for one minute that you were dishonest, I wouldn't have given you the job.'

I became really angry with him and said, 'You dopey bastard. Don't ever do that to me again, as a human being you're first class, but you'll never make a businessman's arse at this rate.'

Steve looked at me burst out laughing and said, 'Sorry, Mum, I won't do that again.'

Steve had an apprentice Brad and a casual butcher George working for him and the four of them got along like a house on fire. Frank, Steve and Brad always seemed to be into mischief and having fun with the customers.

George on the other hand was at first, very conservative and would often be in the back of the shop shaking his head in disapproval and could be heard tut tutting and muttering, 'That's dreadful.'

But before too long George joined in the fun and quite often shocked the others with some of his suggestions of tomfoolery. Some of the antics they got up to defy explanation.

I walked into the back of the shop one afternoon and became hysterical. Brad was hanging from the steel bar where the carcasses of meat usually hung. His hands were tied behind his back, there was a length of twine around his throat and his face was turning purple. Frank and Steve were laughing and saying, 'Go on smart arse, show us how it's done, ya can't can ya?'

I began screaming, 'Cut him down you mad bastards, he's dying. What in the fuckin' name of God, are you trying to do?'

Frank slashed through the twine with his knife and Brad fell to the floor gasping for air. I somehow managed to get the twine off Brad's hands and it took him quite a few minutes to compose himself. Frank and Steve were laughing and saying things like 'It serves the silly little bastard right. It's his own fault.' and 'That should make him learn, that it's impossible.'

I subsequently learnt that they had all been discussing a case of a prisoner in a NSW jail who had supposedly hung himself. It had been reported in the paper that the prisoner had been found with his hands tied behind his back, and the chair he had stepped on had been kicked over.

Frank and Steve had tried to explain to Brad that they thought the prisoner had been murdered. Brad believed that it was suicide, so Steve and Frank told him to convince them. Brad was unable to prove his point, so Frank and Steve assisted him to swing. God only knows what the outcome would have been if I hadn't walked in when I did. As far as I was (and still am) concerned, they both should have been certified for their actions.

I still shake my head in amazement when I think about that day. On another occasion, I walked in to discover Steve and Frank standing over the barrel of brine. Both of them were in fits of laughter. I said, 'What's going on?'

All of a sudden Brad's head emerged from the barrel coughing and spluttering.

Frank and Steve had decided to have some 'fun' and so they just shoved him into the brine and held him down. The reason they were laughing was they could see the whites of Brad's eyes. He didn't have the chance to close them as he went in.

Brad was such a lovely young man albeit somewhat gullible and naïve especially to Frank and Steve's whacky ideas. Fortunately, he managed to survive their madness and probably because of, instead of in spite of, he gave butchering away and became a paramedic.

Frank had worked at the shop for about two years when Steve decided to buy another little shop. Much to our surprise, Steve asked Frank to be manager of the shop. That was one of the worst decisions Steve ever made. The shop was a non-starter and Frank had too much time on his hands and he began drinking during the day. I felt as if I was sitting on the precipice of a cliff with bundles of gelignite around me and someone was about ready to light the wicks.

Fortunately, Steve sold the second shop within twelve months and Frank went back to the main shop. But I think Frank blamed himself for the failure of the second shop.

We sold the house and bought a big four bedroom home six kilometres away. Most people, when they sell and buy a new home, everything falls into place smoothly. Not so with us. As soon as we signed the contract to sell, I phoned different agents about homes and none of them seemed too keen on taking us around to look at any on the market.

One fellow had said to me that there was a house in Long Street, but he didn't give me the number of the house. I drove up and down the street and as the name of the street implies, it is a long street and it's divided into three sections. I went up and down each section at least three times but none of the homes had a for sale sign outside. A few days later another real estate agent took us to the house and I fell in love with it and we signed the papers. The following afternoon as I drove back from seeing the solicitor, the rain was so blinding that I couldn't see beyond the bonnet of the car. That rain was the beginning of the 1974 Brisbane floods. For the next few days, we were housebound whilst we watched our surrounding area go under water. Our suburb was one of the worst flooded areas and we were very concerned that the house we had signed up for may also be badly affected. As luck had it, the water came up to six inches below the floorboards. The laundry, toilet garage and spare room which were under the house were completely submerged however, the rest of the home was unaffected.

We had the option of pulling out of the sale, but we were satisfied that the house was intact. Somehow or other there was a discrepancy of a week in the dates of the sale of the home and the date we were to shift into the new home. The people we were buying the place from wouldn't shift out early for love nor money, and we had to shift into a motel for the week. Fortunately, the sellers were lenient enough to let us store our furniture under the house for that week.

The Forest Lodge Motel's management could be classified as Basil Fawlty and his wife Sibyl, but for one small' difference, Basil and Sibyl were funny, this couple wasn't. Their attitude was to make everyone who stayed at the motel as miserable as possible, and they succeeded. The Saturday we were to shift into our new home couldn't come quick enough, having three young children in a three-room motel suite was bad enough. Having the management walking into the rooms whenever they felt like it was almost reason for murder.

On the Friday night, Frank was extremely late arriving home. It didn't take a genius mind to work out that he had gone to the pub. He finally staggered in at about eight-thirty as I was settling down in front of the TV to watch the event of the year, The Logies. I used to love watching that annual event and I had been looking forward to it for weeks. I had never seen Frank as drunk as he was for quite some time. The frightening thing was, he had driven home in that state. I was very relieved when he went to bed almost immediately. He didn't have a bath or shower, he just flaked out onto the bed fully clothed and I returned to watching TV.

Less than an hour later, I heard this unmerciful scream coming from the bedroom. I raced in as fast as my little legs could take me. By the time I got into the room, I was convinced that an axe murderer had broken into the unit and had felled Frank with one blow. I looked down into his face and all I could see was pure terror, and he screamed another blood curdling screech.

Amelia 'What's the matter with you?'

In another terrified scream

Frank 'Quick, get them off me, Amelia, they're crawling all over me'.

Amelia 'What's crawling over you? There's nothing there.'

Frank (screaming again) 'All the spiders, see them, they're everywhere.'

I brushed him down, told him they had gone and I went back to the TV. I had no sooner settled down and he was screeching again. This scene was enacted out, over and over for the best part of an hour. I was exasperated and exhausted so

I sat down alongside him for the rest of the night and every time he started to scream I brushed his imaginary spiders off him.

Many times, I have thought about that night, and each time I remember it, I always wonder, who out of the two of us was the bigger nit-wit? Admittedly he was in the horrors from alcohol and imagined he had spiders crawling all over him. But I was cold stone sober and had all my faculties intact, yet I sat there all night, brushing imaginary spiders off a drunken fool.

The following day he was as right as rain, he showered early and went to work as if nothing was amiss, leaving me, feeling like death reheated several times over. We had only been in the house a week when the real estate salesman who had sent me to Long Street without giving me the house number, came knocking on the door.

On answering the door, he bombarded me with abuse calling me the biggest bitch he had ever met. I was stunned beyond belief. He went on to say that I should have bought the house from him considering that it was he who had sent me to the house in the first place. I asked him how he had come to that conclusion, considering that he had only given me the street name and that there weren't any signs. He told me that I should have come back to him and asked him for the number. In the course of the conversation he told me that he could have done with the commission because his home had been completely submerged in the floods. I think that this information was supposed to make my cold heart soften and that I should feel very sorry for him. Instead, I looked him straight in the face and said, 'Well, mate, if you had done your job properly in the first place, you would have had the commission. And if you go around to people's homes calling them bitches, God obviously thought you deserved to lose your home, so it serves yourself right.' I slammed the door in his face and went inside and shook like a leaf in both anger and fear.

On Mother's Day of that year (1974) I awoke feeling like death warmed up several times over. I could hardly lift my head off the pillow but when I did manage to, I was violently ill. Frank was not impressed at all. Whenever I became ill, he always got in a very shitty mood with me. I think it may have been that he was at a loss as to what to do whenever I was ill. He'd get angry with himself, which he would then turn it around onto me. I had to practically beg him to ring the doctor.

I would have rung him myself, but I was so ill and dehydrated I couldn't even walk the twenty steps to the phone. Our usual doctor was not on duty, being a

Sunday, and a locum arrived. He said that he had been called to a couple of other cases like me that day and he said that there was obviously a twenty-four hour virus going around. He gave me an injection to stop the vomiting and I said, 'I can put up with the vomiting but the headache was too severe for me to handle.'

He assured me that the needle would make me sleep and that when I awoke, the headache would be gone as well. By the time I awoke some four hours later, the headache and vomiting had gone, however, I felt as if I had been run over by a steamroller. I felt so washed out and completely drained. Normally I would be only too pleased to have visitors, but not that day. I was somewhat upset to hear Jenny and Timmy talking and laughing out in the lounge room. We had met Jen and Tim at Pav 4 two years previously and had become good friends and had had many get-togethers during the past two years. I struggled out of bed, got dressed and went out to join them. The look on Frank's face was enough to tell me that he was really pissed off with me as if he thought I had been bunging a sickie on. When they eventually left later in the day, Frank actually accused me of overdramatising my illness, just so that I could have an extra camp. (sleep)

He said, 'If you were so bloody sick, ya wouldn't have come out and talked and laughed ya silly bloody head off, ya would've stayed in bed.'

I tried to protest and explain that I didn't like to ignore our guests, but it was like talking to a brick wall. As it turned out, my overdramatised illness wasn't a twenty-four hour virus. It was a migraine and unfortunately, they became a regular occurrence every two to three weeks for the next twenty-two years.

From that day on, I had to live with a new fear. Each night before I went to bed, I would worry about waking with the worst pain any human could possibly endure. Many times, if I could have gotten hold of a gun, I would have blown my brains out whilst suffering a migraine attack. Only a person who has suffered from severe migraine could know how agonising and debilitating they are.

Chapter 40

Land of the Long Black Cloud

A few months went by and Frank received a very healthy tax return. He had been taxed as a single man and had gotten most of it back. Frank insisted that I take the girls to New Zealand for a three week holiday, to visit Tim and Andrea whom I hadn't seen for nine years. Frank didn't want to go to New Zealand he wanted to go down to Sydney to meet up with Tom who had been living there for the past couple of years. I knew instinctively that he had intentions of getting himself blind for the entire time he was there, but I wasn't the least bit concerned. I was going over to New Zealand to see my friends and that was all that mattered. As it turned out, I couldn't get a flight from Brisbane to Wellington, I had to fly out from Sydney on a Thursday in the September of 74.

We drove to Sydney and we had a few days there together before our flight left. Tom's accommodation was a huge brick garage that had been converted into a lovely, homey flat. You'd think that three adults and three kids would be very cramped, but it wasn't. There were two good size bedrooms and a combined lounge/kitchen/dining area. Tom made himself a bed on the sofa and Frank and I had the main bedroom and the girls shared the other bedroom. The flat was covered in honeysuckle and each morning we would be awakened by the many birds that came to feast on the nectar.

I thought it was an idyllic place to live. Tom on the other hand, didn't share my enthusiasm for nature and called the birds a fuckin' curse. He certainly hadn't lost his masterful grasp of the English language. We saw more of Sydney in the few days we spent with Tom than what we had seen on our first trip there. Tom arranged for a babysitter to look after the girls and took Frank and I to Kings Cross.

As far as I was concerned, we had entered the world of Sodom and Gomorrah and I walked between Frank and Tom, holding onto their arms for grim death. I was beyond fear I was in total terror. My eyes widened with every step we took as the men standing outside the different doorways yelled at us to come in and view the varied sized vaginas of the women on display. I was not only in sheer terror. I was also in deep shock at what they were saying. Both Tom and Frank were pissing themselves with laughter. The more they laughed, the tighter I gripped their arms.

It didn't seem to bother anyone that I had a bodyguard either side of me, I was approached by a couple of men at different times to go with them and they would show me paradise. I jokingly said to Tom, 'Well, the silly bitch has won a couple of hearts.'

To which he replied, 'Yeah, but didn't ya notice that both of them were pissed out of their brains.'

I was just about to beg Frank and Tom to get me out of this den of iniquity when one of the doormen yelled out to me, 'Come on in and see the man with the eighteen-inch penis. Frank and Tom both laughed out loud and we walked a few more steps before I turned to them and said, 'Come on, this I have got to see.'

Both of them absolutely roared with laughter and couldn't believe it when I steered them over to the ticket box. We had to pay three dollars each to watch a fellow parade around on stage dragging and swinging a paper-mache penis around and above his head. No sooner had we entered, I wanted to leave. But to Frank and Tom's disbelief, I also wanted to complain to management and ask for our money back.

I have always had an inherent fear of heights, so it came as no surprise to Frank and Tom when we went to Luna Park and I refused to go on the Big Dipper. We walked around the park enjoying all there was to see from the safety of the ground. We had fairy floss, ice creams, hot dogs and drinks and the kids had a wonderful day. We were getting ready to leave and Frank said,

'Would you like to go on the scenic tour before we go? It's a little train ride and you can see a lot of the sights including the harbour and the Opera House'.

Well I certainly couldn't miss seeing that, that was for sure. Tom stayed on the ground minding Heather and Claire whilst Vivian, Frank and I jumped onto the train. As the train started, Frank and Vivian started to giggle I thought to myself, I'm pleased that they're enjoying themselves. We started to ascend and I looked down at Tom and he was fit to kill himself with laughter and Heather and Claire began to scream out, 'Mum, Mum, Mummeeeeee.'

Then the realisation hit me that we weren't on a scenic tour at all, we were on the dreaded Big Dipper. I always made sure that the children never heard me swear when they were young. But on this occasion, I couldn't contain myself I screamed out top note, 'I'm going to kill you pack of bastards if it's the last thing I do.'

Then we reached the top and we started to descend. The faster we went the louder I screamed. The louder I screamed the louder Vivian and Frank laughed. The funny part was, I never saw a thing I had my mouth wide open screaming, and my eyes were shut tight every inch of the way.

On arrival at Wellington airport, I was beside myself with excitement and anticipation of seeing Tim and Andrea again. I walked across the tarmac and I caught a glimpse of Andrea's face as the glass doors opened and closed as another passenger entered the airport lounge. My immediate thought was, Oh no. What the hell have I done? I've wasted all this money to come over to visit someone who doesn't want to see me.

Andrea and I had been corresponding at least once a month for the entire nine years since she had left Australia to go to New Zealand. As far as I was concerned, I wasn't going to visit friends, I was going to visit my sister and brother. I felt closer to them than I did to my own siblings. We had shared so many of our innermost thoughts and secrets. There was only ten days difference in our birthdays although I was a year older and Andrea and Tim had been married a week before Frank and I had. We had even had to have hysterectomies within weeks of each other. We had so many things in common, it was uncanny.

By the time I reached the glass doors, I had convinced myself that I must be overtired. I had caught the flu a couple of days before I was due to fly out, and had to spend the day before in bed. I think Frank was getting a bit concerned that I might not be well enough to fly, not that he was worried about me he was worried that I was going to spoil his fun. I was convinced that I was allowing my imagination to run amok.

As the glass doors opened again, I greeted Tim and Andrea with as much love as I could show. Tim gave me a big bear hug and welcomed me warmly, telling me I hadn't changed a bit. Andrea was very reserved in her greeting and I knew then, that what I had witnessed from the tarmac was correct. It was painfully obvious that she was almost green with jealousy. I had taken the trouble to dress in my best frock and even if I do say so myself, I looked pretty good for an old, almost thirty-one year old, mother of three. Andrea had certainly aged and her mode of dress was bordering on poverty. The thought went through my mind that she probably resents the fact that I can afford to fly over to visit her and also bring my kids, but she couldn't afford to fly over to Australia, As we drove along

the motorway to Upper Hutt in their old Kombi van, Andrea exclaimed 'I don't
know what we'll have for tea tonight.'

I suppressed a little smirk whilst thinking, she must be arranging a get
together for me to meet all her brothers and her father, and she's pretending that
there's nothing special going to happen. I knew one thing was for sure, that if the
shoe had've been on the other foot and I was welcoming her back to Australia, I
would have been planning our welcome home meal for weeks before her arrival.
I think you could've knocked me over when the realisation hit me that nothing
had been planned at all. In fact, on arriving at their home, she took three pieces
of Haddock from the freezer and she boiled them almost to a mushie pulp along
with some mashed potato for Tim, Andrea and me and the kids were given baked
beans on toast. I sarcastically said to myself, welcome to New Zealand, this is
going to be one hell of a fun holiday.

The next three weeks were an absolute nightmare, and I would never wish
the same on anyone, no matter how badly they had treated me. That night after
dinner, I volunteered to make a cup of coffee. I had only been in the kitchen
a short while when Tim came in to see if I needed a hand. He put his arm
around me to give me a hug and told me how good it was to see me. Tim
had always seemed like a brother to me and I had no hesitation in returning his
hug and telling him how pleased I was to be there. But as the embrace lasted
longer than usual, I began to feel uncomfortable and I thought to myself, this is
not a brotherly/sisterly type hug. The door flew open and Andrea exclaimed, 'I
thought I'd find you two at it.'

I couldn't believe my ears, and I said, 'Turn it up, Tim's just telling me how
pleased he is to see me, there's nothing funny going on.'

Andrea replied, 'Yeah, I know.'

She had said it in a manner that could be taken as either she was only having
a joke or that it was in sarcasm. I knew in my heart that she was being sarcastic,
but rather than cause a scene I pretended that I knew she was only kidding.

From that moment on, I was on my guard with Tim, who was hell bent on
getting me into bed. He even had the audacity and gall to actually promise me
that he would get me into bed before I went back to Australia. As for Andrea, it
was painfully obvious to a blind person that she regarded me as someone not to
be trusted. She worked as a cleaner and was away most days, so I was more than
happy to find my own way around, taking the kids out and amusing ourselves
shopping etc.

After the first week, I became very homesick and I desperately wanted to return home. Frank hadn't enjoyed Sydney and had driven back to Brisbane. Every night he would ring me to make sure that I was okay. I couldn't tell him how I was being treated because the phone was in the central part of the house and everyone in the house could hear every word that was being said. But Frank wasn't completely stupid, he knew that I wasn't having a good time and kept urging me to contact the airlines and get an earlier flight home. Tim's advances were so bad, I made a habit of having Vivian with me every moment that he was in the house. She even slept in the same single bed with me, in order to protect me from him.

One afternoon, Andrea's three brothers came over with a couple of their mates and we all sat around the kitchen table talking and having cups of tea. I remember it as being a really good day and I thoroughly enjoyed their company. We talked about anything and everything, but they were mainly interested in learning about Australia. They had only been young lads when their father had taken them away from Australia.

Reggie of course had come over and stayed with us but had been deported back to New Zealand. But Mark and Troy were eager to learn as much as they could, as they wanted to return to Australia and hopefully find a permanent home back there. We were all laughing and talking about Reggie's hapless exploits and how I had said that I was going to turn the hose on him to get him to have a shower, when Andrea came through the back door. Her face was as black as thunder and she started screaming at us all, 'Get out of my fucking house, ya pack of fucking bastards, this isn't a fucking brothel.'

I jumped up and said, 'What did you say?'

She scowled at me and scurried out through the door into the lounge room. Reggie and Mark stood up and I said, 'No, don't leave, none of us have done anything wrong, I'll sort this out.'

I went into her and asked her what the hell was eating her. She said, 'I don't like those fuckin', thieving bastards in my home, especially not that fuckin' Mark.'

When I asked her why not, she said, 'He only wants to root Chrystal.'

I looked at her in total disbelief and said, 'Are you fair dinkum? We're talking about your nineteen year old brother and your eleven year old daughter do you honestly believe he would touch her?'

She sheepishly replied, 'N ... no, don't take any notice of me, I'm just on edge at the moment, but will you ask them to leave, I'm not in the mood for them now.'

I went back and said to all of them, 'She's a froot loop short of a breakfast, and if I were you, I would get out whilst you can. If she starts anything with me, I'll put her out of her misery.'

Troy said, 'I can usually calm her down I'll go in and have a word with her.'

Whilst he was in talking to her, Reggie and Mark told me that she had been acting strange for quite a while, Troy came out a few minutes later and told the others that it was a waste of time and that they had all better go. It really made me wonder, how she could present herself in her letters for nine years, as the person I once knew and in reality, she was a complete out and out kook.

I thought back to when I first met Andrea and how she had accused her own father as being a sex offender to her as a child, and how she had maintained that Don (her father) had broken Chrystal's arm when she was only two years old. I had met Ben when he came over to visit Tim, Andrea and the two kids. He came over with his arms filled with presents for them all. He worked on the boats and was often away for weeks at a time, I learnt from Chrystal and Richard. Both children absolutely adored their grandfather and he obviously thought the world of them.

Ben was a happy-go lucky sort of fellow and I remember him with great affection. My three kids were always very wary of people they didn't know very well, but he had them clambering to sit on his lap and they were only too willing to call him Grandpa Don in next door to no time at all. I found it extremely difficult to believe that this man could ever think about harming a child, let alone touching them inappropriately.

After I had met him a few times, he came up to me whilst I was alone and said, 'If I can get Chrystal over to Australia would you look after her?'

I, believing that he meant that he wanted to send her on a holiday agreed. He said, 'Good, I thought you'd look after her well, the poor little bugger is treated like shit over here.'

I think my eyes widened as large as saucers when I realised that he wanted to smuggle his granddaughter away from his only daughter. In the three weeks I was in Andrea's home I witnessed Chrystal being thrashed with the jug cord by Andrea on several occasions. I also saw Richard being punched severely all over his body and head. I intervened a few times and told Andrea to wake up to herself and I came within a hair's breadth of punching her lights out.

Reggie and his girlfriend Kate hastily decided on the second Sunday I was there, that they would get married the following Thursday. At first, I thought that they were only joking, but I soon learnt that they meant business. If you know the true meaning of chaos and farcical, you'll get some idea what this wedding planning was like.

On the night before the wedding, Andrea expected everyone to attend a school concert that had Richard playing a tree. I'm going to be as kind as I possibly can here, to know Richard, is to know that his acting ability was to say the least spot on. It would be only fair to say that poor little Richard had had far too many punches to the scone, because he was as thick as two planks. So, for him to be chosen to play a tree, was, in my estimation a true characterisation.

Kate and I sat and suffered the first half of the concert and we stifled our laughter with great style and dignity. I leant over to Kate and said, 'This is downright cruelty of the worst kind to us poor dumb animals, and I really think that your last night of freedom should be spent in a better place than this.'

She agreed wholeheartedly and I said, 'Andrea's not going to be too happy about this, but who gives a stuff?'

I leant over to Andrea and announced that Kate and I were going to the pub to celebrate her last night of freedom. I added that I'd leave the kids there with her and that we'd be back before the concert finished. We took off like Bondi trams, leaving Andrea there to babysit on her own and boy was she fuming.

We found a little pub and I fronted the bar as if I knew what I was doing. The truth was I had never been into a bar on my own, in my life. I had waited outside plenty, for Frank on many occasions, but to actually order something, was a totally new experience for me. Andrea had told me what to order, and when the barman asked me what I wanted, I said with all the bravado I could muster:

'Two fluffy ducks and you'd better make them strong, because she's getting married in the morning and I'm going back to Australia on Sunday.'

I went over to the table where Kate was sitting and the barman came over with the fluffy ducks and another glass of liquid, which he put down in front of me. He said, 'If you're a fair dinkum Aussie, you'll drink this in one go.'

I said, 'What is it?'

He replied, 'Never mind what it is, but if you're a fair dinkum Aussie, you'll throw it down your neck in one hit and I promise you that if you can still stand after drinking it, your drinks are on the house for the night.'

After assuring me that it wasn't poison nor was it spiked (whatever that meant) I tossed it down and it nearly took my breath away but it felt good. I then stood up and said, 'Well I've passed the test, so now tell me what it was.'

He replied, 'It's a concoction with cointreau, I used to drink it with the blacks in Arnhem Land.'

Well by the end of the night Kate and I were feeling no pain what so ever. We were beyond caring what the rest of the world was doing, especially Andrea. We finally staggered out of the pub at about 10.30 pm and we wended our way to the Civic Centre where the concert was being held. On our way there, I saw a beautiful garden absolutely filled to brimming with beautiful tulips. I was hell bent on picking them for Kate's bouquet. The only thing that stopped me was Kate telling me that if I was caught, I'd probably get three months in jail. I didn't believe her, but I thought I couldn't risk another day in New Zealand let alone three more bloody months.

When we caught sight of Andrea's face, both Kate and I collapsed onto the footpath in total hysterics. Believe me she was far from being amused. She was fit to be tied, but she knew not to say too much to me, because I had had more than enough of her nonsense to last me ten lifetimes.

The wedding, surprisingly enough, went off quite well, considering that the least amount of preparation went into its planning. Unfortunately, not everything went extra smooth. The reception was held at Leanne's home, Kate's eldest sister. Leanne started to cause a bit of a ruckus by trying to throw her weight around. Reggie had gone to the pub to get another keg, and Leanne had said something to Kate and Kate burst into tears. I figured that I was only going to be in the country another two days before I left for good, and I'd probably never see this snotty nosed bitch again. So, I let forth and told her off in front of everyone. You could have heard a pin drop after I went off the brain, then someone said, 'Good on ya love, it's about time someone put her in her place.'

With that Leanne took off and never returned. When Reggie returned, I told him I had some bad news to report and I told him what had happened. Well you should have heard him he was over the moon with delight. He patted me on the back and told me how pleased and proud he was of me. He said he thought it was the best news he'd ever heard.

On the last night I was in New Zealand, Tim and Andrea threw a party. Not to farewell me, but to christen the completion of their new lounge room extension. I met a number of people that night who were completely shocked to find out that I had been there for the past three weeks. Some of them had heard of Andrea's friend in Australia, but none knew that I had come over to visit. I decided to really let my hair down that night and I got myself absolutely blotto on Harvey Wall Bangers, (a very lethal concoction of Galliano Vodka and Orange.)

The worst part about me getting legless is, I always have total recall the next day. I remember only too well counting the Harvey Wall Bangers, but I lost count after sixteen. Then trying to teach Troy to Jive and Rock and Roll in the fifties style. He almost had heart failure and died of embarrassment when I jumped on either side of his hips and for the finale. I did the splits with my legs either side of his waist. Then to an upbeat version of Ma He's Makin' Eyes at Me by Lena Zavaroni,. I did a very sexy routine whereby I stripped down to my bra, much to the delight of all the guys there, who were chanting, 'Go, Amelia.'

I knew that I wouldn't have stripped down any further, but I was quickly brought back to reality when I heard Vivian's voice call out, 'No, Mum, that's enough, please don't take any more off.'

I was proud of myself, that not once during my stay had I complained to anyone about how miserable I was and how horrible Tim and Andrea had treated me. To add fuel to the fire, Tim had tried to humiliate me by crying me down for being an Australian on several occasions. It came as a complete surprise when Tim said to me that he thought I was a bloody good sport for not retaliating and for copping all his shit without one complaint. But instead of being gracious at his compliment I replied, 'That's what it means to be a True Blue Aussie, we can cop all the shit from you peasants because we know that we're head and shoulders above all you riff raff and that we'll always win in the end.'

Sunday finally arrived when I was to fly back home, I had been counting the days from the time I had arrived in New Zealand. Apart from the fact that Tim and Andrea hadn't made me feel welcome, I had been chief cook and bottle washer for the entire three weeks. Not only had I cooked and cleaned every day, I had supplied the food for the entire household. The first day I had bought T-bone steaks and Richard and Chrystal didn't even know what they were.

It was painfully obvious that they weren't used to eating meat, other than mince, stew or sausages. So, not only was I worn out from doing all the housework and cooking, I was also as poor as a pauper. I had exactly three dollars left in my wallet. I got up bright and early and prepared everybody's breakfast and I couldn't help but think, Thank God, this will be the last time I do this. Tim and Andrea ate their breakfast and Andrea made a phone call. She was on the phone for at least half an hour and on hanging up she proceeded to issue orders for Chrystal to do the housework. About an hour went by and Tim asked me what time my flight was. I told him it was due to depart at two pm and I asked him what time we would be leaving to go to the airport. It was ten minutes to eleven o'clock at that stage, and I knew we'd have to leave within the hour as it was a good forty-five to sixty-minute drive to Wellington airport. Andrea piped up and said, 'We're not taking you to the airport we're going on a picnic.'

I looked at Tim, and he gave me a look as if to say, Sorry, I've got no say in the matter. I could feel the tears welling in the back of my eyes and they began to sting the backs of my eyeballs. But I was determined not to allow them to spill down my cheeks. Andrea walked away and I turned to Chrystal and asked her for her grandfather's phone number. As I dialled, I said a silent prayer, Please God, let Don be home, don't let me down PLEASE.

I whispered a very grateful Thank You, when Don finally answered the call. In my most, calmest voice I asked Don if he could arrange for Mark or Reggie to pick me up and take me to the airport. I explained that they had told me they were going to the airport to say goodbye to me, anyway. When he asked why Tim and Andrea weren't taking me, I simply told him that they were going on a picnic. He bombarded me with questions of how I had been treated during my stay, if they had taken me to see any of the sights, had I enjoyed being there etc. I answered truthfully that I had had a lousy time, that I had been treated like a leper and that the only place they had taken me to, apart from the school concert, was to deliver a lounge suite to Palmerston North. He said, 'Christ almighty, love, why didn't you say something? Look, if you like, you can stay at my home and I'll get the boys to take you around and show you all of New Zealand.'

The tears just flowed out of my eyes like a torrential downpour. And all I could manage to say was, 'Thank you, but I can't, I want to go home.'

He assured me he would get a car to me within half an hour even if it meant he'd have to beg, borrow or steal one to get me to the airport. Less than ten minutes later, Don, Mark, Reggie and young Troy pulled up outside in two cars. Mark's fiancé Michelle, and Kate were with them. Andrea came out and told them all that they weren't welcome in her home and I had to struggle with my entire luggage down the stairs and driveway to get them to the cars. Mark started to abuse his sister by calling her a slimy slut and every name he could think of. I intervened and told him not to worry about it saying to him that blood was thicker than water. He screamed at her, 'That fuckin' moll isn't a sister of mine.'

As I walked down their driveway for the last time Andrea put her head out the window and screamed at me, 'I hope Frank shoots you ya stuck up moll.'

I shook my head in disbelief at her but couldn't resist saying, 'He won't, my husband loves me, but yours doesn't love you, he loves me too.'

She then screeched top note, 'I hope the plane falls out of the sky ya bloody bitch.'

I smiled sweetly at her and said, 'So do I and I hope it lands in your big, fat, ugly, mouth.'

Don and the rest of them burst into fits of laughter, and I walked to the car with my head held high and a smug smirk on my face. We wended our way to the airport and Mark and Michelle pointed out places of interest on the way. Unfortunately, I didn't see too many of them because I was crying too hard. They tried to talk me into staying another two weeks so that they could show me all the places, but that only made me cry longer and harder. On our arrival at the airport, I discovered another two couples had arrived to farewell me. Don had rung them as well and told them about my plight. I had met them at Kate's wedding, but the funny part was, I couldn't remember meeting them. I went to the check-in counter to get my boarding pass and I almost died of shock. I learnt I had to pay a ten-dollar departure tax to get out of the country. I felt so embarrassed having to ask Don to lend me the money. He didn't seem to mind in the least, in fact he was only too pleased that he was able to help me in any way that he could.

By the time the last boarding call was announced, part of me was urging me to stay and the other part was cheering that I was finally leaving. Naturally, I was bawling my guts out as I kissed and hugged everyone goodbye. But I couldn't help but laugh when Troy said, 'One thing's for sure, we won't forget you in a hurry, because we've never seen anyone who can cry as much as you.'

By the time I got back to Brisbane, I thought I had cried myself out, but as soon as I saw Frank standing at the airport with a big bunch of flowers in his arms, I started up again. I sent Don the ten dollars I had borrowed from him, the following day. I also sent a telegram which said, 'Arrived safely. The plane didn't fall, thanks again for your kindness.'

Michelle and Mark got married the following May. I received an invitation but I was unable to go. I would've given my eyeteeth to turn up just to see the look on Andrea's face. I was saddened to learn that Don died on Michelle and Mark's first wedding anniversary. He had developed diabetes and had had to have both his legs amputated after developing blood clots. I think the shock of losing both his legs was too much of a shock for him to contend with. He had left everything to his three sons to be divided equally and Andrea got ZIP. However, she contested the will and three years later the courts ruled that she should inherit bugger all. When I heard that news, I had the best laugh I had had in a long time. I hope that Don's decision of not including Andrea in his will was because of how she had treated me. But in all probability, it was because of the way she had ill-treated Chrystal. Unfortunately, Don never achieved his wish of sending Chrystal over to Australia. Perhaps it was only a fairy tale dream, but I know that Don's heart was in the right place. Chrystal certainly deserved a better life than what she had been given. I only wish that he could have sent her to me, even if it was only for a short holiday.

I often think of the rude crude and ugly story Don told at Kate's wedding reception. When Don lived in Australia, he worked in the Mount Isa mines. He said that on one particular day Prime Minister Bob Menzies (Pig Iron Bob, as he was known) went there to address the workers and give them a political speech. There were quite a few hundred men standing there waiting to hear Menzies speak, Don was one of them. Menzies started off with, 'I am a Country Member.'

Before he could say another word, Don yelled out to him, 'Yes, we remember.'

Everyone absolutely roared with laughter, but I think I laughed the loudest and longest.

Michelle and Mark arrived in Australia soon after the distribution of the will and have made Australia their home. Andrea came over to Australia for a brief visit in 1980 in the hope of reconciling with Michelle and Mark but to no avail.

The irony was, we all saw her at the airport as she was leaving, because we were there awaiting the arrival of Michelle's parents. It took all my inner strength to stop myself from going up to her and punching her ugly face to a pulp. The funny part is, if I had, no one would have noticed the difference.

Chapter 41

Good True Friends

In January 1975, I began working for The Sunday Sun newspaper again for four days a week. This time I was in charge of the second biggest column of the Reader's Mart, the motor car column. I can honestly tell you that everything you always suspected about car salesmen is absolutely true. In those days though, there was no RWC's (Road Worthy Certificates) for used cars as there is now. If there had've been, there would've only been about one out of twenty used cars on the road in 1975. The women who worked at Sunday Sun this time around were certainly different than the ones who worked there three years previously. The majority of my co-workers brought a balance into my life, for different reasons.

Phoebe was an extremely pretty and very petite twenty-four year old. She had the world at her feet, or so it seemed. She was engaged to be married to a handsome Maori entertainer. Seeing them together was eye opening, to say the least.

They truly made a stunning looking couple. He, tall, handsome with chocolate coloured skin. She was tiny with platinum blonde hair and peaches and cream complexion. Unfortunately, neither of them had an ounce of common sense between them. Both were madly in love with themselves. I know that sounds unkind, but it's the honest to God truth. Phoebe was a lovely person, but she was obsessed with the thought that she and Dean would have beautiful babies together. Everything else in Phoebe's life always seemed to be an overpowering drama. She would moan from the moment she got into the office until she left every afternoon. The alarm didn't wake her, the toaster burnt her bread, the iron scorched her beautiful blouse etc, etc, etc. The list was always endless. After the first three days of sitting alongside of her, I nicknamed her Whinge.

Despite her whingeing, I liked Phoebe and we remained friends for a number of years. Unfortunately, we lost contact about thirty years ago and I often wonder how she is. No doubt, she'll be still whingeing.

Trish the dish was the temp typist who typed all our copy every Saturday. Trish never got flustered and she was super cool under every major drama that erupted in the office. I might add, most of the dramas, were created by myself around two o'clock in the afternoon as the close of day loomed.

I would get myself into a mad hysteria threatening to throw a tantrum if this, that or the other didn't happen immediately or sooner. Trish would sit there with a bemused smirk on her face as if to say this woman has really lost the plot. Normally, a meek little mouse like lady as Trish was, she would never hold my attention for more than twenty seconds, however, Trish intrigued me. She was so nice and demure that she won my admiration for just merely being, *Trish the dish* which I had named her. I am very proud to say that she remained one of my dearest friends and confidantes until she passed away six yrs ago.

Beryl had seven children. I immediately judged her as being a desperate bedraggled housewife who had a brute of a husband who beat her and kept her pregnant. I also imagined that she came from the backblocks of Woodridge. How wrong could I have been? Beryl was one of the most wonderful human beings God has ever put on this earth. She was kindness itself, had more patience and understanding in her little finger than what I would ever have in a million lifetimes. I will always be in debt to Beryl who has had the most calming effect on me more times than I could ever remember. The amount of times she placed her hands on my head to pass peace through me is uncountable. I last saw her two years ago when I visited her and unfortunately it was obvious, she was in the early stages of dementia.

Anastasia was a young twenty-three year old from England, who came out to Australia on a working holiday and decided to stay. I would like to say that she and I were firm friends from the day we met, but we weren't. We were workmates. I don't think it would have crossed either of our minds to even have lunch together, let alone contemplate going out to a movie. Anne (as she preferred to be known) enjoyed going out to nightclubs and would sometimes mention that she had enjoyed a big night out. I felt a bit sorry for her because she was an orphan and an only child! For some unknown reason the head woman of the Reader's Mart disliked her intensely. I guess in a way I looked upon her as a daughter figure, and I would often tell her to be careful when she went out and to not be so trusting with people she hardly knew.

She arrived at work one morning and announced to me that her girlfriend in London was getting married and that she was flying back to England in a few weeks to be her friend's bridesmaid. I have no idea why, but I just looked at her in shock and said, 'Don't go, Anne, it's not safe.'

She laughed and told me that I worry too much, she said that she was only going to be away about twelve months at the most and would be back in Australia before I'd realise she had gone. I had tears in my eyes as I said, 'It's not safe, Anne, please don't go.'

Over the ensuing weeks, I would try and talk her out of going at least six times a day. I was like a broken record and every time I went near Anne she would laugh and tell me that she was still going. Finally, the day of her departure arrived and I took time off work to go with her to the airport. I was sick with worry about her safety, almost to the point of madness. For the entire time we sat talking in the airport lounge, I repeatedly told her that it wasn't too late to change her mind. Anne just shook her head and told me that she would be okay. Her flight was announced over the loud speaker and when the announcement that it was the last call, we both walked slowly towards the departure door. As she hugged me tight, my tears fell like torrential rain down my face and I said, 'I'll never see you again, Anne.'

She smiled and replied, 'I promise, as soon as I return, you'll be the first person I'll visit.'

We corresponded on a regular basis and although I was very apprehensive about her safety, I had begun to doubt my own intelligence about how obsessed I had been about her returning to England. Then one morning the following May, (seven months after her departure), I walked down to my letterbox and the most dreadful feeling overcame me. Before I took the letters from the box, I instinctively began to cry. Instead of a letter from Anne, which I had anticipated, it was from a friend of Anne's. He explained that he had found my address amongst her possessions and he regretfully notified me that she had been killed in a motorcar crash two weeks previously. I was inconsolable.

Over the next nineteen years I was unable to speak about Anne and my fear for her, without breaking down.

In March 1995, I was fortunate enough to visit England and I took a photo of the house Anne lived in. It was what they called a semi-detached building and I had no idea which side of the house she lived in. On the day I took the photo, the weather was clear with a bright blue sky, however when the film was developed it showed a rainbow over one side of the roof. On my return to Australia I wrote to a weekly magazine telling them the eerie story. For some unknown reason, my letter was misplaced and eventually was found months later. An article appeared in the magazine on Wednesday 8th May, 1996, twenty years exactly to the day of Anne's death.

In the September of 1975, Frank was due for his annual holidays and we decided to drive up to Cairns to see the Barrier Reef. Frank finished work at about one pm on the Saturday and as he was about to leave, Steve told Frank that he was going to sell the shop, and he gave Frank first option of buying the business. When Frank asked him what would happen if he decided not to buy it, Steve said that he'd have no alternative other than to put him off.

When Frank arrived home and told me, I was absolutely livid. I thought what a mongrel of a time to drop that news on us just as we were going on holidays. It certainly put a cloud over our excitement of going away. Frank said that we could think about the option of buying the shop on the way to Cairns and that Steve wanted us to send him a telegram on Monday morning. As far as I was concerned, there was only one thing to think about: Frank had to find another job as soon as we got back. There was no way known that I would borrow the money from the bank and rely on Frank to take the responsibility of running his own shop. There was just too much at stake. As soon as he loaded the car with our luggage we set off.

I remember looking at my watch as we departed and it was ten past two. The only time we stopped on the way to Cairns was to buy food, refuel and have a shower at a service station in Mackay. Frank did all the driving, and yes, just in case you were wondering, he stayed sober. As I have said previously, he had never had a drink of alcohol in front of the kids or me since he had gone to Pav 4, three years previously. Ironically, whenever we went on holidays he never once drank so much as an eyedropper full.

During the journey I had swapped places with Heather. Vivian, Claire and I had dropped off to sleep between Mackay and Bowen. I was awakened by Frank's exclamation to Heather, 'Jesus, did you see that, kid? Pass me a Bex will ya.'

I said, 'What happened?'

He answered in total shock, 'I just saw a train reversing full pelt at us, in the main street.'

When I asked where the train was, Frank said, 'Just back there.'

I looked back and saw a stationary train to the side of the highway and said, 'I think you should stop for a while because you're hallucinating.'

He swallowed the Bex that Heather had handed him and laughed and said, 'We'll be right to go a few more miles, now that I've had breakfast.' (Bex was a common analgesic powder, which could be bought at any shop in those days.)

We eventually arrived in Cairns at ten past two on the Sunday afternoon, it had taken us exactly twenty-four hours to get there. (Brisbane-Cairns is approximately 1,700klms.)

On the Monday morning, I told Frank that I didn't want to buy the shop as it was far too much responsibility. He was very disappointed and tried to delay my sending Steve the telegram. I had worded the telegram in my mind the moment Frank had told me that Steve expected a telegram. My only regret was I wasn't able to see his face when he received it. It read, 'No money, no job, no thanks.'

On our return, Steve contacted Frank and said that Frank could stay on until he found another job. It was obvious that I wasn't in Steve's good books. It didn't take Frank long to find another job but the only word that comes to mind in describing the owner of that shop is, sleaze. He seemed to be only half a step, in front of the law, in everything he did. To make matters worse, he and all the butchers who worked for him were always on the grog most of the day. Every afternoon, I would pick Frank up from work in an attempt to stop him going to the pub with the boys. I remember only too well saying a prayer every day, 'Please God don't let him be drunk today.' Nine times out of ten God never listened.

One afternoon, a thunderstorm was looming, so I left the kids at home. Vivian was a couple of months away from her 14th Birthday and she was making sure that the other two were behaving themselves. When Frank came out of the shop the rain was teeming down in buckets, he introduced me to a young fellow and told me that he had promised him a lift home. We had to drive past our place on the way to the other fellows' home and I decided to call in at home to get a towel. I had to wipe the inside of the windows as the steam was causing everything to fog over. I tooted the horn as I pulled up in the driveway, and Heather popped her head out the window. I called out, 'Quick, go and get me an old towel will you love.'

The next thing I heard her screaming at the top of her lungs, 'Vivian, quick get a towel, quickly, Mum's just killed something.'

Frank and I burst into fits of laughter as we realised what she meant. Whilst we were up on holidays, we went out onto the Atherton Tablelands and I took over the driving to give Frank a break. I had only been at the wheel ten minutes when a gigantic red kangaroo came bounding out of nowhere and it suicided in front of the car. How I managed to keep the car on the road let alone not do untold damage to it is still a mystery to me. There was blood and guts everywhere and to make matters worse there was also a Joey in the pouch and the mother had tried to throw it clear. In Heather's mind, I went around killing animals willy-nilly, on a regular basis.

I resigned from the Sunday Sun around November of that year after working there eleven months. I won't go into details as to why I resigned. Suffice to say, I objected to a few articles that had been featured in the paper and I wanted to distance myself from the paper.

It was a month before that fateful Christmas day when Frank was stabbed.

Chapter 42

Evil in Disguise

There are a number of stories that I haven't written that I thought were not worth mentioning. Most of them were memorable and unusual happenings to me, but time and space prevented me from telling them. But one very memorable occurrence that I know happened, not to me, but to my mother Edith that I struggled with telling the story because of the delicacy of the subject. I feel that the story should be told so that hopefully others may learn not to allow it to happen to them.

It happened in the late 1950s but I didn't learn of the incident until 1973, I went down to visit Edith and Dad one morning after taking Vivian and Heather to school. Claire was with me and as per usual she went straight to the toy box that was kept there for her. Dad had gone to the city for his weekly haircut and Edith was sitting on the lounge crocheting.

Amelia 'Edith, they've deported that bastard Hank Plomp.'

Edith very quietly, 'I know.'

Plomp a Dutch migrant had been convicted in 1962 for drowning his wife in an area of the Pacific Ocean at Southport on the Gold Coast known as The Spit. He had also been convicted of raping another woman at St Lucia, Brisbane but that conviction was later quashed because of some loophole in the judicial system. I remembered the case very well because I had overheard Dad talking about the case to someone at the time of Plomp's rape conviction that a detective friend of Dad's who worked on the case had told Dad, 'The bastard bit the poor woman's nipples off.'

That information would never have been reported in the papers then, not even on page thirteen of the Melbourne Truth newspaper which was the shock horror paper in those days. I doubt that it would even be reported in the media now.

Edith seemed very subdued and when I asked her what was wrong she very quietly said, 'I knew Plomp.'

My eyes went as big as saucers at learning this information.

Amelia 'How, when did you know him, where did you meet him? Don't tell me you think he's innocent.'

She looked up and in a very quivering angry voice said

'Oh. I know that bastard is as guilty as sin and I only wish he had've hung.'

My curiosity had been well and truly whetted and I was very keen to learn more. In the late 1950s and early 1960s Edith had worked part-time of an evening in the bottle shop at a hotel in Brisbane. The publican had been a family friend for a number of years and had previously been the licensee at the Regatta hotel at Toowong.

Edith explained how Plomp had been a regular patron of the hotel for quite some time. **Edith** 'He used to come into the bottle shop in his Brisbane City Council uniform he was either a tram conductor or tram or bus driver and he'd buy a bottle of beer almost every night after work. He was always very polite he was never uncouth and if I wasn't busy, he would always stay and have a chat about his wife and children.'

Amelia 'Did he know you were married with kids?'

Edith 'Yes, but I didn't volunteer too much information about myself.'

I had to stifle a smile because she didn't have to tell me that. Edith was a very reserved, quietly spoken woman who kept everything secret. Dad had nicknamed her the Legal Brain because she wouldn't divulge anything.

Edith 'He came in one night just as I was knocking off work and he offered to drive me home because it was so late. I told him no thanks the tram passes the door and I'll be home within half an hour. He asked me what area I lived in and I told him and he said he lived in the next suburb and that he'd have to drive past my place to go home. I thought he's such a nice clean cut fellow with a respectable job, so like a bloody fool I agreed'. By this time, she was becoming extremely upset as she was telling me

Amelia 'Do you want a cuppa?'

She nodded but typical Edith she had to go and make it herself. She was at sixes and sevens and although I offered to help her

Edith 'I can do this, just be patient.'

She often said that to me because like my father I have no patience whatsoever. Normally I would've jokingly answered, 'No I want it now.'

But that day I knew she was too touchy and I figured, shut your trap, Amelia or you won't get to hear the rest of the story. We sat down and sipped our tea and I could tell she was agitated so I didn't push the issue. Eventually she said

'Christ I was lucky. We drove towards home and he was chatting away to me about anything and everything and I was thinking how lucky his wife and kids were to have a husband and father like him. When we got over the crest of the hill near St Alban's Church of England church in Weinholt Street (where I went to Sunday school) I said to him turn left at the next street past the shops, but he didn't he just kept driving past.'

(I immediately had a flashback of the time when I had, had the same experience which would have been only about one or two years later. I wasn't angry at the time she was telling me the story, but now almost forty odd years down the track I feel angry remembering how she didn't believe me when it had happened to me.)

Edith 'He started to drive faster and we went over the next hill and down past Swartz' corner. (in the 1930's people by the name of Swartz had owned a shop on the corner of Jones Street) We got halfway up the next hill and I opened the car door and jumped out. I hit my head on the gutter, I was lucky I didn't lose consciousness but my head was bleeding quite badly. I had a gravel rash all down my legs and my coat was ripped on the shoulder and the bastard stopped the car. I don't know how I did it, but I jumped to my feet and I ran down the street as fast as my legs would go, and I ran all the way home.'

(Approximately a kilometre.)

When she told me about her head and coat, I remembered her having a gash on her head all those years previously and she had explained to me the following day that she had fallen over.

Amelia 'Who knows about this?'

Edith 'James knew as soon as I walked in that night because he was up and I told him. You and Edward were in bed asleep. Your father was away at the time'.

(I would have been about 13-14.)

Amelia 'Did you ever tell Dad?'

Edith 'Yes, when he came back home'.

Amelia 'What did he say?'

Edith 'He told me I was a bloody idiot for getting in the car in the first place. When Plomp was charged with murdering his wife I knew he had done it. Then when the other lady came forward and accused him of rape and your father was told that Plomp had bitten her nipples off I knew how lucky I had been.'

Amelia , 'Did you report it to the police at the time?'

Edith 'No I didn't want anyone to know how stupid I was.'

Amelia 'Why didn't you go to the police after he'd been accused of raping the other lady?'

Edith 'Because I didn't want to go through a trial, I would've been made out to be of low class by the defence solicitor in a court of law. Even though I wasn't a barmaid, I worked at a hotel and women who worked in pubs didn't have a very good reputation in those days.'

I've often wondered if Plomp at the age of 21 was an employee of the Brisbane City Council when Betty Shanks was murdered in 1952.

Betty Shanks aged 22, had gotten off a tram near The Grange tram terminus and was murdered in a dark side street near The Grange School. She had been badly mutilated.

Her murder was never solved and her murder has always been a mystery.

Chapter 43

The Not So Shiny Stars

After all the excitement of the Christmas fiasco, I was looking for an interest that would help keep my mind off what had happened. Frank had returned to casual butchering and I was stuck at home with just my thoughts and I was not coping very well with the realisation of what had taken place. I used to sit and watch daytime television to try and block out all my memories of that fateful Christmas day.

Unfortunately, nothing seemed to work until I tuned in one afternoon to a show called Pot of Gold which was a talent programme hosted by Tommy Hanlon Junior with resident critic Bernard King. I guess it would be best described as a non-talent show, where all these dreadful acts would vie against each other and Bernard King would castigate them mercilessly. I would cringe at some of the performers, they were so humiliatingly bad. Sometimes I would even run out of the room, I felt so embarrassed for the people making fools of themselves on national television, but I would rush back to hear Bernard's comments and I found myself absolutely screaming with laughter as he tore strips off them. The thing that I found particularly funny was that the contestants always seemed to be totally unaware of how bad they really were.

Every day I would find myself glued to the TV waiting for the show to come on. I was never disappointed there was always at least one act that was so dreadful, that I would invariably say to myself, Christ even I could do better than that. They were always advertising that they wanted more contestants, so I thought, bugger it, I'll write my own script and go on the show, what have I got to lose?

I didn't have a great deal of self-respect and I was eager to upset Bernard's ego. He seemed such an arrogant S.O, B. Even though I agreed with him most times, I still felt like I wanted to put him in his place. I had watched the show enough to know what irked him the most. He absolutely hated guitars, bad grammar and anyone who sang off key. His most hated songs were, Tie a Yellow Ribbon 'round the Old Oak Tree, My Way and Ave Maria.

Vivian had arrived home one day with a friend's guitar and I started to strum it and I made the worst sounds I could possibly think of, as I rehearsed singing off key.

The kids and I thought it was hysterically funny and we'd roll about with laughter. I sat down one day and wrote a monologue and my own words to the song Kansas City from the movie Oklahoma. Even if I had to say so myself, I thought the words were very funny. I abandoned the idea of the guitar and concentrated on rehearsing the words until I knew them off by heart. Before too long I had them down pat and I would rehearse in front of the mirror pulling all different faces getting the best expressions possible. By the time I had mastered the act, I was totally convinced the act was so lousy, that I was going to make a complete idiot of myself. I also convinced myself that I deserved that, too. I went to the auditions and although the audience consisted of other contestants and their family and friends, I got a lot of laughs and a good round of applause. Although I was nervous, I felt like a million dollars. I thoroughly enjoyed making everybody laugh. Forget alcohol, cigarettes or drugs, this was the best addiction in the world, and I was completely hooked.

The big day eventually arrived. I dressed appropriately for my big moment. I wore a daggy old pair of jeans with holes in them. (Jeans with holes in them didn't become a trendy piece of attire until many years later.) The shirt I had on was a relic from my teens. I purposely had not buttoned it around my stomach area and I tied the two sides together, leaving my then very slim tummy exposed. I had a bandaid covering my navel with the word *censored* written over it, and I had a stupid hillbilly type hat and a pair of equally silly shoes on. I figured if I was going to make an idiot of myself, I might as well do a complete job of it. I bowed to Bernard as if to say, I'm ready for any crap you can dish up to me, Sonny Jim.

I had submitted my stage name as Schyzo Paranoid and when Tommy Hanlon baulked over the pronunciation of the word Schyzo and announced me as Skeezo Paranoid I thought that was appropriate too. Without hesitation I went straight into my routine.

The applause I got was nothing short of sensational. I couldn't have cared two hoots about anything at that moment. Getting that boost to my confidence was more exhilarating than anything I had ever experienced. I was on cloud nine and feeling no pain what so ever. Whatever Bernard said to me now, no matter how caustic, would mean bugger all. As a matter of fact, I don't even remember what he said, except at the end he told me, 'I would like to see you back again.'

I didn't win, but I came third, which gave me a prize of twenty LP records. I didn't need to be invited back I had full intentions of going on again even if it killed me. The one thing that I had to learn to overcome was keeping my mouth moist. I had never experienced such dryness in my mouth before. The adrenalin was pumping so much, every last drop of moisture was totally drained from my mouth and I felt as if my speech was completely unintelligible.

As soon as I got home, I began to write more sketches. I was determined to win through to the semi-finals, which included a return flight to Sydney. I would have loved to have believed I was good enough to win the semi-final, which would automatically get me into the grand final. The grand final prize was a cruise on a Russian ship the Rasa Sayang from Singapore and the runner's up prize was furniture. But that would be far too much to hope for. Everyone kept telling me that I was good and that Bernard King knew what he was talking about. They kept saying things like, 'You're going to win you can do it, just wait and see.'

During all this madness, we were continuing to live a normal existence. I continued to try and seek help for Heather whose behaviour continued to be more than unacceptable. I felt that I had exhausted every avenue as far as medical and psychiatric advice was concerned. No amount of advice and treatment had any effect on her whatsoever.

I decided to resort to divine intervention. I figured that by sending the three kids to Sunday school would be of great benefit to them all. On their arrival home that Sunday morning, I enquired enthusiastically from Heather and Claire if they had enjoyed themselves Heather replied rather surly 'It was alright I suppose.'

Claire was full of happiness and told me that she loved it. I couldn't help but notice that Vivian rolled her eyes skyward as she gave out an exasperated groan, as her youngest sister continued to praise her experience in glowing terms. Heather just shook her head and marched off in total disbelief at hearing Claire's account of the morning. When Claire finally went into her room to change out of her Sunday best, I asked Vivian to tell me what had happened.

Vivian 'I'm never going back, Mum. I've never been so embarrassed in my life.'

Amelia 'What happened, what did Heather say or do?'

Vivian 'Heather was really good, it was Claire. Heather and I nearly died with embarrassment. We all had to get up and sing hymns from the books that they gave us, but of course Claire's too young to read, so she sang her own hymn above everyone else's voices.'

I had to stifle a smirk as I pictured the scene.

Vivian continued, 'Claire's hymn was, she'll be comin' round the mountain when she comes, she'll be wearin' pink pyjamas when she comes Ye Ha, and to make it even worse she lifted her leg in the air and hit herself on the backside.'

I absolutely roared with laughter much to Vivian's horror

Vivian 'Mum, it wasn't funny, she wouldn't shut up, the more we tried to keep her quiet the louder she got.'.

No need to be told, they never went back to Sunday school again.

Not long after that momentous incident, one of the commercial TV stations had a telethon in aid of a Christian group who helped teenagers by keeping them off the streets and out of trouble. Although Heather was only ten, and by no means into trouble with the law or going out onto the streets, I figured it would be worth contacting the group to see if they could help her as well. On hearing my plight, the co-ordinator was a little apprehensive in accepting Heather into their fold because of her age, but she agreed on the condition that Vivian attended the group meetings as well. The group held their meetings every Wednesday night at a home in Tennyson, which was a ten-minute drive from our home. After attending their first meeting, both girls informed me that they had enjoyed themselves, although neither of them was overly enthusiastic. The one thing they were both very pleased about was the fact that Claire couldn't go too which was for obvious reasons as previously mentioned. After they had attended their third meeting, I received a telephone call from the co-ordinator inviting the entire family to attend one of their church services. I was very apprehensive because of my encounters with the Catholic faith as a child. I was assured that their services were totally different and that I would come away feeling energised and stimulated by the experience. If either of the TV stations had've had a decent movie on that Sunday night I could've been spared from the fate that awaited me. Frank refused to go and I was rather pissed off about that. He had come to the conclusion that it was I who had agreed to go not him. But he had suggested that I leave Claire at home just in case she wanted to sing her own hymns! I figured that Claire could only benefit by experiencing the religious service.

The service began at 7.30. The first half an hour wasn't too bad the preacher had delivered a short sermon and the congregation sang a few hymns. I managed to stop Claire from going into her routine by promising her an ice cream the following day. If nothing else, my kids were easily bribed. After the singing stopped the preacher called upon anyone to come up to the altar to receive Jesus into their lives. For the next two hours I witnessed what I could best describe as mass hysteria. People of all ages were approaching the altar and after a word in their ear, all of them, one by one dropped to the floor writhing, screaming, groaning and moaning. As they fell to the ground, some on their backs, others forward and face down and others hitting themselves on the pews as they fell sideways. The rest of the congregation would throw their arms skyward yelling, 'Praise be to Jesus, thank you God, Hallelujah'.

I wanted to run out the front door after the first one hit the deck, but I sat there thinking, Christ Almighty, I'm in a cesspit of lunatics, it must be a full moon. I could have left, I should have left, but I felt that I had to stay because I didn't want to let on that I believed that what I was witnessing was abnormal. I finally escaped with the three kids at about ten o'clock, although the service was still in progress. I mumbled my excuse to the person sitting next to me that Claire was extremely tired and that I had to get her to bed. I wished I had thought of that excuse two hours earlier. But the truth was Claire was completely bug eyed at witnessing the events.

We piled into the car and I apologised to the kids for having sent them to the group meetings and for taking them to that nut house. We had only gone about fifty metres down the road when Claire threw her arms in the air and started swaying to and fro, emulating the congregation. Before I could tell her to stop, she started to yell at top note, 'We want Gough.'

Prime Minister Gough Whitlam of course had been sacked only a few months beforehand and the scenes of the crowds chanting for Gough had been a regular occurrence on television. I laughed so hard I had tears rolling down my cheeks and I had to pull over on the side of the road for ten minutes until I composed myself. I still have a good chuckle whenever I remember that incident.

I guess, if the TV channels had've had a decent movie on that night I wouldn't have remembered one moment of it.

•••

We had heard about a warehouse that sold boxes of variety goods to the general public for fifty dollars a box. We thought that a small investment like that was worth the risk and we could start our own stall selling at the flea market each Sunday. We did that for a few weeks and netted quite a good little profit. We weren't millionaires but the extra cash certainly came in handy. When we went to buy our third box full of goodies, the manager of the warehouse asked us to show him identification for the charity we belonged to. Charity? What did he mean charity? I was so embarrassed I could have died. How were we to know that the warehouse only sold the boxes to charitable organisations? Our little money-earning, venture had come to a full stop.

On the last Sunday that we traded at the flea market, Frank had placed the remainder of our goods into the boot and slammed the boot door down hard. Unfortunately, in doing so, he didn't realise a cardboard box had gotten jammed near the hinge and it buckled the boot door. I took the car to the local panel beater who gave me a quote, which I thought fairly reasonable, and I duly booked the car in to have the repair done.

On the quote, it stated that he had to remove and replace the chrome trim. Verbally, he had explained that he had to remove the rear window and the chrome surrounds to enable him access to the boot door. I had said that I didn't care what he had to do so long as he did the job properly and returned it in the same condition it was in before Frank had buggered the boot door. He laughed and said, 'You won't even know that there's been any damage, we'll get it back like new'.

I went back a few days later and I was satisfied that the boot door was perfect and paid him for the work. As I walked over to get into the car, I noticed that the chrome surround on the window had not been replaced. When I asked him about it, he looked stunned momentarily, but then just shrugged and told me he hadn't quoted for its replacement.

Amelia 'Pigs arse. I've still got the written quote at home'.

He sneeringly laughed at me

Panel Beater 'So what are you going to do, sue me?'

I was fuming, I went home and got the quote and took it back to him, and he just shrugged and told me there was nothing that I or anyone else could do about the matter.

I contacted the Small Claims Bureau and for a small fee, I put in my claim. Eventually, I was given a date for my hearing and armed with my quote I went in to do battle. The panel beater made his grand entrance by walking into the room as if he was God's gift to the universe. As he sat down, he glanced around the room and then he sat back in the chair as if to say I am going to win this case, because I am an expert in my field. The adjudicator turned to him and said, 'Mr Green, please remove those sunglasses, you are in a courtroom now, not on the beach'.

I had to stifle a good chuckle and I thought to myself, bewdy, that'll teach you, ya smug bastard. Green tried to convince the adjudicator that the chrome surround actually meant the Ford insignia. He tried to make out I had misunderstood him. The adjudicator found in my favour and ordered Green to reimburse me the money I had paid him. The money was to be paid within thirty days and if after the thirty days the money was not reimbursed the bailiff would confiscate equipment from Green's business to the value of the money owed. Green jumped to his feet and told the adjudicator that he would not pay and that he would be appealing the decision. The adjudicator told Green that this decision was final and again reminded Green about the bailiff confiscating his goods.

When the money was not paid within the thirty days, I went up to the workshop. Green wasn't there and when I told one of his employers why I was there, he was stunned. **Amelia** 'Did he forget to tell you that I won the case?'

The employer told me that Green had told them that not only had he won but that I had to pay Green's appearance fee. I roared laughing and told him that I didn't think that Green could lie straight in bed. I went on further to say that I would return the following day and for the guy to tell Green if my money wasn't ready, I would have the bailiff out within twenty-four hours. Green was not happy to see me when I returned the following day and very begrudgingly paid me by cheque. Waving it above my head for his employees to see I said quite cheerily, 'Nice doing business with you, I just hope that this doesn't bounce.'

The other three fellows were absolutely pissing themselves with laughter, but Green was livid. A few weeks later we traded the car in on a brand-new bright red station wagon and the day after we took delivery of it, I was held up at the traffic lights directly outside Green's panel beating shop. Green and his employees were all sitting out on the footpath having their morning tea, I could feel four sets of eyes looking my way and I turned to look at them, I wound the window down and smiled sweetly at Green and said, 'I won it in a court case.'

The lights turned green and I drove away with the sound of roaring laughter filling the street. I'm willing to bet crowns, pounds and bars of gold that it wasn't Green's laughter I heard.

Back to the auditions I went, and Hal Croxon the producer greeted me as if I was an old friend. Many people in the audience recognised me and came up to congratulate me on my previous appearance. Quite a few contestants said things like, 'If I get on the show, I hope I'm not on the same one as you, because you're too good, you'll win hands down.'

I can't even begin to tell you how that made me feel. The word good doesn't come within cooee of how I felt. One thing I do recall vividly as if it was yesterday was how snotty some of the so-called professional singing and dance teachers were speaking about the other acts to their pupils. I had heard how bitchy and competitive show business was, but I didn't think it would be a big part of the amateur scene as well. Watching the show at home and laughing my head off at some of the acts, and actually being on the show was as different as chalk is to cheese. I found myself encouraging some of the acts to try and improve themselves before they went on camera. The bitchy contestants, however, were a different kettle of fish. If they were dancers, I secretly wished that they'd fall on their arses and make a complete holy show of themselves. If they were singers, I'd hope that they're voices would crack a sour note, or that they'd forget the words of the songs. In all probability they more than likely thought the same about me. I experimented with a little idea that I had and I placed a Tic-Tac on either side of my back teeth, top and bottom to see if that would help to retain the moisture in my mouth. It worked perfectly and I highly recommend this idea to anyone going on TV. There's nothing worse than watching someone speaking on TV and his or her tongue is coming out on a regular basis like a blue tongue lizard. I have often wondered why the stars haven't passed this type of information to guests on their shows. I can only assume that the stars want to look superior to their guests. After the audition was over, I heard one woman commenting to another about me, 'I think this show is rigged I reckon she's a professional, she's too good to be just an amateur'. That was it for me I wouldn't have gotten a ten-gallon hat on my skull even with a sledgehammer. I had to wait a few weeks before I had to appear on the show. If people thought I looked bad on the last appearance, this time I looked atrocious. I was dressed in bright yellow from top to toe, Edith had made this dreadful outfit of bright yellow ribbons, I had bright yellow stockings and yellow ribbons tied to my wrists, I even had yellow eye shadow all over my face and yellow nail polish. I just looked like a giant canary. I again bowed to Bernard as if in defiance saying come on, humiliate me, and see if I care.

When Tommy announced me as the next act he added, 'And she's good.'

I had changed the tempo of Tie a Yellow Ribbon Round the Old Oak Tree, to fit the music to my words of Tie a Yellow Ribbon Round Bernard's Throat. I had also employed the musical director of Pot of Gold to write the arrangements. When I finished, I couldn't believe my eyes, I turned to face Bernard and he was laughing and clapping. He gave me a score of forty, and I along with everyone else gasped in total disbelief. The only people who ever got scores above thirty-seven were very talented singers or dancers. Then at the end of his score he asked me to see him after the show. I was shocked. I got the highest score on the day and I had gotten my wish. Not only had I won, I was going to fly to Sydney to appear on the semi-finals. I was over the moon, but I was very nervous about having a chat with Bernard after the show. I soon found out that to speak to Bernard King was to speak to a thorough gentleman. I was extremely flattered when he asked me to write a sketch for him for his Roxy Theatre Restaurant. He explained that he wanted the sketch for his Christmas show and that the sketch must be an ocker Christmas theme. I thought, great, I've come on this bloody show to try to get over and forget last Christmas and now I've got to think about next Christmas. Talk about ghosts of Christmas past.

Johnny Pace had been the other judge, he asked me to come to Sydney to see his stage act as well, to get an idea of what type of sketch that I could write, which would be good for his show. I couldn't believe my luck. In the meantime, I had to concentrate on my semi-final performance. Fortunately, I had rehearsed two sketches in the hope that I would get through to the semis. My appearance on the semi-finals was to be in two weeks. The way that the show worked, the production team would audition in seven capital cities and tape five daily shows in those cities every seventh week. This meant that there were thirty-five acts on each week from all around Australia, plus every eighth week the semi-finals would be taped. After two semi-finals had been taped, they would then tape the grand final with ten contestants.

Now that I was a star in Edith's eyes, not only did she brag to everyone about my so-called stardom she decided to fly with me to Sydney, to be in the audience there.

No doubt she wanted to take the credit of being seen to be the mother of a bright light. Edith never parted with a penny of her precious money unless it was absolutely necessary. The funny part was, when I had first told her that I was going to appear on the show she was totally horrified and said to me, 'Oh. Don't be so silly. You'll make a complete fool of yourself and everyone in the family.'

So much for motherly love and giving me a boost to my morale, Dad on the other hand laughed at me and said, 'You clot.' I laughed and said to him, 'I'm going to announce that I'm the daughter of Rob Long.' He looked at me with mock horror and said

'You little mongrel, I'll kill you if you do, and I'll get the police onto you for telling filthy lies.' We both burst out laughing, but I never did query how he was going to get the police onto me after he had killed me.

In Sydney I was beaten by only one point. I was so disappointed I felt like having a little cry. But I didn't, I just vowed that I'd keep on trying. I was so desperate to keep appearing on the show, I went to the next auditions and shocked Hal Croxon and the entire audience with my version of Waltzing Matilda which was about Gough Whitlam being sacked and what a mongrel Malcolm Frazer was. All Hal could do was say, 'No way is that going to air.' Undeterred, I asked him if I could do another audition that day. When he agreed, I sang I'm Sorry which is a beautiful Della Reece song.

I thought I had warbled beautifully, but I was shocked when Hal Croxon told me that he wouldn't put me on the next show. I asked very indignantly, 'Why not?'

He replied with a silly smirk, 'Let's face it, Amelia, your voice isn't the best, you're much better doing comedy.'

Well if that wasn't a slap in the face, I don't know what was. The thought went through my mind, well, how come all those other morons who couldn't sing for nuts, get on the show? I knew I wasn't anywhere as bad, as some of those poor saps, but I took his words to heart, and never sang solo in public again.

Although money was still very tight, we decided to take up Bernard and Johnny Pace's suggestion and go to Sydney to see their shows. We stayed at my cousin Vonnie and her husband Reg's home in Erskineville. We had bought our new car from Ipswich and we had to wait six weeks for the registration sticker to come through. Ipswich was regarded as being a country area and in those days the country areas had to wait for the registration papers to be sorted out. We had what was called an interim sticker, which allowed us to drive the car until the rego sticker came through.

Erskineville homes do not have the luxury of garages and/or carports so we reluctantly had to park in the street directly behind Vonnie's home. We locked it as tight as a drum and hoped that it would still be there the following day.

Reg, Vonnie, Frank and I were all enjoying breakfast the next morning, when we were surprised by a loud knock on the back door. Reg opened the door and was taken back at the sight of two police officers enquiring if he knew the owner of the red Falcon station wagon parked in the back street. Frank went to the door and said that it was his car and asked them what the problem was. The young cop asked Frank why he was driving an unregistered vehicle. Frank very indignantly told him that the vehicle was registered, and that if the cop had've looked hard enough he would've realised the vehicle had an interim sticker on it.

The cop 'I'm sorry sir, but we've successfully broken into your car to try and find some identification in the car.'

Frank threw his arms in the air and then placed them on his head

Frank 'My God. We were warned that we could get broken into in the big smoke but they didn't tell us it would be by the cops.'

The cop apologised again and told Frank that the next-door neighbours had made the complaint about a stolen car that was parked in their usual car space. He went on further to say that in all probability we would be pulled over again and asked to show cause why we were driving an unregistered car.

The Cop 'Just tell them to contact me, at the Newtown police station, my name is Constable Trotter'.

Without batting an eyelid

Frank 'Constable Trotter, as in *PIGS* ?. '

I could have choked him on the spot, but Vonnie and Reg burst into fits of laughter and I couldn't help having a good guffaw with them.

The four of us booked a table at the Roxy Theatre Restaurant where Bernard King was performing. We ate our meal before the show began and when Bernard appeared on stage he just stood there and waited until the audience ceased their chatter.

Much to our amazement

Bernard 'Ladies and Gentlemen I want you to give a warm welcome to a very talented young lady whom I believe is an up and coming writer. She has appeared on Pot of Gold in recent weeks, please welcome Amelia Williams. Amelia stand up and take a bow'.

Vonnie let out a gasp and Frank uttered the word 'Shiiit.'

I was stunned beyond belief and very, very flattered to say the least. I couldn't fathom how he had even known I was in the audience. I stumbled to my feet to tumultuous applause and I was on cloud nine. I was truly overwhelmed. Bernard had a chat with me after the show and in the conversation, he told me that one of the main cast members had given him notice to quit the show. I thought he meant Ross Hutchinson the dancer, Bernard was very angry and said 'I could willingly choke her.' As soon as he said the word her, I realised he meant Judi Connelli I thought at the time, Jees I bet she doesn't know how angry he is. I had never seen Judy Connelli in my life before, but I thought she had one of the most amazing voices I'd ever heard.

A few nights later, we went to the Epping RSL Club to see Johnny Pace and his partner Harriet on stage, and he too acknowledged me to his audience. He took Frank and me backstage to their dressing room where we talked for ages about the type of sketches he wanted me to write. We were both made to feel so welcome that we just felt as if we were royalty. One of the things Johnny Pace asked me to write was a parody on the song Who wants to be a Millionaire from the movie High Society. He even gave me his home address at Frenches Forrest and his private phone number to call him at any time. I wasn't sure that I'd be able to deliver the requests of both performers but I was as sure as hell going to do my best. I felt like a million dollars and deemed it a great honour to be asked to write for both men.

On our way back to Brisbane, I took over the driving and experienced one of the most terrifying rides of my life. We were between Kempsey and Coffs Harbour and a semitrailer seemed to appear from nowhere and began tailgating us. No matter how hard I tried to get rid of him, he pursued me like a madman stalks his victim. For well over an hour in the dead of night he stayed only a few inches from the back of our car. I couldn't pull over to allow him to pass because as soon as I left the bitumen he would too. If I accelerated to over one hundred and twenty kilometres an hour, so would he. Anyone who has ever seen the movie, Duel starring Dennis Weaver, will know what I experienced. To be perfectly honest with you, I feel sure that this madman was enacting out that movie.

We finally came to a little town with an all-night cafe on the opposite side of the road. There was a hitchhiker sitting on his suitcase directly opposite the cafe and I pulled up approximately ten feet past him. The semitrailer driver came up so fast and pulled up behind me that the hitchhiker had to jump off his suitcase and landed onto the footpath. We got out of the car, and pretended to lock the car doors, whilst the madman walked across the road. We called out to the hitchhiker asking him if he was okay. When he said he was but that his bag was squashed. We apologised to him that we couldn't hang around to be his witness and we jumped back in the car and took off like a bat out of hell. As tired as I was, when we got home, I sat down and wrote Who wants to be in Politics for Johnny Pace. It was all about the current political turmoil of the day. For Bernard I wrote, The Ocker Santa Claus and the Ocker Christmas Tree Fairy. Both poems could be either said singularly or enacted out together. I knew Ross Hutchinson would have been perfect for the role of the Ocker Christmas Tree Fairy.

I sent the two poems to Bernard and the song to Johnny as soon as I had finished them. I had also come up with what I thought was an ingenious idea that would get me into the grand final. I wrote three, three-minute sketches, which were a continuing story. I figured that everyone who watched the show on a regular basis would want to hear the ending, once they heard the beginning. Once I had learnt all the words of the three skits parrot fashion, I auditioned for the show again.

Hal Croxon told me that I should wear a funny hat or something on the day of taping, so that I could be entered into the special category of novelty act which was the theme for the next series. As I hadn't auditioned in full dress rehearsal, Hal had no idea what I had planned to wear on the day of taping. I looked at him and with a twinkle in my eye I said, 'Forget the funny hat Hal I've got the perfect novelty attire that will rock you to your boot straps.' He tried his hardest to get me to tell him what I was going to wear, but all I'd divulge was that I would be respectably attired and that I wouldn't be wearing anything risqué. The lights in a studio are very high voltage and anyone who has been on camera in any studio will agree that it's like sitting in the blazing noon day sun. It was a great surprise to everyone to see me walk out wearing a flowing overcoat. I'm here to tell you that the Tic-Tac's were really working overtime under those lights. I would have given my right arm to be able to have had a lovely cold glass of iced water to throw over myself that day. I really questioned my sanity standing there, the adrenalin pumping, my nerves were jumping, my hands pouring with sweat and I was wearing an overcoat. But there was a very good reason, which I wanted to surprise everyone with. I was ready raring to go into my routine when someone yelled, 'Cut.' There was a technical problem, which seemed to take an eternity to fix. Finally, Tommy announced, 'Skeezo Paranoid performing Episode One of The Pot of Gold Soap Opera, The Impossible'.

'Me and Bernard were at the pub just the other night

When in walks old Gert, who's on the dole, wantin' to put on the bite

She says 'G'day there me old chinas, how are youse goin

Well we'd hit the jackpot, but we didn't want her bloody knowin''.

As I said the word jackpot, I dropped the overcoat revealing I was nine months pregnant to Bernard. The maternity dress I wore was in fact a long, pink, nightdress with a blue bird and a broken heart insignia over the chest with the words NEVER AGAIN written under the insignia. My pregnancy was a small round cushion that was held on by a leather belt. Everyone erupted into absolute fits of laughter and I wanted to have a good laugh with them as well, but somehow, I managed to keep a straight face and continue with the sketch. When I finished, I felt like a squillion-dollars hearing the applause and I was so proud of myself that I hadn't faltered once. But I was almost bursting when I saw Bernard and Tommy absolutely killing themselves with laughter. I stood there with the biggest smirk on my face, but I really wanted to join in with all their laughter. Tommy finally said, 'Fancy being married to that voice.'

And a lone clapping of hands was heard above the laughter. Tommy looked over at Frank and exclaimed, 'Oh! You are.'

I can't remember the score that day, but I won, which meant I was again going to Sydney for the semi-finals. 1975 had been such a disaster, but 1976 seemed like it was my year. I couldn't seem to put a foot wrong. Edith again accompanied me back to Sydney for the semi-finals, I was on top of the world and she was in her glory as the mother of the so-called star. I won the semi-final as well and I had to wait another three months until February 1977 before the taping of the grand-final.

The following month at the end of November, Vonnie got in touch with me to tell me that she and Reg had gone back to the Roxy Theatre Restaurant. She told me how proud she was of me that Bernard and his sidekick were performing The Ocker Santa Claus and The Ocker Christmas Tree Fairy. I was totally shocked because Bernard had rung me a couple of weeks previously and told me that both sketches were too racy for his show.

We had planned on driving to Adelaide for Christmas that year to meet a lady called Karin who had written to me after I'd appeared on the first episode of Pot of Gold. Karin had appeared on the show as Cilly, but her comedy wasn't up to par. Karin and I kept in contact and I wrote her a couple of sketches free of charge I hasten to add, which got her into the semi-finals. Bernard complimented her on the improvement to her sketches and she told him on air that I had written them, which I thought was nice. Frank and I had all intentions of bypassing Sydney and going directly to Adelaide but on hearing the news that Bernard was using my sketches I had to go to see the show.

We again stayed with Vonnie and Reg. I didn't want to book the table over the phone so we drove to the theatre restaurant which had a little booking office on the side. I was very cautious walking in because I didn't want anyone to recognise me. Frank thought I was nuts and basically told me so, saying, 'It's not a big deal because you're not well known, you're not a STAR!.' I must admit when he said that, I felt like a prize gooseberry for acting like a temperamental star. I got the tickets for that nights show and handed over my money and the girl behind the desk gave me our tickets and change. I was just about to turn around to walk out the door when Ross Hutchinson walked to the door behind the desk. He looked at me and walked away without saying a word. I knew immediately that I would pay the price for having the audacity to turn up at the restaurant unannounced. As we walked out

Amelia 'I'll be in deep shit for this'.

Frank 'You're imagining things, he wouldn't have known who you are, and in fact I don't think he even saw you.'

Amelia 'You're wrong, he saw me alright and he recognised me as well.'

Vonnie, Reg and Frank tried to convince me that I was imagining things but I was just as adamant that I knew my gut feeling was right. We were seated in the middle of the theatre restaurant almost at the same table as we had been a few months previously. We were in the middle of eating our meal when I heard a loud 'Ooh.' from some of the other patrons seated behind us near the front door. I looked up to see Bernard walking through the front door. Although he was a good twenty feet away from me our eyes met but he showed no recognition. I said to Frank, 'This is it. This is where the shit starts.'

Bernard swished his way through the tables greeting people at random saying things like, 'Hello darlings'. and 'Thanks for coming'. He wended his way through the tables until he got to ours and with a flurry of his hands as if in deep shock at seeing me

Bernard 'Amelia darling, you dear little prostitute what are you doing here?'

Amelia 'We've just come to see the show, Bernard,'

And without another word he walked directly to the back of the stage. The show was good but it wasn't as long as the show he had staged six months beforehand and I knew he had purposely cut out, The Ocker Santa Claus and The Ocker Christmas Tree Fairy. The irony was, in those days I probably would've only gotten about fifty dollars per sketch but to sue him over the copyright of them would've cost me an arm and a leg.

As we walked out of the Roxy

Amelia 'Well there goes any chance I ever had of winning the cruise or the furniture in the grand final.'

I don't know if it was naivety, wishful thinking or if he just didn't want to believe it **Frank** 'No you don't want to think like that, everything's going to be okay. You're going to win.'

But I knew differently.

On our way to Adelaide I asked Frank if we would be going to Melbourne. Neither of us had been there before, but we had been told many times that Melbourne was a dump of a place.

Frank 'No we're not going to that hole of a place.'

Amelia 'We can't just by-pass a major city'.

Frank 'Well just watch me as we do.'

But we did head to Melbourne and on our way down Frank emphasized that we'd be

only driving through the dump of a place so we could say that we had been there. As we approached the city, we were very impressed with its cleanliness and beauty and by the time we got into the city we couldn't find accommodation quick enough. The following day we heard Tommy Hanlon on the radio so we decided to call in to the radio station to see if we could say hello. When we got to the reception desk I asked if it was possible to see Tommy. The receptionist hurried away and returned within minutes with another lady. I recognised her instantly as Tommy's wife.

Amelia 'Hello Murphy it's nice to finally meet you.'

She greeted me as if she had known me for years. She grabbed my hand and told us all to follow her and we walked through the corridors until we came to a big window and we could see Tommy sitting in front of the microphone. When he looked over, he exclaimed on air, 'Oh look whose here, it's Amelia Williams but you'll all know her as Skeezo Paranoid.'.He went on and on how funny I was and how he was trying to get me some work with Paul Hogan. I was stunned.

Murphy 'Tommy really likes you he thinks you're the funniest he's ever seen on any show.'

I was completely stunned by that comment. We waved goodbye to Tommy and I just floated out of the radio station. We stayed four nights in Melbourne and we were all very disgruntled at having to leave. If Melbourne had better weather, we would've shifted there in 1977.

We spent a few days with Karin at her home in Christies Beach and met a few of her friends at a New Year's Eve party. Although Karin was very nice, we thought her friends were very pretentious people. It was very obvious that they judged everybody by their occupation. When they asked Frank what he did for a living, before he could answer I replied, 'He's a Managing Director.'

They didn't ask where but they seemed very pleased about that. Well I wasn't lying because Frank was managing the local dump every weekend. The rubbish dump in those days wasn't manned by the City Council. People would just take their rubbish to this particular area and dump it. Frank wasn't employed by anyone there he just used to go regularly to the dump to see what he could find. Whenever anyone drove in, he would direct them where to put their rubbish so that he could sift through it. So as far as I was concerned, he was a managing director. We all had a good laugh over that after everyone had gone home.

I'm afraid the people from Christies Beach didn't help to endear us to Adelaide we just thought everyone from Adelaide must be boorish snobs. We came home with the belief that Melbourne people are the friendliest in the nation and we went to Melbourne many times and we never changed our opinion. Unfortunately, it's no longer the cleanest part of the country but I maintain it's the only place where you can stand on the street corner waiting for the lights to change and the person standing next to you will tell you their life story.

February finally arrived and we all headed to Sydney for the Pot of Gold grand-final. The rehearsals for the show were extremely tiring and they took all day to get through. Claire was in her glory sitting front row watching everything that was going on. She hadn't yet turned six but she didn't miss a thing. At one stage of the day I sat down alongside of her and she introduced me to everyone within earshot, 'This is my mother, Amelia, she's the star of this show'. I could've quite easily choked her on the spot and I wanted the earth to open up and swallow me. But I was laughing so much I was rendered speechless. What really surprised me was Tommy Hanlon's obvious aloofness on the day. I was amazed at his change in attitude towards me. Six weeks previously I was the best thing since sliced bread and then on the big day, I felt as if I was the mould on a two-week old slice of bread. When I found out that Graham Kennedy was to be the other judge, I was quite pleased and excited. I had always liked Graham's sense of humour but Frank had never liked him, so Frank wasn't impressed by any stretch of the imagination. I was able to observe Graham for most of the day and I came to the conclusion that he was the most insecure man I'd ever seen. For the entire day he sat in his chair brushing imaginary things off the shoulder of his suit coat. When he wasn't doing that, he fiddled with his packet of Kool cigarettes and his lighter. He seemed to be forever placing the packet of cigarettes in one particular position and he would place the cigarette lighter on top of the cigarettes and tap it into place. This procedure went on for hours.

When it was my turn to perform, I took particular notice of both Graham and Bernard and not once during my performance did either of them look at me. It came as no surprise to me at the end of the night when I didn't get a placing. Even under the hot lights of the studio I could feel the iciness towards me. It was painfully obvious that Amelia Williams had blotted her copybook by finding out that Bernard King had used my material without payment. To add insult to injury a female contortionist had won the furniture, the prize I should have won as the novelty act, or as someone said to me later, 'She won because she showed her all to the world.' Some may say its sour grapes on my part I can only say to them that it isn't, I know what I experienced and it wasn't pleasant. I was very determined to prove that I could make it in the world of show biz with or without Bernard King's approval. That was until about two weeks later when Frank announced to me that he'd be my manager.

That was it for me, I knew then I was defeated so I decided then and there that it was time to move on and just get on with life.

Chapter 44

Sanity Does Not Prevail

Unfortunately, life has a bad habit of kicking you when you least expect it and the kick we got on Friday 3rd June 1977 was horrendous.

Firstly, I'd like to say that I have the utmost respect for the medical profession. I have had the privilege of dealing with some of the most wonderful doctors Australia has. But some of the specialists have proven beyond a shadow of doubt that they truly believe they are God's gift to the universe and should be revered at all times. But just because some specialists have the personality of a cane toad, doesn't mean that I don't respect their extraordinary abilities. I have also had the misfortune of having to consult with a small number of specialised dickheads.

In the May of 1977, I had been advised by Doctor Webber, Heather's psychiatrist, that it would be best if I placed Heather in Montrose home for crippled children. I should have ignored him because I thought then and still believe now (and I have many reasons) that the man was a kook. Heather's behaviour had become almost intolerable. She was anti-social, argumentative and generally a huge pain in the arse. I think these days she would probably be diagnosed as having ADHD and given Ritalin, thank God that didn't happen. Nothing anyone did could seem to quell her odd behaviour and I was just about at my wits end trying to cope with her. Even so, I was very reluctant to letting her go to Montrose, but I figured that their professional guidance may be beneficial to her. She was to stay there from Sunday night to Friday afternoon and could come home every weekend. She had only been there two nights and I was called in to have a talk with the matron about her behaviour. Ever the optimist I was hopeful they had discovered a magic cure for her behaviour. I was wrong, the reason I was called in, she had taunted the other children with, 'The reason you're in here is you're a cripple but I'm not.' What the matron thought I was going to do is beyond me, all I could do was say that I was sorry for her behaviour and reiterated that this was the reason she had been placed in their care in the first place.

Every weekend Heather was a perfect angel for us but she bellowed like a Brahman bull every Sunday when it was time to return her to the home. She would be kicking and screaming and pleading and begging to stay with us. I started to plead and beg with Doctor Webber to allow her to come home but the more I insisted the more he was adamant that she was to stay there.

Then on that fateful Friday I had made an appointment with the local dentist for her to have a tooth extracted at three pm. When she came out of the surgery, I was shocked to see how swollen her face was. The dentist assured me that the swelling was normal considering the size of the roots of the tooth and he told me that the swelling would subside over the weekend. The following morning her face seemed to be more swollen and I was getting more concerned. Frank thought it had gone down slightly but I could tell he was concerned. By the Sunday morning I was more convinced that her face had swollen more. It sure as hell hadn't gone down at all. I didn't want to alarm Heather by saying too much but I called her over and asked her if her mouth was sore. She said that it wasn't, but I could see that she was worried that it was still swollen. I touched her face and the swelling felt as hard as Ayers Rock. That night when I took her back to Montrose, she was very quiet and didn't rebel about going back. I showed the sister on duty that evening how swollen Heather's face was and very matter of factly she told me that if there's any problem they'd get her back to the dentist.

I told her very adamantly that if there was a problem, they will notify me and I would take her back to the dentist.

When I hadn't heard anything from anyone from Montrose by three pm on the Monday, I rang them and was told that her face was still swollen but she's not complaining so it must be alright. I told the nurse that I would ring the dentist immediately and get him to see her as soon as possible. The dentist told me to bring her in at nine am the following day. The Matron at Montrose was not happy when I arrived at eight-thirty the following morning to take Heather out. She told me it was disrupting her class. I told her that I didn't give a stuff that the class was disrupted, Heather's face had been swollen for nearly four days and I was having it seen to at nine o'clock.

The dentist came out after about five minutes and advised me that I'd best take her to an Orthodontic specialist. When I asked whom he could recommend he said, 'I know someone at the Children's Dental Hospital I'll ring him now.'

By midday the Orthodontist was telling me that I had better get her to a paediatrician as quick as I can. I told him that I had been taking all my children to Doctor Kenneth since their birth. He smiled and said, 'He's my brother-in law I'll ring him now for you.'

He came back and said, 'He's waiting for you. He'll see you as soon as you get there.'

I could tell that Doctor Kenneth was very concerned as he looked at the x-rays that had been taken at the dental hospital. Doctor Kenneth raised his eyebrows very quickly quite a few times as he studied the films. He turned to me and very quietly said, 'I'm so sorry to tell you, Mrs Williams, but Heather has a very rare tumour on her left mandible (jaw)'.

As gentle as his voice was, it seemed to me that he had screamed the word tumour in my ear. I sat there clenching my teeth trying my hardest not to cry. All I could think was, is Heather going to die?

Amelia 'When can it be removed?'

He shook his head

Dr Kenneth 'I'm not sure that it can be. It's a fibrous dysplasia tumour and that's where the problem is.'

I looked at him completely overwhelmed and totally dumbfounded and all I could do was shake my head in disbelief. He went on to say that he believed Heather had been born with the tumour but it had lain dormant for ten years. The tooth she had had extracted had grown in the centre of the tumour and when it was removed all the fibres that formed the tumour had expanded and became entangled around her mandible. He said he believed it to be benign but he couldn't guarantee that it was.

I left his surgery with my head spinning with words I had never heard in my life before and I kept repeating them over and over so that I didn't forget them when I went back home to tell Frank and my parents. The two things that I was certain of that day were that Heather was never going back to Montrose home or to Doctor Webber. I promised myself that I'd fight for her in every court in Australia if necessary.

Ironically the Matron at Montrose didn't argue when I told her Heather would never be back. I rang Doctor Webber and told him what had happened. He said that he wanted to see her and I took great pleasure in telling him that he was a moron and that whilst my arse pointed to the ground, he would never see her again. I was kicking myself for ever having gone along with his crackpot idea in the first place. I had assumed that his word was law and that by agreeing to his law I had given up my parental rights. I also promised myself that I would do whatever it took to get the best medical assistance we could find.

There was a lot of talk at the time about a fellow by the name of Doctor Milan Bric in the Cook Islands who had a so-called cure for cancer. He claimed he had a wonderful success rate and our then National Party Premier of Queensland, Joh Bjelke Petersen was backing him by donating substantial sums of money to him. At one stage not long after the onset of the tumour I said to Frank

'If Heather's tumour is cancerous, when we sell the house, we can put the money into the bank and if necessary we'll take her to the Cook Islands to see Milan Bric.'

Frank 'Like hell we will. Amelia, you know as well as I do that the bastard is a shonk and so is Bjelke.'

I'm glad that Frank was the sense of reason and let sanity prevail because Bric was proven to be one of the worst conmen known to Australia. Bric also gained the nickname of shit a brick. Unfortunately, Joh got off more lightly, even though years later he was sent to trial for underhanded dealings he was acquitted because the head juror was a Joh supporter and a National Party member. What a joke.

The following months were just a blur of medical consultants and Heather being hospitalised for test after test after test. She became a human pin cushion with all the needles she had to endure. I learnt more about syndromes and more medical jargon than many GP's have ever heard of. The little girl who had been such a pain in the arse to everyone she encountered, became very quiet and introverted. I can truthfully say that not once did I ever hear her complain about all the medical tests she had to endure.

One faciomaxillary reconstructive plastic and orthodontic surgeon we had to see (whom I shall call Doctor Scotch which will become obvious) told me emphatically that the tumour would not grow any larger than what it already had. By September, within three months of his consultation the tumour had gone from the size of a small mandarin to the size of a grapefruit. Many days during this time will be forever etched in my mind.

On one particular morning Heather had to undergo a bone marrow biopsy. I had no idea what she was about to experience. I had been sitting with her in the hospital when a tribe of medical staff entered the room. They asked me to step aside which I did and they drew the curtain around her bed. In the next instant I heard Heather scream the most excruciating screech I have ever heard in my life. She kept screaming out 'Mum, Mum, Mum' and all I could do was stand there and sob. (These days patients are anaesthetised before undergoing bone marrow biopsy.)

The following day she was discharged, we were in the lift going down to the foyer. The doors of the lift opened at the floor below and a nursing sister walked in. She took one look at Heather's face and said, 'Ooh. Who hit you in the face with a baseball bat?'

I was totally flabbergasted that someone in her profession could be so insensitive. I looked down at Heather and her eyes were filled with tears. I wanted to scream at the woman and say, you fucking senseless bitch. But I never said a word and when we alighted from the lift, I held Heather's hand tight and said,

'Hold your head up high, kid, you've got nothing to be ashamed of.'

Another time when she was hospitalised, I had asked different doctors who were traipsing in and out of her room, 'Can you please tell me what is happening?'

No one would give me an answer. Finally I saw Doctor Kenneth walking towards me and as embarrassing as it is for me to say this, I just lost my patience and flew at him like a complete lunatic and I grabbed him by the lapels of his white coat and demanded, 'What in the name of Christ is happening, no bastard will tell me anything.'

I vaguely remember his eyebrows shooting upwards but I can't remember a thing he told me other than he spoke in a very soothing voice. I apologised very profusely and he just replied, 'I can understand your frustration, Mrs Williams, it can't be easy for you.'

It was not unusual for Heather and I to be walking down the street and people would pat the arms of their friends or partner and point at Heather. We grew used to hearing, 'Look at that kid.' Or 'Oh yuk, look at her face.'

One sweet mother in Ipswich yelled to her tribe of snotty nosed offspring, 'Look, kids. Look at the kid with the fat face, quick get in front of her so you can see it.'

On these occasions Heather would glance at me and I'd stick my head up in the air to indicate to her what I'd told her privately, hold your head up and be proud.

But two separate incidents at the Indooroopilly shopping centre absolutely floored me. We were walking along the ground floor away from Target towards Myers and I became aware of a mob of about twenty people following us. I told Heather what was happening and I started to laugh.

Amelia 'Come on we're going to hurry up a bit.'

She looked at me knowing I could be capable of some very strange behaviour

Heather 'What are you going to do, Mum?'

Amelia 'Just go with it, trust me, okay?'

The more we hurried the more the mob following us hurried too. We reached the stage outside Myers where many fashion parades and special events were performed. I lifted Heather onto the podium and turned to the madding crowd and yelled 'Roll up, roll up, roll up, come and see the kid with the fat face all photos are a dollar, autographed photos are an extra fifty cents.'

We have never witnessed an embarrassed mob scatter in so many directions as what we saw that day. Heather and I looked at each other and just burst into fits of laughter until tears rolled down our cheeks. On the other occasion we were in the kitchenware department of Myer we went to the counter to pay for my purchases. As I handed over my money the woman behind the counter said, as if it was her God given right to do so, 'What's wrong with her face?' I ignored her question and looked blankly into her eyes. Unperturbed she again said, 'What's wrong with her face?' I stood there just looking at the woman. She repeated the question about three more times getting louder each time as if I was completely deaf or unable to understand the question. She put the money in the till gave me my change, handed me my goods and again very animatedly as if I had to lip read said, 'What is wrong with her face?'

I replied slowly and deliberately, 'I don't know.' I gently stroked Heather's tumour and reached over and wiped my hand on the woman's face and said, 'But it could be catching.' We strolled out of the store and we witnessed the woman scurrying as fast as she could, towards the toilets probably to wash away any possibility of contamination.

In the midst of all this mayhem we had sold our home because I could envisage our mortgage repayments rocketing to two hundred dollars per month. I know that sounds funny in this day and age but in 1977 that was very high. We bought an old Queenslander home in Booval Ipswich with the intention of renovating it. As if we didn't have enough on our plate, we encountered another huge problem. The tenants living in the house had no intentions whatsoever of shifting out. If that wasn't bad enough, the real estate agent who sold the property to us was as bent as a rusty nail. I remember that his last name was Hayden and he skited to us that he loved fooling people into believing he was a relative of Bill Hayden the then leader of the Australian Labor Party and also Haydn Sargeant who was on Brisbane's talkback radio in those days. This Hayden worked for Queen Street Realty which later became known as a company to steer clear of. We signed the contract to buy the house and on Hayden's advice we took the contract to the manager of the Booval branch of the Bank of New South Wales (later to become Westpac.) We had never had bank finance before we had always had Metropolitan Permanent Building Society finance and we banked with them as well. We waited a couple of weeks for the bank manager's decision to finance us and we got no reply. When I rang to find out what was happening the manager told us he knew nothing about the contract. I thought, either I'm living in the twilight zone or he is. Dad knew someone high up in the NSW bank and he rang him to look into the matter for us. Surprise, surprise the contract came to light and it had been altered. We had had to initial changes in the contract and someone had written on the margin near our initials that we had agreed to borrow the money from Queen Street Realty if the bank of NSW refused to finance us. The interest rate Queen Street Realty was charging was astronomical and we would never have borrowed from them if our life depended on it.

We took the contract to a solicitor and he discovered that the New South Wales bank manager had made some sort of a deal with Hayden. The only way we were able to get out of taking the finance from Queen Street Realty was the fact that our initials were face on, on the contract whereas the amendment on the margin had been written sideways. I'd love to know how many times they had gotten away with that scam.

I didn't want to deal with the Bank of New South Wales again so I went to the National Australia Bank (NAB.) At the time I didn't take much notice of the initials of the NAB but I grew to realise it was appropriate. That problem sorted, we then had to deal with the tenants. I had visions of shifting in holus bolus and throwing their belongings out onto the street. I had every intentions of carrying that out, until the solicitor told me that I would be arrested. The people who bought our home didn't want to shift in for another month so we had a verbal agreement with them that we could stay there an extra three weeks and pay them rent. The extra three weeks were nearly over and still the tenants in Booval refused to budge. Dad again came to the rescue he was a good mate of Kev Hooper MLA. Dad rang him and an appointment was made for me to see Mr Hooper in his Inala office two days before we were to shift. I told Mr Hooper my predicament and he seemed very concerned about the situation. I was beside myself with worry and just sitting in his office I was becoming increasingly agitated because his phone never stopped ringing and we were constantly being interrupted by people who had petty complaints. One call I remember hearing was to a Mrs Harvey and Mr Hooper saying 'I'll get onto it straight away Mrs Harvey.' He got off the phone and burst out laughing and shaking his head in disbelief. He told me that someone had opened a brothel in the main street of Inala. He said 'You'd think they'd have the good sense to open it in a side street. Now I've got to try and close it down what a pain in the arse.' I had to laugh at his funny sense of humour but at the same token I was concerned that he may think my situation was also a pain in his arse as well. He told his receptionist to hold all other calls and to get Joe Sciacca on the line. He explained to me that Joe was the Labor candidate for Ipswich and that he'd have a word to him about the tenants. I thought, what the hell is that going to achieve he's only the candidate, the sitting member was the Deputy Premier of Queensland. The phone rang and Mr Hooper said, 'Joe, how are things going there?' For the next five minutes they spoke party politics. I sat there thinking, Jesus what the hell is he doing? I want to get this sorted now.

Finally, Mr Hooper said, 'Yeah well, I didn't really call you to talk party politics, Joe. I've got a very dear friend of mine sitting with me now and she's having difficulty getting tenants out of a property she's bought in Ipswich. Yeah they're a pack of no hopers apparently and wouldn't move with a stick of gelignite. Tomorrow morning, first thing for sure, sounds good to me.' I thought, Christ I've got to go to Ipswich first thing in the morning to meet this Joe Sciacca. Mr Hooper got off the phone

Mr Hooper 'Amelia the tenants will be out of your home first thing tomorrow morning.'

I sat there with my mouth agape when I finally found my voice

Amelia 'Are you sure?'

Mr Hooper 'You can bank on it they will definitely be out of your house before ten am.'

I went home in total disbelief and told Frank that night that I hoped to Christ he wasn't joking because we'd be up shit creek without a paddle if they didn't go.'

I rang Dad and told him about the morning's events in Mr Hooper's office and Dad said, 'You can depend on anything he tells you.' I still wasn't convinced.

There was a mechanic's workshop and an upholstery repair shop directly opposite the house in Booval. I tried ringing the mechanic at seven the following morning but there was no answer so I rang the upholsterer. I explained who I was and asked him if the tenants were shifting out. He was a real rough bushie sounding fellow and said

'No luv they're not shiftin' now.'

I was gutted

Upholsterer 'They pissed off about an hour ago.'

Amelia 'They've already gone?'

Upholsterer 'Yep, the truck got here at sparrow fart and loaded everything and they left.'

Again, I was totally stunned. I honestly do not know how Joe Sciacca got them out but whatever he did I was extremely grateful to him. It was our sixteenth wedding anniversary and I thought it was the best present anyone could have given us.

We shifted into the Booval home the following day and the place was an absolute shambles. Not only was it filthy, the tenants had kindly pulled the wiring which held the old-fashioned lights down from the ceiling. The house was a potential death trap and we had to live there without electricity for a few days before we could get an electrician to rewire the entire house. To make matters worse it was the middle of winter and Ipswich is as cold as charity in winter and we nearly froze to death without any heaters or hot water. The house had never had a phone installation and we had to wait another six weeks for the linesmen to come and install our phone. It would have been a lot longer if we weren't classified as a priority case because of Heather's condition. The nearest public telephone was approximately a kilometre away. What a nightmare.

Not everything was doom and gloom in that house we had more than our fair share of other sheer madness, mainly on my part. I truly believed that Ipswich was way out in the country and that we had become hillbillies by shifting there. I awoke on the Monday morning about four o'clock to the sound of clip clop, clip clop, clip clop

Amelia 'Does the milkman still deliver on horse and cart here?'

Frank 'What? Jesus fuckin' Christ.'

Then he burst out into loud guffawing laughter.

I started to laugh at him laughing

Amelia 'What are you laughing about?'

It took him about five minutes to compose himself,

Frank 'Those horses are the race horses going to the track for their morning gallop.'

I nearly wet my pants and almost fell out of bed I laughed so much. Later that morning there was a knock at the door, when I answered it, there was a young woman there and when she saw me she gasped, 'You were on Pot of Gold.'

I nodded quite flattered that someone remembered me from what seemed like an eternity ago. She introduced herself and looked around as if she expected me to invite her in, which I had no intentions of because the house was a shambles with belongings scattered everywhere. There was a pause whilst I waited for her to tell me what she wanted

Woman 'Are you for or against?'

Amelia 'For or against what?'

Woman 'The racetrack and the racing fraternity.'

Amelia 'I'm neither for nor against, so I guess I'm neutral.'

She was as stunned as I was

Woman 'If you're not a trainer or you don't own a horse, do you want to join our group to close the track down?'

Amelia 'No, why would I?'

Woman 'Because the track is an eyesore and we want it closed down.'

Amelia 'Sorry, love, but I'm not interested I've got more on my plate than that nonsense. I don't give a rat's arse about racing or not racing it's got nothing to do with me.'

I mentioned it to my next-door neighbour a few days later and before we knew it the word had been spread around that the Williams were classified as being very suspect. Welcome to Ipswich.

It wasn't long after that, that the local paper The Queensland Times (locally known as the QT) screamed the headlines, Ipswich should be lacerated, says Bernard King. Bernard had been a school teacher in Ipswich before he became a TV personality and he obviously hated Ipswich with a passion almost as much as I had begun to detest living there. The Ippy peasants as I had begun to refer to them as were ready to lynch Bernard to the nearest tree. I too was hoping they'd achieve their goal but for different reasons. But secretly I thought good on ya Bernard, give 'em heaps.

Frank for some unknown reason had always maintained that he was going to die on his fortieth birthday. And on the morning of his thirty ninth birthday I awoke to find him

lying on the floor and in my dreamtime haze I thought, Oh he's a year early. And I promptly went back to sleep. When I awoke about an hour later,

I discovered his body had left the building. He had only been reaching under the bed to get his work boots. But it just goes to show how my sharing, caring kindness comes to the fore every so often.

I walked to the phone box one particular day and there were two ladies waiting at the bus stop. As I walked past them, I overheard one say that it was true there was a murder committed in the house and she mentioned exactly where I lived. I have no idea if she had known that I was the new resident there or if it was just a coincidence that I'd overheard part of their conversation. I wanted to stop and ask her more about the murder, but I didn't want to intrude on a private conversation and I was in a hurry to make the phone call. But some really strange things happened in that house and I swear to this day that the joint was haunted. I would often wake in the middle of the night from our bed shaking. Frank didn't believe in whizzers (his term for the spirit world) he said, 'You're imagining it.'

Or he'd tell me that the house was probably built over an old mine shaft and the earth's shifting a bit. I was sitting in the lounge one afternoon and our little Australian Terrier Skeezo came running towards me. The next thing he just stopped dead in his tracks and I will swear on any religious book that I saw, Skee stand on his front legs as if he was being held up by his stumpy tail and I nearly shit myself. Frank didn't believe it when I told him.

We took the kids to the Brisbane Ekka that August as we always did, and in one of their sample bags there was a cardboard mobile that they had to string together. It was a rather unusual mobile because it consisted of at least ten scary things including a witch, a skeleton and a coffin. Vivian hung it in the middle of the hallway and the bloody thing started to move around as if it was blowing in the wind but there was no breeze coming through the house at all. We all went back to the Ekka again the following day and on our return that night I turned on the lights and I stopped dead in total disbelief. All the cardboard cut-outs were on the floor except for the witch. She was swaying back and forth on her broomstick as if she was flying through the air. I pulled the witch and the string that she was attached to off the ceiling, gathered all the other cut-outs and tossed them into the burner. Very eerie.

A previous owner had put masonite sheets around the surrounds of the bathtub. Well clearly masonite sheeting hadn't been invented when the house was built. It was a hideous colour, white with blue speckles so I painted it black. It looked good too, even if I do say so myself. A couple of weeks went by and I went out grocery shopping, on my return I put all the groceries away and I went into the bathroom to put the soap in the cupboard and I couldn't believe my eyes. There were pieces of black paint all over the sides and bottom of the bath as if someone had chipped away removing the paint from above the taps. I could handle that, there was no problem about that, but what I couldn't handle was the shape on the wall where the paint had come from, was unbelievable. I'm not exaggerating the shape looked like the devil with flames surrounding him. My friend Beryl and her husband Bill were coming to dinner the following night, both of them were devout Catholics When I showed Beryl the shape in the bathroom her eyes were agog and she immediately started to pray. She advised me to remove all the paint tomorrow if possible, I told her I would've removed it as soon as I saw it yesterday but I wanted you to see it so that you knew I wasn't exaggerating.

We had gotten a whole heap of louvre windows from a house that was being demolished and in order to fit them into the area to enclose the side veranda Frank had to cut quite a few of them down to size. Someone had told him that the best way to cut them was to soak string in petrol and wind the string several times around the area that had to be cut and to set the string alight. Keep in mind that the home was at least seventy years old so the timber was ripe for burning if it ever caught on fire. I have always had a very bad habit of giving advice to Frank whenever he was doing a job. Well I didn't see it as a bad habit and Frank didn't see it as me giving him advice, he called it criticism. Because he had told me to shut my mouth earlier when I had given some advice, I did as I was told, even though this is the scene that I witnessed.

We were both standing on the side veranda at the time. He poured a small amount of petrol onto a plastic three litre ice cream lid, and soaked about two metres of string into the petrol. His tongue was outside the corner of his mouth as he wound the string as tightly as he could around the marked piece of the glass louvre. In doing so, he inadvertently placed his foot onto the plastic lid. He took his lighter out and lit the thirty centimetres piece of string that he'd left hanging down off the louvre. The flame went up the string and the sparks fell down onto the ice cream lid. He was totally engrossed in watching the string on the louvre burning he didn't notice the flame of the petrol burning on the lid until he felt the burning sensation on his foot. I was biting my teeth together so tight so as not to laugh I gave myself a headache. He started to jump around on the foot that wasn't burning, holding the burning piece of glass in one hand and trying to douse the fire on his foot with the other hand. He looked over at me and the tears were streaming down my face and I hadn't uttered a sound. As soon as he saw me we both absolutely howled with laughter. We were lucky to douse the fire without any damage to the house. When we'd finished, I suggested that he take the rest of the louvres down to the backyard.

Frank Why didn't you warn me?

Amelia 'You told me to shut my mouth before, and besides I wouldn't have wanted to miss that sight for all the rice in China'.

He finished enclosing the veranda in time for the arrival of Michelle and Mark who had helped me when I was in New Zealand three and a half years earlier. I hadn't kept in touch with them since receiving an invitation to their wedding three years previously but a mutual friend had told us that they were arriving, so we headed to the airport to greet them. Michelle didn't recognise me and as I later found out she had wondered who the hell the woman was kissing her husband when he walked through the arrival gates. I found out much later that she was really upset because Mark had had an affair and had dabbled with heroin just prior to coming to Australia. The main reason they had come to Australia was for a fresh start. Another couple were supposed to come to meet Michelle and Mark and they were meant to stay with the other couple until they found their own place to live. Although we all waited for a while the other couple never showed up and we brought Michelle and Mark to our home to show them some true Australian hospitality. Michelle told us later when I explained to them about Heather's tumour that she had thought Heather had a few huge gobstopper lollies in her mouth. I thought, hello we have a brain surgeon amongst us here. It didn't take them long to get a nice unit and they both found good jobs within two weeks. Mark had completed two apprenticeships as a fitter and turner and motor mechanic and he started with a firm as a fitter and turner. Michelle had worked a number of years at the ANZ bank in New Zealand and she got a job at the main branch in Brisbane. I hadn't really warmed to Michelle when I was in New Zealand but I liked Mark. In fact, I had nicknamed Michelle 'Princess I love me' when I first clapped eyes on her. It took me awhile for me to get to know and trust her she seemed so aloof, but over time I realised that she was quite an insecure person who didn't trust people easily. They'd only been in Australia two months and in the course of conversation Mark told me that he had applied for a car loan. Even though Michelle worked at the bank they had knocked him back because they told him he'd have to be in the country twelve months before they were eligible for a loan. Frank and I didn't hesitate to go as guarantor for them.

I told him that if he let us down and reneged on the payments, we'd hunt him down. They didn't let us down and they paid it off as soon as they could.

I used to pray every day that a horse trainer from down south would miraculously arrive and want to buy the house from us. When I say pray my idea of praying is begging for whatever I want, I reckon whenever I ask God for something He says, 'here she is, she thinks its ring a request time again'.

I knew that we would never get our money back what we'd paid for the house from a local buyer because we had paid too much for it thanks to our stupidity and Queen Street Realty. Believe it or not my prayers were answered, though I had to wait another three years. A fellow from Wiseman's Ferry in NSW knocked on my door and practically begged me to sell him the house. I sold it to him for about ten thousand dollars more than what it was worth. So that's proof that God does answer your prayers but He doesn't believe in hurrying.

Chapter 45

Physicians Heal Thyself

All of Heather's tests proved nothing which meant we were getting nowhere fast I was becoming so anxious that I was almost at the point of ripping my hair out. I continued to see Doctor Orford who had been my GP for a number of years. On one particular occasion I burst into tears from sheer frustration and said we were getting nowhere fast with all the tests. He told me to leave it with him that he couldn't promise anything but he'd see what he could do. I had no idea what he was talking about and on returning home to Booval, a half an hour drive from his surgery, I walked in and the phone started ringing. I was surprised to hear it was Doctor Orford. He told me he'd just been talking to a colleague in Perth who thought he may be able to help me but I'd have to get the x-rays over to him in Perth.

I found it incredible that he had rung Perth on my behalf, ringing interstate in those days cost a small fortune.

Amelia 'You rang Perth?'

He laughed

Dr Orford 'As you do.'

When I got off the phone, I just stood there shaking my head in total disbelief saying to myself, this is unbelievable. I rang Qantas to ask if they could take the x-rays to Perth. No, they wouldn't. I then asked how much it would be for us to fly there, it was an exorbitant amount, and if my memory serves me correctly it was sixteen hundred dollars each for Heather and me just to fly there. On top of that we'd have to have accommodation and enough money for food. We couldn't afford that under any circumstances.

I rang Doctor Kenneth and told him about the doctor in Perth he was very interested and said he'd see what he could arrange. He rang me back a few minutes later to inform me that his brother-in-law, the orthodontist we had seen months previously, was flying to Perth the following day on his holidays. If I could get the x-rays to him first thing the next day his brother-in-law would personally take them to the doctor in Perth. I looked to Heaven and said, 'Thank you' to God and my grandmother.

I was totally convinced that she was organising all these wonderful coincidences. The x-rays were taken to Perth and the doctor over there gave them to Dr Kenneth's brother-in-law who flew to a doctor in Adelaide. He in turn rang Doctor Kenneth and advised what procedures could be done. I never found out the names of the doctors in Perth or Adelaide but I will be forever in their debt. Doctor Kenneth patiently explained that he had to find the surgeon who would in his opinion be the right one to operate on Heather. I said, 'Aren't all surgeons as good as each other?'

He replied, 'You'd be surprised, Mrs Williams that they are not.'

He went on further to explain, 'Some surgeons would want to do the job for the sake of doing it others will want to operate for their own agenda. I want to find the one whom I consider will want to operate for Heather's sake.'

Operation 'find the surgeon' began.

I have no recall how many plastic reconstructive surgeons we went to but the list was like a who's who on Wickham Terrace. A copy of the x-ray results was forwarded to other plastic reconstructive surgeons in other parts of Queensland and New South Wales. One *lovely* fellow told me I was a liar when I told him the tumour had developed immediately after the tooth was extracted. He told me that it was *impossible* and that any doctor who believed that story was a fool. I said, 'Really? Well, Doctor, I think you might feel the foolish one, because Heather has been a regular patient of Doctor Kenneth since birth, in fact he saw her ten days before the tumour developed and he saw her four days after the tumour developed. Heather was in the care of Montrose home for a month up until the tumour developed. So, who's the fool now?'

Needless to say, Doctor Kenneth's eyebrows rose rapidly on hearing what that doctor had said.

I remember taking a copy of the results to one of the specialists and he requested I get the original x-rays off Doctor Kenneth and bring them to his surgery. I trudged along Wickham Terrace to Doctor Kenneth's surgery and told him the doctor wanted them. Doctor Kenneth laughed and said, 'I'm sure he does want them, Mrs Williams, but he's going to have to *want* . Heather's x-rays are the most wanted x-rays on Wickham Terrace because her tumour is extremely rare. We would never get them back if we lend them to *anyone* .'

Around about the same time, I heard about an acquaintance's son who had developed a brain tumour. I told Doctor Kenneth about the boy and how upsetting it must be for them. He replied, 'Mrs Williams a brain tumour is nothing in comparison with what Heather's got. Surgeons remove brain tumours every day of the week, it's a common occurrence, Heather's tumour is uniquely rare.'

Unfortunately, the lad died from complications about twelve months later.

During all this time Heather announced that she could feel something *funny* in the left side of her mouth. We discovered another tooth was growing through the centre of the tumour. We saw a number of highly qualified dental surgeons but none of them would perform the tooth extraction. I remember one of them coming out of his surgery he was sweating profusely his hands were shaking and he was as white as a sheet. All he could say was, 'I'm sorry I can't do this and I don't know anyone who could.'

Initially Doctor Kenneth had suggested we go back to Doctor Scotch and I refused because I had no faith in him whatsoever. After seeing four other Orthodontic surgeons, Doctor Kenneth insisted that I go back to Doctor Scotch. Reluctantly I agreed and Doctor Scotch told me to bring Heather into his surgery at eight o'clock the following morning. I could tell that Doctor Scotch was very nervous the next day and I thought, God I hope this bastard knows what he's doing. Heather emerged about half an hour later and she looked at me and rolled her eyes skyward. All Doctor Scotch said to me was, 'It went well.'

We got to the lift

Heather 'Mum, he was really scared his hands were shaking and he stunk of grog too.'

Amelia 'What?'

She nodded

Heather 'It's true his hands were shaking and I could smell the grog on his breath it really stunk.'

I was just thankful that we didn't need to see him again. But to add insult to injury when I took his bill to my medical benefits fund, they paid me back everything except for ten cents. Having to pay him ten cents stuck in my craw for a long time.

Doctor Peter Catt was another plastic reconstructive surgeon we had consulted and I thought he was a cocky little upstart of a man. He didn't seem to appreciate anything I had to say and I felt very annoyed as we walked out of his surgery. I thought, to myself, he's up himself I don't like him at all.

Seventeen months after the tumour had developed Doctor Kenneth called me to come to his surgery to tell me that he had chosen the surgeon. I was so excited I could hardly wait.

Dr Kenneth 'After weighing up all the pros and cons, I've decided that Doctor Peter Catt is the best surgeon to operate.'

I almost fell off the chair.

Amelia 'Why him?'

Dr Kenneth 'He ticked all the right boxes, he's young, enthusiastic and he has Heather's best interest at heart and his credentials are impeccable.'

I must've had a stunned look on my face because he said, 'Do you have any questions or reservations?'

Amelia 'I trust your opinion Doctor but I found Doctor Catt to be downright rude.'

He laughed

Dr Kenneth 'I admire your forthright manner, Mrs Williams, but what you see as rude I see as determination to get the best possible result.'

We had several consultations with Doctor Catt and on one occasion he expressed his concern that he would be unable to remove the tumour without removing the jaw bone. He explained that if he had to, he would have to build her jaw with her hip bone. That would not only make her face grotesque but it would also leave her with a permanent limp. I said, 'If it's necessary to remove her jaw bone and use a hip bone then I want to volunteer my hip bone to rebuild her face'.

He replied, 'That's very admirable of you, Mrs Williams.'

I said, 'There's nothing admirable about that at all, any mother would do the same thing.'

He said, 'No they wouldn't.'

I said, 'Oh they would so.'

He cocked his head on one side and looked at me as if he was trying to fathom what makes this woman tick. I looked back at him and thought, what a strange little man you are. It was a moment I'll never forget.

He went over every scenario of what could go wrong and he explained every aspect of what he hoped would and would not happen during the surgery. Eventually he came to the decision that the only way to do it was to cut Heather's throat from under her left ear down to below the centre of her chin and peel back the skin to reveal the tumour. Having done that, he would have to resect the tumour (shave it down) bit by bit.

The chances of him cutting a major nerve causing Heather's face to droop were extremely high. Every nerve, sinew and fibre were criss-crossed like a giant ball of fine crochet cotton. I didn't envy his position at all, but by God I admired his courage to try and achieve the impossible. I began to see the human side of Doctor Catt and the more I met him the more I learned to respect him but he still displayed a superior air about him.

I think we both learnt to admire and respect each other's point of view but it seemed I used to push his buttons by asking far too many questions. But I have the ability to do that to everyone. I guess in a way we had a love/hate relationship, he loved to hate me and I hated to love him.

Heather was booked into the private section of the Royal Brisbane Hospital in February, 1979, twenty months after the tumour had developed. I went to Doctor Orford to tell him the good news and he was over the moon. I said, 'Seeing as you got the ball rolling, I'm inviting you to be in the operating theatre to witness the surgery.'

He burst out laughing and I said, 'What's so funny?'

He said, 'You can't invite me it's not up to you to invite me.'

I was shocked and said, 'Why not, I'm her mother and you're our GP. Don't you want to be there?'

He said, 'Of course I'd want to be there every GP in Australia would want to witness surgery like that.'

'Well what's stopping you?'

'It's just not etiquette, Doctor Catt would have to invite me and specialists do not invite ordinary GP's into their world, especially an operation of this magnitude.'

I said, 'Well we'll soon see about that. I'll see Doctor Catt as soon as I can and tell him I've invited you and that I want you there.'

He laughed heartily and scoffed, 'You will not.'

I said, 'I'll bet you my house that I do. It's about time someone pulled him down a peg or two.'

I went into Doctor Catt the following day and told him that I'd invited Doctor Orford to attend the operation. He very indignantly said, 'You can't do that.'

I said, 'So I've been told but I did it anyway.'

Dr Catt looked at me as if I was an alien from outer space took a deep breath and said, 'I've already chosen Doctor Scotch to assist me in the surgery.'

I gasped, 'That drunk, he was as full as tick the day he extracted Heather's tooth at eight o'clock in the morning.'

He looked stunned and said, 'I know nothing about that.'

I said, 'You do now because I just told you, but I didn't say that Doctor Orford was going to *assist* you. I said I want him to be present to witness the operation and considering that Doctor Scotch will be there I'll need a witness to make sure Doctor Scotch doesn't do anything wrong.'

The following week Doctor Orford rang to thank me because he had just received a written invitation from Doctor Catt to be in the operating theatre to witness Heather's surgery. He said, 'You are unbelievable.'

Unfortunately, Doctor Kenneth was unable to attend the operating theatre because of his workload. If I had've had my way I would have invited myself into the theatre as well. That would have set the cat amongst the pigeons (No pun intended.)

The surgery seemed to take an eternity and Frank and I sat outside on the veranda of the hospital nearest to the operating theatre just waiting and pacing. Approximately six hours went by and when I saw Doctor Catt approaching. I almost broke my neck to get to him as fast as I could. When he smiled (probably at witnessing me almost falling arse over tit) I thought, Oh that's a good sign.

He said the magic words, 'I'm very pleased with everything it all went well, no major hiccups.'

I said, 'What about the nerves are they all intact?'

He said, 'All the major nerves are, but we'll just have to wait and see over the next few days.'

I could have flung my arms around him and given him a big sloppy kiss but I just humbly thanked him and burst into tears. As it turned out, one of the nerves had been badly bruised from the severe onslaught and even to this day over forty years later she still suffers total numbness from the left corner of her mouth down to her chin. But that's a minor problem considering the magnitude of the surgery. I could finally heave a sigh of relief and I thought, thank Christ I can finally get back to some form of normality. Yeah right.

I was taught many years previously to never let my guard down and to always expect the unexpected. What would possess me to think otherwise? Because let's face it my life seemed to be possessed by Satan. You've heard the saying some people have the Midas touch and everything they touch turns to nuggets of gold. Well, I have the ability to turn everything I touch, into nuggets of shit.

Frank had been working at the abattoirs in Ipswich for quite some time and one morning in March 1980 he slipped on the back steps on his way to work. He somehow jarred his back and ended up in the Ipswich Hospital. He should have by rights started a new claim with Worker's Compensation but instead he tried to re-open the old claim he had opened in 1960. In hindsight it was plain stupidity especially after he got knocked back and we asked Bob Gibbs the then minister for trades and work relations to look into the matter for us. Gibbs was about as useless as tits on a bull and only made the situation worse.

Frank had to go on sickness benefit payments and was facing major surgery. To put it mildly, his back was completely stuffed. It was a nightmare trying to feed a family of five and pay the mortgage on the pittance the Federal Government paid us. Frank went back to the meatworks to work but almost killed himself doing it.

I saw an ad in the Queensland Times for Residential Care Assistants (RCA) in training to work at Challinor Centre for the Intellectually Handicapped so I decided to apply for a position there. After having completed the written test which consisted of questions such as, *if there were three parrots, seven pigeons eight doves and seventy three peaches on the branches of the tree and x amount of birds flew away blah, blah, blah---*' All the questions were about twenty lines long which I thought had no relevance to anything but I guess to the powers that be, they were classified as IQ tests.

I received a letter stating that I had passed the test and I had to supply three letters of reference from citizens of good standing. My dear friend Beryl gave me a beautiful letter, and I got another reference from one of Dad's friends, I don't know what possessed me but I decided to ask Doctor Kenneth for a reference. I made an appointment to see him in his surgery because I didn't want to take up his precious time without him being paid for it. I didn't tell his secretary that it wasn't for Heather she just assumed it was. When I arrived, she was surprised to see that I was on my own and I explained why I was there. She apologised profusely and said, 'Look, Amelia, I'll be completely honest with you Doctor Kenneth doesn't write personal references for anyone. Many doctors have asked for references and he's always refused, he never gives out personal references.'

I was crestfallen because I thought a letter from him would be ideal to prove to the Government that I was at the very least capable of trying to be a caring parent. His secretary said, 'I'll go in and tell him you're here and why, but don't hold too many hopes, okay?'

I nodded and she entered his surgery, as I waited, I thought, Christ you're an idiot what on God's earth possessed you to believe he'd give you a reference? After all you grabbed him by the lapels one day and manhandled the poor man.

I felt like running out the door for being so stupid. It seemed like an eternity before his secretary came out with a blank expression on her face. I stood up and shrugged my shoulders and said, 'Thanks you did your best.'

She continued to look at me and finally said, 'Amelia, he's written you a beautiful reference go home and frame it because he said he wouldn't do this for anyone else.'

I burst into tears I was so proud I was bursting. I didn't dare open the envelope to read the reference for fear that I would spoil it by spilling tears all over the writing.

It was a beautiful reference and although I didn't frame it I vowed I would treasure it forever.

Chapter 46

More Than One Flew Over the Cuckoo's Nest

I started at Challinor (as an RCA Residential Care Assistant in training) at nine am on Monday 26th November, 1979. By ten past nine, I was handing out medication to sixteen residents in the area I had been assigned to, which consisted of three modules.

There were seven mixed residents in one module, four ladies in my module and five men in the other. I was shitting razor blades I was so nervous. I had never administered medication to anyone in my life, other than to my children. I had no idea who was who, including my co-workers and two of them were new recruits. I had to rely on a woman RCA by the name of Sandra to make sure I was giving the right residents the correct medication.

Sandra was about as helpful as a bully is to the vulnerable. I didn't like her from the moment I clapped eyes on her. Nor did I like the two other RCA's Mandy and Peter. The two other new RCA's in training were nice. Krys was only seventeen and although I thought she was far too young for that type of job and not really the brightest crayon in the box, I liked her, she was a really good kid.

The other lady, Janice was about fifty but she was an old fifty and was the type who wore an apron. I guess there's nothing wrong with wearing an apron but it just didn't seem to be the place to walk around with a mumsy apron wrapped around your waist.

The four residents in my module were Hilda (Happy), Beryl, Rene and Greta. Happy was in her sixties and so named because she always seemed to be smiling and constantly drooling. She was mute but was able to hear, she also had club feet and wheeled herself around in her wheelchair. Although Sandra had told me differently, Happy was able to understand almost everything you said to her.

Beryl was in her late fifties she too was a happy soul but she didn't have a great vocabulary she constantly sang more than spoke the words '*I love you*'. After a few days of me being there, if I showed signs of tiredness or groaned for any reason, she would clasp her hands together as if in prayer for me.

Rene weighed between sixteen and twenty stone and was in her thirties. She was blind, bedridden and loved to play with dolls. She also loved to sing and she had a phenomenal memory for the words of all the songs. She'd only have to hear a song once and she would remember the words. It was extraordinary.

Greta was only about sixteen she was a very pretty girl but she had absolutely no ability to communicate with anyone and she was a biter which made everyone want to steer clear from her as much as possible.

I'd only been there about an hour, and a very angry looking resident from another module across the aisle came towards me with his fists up to his chest moving them around in a circular motion. I thought, this is it, I'm going to be knocked out, I'll be in hospital and on bloody compo and I've only been here for an hour.

As it turned out Poppy was a harmless poor, old bugger, his RCA came over to fetch him back to his module and she explained that he wasn't looking for a fight he was

begging for biscuits. *What a relief that was* .

Later that day I noticed that Happy had a sore on the nape of her neck which was very raw and angry looking. I asked Sandra what it was because I thought at first it was ringworm. Sandra very matter of factly said it was a burn from the curling wand. She said, 'Happy can be an old bitch and put on a turn when you least expect it, she played up the other day when I was fixing her hair and she accidently got burnt'.

She went on to say, 'If she stacks on a blue, just take her into the bathroom and put the fire hose on the old bitch.'

I was bug eyed at this statement. I thought to myself, pig's arse I'll do that, if Happy starts throwing punches or has a tantrum I'll just step aside.

A couple of days went by and I was the only one who was applying cream to Happy's neck. I'd been told to leave it alone because she's likely to turn nasty but I thought, if I had a sore like this and I was unable to soothe it myself I'd hope that someone would try and help me. Just as I was about to apply some cream, I looked at the sore and had an idea. I took the curling wand out of the cupboard and placed it close to the sore. The curling wand was far too big to have caused the burn. Then I took a cigarette out of my bag and bingo exactly the right size.

I thought, Sandra you slaggy slut you burnt her with your cigarette, you low class moll. But I had no proof of how it had happened because it happened before I started there, so there was nothing I could do or say. But I knew my first gut instinct about Sandra was right.

Everyone was assigned to doing three shifts on a weekly basis, six am to two pm the first week, two pm to ten pm the second week, and ten pm to six am the third week. We were entitled to half an hour for our meal break and fifteen minutes each for two tea breaks per shift. There were other RCA's who worked in our module Vanessa, Margaret, Brian, Malcolm, Les and a few others but I never had an issue with any of them. They all treated the residents well and they were friendly enough to me.

I had been there less than three weeks and working the ten pm to six am shift with Mandy and Peter. I had learnt to dislike Peter more and more every day. It wasn't because he was obviously gay, a person's sexual preference is their business and doesn't worry me in the slightest. Peter had an awful attitude and was just downright rude. He was equally balanced because he had a chip on each shoulder. Actually, he was so agro he had a block on each shoulder not just a chip.

Mandy wasn't too bad, though she could be quite bitchy at times. But she was on very friendly terms with Peter and Sandra and they were all as thick as thieves. I didn't think much of her because of her association with them.

It was about eleven pm and both Mandy and Peter had disappeared without even saying a word, leaving me to look after the sixteen residents on my own. That was definitely a big no, no. It was a really hot night and two of Mandy's residents had epileptic seizures. I managed to get them both on the floor so they could sleep after they had fitted. I was unable to go looking for Mandy because that would've meant leaving the sixteen residents completely unattended. To say I was beside myself would be an understatement. I was not only packing death I was fit to be tied, I was so angry.

Then the unthinkable happened, a massive power failure hit. The South East Queensland Electricity Board (SEQEB) had been on strike for a while and South East Queensland had been experiencing intermittent blackouts that could last for hours. I was running around for over an hour like a chook with its head cut off trying to settle all the residents down. I kept counting them to make sure that none of them wandered away. Then I discovered Happy had disappeared. I was almost hysterical. Somehow, I managed to get the other fifteen settled in their beds. Then I broke the rules by leaving the area unattended.

I ran as fast as I could down the hall past the staffroom to another module where Happy often went to visit another lady. I found her and I scolded her for going away. I started to hurry back pushing her wheelchair back to her module. As I ran pushing her, I said, 'You're a very naughty girl for leaving.'

And the next thing I had difficulty pushing the wheelchair the wheels wouldn't budge and Happy was making this awful sound as if she was trying to scream. She was jumping around on her backside and I thought, Oh Christ she's having some sort of fit too I'm going to have to try and carry her back.

I put my arms under her armpits and tried to grab her hands to lift her and that's when I realised that she had hold of the wheels and was stopping me from pushing her wheelchair. I grabbed her arms placed them around her as if she was hugging herself and I bear hugged her and nudged the chair along with my face. I don't know how long it took me to get her back to her bed but I was sweating like a pig and completely exhausted but oh so bloody angry.

I wasn't angry with Happy though I was annoyed with her but I could see the funny side of it as well. Poor old bugger she didn't think she'd done anything wrong by visiting her friend. I had passed the staffroom twice and each time I heard Peter and Mandy in there laughing and talking. By the time they returned, they had been out of their modules for an hour and forty minutes and they only returned when the lights came back on.

I was ready to rock and roll and I wanted so badly to punch Peter in the face when he came in and sneered at me. I took one look at him and I snarled at him, 'You are nothing but a cunt and that's insulting a cunt.'

He said, 'What did you call me?

I said, 'I called you a cunt, are you deaf as well as being a stupid ignoramus?'

I walked out down to the staffroom to have my break and I was pleased to see Malcolm sitting there having his coffee. He had been called in to take over another module because another RCA had called in sick. I told him what had happened and he warned me, 'Be very careful with Peter he's not on an even keel, he can be extremely dangerous.'

I said, 'Great that's all I need, another resident to watch carefully.'

I have never thought for one moment that I am an intelligent person because I often do some incredibly stupid things. And I never stop to think, I just blurt out whatever comes to mind. I tell people, 'I have no co-ordination between hand and foot and no co-ordination or filter between brain and tongue.'

I was told by a psychologist I knew a few years ago that I am a mosaic thinker and the majority of the world are linear thinkers. But considering that the he was a pot smoker and later ended up in Boggo Road for possession and dealing, he was probably blowing steam out of his rear end.

But weighing up the pros and cons of the individuals whom I was working with at Challinor I became concerned about how dumb I really was. Seriously, I began to question my sanity or should I say lack of sanity because I truly believed that some of the residents were smarter than the workers and that included the hierarchy. I thought If this is the type of people the Government employ here where does that put me? I'm in the same category. I am an unintelligent moron just like them.

I'm not joking the majority of people I was working with were trailer trash. The so-called intelligent hierarchy were a bunch of dickheads with so-called degrees but they had not one ounce of common sense between all of them. I worried about the IQ test that I had done to get into the job. Did I actually pass it? Or did they only employ the morons who failed it? Or was I employed because I had a beautiful letter of reference from Doctor Kenneth? These questions played heavily on my mind all the time.

Mary was a triple certificated nursing sister and she had about as much common sense as a retarded flea. On one particular occasion she sat down with Johnny a forty-eight year old guy who had Down's Syndrome.

Johnny was an absolute treasure, sometimes his speech was a bit hard to understand because not only did he have poor vocabulary, he also had a slight lisp. But you'd get the gist of what he was talking about after a while. He would often tell whoever was within earshot about the fire that destroyed his parent's shop. He would say, 'They burnt the butthe thop (butcher shop) and the flameth (flames) he'd fling his arms in the air to display how high the flames went and the truck clang, clang, clang, clang and they blame me.'

He'd hit his chest and repeat over and over, 'And they blame me.'

The poor little bugger would cry his heart out. You didn't have to be Einstein to realise that the parents must've burnt the butcher shop down to get the insurance, they blamed Johnny and he was put into Challinor, killing two birds with one stone.

Anyhow on this particular morning Johnny had been sitting quietly just flicking through a magazine. Mary plonked herself down alongside of him and for over an hour she tried to coax him to go out into the solarium. Johnny wasn't having a bar of it.

Mary 'Come along, Johnny, come and sit in the solarium.

Johnny 'No.'

Mary 'Johnny, would you like to come outside with me?'

Johnny 'No.'

Finally, Mary told me that she was going to have her morning tea, and that she'd be back later to try again to get Johnny outside.'

Amelia 'Righto, Mary, I'll see you shortly.'

As soon as she had turned the corner I walked over to Johnny and asked 'What have you got there, kiddo? Oh! a magazine that's terrific, Johnny, is there anything good to look at?' I flicked over a few pages and found a photo of a car and said, 'Look at that, mate, isn't that fantastic?' Johnny squinted and put his face close to the book. I said, 'Why don't you take it outside into the solarium and you'll be able to see it much better'. He picked the book up and went straight outside and sat in the sun and studied the car. I said to him, 'Now when Mary comes back, you tell her to go away and stop annoying you'. He never looked at me and I thought no more of it. Mary returned about an hour later and said, 'Where's Johnny?' I pointed out towards the solarium.

Mary 'How did you get him out there, Amelia?'

Amelia 'I used a bit of what I call common sense, Mary.'

She looked at me as if I was off my trolley and scurried out into the solarium. As soon as Johnny saw her, he yelled at her at top note, 'Fuck off.' I nearly wet myself, but I kept a very straight face and pretended I hadn't heard and when she hurried out of the area I sat down in the office and howled with laughter. When I finally stopped laughing, I walked out to Johnny and said, 'Good boy, mate.'

Because I had gone off the brain at Peter. I noticed that many of the RCA's would get up and walk out of the staffroom when I walked in. If they thought I was worried by this, they were sadly mistaken because I was a bit above listening to the stories about their sex life and/or how they'd got pissed the night before. I walked into the staffroom one day and there wasn't a soul to be seen but there was a note pinned to the notice board. I don't remember the exact words but basically it said,

Use your brain before you open your mouth . It didn't mention my name but you'd have to be a complete dunce not to know it was meant for me. I sat down and wrote,

TO THE PHANTOM GRAFITTI WRITER

I know who you are, you should know that I know, and I know that I know that you know—which means —I know you know that I know, and you know that I know. A bit confused? Now everyone knows.

And what I know beats what you know.

To stand out in a crowd one needs to display love, kindness and pity
Especially to those less fortunate than I who can't even sign their graffiti.
And I signed my name.

PS I'm glad that you acknowledged the fact that I do have a brain. I'd love for you to join my debating team. If you've got five minutes to spare then you can tell me all you know.

The following day I came into the staffroom to find another note which read, *SMART ARSED BITCH*. I replied,

The Hallowed walls of the staffroom doth have one gigantic ear
Flapping and constantly listening to anything it can hear
There's also one evil beady eye, peering and watching you
It never bats its one long lash, as it watches all you do
The mouth, an enormous cavity swallows every tiny sound
It adds and subtracts, then regurgitates each word,
Around and around and around
So, when you walk out through the door please give the wall a kick
Eventually you'll destroy its vile ways, brick by bloody brick.
And again, I signed it.

No need to be told I was hauled into the headquarters of the brain trust (laughingly called the hierarchy) and I was given a dressing down for writing notices on the staffroom noticeboard. (?)

I always tried to show some form of affection to every one of the sixteen residents in the module. I feel even now forty years later that I was rewarded with their affection in return. There were a couple of them whom I couldn't warm to but I can truthfully say I did my best.

Alan was a sweet little Downie he used to call everyone Mickey Mummy but for some unknown reason from the day I walked into the module he called me Queen Elizabeth. Everyone laughed the first time he said it, but they didn't seem to appreciate it when he continued calling me that. Especially Peter, because he favoured Alan and treated all the other residents with disdain. Every day Alan would want to dance with me and he'd pat my face and say, 'I love you Queen Elizabeth.'

Billy was the most beautiful natured of them all, he had the worst case of cerebral palsy I've ever seen he had all of his faculties and a twinkle in his eyes all the time. He was also mute and would communicate by honking a horn like Harpo Marx which was attached to his special wheelchair. He loved to sit outside the module and watch for any pretty girl that might walk by and he'd honk the horn at them.

I used to smoke in those days but smoking was forbidden in the modules. Billy became my special guard, I asked him to only honk twice at the pretty girls but honk more than three times if he saw the shit kickers coming so I could get rid of my cigarette. He had a funny laugh it was something like the noise a seal makes but he would inhale and exhale the laugh. When I said shit kickers to him, I thought he was going to choke he laughed so loud. He'd honk that horn as long and as loud as he could and the shit kickers always thought he was greeting them.

I could wax lyrical about most of the residents, they all brought joy to my heart, yet before I started at Challinor I would've said things like, 'They should all have been put to sleep at birth.'

If for no other reason they were put on this earth to teach me a thing or two about severely handicapped people. And that can't be a bad thing.

Christmas Day arrived and I had to start work at two pm. I always liked to be at work well before time and I got there at about one-thirty just in time to see Peter taking Alan away from the module. Peter smiled at me and nodded so I smiled back at him and said, 'Hello, Merry Christmas.'

I thought, Obviously Christmas agrees with Peter, I've never seen him look so happy. I asked someone where Peter was taking Alan and I was told he was going to Peter's home. That concerned me, Peter was gay but not happy Alan was a happy fellow but couldn't communicate. In my opinion it was not a good combination and I wondered what bright spark gave permission for that leave of absence.

Alan was returned by another RCA at six pm and he was blind drunk. Although he wasn't my resident, I got him into his bed because Alan's RCA had disappeared along with the other RCA on duty with me. All the residents were exceptionally good that day and I had them all fed, bathed and dressed and in bed sound asleep by seven-thirty pm.

I'd become confident enough to leave the module unattended and I went to the staffroom, it was in darkness and I thought, that's odd, the staffroom light never goes off. It was a rather dark room and never got any sunlight. I turned the light on and made myself a coffee. One of the RCA's walked past and I said, 'Where is everyone?'

She grumbled 'dunno' and hurried away

I said under my breath, 'Yes, Merry Christmas to you too sweetheart.'

I went back to the module with my coffee and the other two RCA's had not returned. I thought, Oh well, here we go again. It was eerie there that night on my own, more so than the night I'd been in the blackout because the night of the blackout I had been rushed off my feet. I walked out into the hall and I heard voices in the staffroom and I saw another RCA walk out and down the other way.

I walked across the hall to the other module and I asked one of the RCA's there, 'Can you keep an eye on them over here please, they're all asleep, I just want to go down the hall.'

He agreed and I went to the staffroom. I was surprised to see Malcolm sitting there with a writing pad and writing what I thought was a letter.

Amelia 'G'day mate where is everyone, what's going on?'

He looked at me in total disbelief

Malcolm 'Hasn't anyone told you?'

Amelia 'Nuh. Told me what?'

Malcolm 'Jesus Christ.'

Amelia 'What. What's wrong?'

He put the pen down took a deep breath sighed and said, 'Sit Down.'

I did as he said, and I almost fainted at learning the story that unfolded and no one had bothered to tell me.

Peter had brought Alan back at about six pm alright, but he had also brought a loaded gun to the centre. He had been ranting and raving and waving it around and threatening to kill Lana Voltz, Dora Dench and Amelia Williams (Lana was the Manager of Challinor centre and Dora was a Residential Care Officer (RCO.) So, I was in *good* company. Malcolm had tackled Paul to the ground and disarmed him he had held him until someone else rang the police and ambulance. Peter had been taken to Wacol Special Hospital (formerly Goodna Mental Institution) I was told later that he had been diagnosed as a drug addicted, paranoid schizophrenic, and an alcoholic, homosexual.

He was discharged nine months later to the unsuspecting world because the Government and Challinor kept it hush, hush. He wasn't discharged from the public service instead he was given a job in the Queensland Railway Department.

Malcolm should have received a bravery award for his actions but to do that the Bjelke Petersen Government would have had a lot of egg on their faces trying to explain the situation. No need to be told, I had to face the hierarchy firing squad again, this time to explain why Peter was gunning for me. And guess what? When I told them the truth about that blackout night in November, they told me

I should be charged with assault for holding Happy's arms down against her will, and that I should be on a disciplinary charge for leaving the module unattended. I looked at them in total disbelief and laughed in their faces.

And I always thought Christmas Day was supposed to be the happiest day of the year. Maybe I'm a Jewish Muslim and don't realise it.

I didn't get fired (no pun intended) instead Graeme, (another RCO) came to me the following day and told me I had to go to the children's module to work there. It was the worst module in the entire centre. I felt physically ill when I walked in the sights of some of those poor little bastards were indescribable.

One of the children I was assigned to look after, was a little girl called Robyn. Robyn was three years old and her body was the size of a six-month old baby, but her head was the size of an elongated watermelon. What can I possibly say that would soften the blow of my saying, I wanted to smother Robyn to put her out of her misery? I was feeding, caring and bathing a baby who had no future whatsoever. I was well out of my depth.

The hierarchy must've been rubbing their hands with glee with the thoughts that they had broken me. Almost every hour Graeme would come around to ask me how I was coping, each time I would smile and say something like, 'I absolutely love working here.' Or I'd say, 'I feel so rewarded and fulfilled being here.'

I'd go home at the end of each day and cry my guts out. Thank Christ I was only there for a week. Little did the hierarchy know that I came very close to tossing the job in, at the end of that week. But Graeme came again on the Friday afternoon and told me that I'd be going back to my usual module the following Monday.

I got to work one morning for the six am start and it had been pre-arranged that we were taking some of the residents to the Ipswich Show in the park next door to Challinor and the residents were all excited. Rene couldn't go because we were unable to put her in her wheelchair. They had a hoist to lift her, but apparently there was a part that had been missing for at least eighteen months and although the replacement part was supposed to have been ordered, it had never arrived. Other staff had been called in to watch the residents left in the module whilst we took the wheelies out. We'd only been at the show for about ten minutes when an RCA came and told me that I had to go and see Marjorie Brown (she was another one of the hierarchy, and second in charge to Lana.) When I got to Marjorie's room Dora was there and I thought, Shit, the shit kickers are out in force today, Peter must've broken out of Wacol. I was ordered (not asked nicely) to sit down. It went through my mind, Jesus, Peter must've gotten a machine gun this looks serious.

Marjorie barked, 'You didn't clean Rene's false teeth this morning.'

Amelia 'Huh.?'

She repeated the question only louder, and I tried not to laugh.

Amelia 'No I couldn't find them, I looked for them, but they weren't in the glass and I was in a hurry and I was going to look for them when I got back.'

Marjorie 'They were in her bed.'

I looked at them both and wondered what the hell they expected me to say or do. I just sat there waiting for the next instalment.

Dora 'She slept with them in her mouth, she could have choked to death, you are lucky you're not on a manslaughter charge.'

Amelia 'How did you work that one out?'

Dora 'She's your responsibility you should have reported they were missing before you left the module.'

Amelia 'I never left her teeth in her head overnight.'

And in saying that, I remembered that young Krys had been on night duty and I immediately wished that I hadn't dobbed her in. But they didn't seem to care that someone else had made the mistake of not taking Rene's teeth out, they were hell bent on trying to accuse me of almost killing her. All I could think was these people are fucked in the head.

Dora 'I met your daughter last night at college.'

Vivian had started to go to Night College to learn more about the intellectually disabled so that she could get a job at Challinor as well. I smiled

Amelia 'Yes she told me you were there.'

Dora 'She made some very derogatory comments about Challinor in the class.'

My back straightened and I could feel the hairs on the nape of my neck stand to attention. Anyone can pull me to pieces and accuse me of rubbish, but start on my kids and them's fighting words.

Amelia 'Vivian would never say anything derogatory about Challinor, she's met all the residents in my module and she loves them.'

We argued back and forth for the best part of an hour about Vivian's so-called derogatory comments until Marjorie dismissed me with, 'Obviously she's a red neck with a rebellious streak like her mother.' I wanted to spit in their eyes. But what made me most upset was that I knew that Vivian would never get a job at Challinor. At the time I thought it was a crying shame, but looking back now with hindsight I know she would never have handled the pressure. The funny part of that incident Krys never had to face the Spanish Inquisition about the teeth. Funny that.

I witnessed an incident one night where another resident from across the hall was thrown out of his wheelchair onto the ground and kicked by his RCA. I should have reported it to Lana or Marjorie or at the very least written it in the incident book. But by this time, I had no faith in them whatsoever. I decided to go to our state member who was also Minister for Health. He said he would look into the matter, but I had the feeling he was about as interested in it as he would have been to walk backwards from Brisbane to the back of Burke.

No need to be told, he told the hierarchy about my report, I was hauled over the coals once again by the hierarchy for not reporting the incident in the book. My word wasn't good enough anyway, because I was told it would be my word against the RCA. The Minister for Health was Dr Orford's best mate so I had lost confidence in going to Dr Orford as well.

I was really surprised when I requested a pass to take Happy home for the weekend and they approved it. Everyone including the co-workers I was on speaking terms with told me I was mad. After the night of the blackout Happy showed me a great deal of affection and she displayed to me that she was extremely sorry for what she had done. A few days after the incident I pointed to myself and said, 'I'm Happy' I threw myself around waving my arms like she had behaved and she bowed her head in shame. I thought, Oh. You poor little bugger and I patted her and gave her a hug and said, 'It's okay don't worry about it.'

Her face would light up like a Christmas tree whenever I'd walk into the module after that, she'd hold her arms up for me to give her a cuddle. Some days I'd get tears in my eyes when I thought about what sort of a life she must have had in that institution. Christ knows what sort of atrocities she had endured and seen over the years. Even now thinking about her I hope there is a heaven because she deserves to be a beautiful angel.

I'm not looking for praise or recognition for the way I treated her but I wanted to show her as much love as I possibly could. I truly believe that I was the only person who ever did. If for nothing else in my life, I am proud of myself for achieving that for the short time I knew her. I unashamedly say that I loved her dearly she truly melted my heart.

Our home had the toilet downstairs and I knew that there was no way in hell that I could take her up and down those stairs of a night. I had placed heavy plastic under the sheets because I knew she'd wet the bed as she often did in the module. The other RCA's used to scream at her for pissing the bed just because it meant that they'd have to put clean sheets on her bed. Anyone would've thought that they had to wash them by hand as well, the way they carried on. Anyhow, I placed a huge porcelain pot under the spare bed and told her to try and go on that. The following morning no one was more shocked than me when I went into the room to discover she had filled the pot to almost brimming during the night. The bed was bone dry and there wasn't a drop of urine on the floor. I was absolutely totally gobsmacked as was Frank and the kids. I don't know how she managed that with two club feet. She was extremely proud of herself when I praised her for being so good.

The other thing that sticks in my mind about that weekend was the way her face lit up and then she cried when I gave her a bath and I brought in a big red towel and wrapped it around her. She patted the towel as if it was the royal cloak. The realisation hit me that she would've only seen white towels with blue writing stating they were the property of the Queensland Government. I don't think anyone believed me when I took her back to Challinor and told them how she had peed in the pot.

Apart from Malcolm, I got on very well with Margaret. She and I had a similar sense of humour which bordered on crude at times. Whenever we worked together, we had a lot of laughs. Margaret was separated from her husband and she had four kids to rear on her own and she was really doing it tough trying to juggle the kids, the home and work full-time. Her stove had packed it in and they had to resort to eating takeaways because she couldn't afford to buy a new stove. We had an old wood stove that had been in the house when we shifted in which we didn't want, so we gave her that and you would've thought it was Christmas she was so thrilled. The one thing I didn't like about Margaret she was always talking about wanting sex. I'd never known a woman as obsessed as she was about wanting sex. I used to tell her all the time to shut up about it.

One of the residents from across the hall whom we called little Peter so as not to confuse him with horrible Peter used to come over to our module all the time. He couldn't walk in the true sense of the word he would tip toe everywhere but in a jogging way. If you didn't see him coming, and you turned around and there he was tippy toeing near you, it'd give you a hell of a fright, quite a few times

I yelled out in fright. He was a harmless poor little bugger but it used to drive everyone up the wall having to take him home again. I came up with the plan of just turning him around and he'd jog back on his own accord. This particular night Margaret was in the bathroom showering one of her residents and I saw little Peter jogging into our module. The only difference about that night, he had his fully erected penis in his hand. For a little six stone weakling that he was, it was massive. I could hardly stop myself from laughing but I had to, because I didn't want Margaret to come running out to see what I was laughing at. Instead of turning him around I said, 'Go in to the bathroom, Peter, that's a good boy.'

Off he jogged as pleased as punch that I hadn't yelled at him. Then I heard this ungodly blood curdling scream from Margaret and she yelled at him to get out. Then she bellowed, 'Williams, you bitch, you're responsible for this I'm gunna kill ya.'

Poor little Peter jogged past me on his way home still with his penis in his hand and I sat down in the office and cried with laughter. Margaret came out a moment later she was doubled up with laughter and when she could finally speak, she said, 'Fuck, what a pity he's a resident, I'd have taken him on otherwise.'

I think we laughed the entire shift that night.

Another RCA, Brad was a nice kid too but someone had told me he was into drugs. I confronted him one night and he admitted that he smoked marijuana but I had heard he also stuck needles in his arm. I had a long talk with him one night and told him he would end up like Peter if he didn't stop. I tried to get him to see it from a mother's point of view by saying, 'It will kill your mother if she has to visit you in Goodna or worse if she has to go to the morgue to identify your body.' But it fell on deaf ears he continued to dabble with the deadly poison. He was such a nice, well-mannered young man, it was a crying shame that someone like him (well anyone for that matter) would feel the need to take drugs to make themselves feel better.

As an RCA in training I had to go to lessons on a weekly basis to learn a number of things that I had already learnt as a mother. The relevant things I was supposed to learn at these lessons pertaining to the job I had already learnt by being hands on. I had also learnt what not to do by seeing some of the RCA's doing what you weren't supposed to do. All the other fledglings would ask inane, obvious to the brain dead, questions of the teachers and they in turn would delight in going into the ins and outs of the duck's bum in monotonous tones. I sat through two lessons just listening to them all waffle on about nothing. By the third lesson I had had enough so to amuse myself I decided to ask questions too and although I cannot remember what I asked, I know they required complicated answers and after a while they stopped trying to answer. I guess it's just my nature to try and challenge people.

Frank went into hospital on Sunday 2nd March of that year (1980) and had spinal fusion surgery to five vertebrae the following day. He was placed in a rotor bed for ten days. On his discharge he was in neck to knee plaster for another six weeks. The plaster went down to his knee on his left leg but ended at the top of his thigh on the right leg. He had to hold the plaster on his right leg to enable him to keep his balance and hobble around. Do you think he'd stay still? Not on your Nellie. He was out mowing the lawn and trying to do all the housework whilst I went to work. He looked like an upright snail the way he got around in his shell. He was the talk of the street and beyond the way he got around especially when he mowed the lawn.

When he was hospitalised, I told Billy and Happy who were very concerned, they'd listen to everything I told them about Frank's progress. They cheered as best as they could when I told them he was home. Frank was only out of hospital about two weeks and Heather had to go into Greenslopes Hospital to undergo further surgery on her face.

Doctor Catt was a perfectionist, he thought that Heather's face wasn't symmetrical and he had decided that he had to improve on his work of art (my terminology not his.)

I had continued to take Heather back and forth to his and Doctor Kenneth's surgeries in Brisbane when I was on the afternoon shifts. I'd have to make the appointments before ten am which was the only time, I was able to, because I had to be back in Ipswich to start work by two pm.

Heather had continued to undergo tests and from those tests they came to the decision that her tumour finally had a name. It wasn't just a fibrous dysplasia tumour it was called Neurofibromatosis. When Doctor Kenneth mentioned Neurofibromatosis, I recognised the name but didn't question its origin. On the drive home it hit me like a ton of bricks. I had seen the movie The Elephant Man and I realised that Neurofibromatosis was the condition that Joseph Merrick had suffered from. I felt sick in the guts. I rang Doctor Kenneth to ask him if my thoughts had been right. He confirmed it and as per usual he allayed my fears by assuring me that Heather was in good hands with Doctor Catt. I had no doubt about that and I had no doubt that we also had the best paediatrician in the world and I told him so, to which he had a good chuckle.

On one visit to Doctor Catt I told him about an article I had read, about a doctor at the Mayo clinic in America who was performing surgery on a patient with Neurofibromatosis. Dr Catt got very annoyed and like a kid who had his favourite toy taken from him, he said

'Well if you want to take Heather over there go ahead, there's nothing I can do to stop you.'

Amelia 'Keep your hair on, I was just making bloody conversation telling you about what I had read, I can't afford to fly to America and I've got no intentions of even trying to go there.'

Talk about being a spoilt brat.

Before Frank had gone into hospital, we had put an old rubber mattress down on the back of the station wagon so that I could transport him home. It wasn't legal and if the police had've stopped us I would've been in a bit of trouble.

On Thursday March 27th , I had to load Frank into the back of the station wagon. On arrival at the Greenslopes hospital I couldn't find a car park close by and we had to walk about one hundred metres up the street. We must've looked a peculiar sight because people were staring at us as we walked along. We were stopped by a nurse when we got near Heather's ward, she thought we were lost and gave us directions to the orthopaedic ward obviously thinking Frank was a patient there. We arrived just as Heather was getting ready to be prepped for surgery with a pre-op needle at ten am. Before the sister gave her the needle

Amelia 'Hang on, Heather's surgery isn't until three o'clock.'

Nurse 'No she's to be operated on at eleven o'clock.'

Amelia 'Well no one told us that.'

Nurse 'Well that's what time she's having her operation'.

Then she administered the needle. No need to be told Heather went into surgery at three pm and of course the pre-op needle had well and truly worn off by then. The poor little bugger was terrified. We stayed outside the operating theatre for the entire time during the surgery. There were no chairs and poor Frank had to lie on the floor and Vivian, Claire and I had to help him turn over every so often. He said he felt as if he was like a roast chicken. When Doctor Catt came out of the operating theatre, he burst out laughing at seeing such a motley looking crew as we were. He again assured us that he was pleased with what he had done and we all gave out a collective sigh together. We waited until Heather came to before heading home late that night. She was discharged only after a couple of days and I went back to work even though I should have been at home looking after both Frank and Heather. We had to have money to eat and pay the mortgage.

Three doors up the street lived a couple John and Fay with two kids whom Heather and Claire sometimes played with. Prior to them buying the house, Fay had worked with Frank at the abattoirs. She had come to our place unannounced one day and asked Frank if he would corn a piece of silverside for her. I thought she was a bit of an odd bod, Frank said he'd do it for her. I showed her through the house and she didn't say anything about the place. Usually when a person shows me through their home, I pass comment how I like a particular room or whatever. She never said a word. The following afternoon she rang and asked to speak to Frank and I told her that he was way down the backyard (we had a quarter of an acre of land, so he was quite a fair way away.) She said, 'I'll wait.' I trekked down to where he was and told him Fay wanted to speak to him. When he picked up the phone, I heard him say, 'No I don't think so, I'm sure she won't, okay I'll ask her but I'm certain she won't, okay I'll hear from you later today.'

Amelia 'What was all that about?'

He shrugged and laughed

Frank 'She wants to know if you'll sell her Vivian's Queen Anne bedroom suite.'

Amelia 'What? Why couldn't she have asked me herself, instead of making me trudge all the way down the bloody backyard to fetch you, the stupid bitch?'

Frank 'I dunno you can ask her. She's ringing back later to find out if you'll agree to sell it to her.'

About an hour later she rang again and asked to speak to Frank.

Amelia 'Fay, he's way down the backyard.'

Fay 'Okay, I'll wait'.

Amelia 'Fay, I'm not going down there to ask him to come up to answer you if I'll sell you our furniture. The answer is no, I bought the bedroom suite for our daughter and we intend to keep it, but thanks for calling.'

To say I thought she pushed the strange barrier was an understatement.

I came home from work one Sunday afternoon and Frank had a big grin on his face **Frank** 'You're not going to believe this.'

Amelia 'What's happened?'

Frank 'Fay's husband wants to fight me.'

I burst out laughing because I thought he was joking.

Frank 'I'm serious, Heather and Claire had a tiff with his kids and he came down yelling, ranting and raving telling me he wanted me to come out and fight. I told him to go home and wake up to himself because I don't get involved in kids squabbles.'

Amelia 'But you're in neck to knee plaster he must've been joking surely, or was he pissed?'

Frank 'No he wasn't pissed and he was fair dinkum.'

We both had a good laugh and about an hour later there was a hell of a commotion outside. We all went out onto the veranda and there was Johnny on horseback on the footpath with a gigantic whip in his hand. He cracked it a few times and kept yelling, 'Come out and fight like a man you prick.' I couldn't believe my eyes let alone my ears **Amelia** 'For Christ sake man, wake up to yourself go home and sleep it off.

Johnny 'I'm not drunk and I don't take drugs, I don't need to sleep anything off.'

he yelled at Frank, 'Stop hiding behind ya Mrs.' I whispered to Frank 'Don't answer him he's off his head.'

The next thing Skeezo raced up to the fence and started barking at the horse and I thought, Oh Christ Skee's going to get killed, if the horse doesn't trample him Johnny will whack him with the whip. I called Skee but he wouldn't come back inside, Johnny cracked the whip again and Skee barked louder. The next thing, the horse reared up on its back legs Johnny fell off, and the horse bolted down the road with Johnny in hot pursuit. We stood there watching until they got out of sight and we were shaking our heads in total disbelief and fit to kill ourselves with laughter. We went inside and I said, 'From now on, we're going to lock this place up like Fort Knox even when we are inside.'

About eighteen months later, after we'd sold the house, we heard that Johnny had stabbed Fay several times in the chest and she was dangerously ill for quite a long time. Johnny was put in Wacol for the criminally insane.

In the April of that year Happy had put her arms around my neck to give me a hug and in doing so she pulled my head down rather hard towards her. My neck cracked really loudly and it was extremely painful. I went to see Doctor Orford who put me on two weeks Worker's Compensation. Our house was fast becoming the busiest hospital in Australia. Although my neck was still rather sore, I returned to work without hesitation. I never thought for one minute that years down the track I would suffer arthritis in my neck as I do now from such a simple action. I can only say that if someone injures themselves no matter how mild they think it is, they should always keep all records of the injury, just in case.

Two weeks compensation is not enough for many years of suffering.

It was during this time that I was off work that I had received a phone call from the Manager of the NAB asking me if I could come in to see him. I asked him what was it about?' He said, 'I'd like to speak to you about your mortgage repayments.'

On my arrival there I was ushered into the Manager's office

The Manager 'Mrs Williams, one of the payments you made the other week, the teller gave you two receipts for two payments and you only paid one payment.'

Amelia 'I've been paying two payments every fortnight since November as soon as I get my wage.'

The Manager 'Ah yes. But you only paid one payment the other week.'

Amelia 'No. I have paid two payments every fortnight since last November, because I want to pay it off as soon as I can.'

He then asked me if I had my payment book with me. I took it out of my handbag and he asked me if he could have the book. I told him, 'No. But I'll get you a photocopy of it.'

(After the experience with the Manager at the Bank of New South Wales, I had no trust in anyone from any bank!)

The Manager 'I'll get it photocopied here.'

Amelia 'No, I'll take it across the road to the photocopier and get it photocopied there.'

He was getting really agro with me and demanded to know why I wouldn't hand it to him.

Amelia 'Well basically you're more or less accusing me of ripping you off and I've got no idea why.'

The Manager 'The teller was down in her money and she believes she had written you two receipts instead of one.'

Amelia 'I don't give a rats what she or you believe. I know that I've paid this bank *two* mortgage payments each fortnight instead of one every fortnight and I have the receipts to prove it. If she's down in her money I'm not the one who is responsible. It's preposterous that she'd write out two receipts for one payment.'

I took my repayment book over to the photocopier and went back and handed the manager the photocopy and said, 'Try looking for the lost money elsewhere.'

Frank had only been out of his plaster nine days, on the first couple of days he was a bit unsteady on his feet but he gradually improved every day. Then at about eight pm on Sunday 3rd May 1980, whilst I was on the afternoon shift Rene wet her bed. Brad and Margaret were the other RCA's on duty with me that night. The part for the hoist still had not been replaced so we all had to lift her ourselves and try and dry the plastic and place a dry sheet underneath her.

Brad was only about twenty years old and quite a small framed young man. Margaret was about five feet tall the same height as me but she was fairly plump whereas I was only about seven stone then. (Those were the days.) Rene was a huge bulk of a woman and because she was totally immobile and unable to help to lever herself, she seemed to be even heavier. We all counted to three before heaving her up and as we lifted her, I heard more than felt, a cracking sound in my back. We somehow managed to get the job done and as we walked away, I felt a surge of pain in my spine. I said, 'Shit I think I've busted the poofoo valve in my back.' Everyone had a chuckle at my new made up word. **Brad** 'You'd better write it down in the incident book just in case you've hurt yourself badly.'

Amelia 'Ah its nuthin' not worth mentioning.'

Because he kept insisting I ended up writing it down. The following day was the May Day holiday and I was rostered on which meant I would be paid double time, plus I was also on night duty which also meant extra money. I'd had a restless night because by the time I'd finished my shift and drove home, my back was really aching. The following morning, I went to get out of bed and I could hardly move my legs I thought, Christ I'm crippled. I called to Vivian to come and help me and it was so painful to put the weight on my feet. Somehow, I managed to hobble around but I knew I wouldn't be able to go to work that day, so I rang in sick. I would've rung to get in to see Doctor Orford but because it was a holiday, I knew he wouldn't be there. Frank wanted me to go to the Ipswich hospital but I couldn't have sat in a chair for ten minutes let alone an hour waiting to see a doctor, there. I spent the rest of the day in bed. The following morning. I felt worse so I rang Doctor Orford's surgery and Frank helped me into the car and we drove to Dr Orford's surgery with me lying on the back seat. Doctor Orford had gone on holidays for a week and I had to see a locum who told me to go home and stay in bed and rest for a week. The week went by and I still felt like shit, but

I managed to get in the car this time in the passenger's seat and we went back to Doctor Orford.

He rang the physiotherapist across the road from his surgery and told them I lived in Ipswich and could they fit me in straight away. He got off the phone and said, 'Go straight over and they'll manipulate your spine now.'

When I came out of the physiotherapist I felt absolutely shattered and I could hardly walk. If Frank hadn't been with me I would've been run over by one of the cars.

I stumbled onto the ground when I tried to cross the street. Frank couldn't lift me but he held his hand up to stop the traffic. I couldn't stand up and I had to slowly crawl across the street on all fours. It was a case of the maimed helping the lame. I finally got back into see Doctor Orford he gave me pain killers and he ordered more bed rest. He gave me six weeks on Worker's Compensation. I went back and forth to see Doctor Orford during the six weeks, the initial pain had subsided somewhat but I was still in agony and he finally sent me for x-rays. The x-rays showed that I had three crush-fractured vertebrae in my Thoracic spine (T9, T10 and T12.) I knew it before he said, 'You'll never be able to go back to Challinor again because of all the heavy lifting you have to do there.'

I was gutted, I really loved my job, in spite of the hierarchy and some of my co-workers and I just shook my head in disbelief.

I sent my certificates for Worker's Compensation to Lana by registered mail so that it didn't go astray and I had proof of sending it.

Malcolm rang me a few days later to see how I was going.

When I told him about my three crush-fractures, he said

'Shit. We were told you were bungin' it on.'

Amelia 'Who told you that?'

Malcolm 'Jan.'

(Jan believe it or not was one of the psychologists at Challinor.)

Amelia 'What did she say and who did she say it to?'

Malcolm 'Amelia Williams is bunging on a back complaint and she announced it to everyone in the staffroom one morning.'

Amelia 'That's interesting.' And I thanked him for telling me.

I got a letter from Doctor Orford stating the full extent of my injuries and I took it personally to Challinor. Lo and behold the first person I saw was Jan. She smiled so sweetly at me and said,

'Hello, Amelia how are you dear?'

Amelia 'You're just the person I want to see, Jan.'

Jan 'How can I help you, dear?'

I shoved the letter in her hand and said, 'There you go, read that'.

She read it and as she handed it back to me. she said, 'Oh.'

Amelia 'Oh indeed. I'm here to tell you if you continue spreading lies about me saying that I'm bunging it on, I can assure you, you will be in deep shit.'

She gulped

Jan 'I can't stay and chat, I'm very busy, Amelia, I must go.'

And she scurried away like the little rat that she was.

I took the letter up to Lana and handed it to her and without her saying a word she walked off. I had a photo copy of the letter but I had handed her the original letter. I waited and waited but never got anything from Worker's Comp. I eventually rang them and I was told that they didn't have any record of my claim. I said, 'But it's been twelve weeks since I hurt myself, it must be there somewhere.'

The fellow apologised and said, 'You had better ring your employer to see when they sent in the claim.' When I rang Challinor, fortunately someone who seemed very nice answered and she said Lana was unable to speak to me because she was in a meeting. She whispered, 'I don't remember sending any forms in your name to Worker's Comp but I'll look around and see if I can find your file.' She rang me back and said, 'All the paperwork was on Lana's desk under a lot of other files so it must've been there since you sent them in, I'll post everything off straight away.'

If it wasn't for that lady I'd probably be still waiting.

It was four months after my injury before I started to get paid by Worker's Comp. What a pack of bastards that ran that place. They obviously didn't like a little upstart with no qualifications showing them up as swill.

I was on full pay on Worker's Compensation for six months and then on half pay for the following six months minus all my overtime and bonuses of course. So financially we were up the creek without a paddle. Luckily, we were about eight months in front with the mortgage payments by the time I went on half pay from compo. I told Frank, that we could afford to not make the mortgage payments for a while.

A fortnight went by and I got a terse letter from the Manager of the NAB which stated that we were behind in our payments. I went in to see him again and I threw the letter on his desk.

Amelia 'How did you work this one out? I'm eight months ahead with my repayments.'

The Manager 'Technically you are behind because you agreed to pay on or before the first of every month and you didn't pay before the first of this month. I could repossess your house.'

I yelled, 'Just you try that, pal, and see how far you get, I've had enough shit in my life to last me three lifetimes and it won't faze me one bit to take you on as well.'

He meekly told me to make sure that I made the payments every month before the first of the month in future and bade me a good day. I was convinced that I was completely jinxed.

Frank soon bounced back after his surgery and he reapplied and went back to the meatworks. We were back to getting a full wage every week which was a huge relief. We had budgeted so much on the small pittance I had been getting that we felt like millionaires getting his full weekly pay packet. I made sure that we weren't going to squander it willy-nilly. I continued what I had started when I was working and that was to continue paying the house off as quickly as we could. I had a wonderful feeling the following year when I went into the bank to make the last mortgage payment. I had envisaged that it would be like party central with a presentation of a magnum of champagne and as the corks popped the cameras would click as the manager handed me our deeds. Sometimes I should get a grip on reality.

At the very least I thought I'd be congratulated by the teller. Instead I was just handed the receipt for my payment, I was underwhelmed. I've since learnt that the banks prefer you to be in their debt for the rest of your natural life and beyond.

I was told by a bank manager in recent years that we are classified as problem customers because we've always paid our credit card in full each month and the bank never gets any interest out of us.

Chapter 47

Jubilation

I had applied to go on Bert Newton's New Faces and had received a letter that there was a huge waiting list. I thought, that's it I won't get on and promptly forgot all about my application. I was more than surprised when I got a letter a short time later to say they were flying me to Melbourne to appear on the show. The reason I was chosen to jump the queue was my act was comedy and they had more than enough singers and dancers applying to go on. I was also surprised that I didn't have to audition I was flown down on the Friday morning in August 1980, booked into a motel taken to the studio with the other contestants in hire cars. We all rehearsed in the afternoon and performed the show live to air that night.

I was voted by the judges to return for the Judges choice programme. I got another trip to Melbourne which was rather exciting.

Then I was voted to return by the viewers for the public choice programme.

Everyone kept asking me,

'What's Bert really like?'

I could only reply, 'How would I know? He's such a private person, I think he spoke about fifty words to me the entire three times I was on his show.'.

From my first appearance on New Faces I got heaps of congratulatory mail from around the country which was extremely flattering.

One lady Mollie from Chermside sent me an entry form to win a cruise to the Caribbean. The second prize was a cruise to Fiji. She insisted that I should enter it because she was convinced, I could win it. I had a good laugh when I read the conditions of the competition.

Write twenty-five words or less why you want the cruise and why you are lucky in love, plus send in a receipt of a particular brand of expensive chocolates and the winner will receive a set of luggage. I checked out the price of a box of the chocolates and nearly fell over they were almost eight dollars and I thought, I can't afford that but what the hell I'll write an entry anyway.

A Caribbean cruise would be ideal, to show my husband how I feel

I'm lucky in love with someone kind, a truer friend would be hard to find.

When I read it out to Frank he laughed and said, 'You're going to jail for telling lies.'

I promptly forgot all about the competition once I had sent it off, we had so much more to think about that was going on in our lives.

On the morning of Friday 17th October 1980, Frank and I had a huge argument and he stamped off in a really bad mood. Then mid-morning I received a telegram asking me to ring a number in Melbourne. Long distance phone calls were still a big thing in those days and I was hesitant to waste my money ringing the number, but curiosity got the better of me. I had secretly hoped that I'd won a prize, and I was trying to remember if there had been other prizes involved, maybe a few boxes of chocolates which would be really nice. When I told the girl that I'd received a telegram that morning, she put me through to a fellow

The Man 'Mrs Williams, did you get a telegram today?'

When I said that I had he replied, 'I'm so sorry.'

I was crestfallen thinking they've made a mistake I've won a big fat zero.

He said, 'I sent that telegram yesterday morning you should have received it over twenty-four hours ago.' By this time my heart started to skip a little beat and he continued, 'Congratulations you've won an all expenses nine night cruise to Fiji departing on January 31st next year.' I was so excited I screamed, cried and laughed all at the same time.

The Man 'Oh, Mrs Williams, you're the most excited person I've ever spoken to telling them they've won a prize.'

Amelia 'I've never won anything like this before in my whole life and I can't even begin to say how much it means to me.'

The Man 'I'll be sending you a letter in the next couple of weeks confirming your win.'

I hung up and I couldn't remember a word he had said other than I'd won a cruise. I was still crying when I drove to the meatworks and asked the fellow at the gate to get Frank. Frank came towards me and I could see he was still angry from the argument we'd had earlier. As soon as he saw I was crying

Frank 'W ... what's wrong?'

Amelia still bawling, 'I won.'

Frank 'What?'

All I could do was cry and repeat, 'I won, I won, I won.'

Frank 'What the hell are you talking about?'

He put his arm around me and I blubbered like a baby onto his shoulder. When I composed myself I started to laugh

Amelia 'I'm not going to jail.'

He was looking at me as if I had completely flipped my lid, he already thought I was nuts, but by this time he was convinced that I was.

Amelia 'I won the cruise, that poem I sent about being lucky in love, I won the cruise.'

We both hugged each other and Frank was patting me telling me not to cry because it's good news. I looked over at the guard at the gate and he was looking at us as if we had both gone nuts. When Frank came home that day, he said that everyone he knew at the meatworks had been looking out at us. They knew I was crying and they all thought Heather was sick or worse. Heather's jaw was extremely fragile and the least little bump could have shattered her jawbone and that's what they had all feared might have happened. When they saw us both hugging, they thought I was having some sort of stress attack and that Frank was trying to calm me down.

I got the letter confirming my win and I had to appear on the People's Choice show the following week. When I was flown back to Melbourne for the show, I went to the address on the letterhead to thank the man whom I had spoken to. I was amazed to see that it was a central office for numerous competitions and there were many people sifting through piles of entries for various competitions. He showed me how some people wrote their entries on cakes and sent them in. He said, 'Bribery gets you nowhere in this business, we go on talented entries and yours was very good, you came very close to winning the Caribbean cruise.' I was extremely flattered and more than happy with the cruise to Fiji. I received the beautiful luggage too even though I hadn't sent in a receipt for the chocolates.

When January finally rolled around, we flew to Sydney and boarded the (original) Oriana. Our cabin was on C deck with ocean views and well before the movie Titanic was made, we thought we were King and Queen of the world. It was magic. Everything about that cruise was a wonderful new experience for us. The food was sensational, the entertainment was excellent (with one exception) and the service was second to none. It was classified as a Rock Cruise and P&O had hired Darryl Braithwaite from Sherbet and John Paul Young as guest entertainers and of course they were excellent entertainers.

Unfortunately, P&O had also employed a band called Bland Frenzy. I love all music from Opera down to Hillbilly, but what Bland Frenzy played was not music. It was a downright insult to my ears. They were the warm up group for both Darryl and JPY on alternative nights. To make matters worse they never knew when to get off stage, the compare would start walking out to introduce Darryl or JPY and they'd start playing another song and would end up being on stage for an hour and a half. By the third night I'd had enough of bloody Bland Frenzy if I had've had my way I would have made them walk the plank. So after about a half hour of suffering there cacophony of noise I yelled, 'Get off' Frank started to laugh and joined me chanting, 'Get off' Before too long a few people joined the chant with us and the leader of Bland Frenzy said, 'We're getting paid to play.' I yelled, 'I'll pay you double what you're getting to get off.' They played another tune and the compare ran on stage and announced JPY was going to perform and everyone cheered as if it was New Year's Eve all over again.

A few days later whilst we were strolling around one of the islands Frank noticed the singer from Bland Frenzy in one of the shops. Frank put his head inside the door and called out, 'Get off.' The guy flew out the door and stood in front of us and screamed at Frank 'I'll do you.' I pushed myself between them and looked up to the guy who was over six feet tall and I said, 'My husband's not that way inclined.'

There were a number of passengers from the ship nearby who burst out laughing. The singer looked around and his band mates were behind him laughing too. They told him to get back inside the shop. That night we were sitting in one of the lounge areas and two of the high-ranking officers sat down with us and were chatting away to us as if we were Lord and Lady Nuffield. The singer from Bland Frenzy walked in took one look at the four of us and you could tell he was shitting razor blades, he was so scared. He came up bowed and apologised for his behaviour I nodded and told him it was okay and Frank shook his hand and the poor bastard skulked away. The big brass wanted to know what that was all about and I said 'I don't know maybe it was mistaken identity.'

After the officers left Frank said, 'You're going to get us hung.' I said 'ME? You're the one who yelled at him in the shop.' And we cracked up again.

We got to Fiji and a huge military band played for our arrival in Suva. Some dignitary stood on a stage and announced over a microphone that unfortunately there were conmen in his country and that they would shake our hands offer us gifts and ask our names. He advised that we were to ignore them and walk away because once they get your name, they will write it on the gift and you are obliged to pay for the writing.

We got about one hundred metres from the ship I was about three metres in front of Frank and our new ship mates and a Fijian fellow grabbed me by my right hand and started to shake it thrusting a wooden sword into my left hand telling me it was my gift and asking me my name. I tried to break free but he wouldn't let go. I kept tugging my hand away and he held onto like it was stuck with super glue. By this time Frank and our friends had come up alongside of me and I looked at Frank as if to say, come on get me out of this. He walked past me and called back over his shoulder, 'You're on ya own. You got yourself into it.' I would've started laughing but I knew it was a serious situation. I did the first thing that came to mind I pretended I was fainting. I rolled my eyes back and started to sway back and forth and dropped the sword. The fellow let go of my hand and I ran for the lick of my life. When I caught up with Frank, I threatened him with a fate worse than death. Everyone roared with laughter when I re-enacted how I had escaped. We separated from our friends and said we'd meet them back at the ship. Then we shopped like we were multi-millionaires everything was so cheap there in 1981. We bought a movie camera, a ghetto blaster and a heap of other things. But the one treasure I bought that I still have and it worked for over thirty years was a little Casio electronic, musical calculator and clock. It was my most treasured possession and I cried when it eventually died. Some passengers stopped us to tell us how they nearly got ripped off by the conman and that they had seen an elderly lady who hadn't heard the warning and the conman had ripped her off of sixty dollars. Frank was loaded up carrying all of our goodies and I had had enough bartering so we headed back to the ship. We walked on the other side of the dock to avoid the conman. As we got closer to the area I looked over and the conman had some young fellows bailed up.

I said to Frank, 'Shit those young guys mustn't have heard the warning they're going to get ripped off too. We'd better warn them.'

Frank 'Don't worry about them, it's their problem.'

Amelia 'Oh we can't let the poor bastards be ripped off.'

I yelled out, 'He's a conman.'

Frank looked over and we saw the conman starting to run towards us.

Frank yelled at me, 'Run.' We both took off as fast as we could but both with back injuries was like a fast walk. Frank could hardly see where he was going because of the movie camera and ghetto blaster boxes he was carrying but he was a country mile ahead of me. My little legs were pumping like the Lithgow

Flash but I can't run for nuts and I could hear the fellow coming up right behind me. My back was screaming in pain and I thought, Jesus he's going to grab me any tick of the clock and drag me down like a lion would grab a gazelle. Frank was screaming at me, 'Run for Christ sake, run.' I screamed back, 'I'm goin as fast as I can.' The next thing this big, dark skinned fellow in a khaki uniform stepped out of nowhere. He had a gun in his hand and he held it fully cocked and his arm was stretched to the limit pointing it at the conman. In a very deep menacing voice he ordered, 'Halt.' I'm not exaggerating the conman stopped only centimetres from the barrel of the gun and it was pointed at the centre of his forehead. The soldier asked us what had happened and he never took his eyes off the conman. I explained as quickly as I could what had happened to me earlier and that I'd yelled out a warning to the young passengers. He told us to get back on the ship and not to come back down because our lives would be in danger. We couldn't climb the gangplank quickly enough. We got to the cabin collapsed on our bunks with complete exhaustion and absolutely pissed ourselves with laughter. It was the most frightening yet funniest experience, and we never found out what happened to the conman.

You could take us anywhere once but never back to apologise.

There was a young couple we had observed on board who were very much in love and obviously on their honeymoon. Everywhere they went they were holding hands and kissing and cuddling and I was often tempted to say go back to your cabinwhen they got so hot and passionate. She was a very pretty girl and Frank and I referred to her as Marie Osmond because that's who she looked like. He was quite a handsome fellow and looked like an up and coming go getter. When we docked in Sydney after the cruise, we noticed them again having a very passionate embrace. He was dressed in a business suit and I assumed that he had a business appointment that morning. We were a bit surprised to see him leave her and I remember saying to Frank, 'He must have some business to attend to here in Sydney.' She caught the same bus as us to the airport and the same plane back to Brisbane and was crying most of the way. When we got off our flight Frank and I were dumbstruck to witness her running to her boyfriend who was crying with happiness at seeing her. He presented her with the biggest bouquet of flowers and we heard him say, 'Darling, I missed you so much will you marry me'.

Frank looked at me and said,

'Amelia, leave well alone, do not say one word.'

Chapter 48

Motherly Love Can Be Very Blind

Vivian had turned eighteen at the beginning of that year I always thought she had been a very responsible girl except for one particular night a few months previously. She had gone out with a number of her friends to the Palais club in Ipswich. The Palais was the hub and the place to be as far as the teenagers were concerned. She had been there a few times and just to make sure she was where she was supposed to be, Frank had turned up at the front door a couple of times and looked in, much to her embarrassment. But all of the other kids with Vivian tried to encourage Frank to come in and dance. They thought Frank was the bee's knees and some had often commented to me that they thought he was a really cool guy.

I had always stipulated that Vivian had to be in by midnight but this particular night she arrived home at quarter to three am and I was beside myself with worry. When she walked in and I saw that she had been drinking, I was livid. I yelled at her, 'What time do you call this?' She just shrugged and grinned at me, knowing that she could melt me with her smile. But not that night it only made me even more furious. I said, 'It's the slut's hour, that's what time it is.' She was totally shocked that I had yelled at her. I would learn to regret saying that, years down the track, because Vivian in her stupor recalled the conversation as me calling her a slut. As far as I'm concerned and I'll go to my grave saying, I was making the point that good girls should not be out at that hour, nothing more. If I had've thought she was irresponsible and of low morals I would never have called her a slut anyway. I had unconditionally idolised her from the moment she was conceived. The pedestal I placed Vivian on wasn't high enough. I would tell anyone who was prepared to listen, 'Every mother should have a daughter like Vivian.' I don't think a week went past that I didn't say that to someone. She could do no wrong in my eyes and everyone who has known me for years would confirm that.

At the time she never indicated that she was traumatised by what I had said. In fact, she apologised profusely when she awoke and gave me a story why she was so late (which I don't even remember now) but I had no reason to disbelieve her. She could have told me that aliens had invaded and taken her to Mars and I would've believed her, I loved her so much.

Frank and I had bought her a little Mini Cooper S when she had gotten her licence and she told us that it kept on breaking down and she wanted to trade it in because she feared driving it. Whenever Frank drove it to find out what was wrong with it, it never faltered. But I believed her, so we sold it privately much to Frank's annoyance. We put a deposit on a red Mazda sports coupe for her and she felt like a million dollars and I thought she deserved a million dollars. We went guarantor for her to get the car but we stipulated that she had to keep the payments up. To her credit she did do that.

The day after she got the Mazda, Andrew McKenzie one of the jockeys who lived up the road came down to ask her for a date. We joked at the time, 'We've bought ourselves a son-in-law.' A couple of months later I trusted her so much that for her eighteenth birthday I gave her the biggest and best party we could afford. There were at least fifty teenagers at our home that night and all of them (including Vivian) thanked me for the best party they'd ever been to. If I didn't trust her, I wouldn't have left her in charge of Heather and Claire when we went on the cruise. The three of them would have gone to their grandparent's home. Vivian had lost her job as a receptionist at a local Real Estate Agency. The owner had asked her to leave because there was a discrepancy in the rent money that had been collected from tenants. We thought it was grossly unfair without proof of any misdoing. She had done an excellent job caring for her sisters and we came back to a spotless home and a home cooked meal of chops and vegies. Unfortunately, we didn't really enjoy them, (though we didn't tell her that) because we had become accustomed to eating fine cuisine fit for a king and queen.

We had met Andrew's parents Jock and Dora and Andrew's sister, Deanne, a few months previously they seemed a nice enough family but Frank and I couldn't help but see the resemblance to the Clampetts from the Beverly Hillbillies. Jock wasn't as tall as Jed but he did look a bit like him. Dora was a dead ringer for Granny and Deanne had long blonde hair like Elly-May. So as far as we were concerned that meant Andrew must've been Jethro. Andrew told Vivian that he was moving to Mullumbimby and Vivian was heartbroken. She told me that Andrew wanted her to go with him but Frank and I both said, 'No way, under any circumstances.' For days she screamed and cried like a banshee and I feared that she would have a nervous breakdown the way she was carrying on. I finally relented on the condition that Frank agreed. He reluctantly gave in because I had. Legally she could have moved out if she wanted to but she didn't want to go without my blessing. At the time I thought that showed me how much she respected my opinion. In hindsight I don't think Andrew cared one way or the other if she had moved in with him. I think she was obsessed or possessed or maybe both. Vivian moved out on a Sunday in February, 1981 the day before Heather's fifteenth birthday to live in the backblocks of nowhere in the Mullumbimby area in a caravan that should have been sent to the dump many years before. I couldn't believe that my beautiful daughter had lowered herself to living like trailer trash. I have no idea if Andrew was earning any money at the time but Vivian got a job as a checkout chic at the local supermarket.

We took some visitors Val and Vic from Western Australia down to visit Vivian and Andrew a few weeks later and we were appalled at the conditions they were living in. Vivian had arranged for us to stay in other caravans. I never found out where the other caravans came from. We took everyone out to dinner at the local RSL club and had a huge Chinese banquet meal. We went back to their caravan later that night and were all sitting around talking and laughing when all of a sudden Andrew demanded, 'Get me a T-bone I'm hungry.' I looked at my watch and it was five minutes past midnight. 'It's a bit late to be eating again now isn't it?'

Andrew 'I'm hungry.'

Vivian 'The T-bones are frozen, I can get you some sausages, does anyone want sausages?'

Everyone shook their heads no and Andrew demanded again, 'I said I want a T-Bone.'

Vivian took a T-bone out of the freezer and started to get a frypan out of the tiny cupboard. She was just about to turn the hotplate on and Andrew said, 'Ah it doesn't matter I won't have it now.' Frank, Val, Vic and I never said a word for a minute or so and I broke the silence with, 'I'm buggered I'm going to bed.' Everyone else agreed and we all went to the other vans. The following morning, I awoke with a dreadful migraine which I'd been suffering from on a regular basis since Mother's Day 1972. I could hardly lift my head off the pillow but I wanted to get as far away from Andrew as possible. I also dearly wanted to kidnap Vivian and bring her home, but I knew we couldn't do that. As soon as I stepped foot outside the van I started to throw up. I tried desperately to get as far away from everyone as I could with my back to them. I think I must've vomited for at least ten minutes that morning.

When I finally stopped, I turned to go back to where everyone was standing and I started heaving again. There was fluid spurting out of my nose I vomited so violently. I was aghast when I finally stopped and I looked over at Vivian and she was killing herself with laughter at me. I was too ill to say anything I just waved my hand goodbye and got in the car holding a plastic bag that Frank had handed to me.

On the way home I heard bits of the conversation as I dosed in fits and starts and I heard Vic say, 'If that T-bone had've hit the frypan I was going to punch his lights out.'

Frank replied, 'So was I and I was getting ready to as well.' I muttered, 'I wish to Christ it had've hit the pan, then.' I'm willing to bet Jethro had sensed he may have been in deep shit and that's why he changed his mind so quickly.

It was a few weeks after that that Vivian told me Andrew had taken out two life insurance policies. His policy was to be paid to her if anything happened to him and her policy was to be paid to him if anything happened to her. That more than worried me and that particular day we came within a hair's breadth of whisking her back home. But I figured that she would in all probability return to Andrew. I would have failed as a mother if I hadn't told her that I was very concerned about him taking out the policy against her life. I said, 'You can tell him from me that if anything should happen to you, I guarantee that he will never enjoy one cent of his ill-gotten gains.' She laughed and said, 'I'll tell him, Mum, but you don't have to worry because he really does love me he looks after me so well.' I didn't believe her but said, 'He had better.'

In the early part of September one of the horse trainers from up the road died of an asthma attack. He left a widow and five kids. The eldest two were good friends of Vivian and Andrew. Vivian couldn't come up for the funeral but Andrew had agreed to meet us at our place an hour before the funeral. We waited until twenty minutes before the funeral started and I said to Frank, 'I'm not waiting any longer we can't all walk into the church late.' Andrew arrived about five minutes after the service had started and I could have died too, I was so embarrassed. He was wearing his one and only good shirt and trousers and they were so crinkled he looked as if he'd been sleeping in them for months. Vivian must've washed them and wrung them by hand. I wasn't so much embarrassed that he looked as if the cat wouldn't drag him in. It was knowing that Vivian hadn't bothered to even try to iron the clothes.

As mentioned before, we sold the house to a horse trainer from Wiseman's Ferry.

Naturally, being us, it wasn't as easy as that. I had gotten a knock on the back door and the fellow asked me if I knew of any homes in the area that was up for sale.

Amelia 'Are you a real estate salesman?'

Man 'No I'm a horse trainer from down south.'

My prayers had finally been answered.

Amelia 'If you're interested this one can be bought at the right price.'

He introduced himself as Eric Verity and showed me his card and I said, 'Come in and I'll show you around.' He said that he liked the place and the position and asked me how much I'd want for it. Without hesitation I told him the price I wanted. I had hoped to sell it for six thousand dollars less than what I had told him, but no locals would have never paid that much. But because he wasn't a local and didn't know how cheap houses were in Ipswich, I thought You only get God's gift once in a blue moon so make the most of it. Without hesitation he said, 'Sounds good to me, but before we sign any papers, I'd like you to check with the council to see if they will change the land from urban to rural.' I agreed to do so.

More than three months went by and I had spoken to every dill in the Ipswich Council in several phone calls, and each of them had given me the run around and a different answer. I was furious, not only at the idiots at the Ipswich council, but also at Eric Verity, because he hadn't bothered to ring me to see what was happening. I sure as hell wasn't going to waste my money chasing him. I said to Frank, 'Bugger it I'm not selling, he can take a running jump at himself, I've wasted my breath and time on a pack of idiots at the council so they can all go to buggery.'

The following night out of the blue as if he had sensed my reluctance to sell, Mr Verity rang. I was really riled when I heard who it was.

I said, 'No I'm not interested in selling now, I've been running around like a chook with its head cut off trying to get some sense out of a pack of dimwits at the council for the best part of four months and you haven't had the decency to even call me in that time.'

And I hung up in his ear. Ten minutes later the phone rang again it was Mr Verity he said, 'Please don't hang up until you hear what I've got to say, I'll give you another four thousand dollars for the trouble you've gone through.'

My heart almost leapt out of my chest, my hands were dripping great globs of sweat but I very coolly said, 'I'll have to speak to my husband about this and you'll have to ring back in twenty minutes time'.

He agreed and I hung up and I felt like falling to my knees and thanking God. I said to Frank, 'He's just offered us another four thousand dollars.

Frank 'What? Did you say yes please?'

Amelia 'Nuh, I told him I had to talk it over with you and to ring back in twenty minutes time.'

Frank 'Are you nuts or what? What if he changes his mind and doesn't ring?'

I started to panic when the twenty minutes became thirty minutes and I thought, Shit what have I done? But he eventually rang and we made the arrangements to get the papers signed and we shifted out on the Wednesday 23 September, 1981. We had suffered it there for four years and two months and yet it had only seemed like twenty-four years. Getting another home wasn't easy either. Nothing we ever did was easy God makes sure of that. I'm sure He has nothing better to do than say to himself, 'Okay I got them out of that little scrape, now I'll give them a harder task and see how long it takes them and what sort of trouble they can get themselves into.'

We found a nice little home back in Long Street just a few houses down from where we had lived until July 1977. The owner had decided to go on a holiday to New Zealand a week before we looked at the house and wasn't due back for another two weeks. Who in their right minds puts their bloody house on the market then decides to go away for three weeks? This goose of a woman did. When she finally came back, she bunged on all of the airs and graces about what a wonderful time she'd had *abroad* . I know I shouldn't have said it, but I couldn't help myself, I detest pretentious people and I like taking the piss out of them by playing their silly games back at them. I said to her in my best elocution voice, 'Yes New Zealand is lovely, especially at this time of year we went there in the September almost ten years ago now. But if you really want to broaden your horizons you should take yourself on a cruise. We've not long come back from our last cruise.'.

I wasn't telling a lie by not stating it was our only cruise which I had won. But because of that comment she didn't want to accept our offer.

The real estate agent was visibly upset when I said, 'I'm not paying her what she wants, if she doesn't want to drop the price, she can whistle Dixie, I'll look elsewhere.'

Frank said later to me, 'Christ woman we're up shit creek with hardly any time left to find another place and you want to play stupid one upmanship games with her just because she used the word abroad when she was talking about New Zealand.'

Amelia 'It's good fun, it's amusing me.'

Frank 'Well I can't see the funny side.'

Later that day the agent told us that she had agreed to our offer but to be perfectly honest if we had've had more time I would've said, 'I've changed my mind.'

And I would have tried to bring the price down another two thousand dollars but time was against us.

I was going to ring the nearest NAB the following Monday to make an appointment to see the manager. We needed to borrow ten thousand dollars to cover the legals shifting expenses and to get a few incidentals for the new place. But Heather became quite distressed with stomach cramps on the Sunday night whilst having her bath. I raced her to the Ipswich Hospital and the Doctor on duty said her appendix was about to burst. He said, 'We'll take her straight in for surgery now.'

I just had a feeling that he was wrong I can't explain why, I just did.

Amelia 'I want a second opinion.'

Doctor 'There's no one else to consult.'

Amelia 'Her paediatrician is Doctor Kenneth from Wickham Terrace in Brisbane I have his home phone number in my bag.'

He and the nurse both looked at me as if I was completely off my face and both burst out laughing.

Doctor 'You can't ring a specialist at his home, especially not at this hour on a Sunday night.'

Amelia 'I can. Doctor Kenneth won't mind.'

No matter how much I tried to convince him, he wouldn't believe that a specialist would consult a patient after hours.

Amelia 'Look if I'm wrong and you're right you'll have nothing to worry about. If I'm right and you're wrong you still won't have anything to worry about I'm the one who'll be in the shit either way.'

He finally agreed to ring the number and I'm not exaggerating he was practically bowing on the phone he grovelled so much. When he hung up

Doctor 'Doctor Kenneth's a lovely man to talk with, isn't he? He said that he'll meet you at St Andrews Hospital in Brisbane in an hour.'

It was almost midnight when we arrived at St Andrews Hospital and Doctor Kenneth arrived within five minutes. Heather was booked in and he examined her and by twelve-thirty am he had diagnosed her as having a bowel infection. Frank and I were totally knackered on the Monday, we had driven back home and then back to the hospital by ten am but Heather had to stay in for another twenty-four hours. As we headed back to Ipswich, I decided to go in to the Indooroopilly bank on spec. We both looked like the wreck of the Hesperus. I asked the girl at the front desk if we could see the manager or the accountant. She asked why we wanted to see them and I said, 'To borrow ten thousand dollars for a house.' We had to wait for nearly an hour while he had his lunch. The seats were very hard and both our spines were screaming in agony and we were so bloody tired. Finally, we both limped into his office and he sat back with an exasperated look on his face, his eyes were closed and he said, 'You should make an appointment to see me you know.'

I apologised and before I could explain why we didn't make the appointment

The Manager 'So you want to borrow ten thousand dollars for a house?'

Amelia 'Yes.'

The Manager 'Where's the house?'

I told him the address

The Manager 'We don't lend money for deposits on homes.'

Amelia 'I know that.'

The Manager 'So what do you mean that you want ten thousand dollars?'

Amelia 'That's all we need.'

The Manager 'How much is the house?'

I told him how much we would be paying for the place and still he persisted

The Manager 'So where are you getting the rest of the money from?'

Amelia 'From our bank account once the sale of our house in Ipswich is finalised.'

His eyes snapped open, he sat bolt upright,

The Manager 'All you need is ten thousand dollars to buy a home in that beautiful suburb?'

Amelia 'Yes.'

He burst out laughing

The Manager 'Oh my God, I wish I could go into a bank and say that. I'm so sorry I thought you were confused thinking you could borrow the deposit for a house.'

Amelia 'I know we look like deadbeats but there's a good reason.'

I told him what had transpired and he was so apologetic for his behaviour. Every time I went into the bank after that he greeted me as if I was his best friend.

Although I had continued to go down to visit my parents on a regular basis from Ipswich, and as much as Dad used to mock protest at my arrival whenever I visited, he was really pleased that we had shifted back to Brisbane. He said, 'It will be good for your mother that you're close by.' I never gave that statement any thought whatsoever at the time. We had only been in the new house a couple of days and the kid from next door came over with an Avon book and told me that the neighbour on the other side of her was an Avon rep and wanted to know if I would order anything. I thought it was a bit rude asking the kid to come and see me instead of coming to see me herself. I said to the girl, 'I'm sorry, sweetheart, I don't buy much makeup and I prefer other perfumes. Tell the lady thanks but no thanks.' Sweet Jesus that was enough to set the woman on a hate campaign against us. Her name was Janine and her husband Kerry, believe me when I say that they deserved each other. They were nuts with a capital N. They had two little boys Jack and Jerry aged about seven and eight. I guess they couldn't help it that their parents were complete morons but unfortunately the parents had taught them to be as crazy as they were. Heather and I appeared on The Mike Walsh Show and This Day Tonight because of Heather's Neurofibromatosis. Neurofibromatosis was what Joseph Merrick the elephant man had, of course both programmes had to mention this in the interviews. After both programmes Jack and Jerry threw stones at Heather and would yell out at her on a regular basis, 'Get out of our street elephant girl.' There was no way on God's earth that they saw her on The Mike Walsh Show because it was on at midday when they were at school. The only way that they knew to call her elephant girl was that their mother and/or father had told them to. I told Heather to ignore them and they'd soon tire of it, but they didn't, it went on for months.

Frank tried talking to both Kerry and Janine but they told him to fuck off. Kerry worked at a big car yard a couple of suburbs away and an advertisement came on television that they were having a massive clearance sale of their cars. The ad said that there was to be a sausage sizzle and all the trimmings of a fun day. Frank rang Kerry at the car yard a few days before the big day and said, 'I'm only going to say this once, if you don't stop your boys from abusing my daughter, I'm coming down to the caryard on Saturday with a megaphone and I'll announce to the crowd what an arsehole you are and what you've been teaching your kids to do. If the name calling and stone throwing continues after your big day, I will not only ring your boss, I'll ring the Ford Company in Melbourne as well'. The kids never bothered Heather again however that wasn't the end of Kerry and Janine's vindictiveness. Frank had chipped out every blade of grass around our home and had planted Queensland blue couch seed. He had also planted it on the footpath as well. To stop people walking on it until the grass was established, Frank had roped off the footpath outside our home. The postman would come into our driveway and put the letters on our front steps. I had asked the postie if it was a problem to him and he said, 'Not at all, I'm a gardener too so I can appreciate what you're doing.'

The City Council inspector came around

City Council inspector 'We appreciate what you are doing we know you are trying to beautify our land as well as yours but we've had a complaint and we have to ask you to remove the ropes.'

Amelia 'I know you can't tell me who it was, but I already know it's the idiots two doors down the road isn't it?'

He just grinned and winked

City Council inspector 'We wouldn't have even known about the ropes here if we hadn't gotten the call.'

Amelia 'No problem, I'll remove the ropes immediately.'

They say that Karma gets you one way or the other and less than a week went by and a huge amount of timber was delivered for Kerry and Janine. As luck had it, no one was home at the time of the delivery, Kerry was at work and Janine had driven the boys to school, so the timber was left on their footpath. Frank was home at the time and as soon as he saw the timber arrive, he immediately rang the City Council to tell them that there was a massive amount of timber blocking the footpath. The inspector came out almost immediately and we saw Janine arrive home and he spoke to her. Within the hour Kerry came home and he worked his backside off until after nine pm lugging every piece of timber into his yard on his own.

During the time I was on Compo I kept getting letters from Challinor to resign. Hey. I might be dumb but I'm not completely stupid. I didn't want to be

CLEAN HANDS, CLEAR CONSCIENCE

on Compo, I didn't purposefully crush fracture three vertebrae I wanted to be gainfully employed. As far as I was concerned, if they could find Peter a job after he had wielded a loaded gun around and threatening to kill three people they could find me a job as well. But persist they did.

I was shocked one morning just before lunchtime when I answered a knock at the door. A taxi driver had driven from Ipswich (approximately a return trip of 100 kilometres) to deliver a letter to me personally. The letter was another request for me to resign from the Public Service. I was supposed to sign a document in front of the driver that I had personally received the letter and that I had read it and I was to sign another document acknowledging that I agreed to resign from the Public Service. I looked at the driver shaking my head in total disbelief and he shook his head as well.

Taxi Driver 'Who did you kill?'

Amelia 'Oh mate I can only wish it had've been every nut job in that dump and I aint talkin' about the residents.'

I rang Challinor and said to the person who answered the phone, 'It's Amelia Williams here'. Whomever I was speaking to said excitedly to someone else, 'It's Amelia Williams.' I could hear a voice in the background and then the person whom I was speaking to said to me, 'Did you sign the document?'

I answered, 'Yes'. The voice whispered to the other person, 'She's signed it.'

I laughed out loud and said, 'What numbskull thought this crap up? As if I'd resign, tell them to wake up to themselves.'

The phone call was terminated abruptly, but not by me. That was the last I ever heard from anyone at Challinor regarding my resignation. But they were in for a surprise if not a big shock.

Chapter 49

Marriage and Madness

Vivian and Andrew had shifted back to Brisbane and were living in a tiny one-bedroom cottage at Underwood. It wasn't a palace but in comparison to the hovel they had been living in down at Mullumbimby the cottage was the closest thing to a palace.

Dad rang me one morning to tell me Vivian had been in a car crash down at Fortitude Valley not far from the Import/Export business she was employed at as a receptionist/cashier. I thought it was rather strange that Vivian had rung Dad and not me, and I said, 'Why didn't she ring me?' He replied, 'I guess she didn't want you to worry.' I thought that it was more than odd, she didn't want me a thirty-eight year old to worry, but she rang a sixty-eight year old man who would worry himself sick. I picked Dad up and we drove to where the accident was. Dad had never been in the car whilst I was driving, whenever Heather needed to go to an appointment I'd drive to his home and he would drive me into Wickham Terrace and after the appointment I'd ring him and he'd pick us up. He would never drive our car he always insisted on driving his own Torana. We were wending our way through traffic and I was telling the other drivers to get out of my way calling them idiots and generally being my impatient self.

Dad 'Who are you talking to?'

Amelia 'The morons in the other cars.'

He blessed himself and pretended to say his prayers and muttered, 'Please God don't let this be a case of a funny thing happened on the way to the forum'. I had a good chuckle at that. When we got to the accident Vivian looked at me and said, 'What did you have to come and stick your nose in for?' I was shocked and just matter of factly said, 'Your grandfather rang me because his car is at the mechanics being serviced'. She said, 'I know he told me that, and I told him I didn't want you to come here'. I said, 'Well he didn't tell me, he rang to tell me you wanted him down here, how else did you think he would get here?' I put her anger down to her being in shock. I always had an excuse for Vivian's behaviour. She was taken to the hospital and Dad told me that he didn't want to go to the hospital, he was satisfied she wasn't badly hurt so I drove him back home. When we got to his place Dad got out and kissed the ground and looked up to the sky and said, 'Thank you God'. I had the best laugh at that. I drove to the hospital and by the time I got there Andrew was there and Vivian was doing the dying swan act. Admittedly she was extremely lucky that she hadn't injured herself badly or been killed for that matter, because she must've been moving at a rapid pace, the car had spun over on its lid. She told me to get out of the booth she was in because she wanted to speak to Andrew privately. I walked out and sat outside and a nurse came out and told me, 'Madam, you'll have to leave, the young lady in there said you were distressing her'.

I wanted to yell, 'I'm distressing her?' But I kept quiet and went home.

A few weeks later Vivian told us that she and Andrew had decided to get married. Unfortunately, it was she who had proposed to him. I honestly believe that the reason he agreed to marry her was to have a big party at our expense. The year before on our twentieth anniversary, Andrew had invited us to have dinner at the Blue Ensign Restaurant at Underwood where he had been working as a bar tender. The dinner was to be their Anniversary gift to us. When we arrived, we were surprised to see Jock and Dora with a friend who was visiting them from Bundaberg there as well. We all ordered different meals and for some inexplicable reason I took notice of the fact that Frank and I were the only ones who had ordered the cheapest meals. Andrew kept ordering jugs of beer like they were going out of fashion and Frank and I had had one glass of coke each. At around eleven pm Andrew said to the waitress, 'Take the jug of beer away, and bring a bottle of Scotch'. The jug of beer was over half full and Frank and I glanced at each other but never uttered a word. Another bottle of Scotch was brought about an hour later and of course by this time Andrew was fuller than the Marist Brother's College. At quarter to one in the morning the waitress came and told us that they had to close in fifteen minutes and she handed Andrew the bill. He was staggering around shaking his head saying, 'Oh No.' and he handed me the bill. I looked at it and it was over two hundred and twenty-five dollars which in 1981 was exorbitant. I said, 'Well our meals were seven dollars and ninety-five cents each and we only had the one coke each so our portion of the bill is eighteen dollars forty but here's twenty dollars keep the change.'

Vivian 'Mum, do you have your bankcard with you, we'll pay you back.'

I lied through my teeth 'No it's lucky I brought the twenty dollars with me.'

I felt embarrassed, ashamed and bloody ropeable all at the same time. They were all scraping around trying to come up with the rest of the money and Frank said, 'Let's go'.

We left and I believe that Jock and Dora's friend paid most of the bill.

The wedding of the century was about to be planned and I made sure that I stipulated that all grog over a certain limit would be paid for by Andrew and/ or whomever drank it. Andrew came up with the idea that it would be nice to have the wedding and reception on board a riverboat. Vivian and Andrew had arranged for us all to have a meeting with the woman who ran the riverboat. It was the most revolting looking boat that ever sailed any river anywhere in the world. In my opinion it was built for a three ringed circus (come to think of it I should have hired it on the spot.) But to make matters worse the woman whom we met absolutely reeked of stale grog and I think if I'd lit a match near her, she would have exploded. Andrew was all for having the reception on board, and I said, 'Okay but don't expect me to pay for it, I wouldn't want to sail six inches off shore in that tub, especially with that woman in charge.'

I rang a number of wedding reception places and all were so expensive, we finally chose Wanganui Gardens at Tennyson. All we had to do was let them know how many people would be attending. I made up the list on our side of the family and we went over to Jock and Dora's place to discuss whom they wanted to invite. The list was endless. I seemed to be writing names down for hours. But what really stunned me beyond belief was when I asked for the addresses of their friends and family, they had no idea whatsoever. Most of them we had to look up in various telephone books between Rockhampton and Sydney. We later found out that they hadn't seen most of the people for nearly twenty years. Frank and I were totally gobsmacked. Vivian told me that she would hire her dress to save us money. She picked me up and we drove into the city to look at bridal wear at the hire shop, but 'somehow', we just happened to walk past a bridal shop and she took me in just to show me a dress she had admired a few days beforehand. It had a price tag of twelve hundred dollars. She needed no encouragement from the sales woman to try it on *again* . She swished and sashayed around in it and kept giving me glances to see my reaction. No doubt Vivian was a very pretty girl and she did look lovely in it but there was no way on earth, in heaven or hell that I was going to buy her that dress.

To hire a dress in those days was quite reasonable and I thought to myself, she's not going to pay for a hire dress. She tried on another dress which was a hundred and thirty dollars which still was a lot of money then, but I agreed to buy it for her. I was the best mother in the world that night. I might add I have never paid that much for a dress for myself even in this day and age.

Vivian had arranged to meet Andrew and they invited me to a restaurant to have dinner. I had never had wine in my life and I had two glasses that night and I was feeling no pain. No need to tell you who coughed up for the bill. Luckily, I hadn't been driving. On our way home we called in to see Dad and Edith. Dad and I spent a couple of hours singing our favourite songs that we had often done when I was a little girl. I was the happiest I'd been in a long time. Then I heard Dad saying to Andrew, 'Get her home she's blotto.' I almost fell on the floor I laughed so much. Dad and I were like two peas in a pod, far too much alike for either of us to want to admit to.

I had to work out who would sit near whom and who could not sit near whom on the McKenzie's side of the nuptials. It seemed to me that the Clampetts seemed to be better bred than the McKenzies. The week before the wedding we held a pre-wedding party so the two families could get to know each other better and for the McKenzies to meet some of our friends. During the course of the evening I needed Vivian to help me with something (I can't remember what it was now) but I called out, 'Number one daughter, can you come into the bedroom please?' Michelle and Vivian raced to the door and Michelle edged her way through the door in front of Vivian with Heather and Claire in hot pursuit. We all had a good laugh at that and I deemed it as a great honour that Michelle had thought of me as her mum. Especially considering that she had lost her much loved mother, Mary, to breast cancer less than two months earlier. But I couldn't help but notice that although Vivian was laughing her eyes flashed with anger. From that day on Vivian hated Michelle with a passion and every chance she could, she would say derogatory things about Michelle and how much she hated her.

Vivian stayed with us the night before the wedding and I felt really content that my little girl was home with me where I felt she belonged. She was very concerned that Andrew wasn't going to turn up for the wedding because they had had a big fight that morning and he had told her he didn't want to marry her. Although I soothed her and told her he'd be there I secretly hoped that he wouldn't. She told us that she loved us all so very much and I really didn't want that night to end.

The big day finally arrived and surprisingly everything went very smoothly without any problems. The only upset I had on the day other than Andrew turning up for his own wedding, was when one of Andrew's mates found out that I had given up smoking six months earlier he persisted in blowing his cigarette smoke in my face several times. I somehow resisted the urge of punching his head in and kicking the little bastard in the nuts. My sister-in-law Judy also upset my peptic system somewhat when Vivian and Andrew said their vows Judy whispered to me, 'You can see that she's truly in love by the look on her face.' I wanted to scream, 'That's not love, that's an obsession.' Frank and I truly believed that somehow Andrew had some sort of Svengali type hold over Vivian. We could not for the life of us work out what she saw in him. I guess my parents probably thought the same about Frank but at least Frank had a personality and good sense of humour and was reasonably intelligent although uneducated and was quite good-looking. Andrew had no personality was as dumb as a box of rocks (He thought Karl Marx was Groucho's and Harpo's brother.) He had a very long nose and wide mouth and his sense of humour was zero and dropping. When it came time for Frank to give his speech as father of the bride, I had no idea what he was about to say. He was very nervous as he rose from his seat and asked everyone to raise their glasses to the bride and groom. He went on, 'This has been a true fairy tale wedding.' Everyone went, 'AWWW' He then said, 'Yes Cinderella has just married Pinocchio.'

Everybody clapped, laughed and cheered, well everyone except Vivian and Andrew. Dad rang me the following day to thank and congratulate me for hosting such a wonderful day. I was extremely touched by that call. On their return from their Cairns honeymoon, Vivian became very aloof whenever I tried to speak to her it was always the wrong time because she was so busy. I thought, Okay I'll wait for you to contact me. Six weeks after the wedding I drove Claire up to Channel Nine studios as had become a bit of a ritual over the last few months. She loved going on the Channel Niners kids' TV show every Saturday morning. The host of the show Gibbo must have loved Claire too because he always chose her out of the hundreds of kids in the audience to try and win prizes. She had so many fluffy toys that she'd won sitting on her bed, it was almost impossible for her to get into bed of a night. On one occasion she was called out to tell a joke to win a prize

Claire 'What wood won't float?'

Gibbo 'I don't know, Claire, what wood won't float.'

Claire 'Natalie Wood.'

Natalie Wood had only drowned a few days earlier. Gibbo laughed so much he staggered off camera leaving Claire standing in front of the camera on her own with the biggest smile on her face. The following week when we took her to the Channel Niners we were absolutely shocked to see a huge photo of Claire on the wall alongside all the other stars of Channel Nine. That photo was a still of her when Gibbo left her in front of the camera alone. It would have easily been 200cm wide x 100cm high and it stayed there for the entire time Channel Niners was on the air.

On this particular day the theme was for the kids to dress as aliens. Claire was dressed in her green velvet track suit and I had covered her face and hands with green eye shadow and made antennas for her out of silver foil. I had also painted her face to look alien like. No need to be told she won first prize. On our way home I decided to call in to the RSL Club where Dad was, to show him what Claire looked like. Dad always had to be early at the club because he was second in charge (well that was his excuse anyway.) I was quite shocked to see Vivian and Andrew sitting there with him and I could tell by the look on their faces that they were not pleased to see me arrive. I pretended not to notice their disappointment at seeing me, but I couldn't help but wonder why they would be there at eleven o'clock in the morning. Especially considering that they had to drive from Underwood a distance of about twenty-five klms to get there. I immediately thought, you're on the hum for something, and if its money you are barking up the wrong tree. I had only intended staying a moment but seeing Vivian and Andrew there and knowing they were not happy to see me I decided to stay there for an hour or so just to annoy them even more. Dad and I never had any secrets and when I had expressed my concern to him about Andrew months previously, he said, 'I've already had him and his family checked out and there's no criminal record, but if he does the wrong thing by Vivian he'll regret it.' Dad wasn't silly enough to part with any money if they asked, not that he had any because Edith had a very tight hold on the purse strings.

I remember commenting to Dad that day about the mark on the side of his temple where he had had a skin cancer burnt off a couple of days before. I said 'You look as if you've been shot it looks like you've had bullet to your head.' Normally he would have made a funny remark back to me but that day he just nodded and quietly said, 'Yeah I know.'

I recall being shocked at the way he said it as if it really was a bullet in his head.

The following Tuesday I went to pick Edith up to take her to lunch to my friend Beryl's home. Before we left, Edith and I had an argument in front of Dad about a pair of pearl earrings Vivian had given Heather for being bridesmaid. Vivian had borrowed them to wear on her honeymoon and hadn't returned them. She had eventually given them to Edith which meant Vivian would have had to have driven past our house to give them to Edith. Edith had misplaced them which made me extremely annoyed.

On our return back to Edith's home Dad had left a note saying he had searched the joint and finally found the earrings before heading to the club. I had all intentions of calling into the club on my way home to thank him, but the traffic was so heavy it was almost impossible to turn into the club so I continued on my way home. I didn't call in to see them the following day and I forgot to ring Dad to thank him for finding the earrings.

Thursday 30th September 1982 was a public holiday for the opening of the Brisbane Commonwealth Games, so again I didn't go down to see Dad and Edith. Along with most of the nation and half the world Frank, Heather, Claire and I sat glued to the TV watching the opening ceremony. At the closing of the opening ceremony Frank went into have his shower and I started to prepare dinner when the phone rang. Edith was near hysterics crying that Dad had collapsed, I told her to ring the doctor and ambulance and she assured me that she had already done so. I hurried into the bathroom and told Frank and I remember him exclaiming, 'Oh shit.' He got dressed and was still dripping wet and we practically flew to Dad's home. By the time we got there the doctor was kneeling over dad frantically pumping Dad's chest and giving him mouth to mouth. The doctor said to me, 'Ring the ambulance again.' He continued the mouth to mouth resuscitation for another fifty-five minutes before calling the time of death at six pm. The ambulance failed to show until ten past six. Even though Edith had rung them at four forty-five and I had rung them three times between 5.05 and 5.45 pm. To say I was hysterical would be the understatement of the millennium. I had just lost the man who had fought for his country, the man who had sung me to sleep, the man who called me his Princess, the man who had been my backbone, the man who drove Heather and I to every doctor's appointment and picked us up afterwards, the man who called me his shadow and the eternal flame (because I was always there and I never went out.) The man I had adored all my life. I wanted to die too.

I felt so sorry for Edith she was overwhelmed with grief and she was completely out of her depth not knowing what to do. It was up to James to make the arrangements for the funeral. Edith suggested that we have a private funeral but I was adamant that he should have a funeral befitting a war veteran.

The following Tuesday exactly one week to the minute since I had seen him, he was cremated at Mt Thompson Crematorium. More than two hundred people came to pay their respects and his RSL mates formed a guard of honour for us as we left the chapel. After the funeral we went back to Edith's house and I was stunned beyond belief to see Edward trying to put Dad's shoes on. God only knows what was going through his mind. Edward wore size seven shoes and Dad had worn size five. But the day wasn't over I was still in for more shocks. Vivian started to complain to me that Edith had really upset her on the Friday by ringing her and saying, 'Your grandfather's dead.'

Vivian said to me, 'Wouldn't you think the old bitch would have broken the news better than that?' I have no idea how Edith was supposed to tell Vivian gently that her husband of forty-seven years had died. Maybe Edith should have said, 'Although I've been married to your grandfather for forty-seven years it's all about you and your pain so it's my duty to break the news gently to you that your Granddad's gone to visit God permanently.' Edward summoned me out onto the back veranda as if he was king of the house and informed me that he was going to take Dad's Torana and give it to his son. I thought, Christ the poor bastard's only been cremated an hour ago and I have to deal with a pack of village idiots.

Amelia ' Edward, wake up to yourself. It's Mum's car now, you don't have the right to give the car to anyone.'

Edward 'It's a bomb she can't drive it, and she won't be able to sell it because no one would pay anything for it, it's not even worth a thousand dollars.'

Amelia 'If it's a bomb why would you want your son to be driving it?'

I walked inside and said to Edith, 'Edward just said the car isn't worth a thousand dollars and he wants to give it to Mark, I'll give you fifteen hundred dollars for it because Frank needs another car to get to work.'

Edith agreed to sell it to me for a thousand dollars and Edward protested by saying, 'Oh I'll pay the thousand dollars, I'll get it from the bank tomorrow.'

I thought, two can play this idiotic game so I lied and said, 'I'll get it out of the bank machine now if necessary.' ATM's had only been introduced a few weeks earlier but I had no idea how to work them. About five minutes or so went by and Edward went outside and drove off in the Torana. When he came back ten minutes later, I said, 'Why did you drive away in the Torana?' He replied, 'I wanted to take it for a test run to see if it was safe to drive.'.Dad had bought the Torana in 1974 and had kept it in perfect condition and had only driven it the day before he died. I thought, this is absolute madness I'm dealing with a complete basket case. I just wanted the world to stop.

We subsequently found out Dad had had an aortic aneurysm for about five years and had been told it was inoperable. He hadn't told anyone except one of his mates because he didn't want us to worry. For the next six weeks I spent every day with Edith from nine am to three pm and after the first week I felt stifled. As much as I felt sorry for her she didn't seem to understand that I was grieving too. Out of my two brothers and myself I was the only one most like Dad and she relied on me to be there. When I finally pulled away, she felt that I had left her in the lurch. The truth was I needed to mourn on my own. The sad part is, almost forty years later I am still mourning his loss. I have his and my grandmother's photo as my screen saver on my computer and never a day goes by that I don't talk to them.

It had been some time since I'd heard from Vivian so I rang her at her work. When I asked Sharon her co-worker if I could speak to Vivian there was a deathly silence. After what seemed like an eternity Sharon said, 'Vivian isn't here.' I asked if she was sick?'

I was stunned when Sharon said, 'Vivian got the sack because a lot of money went missing, didn't she tell you?' I stammered, 'No I haven't heard from her for weeks.'

I was totally shocked I rang Vivian at home and her version of things was that she was convinced that Sharon had taken the money but because she was the boss' daughter-in-law she could get away with it. I didn't know what to believe, but I couldn't help but recall that money had gone missing from her first job as receptionist at a real estate firm in Ipswich. She had been under suspicion there and was terminated from that job as well. She had also left the checkout chic's job at Mullumbimby in a hurry as well and she and Andrew had returned to Brisbane quite quickly.

Another couple of weeks later, Vivian announced that she was pregnant and Frank and I were over the moon to think we were to become grandparents. As my grandmother had provided Frank and me with love and comfort, we too were preparing to provide as much as we could afford for our grandchild. We bought everything a baby could possibly need or want. Vivian started a new job as a saleswoman at a waterbed company at Mt Gravatt she was only there a short time before it was broken into and money was stolen from a cash box hidden under a desk. Frank and I called in to see her at work a few days after the break in and we couldn't help but notice that the window that had been smashed was rather small for anyone to crawl through. We got the impression that the window had been smashed to make it look as if there had been a break in. But we kept our suspicions to ourselves.

Vivian rang me on a Tuesday in June 1983 to say that she was going into the Mater hospital, I desperately wanted to race to the hospital to be there with her but she told me to stay away. She assured me Andrew would ring me after the birth. I lay alongside the telephone in the lounge room waiting for the call. The phone only gave a tinkle and I answered it immediately. Andrew McKenzie had arrived into the world on the Wednesday in 1983 at 3.33am and I was on cloud nine.

We visited Vivian and saw baby Andrew and he was perfect he was so handsome. Vivian seemed very distant in her manner towards me but as per usual I dismissed it as her being tired after the birth. She was discharged a couple of days later and although I was anxious to go and visit them, I thought it wiser to allow them time to adjust as a family. The following Monday Vivian rang me to tell me that the baby was very unsettled. She asked if I would come over to help her. I had to drive twenty-five kilometres to their new rental home and I drove with Heather at breakneck speed to get there. On our arrival I was more than a bit surprised at the state of the house it looked as if a bomb had hit. There were empty beer bottles and glasses littering the living room floor and remnants of food scattered around the living room and kitchen area and spilling out of the kitchen tidy bin. I indicated to Heather to start cleaning the mess and I went into the bedroom where the baby was. The room reeked I don't know what of but it wasn't pleasant. Andrew was crying his little heart out. I picked him up and took him into the living room and asked Vivian if he'd been fed, she replied that he had. I then asked if she'd given him any water. She looked at me as if I was speaking gibberish

Vivian 'No, why would I?'

Amelia 'He may be thirsty'. I then explained as if to a three-year old, that milk was food and water was for thirst. She hurried into the kitchen and within a moment brought back one of his bottles filled with water. I said surprised, 'Did you have this prepared?' She laughed and said in a tone that surprised me, 'No. I just filled it up from the tap.' Heather flashed a look of horror on her face at me and I stood looking at Vivian with my mouth agape.

Vivian 'What?'

Amelia 'Vivian, you don't give babies water from the tap you have to boil the water to get any germs out of it'.

Vivian 'It'd be too hot to give him.'

Amelia 'For God's sake you allow it to cool down first, you should always have it prepared in a sterilised glass container in the fridge and warm it in a jug of hot water when needed'.

Vivian 'I never knew that.'

Heather 'That's one of the first things they teach you in mothercraft at school even a dummy like me knew that.'

Heather boiled the water sterilised all the bottles half-filled one bottle and placed it in cold water to cool explaining it all to Vivian as she did so. I thought to myself, I never thought I'd see the day when Heather had to teach Vivian what to do. Andrew drank it with gusto. After showing Vivian how to burp him I asked her to get me a nappy. As soon as I undressed him, I almost had a blue fit. The nappy was saturated and his penis was red raw and the skin was peeling off it. I was shocked to my back molars

Amelia 'Christ we'll have to get him to a doctor.'

She said that she didn't want to go because she was too tired.

Amelia 'Well you had better start putting some sort of cream on him to clear that up before it becomes infected.'

I bathed him changed his bedding gave him his bottle and put him back into his cot. Heather and I left after we'd finished cleaning the house and on the way home, Heather said 'Mum, I can't believe how slack Vivian was not looking after Andrew properly.'

I couldn't have agreed with her more. Three days later I went back over and I was sick to the pit of my stomach when I saw Andrew. He was still in the same clothes I had put on him.

Amelia 'Vivian, haven't you bathed Andrew for three days?'

Vivian 'Y … yes'.

Amelia 'No you haven't he's still in the same clothes that I put on him.'

Vivian 'I've washed them in the meantime.'

Amelia 'Bullshit, he absolutely reeks of stale vomit.'

I removed his clothes and his nappy was saturated again and his penis was almost purple it was so sore looking. I gave him a quick sponge changed him and we hurried to the car and I drove to Doctor Orford's surgery. Doctor Orford was as horrified as I had been when he examined him. In true boy style Andrew peed up and over his head splattering Doctor Orford and the wall. Doctor Orford cleaned both him and Andrew and asked Vivian for a clean nappy. Vivian looked at us with total bewilderment and said, 'I didn't think I'd need any I didn't bring any with me.' Doctor Orford looked at me his eyes were as big as saucers and we both shook our heads in total disbelief. He had to put the wet nappy back on Andrew and the urine must have stung like buggery again and he screamed in pain. Doctor Orford wrote a script and instructed to get it straight away and apply it immediately. I paid for the consultation and we left.

Although there were a number of chemists near Dr Orford's surgery, Vivian was adamant that we had to wait until we got to a chemist near her home. I insisted that we go to Edith's place to rinse the nappy and dry it in the dryer before driving the twenty-five kilometres back to her home. Luckily for Vivian, Edith wasn't home, if she had've been home I think Edith would've had more than a blue fit. I let us in with my key got a clean towel and lay Andrew on it and washed and dried the nappy before heading back to Underwood. What happened next defies belief but I lived the experience so I know it definitely happened.

We arrived at the shopping centre and I parked directly outside the chemist Vivian got out and made a beeline to the supermarket. I said, 'Aren't you getting the script filled?'

She replied, 'I want to get a few things at the supermarket first.' I followed her into the supermarket and she placed bottles of soft drink, packets of chips, lollies and salami sausage into the trolley. I asked, 'Are you having another party?'

'No Andrew likes these things.' She then went over to the electric appliances and said, 'I'd like to get a heater, what do you reckon, are they too expensive?' I said, 'Well that's up to you if you can afford it or not.' I thought, this is going to be interesting if she thinks I'm paying for shit for that turd. When we got to the cashier she hesitated to see if I was going for my wallet and I just said, 'I'll wait for you outside.' She got to the car put her purchases into the boot and sat in the car. I said 'Andrew's prescription.'

She replied, 'I haven't got any money left.' I grabbed the script and went in and got the cream. As we drove to her home I said, 'Vivian, I don't know where your brain is at but I've got to tell you your baby has to come first, second, third, fourth and every other number you can think of before you start buying that shit for Andrew.' Over the next seven weeks I drove over as often as I could and I invariably ended up doing all the housework as well as bathing and caring for Andrew as much as I could. I tried to teach Vivian everything I could possibly think of in caring for the baby, but nothing seemed to penetrate. Each time I went there he always looked grubby and stunk of stale vomit or dirty nappy. On one occasion there was a cat in a cage on the back veranda in the sun. I said, 'What the hell's going on here?' I ran out and was about to let it out and she cried, 'No, Mum, please don't, Andrew will go off the brain if you let it out. The cat's been running in looking for food and he wants to teach it a lesson.'

Almost forty years later I still feel guilty that I didn't release that poor animal and I regret that I didn't call the RSPCA and dob the pair of them in.

On Saturday July 30 1983 Vivian and Andrew were going to a work function at Archerfield Aerodrome where Andrew was to receive an award. He had been working for a well-known pest control company and he was to receive the award for being the most conscientious new employee or some such nonsense. They brought Andy (as he had been nicknamed to avoid confusion) to me to look after and before they left, I asked Vivian if she had brought enough formula for him and she said she had and that she had put it in the fridge. She added that he had just finished his bottle before they left home.

They left at six-thirty pm and I don't think they would have gotten one kilometre away and Andy started to cry. I gave him some water but he wasn't thirsty he kept spitting his dummy out and over the next hour and a half I tried everything I could to soothe him but nothing worked. In desperation I decided to give him his bottle. I went to the fridge and I was stunned when I saw there was only one ounce in the bottle. I warmed it and he drank it as if he hadn't been fed for hours. As soon as he finished, he cried for more.

In those days there were no after-hours chemists to get more formula nor were there any supermarkets open. I couldn't just give him ordinary milk because to change from his regular formula to cow's milk suddenly, would only have given him a gripe belly. The poor little mite was starving and he did not stop crying. At about nine pm I drove to the Archerfield Aerodrome in search of the venue but the entire place was in darkness. I was beside myself with worry over the way his little heart was breaking from wanting a feed. Vivian and Andrew finally got back at two-fifteen am and I was absolutely livid but all I said to Vivian was 'Andy is starving and you only left an ounce of milk for the poor little bugger he's been crying for almost eight hours.'

Andrew 'That's it, you'll never see your grandson again, and I've won'.

I looked at him in total disbelief

Amelia 'What are you talking about, Andrew, what have you won?'

He just kept repeating over and over, 'I've won, I've won, I've won'.

Amelia 'You're half pissed, Andrew, so stop talking shit.'

And he again repeated with a smirk on his face, 'I've won.'

He turned to Vivian and said, 'Let's go.'

And they left. I went into the bedroom

Frank 'Did you tell Vivian the little fellah's been cryin' all night?'

Amelia 'Have you been awake all the time?'

Frank 'Yeah why?'

Amelia 'You're not going to believe this'.

I told him what had transpired.

Frank 'He's talking through his arse don't worry about it.'

The following day Andrew and Vivian arrived and demanded their belongings. They had left a few bits and pieces which were probably worth about twenty dollars and I went inside to get them. I invited them to come in but they both refused. Frank went to the door and said hello to them but they both ignored him.

Frank 'What's your problem, Andrew?'

To which he replied, 'I don't have one.'

I handed their belongings over and they walked down the stairs. Frank followed them. They got in the car and Andrew started the engine Frank walked up to the driver's side window and Andrew grabbed Andy from Vivian and held him up in front of his (Andrew's) face thinking Frank was about to punch him. Frank grabbed the steering wheel and said, 'Turn the motor off I want to talk.'

Andrew wound the window up and Frank wasn't quick enough pulling his hand out and was caught like a trapped animal. I was standing on the front veranda and I watched Andrew fling Andy over to Vivian he put the car in reverse and took off with Frank running alongside trying to pull his hand out. Andrew swung the car around into drive and sped up the hill with Frank running full speed alongside unable to remove his hand.

They got about thirty metres up the hill before Andrew wound the window down far enough to release Frank's hand. Frank fell to the ground and I watched in horror as the back wheels of the car missed him by centimetres. I thought the car had run over him because Frank lay on the bitumen until I ran up to him. He was okay but he was completely exhausted from the ordeal. I wanted to ring the police and have the little prick charged, but Frank said that he wouldn't do that.

Vivian refused to take my calls and she eventually changed her phone number to a private listing. I had visions of going over to confront her but I didn't. I wanted her to contact me first but she didn't. She kept in touch with Edith and had given Edith a cock and bull story that I had interfered with Andy's upbringing and I had caused the argument with Andrew by screaming abuse at him that fateful night. The irony was that our voices hadn't been raised, if they had've been, Frank would have jumped out of bed to come and see what the commotion was. He had been a mere six metres from where Andrew, Vivian and I had stood and he hadn't heard a peep.

I got the shock of my life one afternoon the following March when Andy was nine months old, Vivian arrived with Andy and spent about twenty minutes with me. In that time, she wistfully looked at the swimming pool we had recently installed and she quietly said, 'You've always wanted a pool and you deserve it Mum.' I replied, 'What we don't deserve is to be treated the way you and Andrew have treated us.' She agreed with me and she begged me to never tell Andrew that she had called around and then she left.

Frank, Heather, Claire and I continued our lives as a family as best as we could. Vivian eventually allowed Heather and Claire to visit them occasionally. I pretended to be enthusiastic at them going over to visit but I had a deep-seated feeling of reluctance. I couldn't pinpoint what it was I just felt an uneasiness that something sinister was going to happen. I tried talking to the girls about being very careful whilst they were over there, but Heather in particular took umbrage at everything I said. She kept insisting that Vivian and Andrew were alright and she implied that she thought we were totally wrong in the way we had treated them. I used to worry myself sick that Heather was being brainwashed by them. She was, and still is a very vulnerable person who can be easily swayed. One particular Sunday she arrived home from visiting Vivian and Andrew and she seemed on edge. She was very reluctant to tell me what she was concerned about, I got the distinct feeling she felt guilty about being disloyal to Vivian and Andrew. I didn't pressure her into telling me what was troubling her I thought it best to wait until she was good and ready to talk. Later in the evening

Heather 'Mum, I'm worried about Andy's safety.'

My heart started pounding but I very nonchalantly said, 'Why?'

Heather 'We went to dinner at the Pizza Hut last night and Vivian and Andrew locked Andy in the car in the car park. I was packing death worrying about him that he might suffocate and when I told them that and they just laughed at me. I kept telling them I had to go to the toilet but I'd go down to the car to check on him every ten minutes or so.'

I wanted to scream, I told you so. Instead I said, 'You did the right thing kiddo that was a very wise thing to do and I'm very proud of you.' As much as I wanted Heather to continue a relationship with Vivian I knew that this was the first chink in the armour and that there would be more problems to follow. Claire wasn't all that interested in visiting Vivian regularly but Heather continued to go over to visit them on a regular basis. Each time she would take at least two bags of groceries she had bought for them. No matter what I said or did to try and stop her from spending as much as she did, she would ignore me. She arrived home a couple of months after the Pizza Hut incident and was in a very good mood about how much Vivian and Andrew had praised her for her kindness. She'd only been home about an hour when the phone rang. It was Vivian. She said, 'I don't want Heather or Claire over here again'.

Amelia 'Why not?'

Vivian 'Heather has stolen fifty dollars out of Andrew's wallet.'

Amelia 'I don't believe you she'd rather give you a hundred dollars than take anything from you and you know that.'

She screamed, 'Don't you call me a fuckin liar you old bitch.' She slammed the receiver down in my ear. I was shell shocked and really upset at having to tell Heather what Vivian had accused her of. I called Heather out of her bedroom and said, 'That was Vivian on the phone she's just accused you of stealing fifty dollars from Andrew's wallet'. Heather looked at me as if I had told a lie and said, 'She did not.'

I said, 'Heather, I'm fair dinkum she said you and Claire can't go over there again because you stole fifty dollars out of Andrew's wallet.' Heather burst into tears and was inconsolable. When she was finally able to speak, she said, 'Mum, I've given Vivian money nearly every time I went over there, I felt sorry for her because she told me she never had enough money to buy things. I would never take anything from either of them. Why does she do these things?' I couldn't answer that then, any more than I can now.

Chapter 50

Premonitions or Coincidences

There's an old saying everyone knows — You can lead a horse to water but you can't make it drink.

This was the case with Michelle and Mark. We had advised them which were the best suburbs to look at and what suburbs not to look at when they decided to buy their home. Michelle and Mark bought a home in one of the worst suburbs anyway. It was a nice enough home but even in the right suburb I would have avoided it like the plague. Solely for the fact that the previous owner had painted the brick wall of the inside of the garage, Kelly green. The cement between the bricks were white, it was a shocker. But they were happy enough with their purchase, so I guess that was the main thing.

On Thursday 26th January 1984 Michelle gave birth to a beautiful baby boy whom they named Beau. When we visited her that night I said, 'No doubt about you Kiwis you've got more hide than Jessie the elephant giving birth on Australia Day of all days, nothing's sacred to you lot'. What amazed me about Beau he had the most gorgeous big brown eyes and his skin had a beautiful bronze glow. I commented to both Michelle and Mark that Beau was a beautiful colour and Mark ever the racist said, 'Yes he's white.'

But to be perfectly honest with you I thought Beau looked Vietnamese. Not that I thought for one moment that Mark wasn't the father, Beau just had a special glow about him. I also had this feeling that he had been on this earth before. I know that sounds crazy but that's one of the first things I thought. Michelle and Mark were over the moon, they had been married almost nine years and had just about given up hope of ever having a family. Where Vivian had been neglectful as a mother, Michelle was the complete opposite. She was almost an obsessively neurotic in caring for Beau. She wrote down every detail of Beau's existence. She recorded in her diary how much milk he had drunk, how long it took him to feed, what time he had a bath how long he slept, how many stools he passed what the consistency was. It was unreal. She justified her behaviour by telling me that Beau would be interested in reading it all when he got older. I didn't comment about it because although I thought she was going over the top, I felt it was by far better than the way Vivian had treated Andy.

Michelle was irate when her brother Robert made fun of her about her compulsive behaviour and especially when he called Beau Mr Bo Jangles and Buttons and Bow. Beau grew to be a delightful little boy with a very gentle nature and although Michelle and Mark taught him to call Frank and I Granddad and Grandma, Beau insisted on calling me Doan or Dabbar and he called Heather Tin Tin. The irony of those names I learnt much later, both Doan and Tin Tin are Vietnamese words Dabbar is Arabic. I never told Michelle and Mark that though because Mark would have gone off the brain. Beau and I used to have pretend standoffs, I'd tell him, 'Not Doan.' Because I thought it sounded too much like Joan and I didn't particularly like the name Joan. Beau would laugh and say defiantly, 'Doan.' Everyone would crack up. It was nothing unusual for us to spend at least one day of the weekend together. If they weren't at our place for dinner or a BBQ, we'd be visiting them at their place. It had been like that ever since they arrived from NZ. As far as we were all concerned, we were family and now Beau was the icing on the cake.

I had become a bit obsessed over the last four years of having my chest x-rayed. Every twelve months I would go in like clockwork to have my free x-ray. Fortunately, I got a clean bill of health each time but I'd become so conscientious about having it done I think I would've had the x-rays more regularly if it was allowed.

Then in November 1984 I received notification from the Queensland Government to go in for an interview about a position that had become available in the Health Department in Brisbane. I was excited and annoyed at the same time. Excited at the prospect of the possibility at long last of getting a new position but annoyed to think I had to apply for a position considering I was already an employee of the Health Department. Albeit that I hadn't received a red razoo from the Government since 1981. After my half pay fortnightly Worker's Compensation payments ceased, I was awarded a fifteen per cent lump sum payout on my spinal injury but I hadn't heard a peep from the Health Department for almost four years apart from all the geese at Challinor pestering me for my resignation.

When I went in for my interview I was questioned like a criminal about where I'd worked previously, where I'd been since then, why I hadn't worked in the past five years. Why did I want to re-join the workforce etc, etc. The questions seemed to go on forever. I have no idea if the fellow who interviewed me had any information re my Challinor position or if he was just a pawn in the system who was trying to be a smart arse. Whatever his reason it wasn't good enough for me. I snapped. I went off the brain big time telling him I had had a gutful of him and the Bjelke Peterson Queensland Government and that I was entitled to a job and that this interview was just a load of bullshit. He didn't know what to say and he excused himself and hurried out of the office. I thought good on ya Amelia you've just dug your own grave he's gone to get the cops to arrest you for being an idiot. On his return he said, 'I've arranged for you to start at the Chest Clinic in George Street, you'll have to ring there and speak to a Mr Gray to confirm your starting date.' What a strange coincidence. I must've had an inner premonition about the chest clinic. I marched out of the fellow's office like a soldier ready to take on Mohamed Ali if necessary. As soon as I arrived home, I rang Mr Gray and I said, 'Good afternoon its Amelia Williams speaking, I've just been informed that I've been given a position at the Chest Clinic and I'd like to know when you'd like me to start.'

Mr Gray 'I will have to interview you first to see if you are suitable for the position'.

I thought this is my Mohamed Ali. I said, 'Don't give me that bullshit you do not interview me. I have been appointed to start there and whether you like it or not I will be starting so what day am I to come in, tomorrow or next Monday?'

He coughed and spluttered

Mr Gray 'You can start on Monday, Mrs Williams.'

Amelia 'Good. And what position do you hold Mr Gray?'

Mr Gray 'I'm the Chief Radiographer.'

Amelia 'Well I'm glad I'm not just talking to a pen pusher.'

I got off the phone shaking my head in total disbelief at my attitude and thought

Jesus Christ, you really do push your luck at times you foolish woman.

When I met Mr Gray on the Monday it was painfully obvious, he was not impressed with this little upstart and I could not have given two hoots. I didn't like the look of him either he was obviously a chauvinistic old fart who had never had a woman stand up to him in his life. What a challenge. One of the first things Mr Gray did was to call me all of the women I was to work with and he gave us all a pep talk about how we were all to behave and be ladylike and non-aggressive. It took me all my time not to laugh and say 'Fuck off dickhead.' I felt very strongly that I wanted to be really anti-social just to get up his nose. After he left, the others were all abuzz, 'Oh I wonder what that was all about?' I thought God is really testing my patience here. I have landed in purgatory or possibly hell, I had nothing whatsoever in common with any of these people. I had waited four bloody long years for this.

The majority of the women I worked with were all narrow minded, staid old maids who had worked at the Chest Clinic for many years. I use the word work very loosely. It didn't take me long to work out their personalities and it wasn't a pretty sight. I could not believe that I had been jettisoned onto yet another planet of a different form of losers. I know that sounds pretentious and egotistical but seriously you had to be there to understand how I felt but at least they weren't trailer trash.

Beatrice was in her fifties and was the only married woman there. She was opinionated on every subject known to mankind and wrong on every one of them. Her favourite pastime was wandering through cemeteries reading headstones. She pretended to read books during her lunch break. What she didn't realise, I observed that she'd alternate three books and would always open them onto the same page.

Wanda was overweight and in her mid-thirties her mannerisms and her dress sense belied her age. She was more like a woman in her late fifties from the 1940s she was so old fashioned. The sad part was she thought she was a woman of the world who had personality plus. She spent most of her working days socializing by wandering around to each department with the same file under her arm. Anita was an identical twin. She was in her late thirties, quietly spoken and definitely the pick of the bunch but her education level was decidedly below standard. I felt sorry for Anita because I think out of all of them, she was the most genuine one. She was very family orientated and I think it was unfortunate that she hadn't met her Prince Charming. Instead she began dating Todd who worked in the dark room and he had the personality of a cane toad. Mary was in her fifties and also an identical twin. She was quietly spoken and second pick of the bunch. It's a pity that she wasn't brave enough to come out of the closet. She was deluding herself if she thought no one realised that her housemate was her girlfriend. One of the young women in the back office was an amputee and Mary loved to be organizing outings with Wanda and Anita for the amputee association. Mary spent most of her work days knitting, sewing and organising outings for the association.

Joan thankfully was close to retirement age. She was a vexatious, horrible, mean spirited, old crone who loved nothing more than to be as spiteful as she could possibly be. Everyone detested Joan and were all shit scared of her and rightly so. But I wouldn't let on that she frightened me. I was the only one who would dare to stand up to her when she tried to put shit on me. Unfortunately, every time I stood up to her I'd end up with a migraine for days. Sometimes I think I deserved the migraines because just to get back at her for something she had said days beforehand, I'd have a little dig at her.

For example she was forever eating rice cakes and big slices of carrot cake supposedly to try and keep her weight down. But she'd slather an inch of butter on top of them. One particular day I said, 'Would you like a piece of cake with your butter, Joan?' Honest to God if one of the radiographers hadn't been there, I think she would have tried to crush me as if I was a bug. She had the ability to undermine everybody by continually needling away at anything, anyone said or did, and baiting them into a confrontation. She also had the ability to twist every word someone said to make it sound sinister. She would completely frustrate the living hell out of anyone to the point where you would feel totally exhausted. I went to Doctor Coral around the corner from the Chest Clinic on one occasion with an excruciating migraine and she gave me a script. I went home took two of the tablets as prescribed and I was unconscious for two days and semi-conscious for another two days. Frank had rung the doctor because he was so worried about me and she told him it was a normal reaction and that he was to make sure I continued taking them. When I finally came out my stupor, I vowed I'd never take another one. They were called Rohypnol which I found out many years later that they were known as the date rape drug.

Our job was to sit around a table in a little back room where we ate our lunch and waited for patients to come in for their x-rays. We all took it in turns to go out and take the person's details, write them on a little blue card and usher them through to the next room. Some days we would only get about ten people through. But if we got a lot of people coming in, all hell would break loose they'd be running around like ants at a picnic. Talk about rush hour. After the first week I felt as if I was in the twilight zone. After a couple of weeks, I made the dreadful mistake of looking for things to do. I started to pull out all the drawers filled with the patient's files and going through them to make sure they were all in alphabetical order. What a hide I had, to actually try and earn my money. After I had completed that task, I went up to the first floor and asked the nursing sisters if they needed their files sorted out. I thought they were going to kiss my feet. I had the audacity and gall to bring their files down to the table and I started to put them in order. This went on for a few weeks until Mr Gray told me a complaint had been made that I hadn't been doing my regular job and I was doing the wrong thing by bringing another department's files into the office. I just looked at him and burst out laughing and I shook my head in total disbelief. I thought what the hell is my regular job? Sitting listening to them knitting and what bloody office? It was a friggin table with six chairs in a pokey makeshift room.

I finished the box of files I was sorting, took them up to the sisters and told them that I wasn't allowed to help them anymore and they were totally flabbergasted. They couldn't thank me enough for the work I had done for them. From that day on I would take magazines and books in to while away my eight hours a day. No wonder the general public hate public servants, so do I.

I was thrilled out of my brain one morning when Mr Gray came up to me and told me that the following week, I was to accompany Susan the female radiographer to go to Challinor Centre. We had to get the details of all the residents in preparation of them having their x-rays. I don't know if he thought I'd be packing death over it or if he thought it would be some form of punishment to me or if he just wanted me out of his sight. It just seemed a bit strange that he had chosen me to go instead of one of his favourites. I was in my glory.

When we got there, I was taken to their main filing room and basically given the keys to the kingdom. I was in charge and I could go anywhere I wanted and there wasn't a bloody thing that the hierarchy could do. During my lunch break I went and visited Happy. When she saw me walking towards her, I got tears in my eyes she was so overcome with joy. She covered her face with her hands and I could tell she was crying and as I got closer her arms went up in the air for me to give her a big hug. I held her in my arms for about five minutes and she kept kissing me with all of her drool. It was just magical being with her again. I wanted to take her home with me. I squatted down alongside of her and she put her hands on my back and started to rub the base of my spine as if she knew that was the reason, I hadn't been back to be with her. She must've overheard the other Residential Care Assistants talking about me because I hadn't been back to see Happy since I'd injured my back.

Beryl wheeled herself over to where I was and she sang, 'I love you' and she put her arms around my neck and gave me a big kiss and put her hands together in prayer for me. I went over to Rene's bed and I changed my voice into a squeaky sound and said, 'Hello, Rene do you know who I am?' She hesitated and frowned for a moment then laughed and yelled, 'It's Amelia.' Unbelievable but the honest to God truth. I was at Challinor for two weeks sorting out all the files and I visited my girls every lunch hour. The poor buggers greeted me each day with great excitement. On the last day I never told them goodbye I just said, 'I'll see you all later.' It nearly broke my heart knowing I would never see them again. The one thing I had noticed whilst I was there, most of the mongrel RCA's whom I had known when I worked there, were nowhere to be seen. The ones who were there couldn't believe their eyes when they saw me wandering around with files in my arms. I never encountered any of the hierarchy whilst I was there either. They must've had their noses put out of joint though.

Not long after that, I awoke one morning and said to Frank, 'I had the queerest dream last night, you fell into the water and you were drowning. I dived in and tried to save you but I couldn't dive deep enough. When I surfaced, I could see Bob Hawke (the Prime Minister at that time) and on the other bank I could see the Opera House'.

I couldn't get the dream out of my mind and about an hour went by and a light bulb moment hit me like a tonne of bricks.

Amelia 'Frank, the taxation department is checking you out that's why you haven't received your tax cheque this year.'

Frank 'How do you know?'

Amelia 'That dream you were at the bottom of the harbour.'

At the time the ATO was checking a lot of wealthy business men's tax files and they called the operation The Bottom of the Harbour Scheme. Admittedly Frank wasn't a wealthy business man but I was convinced my dream was an omen telling me that he was being audited. I urged him to contact the ATO to see what was happening and the fellow he spoke to told him he was going to ring him that day because they wanted Frank to come in to see them. Frank went in the following day armed with all the receipts etc. The fellow was extremely nice and after going through everything with a fine-tooth comb he said to Frank that he was satisfied that everything was in order. Frank asked if they had received a phone call or if his file had been pulled out at random and the fellow said, 'I'm not at liberty to say.'

The goy stood up and said, 'I won't be long, Mr Williams, I'll be back in a moment.' As he stood up he pressed his hand on a piece of paper and twisted it around. In doing so, he told Frank not to read anything on his desk. Frank was able to clearly read Vivian's name on the piece of paper.

The fellow came back and said, 'You can go now, Mr Williams, you'll receive a cheque in the mail in the next few days.' When he came home and told me I was totally shocked.

Chapter 51

Another Chance

The butcher shop where Frank had worked with Steve and the apprentice Brad in 1975, had come on the market once again. Frank was very keen to buy it but I had grave reservations about taking on such a huge financial burden. Frank had been sober for ten years and I thought the pressure of taking on all that responsibility may cause him to start hitting the bottle again. But at the same token I didn't want him to think I didn't have faith in his ability, so against my better judgement I agreed to get the shop.

He opened up for business on Monday 17 March 1986.

My friend Beryl was phenomenal in finding four leaf clovers in any garden and she presented Frank with a huge one for good luck. Although business was slow it was gradually picking up over the following months. He wasn't earning a fortune but he was making an average income from it. And many of his customers became regulars who often praised him of the quality of the meat. Frank was pedantic at choosing the best quality beef, lamb and pork. Heather and Claire would often help Frank in the shop.

Heather would often spend the entire day with Frank helping in any way that she could. Claire would try to help after school but sometimes would get things a bit muddled. One incident that we've told over the years always gets a laugh. Frank had asked Claire to put some rissoles in the breadcrumbs for him. She told him about a half an hour later that she had done the job and she went off to spend her pocket money that he gave her. He thought no more of it until a couple of days later when he went looking in the freezer room for the rissoles and couldn't find them. He thought to himself, I'd better make some more. He got the big bag of breadcrumbs out from the cupboard and there were the rissoles still sitting in the bag of breadcrumbs. Luckily Frank had another unopened bag of breadcrumbs to start again and do the job properly. She said later, 'You didn't tell me that I had to roll them in the breadcrumbs and put them in the fridge'.

A smokehouse oven had been installed by the previous owner and Frank would cook at least two hams a week and the smell was delicious. Everyone who came in when they were cooking would order some. The smell would waft through to the ANZ bank next door and the manager would come in through the back door for a sample every day.

He would tell Frank and Heather to never tell his wife because she had him on a strict diet. On one occasion he slopped warm fat from the ham on his shirt and Heather got it off by dabbing it quickly with detergent on a clean cloth. He was as happy as a pig in mud and told them the following day that his wife didn't suspect a thing.

A couple of weeks later the same thing happened this time the fat fell on his shirt pocket. Heather was getting the detergent out again when he yelled, 'Oh shit my wife has just pulled up across the road.'Heather as quick as a wink said,

'Quick come over here.'

She cut a biro pen open and wiped ink on the fat stain and put another pen in his pocket and said, 'Get going hurry up.' He came back an hour later and couldn't thank Heather enough he said, 'You saved me from a fate worse than death. She wasn't happy that I had ink all over me but she would've skinned me alive if she had've known it was hiding ham fat.'

Every day after work I'd hurry to the shop to help Frank as much as I could. On one particular day I was hurrying to catch the train and I ran across Edward Street and kicked the top of the sole of my left foot on the kerb. I thought I'd broken my toe it was so painful I limped around on it for weeks. I should have gone on compo but I didn't. My toes were as black as the ace of spades. The end result is now thirty odd years down the track my middle toe has shrunk and I have to wear a padded insole because of the damage to my metatarsal bone. I'm an awkward bugger.

I would come home exhausted and sort out the money and the bills from the shop and house. Each Sunday I'd write out all the cheques making sure every bill was paid on or before they were due. Frank would often tell me that his creditors would praise him for being so prompt in paying. They would tell him that he was the only butcher in Brisbane who paid on time. He told me that he would say to them, 'My wife is the one who's responsible for that.' Every Friday without fail Frank would buy me a bunch of flowers from the local florist to thank me for all my work.

An American lady came in one morning in November and asked Frank to order her a twenty-kilo turkey for Thanksgiving. She insisted that it had to be fresh not a frozen one. She said, 'I'll know if it's a frozen one, Frank, because they have a different look and a different taste, it has to be a fresh one.'

Frank rang everyone he could think of in search of a huge fresh turkey. But no one could help him. In desperation he decided to leave Heather in charge of the shop and he drove to Indooroopilly shopping centre and bought a frozen turkey from Woolworths. Two days before Thanksgiving he rang the woman and told her the turkey would be delivered to the shop the following day and she came straight down with her own seasoning for the turkey. Frank baked it in the smokehouse and she picked it up on Thanksgiving afternoon. The following day she turned up and Frank thought,

Oh-oh here's trouble she's going to go off the brain now.

Customer 'Frank that was the best turkey we've ever had in our life.'

Frank 'I worked hard getting it.'

The crunch came, just before Christmas of that year. A three-storey shopping complex two km from Frank's shop opened its doors. The decline in his business was immediate. We were seriously facing bankruptcy. If I hadn't been working, we would've lost the shop and our house by Christmas that's how bad it was. I was putting my entire wage into the shop to keep it afloat. The manager from the ANZ Bank told Frank that his head office was looking to expand his branch and were looking at our shop as a way of expanding. We kept hoping and praying that they'd make an offer but by the time New Year had passed there was no communication from head office whatsoever. Frank was honest and told the manager in mid-February that he didn't think he could hang on much longer and the manager promised that he would see what he could do.

On the morning of Thursday 19th March 1987 Frank rang me at work and said, 'Can you get off work by two pm to pick me up?' I said, 'What's wrong?' The bank manager had told him that he had told head office that we were trading well and not likely to close the doors after all. Head office of the bank made an offer and Frank agreed and we had to go into the city to sign some papers at four o'clock. I wanted to jump through the phone and kiss and hug him. The relief we both felt was unbelievable. When we signed the papers the head honcho asked Frank when he could vacate the shop and Frank said, 'I already have, it's yours now mate, I'll have all the meat out by tonight.' More than thirty years later I still feel so grateful to that wonderful bank manager. Frank reckoned that he thought about how lucky he was at least once every two months or so. He would often say, 'I'll never win lotto because I used up all my luck on that shop.'

On Friday 8th May 1987, it was raining and I was hurrying down George Street from Roma Street railway station on my way to the Chest Clinic and I slipped on the footpath on the corner of Adelaide Street. I skinned both knees and gravel-rashed the base of both my hands trying to stop myself from falling flat on my face. I was literally a bloody mess by the time I got to the Chest Clinic and I just knew that I had done more damage to my back because I had a stinging sensation around my coccyx. Mary took me to Doctor Coral who sent me home immediately. I was just thankful she didn't prescribe any more drugs. It was another ten days before it was discovered that I had popped the disc of another vertebrae. Doctor Coral referred me to an orthopaedic surgeon Doctor Peters ordered x-rays of my entire spine. When he saw them, he told me I would never work again. He also said that I had the early stages of arthritis in my neck from the injury in March 1980 and it was in my upper and lower spine as well.

Chapter 52

Claire's Nightmare

Claire had stayed over at one of her school friend's home for a weekend the previous year and on her return on the Sunday she very matter of factly announced, 'Kristy, Cara and I got held for shop lifting on Friday night.'.

Without asking for an explanation I went right off the brain. When I stopped ranting, she said, 'But, Mum, we didn't do anything.'

I said, 'Well what do you mean you got held for shop lifting?'

She replied, 'I went with Kristy and Cara into town to do some late-night shopping. When we went into a Sportsgirl clothing store I decided to try on a top and we all went into the change room together. The top was too big so Kristy went and got another one for me and the lady at the counter said that it was okay to take the extra top into the room. I liked the top and it fitted me so I decided to get it but I wanted to see what it would be like with some shorts. Cara went and got a pair of shorts but they were too big so she got another pair but I didn't like them anyway, so we just put them all back on the coat hangers and I paid for the top and we left the shop.'

The girls had inadvertently put the items on the wrong hangers and the shop assistant had thought they had done that to try and steal clothes.

Claire continued, 'When we got outside, we walked about ten feet from the door and someone caught the back of my dress and a big arm came around the three of us and dragged us back to the door. I didn't know who it was until we got back to the doorway and it was this big fat lady who kept yelling at us that we were shoplifters and she pushed us up a flight of stairs. Mum she kept yelling at us as she pushed us that we were thieves and I was really scared because I thought Kristy or Cara had taken something. She shoved us into this little room and told us to lift our dresses'. Gobsmacked I said, 'What?'

Claire 'She told us to lift our dresses.'

Amelia 'You didn't, did you?'

Claire 'Yes because she was really angry and I thought she was going to hit us, she told us that if we didn't lift our dresses, she'd lift them and take our panties down as well.'

Amelia 'What happened then?'

Claire 'She knew we didn't have anything other than our undies on under our dresses so she grabbed our bags and ratted through them. She grabbed a jacket that Kristy had and demanded to know where she had gotten it and Kristy told her that her mother had bought it in America. But she didn't believe Kristy and she kept demanding where Kristy had stolen it from.'

Amelia 'Was there anyone else to witness all this?'

Claire 'There was a big man standing outside the door and the door wasn't closed. I was really frightened Mum I didn't know what to do.'

Amelia 'How long were you in that room?'

Claire 'I reckon it was almost an hour before she pushed us out and back down the stairs. There were people everywhere looking at us it was really embarrassing and scary.'

Amelia 'Did she apologise.'

Claire 'No she kept saying she knew we had taken something and that we were cunning little bitches by hiding the stuff we'd pinched.'

The following morning on my way to work I went into the store and spoke to the staff on duty registering my complaint about the treatment the security officer had meted out to my daughter. I was told the Manageress was not available and that I should come back during my lunch break. When I returned at one pm the Manageress refused to speak to me so I went back to work and rang the solicitor Peter Channel whom I had met at a Labor Party meeting I had attended.

Peter was also the solicitor for the Queensland Labor Party.

Initially the store had offered Claire a five-hundred dollar voucher to spend in any of their stores. We refused that offer, then six months later they offered Claire five hundred dollars cash and we refused that. By then the legal bill had skyrocketed and even a thousand dollars wouldn't come anywhere near the legal cost. Approximately two years later just before we got to court the store made an offer to pay the legal costs and compensation to Claire. I was hell bent on continuing to taking them through court but Claire was having nightmares because of the incident and at the prospect of seeing the security officer again so reluctantly I agreed to accept. Because of the terms of the payout I am unable to divulge the amount. It wasn't an enormous amount and certainly nowhere near the payout an American woman was paid for a lesser incident that she had experienced which was reported in the paper around the same time. The best news was the security officer had been sacked over the incident. We were told by Peter that if Claire had refused to lift her dress and the security officer had lifted her dress the security officer would have faced a sexual assault charge. I have never entered a Sportsgirl store since and while my backside points to the ground I never will.

Because of that incident, if I'm asked aggressively to show the contents of my bag as I'm leaving a shop I will say, 'No if you think I've stolen something, I'll sit here on the floor inside the shop while you ring the police. I look forward to suing you and the store for wrongful accusation.'

I've never had to sit on the floor yet but I look forward to being wrongfully accused. I wouldn't back down before going to court if there's ever a next time.

A store has to clearly display a sign to say it's a condition of entry into the store that they intend to conduct bag checks.

Chapter 53

Politics and Legality

Unbeknown to me I now faced a battle that had I had never been fought before. Why not? God obviously loves to throw me challenges and I have to respond as best as I can.

I was back on heavy duty pain killing medication and far from happy about life in general. Dr Peters hadn't given me a great deal to be over the moon about. He told me that although I hadn't crush fractured another vertebrae, I had actually popped the disc near my coccyx and that full-time work in the future was totally out of the question. Although he was really of no further use to me, I continued to see him regularly because that was what was required for Worker's Compensation.

The Health Department had already told me that they would retire me on the grounds of ill health once they read Doctor Peter's report on my spinal injury. All I had to do was sit back and wait for them to pay me out. But no not me I wanted the magic cure so when I saw a story on ABC Channel two about a back-pain clinic which was being run from a Belmont Private Hospital. I couldn't get into see Doctor Peters quick enough to get a referral. What a big mistake that was.

I went to the clinic in the September of 1987 and I soon realised that this programme was a rort by the Bjelke Petersen government. It was a psychiatric hospital and secondly the back pain clinic staff consisted of an Orthopaedic Surgeon who was never available, a nursing sister whose qualifications were questionable and a psychiatrist. They had access to a gymnasium two klms down the road where they would march the spinal injured patients to every day. Anyone who has ever suffered from even a minor twinge of back pain will know that it's difficult to get motivated, but to walk two klms in searing morning heat is pure torture. Especially considering that they hadn't even received our medical history. Medical documents are not transferrable without authorisation and on speaking to most of the patients I became aware that none of them had given permission for their files to be sent to the hospital either.

Did they have them? Who knows?

On one morning after our two kilometres march one of the patients had collapsed in the gymnasium's swimming pool. After I helped him out of the water, I went looking for Pam the nursing sister, she was nowhere to be found. I rang for an ambulance from the office. After the ambulance had taken the fellow away, Jane turned up and told me I had over reacted. She told me the fellow had only suffered a bit of heat exhaustion. Yeah right that's why we never saw him again. For all I know the poor bastard could have died from a heart attack.

On another occasion Jane told me to work out on a machine on which I had to lift weights with my legs. There was no supervision she just told me what I was to do and she walked away. I tried to lift the weights and it nearly killed me. Another patient came to my assistance and explained that there were too many 'bricks' on the machine for a person my size and that I should only have only had about two at the very most and there were at least six bricks on it. When I complained to Jane, she told me that I should have known not to be so stupid. That was it for me I'd had enough.

It was time to ask around to find out where some of the other patients were and why they hadn't returned especially considering that they had shown interest in really getting into the program. I soon learnt that Jane, the psychiatrist and Orthopaedic Surgeon were encouraging patients to go off worker's compensation and go on unemployment benefits. As soon as I heard this, I let Jane know that what they were doing was totally wrong. She said, 'What business is it of yours if they're on compo or unemployment?'

I said, 'Plenty, I'm a taxpayer and you and your cronies are taking these poor bastards off what they are entitled to and making the Australian taxpayer pay for their incapacity when it's the Queensland Government who should be paying.' I was called into a huge room the following morning and I had to sit at a beautiful mahogany table which had at least twenty matching chairs. I finally got to meet face to face with the Orthopaedic Surgeon who ran the show. I cannot recall his name now, if I could I would name and shame him, but what I do remember being told was that he had been Doctor Peter's partner until he opened the back pain clinic.

Terrific I was at loggerheads with the ex-partner of my own orthopaedic surgeon. How was that going to affect me?

Doctor Nameless started off by telling me how Wally Lewis had overcome a back injury by getting back on the field and playing football. I responded with, 'That's great for Wally but his back injury has nothing to do with my back injury.

He then said, 'Greg Norman had injured his spine but he's gone back to playing golf.'

I looked him square in the eyes and said, 'Terrific I'm pleased for both of them but I don't play football or golf.' I could tell he was getting pissed off with me by the way he was sitting and I can truthfully say I enjoyed getting up his nose. He could not stand to be in the same room with this smart arsed piece of dirt beneath his feet and it showed. He finally said very aggressively, 'You're sacked from this clinic we don't like trouble makers around here.' I laughed and said, 'Well you had better sack yourself and the other two out there because you are all causing more trouble to the Australian taxpayers not to mention the poor bastards you've put off their rightful entitlements.' He then told me he would make it his business to make sure I got nothing more from the Queensland Government. I laughed again but I knew that this bastard was going to be trouble with a capital T.

I went back to Doctor Peters who told me in no uncertain terms that I had done the wrong thing and that he didn't want me as his patient. Wonderful. Doctor Coral didn't want me as her patient either, it seems she was a friend of Doctor Peters and as I've explained before, GP's are very reluctant to go against the specialists for fear of reprisals. Specialists think they are Gods and ordinary GP's can never speak ill of the Gods. I had become a pariah amongst some in the inner sanctum of their little kingdom.

Doctor Watson who was the doyen of Orthopaedic Surgeons and had been my Ortho when I crush fractured my vertebrae had since passed away so I was up the proverbial without a paddle. I soon received a letter from the Workers Compensation Board asking me to come in and see them. I recall the Compo Doctor was a nice bloke and he just advised me to find another Ortho.

The letter from Worker's Comp was followed by a letter from the Health Department requesting the pleasure of my company to visit three of their doctors. I'm not lying when I say this: All three of the doctors I had to see in the Health Department were at least eighty years old. They all wore very dark three-piece pin striped suits and bow ties and I reckon they had all been dragged out of retirement possibly from the nursing home for retired doctors for that consultation. They were all extremely doddery and although I can't remember everything they asked me, I do recall that most of the questions had nothing to do with my spinal injury. One thing I do remember one of them saying, 'Mrs Williams you are not going to die of cancer.'

I thought Jees, thanks Doc, you are a fucking mind of information, you silly old fart.

I received another letter from the Health Department telling me an appointment had been made with a Doctor from New South Wales. I cannot remember his name now but I'll call him Doctor Sydney from whence he came, he was important to my case later on. He was flown to Queensland just to see me. Boy I was beginning to think I was really someone important for all this attention.

I consulted Peter Channel regarding my position with the Health Department because it was becoming evident to blind Freddy that the shit had really hit the fan. Joh Bjelke Petersen and the National Party were still in Government so I figured that the best way to fight them was with the opposition. Peter advised me to consult an Orthopaedic Surgeon (Dr Wilson), so I had to find a new GP as well to get the referral, I went to a local GP. Two problems solved, f only all of my life was that easy.

Dr Wilson could not believe his eyes when he saw my x-rays. He said, 'Lass, you're lucky to be still walking.' When I told him about the hoo-hah I'd encountered, he shook his head and said, 'There are some cowboys around.'

He went on to say that if it came to a court of law, he had no hesitation to tell the truth on my behalf. What a relief to hear that.

Chapter 54

A New Beginning

I didn't see Vivian again until Friday October 9th 1987 when I decided to arrive unannounced at SEQEB where she worked as a cashier. By that time Andy was four years and four months old. She promised me that she would contact me in the next few days and arrange to meet me for coffee somewhere. She kept her word and we met in the city but I was extremely disappointed that she hadn't brought Andy with her. She told me that she had intended contacting me because she and Andrew were on the verge of splitting up. I showed sympathy to her but underneath I was very hopeful.

We met again at Garden City the following week and I was so overcome with joy when I saw my grandson for the first time in three and a half years I wept like a baby. Although I loved him with all my heart there was no bond with him, I was a stranger to him and he was a stranger to me.

Over the next few months, I tried my hardest to bond with him but he was a very strange little boy and I thought his behaviour at times was decidedly odd. He had the most piercing stare I've ever seen on anyone. If he didn't like something someone did, he would just stare at them and no one could outstare him. I subsequently learnt from Dora and Jock that they had reared Andy for the past four years. Vivian would leave him in their care, for days and weeks at a time without nappies or formula. Vivian would only take him home on rare occasions when it suited her. He had grown up without any contact with other children. Two rather strange incidents that come to mind about Andy as a four-year old, I had taken Vivian, Heather, Claire and Andy out to lunch on Melbourne Cup Day and a little girl about the same age as Andy came up to our table. She stood there waiting for Andy to come and play with her and he sat staring at her as if she was an alien. The little girl eventually left and he watched her leave. I said to him, 'Why didn't you play with her? She could have been your friend.' He looked at me in complete amazement and said, 'Could she?' Claire remarked later in the day after we had left Vivian, 'Mum, there's something radically wrong with Andy.'

We had a time share unit at Beach House at Coolangatta and I took Andy down to the beach one afternoon. He pointed his fingers at me and shot me so I lay on the sand.

He then threw sand over me as if he was burying me. I thought this is a bit strange. He then started to run away from me so I jumped up he looked at me completely shocked

Andy 'You're alive?'

Amelia 'Did you really think you had killed me?'

Andy 'Yes.'

Amelia 'But mate if you had killed me how would you have gotten back?'

Andy 'I would've run fast across the road.'

I don't think that was a normal response from a four-year old child then, any more than I do today.

Frank had been working as a casual/relief butcher through a butchering agency and although he had an excellent reputation for being extremely reliable it was obvious that the work availability was drying up. Vince Channer the fellow who ran the butchering agency was retiring and we felt that the best thing to do was to sell the house and shift farther south where Frank could get full-time employment. I heard on the grapevine that our move had set everyone in the Government ranks into a frenzy. It seemed everybody and his dog had a theory as to why we shifted. I was running away in shame and/or in hiding for some inexplicable reason. The rumours were rife as they always are when you get a gaggle of women with nothing better to do than sit doing absolutely nothing and getting paid for it. To add fuel to their fire I entered a competition on Channel seven to win a house. The competition was run over five weeks and each week for five weeks they pulled a name out of the pile of entries and each name called, won a two-night stay at SeaWorld Resort and the five names were in the draw for the house. My name was the first name pulled out and for five weeks seemingly every five minutes my name was plastered across the screen and the voice over man screamed out, 'Amelia Williams is a winner in the Win a House competition.'

From what I was told, the Government employees were absolutely filthy on me for winning the house when in actual fact all I had won was two night's accommodation at SeaWorld. I had a one in five chance of winning the house but God isn't that kind to me he just wanted me to get all churned up in the hope of winning it.

I had also entered a competition on Channel nine around the same time to win a trip for two to England. Again, I was a one in five contenders to win, but once again God said, 'No kiddo you aint going to win.' But that didn't stop the gossip mongers when my name was again announced on TV.

One afternoon I even received an unannounced visit from one of the Health Department employees. I thought she was there to offer me moral support but I soon realised she was there at the request of the hierarchy to check out as much as she could possibly report back to them which I might add was zero. What a shame they couldn't put their money into actually helping people instead of wasting money trying to stalk them for no reason. I have no objection to Workers Compensation Board checking out cheats but this wasn't the Worker's Compensation Board this was the Queensland Health Department trying to pry into my private life. I had a genuine reason not to be working, with two Orthopaedic Surgeons reports stating that my spine was a complete mess.

But still the Health Department insisted that I had to re-join their ranks and I was forced to return to work in the epidemiology department in Brisbane. I was assured that I would have an ergonomic chair and that my position would be of great importance in helping the professors in the epidemiology department. I truly believed that by my accepting the position it would not only be detrimental to my health but that it would jeopardise my chances of applying for early retirement if the position was not to my total satisfaction. My union reps were about as helpful as the proverbial on a bull. They cow-towed to the Health Departments demands and agreed that I should return to work or face the prospect of being dismissed for insubordination.

Reluctantly on Monday 4th December 1989 I travelled to Brisbane by bus to start work in the epidemiology department, to say that I was knackered by the time I arrived would be the understatement of the year. The bus ride alone was enough to jar the spine of a physically fit person so you can imagine how I was feeling. My ergonomic chair believe it or not, was a plastic chair which was the common garden variety. I was placed in front of a computer and told to enter names which were typed out on A4 paper. That may not seem too bad except for one thing, in 1989 I had never used a computer in my life, I couldn't even turn it on. When I told the girl, who placed me in front of the computer that I had never used a computer before, she looked at me as if I was an alien, turned it on and walked away. I was in agony and I was typing away probably making mistakes by the thousand and I couldn't have given a stuff. In all probability the names weren't of any importance. I truly believe I was being made an example of and this was my punishment. The following day I told someone whom I thought may have some sort of authority that I was not going to sit at that computer again or on that rickety chair and that I had better be given a decent job or I would find the lunch room and stay there for the duration. I was told I shouldn't have been put in the computer room in the first place because I had been hired for another position. I was ushered into another room and was told I had been appointed to filling plastic bags with important information. The bags were like the sample bags you get at the Ekka and my job was to stuff them with pamphlets about the health department which would be sent to schools. My chair was an 'upgrade' to an office chair with a rickety back. On the Wednesday I was told I'd be given my ergonomic chair by the end of the week. I was driven out Zillmere way, to a chair manufacturer and the fellow at the factory told me there were no ergonomic chairs available and even if they could manufacture one that would be of great comfort to me it wouldn't be ready for at least two months because of the Christmas/New Year break. *Joy to the World* . I went home early on Wednesday 11th December after suffering migraine and throwing up in the bathroom for twenty minutes. Frank rang the department on the Thursday and told them I would never return to the epidemiology department or any other department again. Almost two years went by and finally the Health Department agreed to retire me on the grounds of ill health. Two days later the news was announced that Christopher Skase had absconded to Spain with thirteen million dollars of the Queensland Government Superannuation money. I believe it was much more than what was reported. Less than a week later I received notification from the Superannuation Department that they felt that I was not ill enough to be retired and they were refusing to pay me my superannuation. I now faced a court action fighting one Government Department against another Government Department with the now Government's solicitor, because Wayne Goss had been elected as the Labor Premier. I was broke, so I was using Government funding namely Legal Aid. To add fuel to the fire I had to be reviewed by Legal Aid every three months and they were getting very cheesed off because the case dragged on seemingly forever. Eventually they refused to fund my case stating that it had gone on too long and that they had other more pressing cases to attend to. I told Peter Channel my solicitor that I'd have to drop the case because I was unable to find the money to cover the cost.

They say miracles happen every day and the following day I experienced one when the Courier Mail front-page headline read that a couple were both getting Legal Aid to fight for custody of their dog. I immediately rang Legal Aid and went off the brain. I was reinstated as a recipient of Legal Aid immediately and to the best of my recollection I was never reviewed again.

Frank had undergone numerous tests on his back and x-rays showed that his spinal fusion operation was slowly crumbling he had pieces of the plastic fusion floating throughout his spine. He was told that to continue working was sheer folly and in October of 1992 he began receiving the disability pension and I as his wife received the wife pension.

Unfortunately, Peter Channel was killed in a freak accident in September 1993 whilst on his honeymoon. He had been driving along a country road in Victoria with his wife when a tree on the side of the road fell out of the ground and crashed onto their car killing Peter instantly. His wife was trapped in the car for three hours before being released by the jaws of life. Fortunately, she was unhurt.

I didn't have a great rapport with Peter's successor but it was too late in the proceedings to try finding someone else. After almost seven years of legal wrangling I was given the date when my case would be heard in court, Thursday March 24, 1994. I thought, no matter what the finding, I'm taking Frank and myself on a holiday.

We had never been to Perth and Qantas had a special deal going. (Ever since Compass Airline started the cost of airfares had dropped drastically!) I booked us on a three-night stay departing Saturday March 26, 1994. I had been saving for ages and it cost our entire savings of one thousand dollars and that was spending money included. Talk about living it up, the rich and famous had nothing on the Williams.

I recall reading about a case two years earlier in the Courier that had a Judge Williamson presiding over it and I said to Frank, 'I want Judge Williamson to preside over my case when it ever gets to court.'

Frank 'Why?'

Amelia 'Because I like his name it's almost the same as ours.'

Frank shook his head and muttered something about me being nuts.

On the morning of March 24th, I met my barrister for the first time. He had been appointed more or less at the last minute, which was a bit of a disappointment to say the least. But what pissed me off completely was the fact that my solicitor hadn't bothered to turn up, he just sent a junior female solicitor in his place. I got the impression that he didn't want to be seen as the one to wear the blame for losing the case. A judge was appointed to the case but on reading some of the transcripts he said, 'This will take at least two days and I'm due in another court tomorrow, so the second day will have to be in a few weeks.' I was asked if this would be to my satisfaction and I told them it wasn't as I had waited long enough. I didn't want to wait another minute I just wanted it over and done with so I could get on with the rest of my life. Just then another Judge walked past the court room and he was asked if he could preside over the case. He said he had just that minute arrived back from Toowoomba but he added, 'As soon as I've had morning tea I will.' At approximately eleven am we were told to stand and as the judge entered the room the official announced, 'Judge Williamson presiding.' I looked at Frank and I could hardly contain myself from bursting into laughter as he stood shaking his head in disbelief. My mind after that went into shutdown mode, I couldn't tell you a thing that was said before I was called to the stand. I can't remember what I said whilst I was on the stand for that matter. I do recall having tears in my eyes when the opposing counsel fired questions at me. Then Judge Williamson told me I was to leave the court room because he thought I shouldn't be a witness to hearing about my ailments. I still cannot for the life of me understand his reasoning for that especially considering I live with my ailments 24/7. Dr Wilson was one of the first witnesses and he went into great detail about my height and weight and how the strain put on my lower back was detrimental to my overall wellbeing. Dr Sydney was called to the stand as the opposition's expert witness. He testified that he had been told by someone in the Queensland Health Department that I was a belligerent, aggressive and a rude individual (by whom I have often wondered) but he said he had found me to be polite, honest and extremely co-operative. He agreed with Dr Wilson that my spinal injury was restrictive and he too would advise that I should not work in a full-time capacity. I kept looking through the small window to get Frank's reaction at the proceedings and whenever he looked over at me, he would pull a face and shrug his shoulders to indicate that it didn't look good. When they stopped for lunch, I was told that although Dr Wilson and Dr Sydney had given me a glowing report the other opposition witnesses were equally as convincing.

At the end of the day I was advised that I should agree to settle out of court and only ask for half of what I was entitled to. I argued that I hadn't waited seven years to walk away with only half I said, 'It's all or nothing.' The barrister, solicitor and Frank kept browbeating me until I reluctantly agreed. The barrister said it was for the best and he'd have their answer by nine o'clock the next day. I was far from happy. When we arrived at the motel we were booked into, (within ten minutes of leaving the barrister) I rang him and told him I had changed my mind and that he was not to approach the opposition at all. He told me it was too late he had already put the proposal to them. Frank and I sat up late, arguing about what had transpired. I was extremely annoyed to say the least but Frank was just as adamant that I didn't hear all the testimony and that it didn't look good at all.

At ten o'clock just as the court was about to start, the barrister told me the opposition had rejected the proposal and I was as happy as a pig in mud. All or nothing at all, I just wanted to go out knowing I'd tried my best.

At one o'clock the doors opened and the barrister, solicitor and Frank came out and I could tell by their faces that I hadn't been successful. I shrugged and had tears in my eyes I thanked the barrister and solicitor for doing their best and I went to put my arms out to hug Frank and the young solicitor broke into a big grin and said 'Amelia you won.' I looked at her in total disbelief and I looked at Frank and the barrister and they were nodding and laughing. I just let out a blood curdling scream and burst out laughing and crying at the same time. I looked over at the courtroom door and saw three opposing counsel walk through the door and their faces were furious. I couldn't help myself I pointed at them and cackled like a clucky hen. Not only had the judge awarded in my favour the barrister had asked for interest on the money dating back to when I had last injured my spine. Judge Williamson calculated it at an average of nine percent over seven years. I'm not talking hundreds of thousands of dollars here, the total amount with interest was eighty thousand dollars and out of that the solicitor who hadn't bothered to show up took twelve thousand dollars which he maintained was out of pocket expenses that Legal Aid hadn't paid. *Yeah right* . But you cannot argue with those bastards. At a rough estimation I reckon it would have cost the Queensland Government at least five hundred thousand dollars in legal and medical costs taking me to court.

It was a bit like trying to crack a peanut shell with a steamroller.

Our holiday to Perth was not really memorable, because I was on cloud nine for the entire three days!

One thing I do remember: We went to the casino one night and I went to the automatic machine to get change for the pokies. There was a man at the machine and he grabbed his cup full of change and walked away into the crowd. I stepped towards the machine and sixteen one-dollar coins spat out onto the floor at my feet. I picked them up walked back to John and said 'No need to play the pokies I've just won another sixteen bucks.'

Talk about being shot in the arse with a rainbow.

Chapter 55

Once Bitten Twice Shy

In March 1990 much to our dismay Claire had decided to go to Sydney to live after finishing her apprenticeship as a hairdresser. Heather had been working at a Tweed Heads Solicitor's office for about eighteen months and had been invited to a friend's wedding in Sydney in the July of that year. As I hadn't seen Claire for four months and I missed her greatly I decided to go with Heather and we stayed with relatives of the McKenzies, another momentous mistake. Will I never learn? All I can say is that it was another holiday from hell.

Vivian gave birth to a beautiful baby daughter Emma on a Thursday July 1990, whilst we were in Sydney. Heather and I arrived back the following Sunday and we went to where Vivian was living. Andrew's mother Dora had been looking after Andrew and Andy and was still at the house. Dora didn't look well, she told me that she had had the flu the entire time she had been at Vivian's. She said she didn't want to give Emma the flu so she had rung her other son Ronan to come and pick her up. Her husband Jock had flown to Scotland for a holiday on the Saturday. I can still here her saying very wistfully, 'My Jock is on the other side of the world now.' I said, 'Why didn't you get Andrew to drive you home earlier?' She whispered, 'He said he didn't want to, he wouldn't even go to the chemist to get me some cough syrup for me.' No sooner had Ronan picked her up and I farewelled them, Vivian arrived home with Emma. Vivian went off the brain at me for being in Sydney when she went into labour. Saying, 'What sort of mother are you that you're not here for your daughter and granddaughter?' I replied, 'Considering you didn't want me at the birth of Andy, and you had Emma two weeks early, you can't really blame me for not being here. I'm not a mind reader.' She then focused on the fact that Dora wasn't there! I told her that she had gone home sick Vivian went off the brain again accusing Dora of bunging it on. I told her that Dora looked like death warmed up and that Dora had said Andrew wouldn't go to the chemist for cough syrup for her and Vivian screamed, 'She's a fuckin liar the old bitch.'

Dora died in her sleep three nights later. When she hadn't come out of her room for breakfast, her son Ronan found her at ten am on Thursday 19 July, 1990.

Vivian showed no remorse at what she had said about Dora instead she played the grieving doting daughter-in-law at Dora's funeral. Vivian played the dying swan act with me and I like a fool believed her. Almost every day I would drive over to Vivian's and look after Emma. Apart from almost wearing me out driving the one-hundred kilometre round trip, it was exhausting my finances as well because I was also helping to buy their groceries, not to mention my petrol bill. It became apparent that I was right in my belief that Vivian had only fallen pregnant in an effort to keep her failing marriage together. They had had a nice home on the southside of Brisbane which they sold to buy the acreage so that Andrew could pursue a career as a horse trainer. Vivian had convinced herself and tried to convince us that she and Andrew would be better trainers than Tommy Smith and Bart Cummings. She even said to us, 'I'll overtake Gay Waterhouse before too long.'

From our observation Andrew couldn't train a horse on a merry-go-round.

Financially for them, things went from bad to worse and Vivian got a job with a local kitchen builder. She had only been there a short time before the fellow went broke. I never found out if he had had money missing but it would not have surprised me if he had. She then got a position with the local council and was only there for a short while before she fell down the stairs after enrolling Andy at the local State School. I'm not going to say that it wasn't an accident but she went on compo with an injured spine and made sure she got a consultation with my orthopaedic specialist Dr Wilson. He couldn't find much wrong with her so she was only on compo for a short period of time. I do know for certain that something must have happened at the council because she never returned to their employ.

On our thirtieth wedding anniversary in 1991 I was summoned to help Vivian because she had had a miscarriage and was bedridden. I spent the next two days at her beck and call. Apart from taking her cups of tea and preparing meals etc. I was caring for Emma, washing and ironing and generally being a slave. Ninety percent of the time whilst she stayed in bed, she was on the phone, who she was talking to is still a mystery. She summoned me to the bedroom and told me to take an envelope to an address behind the main shopping centre of the town. She insisted that it was urgent and I had to go immediately. Emma was asleep in her cot but Vivian insisted that I had to take her with me because she wasn't well enough to get out of bed to tend to her if she woke whilst I was away. Reluctantly I had to wake the poor little mite to take her with me.

I found the street but I couldn't find the house number that Vivian had given me it just didn't exist. I didn't want to drive all the way back so I tried ringing her from the public phone. That took me at least ten minutes because the phone was constantly engaged. When I finally got through to her she went off the brain telling me I was a moron and to go back and look again. I was tempted to drop the envelope in anyone's letter box when I still couldn't find the right house. I thought, bugger it I'm going back and suffer the consequences. On my return she again abused me telling me to piss off out of her home. I tried to reason with her that there was no such an address and she screamed, 'I know I gave you the wrong street address okay, now piss off.' I cried my guts out all the way back home. I could not believe how stupid I was to put up with that sort of crap. I wouldn't have, if it hadn't been for the love of my grandchildren. I found out much later that Vivian hadn't had a miscarriage at all. She had had an abortion at Andrew's insistence.

On another occasion I was summoned to babysit both my grandchildren for the weekend whilst Vivian and Andrew attended a race meeting in New South Wales. They left as soon as I arrived. I went into the kitchen and was shocked to my back molars at finding syringes on the floor. Andy told me that they were the needles that Andrew gave the horses. Apart from the fact that I wasn't totally convinced about that, Emma was crawling around amongst the needles as well. She and Andy didn't look as if they'd had a bath for days so I gave them both a bath fed them and started to clean the filthy house. The laundry was in a separate building away from the house and I took the kids clothes out to put in the washing machine. I was sickened to the pit of my stomach by the sight that I was confronted with. Without a word of a lie there were shit filled disposable and cloth nappies piled on top of each other in the corner of the laundry, the pile was over two foot high. There were maggots by the thousands crawling everywhere. I felt like throwing up. I sorted out the cloth nappies and found plastic bags for the disposables. But before I could put them into the bags to take to the bin, I had to hose out the shit and maggots making sure I killed them all. When I finally took the plastic bags to the garbage bin on the other side of the house, I discovered the garbage bin was filled with maggots. I have no idea how long it took me to clean everything but I can tell you it seemed like an eternity. Later that day I remember making a phone call to my friend Kay and saying to her, 'I'm in downtown Bangladesh.'

I really think Kay thought I was exaggerating when I described the filth of the place to her. It was pointless me saying anything to Vivian when she returned, I knew only too well that I'd only get abused and possibly banned from seeing the kids again.

I arrived over at Vivian's one morning and she was on the phone. She hurried out of the office area and whispered 'Don't tell, Andrew, but I've just rung the child welfare department, that kiwi bitch Tracy around the corner has stuck a fork in her little girl Chloe's face. She reckons a dog bit the kid but I know a fork attack when I see it.'

Incredulously I said, 'Are you a hundred percent positive because that's a terrible accusation to make if you're not.'

'I'm a thousand percent positive, Mum, a couple of months ago poor Chloe was taken to hospital because of a so-called kick in the head by one of their horses. I'm positive she hit Chloe on the head with a hammer.'

The child welfare department was hell bent on taking the child off Steve and Tracy but fortunately the medical practitioner at the local hospital stated emphatically that Chloe had in fact been kicked by a horse and bitten by a dog.

Chapter 56

Betrayal

It was becoming a tradition to hold an Australia day/birthday party weekend for Beau and Michelle whose birthday was two days after Beau's. When she turned thirty in the February of 1986 the party was even bigger. She had given birth to another son in the June of 1985 and named him Don after his paternal grandfather. Don was the opposite of Beau. Beau was sweet and gentle and Don was shall we say more outgoing.

Unfortunately, Mark had been in a very bad mood most of the day which wasn't unusual for him he could turn quite nasty very quickly. Although they were supposed to stay the night Michelle decided to take the boys home early. When I say early, I guess it was close to ten-thirty pm. Mark and a few others stayed out in the pool area drinking and we said, 'Mark, if you want to crash you can have Heather's double bed, she's going to sleep on the lounge.' Heather's room was at the back of the house and overlooked the pool and I left her back door unlocked for Mark to come in when the others went home.

I don't know what made me wake at about two-fifteen am, in those days I could sleep through a thunderstorm and not stir. I jumped out of bed and crept silently out to the lounge room. The curtains had not been pulled and I could see quite clearly by the light of the moon. Heather was fast asleep and Mark was kneeling at the lounge, with his left hand lifting her nightie and his right hand was moving slowly along the lounge towards her crotch. His head was almost on the lounge and I will swear in any court that he was looking up her nightie. I yelled, 'Heather, Heather, get up and get to bed.' Mark lowered his head further down onto the lounge as if he was asleep and pretended to stir. He sat up and I again told Heather to get to bed. Very sleepily she got up and without realising the danger she had been in got up and staggered to her room. I snarled at Mark, 'Get out before I kill ya.' He apologised and I pushed him out the door. I went around the house checking every nook and cranny and locking every door and window like Fort Knox. When I told Frank the following morning he said, 'Oh you must've been mistaken I don't think he'd do anything like that. He probably crashed on the floor with his head on the lounge chair.'

No matter what I said, Frank could not believe that Mark would have done that. Later that day we went over to their home and Mark was very sheepish and wary. Michelle kept whispering to me asking me what was wrong and what had happened after she had left the party and I said, 'Nothing, everything's fine.' As we left I snarled at Mark, 'You've gotten away with it this time I won't be telling Michelle she doesn't deserve to hear what you did.' He muttered, 'Thanks.'

I said, 'Don't you dare thank me I didn't save you I saved her.' I have regretted that decision for over thirty years. The only person I told about that incident was Vivian when she came back into the family fold. Around August 1990 Michelle rang and said, 'You'll never guess what happened last night'.

I said, 'What?'

She replied, 'I went to bed early and Sharon was asleep on the lounge (Sharon was Michelle's younger sister) Mark came home from the pub and thought Sharon was me and climbed on top of her and tried to have a nooky. She shoved him off and told him to piss off. What do you think of that?' My heart went into my throat and I thought, oh no not again, but I replied, 'Really?' And I pretended to laugh. I have often wondered if Vivian had told Michelle what I'd seen and Michelle had concocted a similar story to get my reaction. Or if in fact Mark had tried the same thing again. I guess I'll never know for sure but my intuition says Vivian told her.

In the February of 1991 Michelle and Mark had brought Beau and Ben down to our home for the weekend. On the Friday night Heather had looked after the boys whilst we all went out to the club for dinner. We had to come home early because Frank had to get up early for work on the Saturday morning. Michelle complained about coming home early she and Mark had wanted to stay out longer. I said, 'There's nothing stopping you from going back out I'll look after the boys and you two can go and enjoy yourselves'.

But they didn't go out and the thought crossed my mind, maybe they wanted us to go out with them so that we could pay for the rest of the evening as well. I had loaned Michelle and Mark a thousand dollars when I was working at the chest clinic to get them out of their credit card debt. Although Michelle had worked at a bank, she had no idea how to manage a household budget and she asked me to sit down with her and help her to work her finances out, which I was only too happy to do. They had promised to pay us our money back in weekly instalments but they didn't pay us a red razoo for over eighteen months until I asked them for the entire amount back. I don't know where they got the money from and I didn't really care, I felt they'd done the wrong thing by not even offering us ten lousy dollars. I subsequently found out that within two weeks of us loaning them the money and me working out a budget for her that they had booked more on their credit card which pissed us right off. I vowed and declared that if someone needed help again, I'd willingly buy groceries for them but I would never loan anyone any money again.

Mark was a marijuana smoker and Frank had told him from the time they arrived in Australia that he was to never bring or smoke that shit in our home ever. Frank had said many times, 'If you have to smoke it go out on the footpath.' Mark had always abided by that rule. Frank had left for work at five am on the Saturday and I had stayed in bed until I smelt a pungent burning odour at about six am. I got out of bed and Mark was sitting in the lounge watching cartoons and smoking marijuana. I said, 'Christ that stinks, take it outside on the footpath.' He didn't, instead he finished the joint and went back to bed. When Frank came home at around one pm Michelle and Mark had taken the kids down to the beach and I told Frank what had happened. I had confiscated the remains of the joint from the ashtray to prove I wasn't imagining things, Frank was ropeable. When they all came back from the beach Frank never said a word to Mark about smoking the marijuana which surprised me. We had lunch

Frank 'I'm not going out tonight you pair can go out with Amelia if you want to'.

Amelia 'If you're not going, I won't go either.'

I could tell that Michelle and Mark weren't happy about that but they agreed to stay in as well. The following morning, they packed their things and left at about ten o'clock. As they drove off, we waved them goodbye and watched until their car was out of sight and as Frank lowered his hand from waving

Frank 'That's the last time we'll ever see them again. If Mark can't respect us and our home, I don't want him back and it breaks my heart that we'd never see the boys again.'

A few months previously we had been at their place and Beau had been playing out on the footpath and he climbed a little sapling tree. It had started to bend and Beau fell onto the ground and began to cry. Mark jumped up off the lounge ran outside grabbed and held Beau up by the arm picked up a tightly rolled up newspaper and kept whacking him on the legs as hard as he could. Mark threw Beau in the house and told him to get to his room. Beau limped past us and I had tears in my eyes over what we'd witnessed. I protested by saying to

Mark, 'Beau could have broken a bone in the fall or you could've broken his leg with that bloody paper.' To which Mark told me to shut up and mind my own fuckin' business. I went down to Beau to see if he was okay and Mark yelled out, 'Keep out of his room, don't molly coddle him he's a big enough fuckin sook as it is.'

Mark came up the hallway yelling at me to get out of Beau's room so I hurried into the toilet and called out, 'I'm nowhere near him I'm on the toilet.'

After that incident we had difficulty having any more to do with Mark. But I think Frank had realised that Mark wasn't the person he thought he was and although he didn't want to believe what I'd witnessed in our lounge room, he finally had his doubts.

After the February farewell Michelle rang me in the May but I wasn't home. She spoke to Heather and asked for me to ring her back. As much as I wanted to see Beau and Ben again, I never rang her. I still think of the boys who are in their thirties now.

Chapter 57

Hey Mr Movin' Man

Around February 1992, Vivian moved out of her home into a rental house in Ocean Shores (approx. 20klms north of Byron Bay. We were over the moon that she had left Andrew but to shift further away wasn't ideal. Frank and I had to help her shift. Anyone who remembers the Beverley Hillbillies arriving into town from the backblocks will get an idea of what the moving van and cars looked like. She was only there a month and she shifted back to her own home without our assistance.

I had a premonition that something bad was going to happen at Easter of that year. I couldn't shake the feeling of déjà vu but I couldn't pin point any one incident. Let's face facts, there had been so many incidents in our lives that even a professional psychic would have difficulty determining what could happen next.

We went over to Vivian's on Easter Sunday morning and when Heather walked in holding the Sunday Mail Vivian exclaimed, 'Oh good we haven't had a chance to get the paper yet, Andrew likes to read the race results, thanks.'

After lunch Vivian suggested we all go to the swings and merry-go round, at the local park. Although we all thought it was unusual for Vivian to be motherly and take the kids to places like that, we thought it was a great idea. Andrew didn't want to come which suited us and as we were leaving he walked down towards the stables. On our arrival at the park I just happened to notice that it was three minutes past one. Vivian complained of feeling thirsty and I said, 'There's a water fountain over there.'

Heather said she'd go down to the shopping centre to get everyone a drink. Typical of Heather she didn't want any money she has always been generous with her money and didn't want me to contribute. She had only been gone a short time yet Vivian seemed anxious and said, 'Heather's a long time, isn't she?' I didn't take much notice of the question then a couple of minutes later Vivian said it again. I replied, 'She won't be too long it's a fair walk there and back, especially if she's carrying bottles of drinks.'

Another couple of minutes went by and Vivian said, 'Christ where the hell is she?'

I felt like saying, you sound like a broken record, but instead I looked at my watch and said, 'It's only seventeen past she left here at five past she's only been gone about ten minutes.'

No sooner had I said that and Heather walked into the park carrying bottles of soft drinks for everyone. We drank our drinks and the kids continued to play on the swings and at around two pm we decided to go back. Vivian seemed to be taking her time walking back to the car and I had the kids buckled in and we were all seated waiting for her. She finally got in and complained that she wasn't feeling well and asked her father to drive slowly. When we got back to the house Andrew was lying down on the bed reading the newspaper. We sat around talking for a short period of time and as we started to say our goodbyes Andrew walked out of the bedroom muttered a goodbye and walked down towards the stables. On our way out, Heather picked up her newspaper. At around six pm that night Vivian rang and said, 'Heather has taken four hundred dollars from my account at the ATM.' My stomach churned and my immediate thought was of my premonition of déjà vu and I remember thinking, I wish I could predict the lotto numbers.

Amelia 'How could she have done that?'

Vivian 'When she went to get the drinks, this afternoon.'

Amelia 'How would she have gotten your card?'

Vivian 'She must have gone into my bedroom and taken it out of my wallet.'

Amelia 'She never went near your bedroom.'

Vivian 'How would you know you weren't watching her the entire time.'

Amelia 'Listen, Vivian, I'm sick and tired of playing these fuckin' stupid games with you. Heather did not I repeat did not take money from your ATM. If there's money missing from your account go and ask Andrew where it is.'

She screamed 'Andrew hasn't left the house all day.'

My mind was racing as I quickly turned the events of the day over in my mind. I said, **Amelia** 'Oh yes he has, when we left to go to the park, his car was in the driveway in front of our car. When we came back his car was down near the stables. Plus, he was lying on the bed reading the newspaper yet when we left Heather picked up the paper she brought with her. it hadn't even been unfolded.'

Vivian screamed top note

'You always take that bitch's side you never believe me.'

And she slammed the receiver down.

The following day I rang the manager of Vivian's local Commonwealth Bank and told him what had happened and I asked him if there were cameras to prove who used

the ATM and if he could check what time any money had been taken from the account. He was very non-committal and reluctant to become involved but I emphasised it meant a great deal to me and I really needed to know the exact time if the money had been withdrawn. He told me it would be at least Wednesday before he could tell me anything. I rang him late on the Wednesday and he confirmed that an amount of money had been withdrawn at one twenty-three pm on the Sunday. He would not say if he had video proof of who had withdrawn the money. But I didn't need that I already knew that it was impossible for Heather to have taken it because she had been back in the park before one-twenty pm.

I immediately rang Vivian and told her what the bank manager had said and she again slammed the receiver in my ear. At the time I thought Andrew was cooking up all these so-called thefts. But in hindsight I realise that Vivian was the one who was setting the scenarios in place and Andrew was the stupid sap who went along with her. But why?

It would be another fourteen years before I came to a sort of reason why.

I hadn't been ordered to keep away from them so although I wasn't made too welcome, I continued to go over on a regular basis making sure that the kids were well fed and cared for. Vivian rang me in August of that year to say that she had again shifted out with the children and they had moved into a flat in the town. I went over to the address she gave me and I was appalled at how small and cramped their conditions were. I encouraged her to come to live near where we lived and she soon found a unit not far from our home. In less than a week of her shifting in she had found herself an office position at a clothing company.

Unfortunately, for the clothing company Vivian had access to the payrolls as well. Money went missing and about twelve months later, although nothing was proven Vivian was dismissed from their employ. According to her it had nothing to do with her, it was the fellow who was in charge of the payroll. It didn't take her long to get a job with a foreign firm which was a subsidiary of an international airline. Not only was she the receptionist she was also in charge of collecting the rent from the many properties and businesses the airline owned.

Frank and I were caring for Emma twenty-four hours a day, seven days a week. Some days, but only when it suited her, Vivian would pick Emma up after five pm and return her to us before seven am the following day. Andy would often stay over at our home but the majority of the time Vivian insisted that he return home after school.

Every weekend she would go over to Andrew's leaving Andy with us but at the time we didn't know where she went. She used to make so many excuses as to where she was going. we got to the stage we were beyond caring. We were only too happy to make sure our grandchildren were well looked after.

I enrolled Emma in the nearest Montessori preschool and Frank and I would drive her almost thirty kilometres to and from every day. She was doing extremely well there and although Frank and I paid for the school fees Vivian would collect a rebate from the Government. Whenever I asked Vivian to contribute something towards the petrol, she would go off the brain. Vivian in her wisdom decided to change Emma from five days a week at the Montessori preschool to three days a week at the local kindergarten. I stopped paying for the fees.

Vivian found a three-bedroom home and it wasn't a moment too soon. She had been reported to child welfare on one of the rare occasions she had the children with her at the unit. The unit was on the first floor and Vivian had gone out leaving them unattended. Emma climbed the balcony railing and had almost fallen approximately thirty feet (ten metres) onto the concrete driveway. Vivian vowed and declared that she'd get even with the person by throwing nail polish remover onto her car and stabbing her tyres. I told her to wake up to herself and I have no idea if she carried out the threat.

We hired a removalist to help her move and Frank sat in the truck with the microwave on his lap. Both he and the driver were complaining of a stench and couldn't work out where it was coming from. On arrival at the house Frank discovered the carcass of a chicken in the microwave and hundreds of maggots feasting on it. Vivian blamed Andy for leaving it there. My skin crawls just thinking about it.

Andy absolutely detested school and would try to keep me occupied by talking constantly to me each morning in the hope that I wouldn't notice the time. He was supposed to ride his bike to and from school but it got to the stage that I would have to drive him there and pick him up every afternoon a distance of about one kilometre each way. Some mornings until I realised what he was up to, he'd distract me so much I'd get him to the gate as the bell went. Vivian later denied that we had cared for Emma twenty-four, seven what she didn't count on was the couple who owned the shop across the road from our home were prepared to vouch for us in any court of law.

One afternoon I made the mistake of telling Vivian that Emma was calling me Mama. She went off the brain saying she didn't want Emma to call me that. I said, 'It's just a shortened form of grandma what my two brothers and I used to call our grandmother when we were little.' That didn't mean a thing to Vivian she found a babysitter to stay in her home to look after them. She told me that the girl was the niece of her employer. I went around and met her and as lovely as Mica was, she could hardly speak a word of English. She attended English classes of an evening and we were able to communicate a lot better with her. Frank and I got on extremely well with her and she always showed Frank and I the utmost respect and called us grandmother and grandfather. Unfortunately, she went back to her own country approximately nine months later. We corresponded for quite a long time after that and I still have some of the letters she wrote and the craft she made for me. She found another girl Cathy from Ireland to mind the kids.

Vivian rang us from the local hospital one night telling us that she had been admitted under observation for having dizzy turns and fainting spells. When we arrived at the hospital, she begged Frank to drive the 120kilometre round trip to tell Andrew. When Frank suggested that he'd ring Andrew she insisted that he drive there. Frank didn't get home until after midnight and he said that Andrew was very guarded in saying too much but kept insisting, 'You don't know your daughter she's not the person you think she is.' He refused to come to the hospital to see her. I being the idiot I am still blamed Andrew for Vivian's behaviour. She discharged herself the following day when she realised Andrew wasn't coming to visit her. It didn't dawn on me for ages that Vivian had actually driven herself to the hospital even though she was supposedly having dizzy turns and fainting spells.

When she was a teenager still going to high school she went through a stage where she maintained she couldn't see and would often walk through the house holding on to the walls for support. Her so called dizzy and fainting spells reminded me of that time and I was really concerned about her mental stability. I actually feared that she was taking after Frank's mother who had obviously had severe mental problems.

I'll never forget one afternoon Andy called in on his way home from school to ask his grandfather if he could help fix a flat tyre on his bike. Andy had only been there about ten minutes when Vivian rang asking if Andy was at our place. I told her he had just arrived with a flat tyre and had asked Frank to help fix it. She screamed, 'Tell the little cunt I said to get home now. I've told him he wasn't to go to your place'.

I placed the phone down and told Andy to get home quickly because his mother had come home early. His face showed pure terror and he ran down the street towards his home which was approximately a kilometre away. I went back and kept talking to Vivian trying to calm her down. I heard Andy run through the door and she screamed abuse at him and I heard her thumping the living daylights out of him and he was screaming and crying. I was gasping trying to stifle my sobs. Vivian came back on the line and said, 'Did you hear that?' I managed to say, 'Yes.' she replied 'Good.'

Once again she slammed the receiver down.

Frank repaired the bike and placed it into the boot and took it around to Vivian's house. Vivian wouldn't allow Andy to ride the bike again he had to walk the two kilometres to and from school. Another incident that happened around the same time, Andy had saved twenty-eight dollars from pocket money we had given him. He came home from school one afternoon to discover Vivian had taken it. He just shrugged and said, 'Mum must've needed it.'

In the meantime, I had won my court case and we sold the house and bought the best home we have ever owned. As per usual, the sale of the house did not go smoothly. We actually sold it twice and bought two homes. The woman who bought the home first, had paid a third deposit on the home and we had actually purchased another home nearby. We held a garage sale on the weekend prior to settlement day and we sold most of the furniture we possessed and we bought new furniture for the new home. Fortunately, we had stipulated in the contract that it was subject to the sale of our home.

The woman who was buying the home had gone to the City Council and was told by some moron there that the Main Roads were going to resume the footpath and some of our land to widen the street. She reneged on the deal and neither she nor her solicitor turned up for the settlement the following Friday. To make matters worse all the furniture we had bought had to be stored under the house because it was far too big to fit into the home. We were entitled to keep the deposit but she threatened to take us through to the supreme court if necessary, to stop us getting the money. Eventually she gave in and she agreed to let us keep half of the deposit.

I wasn't going to let the matter drop so I decided to take on the City Council and the Main Roads Department for the stuff up. Main Roads asked us to get an independent Real Estate Agent to put a value on the property. To cut a long story short the Main Roads Department bought the house for twelve thousand dollars more than the original buyer. We didn't mind that, it was the inconvenience of the whole procedure that was so upsetting at the time. But we still weren't able to shift into our new home! The tenants who lived there weren't willing to shift unless we paid their removal costs. They still had 2months on their lease. We refused their demands and they had to pay us their rent which went directly to Main Roads for the time we were in *their* home. From the time of the first sale to the time we shifted out was approx. 5months, we slept on mattresses on the floor and lived out of suitcases.

In the words of Garfield the cat, WHY ME?

More than twenty-five years down the track, there still has not been any resumption of land or widening of the street.

We shifted into our beautiful new home on Thursday 11 August, 1994 and for the first time in a long time I felt truly contented. We just absolutely loved living there it was such a peaceful area, the neighbours were nice and life was finally looking good for us.

It didn't last long.

We held two house warming parties in the September, the first party was for the Real Estate Agency because the principal had waivered the fees on the first sale of the house. But it was mainly for the agent Frank Fulton (Fully) who had become a close friend. Funnily enough Fully was an ex-detective and although Frank had never told Fully of his criminal past, I always suspected that Fully had an inkling. Fully died exactly eleven years to the day after the party.

The second housewarming was for family and friends and a chance to meet the new neighbours. I hadn't seen my two nephews for many years and I hadn't even met Mike's wife so I thought it would be an excellent opportunity to try and mend a fractured family. Everyone thoroughly enjoyed themselves and surprisingly there wasn't any arguments. We all vowed we'd have another get together but it never happened. Mike told a different story in an affidavit eight years later.

Although I couldn't find fault with Cathy the Irish babysitter, there was just something about her that I didn't particularly like. She was liked by the kids and that was a bonus. In the October Vivian told me that Cathy had to find the money to go back to Ireland her work visa was running out and she had to be out of the country before Christmas. Vivian came to me one day telling me that she couldn't afford to make the payments of her car and needed fifteen hundred dollars to pay it outright. I didn't lend her the money nor did I give it to her, instead I went and paid the car off. Vivian told me, 'Mum, you are without doubt the best mother in the world.' All I could think of was, at least I know she won't squander it on other things in particular Cathy's fare home to Ireland.

Two days later she came back and asked me if I'd look after Emma for four days as she felt worn out and needed a break. I was only too willing to look after my precious granddaughter any time anywhere. Vivian said she was going to take Andy over to his other grandfather for the time she'd be away. I was disappointed about that but I figured that Jock hadn't seen Andy for quite a while and it would be good for the two of them. When Vivian brought Emma to me, I asked her where she was going in case I needed to contact her. I nearly fell over in shock when she said, 'Hamilton Island'. I didn't bat an eyelid and I asked, 'Would Cathy like to come up here for dinner while you're away, seeing as she'll be there on her own?' She said, 'Cathy's coming with me.' I thought, yes muggins you've done it again. You've been conned into paying for this bloody jaunt in a roundabout way. I later found out that Andrew had gone with them for the four nights.

Cathy returned to Ireland on their return from Hamilton Island and Vivian found another babysitter. Tracy was from Melbourne and no doubt had been dragged up in a gutter. To say she was vile is unkind to all the vile people in the world. I subsequently found out that Vivian wasn't hiring babysitters from advertisements in the local paper she had been placing notices on the notice board in a backpacker's hostel offering free board in lieu of babysitting. Mica hadn't been the niece of Vivian's boss she and Cathy had been on working visas. Tracy was just a slurry who was one feed away from being homeless. My grandkids could well have been put in the care of paedophiles, rapists or mass murderers. I wish I had've rung child welfare or gone off the brain at her but surprisingly I didn't. Like the fool that I am I kept quiet because I was terrified of never seeing my grandkids again.

On Monday 5 December, 1994, Vivian rang me from work and told me that someone had rung Andrew's business partners and told them a pack of lies about her and Andrew. I honestly can't recall what was supposed to have been said but Vivian blamed Frank for making the call and she told me that we were never to see Andy or Emma again. I said, 'Vivian, this is lunacy at its worst, your father and I have absolutely no idea what you are talking about. We don't even know Andrew's work partners.'

She screamed, 'You're a fucking liar you old bitch, just keep away from me and my kids.'. She slammed the phone down in my ear. It was exactly six weeks to the day since she had said to me, 'Mum, you are without doubt the best mother in the world.'

I found out that she had shifted to a waterfront home. I thought, obviously her income has improved to be able to afford the rent on that home. I took their Christmas presents around to Vivian and the children and the babysitter told me to leave them on the doorstep. Vivian was inside but she wouldn't come out or let the kids come out. Three weeks after Christmas, Frank went around to Vivian's home and said to her, 'If you honestly believe that I've made a phone call to these people by all means stop me from seeing the kids but not your mother.'

She agreed for me to visit them on Wednesday morning whilst she was at work. I went around at ten-thirty in the morning on Wednesday 18 January, 1995. Andy was a bit apprehensive at first but Emma was over the moon to see me. She hugged and kissed me and ran into the bedroom yelling, 'Tracy my grandma's here, my grandma's here'.

Tracy yelled, 'Shut the fuck up, ya little bitch, I'm not fuckin deaf.'

I was absolutely horrified. Emma came running back to me and said, 'Tracy's still in bed.' Andy asked me if I knew about the earthquake where Mica lived, that had happened the day before. I told him I had heard about it and he then asked if I thought Mica would be ok. I replied, 'I don't know, mate. I hope she is, but I won't know for sure until I hear from her.' I stayed with my grandkids for over an hour just talking and playing and Tracy never surfaced the entire time I was there.

On my arrival home I rang Vivian to tell her what Tracy had said and she replied, 'I don't give a flying fuck what she said. You've upset Andy by telling him Mica is dead, you old bitch. I don't want you going around to my home again.' I tried to say, I said nothing of the sort, but she slammed the receiver down. I tried to ring her back three more times but as soon as she heard my voice she kept hanging up.

In the meantime, Claire had had a nervous breakdown and had returned home a few weeks previously and spent two weeks in the local hospital where she was diagnosed as having Schizophrenia. Vivian refused to visit Claire the entire time she was there. Frank and I had booked months previously to go overseas to Egypt, United Kingdom and Europe and we were on the verge of cancelling the trip to stay with Claire, however, she seemed to make a good recovery and was on Haloperidol an antipsychotic drug to keep her stabilised. I couldn't help thinking that Vivian should start taking the same medication. We paid for Claire's air fare and arranged for her to meet us in England after our seventeen-night tour of Egypt. Frank and I departed on Saturday 11 February, 1995 and Claire met us in England on February 28 we all returned home on Wednesday 4 April 1995, only to learn that Vivian had caused more upset for Heather whilst we were away. Mike had come down from Brisbane in his semi-trailer supposedly for work reasons. He convinced Heather that he had cleared it with us that he could stay at our home and drive our car whilst he was staying in our home uninvited. He talked Vivian into allowing Heather to come around for dinner one evening. Mike drove Heather in our car and Heather told me later that she started to cry when she heard Emma yelling excitedly, 'Grandma's here, Grandma's here.' The dear little mite had seen the car pull up and thought I had come to visit her. It wasn't long before Vivian started an argument with Heather and Vivian told her to piss off. Our holiday should have left us on a high, although we had thoroughly enjoyed ourselves especially in Egypt, I felt completely drained having to face the reality of Vivian's behaviour on our return.

I was so desperate to see my grandchildren that I'd often drive down and park the car in a position where I couldn't be seen, yet I could see the house, but I never caught a glimpse of them. I used to spend most of my days yearning and crying for my grandkids but to no avail. Then one day I drove past the house and I saw a carpet cleaning truck in the driveway. I went home and returned about four hours later and the truck was still there. A few days later, I went to the local real estate agent where I thought Vivian would have had to have paid the rent. I told the Real Estate Agent I'd noticed the carpet cleaners at the house and I wondered if the house was for rent. He said, 'No the owners finally got the tenants out of the place and they're eventually going to shift back in. The place was a shambles the carpet cleaners couldn't get the stains out so the owners have ordered new carpet and they have to get the inside painted as well.'

I decided to do a bit of investigating and I knocked on the door of the house next door to where Vivian had lived but there was no one home. I went to the house two doors from the house. I introduced myself and said I was making enquiries about the people who had lived two doors away. I explained that unfortunately she was my estranged daughter and that I was very concerned about my grandchildren. He told me his name was Eric and introduced me to his wife Betty and for the next hour over a cup of tea they told me horror stories about how Andy and Emma had almost drowned several times in the lake behind their home. When he had called out to Vivian to warn her about keeping an eye on the children, she had come to his front door with two men and they had threatened to do him over. Eric said, 'I called the police but to the best of my knowledge nothing was done because it was her word against mine. The police told me that when they spoke to her she was extremely well mannered and polite.' I nodded and said, 'As if butter wouldn't melt in her mouth.' He assured me that if I needed them to, he and his wife would speak up in court if I ever went for custody of the children. I told him I wouldn't go for custody but I had full intentions of trying to get regular access to them. He said, 'I'm fairly certain that Mary and Louigi (the owners of the house) would be prepared to tell of their nightmare with your daughter as well and if I were you, I'd go for custody she's not fit to be in charge of a guppy.' I spoke to Louigi on the telephone and he agreed to appear in court to tell how Vivian had wrecked his home.

He rang back later and said he feared repercussions if he spoke out about it.

Not long after that, Vivian contacted Claire asking her to come and visit her at her huge new home. God only knows how she was able to afford the rent on these homes. Let alone get access to them, considering her track record of leaving the other homes like pig sties. Though I was sure she was tickling the till at work I really didn't know how, and I didn't have proof.

Claire was again showing signs of being unwell and I didn't like the idea of her having anything to do with Vivian. But there was no way I could stop Claire from visiting her.

I drove Claire over to the house a couple of times and each time she came home she seemed very subdued. One Saturday evening after she arrived home from Vivian's I suggested we all go out to the club for dinner. Claire refused to go but Heather came with us. On our return home Claire was sitting watching television but her eyes were very glassy and she didn't seem to be acting right. I went into the kitchen and there were dirty pots and pans all over the top of the kitchen cupboards. I told Claire to get in and clean the mess up. She didn't move. About ten minutes went by and the kitchen was still in a mess and I again told Claire to clean it up. Frank was sitting in the lounge and he said, 'Claire, do as your mother asks.'

I walked to the front door behind where Frank was sitting taking some rubbish outside to the bin. Claire got up walked out behind me grabbed me by the throat and was squeezing my throat so hard I could not breathe let alone call out. I somehow managed to bend forward and I head butted Frank on the back of his head. Up until that moment he was totally unaware of the scuffle that was taking place. He jumped up grabbed Claire's arms wrapped his and her arms around her in a hugging way and half dragged half carried her to the big lounge chair. He pushed her down onto the lounge and she yelled, 'That's right beat me like you did when I was a kid.'

I said 'Frank she's either not taken her medication or Vivian's given her other drugs. I'm ringing the doctor.' The locum doctor told me there was nothing he could do and that I could ring an ambulance but he didn't think I'd get her admitted. All the while I was on the phone Claire was screeching top note. When I walked out to the lounge room, she ran out the door and down the driveway. By the time we got to the street she was nowhere in sight. Frank, Heather and I ran up and down our street but it was as if she had vanished into thin air. I was sick with worry to the point of almost throwing up. Frank and Heather both kept saying, 'She'll come back don't worry, even if she doesn't, she'll find her own way to Vivian's place.''That's what I'm scared of, I reckon Vivian has given her drugs.' I was convinced by that point that Vivian was on drugs by the way she had been acting and now Claire was going the same way. I would have rung Vivian but she had a silent number and I didn't know what the number was. We didn't want to go to her house because none of us wanted a confrontation with Vivian we never knew what could happen. The following Wednesday 17 May, 1995 there was a knock at the door and I was shocked to see a male and female police officers.

Amelia 'Oh no is Claire alright?'

The male officer 'Are you Amelia Williams?'

Amelia 'Y … yes'.

The male officer 'Is Frank and Heather here?'

Amelia 'Y … yes. Frank, Heather come here.'

By this time I was shaking uncontrollably. Frank and Heather came to the door and the male officer handed me two pieces of paper

The male officer 'I'm here to serve you all with a summons to appear in court next Wednesday 24 May 1995 at two pm.'

I was stunned

Amelia 'What for?'

The male Officer 'Your daughters have both filed for a restraining order for you all to keep away from them'. I said, 'I haven't seen my eldest daughter, Vivian, since January and we have been keeping away from her. My youngest daughter, Claire has been living with us for over six months. She visited her sister on Saturday and I think Vivian gave her drugs because Claire tried to choke me and ran away on Saturday night.'

The female officer 'Claire went to a neighbour's house down the street and rang us for protection and asked to be taken to Vivian's home. Claire didn't seem to be quite right but we took her there and at first Vivian didn't want to take her in. We didn't want to chase around transporting her back and forth so we talked Vivian into taking her in.'

I burst into tears and Frank put his arm around me

Frank 'You have no idea what hell we've been through with our eldest daughter she is off the air completely.'

The female officer 'Claire is in the car and wants to get her belongings. Will you allow her in the house to collect them?'

Amelia 'We've never stopped her from doing anything she's ever wanted to do, if she wants her clothes she can come in and get them.'

Claire never uttered a word to us as she and the two officers went into her room whilst we sat in the lounge. I couldn't help but stifle a laugh when the two police carried all of her belongings to the car whilst Claire walked alongside them like a precious princess empty handed. The officers came back and wished us all the best and left us to try and decipher the allegations. We had all been accused of making nuisance phone calls to Vivian, threatening to take our grandchildren off her, threatening to put Vivian and Claire in a mental institution, and of assaulting both Vivian and Claire. Neither of us could believe what we were reading, I said to both Frank and Heather, 'How the hell could any of us have made phone calls to her, she's got a silent number. And the only time I rang her at work was in January.' Heather said, 'I wish to Christ you had tried to put Vivian in a mental institution because how the hell could any of us have assaulted her when we don't even see her? Mum she is cracked in the skull.'

In the courtroom Claire sat there with her head bowed and never uttered a word. Vivian was dressed impeccably and she spoke with a plum in her mouth and rattled off a litany of lies. I don't know if it was deliberate on Vivian's part or if she made a genuine mistake by continually calling the female magistrate 'Your Worship' and not 'Your Honour' but it seemed to me the magistrate liked what she heard. The magistrate listened carefully to Vivian and she kept looking at us as if we were the family from hell. I stood up and said, 'Your honour this is absolute fantasy and a figment of Vivian's vivid imagination. Neither Frank Heather nor I have ever assaulted any of our daughters. Nor have we made nuisance phone calls and none of us have ever threatened to have them certified, but I really do believe that Vivian has a mental disorder.'

The magistrate was obviously irritated at my outburst and told me to be seated. Heather jumped to her feet and asked the magistrate if she could ask a question and when the magistrate agreed Heather said, 'I'd like to know when the so-called phone calls were made.' Vivian replied, 'I think my mother made them in February and March.' Heather said to the magistrate, 'If I had been receiving nuisance phone calls, your honour, I would have made a list of the exact dates.' I jumped to my feet and said, 'Your honour, my husband and I were in Egypt in February and our daughter Claire joined us in England and Europe at the end of February and we didn't arrive home until April.' The magistrate dismissed the case but gave me a warning that she would issue the restraining order if we came before her again. I couldn't resist saying, 'You'd have to accept new lies from Vivian.' As we walked out of the courtroom Vivian and Claire got into a brand-new Hyundai car with Vivian's initials as the registration. We all said together, 'Where did she get the money to buy a brand-new car?' Frank and I had tried to get Vivian a new car eighteen months previously but she had such bad credit rating the finance company wouldn't even consider her even with us as guarantors.

At eleven-thirty pm Sunday 16 July 1995 the phone rang and Claire was crying she said, 'Mum, Vivian's kicked me out can you come and pick me up please. I'm at the corner of Vivian's street.' It was a freezing cold night and Claire was only wearing shorts and a skimpy top and had no shoes on. She hugged me tight and said, 'I'm sorry, Mum, Vivian is fucked in the head and she really fucked my head in by telling me a lot of bullshit.'.

When I got her home, I drew a warm bath, found some warm clothes for her made her a coffee and the stories she told made our heads spin.

Vivian was living the lifestyle of the rich and famous but treated Claire like an unpaid slave. From what Claire had observed Vivian was paying Andrew money and alcohol. Mike was also there on a regular basis and Vivian had held a fifth birthday party for Emma with a hired clown, horse rides and all the bells and whistles. I said, 'Where's all the money coming from? Claire's eyes widened and she said, 'The company she works for. Mum, she takes people out to dinner at the poshest restaurants, it's unreal.' I said, 'Does she have to entertain clients or something?''No, she takes Andrew and their so-called friends out to dinner. She's a poser. The people she works for don't speak or understand much English and they haven't got a clue what's happening.'

We didn't have to be geniuses to work out what Claire meant, but we had no proof of anything and who the hell would we have reported it to?

We managed to get Claire back on her medication and not long after that Claire returned to Sydney and we were faced with trying to legally get access to Andy and Emma.

Chapter 58

Courting the Legal System

I read an article in the Women's Weekly magazine about a woman who was trying to get access to her grandchild. I contacted her and through her I met another grandmother, Moira who lived nearby. Up until meeting them I truly believed that we were the only grandparents who were denied access to their grandchildren.

Moira, Frank and I started the first grandparent's support group in Queensland and held monthly meetings with other grandparents who were denied access to their grandchildren. I was inundated with phone calls from all over Australia from people whose stories were heartbreaking. There were never two stories the same and I have often said, 'If I threw a handful of hundreds and thousands in the air at a football match and if everyone who caught one of them they would each tell a story of a dislocated family.'

Most of the grandparents who lived near us were too ashamed to come to our meetings they preferred to speak anonymously over the phone. Although my heart was aching and breaking for my own grandchildren I would listen and try to comfort each caller and by the end of their call I would be totally exhausted and a blubbering mess. Some of the things that were told to me was gut-wrenching, and I was completely out of my depth.

I hired a solicitor to try and gain access to Andy and Emma. I would have been better off going on another overseas holiday or just throwing the money down the nearest drain, for all the use the solicitor was. Over a period of about two years we got into a court of law on one occasion and Vivian who had somehow become a Justice of the Peace and later a Commissioner of Declaration had the matter adjourned. All told it cost us almost twenty thousand dollars but that was a drop in the bucket compared to some grandparents who had wasted over fifty thousand dollars in their quest of seeing their grandkids.

Vivian had acquired an affidavit from my nephew Mike and one from my ex friend Michelle. I very rarely throw important documents out and I regard their affidavits as important. If this book is ever published and anyone wishes to sue me for libel, they are welcome to do so. I believe honesty is the best policy and that if you tell the truth you don't have to try and remember what you've said.

In Mike's affidavit he told so many lies that I doubt he could lie straight in bed. I feel sure he made them up as he went along. He had been convicted of heroin and marijuana addiction crimes in the early eighties and I doubt that he would know the truth if it hit him on the head. One of his lies he said that at our housewarming party Frank had bragged about being a criminal and of being in jail. Unlike Mike, Frank was embarrassed about his criminal activities and would never in a million years discuss his past with anyone let alone new neighbours. Again, unlike Mike, Frank had integrity and more finesse in his little finger than what Mike would have in his entire body. If this book is ever published it will shock everyone we know to the soles of their feet. Apart from my immediate family and two very close friends no one we know knows anything about Frank's convictions. Michelle's affidavit was also a total fabrication I will not go into detail what she stated except that in paragraph twenty-four she said she would not allow me anywhere near her children. I have proof where Frank and I have taken her children unaccompanied by their parents on several occasions. As soon as I read Michelle's affidavit, I wrote to her telling her that I could have quite easily sued her for libel over what she had written and that the statute of limitations on that was seven years. I had no intentions of doing that because I felt sorry for her. She was married to someone who was amoral and she was obviously hurt by our abandoning her as a friend without explanation. Although I haven't seen or heard from her for almost thirty years, I still feel sorry for her. We learnt that Vivian had changed her name and had shifted to a unit not far from us. She hated me so much that she had taken to using my maiden name. I could only imagine that she was hiding from something or someone. I rang the company she worked for out of curiosity and a lady with an accent answered. I was prepared to hang up quickly if Vivian had've answered. I knew that Vivian was the only female working in the office so I was quite surprised to hear another female voice. I asked to speak to Vivian and the lady said, 'She not here, she sick.' I said, 'When will she be back?' The lady again said, 'She sick, she really sick.' The way the lady had said it I had the feeling that she meant that Vivian was sick in the head not just sick in the stomach. My gut feeling was that they had found out that Vivian wasn't doing the right thing by the company.

When I read this last paragraph to Frank, he said that he too had rung Vivian's workplace and a lady had said to him, 'Vivian sick, she mad.' Up until that day I had no idea Frank had also rung them.

In desperation to see our grandchildren we hired a car (our car had personalised plates and was easily recognisable) and we followed Vivian from her new address. She dropped Emma off at the zebra crossing near Emma's school, we were directly behind Vivian. We were so close to Emma as we pulled up behind Vivian I could have opened the passenger side door and pulled Emma into the car. I was so excited at seeing my granddaughter I began to cry and I had to hide my face from her because I didn't want her to get upset. I knew Vivian had told so many lies to her that the poor little girl wouldn't have known what to do if she had seen us. We continued following Vivian's car up to a block of flats about 2klms from our home. Vivian parked her car and we parked behind her but at a distance of about fifty metres. We watched her walk across the road to the flats and she entered the downstairs back flat. Because she had a parcel in her hand, we assumed she was delivering something to the occupants of the flat. We waited approximately twenty to thirty minutes but she never came out. We went to the address a few mornings and Vivian's car was always parked outside and opposite the downstairs flat. We even went around late one evening to see if we could see inside the flat but the windows were covered in heavy curtains, but her car wasn't there. We later found out that Vivian had become a prostitute and the flat was her place of business. They say there is no shame in being a prostitute that the prostitute is only providing a service. Tell that to the parents of the prostitutes and I guarantee ninety-nine percent of the parents have a different opinion. I could have notified the authorities and in hindsight I should have but I didn't. I could have gotten custody of my grandkids but I didn't but I should have. My philosophy was that Vivian was our daughter and you should never give up on your own flesh and blood regardless of what they say or do. What I didn't know at the time was that Vivian had done the unthinkable and it would be another ten years before I was to learn of it.

Chapter 59

Another New Beginning

Friday 13th November 1998, we had been up to Brisbane for lunch at the Broncos Leagues Club and I had secretly paid the final payment for Frank's surprise sixtieth birthday party which was to be held the following week.

On our arrival home there was a message on our answering machine from Vivian asking me to ring her. I was in total shock I paced up and down the hallway of our home like a caged lion for the best part of half an hour. I kept saying to Frank and Heather, 'What do I do? Do you think I should ring or do you think I should ignore the message?'

They both kept replying, 'It's up to you.' Not only was I shocked I was terrified. Was this some sort of sick joke? Was she going to fool us and do something cruel to us?

She had put our names down with many nursing homes / retirement villages throughout Australia and for over a year we had been inundated with letters and phone calls telling us how great their establishments were. She had even booked me into having a face lift and liposuction with a local Medical centre. The first I knew of it was when the receptionist rang to remind me of the appointment for the following day.

I wouldn't have minded liposuction if Vivian had've been paying for it.

I had also received two pornographic anonymous letters supposedly from a grandfather who had been denied access to his grandchildren which I took to the Burleigh Heads police. I was flabbergasted when the officer said, 'Mrs Williams, I think you should ask your daughter about these I think she'd be the one who instigated them.'

It went through my mind that Edith was not long for this world and in all probability, Vivian knew it. She'd also know that I'd be inheriting a substantial amount of money once Edith's home was sold. I figured that she probably wanted to try and con me out of some of it!

But the chance of seeing my two grandchildren was the deciding factor and was too hard to resist.

It was with great trepidation that I picked up the phone and called her. I was hoping that this Friday the thirteenth wasn't going to be my folly.

Vivian brought my grandkids around at seven-thirty that evening and Frank and I were over the moon to see them. It was painfully obvious that Emma was absolutely terrified of us when she saw us and Andy was extremely apprehensive. When they saw the jar of lollies on the table and I told them to help themselves they practically had a hoedown. After a while I realised that they hadn't eaten dinner and I asked if they would like something to eat, they couldn't agree quick enough. When I opened the fridge Andy exclaimed, 'Mum, Grandma's got heaps of food in her fridge.'

I cooked sausages, chips and fried egg with salad, and they ate like they hadn't eaten in weeks. When I offered them ice cream for dessert Andy said, 'I'm stayin' here from now on.' Emma said, 'Me too.' Your guess is as good as mine as to how long it had been since they had eaten a home cooked meal or any food for that matter. Everything was a source of amazement to Andy, when I took out the cheese cutter he exclaimed, 'Oh Mum! How rich are they?' When it was time for them to go home Andy and Emma didn't want to leave. Emma threw her arms around my neck and said, 'I love you, Grandma, and I missed you so much and I'm never going to let you go again.' My heart just broke and it took all my will to stop the flow of tears. After they had gone Frank, Heather and I discussed the events of the evening and we all questioned the reason for the reunion. None of us had found out what the real reason was and I distinctly recall saying what I had thought earlier in the day 'I bet she realises that Edith hasn't got a long time on this earth and she wants to get some of the inheritance.' The following day Vivian brought the kids around again, this time with another child Krys, who was Andy's age (fifteen) whom Vivian claimed she had adopted. Krys seemed a lot more worldly than Andy and I wasn't overly enamoured with her. I felt sorry for her because her own mother had kicked her out and that she had found Vivian as a surrogate. Vivian told me that she had to have a colonoscopy because her doctor thought she had bowel cancer. She said, 'Mum, I went home and thought to myself I need my mother to be with me. Because if I'm to die I don't want Andrew looking after the kids and I knew you and Dad would make sure they were well looked after.' I didn't buy the story but I went with her to the doctor's surgery when she underwent the colonoscopy. The bowel cancer turned out to be piles.

The funny part about that day, on the way to the surgery we saw Andrew walking towards us with his pest control equipment in his hands. We ran into a nearby shop and watched him as he walked past and enter another shop.

About a week went by and Vivian asked me to accompany her to a masseuse academy.

The place was closed and Vivian told me that she had signed up for lessons on how to become a masseuse. She didn't finish the course and explained that she owed the woman who owned the company about two hundred and fifty dollars but she couldn't afford to pay the money and they were threatening to sue her. I thought I'm not falling for that old sob story again and I asked why we were there. She said 'I want to pay them their money.'

When she realised that I had no intention of returning when they were open to pay the debt, she pulled a heap of cheques out of her bag and said 'I've made them all out for five dollars and pre dated them a week apart.' I said 'That's not legal.' She replied 'Fuck her, she's got no other choice.'

Vivian continued working as a masseuse at different companies and she also set up a bedroom and took clients at her home. She had printed out a certificate off the internet stating that she was qualified in a number of areas pertaining to the work as a masseuse which she displayed on the wall.

Frank wasn't the only person who was shocked at his surprise sixtieth birthday party everyone else was stunned when they saw Vivian walk in as well. I don't think they could believe we would be so stupid to have taken her back and most of them didn't know even half of the crap she had put us through.

Christmas that year was exceptionally good the only thing that marred it was Claire not being there. She had gotten the time off to come up for Frank's birthday but wasn't able to be with us for Christmas.

Chapter 60

Edith

Edith had been spending Christmas with us for the past four years and that year was no exception. At Christmas lunch as per usual she complained about there being too much food on her plate and we all waited in anticipation of her not eating all of her oysters and prawns. As she swallowed the last few morsels of her lunch, we all fell about in hysterics. She had no idea what we were laughing about.

In November 1994 the month before Vivian told me to keep away, Edith married Harry. She had met him when she was only sixteen when he came to work for my grandfather in his slaughter yards at Kenmore. Harry was keen on Edith way back then but she chose to be the wife of Rob Long the Sydney city slicker.

Harry's wife of about fifty years had died and he joined the same seniors club that Edith had been going to for years and that's how they met up after sixty years. When she announced that she was going to marry Harry there were howls of protest from Edward and I. Edward was concerned that he would be tossed out on his ear to fend for himself. He had been living with Edith almost rent free since the early seventies and I know he thought he was king of the castle and had visions of trying to diddle James and me out of inheriting Edith's house. He had approached me on a couple of occasions and asked me to come up with a plan how to get James out of the will. I can only imagine that he had said the same thing to James about me. I told Edward in no uncertain terms to wake up to himself. Anyway, my reason for not wanting Edith to marry Harry was simple I just didn't like the old coot. As far as I was concerned, he just wanted a cook and bottle washer. As it turned out he not only wanted a cook and bottle washer he also needed to be married so that he could continue being Number two in the Masons. Apparently to hold the top positions in the Masons you have to be married and Harry wasn't.

As far as Edith was concerned Harry was a very important man and she was finally going to live happily ever after. I remember saying to her that Harry was a legend in his own mind. James didn't see any problem with Edith marrying Harry he thought Harry was a nice bloke. No amount of my protesting was going to make Edith see sense and so the wedding took place with James and I as best man and matron of honour.

It didn't take long for Edith to realise that I was right all along especially when she had to go into Wesley hospital for a triple by-pass. She had to undergo two surgeries in two days because of complications and was in ICU for almost a week. She was finally discharged about three weeks later and within two hours of arriving home the old prick told her to cook his dinner. If I had've been there he would've worn the frypan as his marching hat.

We were also concerned that even though he had his own home that if Edith had passed away before him, he would claim her house as well. Edith said that they had had a verbal agreement between them that neither of them would do that. But as far as my two brothers and I were concerned that didn't mean a hill of beans. Harry and Edith used to alternate their living arrangements in both houses every two weeks. Harry was about eighty-seven and Edith was seventy-nine when they got married. After a couple of years, I know for a fact that Edith was calculating how much his house would sell for once he hit croak city and I'll go to my grave saying that she intended to get the lion's share of it.

In the September of 1998 Edith and I had had a very rare heart to heart talk about all the problems we had encountered over the years. It was during this talk when I told her about how Edward had sexually assaulted me when I was eight. I knew she believed me and I could see she was blaming herself for not protecting me. She told me that a doctor had told her when Edward was four that she should put him in an institution and forget about him. I wish I had've had the insight to ask her what his reason was for saying that. But at the time I just accepted what she was saying and not questioning anything. I told her that Edward wasn't the person she thought he was I told her that I knew for a fact that he was inviting prostitutes into the house when she was living at Harry's house. I also told her how he had asked me to come up with a plan to keep James out of the will. She was totally gobsmacked at hearing that. But when I told her that Edward had been paid five thousand dollars from his car insurance company, she was livid. Edward had had a car accident in the March, and his car had been a write off. He had borrowed five thousand dollars off Edith to buy himself another car with the promise that he'd pay her back as soon as the insurance company paid him. He rang me in the April, four weeks after the accident and told me that he'd gotten his money. I had said to him, 'The old girl will be happy that she's got her precious money back.'

He said, 'Don't say anything but I'm not giving it back, she's got plenty of money. She's a lousy old bitch and I've got nothing.' I said, 'Edward, you can't do that, it doesn't matter how much she's got or how lousy she is it's her money, you cannot do that.' It wasn't until that day in September that I found out he hadn't paid the money back. Edith could not comprehend that he had done that. She then told me that she had thirty-six thousand dollars hidden in the house and I went off the brain. I said, 'If he finds out, anything could happen, he could tell Mike or even the prostitutes and the money could disappear and you'd never get it back. You've already had two robberies you don't want another one?' My mind was already ticking over wondering if what I had suspected ages ago that someone in the family already knew that there was big cash in the house and both robberies were inside jobs. She asked me what I thought she should do with the money. I said, 'Is it for anything in particular?' And she replied, 'It's for the three of you'. I said, 'Look, Mum, it's up to you, you either distribute it out to us now or take the risk of having it knocked off.' The result of that heart to heart discussion she decided to distribute the money out to the three of us with Edward getting five thousand dollars less than James and myself. I had been telling her that she needed hospitalisation for months but she was adamant that she didn't. She was stick thin when she came to our home a couple of weeks before Christmas and Harry went to stay with his daughter. Edith told me that she had no intentions of going back to Harry because she was tired of being at his beck and call all day. But on Thursday 7th of January 1999 she insisted on being driven back to Harry's house. She didn't want to go back to her house because Edward was there. I was furious and told her she was an idiot, I knew she wasn't well and I said, 'Stay here until you're feeling better or go to James's place, he and Judy can look after you for a while.' But no she had to go back to sort a few things out, I drove her there and drove straight back home. I didn't even ring her over the next five weeks and she didn't ring me until Thursday 11 February 1999. She seemed quite pleased that she had been put in hospital so that she could be looked after twenty-four, seven. I thought, good it's about bloody time and I told her it'd be a few days before I could get up to see her.

I was looking after Andy and Emma because Vivian had found a full-time job at the local Surf Club. On Thursday 18 February 1999, Frank and I along with Andy and Emma visited Edith in the Greenslopes Hospital. She was in good spirits but she complained about her feet being swollen. When I looked at them, I was shocked to see they were twice the normal size I said, 'Have you shown the doctor and nurses?' She assured me that she had and when I asked what they'd said was the reason for the swelling she said they were checking it out. In the course of conversation, I learnt that they had taken her off all her medication. 'What, all of it?' 'Yes.' I later said to Frank, 'She must be mistaken they wouldn't just take her off all of her medication, that would be too risky.' During the time we were with her, she told us that she was definitely going to leave Harry and go back to her own home when she got out of hospital. She said she was going to tell Edward to get out and find a flat. I told her that was an excellent idea and to make sure she did do it. She said, 'I've had a lot of thinking time and I definitely am going to change things.' We spent over an hour with her before leaving her to have lunch.

At seven o'clock the following morning my sister-in-law Judy rang to tell me that Edith had gone into a coma at three am. The hospital had rung her at two am to say that Edith was deteriorating. When I asked why she hadn't notified me then, she said she didn't want to disturb me. *What* ? My mother was deteriorating at two am and went into a coma at three am and Judy didn't want to disturb me until seven am. I was too upset at that stage to question anything. I just hung up and Frank and I got dressed as quick as we could and took off towards Brisbane. We only got halfway up the highway before finding out that a truck had been involved in an accident and because the road workers were building a new highway the entire highway was blocked. By the time the highway was cleared we didn't arrive at the hospital until after nine am. The nursing sister was shocked when I told her who I was. She said, 'I'm so sorry sweetheart your mother passed away at eight twenty-five am, your brother collected all her belongings. If we had've known you existed we would have notified you at two am'. I was escorted to her bed and I held her hand which was still warm but losing its warmth quickly. Edith, my mother, whom I had fought tooth and nail with most of my life, lay lifeless with no more fight left in her. I kissed her goodbye, told her I loved her and apologised for not being there for her when she passed over. By rights I should have questioned thoroughly why Edith had been taken off all her medication. But I definitely was not thinking coherently for weeks after her death. There are a lot of unanswered questions that will forever remain a mystery.

Chapter 61

Trust and Instinct

James and Edward were sitting in Edith's dining room when Frank and I entered the house. It didn't occur to me that neither of them had bothered to try and contact me about Mum. I was too numb to really think straight I just wanted to console and be consoled by our loss. After hugging each other, Edward handed me a little coin purse which contained Mum's original wedding ring, my grandmother's wedding ring, a ring that my grandfather had had made for my grandmother and a costume jewellery ring that looked as if it had come from Woolworths. He said, 'There wasn't any money except for a few cents.' I never gave that a moment's thought at the time. But hindsight is a wondrous thing and looking back I know for a fact Mum always kept at least five thousand dollars cash in her handbag. I had seen her counting it in her room one night when she stayed with us at Christmas time only eight weeks previously, I had even said to her, 'What the hell are you doing with all that and why are you counting it again. Do you think one of us is going to knock it off when you're outside?'

No sooner had Edward given me the rings, James said to Edward, 'Come on we'll get it done and over with.' As they got up and walked to the door I said, 'Where are you going?' They both said in unison, 'To Harry's house, you can ring everyone and tell them Mum has died.' On their return about forty-five minutes later they walked in carrying bundles of Mum's clothing and belongings. They were both in fits of laughter as they explained that they'd broken into Harry's place because he wasn't there. I said, 'If you had've waited a moment before you left, I could have told you he wasn't there he's staying with his daughter.''We knew that, that's why we went to get Mum's things just in case he wouldn't give them to us.' Frank and I just glanced at each other in total disbelief. I thought what the fuck is going through their skulls? Mum's clothes are from the thrift shop and that's where they'll be going back to. Harry was not a happy chappie at all when he found out that they had broken into his home and rightly so.

Being the eldest, James assumed the responsibility of organising the funeral it didn't occur to me that he and I had both been appointed executors of the will.

In hindsight I remember accompanying Mum into the Public Trustees Office in the June of 1998 where she made the will out to the three of us and naming James and I as executors. In previous wills she had always stipulated that Edward could stay in the home providing that he pay all rates and maintain the home in good order. She said to me at the time, 'Will you see that he gets a decent place to live?' And I promised her faithfully I would.

In that new will she had stipulated that her home should be sold and the money equally divided between the three of us, however, she obviously had a change of heart and approximately two weeks later she changed her will again stipulating that Edward could stay in the home. I must say that I was somewhat surprised by that and even if I had've recalled being co-executor I still would have let James take charge of the funeral arrangements. The funeral was held on Tuesday 23 February 1999 at the church she had married Harry four years earlier. I mentioned in my eulogy that I thought it was an appropriate day because it was the anniversary of my grandmother's (99th) birthday.

It had been told to me on several occasions that there were provisions made for Edith to be buried with Grandma and Granddad. Neither James nor Edward knew where the grave was and they took not a scrap of notice of me when I told them that I knew. James decided to have her cremated and insisted Harry had to pay his share of the expenses. I never saw the bill but I just coughed up what James said was my share of the costs. Edith's ashes were supposed to be buried with Grandma and Granddad but James in his wisdom had decided to keep them in his home. I have never been to his home since her death so I don't even know what the urn looks like.

Over the next two weeks or so, the house was a hive of activity with everyone trying to sort out everything. Edward even invited his girlfriend Jean and her granddaughter to sift through Mum's belongings. I couldn't stand a bar of Jean and neither could Edith but at the time I thought there's nothing to gain by telling her to get out. But it really irked me when Edward was giving her what he claimed was his share of the unused linen that Edith had kept for special occasions which never happened. Like a fool I didn't question James locking himself in Mum's bedroom telling us not to disturb him while he sorted her private papers out. When he came out, I asked him if he'd discovered anything worthwhile and he said that he hadn't and I accepted that. A week or so later he told me that Mum had had a bank book with forty thousand dollars in it and that the solicitor would divide it between the three of us after he had taken his fees out. It makes me wonder what else he may have found that he didn't tell me about. I'm not saying that I think James ripped me off, but again in hindsight I think that everything that happened after Mum's death should have been handled better. James had chosen his solicitor to handle the settlement of the will. I didn't hear from James for a couple of weeks so I rang him one evening to find out what was happening. He told me that he and Edward were going into see the solicitor the next day. I was quite surprised that I hadn't been told and I said, 'I'll be there'. He said, 'There's no need for you to be there, it's just a meeting to get the ball rolling. I said, 'Yeah well I intend to be there for the kick off.' Unbeknown to me when we arrived outside the solicitor's office James said to Frank 'What the hell are you doing here. It's got nothing to do with you.' I never knew about that comment until years later. Frank has never been the type of person to stick his nose in other people's business and the only reason he had come with me we had decided to go to the Broncos Club for lunch after I had been to see the solicitor. I only wish Frank had've given me his opinion on what he thought from the onset because I think I would've removed the rose-coloured glasses. I let James and the solicitor do most of the talking and I watched Edward smugly sitting in his chair when the solicitor mentioned that Edward could stay in the house for the rest of his life providing that he pays the rates etc. Edward was even swinging his legs back and forth as if to say, Ha Ha I've got the upper hand over you mugs. James surprised me by saying, 'The house needs painting, I'm a painter so I'll put in the quote and get that done and that can come out of his share of the money.' I tried not to smirk as I remembered that Mum had asked James to paint the house for her many times after Dad passed away in 1982. James's standard answer was that he was always too busy to do it.

I could see the smirk leave Edward's face when James mentioned the quote to paint the house and he said, 'Will I have to pay the entire cost of the paint job?' The solicitor and James both answered, 'Yes.' I piped up and said, 'I have a question.' James flashed a look at me as if to say, you have no right to even think about speaking. I had been waiting patiently the entire time we'd been there to get the solicitor to answer my question even though I already knew the answer. I said, 'Edward and I are both pensioners but James isn't, will Edward still be entitled to a pensioner discount on the rates?' 'No, he'll have to pay the total amount.' James smirked at me with his eyes and I knew he was thinking, Good on ya Fatso and Edward's legs stopped swinging, he sat bolt upright in his chair then his shoulders slumped and he let out a low guttural groan then said, 'We'll have to sell the place then.' I sat there with a smug look at James and I wanted to say out loud to him, I'm not the idiot you think I am. I went to visit Edward one day only to find that he was sleeping on a mattress on the floor. He told me he had given all the furniture to his sons. I found out later that he had in fact sold everything including some antique furniture to a second-hand dealer for a total of two thousand dollars. The house was eventually sold and I kept my promise to Edith by helping Edward find a nice unit at Southport. A fat lot of good that was he sold it twelve months later and spent it all living with a prostitute, when the money ran out, she kicked him out.

Chapter 62

The Chicken or the Egg

As mentioned before Vivian had started work at the local Surf Life Saving Club in the January of 1999 as Finance and Promotion Assistant and from what she told me she enjoyed her job immensely. She had only been there for a few months when she announced to us that she had been promoted to Promotions Manager and was also in charge of counting the takings. I thought at the time it was like leaving a two year old in charge of the lolly shop. Vivian had 'employed' a sixteen year old girl (Cassie) to keep house for her in lieu of free board. Poor little Cassie wasn't the brightest crayon in the box but from what I observed she wasn't completely stupid either because she only did the basic chores to earn her keep. In the June of that year (approximately two weeks after Andy's sixteenth birthday) Frank and I took Vivian, Heather, Andy and Emma on the P&O Fair Princess cruise to Fiji. I had wanted the entire family to have a get together and enjoy each other's company. Unfortunately, Claire was unable to get time off from her job in Sydney, but we managed to catch up with her before we departed Sydney Harbour. She was not happy when I told her 'NO!' when she asked me to give her the money it would have cost me for her fare. (More about the consequences of that decision later.) No doubt about it most of my 'wonderful' family were mercenary sods. The only ones who weren't was Frank, Heather and me. Years after the cruise I learnt that whilst on the cruise Andy had complained bitterly that he thought I should have paid for him to have a single cabin. I had booked a four berth cabin for Frank and me sharing with Andy and Emma. Vivian and Heather were booked into the cabin next door, sharing with two other young women. Money went missing from Heather's purse and another one of the young ladie's money and belongings went missing as well. The fourth lady got blamed and she was moved to another cabin. Maybe it was her; maybe it wasn't.

Frank and I paid for all the 'goodies' purchased for Vivian, Andy and Emma including a helicopter ride for Emma with me and a jet boat ride for Vivian and Andy with Frank. Andy insisted on me buying name brand name clothing (Tommy Hilfiger in particular.) It wasn't a case of him missing out on anything.

Heather on the other hand insisted on paying for her own 'goodies' and jet boat ride.

We had only been back home a few weeks when the sale of Mum's home was finalised and the house two doors down the road from our home came on the market. I decided that it would be a great investment for Vivian, Heather and Claire and that Vivian, Andy and Emma would have a permanent roof over their head. The home was in perfect condition, not a mark on the walls or carpets and everyone fell in love with it on inspection. Vivian agreed to pay the mortgage, rates etc and to keep the home in good repair. I put forty thousand dollars of my inheritance down as a deposit and I helped Vivian and Heather to obtain finance through my bank. Claire had decided against putting her name on the contract, Frank and I couldn't for the life of us understand why. I found out many years later that Claire thought Vivian would fail to pay the mortgage repayments and she believed that it would be up to her and Heather to pay them. It was always understood that the house was for the three sisters no matter what happened. Vivian, Andy and Emma moved in to the home in November 1999 just twelve months after coming back into the family fold. Everything was falling into place, and finally we didn't have a care in the world. Frank and I became our grandkids carers before and after school which included getting them their breakfast, lunch and dinner and driving them to and from their schools and we cherished every moment. Vivian arrived home from work one afternoon with a large lump on her leg and she told me that she had fallen down the stairs at the club. She said she was going on compo and that she was going to sue the club for everything they had. I immediately knew that this was another one of her scams but I said nothing. She obviously doesn't think her plans out too well because she made an appointment to see the solicitor who had represented us in our trying to gain access to Andy and Emma. We had told him everything we knew about Vivian's conning and cunning ways at the time. No need to be told he told her in no uncertain terms that she didn't have a (pardon the pun) a leg to stand on. He didn't let on that he knew she'd already claimed compo for falling down the school stairs. It became increasingly obvious that Vivian's mood swings were erratic to say the least and rather than say anything to her about her changeable moods everyone kept quiet and put up with her behaviour. I would advise Andy and Emma what not to say or do so as not to get them into trouble. Some days Vivian would fly off the handle for no apparent reason and neither Andy nor Emma knew what they were being abused for. Emma had said to me many times that she wanted to shift in with us and as much as I wanted her to, I knew it would only cause bigger problems. Emma always felt too scared to go against her mother's demands. No matter what Emma did, it was always wrong in Vivian's eyes. The poor little bugger was verbally abused almost daily.

Then in the July of 2000 Vivian told me that her boss had kissed her and had tried to drag her up the stairs to the lifesaver's sleeping quarters a few weeks previously. She again told me she was going to sue the club and the manager. Naturally I was very wary about the allegations and I asked her why she hadn't told me when it happened. She said she didn't want to cause a fuss because she wanted to keep her job. She then showed me a letter addressed to her boss from a woman in Sweden. The woman had sent the letter to the boss' daughter whom she had been friends with for a number of years. The boss' son-in-law had faxed it to the boss and Vivian had photocopied it.

In the letter the woman accused the boss of sexually assaulting her seventeen-year old sister a few weeks previously when her sister was holidaying at the boss' home. This letter of course strengthened Vivian's story of her boss sexually assaulting her at work. What I didn't think of at the time was a chicken and egg scenario 'What came first Vivian's alleged assault or the letter?' The letter could have easily come first giving Vivian enough fodder to accuse her boss of a similar assault. Vivian's boss appeared in the Coolangatta court and admitted kissing Vivian on the forehead for doing a good job but he denied any sexual assault. He was remanded for sentencing and on his next appearance he was represented by a solicitor who withdrew the guilty plea and another new date was set aside for a hearing. That hearing brought out a lot of animosity towards Vivian from some of her co-workers and again the case was adjourned. It never did come before the magistrate's courts again that I was aware of.

As I sit here typing, I've just realised that Vivian could have written that letter then photocopied it to convince me and Frank that her boss was an evil predator! After all, she had written two pornographic letters to me from a supposed grandfather a few years previously. It's certainly a strong possibility.

Vivian seemed to resent Emma's very existence, so much so that she began to order Emma to keep away from our home before and after school. But she allowed Andy to come to our home to use our computers for his homework. Nine times out of ten Andy

only used the computers to play computer games. Vivian's 'rules' changed more regularly than I changed my clothes. Vivian ordered us not to cook the kids their meals but we were still relied upon to drive Emma to and from school. Andy had to find his own way to and from school. Although I didn't agree with the situation I didn't protest because I feared repercussions on a grand scale. I certainly didn't want to lose my grandchildren again. Even though they only lived two doors away that didn't amount to a hill of beans knowing what deviousness Vivian was capable of.

Frank had always wanted to go on a Kangaroo Tour because his beloved Rugby League team the Brisbane Broncos always had at least six players in the International team.

I started to plan a trip after I heard about an organised tour on one of the football programmes. I did the sums on the organised tour and I knew I could organise a tour that would be cheaper than the one they offered. By the time I sorted everything out and included a side trip to Ireland which wasn't on the organised tour I realised I could include Emma in our trip and it would still be a lot cheaper than the organised tour.

Thankfully Vivian thought it was a great opportunity for Emma to go with us and Emma was over the moon about the adventure. Both Frank and I truly believe that Vivian was relieved not to have Emma around. We would have loved to have taken Andy on the tour as well but our finances would not allow that because Andy was well over the child fare stage and his fare and accommodation would have cost us what we were paying for ourselves. Besides that, Andy was in the midst of end of year ten exams. Ironically on our way to Brisbane airport for our departure Vivian received a phone call from Andy telling her that he had been expelled from school for absenteeism. Vivian's screeching at Andy almost caused Frank to crash the car. Andy apparently had to do a lot of grovelling to the principal to get reinstated.

Emma was a fantastic travelling companion, and she, Frank and I had the best five weeks in England, Scotland and Ireland and three days in Bangkok on our way home. Even though we took her for a few more holidays within Australia, for the next six years we still talked about different experiences we had enjoyed together over in the UK and I will always treasure that magical holiday.

To convince the court that she was traumatised by her experience Vivian went to a psychiatrist. After a few visits she encouraged Heather to go and see the psychiatrist as well. Heather has had an inferiority complex ever since she developed the tumour on her mandible when she was ten years old. Vivian offered to drive her to the psychiatrist on her first visit and I thought that it was a good thing that they were able to go together to try and sort out any old grievances that they may have had with each other. Heather never spoke about anything she had discussed with the psychiatrist and I never tried to question her I figured that she'd tell me in her own good time.

Vivian was admitted to a private hospital as a psychiatric patient where she spent two weeks all expenses paid by Worker's Compensation even though she had admitted to me that she had fooled the psychiatrist into getting her in there. Frank and I cleaned her home and cared for the kids and basically ran ourselves ragged doing everything for her including visiting her every day. I recall one evening visit I made to her on my own we were sitting quietly in her room chatting and all of a sudden without any reason she started screeching abuse at me. To say I was stunned would be an understatement but she got the attention she obviously wanted to prove that she had problems. I was escorted out of the hospital by one of the nursing staff. When I told Frank and Heather about the incident, Heather said, 'Mum, I have to tell you something, the first day Vivian took me to the psychiatrist she told me not to tell him that we were sisters. She didn't have an appointment that day and she stayed outside in her car while I went in by myself'. 'Have you told the doctor yet that she's your sister?' 'No, I don't even know how I'd bring the subject up.' I was totally gobsmacked and I wondered why Vivian wouldn't want the doctor to know that Heather was her sister. I sat down and wrote a lengthy letter to the doctor explaining everything. In the meantime, Vivian discharged herself from the hospital and the next time I took Heather to her appointment the doctor called me into his surgery and he told me how shocked he was at learning the truth about Vivian. All he could say was, 'I doubt very much that I'll ever see Vivian again, she obviously got what she wanted, I recommended for her to receive the disability pension and it was awarded to her a few weeks ago'. This was all news to me. God only knows what lies Vivian had told him. Vivian received a letter from Centrelink asking her to explain an overpayment of dole money they had paid her when she had been working at the club. It was obvious that her boss knew about her receiving the money and had decided to contact Centrelink to report her. After weeks of waiting after her initial interview with the Centrelink investigators Vivian was summoned to appear in Southport Magistrate's Court charged with fraudulently taking thirteen thousand dollars from Centrelink. I'm not a hundred percent certain of the date now, but I believe it was in the November of 2003. On the morning of her court appearance she came and asked me to give her a couple of my 'heavy duty' pain killers which was regularly prescribed to me for my back pain. She claimed that she had not slept a wink all night and that she had a bad migraine. Foolishly I gave her the tablets which she threw down her throat without water, much to everyone's amazement.

By the time we arrived at the courthouse it became very obvious that Vivian was disorientated and incoherent. Her speech was slurred and I asked her what other drugs had she taken, she muttered something which I could not understand and I felt as if I wanted to slap her around to bring her to hr senses. She made a complete holy show of herself in front of the female magistrate and I stood alongside of her and whispered to her to shut her mouth and I tried my hardest to plead her case for her. I must have done a fair enough job of it because instead of going to prison Vivian received a three-year suspended sentence and to be of good behaviour for twelve months.

In November 2004 the case against her boss was heard in the Anti-discrimination Tribunal and Vivian was awarded forty thousand dollars but she never received a penny of it because her boss filed for bankruptcy and I believe he put all of his assets into his wife's name. Frank and I had been ordered not to attend the hearing. She rang me panic stricken because Andrew had read about the case and had contacted Vivian's ex-boss and he offered to give evidence of Vivian's behaviour during the time he was married to her.

Vivian became fixated with the belief that she was a witch. She told us she needed bat blood and she asked Frank if he could catch ten bats from the bat colony near our home so that she could bleed them for her project.

During the time Vivian had been working and I wasn't allowed to prepare the kid's meals, I used to go down to the house to check on the kids before Vivian arrived home and on at least two occasions I found Emma standing on a rickety chair teetering over the stove trying to cook herself some chips in a pot filled with boiling oil. I gave Vivian my deep fryer but I didn't let on that I had seen Emma trying to cook the chips. Vivian exclaimed, 'Oh good thanks this is perfect for my cauldron'.

If it hadn't been so pathetic, I would've fallen on the floor with laughter.

Chapter 63

Ivan

In September of 2001 I became a volunteer for an organisation which goes out on the street to feed the homeless. I was assigned to going out every second Friday night and although I was looking forward to this new adventure, I was petrified the first time I went out with the crew of six, not knowing what I was to encounter. But within minutes of meeting the 'streeties' as we affectionately called them, I felt totally at ease. I loved being with these lovable rogues their humour was infectious and their stories were fascinating, exciting and incredibly interesting. My favourite streetie was a Maori guy who was one of the most endearing characters I've ever met. Everyone from the organisation and all the other streeties loved him. All the other streeties called him Uncle and he would help all of them either giving them advice and/or sharing his tobacco and grog. The first time I met him I kept calling him Kiwi because I had been told that some streeties preferred to be anonymous. I knew instantly he and I would be good mates and at the end of the evening I said to him, 'I can't keep calling you Kiwi can I ask you your name'. He replied, 'Ivan.''I'll remember you next time, Ivan.'

And with a twinkle in his eye he said, 'And I'll remember you Amelia.' Ivan and I became great mates and I worried for him like a mother duck would her duckling. So much so that Ivan would often call me 'mum' even though I was only four years older than him. If Ivan wasn't at our designated area when we arrived, I'd be looking out for him waiting, worrying and wondering where he was. As soon as he arrived someone would say, 'Here he is.' And I'd go off the brain at him for making me worry especially if he was drunker than usual. He'd have a grin from ear to ear and announce to everyone, 'She's a good mum, she's number one in my book.''I'll give you number one, I'll kick your arse until your nose bleeds if you don't wake up to yourself, ya Kiwi bastard.' Then I'd proceed in giving him a lecture, and he loved every minute of my ranting and raving. I never saw Ivan in a bad mood, drunk or sober he was always happy go lucky. My team leader was a lovely Irish, lady whom I held in high esteem. I feel sure she must've said at least ten rosaries for me after every Friday night we went out on the street. Everyone knew that Amelia wasn't the average do-gooder that the organisation usually had as a volunteer. Well no-one has ever accused me of being average or normal. I like to make everyone laugh and enjoy themselves; let's face it being on the street isn't fun. Making the streeties forget their lifestyle for a couple of hours by listening to me being an idiot, I felt I had achieved something good. I had only been with the organisation a year when I was asked to help out on the Saturday night team, because they were short staffed and there were problems with the team not getting along. I had met the team leader Graeme a couple of times and I got on well with him, he had been with the organisation for about twelve years. He told me I would be his deputy team leader for the night. I thought, shit I don't like the sound of this I don't like being boss or deputy boss over anyone. But somehow, I managed to muddle my way through the night without too many problems. Then at the end of the night

Graeme , 'Will you come back on Saturday two weeks from tonight?'

I figured that a weekly outing wouldn't kill me Fridays one-week Saturdays the next. **Amelia** 'Okay why not.'

Graeme 'Great when you come in, you'll need these'.

He handed me a set of keys to the front door of the building we used to prepare the food and told me the combination of the security alarm and showed me how to turn it on and off. I looked at him

Amelia 'Will you be running late?'

Graeme 'No I won't be back for a while I'm going on holidays.'

Amelia 'Who'll be the team leader?'

With a big grin on his dial

Graeme 'You will Congratulations we've been watching you for a while you're perfect for the job'.

Amelia 'BULLSHIT.'

Graeme burst out laughing and shook his head

Graeme 'Amelia, you'll do really well there's nothing to worry about'.

Nothing to worry about be buggered the team had some good members but there was two or three who were as useless as the proverbial on a bull. Now that I was team leader I had to try and syphon off the useless ones without being too brutal. For someone with about as much tact as a bull in a china shop, I had my work cut out for me. The following fortnight I asked the quiet Chinese girl Zoe to be my deputy and I was surprised but pleased when she accepted the challenge. Did I say she was 'quiet'? What are those old sayings, still waters run deep and it's the quiet ones you have to watch. Zoe proved to be an excellent choice, unbeknown to me she was studying psychology and has since graduated with flying colours. Good luck was on my side that first night I started as team leader, one of my Friday night team members Liz decided to join my team which I deemed a great honour. Liz was studying to be a social worker and she too blitzed her exams and is now in a well-paid position. She is still a good friend. Robert also joined my team for a short time when he could tear himself away from studying to be a doctor. I still enjoy late night phone conversations with Robert although he's frantically busy. He's now a Psychiatrist. I love him to death as my surrogate son. He's even nuttier than I am if that's possible. Graeme returned to the team whenever he could Graeme is a well sort after Grief Counsellor and was often called upon to go to disaster areas to counsel victims of cyclones, floods and fires. Although we don't see each other regularly we email each other at least once a week. Phillipa has the sweetest nature and my nickname for her was Sweet she became a successful criminologist and to me that seems to be the most bizarre occupation for someone as gentle as she is. We kept in touch for years but unfortunately not any more, life got in the way for both of us. But I'm sure we'll reconnect. Jo, Patti, Heidi, Judy, Raelene, Bruce and Greg were all integral members of the A Team which I named us. I actually chose Jo, Heidi and Raelene from the new recruits. David the chief co-ordinator had chosen me to teach any newcomers at orientation nights what to expect when they went out on the street. Judy I'm ashamed to say I poached from my old Friday night team. A couple of people tried to nuzzle their way onto my team but I was very choosy so if they didn't cut the mustard with me, they didn't get in. Unfortunately, Heidi has passed away and I've lost contact with the others. But I feel certain that one of these days we'll have a get-together and have a few laughs over some of the things we all got up to on the A Team. We were a force to be reckoned with. We used to all have a night out every few weeks. We didn't need to go out for entertainment, we would just book a huge table at different restaurants and we'd have an absolute ball just enjoying each other's company. As for the useless members of the team, I had more than enough members to fill the bus and it gave me the best opportunity to tell the useless ones they'd have to see David, to find another team to go to. David came up to me one day and congratulated me on making the worst team into the best team. He said, 'I think you are without doubt the best team leader on the street'.

I was on cloud nine for yonks after that.

On Saturday 11 October 2003 as I stepped out of the bus, Ivan presented me with a beautiful bunch of yellow roses

Ivan 'These are for you, Mum'

I was so touched by his beautiful gesture but I said, 'Why are you giving me these?'

Ivan 'They're for your birthday.'

Amelia 'But you know as well as I do my birthday isn't for another two months'.

He said very wistfully, 'Yeah but I might not be here.'

Amelia 'Of course you'll be here and you'll be clean and sober because you're coming to the Broncos with us to celebrate.'

I had made arrangements to have a big slap up lunch at the Broncos Club to celebrate my sixtieth birthday and I had invited and paid for over one hundred guests and Ivan was included. But that particular Saturday night Ivan wasn't his usual jovial self and when I asked him what the matter was, he just shrugged my question off. A few minutes later he made everyone laugh by saying out loud to me, 'Amelia, you look like a poodle tonight.' I had placed an orange bow in my hair for remembrance of the first anniversary of the Bali bombing victims. I replied 'Thanks, Ivan, first you give me a beautiful bunch of roses and in the next breath you're telling me I'm a bloody dog. At least try and be consistent.'

The following fortnight Ivan was nowhere to be seen and I was pacing up and down looking out for him when one of the streeties said, 'Hasn't anyone told you that Ivan's in hospital.' 'WHAT? WHERE? WHEN? WHY?'

I rang Heather at home and asked her to ring the hospital to find out what ward he was in and when she rang me back with the news that he was in intensive care with a severe head injury and he wasn't expected to live, I was shattered. I subsequently learnt quite a bit about how and why he got to the hospital but I don't have any proof and all I can say is he didn't fall. A few Streeties witnessed what had happened and oddly no-one bothered to check the CCTV camera footage that was almost directly above what had occurred. Streeties are not classified as being human in certain circles so as far as being reliable witnesses was way out of the question. I know what happened, a number of streeties know what happened, police know what happened but Ivan was only a homeless bum so therefore his death didn't really count in the greater scheme of the universe.

The Indy was on the following day so it was impossible for us to get to the hospital because of the traffic, however, Frank, Phillipa and I sat at his bedside all day on the Monday and I knew once I walked out of that hospital I would never see this amazing man alive again. Ivan passed away at eleven-thirty pm that Monday 27 October.

Within a heartbeat of my placing the phone down after the hospital notified me of Ivan's death, I received a call from a male questioning me about what I knew about the circumstances leading up to Ivan being hospitalised. He said he would ring me the next day but I never heard from him again. Case closed.

Ivan had three funerals, two in Queensland and one in Auckland. Ironically his ex-wife Shirley had been holidaying on the Sunshine Coast with her husband when she was notified of Ivan's death. When I met Shirley at his funerals, I was struck by her beautiful face but she was also a genuinely lovely person. Ivan had often spoken to me about her and I knew that he still loved her with every beat of his heart. As soon as I started talking to Shirley, I could tell that she still loved him as well, but his drinking had caused the rift between them. Some of the stories Ivan had told me of his life in New Zealand and his early days in Australia had seemed exaggerated and pie in the sky bordering on fanciful, however, Shirley confirmed that everything he had told me was true. I won't go into details of his achievements just in case one day his family want to write their own book about him. All I will say is Ivan was a wonderful, amazing, humorous and gentle human being and as I said in his eulogy, 'I am very proud to say I was his friend.' Shirley wanted to donate a large amount of money to the organisation but I told her to keep her money and donate it elsewhere in Ivan's memory.

The hierarchy of the head office in Brisbane were becoming more than a bit strange. I found out that all the other team leaders were having their issues with the hierarchy as well, but I felt that they seemed to be hell bent on making my life unbearable. David went on an extended overseas holiday and on his return the hierarchy gave him his marching orders. To say all the volunteers were stunned would be an understatement. David was the hardest working fellow at the organisation. He was available to the streeties and volunteers twenty-four/ seven and nothing was too much trouble for him. At his farewell party David took me aside and said, 'Amelia, if you really think they are gunning for you, don't wait until they oust you, give them notice first.'

All the team leaders were invited to go to lunch at a well-known exclusive club where a couple were being honoured for their donation of over fifty thousand dollars. I couldn't help but wonder how long that money would last in the coffers but I kept that thought to myself. The thought started out as a tinkling in my brain but when one of the hierarchy had had far too much wine and announced that he would pay for everyone's lunch the alarm bells started to chime like the Town Hall clock at midday to me. To make it even more 'interesting' everyone's lunch order changed from spaghetti bolognaise to T-bone steaks with all the trimmings. David's replacement was one of the biggest dunces God ever allowed to draw breath, but he was one of the in crowd with the hierarchy. The man had no idea what he was doing and unfortunately when he made a decision, we had to abide by it. The hierarchy assigned two new members to my team and from the moment I clapped eyes on them I knew they were hierarchy 'plants.' My team members thought I was being completely paranoid for no valid reason but no matter what my friends said to me I could not trust those two for all the rice in China. It took me another fifteen months before I took David's advice and in May 2005, I reluctantly resigned with most of my team resigning with me as well. I was not surprised to learn that the two team members the hierarchy had placed on my team became part of the hierarchy within days of my resignation though I think they already were, it just hadn't been announced. If they thought that those two were my reason for resigning, they should think again. It didn't come as any great surprise to hear within twelve months that the entire hierarchy of the organisation had been sacked because they had almost sent the organisation broke. I wonder what happened to the fifty-thousand dollar donation. No-one was questioned but I reckon they should have been, everything was swept under the carpet and kept hush hush.

Chapter 64

The Biggest Shock of My Life

On a number of occasions both Heather and I had lamented that we thought we had more money in our purse than what we did. But we dismissed it as thinking we must have spent it. Heather has never been diagnosed with Bi Polar but every so often she goes overboard with buying things that really aren't needed. She has always been very generous to everyone in the family, buying groceries and gifts and she never asks anyone for anything.

We all went to the Broncos Leagues Club for lunch and Heather insisted on paying. She pushed me out of the queue to pay the cashier and as we were about to leave the club, she went to the ATM to withdraw money.

Emma called in after school and she played games on Heather's computer as she often did. The following day we went to the local shopping centre to get groceries & again Heather pushed me out of the queue. She opened her wallet and her mouth was agape. She had no money in her wallet. We didn't need to be Einstein to realise that Emma had stolen the fifty dollars that Heather had gotten the day before.

We confronted her in front of Vivian and she sheepishly admitted to taking it and Vivian handed the fifty dollars back. I asked Emma how often had she taken money from us but all she would do was deny having taken any from me! To say I was devastated with her was an understatement.

Heather had bought her many things and given her money to buy lollies etc.

Frank and I bought her anything her heart desired and we had taken her on numerous holidays including almost a month to England, Scotland, Ireland and Thailand.

I subsequently found out from neighbours that she had regularly gone around asking for money to sponsor her in spelling bees and running races on sports days. Lord only knows how much she had swindled from the neighbours!

Not long after that, in the February of 2006 Andy came to tell Heather that his laptop had broken down again and asked her if she could fix it. Heather found the problem and ordered the replacement part paying fifty dollars for it on her Visa card. Andy offered Heather the money and she told him he could pay her when the account was due at the end of the month. The part arrived and Heather installed it and realised immediately it was faulty and sent it back with the request for a replacement.

It arrived a few days later and she installed it and it worked perfectly. By that time, the Visa payment was due and as promised Andy paid Heather the money. A week or so went by and we hadn't seen Vivian, Andy or Emma which by that time was not unusual. Heather went down to say hi and see how they were, within five minutes Heather stormed through the door and she was so upset she couldn't speak she was fighting back tears and I said, 'What's wrong now?' She just waved her arms in the air shook her head and went to her room. I followed her to her room and I said, 'Crying isn't going to solve it, come out and tell us what's happened' She eventually came out and sat down and fighting back more tears

Heather 'She's done it again'.

Amelia 'What has she done?'

Heather 'Virtually accused me of theft'.

Amelia 'What?'

Heather 'She reckons I ripped Andy off of fifty dollars.'

Amelia 'How did she work that out?'

Heather 'She said that Andy's computer broke down again and that he got an expert out who reckoned that the part I installed was a fake copy replacement part. Mum, I bought that part from a reputable dealer, there was nothing wrong with the part. She's a fuckin liar and I hate her guts, she's such a fuckin bitch.'

Both Frank and I gave out exasperated sighs in unison and I thought, here we go again. Heather was crying almost uncontrollably and sobbed, 'I've given them all everything I can give them and they still treat me like shit.'

I knew the feeling only too well and so did Frank. We just looked at each other and both shook our heads in disbelief and frustration. I put my arm around Heather and said, 'Don't take it to heart we all know that there's something wrong with her.' Both Heather and Frank almost screamed in unison, 'But she knows what she's doing.' **Heather** 'Mum and Dad, I want to sell the house, fuck her she can go homeless.'

I tried to make light of it and said, 'That means I'll have to go back to the organisation and feed them of a Saturday night'. Heather tried to laugh but said, 'No I mean it, Mum, I want them out of that house they've just about wrecked a fantastic investment and I think Claire will agree to sell as well'. I went down to speak to Vivian but all she would say to me was that she had had enough of Heather's bullshit and of me sticking up for her. I thought, Christ, talk about role reversal. I was always sticking up for you and your bullshit not Heather. But I just said, 'You're totally wrong there, Vivian.'

When I got home Heather asked me my opinion of her wanting to sell and I said, 'Heather, I told you on your fortieth birthday (less than a month previously) I've got about twenty years left on this planet if I'm lucky and it's time for you to start making your own decisions because you cannot keep relying on us.' She said, 'Well I want to sell I'll ring Claire tonight and see if she wants to sell as well.' That night Heather came out from the bedroom extension and said, 'Claire said yes, she wants to sell the house as well.' The following day Heather made an appointment to see a solicitor whom she had picked at random from the phone book and she informed me that she would go on her own. Because it was over two kilometres to the nearest bus stop, I insisted that I'd drive her there because she had no idea what stop she would have to get off at. When we arrived at the solicitor's office I said, 'I'll wait in the car.' She said, 'I might be here for an hour you'd better come in and wait in his waiting room'. When the solicitor called her in, she whispered, 'Come in with me I'm scared.' I whispered back, 'He's not going to bite, there's nothing to be scared of.' But he came out a few minutes later and asked me to come into his office, because I was the one who had paid the deposit on the house in the first place, he asked me if I wanted to be reimbursed my deposit and said, 'It can be arranged that it comes out of Vivian's share of the proceeds.' I told him that I've always tried to be a good mother and I've never been an Indian giver and I'm not prepared to change that now. He told us that there wouldn't be any problem selling the property even if Vivian tried to stop it in a court because two of the owners wanted out of the contract. The only concern he had was that there could be a big delay if Vivian decided to fight, but that would only cost her money and Heather and Claire could fight Vivian for her to pay their legal expenses.

Two days later on Thursday March 16th I was in the kitchen, my friend Zoe was coming for lunch and I was starting to prepare the food. Vivian marched in and was almost hysterical. She cried that she had received the letter from the solicitor informing her that both her sisters wanted to sell her house. I said, 'It's not just your house Vivian and it never was it's their house as well.' I told her that it's got nothing to do with me it's up to them. She screamed, 'Of course it's got to do with you, you would have fuckin instigated it and you would have fuckin driven her to the fuckin solicitor in the first fuckin place.'And I suppose I twisted Claire's arm over the phone as well. I think you had better take a long, hard look at yourself. The way you've treated them not to mention your father and I over the years it's taken a while for them to say enough is enough.' She started to calm down and tried to implore on Heather's good nature for her to change her mind. Both Vivian and Heather kept looking over for me to say something and I put my hands up in the air as if I was being held at gunpoint and as if to say not my decision. The argument went on back and forth for ages all the old issues surfaced and were also argued.

Amelia 'Vivian, you even implied in that affidavit when you took us to court for supposedly stalking you that we had sexually assaulted you'.

Vivian 'Implying and saying definitely are two different things.

Amelia 'Not in my book they're not'.

Frank 'Vivian, do you deny that you've ever accused me of sexually assaulting you?'

Vivian 'Of course I emphatically deny it.'

Frank 'Well I've got written proof that you have.'

Vivian 'Show it to me then.'

Frank 'I'll have to go out and get it, it's in the shed, there are a hundred and thirty-two pages of absolute shit that you've written.'

My eyes went as big as saucers. When he came back, he was empty handed and I thought, he mustn't be able to find it and I hoped he was only bluffing to frighten the crap out of her.

Vivian demanded, 'Well where's your proof ya silly old bastard?'

Frank 'It's outside I never wanted your mother to see it, because I feared it would kill her knowing you wrote it.'

He walked out and came back in within seconds holding a number of white pages. He stuck them under her face and said, 'Did you write this?'

She took the papers from his hand looked at them and hesitated then said, 'Y … yes I have to say I did.' She had been sitting approximately two to three metres from where I was sitting, I jumped up and flew across the room grabbed the pages out of her hand and ran up the hallway to my bedroom and hid them under a cushion on my bedroom chair. She had started running behind me crying and repeating, 'Mum, I'm so sorry; I swear I never showed it to anyone.' I walked back out and she kept pleading, 'Please, Mum, don't read it. Please, Mum, I only wrote it because you were going to get custody of the kids.' She must have said it at least a dozen times. I said, 'You know as well as I do Vivian, we weren't going for custody we only wanted to get access. Now get out and don't come back.' Just as she was walked down the driveway, Zoe arrived and they both stood in full view of me as I sat in my lounge chair absolutely sobbing my heart out. Vivian smiled her usual warm, sweet smile at Zoe and asked her how she was and chatted to her as if there was not a care in the world.

When Zoe walked in, she was in shock at seeing my face, I must've looked like a total wreck. I certainly felt like it. I blubbered what had happened and she desperately tried to calm me down. I think all her skills as a psychologist kicked in that day and she managed to get me to stop crying. I honestly don't know how I managed to get lunch ready, let alone eat anything. Zoe left around three pm and I fell on the bed completely spent. I said to Frank and Heather, 'Just let me lie down for half an hour, I need to try and relax and think.' Within five minutes Heather knocked on the door and said, 'Vivian, Andy and Emma are here.' I don't know why I walked out to speak to them I knew it was going to be futile. One of the first things I asked Andy and Emma was, 'Has your mother told you what she's written?'

They both said, 'Yes.' And Andy said, 'But that's in the past, get over it.' From there on it was a six way argument that went on for almost an hour or so. I can't remember anything that was said except at one stage I remember Andy saying, 'One hot day doesn't make a summer.'

Vivian looked at him with pride as if to say, that was clever.

Frank, Heather and I looked at him as if to say, what the hell are you on? Emma stood up and started screeching at top note I cannot remember what she said or for that matter if I even understood what she said but I went over to her and screamed back in her face. She pushed me out of her way and ran out the front door and as she ran past the big glass doors of the lounge room, she turned her face towards me and yelled, 'I hate your fuckin guts ya fuckin old bitch.' Those were the last words I ever heard coming out of my much loved fifteen year old granddaughter's mouth. Andy and Vivian left almost immediately. Andy's parting comment to me was, 'You are going to die a very lonely woman.' Surprisingly, I felt a great sense of relief at finally seeing them all walk out of our lives. What a pity I didn't use Dr Kenneth's advice from all those years ago and given them all a good hard slap and told them to wake up to themselves.

I remember only too clearly that I awoke at four thirty-two am the following day St Patrick's Day after a very fitful sleep. There was just enough first light filtering through the room that I didn't need to flick the touch light on, on my night stand. I reached past the night stand to the pages still under the cushion on the bedroom chair.

I can honestly say that I have never read pornographic literature in my life, until that day. I wanted to vomit. To say that I was shocked doesn't come anywhere near how I felt as I read each vile word of the six pages. I had cried more than twelve months-worth of tears the day before just imagining what she had written about Frank. What I didn't know then, she had gone into explicit detail of how I had sexually abused her as well. This entire putrid diatribe (as I now always refer to it) was supposedly to have happened when she was a baby. I think she may have gotten the idea after reading Roseanne Barr's autobiography. The tears flooded from me as I finished reading it and I curled into the foetal position and I thought of suicide. I felt abandoned because I truly believed that my mother, father and grandmother had watched over and protected me all these years. I desperately wanted them all to hold me until the pain in my soul subsided.

Then the realisation hit me that the past forty-four years since Vivian was born was a complete sham. I didn't know who she was she was definitely not the wonderful loving daughter I thought she was. I had given birth to, cared and nurtured a cold heartless alien and I felt totally violated, physically, mentally and emotionally. I sent her a text message telling her I had read her putrid diatribe and how disgusted I was. She came straight up knocking on the door pleading for forgiveness and begging me to talk Heather into changing her mind. I was numb to her grovelling. I was in shock and I had read and heard more than enough of her lies in twenty-four hours than what I had from hundreds of other people over my sixty-two years. She told me that she loved me so much that she hated the fact that I had chosen Frank over her when I took him back in 1976. She said, 'You always told me I was your right hand and you abandoned me.' I said, 'Vivian, I never chose your father over you at all. Yes, I did tell you, you were my right hand all the time because I felt that you were so helpful in those days. But you weren't my backbone my father was my backbone in those days because I had to lean on him when I thought I'd lose my ability to cope. And I certainly never abandoned you. That is just your interpretation of how much I relied on you and a figment of your imagination.' I felt sorry for her for feeling that way and I promised I would talk to Heather. But Heather was adamant she wasn't going to change her mind.

She said, 'Mum, open your eyes and smell the coffee she's a better actress than Nicole Kidman.'

Later that day I found out from Frank and Heather that Vivian's computer had broken down in 2002 and Vivian had asked Heather to fix it for her. Heather had not only fixed it, she noticed that Vivian had a file called, 'Get the Williams', Heather quickly got a disc, copied the file it she printed it off. Back then Heather had actually put it on my computer for me to read. When she contacted me back in 1998, Vivian had asked me to try and put the past behind us and move onto the future, so I told Heather I didn't want to read it and she took it off my computer. She gave the copy she had printed to Frank and after he read it, he said to her, 'Whatever you do don't show this to your mother because it will just kill her.' They both thought that I would be angry at them for keeping such a terrible secret from me for so long but I can understand why. Part of me still wishes that I hadn't read it, on the other hand, I'm pleased I eventually found out even though it was and still is devastating to me. I have learnt since that dreadful day in March 2006 some horrific things that Vivian has done to Heather and Claire when they were growing up. All of which are their secrets which they want to keep, however, the basis of her actions was she wanted to be the only child and would constantly tell them they should never have been born and that she should have been an only child. So, her telling me she blamed me for abandoning her for Frank was just another bullshit story to try and win me over again and for her to be number one in my life. Frank told me that Vivian had said to him one day 'I'm going to make sure that I'm number one again in Mum's eyes.'

Over the following weeks I was able to call upon my friends to talk everything out. Five of my friends were professionals in the mental health area and I was able to save myself from having a nervous breakdown by just talking to them. Because I was their friend, they wouldn't give advice they just let me talk. One of them encouraged us to speak to a wonderful counsellor at Lifeline. Over a few sessions the counsellor was able to ease the pain somewhat, one thing I remember her saying was, 'Stop blaming yourself for your daughter's appalling behaviour just because you gave birth to her, remember Jack the Ripper and Adolf Hitler would have had wonderful mothers too.'

I sent Andrew McKenzie a letter telling him that I was no longer keeping a watchful eye over his children and that I had tried on several occasions to encourage Emma to come to visit him. Regardless of my feelings towards him I always felt that he, as their father had every right to see them. I truly believe this of all parents and grandparents unless of course they are proven to be paedophiles. I said in my letter to Andrew, 'You may recall I said to you years ago that I had always thought of you as being the better parent and I meant it at the time and I still do.' He rang me the moment he finished reading the letter and we spoke for almost three hours. He admitted that he had acted like a fool in the beginning but he too had believed everything Vivian had told him about us. He said it got to the point that he didn't know what was truth or fiction coming out of her mouth and he had felt like killing her and himself on many occasions when he lived with her. He told how he had tried to get access to the kids when she finally stopped stalking him but it was far too expensive to go through the courts.

He didn't need to tell me that, we were almost twenty thousand dollars poorer because of our trying to get access to Andy and Emma. He went on to explain that Vivian kept hassling and hassling for more and more money so he took out a second mortgage of twenty thousand dollars on his home in 1996 and gave her the lot. He said, 'I'm still paying it off. 'I know she's your daughter and that you probably still love her, but she's bloody evil.'

I realised then where she had gotten the money for the brand-new car, she had at the Southport court when she & Claire had tried to get an AVO back in 1996.

Chapter 65

Finito.

Since completing this (original) epic in 2009 which had a different title and I used everyone's true identity, we went through hell and back again. Frank was diagnosed with aggressive lung cancer, emphysema and an aortic abdominal aneurysm in February 2009. He had undergone every test, X-ray, CT scan, Pet scan, bronchoscopy, known to mankind only to learn that the lung cancer had gone from the size of a 5cent piece to the size of a 50cent piece in less than six months. He had shown no signs of having cancer, not even with blood tests. The only way they discovered it we both had a respiratory infection after being on a cruise. My infection cleared up with antibiotics but Frank's didn't and he had to have a chest Xray. The surgeon removed half his right lung and four ribs, on Friday 13th November 2009 and somehow, he managed to survive. The surgeon said the aneurysm was too small to be operated on and could quite easily have been there for years. The emphysema was extremely bad but his breathing was as good as gold. I had notified Vivian about her father and she arrived at the hospital a day before the operation with Andy and Claire. Andy and Claire didn't say a word to me but Andy made a rehearsed speech to Frank telling him he would never forgive him.

Never forgive him for WHAT?

Frank and I had only ever shown Andy love as every grandparent does for their grandchild. Frank had taught Andy to drive and we had bought him a very good used car after he got his licence. Heather told us after the big argument that Andy had said that he thought we would have bought him a brand-new car. Within a matter of months, he wiped the car out after speeding through an intersection and failing to give way to another car. He tried to convince everyone that it wasn't his fault. Not long after that, he wrecked his mother's car. He dropped a lit cigarette whilst driving and in trying to retrieve it, he ran up the back of a parked car.

I made a foolish investment of $5,500 to a very wealthy businessman in May 2009 and got ripped off. I was promised the world but received nothing. I was told I had to pay another $20,000 which I didn't have. A 'verbal altercation' took place and I was told if I repeated what I had said to him, or to anyone else he would own my home. Because Frank was in for the fight of his life, I backed away with my tail between my legs. I couldn't afford to pay the guy what they wanted and I certainly couldn't afford to go to court to pursue what was rightfully mine. The prospect of losing Frank and my home was far too much to deal with.

In February 2012 Frank was diagnosed with Motor Neurone Disease (ALS).

I nursed him as best as I could and I kept saving every cent I could and as soon as I could afford to, I would book us on a cruise. We managed to go on a total of twenty one cruises between 1981 and 2016, but we really upped the ante between 2010 and 2016 by going on nine cruises in that time. I would save and save until I had enough money and I'd book us on a cruise usually leaving Brisbane to Singapore our favourite city in the world.

My brother James passed away in April 2017 from Mesothelioma which he had contracted as a house painter having unwittingly sanded back hundreds of walls made of asbestos in the 1950's.

Frank succumbed to complications of MND (ALS) forty-six days later, just fifty one days short of our fifty sixth wedding anniversary. I sent a text to Vivian asking her to contact me ASAP when Frank was admitted to the Palliative Care ward of our local hospital. She rang me the following day demanding in a rather aggressive voice 'What's this all about?'

I told her that her father had gone into a coma twice and was not expected to live. She replied 'Okay.' She never came to the hospital to visit him but I notified her after he passed away. I would have shown her more respect if she had've at least made the effort to pay him her last respects.

Claire, the little girl who had adored her father had only visited us about 10 times in 28years since moving to Sydney and then to Melbourne. She had rung to speak to her father about once a month. We subsequently learnt that she had flown up to visit Vivian who lived less than 10klms away, on several occasions. But to her credit she flew up to be with him at his deathbed and again for his memorial twenty-four days later!

I didn't notice, but it was pointed out to me later by family and friends that the eulogy poem she had written was mainly about her.

I would never advocate anyone else to stay in a marriage where any form of domestic violence was happening. The only thing I can say in my defence of staying with Frank: It was a different era back then, of course I had options, but I chose to stay, not only because I loved him, but I truly believed that deep down he was a decent human being with a very dark past and I desperately and genuinely wanted to help him even though he seemed incapable of helping himself.

The first fifteen years was no bed of roses but the last forty years certainly improved between us, we very rarely argued. But whenever we did, I was such a bitch that I'd never let him forget the first fifteen years, but Frank never once brought up the past. Admittedly I felt remorseful for being a bitch but I never once apologised. I used to admonish myself by thinking you're almost as bad as his mother. Mabel was the Queen of evil she had treated Frank abominably.

A few days before his lung operation he admitted to just some of the atrocities Mabel had done to him. This is what he told me:

'When I was about ten she had bought a number of large bottles of soft drink, I got home after school and she wasn't home and I drank one bottle. When she came home and found the empty bottle, she made me drink all the other bottles until I vomited. She forced me to slurp my own vomit off the floor.'

'On another occasion she made me climb up and down the ladder to empty the rain water tank one bucket at a time as soon as I had emptied it, I had to fill it with town water one bucket at a time.'

He said he used to be worried sick all the time because Mabel had told him she had written to the government to ask them to take him and put him away. 'One day I saw a big black car pull up in the school grounds and I thought they had come to take me. I found out much later that she had given the letter to Myrtle (Mabel' sister) to post. Myrtle gave me the letter when I was 17. I never read it, I handed it back to Myrtle and told her to burn it.'

He left school at the end of Grade 5 when he was 12 and he got a job at the local butcher shop. He gave Mabel his unopened pay packet each week.

She went to the butcher shop one day with his lunch, freshly cooked chicken sandwiches. When he got home from work, she asked him if he had enjoyed his lunch and he told her they were delicious and he thanked her. That's when she told him that she had killed and cooked his pet bantam chicken. He said 'I went outside and spewed my guts out.'

I believe that Frank was sexually abused by a Catholic priest when he was an altar boy, but he was too ashamed and embarrassed to admit it. He hated all religions with a passion, in particular Catholicism. I had asked him twice before if he'd been abused by a priest and he had said rather aggressively 'NO!'

I tried to press him for more information about being sexually abused and he replied 'Let it go Amelia, I've told you enough.'

Not a bit of wonder Frank became an alcoholic.

In his first year at school his mother had given him sixpence to put in his school bank book and threepence to buy his lunch at the tuck shop. Frank took his new found school mate to the local shop and spent the sixpence on two ice creams and a bag of lollies which they ate before heading back to school. When they reached the school gate a man that Frank had to later describe as having wickers (whiskers) offered to buy them chocolates and ice creams. Frank didn't want to have any more ice cream but his little friend did. They found the young lad the following day he had been stabbed so viciously that the blade had broken in his back. Frank never found out if he had survived or died because he was never told.

When Frank was 17-18, he and a friend were going from Eukey to Tenterfield his friend offered to take Frank on his motorbike but Frank had just bought a new Morris Minor with a canvas hood and he was keen to show it off to the local girls. His mate took off on his bike and Frank followed a few minutes later. About half way along the road between Wallangarra and Tenterfield, Frank came across a truck stopped on the road and he saw it had a motorbike jammed under the chasis. Frank went searching for his mate he'd been thrown about 50metres into long grass, his mate's head was almost severed but he was still breathing and Frank cradled him. Frank witnessed the blood spurting from his mate's throat as he took his last breath. He said he could never erase that image from his mind.

Many people have asked us over the years 'How come you pair stayed together when other marriages failed?' My answer was 'Neither of us wanted custody of the kids, and we certainly didn't want custody of the grandkids.'

Frank used to say 'Amelia is top shelf and I didn't want to see her left there unwanted gathering dust.'

I used to tell everyone that Frank never had a romantic bone in his body but he proved me wrong on my 60th birthday party when he played 'You Raise me Up' by Josh Groban.

That birthday party was supposed to be a surprise, Frank and Heather had been making arrangements for months. Foolishly they had asked Vivian to send out the invitations. I had gone to see Vivian one particular day and she had a number of envelopes on the table displaying the names of some of my friends who had responded. I didn't need to be a genius to work out why they were writing to Vivian. She took great delight in knowing she had spoilt my surprise birthday party.

Frank made a tape-recorded message for all of us in March 2003 with a song for each of us to remember him by. He had wrapped it and sealed it with my name on it and had hidden it. I found the little package about 10yrs ago in a suitcase whilst packing for one of our cruises and he told me it wasn't to be opened until after he had died. I placed it in his undies drawer and every so often I would give the parcel a shake and it would rattle. I truly believed it held an old coin that would make me wealthy in my old age. As it turned out, I think it was worth more than any valuable old coin. I had no idea it was a tape recording until I opened it the day he passed away. I howled like a banshee when I listened to it. He thanked me for not giving up on him when everyone else had told me to piss him off. I especially cried when I heard the song, he'd chosen for me was, You're Still You by Josh Groban.

After I listened to the tape again, I firmly believe that the reason he had made it at that time, he had intended to suicide. It would have been just after he had read the diatribe papers that Vivian had written. I know that when I read the diatribe, I definitely contemplated suicide for quite some time.

Looking back in hindsight I recall that he was quite depressed for a while around that time.

There weren't many people who met Frank who didn't love his sense of humour and thought of him as a bloody nice bloke. He used to tell me

'I've brought laughter and gaiety into your life and you hadn't lived until you met me.'

In February 2017, I finally admitted in front of all our friends at a surprise party for him that he was right, he had brought a lot of laughter into my life and that he had taught me more about life than anyone else could possibly have.

God really did break the mould when he made Frank, he had the constitution of ten oxen and he never complained once about his obvious pain. I said in my eulogy at his memorial service 'I will never put Frank in the Saint category, he was a little bastard, but he was my little bastard and I'll miss him until the day I die.'

I continue to walk, talk, laugh, make others laugh, but I cry when no one is watching, because inside my entire heart is shattered in a trillion pieces. I truly believed that Frank loved me more than I loved him and I'd often tell friends that. I now realise that I loved him more than I ever knew, because I held so much resentment over his treatment of me during the first fifteen years of our marriage.

He never wanted to deceive anyone about his criminal past, and I know some people will be upset to think that they were deceived. I want them and everyone else to understand that he was very remorseful of his past.

If he could have gone back and changed it he would have in a heartbeat.

Edward has been in a nursing home for the past nine years. After the prostitute kicked him out, he lived on the street for about a week and ironically had been fed by the organisation I was still volunteering with. He hadn't visited my team I think I would have got the shock of my life if he had. Someone had arranged for him to be hospitalised and I had no idea where he was for about five years.

Vivian continues her life of lies. About five years ago she wrote on Facebook that she had been accepted into a university to study medicine. She wrote about how she was enjoying studying for a few weeks then the subject was dropped. Not long after that she started another Facebook page where she uses my mother's maiden name calling herself a psychic/medium/healer and that she lives in the UK. She's visited there a couple of times but she definitely lives in Queensland. She cons people on a global scale now, claiming she's been a psychic for over twenty-five years. That would take her back to when she was living in downtown Bangladesh leaving shit filled nappies in her laundry for the maggots to feast on and for me to clean up. Lately she claims that she's been a practicing psychic since 2006, that's the same year I told her to get out and never come back.

She recently claimed that she's a fourth-generation psychic and that my mother is now her spirit guide. When I read that she was sullying my mother's good name I was saddened and angry and I wanted to comfort Edith. She doesn't deserve to have her impeccable name trashed.

Some of the absolute bullshit stories she has written on Facebook have kept me amused/confused/bemused and angry.

She has changed history by claiming my maternal great-grandparents owned an inn for travellers hundreds of miles from where they originated. I doubt that they would have even heard of the area where Vivian claimed they lived. They were dirt poor farm hands who worked their arses off for a mere pittance and a roof over their heads.

Vivian also told her 'followers' she was in the car with us one night when we drove a country friend to the accommodation he was staying at. The true story is: We had encountered a car full of youths who were tailgating us when they tried to ram the side of our car. I grabbed a heavy steel tool from the back of the station wagon and hit the passenger's arm with it and the driver sped off. Vivian was at home approximately twenty klms away, minding Heather and Claire at the time.

She claims she was cringing in the back seat terrified.

In August 2019 she wrote:

Most of you know that I was involved with breaking my father out of jail when I was about 9 as being in the getaway vehicle. And he was almost stabbed to death in front of my eyes by my mother when I was about 14. It wasn't long after that that I had my first panic attack.

REALLY? How interesting!

Vivian was about seven when I hired a car to visit Frank in Numinbah. She was six days shy of her eighth birthday when he was taken back to Boggo Road jail after Lee had told the authorities that I had taken Frank out of the prison farm.

She recently wrote that I had told her that her father was the balaclava killer. I had never heard of the balaclava killer. I looked about the case online and he apparently raped a number of young women in the Gold Coast/Tweed Heads area during 1979/1980 and one unfortunate girl was murdered. Not only did we live in Ipswich at the time, Frank had injured his spine and was operated on during the time and in neck to knee plaster when the balaclava killer was on his rampage.

All her followers were so sympathetic to her dreadful upbringing and I just sat reading her bullshit not knowing if to laugh or cry.

Do I think she's mad? NO! I think she's pure EVIL.

I can't be hundred percent sure, but IF she has panic attacks, they would have started in 2006 when I ordered her out of my home and I told her I never wanted to see her again. She would have realised that she would never be number one in my book again.

The secret to success is sincerity, once you can fake sincerity you've got it made. Jean Giradoux.

Vivian has taken fake sincerity to the nth degree. She is fooling many people into believing she is a genuinely lovely human being.

I have seen her oozing her charm to many people far too many times, telling them how much she enjoys their company etc and as soon as they leave, she has called them fuckwits and morons.

Most of the people who follow her on Facebook I have met and I've heard her cry them down calling them all the filthiest names you can think of, behind their backs. I'd love to tell them the real truth about Vivian, but I think they would choose not to believe me.

Just by the way they respond to her comments I think they are very lonely people who believe they've finally reconnected with their best friend. One refers to her as a little warrior, another calls her BFF. It's quite sad really.

Vivian has tried to win me over a few times, but I want nothing to do with her. She once told Frank that she'd be number one in my book again. Hell will freeze over before that happens!

Could she have changed? Definitely not, though she tried to convince me she had. I told her that a leopard never changes its spots. Her reply:

'That's because it's a fucking leopard.'

A lie doesn't become truth, wrong doesn't become right, and evil doesn't become good just because it's accepted by the majority. Rick Warren.

I believe that there are some genuine psychics but they are very few and far between. Here's a lesson for all of you if you want to spend your hard-earned money on being told what you want to hear: Never, I repeat never, give the psychic your email address especially if you're on Facebook. Before booking an appointment create another email address altering the spelling of your name. Not only will psychics read your Facebook page they'll read your friends and family's Facebook pages as well before you go to the appointment. That gives them all the details about you and your friends. Don't pay them over the phone or internet with your Visa or Master Card, tell them you don't have one and that you'll send them a bank cheque or deposit it into their account.

Claire came out of the closet in 1997 by ringing me from Sydney one night as drunk as a skunk and screeching down the phone that she was a Dyke on a Bike. Frank and I actually admired her for all the challenges she's gone through. I honestly don't know how she has coped with being schizophrenic having voices in her head telling her horrible things and also knowing she was a lesbian and not being able to admit it.

In 1992, we were notified one night that she had been taken to hospital after almost destroying the flat she had been living in. We drove to Sydney and on our arrival at the psychiatric ward the following morning the attendant didn't believe we had just arrived from Queensland after driving through the night. I overheard her saying to another attendant 'They reckon they're the parents of the one whose going into the locked ward.' The other attendant came over and both Frank and I showed her our driver's licences to prove who we were. I asked if I could take Claire down to have a cup of coffee and a chat so that I could hopefully get her to come to her senses. The attendant agreed and we got Claire into our car and drove her to her flat. We cleaned the flat stayed in Sydney for a few days got her back on her medication and drove back home.

Another night she rang several times, she was extremely drunk. Each time she rang she told me she'd taken more pills then she'd hang up immediately. I had no idea where she was and on about the seventh call a male voice said 'Whoever you are this girl has just collapsed on the barroom floor she's completely wasted.' I told him I was her mother and I lived in Queensland and would he please ring an ambulance because she's been taking pills for the past two hours. We again got to Sydney by morning. By the time we arrived she had had her stomach pumped and was waiting to be transferred to St Vincent's psychiatric ward. This time I didn't try to let her escape.

She had a screeching fit at one of the other patients because he had called her a bitch for making her parents worry about her. It was then that I explained to her in the simplest of terms 'Claire you have to accept that your brain is an organ or like a muscle and it needs to be healed with medication for the rest of your life. It's a part of your body that needs to be fixed. If the muscles in your arms didn't work, you'd need to take medication to have them fixed, if you had a problem with your lungs, you'd need to take medication to have them fixed. Your brain needs medication to have it fixed. It's no big deal just take the medication and be happy.'

After that she continued to take her meds regularly.

What I did have a problem with, she rang me another time to tell me she had a girlfriend she said 'Mum she's really ugly but her parents are very wealthy.' We loved her girlfriend Madeline as if she was our own, she made sure Claire took her medication at the same time every day and she encouraged Claire to get off the disability pension and get a job. Claire had done her apprenticeship as a hairdresser after finishing high school. I was so very proud of her and Maddy, I could have burst. They were together for 13yrs and when they had a big argument, we had to race down to Sydney to comfort Claire after she rang me and was inconsolable. It wasn't until then that we found out Maddy's father had being paying the rent on their unit the entire time and he was occasionally paying for their groceries. To be honest I don't think Claire would have stayed one night with Maddy if Maddy's parents weren't wealthy.

After I refused to give Claire the equivalent of the cost of the cruise fare the rest of us went on, she decided not to speak to Frank, Heather and me for about three years. When she did contact us and I told Vivian we were going to Sydney to visit Claire, it was very obvious Vivian was not happy.

I truly believe that Vivian had influenced Claire into staying away for that period of time. Unbeknown to us, Claire had kept in contact with Vivian after the sale of their home in 2006 and obviously she had reported everything that was happening in our lives to Vivian. Heather had had her suspicions from about 2010 and every time I visited Claire or when we spoke on the phone, she would make little slips of the tongue. Vivian would also drop hints on her Facebook page. Photos went missing and one photo of us all on board the cruise was posted on Vivian's Facebook page minus Frank, Heather and myself. She had cut us out of the photo.

I've never been on Facebook but we managed to read quite a lot one way or another. Frank didn't believe me when I pointed out the reasons for my suspicions because they were only circumstantial.

Claire and Maddy had shifted to Melbourne in 2007. Frank and I drove from Queensland to Sydney and on to Melbourne helping them with their shift. Maddy's father had given Maddy more than enough money to cover the petrol bill for both cars but Claire convinced Maddy to keep our share of the petrol money! Claire and Maddy broke up two years later. Claire found a new girlfriend Danielle. Frank and I weren't overly impressed with Danni, but we figured as long as Claire was happy, we were happy for her.

Claire announced on her Facebook page that she and Danni got married on my birthday in 2014. Whether it's true or not I have no idea, they would've had to go to New Zealand back then. Who knows who cares? To this day they never knew that I found out.

The last time I visited Claire and Danni Claire said 'We're going to take you to the movies Mum.'

Her work gave her two free movie tickets every week, and she had previously told me that they hadn't been to the movies for a couple of weeks so I figured that's good they won't be out of pocket. I soon discovered when we got there when she had said they would *take* me reallymeant they'd take me because Danni drove us there and I had to pay for my own ticket.

Even Edith wasn't that scungy.

When I discovered for certain two years ago that Claire and Danni had been visiting with Vivian, I gave Claire the ultimatum of either having a normal mother/daughter relationship with me or to call it quits and move on. Heather and I didn't hear from her for nine months. She started texting me daily for about 2 months. She never phoned and I had the deja-vu feeling she was getting information about what Heather and I do to report it back to Vivian. I made up a story that we had an appointment at a particular time and we were able to observe a car pull up outside our home at the time we were supposed to have the appointment. Whoever was in the car couldn't see us because I've had mirrored film applied to my bay window. I couldn't tell who the two women were in the car either. But they did an immediate U turn after looking at the house. I never told Claire what we had observed but I asked her some time later why she had contacted me after nine months. She stopped texting after that.

About four years ago Claire had to see a Gynecologist and she was so scared of what she might hear she asked me to fly to Melbourne to accompany her at the visit. Imagine my shock to learn in the course of the conversation with the Dr that she had had two abortions. The first before she left Queensland the second sometime during her time in Sydney.

Emma went to University for three years I have no idea what she studied, she worked at local menial jobs for about 12months after leaving Uni. She shifted to the UK about four years ago and has been working for an international travel agency.

Andy went to University seemingly for about four years. According to Vivian's Facebook page he was studying a business degree and then law.

Yeah Right. Frank Heather and I have always believed that poor Andy had far too many clouts to the head by Vivian. The last bit of news about him he has bought a house with Vivian a few months ago, after being in the UK working with Emma for a short time.

It beggars a few questions where did their university fees come from? Did Vivian, Andy and Emma receive HECS-HELP grants from the Federal Government? If they did, have they began paying the money back?

Have they paid tax to the Australian Government as well as to the UK? Vivian maintains she also worked in the USA so has she also paid tax there as well?

Andrew apparently has finally found happiness with a new wife whom he has two sons with. He fathered another son with a 16yr old girl whilst still married to Vivian.

I will love my daughters until my dying breath but until the day they really seek help I will go to my grave without ever wanting to see or speak to them again. I will not die a lonely old woman. I have friends who accept me for who I am with all my faults. I have my wonderful daughter Heather who still suffers emotionally from her sister's horrible unkindness.

Heather underwent open heart surgery in August 2019 for repair to her mitral valve. She was discharged six days later, feeling the healthiest she had been for quite a long time. The local chemist gave her the wrong medication of four mg of Warfarin instead of 1.5mg. She developed a cyst which bled internally and was readmitted to hospital where they did absolutely nothing for her and was again discharged. I insisted that our GP order another CT scan which found that the cyst had doubled in size to 12cm in less than a week and it had latched onto most of her organs. Heather was again readmitted to hospital and underwent another seven hour surgery where they removed the cyst/her spleen/half her pancreas/part of her large bowel and an adrenal gland. She is coming along nicely and recuperating well.

I've always tried to be honest and forthright, of course there have been a few indiscretions which I readily admit to. I concede that some may say I'm an outspoken big mouth, but it's not my fault that some people can't handle the truth. To those people I say, 'If God didn't want me to speak my mind why did he give me a tongue?' Admittedly I talk tough, I try to act strong but on my own with only my thoughts to haunt me I still shed a few tears though less frequently now for the daughters, grandson and granddaughter who live their lives of lies. I still occasionally wear my favourite T-shirt which Emma bought me when we visited Thailand in 2000 it reads:

Does not play well with others it seems others have a problem with losing.

I may not be everyone's cup of tea but I know I'm a good person and I always try to do the right thing. Many years ago, one of my friends, (I'm not sure who) put a little sticker on my car, Angel with attitude. I thought that was a sweet thing to do. I don't think I'm an angel by any stretch of the imagination but I certainly have attitude.

Since March 2006 I try to live by the quote I once read outside a shop in Sydney, I'd rather trust a known enemy than a sometime friend.

But then again sometimes it's difficult finding out which one is which.

I definitely don't trust easily with most people I meet, knowing what I've been through who could blame me?

Another quote I like:

I no longer look for the good in people, I look for the real. Because good is often dressed in fake clothing, real is naked and proud no matter the scars.

I am a very proud survivor and I classify myself as being extremely lucky not only to survive many threats and mishaps. I've been lucky enough to win a few competitions including two cruises a return coach tour to Ayer's Rock and two diamond rings. One of the rings was what I like to call from a lucky dip. I filled in my name and address for a Sunday Mail competition along with many thousands of other entries and my name was drawn.

The ring was valued at twenty thousand dollars.

Even if I outlive everyone I know, I can still die happy knowing that I have been truly loved unconditionally all my life by my parents, grandmother, husband and my daughter Heather.

What more could one human being want?

* * * * * *

CPSIA information can be obtained
at www.ICGtesting.com
Printed in the USA
LVHW090103290520
656808LV00005B/572